MAGIC SQUARES
&
TREE OF LIFE

WESTERN MANDALAS OF POWER

Nineveh Shadrach

Ishtar Publishing
Vancouver

MAGIC SQUARES AND TREE OF LIFE: WESTERN MANDALAS OF POWER
AN ISHTAR PUBLISHING BOOK:
978-1-926667-06-5

PRINTING HISTORY
Ishtar Publishing edition published 2009
1 3 5 7 9 10 8 6 4 2

Copyright (c) Nineveh Shadrach, 2009
Text Design and Layout (c) Ishtar Publishing, 2009

Ishtar Publishing
141-6200 McKay Ave
Suite 716
Burnaby, BC
Canada V5H4M9

www.ishtarpublishing.com
Printed and bound in the United States.

TABLE OF CONTENTS

Maker of earth and sky, from age to age
Who rul'st the world by reason; at whose word
Time issues from Eternity's abyss:
To all that moves the source of movement, fixed
Thyself and moveless. Thee no cause impelled
Extrinsic this proportioned frame to shape
From shapeless matter; but, deep-set within
Thy inmost being, the form of perfect good,
From envy free; and Thou didst mould the whole
To that supernal pattern. Beauteous
the world in Thee thus imaged, being Thyself
Most beautiful. So Thou the work didst fashion
In that fair likeness, bidding it put on
Perfection through the exquisite perfectness
Of every part's contrivance. Thou dost bind
The elements in balanced harmony,
So that the hot and cold, the moist and dry,
Contend not; nor the pure fire leaping up
Escape, or weight of waters whelm the earth.
Thou joinest and diffusest through the whole,
Linking accordantly its several parts,
A soul of threefold nature, moving all.
This, cleft in twain, and in two circles gathered,
Speeds in a path that on itself returns,
Encompassing mind's limits, and conforms
The heavens to her true semblance. Lesser souls
And lesser lives by a like ordinance
Thou sendest forth, each to its starry car
Affixing, and dost strew them far and wide
O'er earth and heaven. These by a law benign
Thou biddest turn again, and render back
To thee their fires. Oh, grant, almighty Father,
Grant us on reason's wing to soar aloft
To heaven's exalted height; grant us to see
The fount of good; grant us, the true light found,
To fix our steadfast eyes in vision clear
On Thee. Disperse the heavy mists of earth,
And shine in Thine own splendour. For Thou art
The true serenity and perfect rest
Of every pious soul to see Thy face,
The end and the beginning — One the guide,
The traveller, the pathway, and the goal.

The Consolation of Philosophy by Boethius

I

Introduction

Y ou are holding in your hands a book unlike any you may have seen before. Instead of spells, ritual magic techniques or occult philosophy, I am going to reveal a secret more than a thousand years old. This secret is actually not that much of a secret for the wizards of Arabia. However, you will not find a single mention of it in any English esoteric writing before the publication of this book. Whether by intent or circumstance, this knowledge ended up being a secret kept from the Western world. On the surface you will be tempted to dismiss it as too simplistic. Keep in mind things don't need to be complex to have power. Some amazing effects can come from approaching the familiar differently. The familiar in this case is nothing more than numbers.

"Near Constantinople, in a place called Ephiha, there was a certain man, who, instead of Enchantments, made use of certain numbers which he wrote upon the earth; and by means of these he caused certain extravagant and terrifying visions to appear."

– The Book of Sacred Magic of Abramelin

We don't know what numbers this man in Ephiha wrote to create those astonishing miracles. However, we can make an informed guess that most likely they were written down in some pattern possessing mystical or esoteric properties.

The most likely patterns would be the one familiar to occultists of that era. The one pattern with a reoccurring theme in numerical magic is that of the magic square. They have been used in talismanic construction and for magical manifestations since the Vedic times. The earliest known magic square is the Lo Shu from 650 BC. A magic square is basically a square grid with non-repeating numbers organized so that they add up to the same value horizontally, vertically, and diagonally.

4	9	2
3	5	7
8	1	6

It should be obvious by now that the secret to which I was referring earlier is a magic square whose occult properties were considered powerful enough for it to reside in a class of its own. Let me share with you a sample from a manuscript discussing this particular square:

٢

بغراط الحكيم لتلامذته عليكم بوفق العظيمة قالوا وما هو قال الكبريت الأحمر والترياق

الأكبر وهو المئيني وأن جميع الأمر تتعاظم من حمله ويعظم قدره عنده وحامله

يكون آمنا من الطعن والطاعون والجذام والنقرس واللقوة والفالج والموت

فجأة ويصرف الله عنه جميع الأشرار بالغاية بحيث لا تصل إليه العباده وأن

حامله يظفر على الأعداء ويكسر جيوش العدو وكان أرسطو للحكيم يجله ويرفعه

فوق رأسه وقت قيامه إلى حاجته ويقول هذا سيف الله القاطع ودرعه

المانع وكان اسكندر ذو القرنين يضعه على العلم وبه ملكه الله جميع البلاد

والعباد والأقاليم السبعة وصاحبه معظم عند الملوك والعلماء لأن فيه

سر جميع الموفاق إذ جميع الموفاق داخلة فيه و مجتمعة فيه وعدده وحامله

بما شاهد من صنع الله تعالى ما لا ينصفه الألسن ومن خواصه شفاء الأمراض والأبراص

وزوال الأعراض وإقامة المصروع وهزم الجيوش والعساكر ويبطل مواضع

المكنون وإذا كان في بيت لا يدخله الوبا والأمراض الصعبة والطواعين وبأمن

البيت من الحرق والغرق والسرقة ولو كان في بلد لم يظفر به العدو وبإذن الله

تغلب ولو حاصروه مدة طويلة و ذكرته بعض الخواص لسلطان السلاطين

السلطان على الشهيد فلم يظفر به عدو وقد ظفر هو ببلاد لا يحصى

عددها حتى لما أراد الله قتله ضاع منه قبل ذلك بمدة وقيل نزل في الحمام

ليغتسل ودخل الحمام فقتل وكان وقته ليس حامل له و قد شاهدت سره

عند شيخنا الولي الصالح الصوفي الشيخ محمد الذكر وركب لمنازله باسم إسماعيل

بيك الشهيد فرموا عليه بالرصاص فلم يضره ذلك بل دخل في جوانبه

الملبوسة فقط وقد شاهدت منه أيضا أن الحلاق لم يقدر على قطع شعرة

منه وهو حامله نزل لما أزاله عنه حلق جميع شعر رأسه نزل لما أراد الله

شهادته ضاع منه فبلغ منونه سبعة أيام والحاصل أن خواصه كثيرة للبركة

تحصيلها وهو مما يتعلق بالملوك والأمراء وتبسيم وتريح الغاف إيمانة خانه

في مانة خانه وإذا رسم وعلق على الأعلام والصنائق أي البيارق ينبسط

رسمه في الأطلس أو الورق العبادي الذي يأتي من بلاد الهند فينهزم

العدو بإذن الله تغلب وينكسر الجيوش ويظفر بالعدو وحامله وقد

ذكر كل من البوني والغزالي وأكابر الصالحين من خواصه بنزلا نختلها

Here is a translation of parts of this manuscript:

"Hippocrates the wise said to his students: "Hearken to the magical square of majesty!" They said: "What is it?" He said: "The red sulfur and the greatest antidote, which is the centenarian." Its carrier can obtain audiences before all the princes and his status amongst them becomes magnificent. Its carrier is safe from stabbing, plague, leprosy, gout, facial paralysis, hemiplegia and sudden death. God dismisses absolutely all evil things from him, so that sadness doesn't reach him. Its carrier gains victory over enemies and destroys the armies of his foe. The sage Aristo venerated it and raised it above his head at the times he would arise to his affairs. He would say that this is the severing sword of God and His protecting shield. Alexander, who had two horns, would place it on his flag and through it God made him sovereign of many nations and people across the seven regions.

Its possessor is praised among the kings and sages, because it contains the secret of all the magic squares. This is because all the magic squares are inside it and united in its numbers. Whoever carries it will see, from the constructions of God the Exalted, what can't be described by tongues.

Among its properties are treatments of illnesses, leprosy, removal of maladies, awaking from unconsciousness, defeating armies and soldiers, and abolishing the barriers of treasures. If it is in a house, no malady will enter it and neither will serious illnesses nor plagues, and the house will be safe from burning, flooding and theft. If it is in a city, then no enemy will be successful in taking it, by permission of God the Exalted, even if they lay siege to it for a long time. One of the elect wrote it for the Sultan of Sultans, Sultan Ali al-Shaheed, and no enemy could get to him. He was able to attain numerous nations. When God wanted to kill him, he lost it shortly before that. It was said that he went naked to wash in the bath, entered the bath and was killed during the time he wasn't carrying it.

I witnessed its mystery at the hands of our saintly and pious Sufi Sheikh Mohamd al-Dakroree, when he wrote it for the martyr Ismail Bayek. They fired a bullet at him and it didn't harm him at all, but instead lodged in his vest. I also saw how the barber couldn't cut a single strand of hair from him while he bore it. When he put it down, all of his head's hair was shaved. He lost it seven days prior to his death, when God wanted his martyrdom.

In summary, its properties are numerous and beyond reach and are connected with princes and kings. It is known as the square of Qaf, which refers to one hundred cells by one hundred cells. If it is drawn and hung on banners and cymbals, on the condition that is drawn on satin or India paper, then the enemy will be defeated by permission of God the Exalted, and their army will be broken.

Al-Buni, al-Ghazzali, and the greatest of saints have mentioned from its properties an excerpt outside the scope of this letter. There is no doubt that its beneficial qualities are numerous and its carrier is constantly in God's safety, protection, preservation, and blessing, for undoubtedly that the Greatest Name of God is in it. All the beautiful names of God are in it and it contains some of the verses from God's scripture in it as well and God is the source of success."

You would almost get the impression from the author of this manuscript that he is revealing the holy grail of magic squares. Many old masters of our tradition would have agreed with him had he said so. From the manuscript, we know some of its properties and we know its size. What our writer neglects to tell us is why the number 100 in particular is so important that its magical square would possess such a venerated status and occult potency.

The first step in unveiling this mystery is to understand that, influenced by Chaldean and Greek numerology, ancient occultists viewed numbers as more than a measure of quantity. Historically, numbers came into being long before any of the recognized alphabets. Letters of the alphabet are connected with numbers, for numbers constitute an almost universal language. Indeed, the ancient mystery schools saw in numbers the language of nature itself.

Likewise, the Pythagoreans considered arithmetic to be the mother of their sacred science. They believed that geometry, music, and astronomy are dependent on it. Plutarch states: "The Pythagoreans indeed go farther than this, and honour even numbers and geometrical diagrams with the names and titles of the gods." Chaldeans and those who inherited their knowledge from the Hebrews and Arabs likened numbers to Divine emanations. They are part of the language of the Logos through which the universe was shaped and came to be.

> "1. In thirty-two mysterious paths of Wisdom, Yah, Eternal of Hosts [Yod-Vav-Yod], God of Israel, Living Elohim, Almighty God, High and Extolled, Dwelling in Eternity, Holy Be His Name, engraved and created His world in three Sefarim: in writing, number and word. Ten Sefirot out of nothing, twenty-two foundation letters, three mothers, seven doubles and twelve simples." – Sefer Yetzirah

Each letter is a world unto itself. Each letter is composed of spirit, soul and body. The spirit is the number that corresponds to the letter. The soul is the vibration or sound of the letter (music) that is the spoken word. The body is the glyph design (geometry) that is the writing that represents it. From the celestial, each letter has a corresponding body (astronomy). Combining spirit, soul, and body when in harmony with astronomical principles is the ultimate key to magical manifestation. Agrippa similarly proposes that letters derive their efficacy from the numerical geometry of their written symbols combined with the numerical harmony of the voice.

> "Harmony also, and voices have their power by, and consist of numbers and their proportions, and the proportions arising from numbers, do by lines, and points make characters, and figures: and these are proper to magical operations, the middle which is betwixt both being appropriated by declining to the extremes, as in the use of letters."
> – Agrippa's Three Books of Occult Philosophy (p237)

Numbers progress from the Monad or Unity into a multitude of parts. Each part contains all the previous individual parts of the Monad plus itself. Emanations likewise move from the most primordial and subtle to the most dense and tangible. That is why the Tree of Life of the Kabbalah starts with the subtle emanation that represents the primordial light and terminates with an emanation that represents the totality of the Divine's kingdom often associated with Earth. These emanations are cyclical. The first cycle of emanation proceeds mathematically from 1 till 10. These ten digits are referred to as the perfect ten in the Quran. They create the sacred Pythagorean tetractys (10 dots). They are the number of emanations of the Tree of Life as described in the Sepher Yetzirah.

> "Ten Sefirot out of nothing. Ten and not nine, ten and not eleven. Understand in Wisdom and be wise in Understanding. Examine them, investigate them, think clearly and form. Place the word above its creator and reinstate a Creator upon His foundation; and they are ten extending beyond limit. Observe them: they appear like a flash. Their boundary has no limit for His word is with them: "and they ran and returned." And they pursue His saying like a whirlwind; and they prostrate themselves before His throne."
> – Sefer Yetzirah

> "Bless us, divine number, you who generated gods and men. O holy, holy Tetractys, you that contains the root and source of the eternally flowing creation. For the divine number begins with the profound, pure unity until it comes to the holy four; then it produces the mother of all, the all-comprising, all-bounding, the first-born, the never-swerving, the never-tiring holy ten, the keyholder of all."
> – Pythagorean prayer to the Tetractys.

1			Light (Universal Spirit)			Seed (Sperma) and Root (Rhiza)
2		Darkness (Moon)		Light (Sun)		Growth (Auxe)
3	Darkness (Earth)		Water (Mercury)		Light (Sulfur)	Skin (Khroia)
4	Earth	Water		Air	Fire	Body (Soma)
= 10						

The next cycle of numbers proceeds from 10 and ends at 100. The third cycle of numbers proceeds from 100 and ends at 1000. The fourth cycle of numbers proceeds from 1000 and ends with the ends of numbers. The Greek number system is slightly different as it is divided like this:

Single digits (1-9)

Tens or Decad (10-99)

Hundreds or Hekatontad (100-999)

Thousands or Chiliad (1000-9999)

Myriad (10,000+)

The traditional cut-off with the thousand has more to do with the science of letters than pure arithmetic. According to the science of letters, 2000 is (2x1000) and 100,000 is (100x1000) and 1,000,000 is (1000x1000) and so on. This principle is what is used when representing numbers with letters. In Greek numerology, the cut off is at 10,000 upward. For example, 100,000 is counted as 10 x 10000 and written 10,0000 rather than 100,000.

The numbers 10, 100, and 1000 partake of the attribute both of the '0' and the '1' within cyclical transitions. They are the termination of one cycle and the point of birth for the next. It may not make sense at first, when you consider that 10 is a two digit number. However, the number 10 shares much of its properties with the number 1 for (1+0=1). It is the serpent biting its own tail. It is the end of the first cycle, but why is it the start of the second cycle? If we started the next cycle with 11 then we would have started it with (1+1=2). One is thus the initiator of each cycle and in effect its terminator.

The numbers 10, 100, and 100 are considered magnifications of each other and the number one. We find that 100 partakes of the qualities of ten, as it is tenfold ten. It also partakes of the qualities of one just like ten does. This is the principle behind the reductionism explicit in numerology called Pythagorean, which is a parallel to the Hebrew Aiq Bekar system.

Pythagorean Numerology Table

1	2	3	4	5	6	7	8	9
A (1)	B (2)	C (3)	D (4)	E (5)	F (6)	G (7)	H (8)	I (9)
J (10)	K (20)	L (30)	M (40)	N (50)	O (60)	P (70)	Q (80)	R (90)
S (100)	T(200)	U (300)	V (400)	W (500)	X (600)	Y (700)	Z (800)	

Hebrew Aiq Bekar

9	8	7	6	5	4	3	2	1
(9) ט	(8) ח	(7) ז	(6) ו	(5) ה	(4) ד	(3) ג	(2) ב	(1) א
(90) צ	(80) פ	(70) ע	(60) ס	(50) נ	(40) מ	(30) ל	(20) כ	(10) י
					(400) ת	(300) ש	(200) ר	(100) ק

The next point of consideration is that each emanation in a cycle is an increase in density from the one prior. It is the totality of the density of all previous emanations plus the initial emanation. This is illustrated mathematically thus: 1+1=2, 2+1=3, 3+1=4, 4+1=5 and so on. Each cycle is a considered a world of manifestation with various level of dense manifestations of the Unity.

This very basic mathematical model is helpful in understanding the Kabbalistic Tree of Life and the four worlds. Of itself it isn't sufficient, as much of the traditional Kabbalistic imagery is based on Jewish esoteric understanding of the Torah and the Divine mysteries. Still a basic model of associating Divine facets with the mysteries of numbers can be discerned.

Tree of Life Emanation	Emanation Sequence
Kether: Crown	1st
Chokmah: Wisdom	2nd
Binah: Understanding	3rd
Chesed: Mercy	4th
Geburah: Severity	5th
Tiphareth: Beauty	6th
Netzach: Victory	7th
Hod: Splendor	8th
Yesod: Foundation	9th
Malkuth: Kingdom	10th

In the Kabbalah, the Tree of Life is associated with another cosmic model known as the four worlds. The four worlds of the Kabbalah are:

World	Meaning	Golden Dawn Elemental Attribution
Olam ha-Atziluth	World of Emanation	Yod (Fire)
Olam ha-Beri'ah	World of Creation	Heh (Water)
Olam ha-Yetzirah	World of Formation	Vav (Air)
Olam ha-Asiyah	World of Action	Heh (Earth)

The four worlds can be divided among the Elements based on two models. The first relies on the attribution of the four Elements to the Tetragrammaton (YHVH) and the other on elemental weight of cycle of numbers: Fire (the first perfect ten), Air (tens), Water (hundreds) and Earth (thousands). This attribution is based on alchemical density, with Earth being the densest and Fire being the most subtle correlating with the increased density of numbers.

Mathematical Model	Magic Society of the White Flame Attribution Based On Elemental Weight	Kabbalistic Four Worlds	Cosmic Model According to the Ismaili Secret Teachings	Agrippa's Three Books of Occult Philosophy
Single Digits	Fire	World of Emanation	World of Innovation	Divine Things
Decad	Air	World of Creation	World of the Body	Celestial
Hekatontad	Water	World of Formation	World of Religion	Terrestrial
Chiliad	Earth	World of Action	World of Second Emergence	Things That Will Exist In the Future

There are two primary schools of thought within the Kabbalah concerning the integration of the ten emanations of the Tree of Life with the four worlds. The first associates the four worlds with portions of the ten emanations. The other assumes an entire Tree of Life in each of the four worlds.

The mathematical expansion of this model would look something like this:

World	Emanation	Numeric Value
1st World	1st Emanation	1
1st World	2nd Emanation	2
1st World	3rd Emanation	3
1st World	4th Emanation	4
1st World	5th Emanation	5
1st World	6th Emanation	6
1st World	7th Emanation	7
1st World	8th Emanation	8
1st World	9th Emanation	9
1st World and 2nd World	10th Emanation & 1st Emanation	10
2nd World	2nd Emanation	20
2nd World	3rd Emanation	30
2nd World	4th Emanation	40
2nd World	5th Emanation	50
2nd World	6th Emanation	60
2nd World	7th Emanation	70
2nd World	8th Emanation	80
2nd World	9th Emanation	90
2nd World and 3rd World	10th Emanation & 1st Emanation	100
3rd World	2nd Emanation	200
3rd World	3rd Emanation	300
3rd World	4th Emanation	400
3rd World	5th Emanation	500
3rd World	6th Emanation	600
3rd World	7th Emanation	700
3rd World	8th Emanation	800
3rd World	9th Emanation	900
3rd World and 4th World	10th Emanation & 1st Emanation	1000
4th World	2nd Emanation	2000
4th World	3rd Emanation	3000
4th World	4th Emanation	4000
4th World	5th Emanation	5000
4th World	6th Emanation	6000
4th World	7th Emanation	7000
4th World	8th Emanation	8000
4th World	9th Emanation	9000
4th World	10th Emanation	10000

In the preceding structure, the Myriad is the termination of the Chiliad and, as such, it is counted as an extension of it rather than as its own category.

The number one hundred is the termination or final manifestation of the emanations of the second world and the beginning of the third world. If we consider the fourth world, the world of manifestation and materialization, the third world is the world of images in the mind of the Logos. It is the spiritual consciousness (Water) before it takes on form in the universe (Earth). This is the point at which what is created in the Celestial comes to be in the Terresterial. The number one hundred is the crown of this Divine mind in the state of conceptualization and formation. Whatever is created at that juncture will thus manifest.

In addition to the Tree of Life, the esoteric tradition of the Ismaili contains a pattern of cosmology of existence through the four worlds similar to the Kabbalah. They have corresponded their system explicitly to the numerals.

Numeral	Cosmology
1	Innovation (First Mind)
2	Second Mind
3	Third Mind
4	Fourth Mind
5	Fifth Mind
6	Sixth Mind
7	Seventh Mind
8	Eighth Mind
9	Ninth Mind
10	Chief in Charge of Power
20	Angel of the Stars
30	Angel of Saturn
40	Angel of Jupiter
50	Angel of Mars
60	Angel of the Sun
70	Angel of Venus
80	Angel of Mercury
90	Angel of the Moon
100	Chief in Charge of Speaking
200	Chief that is the Foundation
300	Third Completer
400	Fourth Completer
500	Fifth Completer
600	Sixth Completer
700	Seventh Completer
800	Eighth Completer
900	Ninth Completer & All Inconceivable Qualities
1000	Tenth Completer & All that is Endowed with Speech from the Qualities

Various mystery schools and traditions have approached the mysteries of numbers differently. However, much overlap still exists as their understanding of numbers comes primarily from the characteristics of numbers. This is one of the many reasons why the Pythagorean School was so influential. They studied the numbers themselves and their patterns, to figure out their deep layered meaning. They didn't see them as merely mathematical coincidences, but as clues left in nature by the Divine architect.

The number one is associated with Divinity itself, the first principle, and the Hermetic Monad. It represents unity and singularity, which is considered a Divine attribute. In effect number one contains all other numbers and, as such, all numbers are manifestations of one. In his Three Books of Occult Philosophy, Cornelius Agrippa echoes the wisdom of sages past when he also states: "For unity doth most simply go through every number, and is the common measure, fountain, and original of all numbers, contains every number jointed together in itself entirely, the beginner of every multitude, always the same, and unchangeable."

This metaphysical statement can be mathematically demonstrated thus:

$1 \times 1 = 1$
$11 \times 11 = 121$
$111 \times 111 = 12321$
$1111 \times 1111 = 1234321$
$11111 \times 11111 = 123454321$
$111111 \times 111111 = 12345654321$
$1111111 \times 1111111 = 1234567654321$
$11111111 \times 11111111 = 123456787654321$
$111111111 \times 111111111 = 12345678987654321$

Just as the number one can be expanded to generate all other numbers, so can all the digits be expanded to return to a multi-dimensional state of unity. This can be shown using mathematics as such:

$0 \times 9 + 1 = 1$
$1 \times 9 + 2 = 11$
$12 \times 9 + 3 = 111$
$123 \times 9 + 4 = 1111$
$1234 \times 9 + 5 = 11111$
$12345 \times 9 + 6 = 111111$
$123456 \times 9 + 7 = 1111111$
$1234567 \times 9 + 8 = 11111111$
$12345678 \times 9 + 9 = 111111111$
$123456789 \times 9 + 10 = 1111111111$

The number one hundred partakes of the power of the Monad. It can also be described as tenfold ten. Therefore it shares the qualities of the number ten and extenuates them tenfold. The mystery school of Pythagoras saw the number ten as an epitome of perfection.

According to Speusippus, the head of the Pythagorean academy before Xenocrates, ten is an even number that contains an equal amount of even and odd numbers. Anatolius also states that the number ten is generated by an even and an odd number, two times five. It is thus called power and the all-fulfiller because it limits all the numbers. It does so by encompassing within itself the whole nature of odd and even. It contains 1,3,7,9 for odd numbers and 2,4,6,8 for even numbers.

Number ten contains an equal amount of prime and incomposite numbers, as well as secondary and composite numbers. Prime and incomposite numbers are those that can be measured or factored only by 1 and by the number itself. These prime numbers are 1,2,3,5 and 7. The secondary numbers are 4,6,8,9 and 10 itself.

The number 10 also contains all the proportions. It contains one, the point, two, the line, three, the triangle, and four, the pyramid. These are the primary elements in plane and solid figures. The number ten arises out of the combination of the tetraktys of the first numbers (1, 2, 3 and 4). When you add 1, 2, 3 and 4 you end up with the number 10.

Then, after reaching the number 10, the numbers reach their course and turn around as if it is a turning-point. That is, they reach the next stage whereupon 10 is like 1 for the next cycle of numbers. Therefore, the number 10 is like the single monad reoccurring.

The number 10 also generates an important number that is 55 thus: $1+2+3+4+5+6+7+8+9+10 = 55$. The number 55 is the tenth number of the Fibonacci sequence. It is also generated by doubling and tripling the systematic sequence. The doubles are 1, 2, 4 and 8, which add to fifteen. The triples are 1, 3, 9 and 27, which add to forty. The sums of fifteen and forty add up to fifty-five. Obviously, the reduction of 55 (5+5) results in the number 10. I should note out of interest that the number 10 represents Malkuth (the Kingdom) in the Tree of Life emanations. The number 55 is the Gematria or large range of the word Kalah (כלה), which means bride and is a title of Malkuth.

Looking at all the various qualities of this number, which I have touched upon only partially, those ancient philosophers felt justified in referring to it as heaven, eternity, power, trust, necessity, universe and simply all.

As I said earlier, the number one hundred is tenfold ten or the third occurrence of the monad.

The corresponding letter among the Semitic alphabet is the letter Qoph (Hebrew) or Qaf (Arabic). The letter Qoph alludes to the Divine's holiness (קדושה) [Kedushah]. The idea of the Divine being holy conveys the idea that the Divine is exalted without limits. The Divine is boundless and formless. The word holy (קדוש) [Kadosh] has the same large range as the word Omnipresent (מקום), which is 186. Since the Divine is without limitation, then the Divine Spirit can enter into and penetrate every facet of the Universe. Things that are holy have a degree of sanctity that removes them from other things. A person who is holy is in a higher station than others. The Divine is the embodiment of holiness and thus is in a higher station than all other things.

Cycles are the most obvious manifestations of this Divine majesty when it is expressed in nature. The word Qoph (קוף) is related to go around (הקף) and cycle (הקפה). All the various cycles of nature teach us there is a pattern and purpose to the universe.

We can see overlapping associations between the Jewish Kabbalah view of the letter Qoph and the theology of numbers. The number one hundred is associated with holiness, infinity, cycles and total presence and manifestation.

The Arabic esoteric lore states that the letter Qaf (100) resides in the interior of the Pen. The pen is visible on the Tablet. The Tablet is visible by the cosmos. The cosmos is visible due to the emergence. The letter Qaf is the reality of the heart that carries the reality of all things. The heart's ascension through kingship is in a day measured by a thousand years. This is a measure of the multiplication of one hundred by ten. This is the degree of the heart, which is the degree of the interior Divine names, for each of the Divine names administers ten degrees of the celestials and ten corresponding degrees of the lower world.

It is said that the letter Qaf is the light of the Pen, (Qalam), for the Pen contains the letters Qaf (Q), Lam (L), and Meem (M). The letter Qaf is the secret of will, which is fate. It is the reality of all that the Pen has written in summary and in detail. This is why all things in the universe are under the dominion of the one hundred Divine names. This is why the letter Qaf has the mathematical value of one hundred, as the letter Qaf is the interior of the Pen, which is the secret of fate. The letter Lam is the secret of the being of fate that carries Qaf, that is, its secret that is allegorically referred to as secrets of fate. The letter Meem is the secret of its connection with the Tablet, for the letter Meem is from the worlds of the Tablet. Thus it united the Pen with the mystery of its own essence and the secrets of the Tablet. Afterword, the Glorious Quran became visible in the Protected Tablet. This is meaning behind the Quranic verse: "Qaf and the Glorious Quran"

The letter Qaf is also referred to in *Kashef al-Asrar al-Makhfiah* as a letter from the letters of the secret stone that is of plant and animal nature. This is the stone that is referred to by the philosophers as the noble stone. It is the great name of God in the natural lower world and its interior is the great name of God in the spiritual upper world.

Thus, like many other mystery schools, the Arabic esotericists see in the number one hundred and its corresponding letter Qaf, the power of manifestating what resides in the celestial spiritual world into our world.

It is the multiplied power of the Monad and the Decad.

There are no magic squares that can host the monad. The smallest sized magic square is three by three. Most traditional occult texts expand the size of magic squares to nine by nine and stop there. Few Western occult authors have pushed the envelope of common lore and presented the ten by ten, which is the second manifestation of the Monad. However, rarely has that square been used in practical occultism except by very few adepts. Even then, how many were aware of that magnificent magic square identified most with Divine power, holiness, majesty, as well as limitless manifestation? I am referring, of course, to the Hekatontad magic square.

Count yourself fortunate for you are one of them now, but this fortune is merely a potential. It can only really become a full reality in your life, if you create the magic square and release its power.

In this book, I will present you with the original design of the Hekatontad magical square so you can construct it, should you wish to unleash its power in your life. I am also providing you with ten variants specifically attuned to each of the traditional emanations of the Tree of Life. They were constructed based on combinations of the Divine name and the name of the Emanation to identity it as the Divine facet. This is based on the advice of the Sepher Yetzirah:

> "Place the word above its creator and reinstate a Creator upon His foundation; and they are ten extending beyond limit."

The numerical range of each of these constructs is used as progression value between the various numbers in the corresponding magic squares. The reason I chose it as a progression was to emulate the facet of emanation from one level of existence into the next like the flowing of water from one cup into another.

Emanation	Divine Name	Construct	Total Value
Kether: Crown	Eheieh Asher Eheih: I am that I am	Kether ha-Eheieh Asher Ehieh: Crown of I am that I am	1168
Chokmah: Wisdom	Yah	Chokmah ha-Yah: Wisdom of Yah	93
Binah: Understanding	YHVH Elohim: Lord God	Binah ha-YHVH Elohim: Understanding of Lord God	184
Chesed: Mercy	El	Chesed ha-El: Mercy of El	108
Geburah: Severity	Elohim Gibor: Almighty God	Geburah ha-Elohim Gibor: Severity of Almighty God	518
Tiphareth: Beauty	YHVH Eloah va-Daath: Lord God of Knowledge	Tiphareth ha-YHVH Eloah va-Daath: Beauty of Lord God of Knowledge	1634
Netzach: Victory	YHVH Tzabaoth: Lord of Hosts	Netzach ha-YHVH Tzabaoth: Victory of Lord of Hosts	678
Hod: Splendor	Elohim Tzabaoth: God of Hosts	Hod ha-Elohim Tzabaoth: Splendor of God of Hosts	605
Yesod: Foundation	Shaddai El Chai: Almighty Living God	Yesod ha-Shaddai El Chai: Foundation of Almighty Living God	448
Malkuth: Kingdom	Adonai ha-Aretz: Lord of the Earth	Malkuth ha-Adonai ha-Aretz: Kingdom of Lord of the Earth	862

CONSTRUCTING THE 100 x 100 MAGIC SQUARE

There are a number of ways to build the 100x100 magic square. One of the easiest ways to do it is to build a square within a square. We will start first with a magic square of 5x5 as a basis for our construction.

Large 5x5 Square for the 100x100

7	22	5	8	23
6	12	17	10	20
25	11	13	15	1
24	16	9	14	2
3	4	21	18	19

What is unique about this square is that in the middle of the 5x5 is a perfect 3x3 magic square.

Each line of the 5x5 adds up to 65.

Each line of the 3x3 inside the 5x5 adds up to 39.

Each cell in the square will have the designation L.

We will now build a 4x4 square in each of the cells in the 5x5 square:

4	14	15	1
9	7	6	12
5	11	10	18
16	2	3	13

Each cell in the 4x4 square will have the designation M.

We will now take each of those cells and build in it another 5x5 square with the 3x3 in the center of it.

The total will be 5x4x5 = 100 per line or 100x100 square.

The naming of each of the interior 5x5 magic squares will be done according to the follow classification: Ln-Mn where n represents a number.

For example: L2-M5

This means that the 5x5 goes in the 5th cell of the 4x4 pattern that constitutes the 2nd cell in the large 5x5 pattern.

The large pattern of the 100x100 magic square is as follows:

L7-M4	L7-M14	L7-M15	L7-M1	L22-M4	L22-M14	L22-M15	L22-M1	L5-M4	L5-M14	L5-M15	L5-M1	L8-M4	L8-M14	L8-M15	L8-M1	L23-M4	L23-M14	L23-M15	L23-M1
L7-M9	L7-M7	L7-M6	L7-M12	L22-M9	L22-M7	L22-M6	L22-M12	L5-M9	L5-M7	L5-M6	L5-M12	L8-M9	L8-M7	L8-M6	L8-M12	L23-M9	L23-M7	L23-M6	L23-M12
L7-M5	L7-M11	L7-M10	L7-M8	L22-M5	L22-M11	L22-M10	L22-M8	L5-M5	L5-M11	L5-M10	L5-M8	L8-M5	L8-M11	L8-M10	L8-M8	L23-M5	L23-M11	L23-M10	L23-M8
L7-M16	L7-M2	L7-M3	L7-M13	L22-M16	L22-M2	L22-M3	L22-M13	L5-M16	L5-M2	L5-M3	L5-M13	L8-M16	L8-M2	L8-M3	L8-M13	L23-M16	L23-M2	L23-M3	L23-M13
L6-M4	L6-M14	L6-M15	L6-M1	L12-M4	L12-M14	L12-M15	L12-M1	L17-M4	L17-M14	L17-M15	L17-M1	L10-M4	L10-M14	L10-M15	L10-M1	L20-M4	L20-M14	L20-M15	L20-M1
L6-M9	L6-M7	L6-M6	L6-M12	L12-M9	L12-M7	L12-M6	L12-M12	L17-M9	L17-M7	L17-M6	L17-M12	L10-M9	L10-M7	L10-M6	L10-M12	L20-M9	L20-M7	L20-M6	L20-M12
L6-M5	L6-M11	L6-M10	L6-M8	L12-M5	L12-M11	L12-M10	L12-M8	L17-M5	L17-M11	L17-M10	L17-M8	L10-M5	L10-M11	L10-M10	L10-M8	L20-M5	L20-M11	L20-M10	L20-M8
L6-M16	L6-M2	L6-M3	L6-M13	L12-M16	L12-M2	L12-M3	L12-M13	L17-M16	L17-M2	L17-M3	L17-M13	L10-M16	L10-M2	L10-M3	L10-M13	L20-M16	L20-M2	L20-M3	L20-M13
L25-M4	L25-M14	L25-M15	L25-M1	L11-M4	L11-M14	L11-M15	L11-M1	L13-M4	L13-M14	L13-M15	L13-M1	L15-M4	L15-M14	L15-M15	L15-M1	L1-M4	L1-M14	L1-M15	L1-M1
L25-M9	L25-M7	L25-M6	L25-M12	L11-M9	L11-M7	L11-M6	L11-M12	L13-M9	L13-M7	L13-M6	L13-M12	L15-M9	L15-M7	L15-M6	L15-M12	L1-M9	L1-M7	L1-M6	L1-M12
L25-M5	L25-M11	L25-M10	L25-M8	L11-M5	L11-M11	L11-M10	L11-M8	L13-M5	L13-M11	L13-M10	L13-M8	L15-M5	L15-M11	L15-M10	L15-M8	L1-M5	L1-M11	L1-M10	L1-M8
L25-M16	L25-M2	L25-M3	L25-M13	L11-M16	L11-M2	L11-M3	L11-M13	L13-M16	L13-M2	L13-M3	L13-M13	L15-M16	L15-M2	L15-M3	L15-M13	L1-M16	L1-M2	L1-M3	L1-M13
L24-M4	L24-M14	L24-M15	L24-M1	L16-M4	L16-M14	L16-M15	L16-M1	L9-M4	L9-M14	L9-M15	L9-M1	L14-M4	L14-M14	L14-M15	L14-M1	L2-M4	L2-M14	L2-M15	L2-M1
L24-M9	L24-M7	L24-M6	L24-M12	L16-M9	L16-M7	L16-M6	L16-M12	L9-M9	L9-M7	L9-M6	L9-M12	L14-M9	L14-M7	L14-M6	L14-M12	L2-M9	L2-M7	L2-M6	L2-M12
L24-M5	L24-M11	L24-M10	L24-M8	L16-M5	L16-M11	L16-M10	L16-M8	L9-M5	L9-M11	L9-M10	L9-M8	L14-M5	L14-M11	L14-M10	L14-M8	L2-M5	L2-M11	L2-M10	L2-M8
L24-M16	L24-M2	L24-M3	L24-M13	L16-M16	L16-M2	L16-M3	L16-M13	L9-M16	L9-M2	L9-M3	L9-M13	L14-M16	L14-M2	L14-M3	L14-M13	L2-M16	L2-M2	L2-M3	L2-M13
L3-M4	L3-M14	L3-M15	L3-M1	L4-M4	L4-M14	L4-M15	L4-M1	L21-M4	L21-M14	L21-M15	L21-M1	L18-M4	L18-M14	L18-M15	L18-M1	L19-M4	L19-M14	L19-M15	L19-M1
L3-M9	L3-M7	L3-M6	L3-M12	L4-M9	L4-M7	L4-M6	L4-M12	L21-M9	L21-M7	L21-M6	L21-M12	L18-M9	L18-M7	L18-M6	L18-M12	L19-M9	L19-M7	L19-M6	L19-M12
L3-M5	L3-M11	L3-M10	L3-M8	L4-M5	L4-M11	L4-M10	L4-M8	L21-M5	L21-M11	L21-M10	L21-M8	L18-M5	L18-M11	L18-M10	L18-M8	L19-M5	L19-M11	L19-M10	L19-M8
L3-M16	L3-M2	L3-M3	L3-M13	L4-M16	L4-M2	L4-M3	L4-M13	L21-M16	L21-M2	L21-M3	L21-M13	L18-M16	L18-M2	L18-M3	L18-M13	L19-M16	L19-M2	L19-M3	L19-M13

Like a jigsaw puzzle, all that is left is for you to insert each of the 5x5 squares into the cell that fits its label and you have your 100 x 100 magic square.

BIBLIOGRAPHY

al-Mandhri, Omar. <u>Kashef al-Asrar al-Makhfiah</u>. Beirut: Alaalami Library, 2003.

al-Karamani, Ahmed. <u>Rahat al-'qel.</u> Beirut: Dar Al-Andalus, 1983.

al-Toukhi, Abdu al-Fatah. <u>al-Bediah wa al-Nehayah</u>. Beirut: al-Maktabah al-Tahqafiah, 1980

al-Shadhli, Ibrahim. <u>Risalah bi al-Wafeq al-Ma'eeni</u>. Manuscript.

Munk, Michael Rabbi. <u>The Wisdom in the Hebrew Alphabet.</u> New York: Mesorah Publication, Ltd. 1983

Agrippa, Henry Corenlius. <u>Three Books of Occult Philosophy.</u> St. Paul, MI: Llewellyn Publications. 2000

Hall, Manly P. <u>The Secret Teachings of All Ages.</u> Los Angeles, CA: The Philosophical Research Society, Inc. 1988

Waterfield, Robin. <u>The Theology of Arithmetic.</u> Grand Rapids, MI: Phanes Press. 1988

NATURAL 100 x 100

L1-M1

7	22	5	8	23
6	12	17	10	20
25	11	13	15	1
24	16	9	14	2
3	4	21	18	19

L1-M2

32	47	30	33	48
31	37	42	35	45
50	36	38	40	26
49	41	34	39	27
28	29	46	43	44

L1-M3

57	72	55	58	73
56	62	67	60	70
75	61	63	65	51
74	66	59	64	52
53	54	71	68	69

L1-M4

82	97	80	83	98
81	87	92	85	95
100	86	88	90	76
99	91	84	89	77
78	79	96	93	94

L1-M5

107	122	105	108	123
106	112	117	110	120
125	111	113	115	101
124	116	109	114	102
103	104	121	118	119

L1-M6

132	147	130	133	148
131	137	142	135	145
150	136	138	140	126
149	141	134	139	127
128	129	146	143	144

L1-M7

157	172	155	158	173
156	162	167	160	170
175	161	163	165	151
174	166	159	164	152
153	154	171	168	169

L1-M8

182	197	180	183	198
181	187	192	185	195
200	186	188	190	176
199	191	184	189	177
178	179	196	193	194

L1-M9

207	222	205	208	223
206	212	217	210	220
225	211	213	215	201
224	216	209	214	202
203	204	221	218	219

L1-M10

232	247	230	233	248
231	237	242	235	245
250	236	238	240	226
249	241	234	239	227
228	229	246	243	244

L1-M11

257	272	255	258	273
256	262	267	260	270
275	261	263	265	251
274	266	259	264	252
253	254	271	268	269

L1-M12

282	297	280	283	298
281	287	292	285	295
300	286	288	290	276
299	291	284	289	277
278	279	296	293	294

L1-M13

307	322	305	308	323
306	312	317	310	320
325	311	313	315	301
324	316	309	314	302
303	304	321	318	319

L1-M14

332	347	330	333	348
331	337	342	335	345
350	336	338	340	326
349	341	334	339	327
328	329	346	343	344

L1-M15

357	372	355	358	373
356	362	367	360	370
375	361	363	365	351
374	366	359	364	352
353	354	371	368	369

L1-M16

382	397	380	383	398
381	387	392	385	395
400	386	388	390	376
399	391	384	389	377
378	379	396	393	394

L2-M1

407	422	405	408	423
406	412	417	410	420
425	411	413	415	401
424	416	409	414	402
403	404	421	418	419

L2-M2

432	447	430	433	448
431	437	442	435	445
450	436	438	440	426
449	441	434	439	427
428	429	446	443	444

L2-M3

457	472	455	458	473
456	462	467	460	470
475	461	463	465	451
474	466	459	464	452
453	454	471	468	469

L2-M4

482	497	480	483	498
481	487	492	485	495
500	486	488	490	476
499	491	484	489	477
478	479	496	493	494

L2-M5

507	522	505	508	523
506	512	517	510	520
525	511	513	515	501
524	516	509	514	502
503	504	521	518	519

L2-M6

532	547	530	533	548
531	537	542	535	545
550	536	538	540	526
549	541	534	539	527
528	529	546	543	544

L2-M7

557	572	555	558	573
556	562	567	560	570
575	561	563	565	551
574	566	559	564	552
553	554	571	568	569

L2-M8

582	597	580	583	598
581	587	592	585	595
600	586	588	590	576
599	591	584	589	577
578	579	596	593	594

L2-M9

607	622	605	608	623
606	612	617	610	620
625	611	613	615	601
624	616	609	614	602
603	604	621	618	619

L2-M10

632	647	630	633	648
631	637	642	635	645
650	636	638	640	626
649	641	634	639	627
628	629	646	643	644

L2-M11

657	672	655	658	673
656	662	667	660	670
675	661	663	665	651
674	666	659	664	652
653	654	671	668	669

L2-M12

682	697	680	683	698
681	687	692	685	695
700	686	688	690	676
699	691	684	689	677
678	679	696	693	694

L2-M13

707	722	705	708	723
706	712	717	710	720
725	711	713	715	701
724	716	709	714	702
703	704	721	718	719

L2-M14

732	747	730	733	748
731	737	742	735	745
750	736	738	740	726
749	741	734	739	727
728	729	746	743	744

L2-M15

757	772	755	758	773
756	762	767	760	770
775	761	763	765	751
774	766	759	764	752
753	754	771	768	769

L2-M16

782	797	780	783	798
781	787	792	785	795
800	786	788	790	776
799	791	784	789	777
778	779	796	793	794

L3-M1

807	822	805	808	823
806	812	817	810	820
825	811	813	815	801
824	816	809	814	802
803	804	821	818	819

L3-M2

832	847	830	833	848
831	837	842	835	845
850	836	838	840	826
849	841	834	839	827
828	829	846	843	844

L3-M3

857	872	855	858	873
856	862	867	860	870
875	861	863	865	851
874	866	859	864	852
853	854	871	868	869

L3-M4

882	897	880	883	898
881	887	892	885	895
900	886	888	890	876
899	891	884	889	877
878	879	896	893	894

L3-M5

907	922	905	908	923
906	912	917	910	920
925	911	913	915	901
924	916	909	914	902
903	904	921	918	919

L3-M6

932	947	930	933	948
931	937	942	935	945
950	936	938	940	926
949	941	934	939	927
928	929	946	943	944

L3-M7

957	972	955	958	973
956	962	967	960	970
975	961	963	965	951
974	966	959	964	952
953	954	971	968	969

L3-M8

982	997	980	983	998
981	987	992	985	995
1000	986	988	990	976
999	991	984	989	977
978	979	996	993	994

L3-M9

1007	1022	1005	1008	1023
1006	1012	1017	1010	1020
1025	1011	1013	1015	1001
1024	1016	1009	1014	1002
1003	1004	1021	1018	1019

L3-M10

1032	1047	1030	1033	1048
1031	1037	1042	1035	1045
1050	1036	1038	1040	1026
1049	1041	1034	1039	1027
1028	1029	1046	1043	1044

L3-M11

1057	1072	1055	1058	1073
1056	1062	1067	1060	1070
1075	1061	1063	1065	1051
1074	1066	1059	1064	1052
1053	1054	1071	1068	1069

L3-M12

1082	1097	1080	1083	1098
1081	1087	1092	1085	1095
1100	1086	1088	1090	1076
1099	1091	1084	1089	1077
1078	1079	1096	1093	1094

L3-M13

1107	1122	1105	1108	1123
1106	1112	1117	1110	1120
1125	1111	1113	1115	1101
1124	1116	1109	1114	1102
1103	1104	1121	1118	1119

L3-M14

1132	1147	1130	1133	1148
1131	1137	1142	1135	1145
1150	1136	1138	1140	1126
1149	1141	1134	1139	1127
1128	1129	1146	1143	1144

L3-M15

1157	1172	1155	1158	1173
1156	1162	1167	1160	1170
1175	1161	1163	1165	1151
1174	1166	1159	1164	1152
1153	1154	1171	1168	1169

L3-M16

1182	1197	1180	1183	1198
1181	1187	1192	1185	1195
1200	1186	1188	1190	1176
1199	1191	1184	1189	1177
1178	1179	1196	1193	1194

L4-M1

1207	1222	1205	1208	1223
1206	1212	1217	1210	1220
1225	1211	1213	1215	1201
1224	1216	1209	1214	1202
1203	1204	1221	1218	1219

L4-M2

1232	1247	1230	1233	1248
1231	1237	1242	1235	1245
1250	1236	1238	1240	1226
1249	1241	1234	1239	1227
1228	1229	1246	1243	1244

L4-M3

1257	1272	1255	1258	1273
1256	1262	1267	1260	1270
1275	1261	1263	1265	1251
1274	1266	1259	1264	1252
1253	1254	1271	1268	1269

L4-M4

1282	1297	1280	1283	1298
1281	1287	1292	1285	1295
1300	1286	1288	1290	1276
1299	1291	1284	1289	1277
1278	1279	1296	1293	1294

L4-M5

1307	1322	1305	1308	1323
1306	1312	1317	1310	1320
1325	1311	1313	1315	1301
1324	1316	1309	1314	1302
1303	1304	1321	1318	1319

L4-M6

1332	1347	1330	1333	1348
1331	1337	1342	1335	1345
1350	1336	1338	1340	1326
1349	1341	1334	1339	1327
1328	1329	1346	1343	1344

L4-M7

1357	1372	1355	1358	1373
1356	1362	1367	1360	1370
1375	1361	1363	1365	1351
1374	1366	1359	1364	1352
1353	1354	1371	1368	1369

L4-M8

1382	1397	1380	1383	1398
1381	1387	1392	1385	1395
1400	1386	1388	1390	1376
1399	1391	1384	1389	1377
1378	1379	1396	1393	1394

L4-M9

1407	1422	1405	1408	1423
1406	1412	1417	1410	1420
1425	1411	1413	1415	1401
1424	1416	1409	1414	1402
1403	1404	1421	1418	1419

L4-M10

1432	1447	1430	1433	1448
1431	1437	1442	1435	1445
1450	1436	1438	1440	1426
1449	1441	1434	1439	1427
1428	1429	1446	1443	1444

L4-M11

1457	1472	1455	1458	1473
1456	1462	1467	1460	1470
1475	1461	1463	1465	1451
1474	1466	1459	1464	1452
1453	1454	1471	1468	1469

L4-M12

1482	1497	1480	1483	1498
1481	1487	1492	1485	1495
1500	1486	1488	1490	1476
1499	1491	1484	1489	1477
1478	1479	1496	1493	1494

L4-M13

1507	1522	1505	1508	1523
1506	1512	1517	1510	1520
1525	1511	1513	1515	1501
1524	1516	1509	1514	1502
1503	1504	1521	1518	1519

L4-M14

1532	1547	1530	1533	1548
1531	1537	1542	1535	1545
1550	1536	1538	1540	1526
1549	1541	1534	1539	1527
1528	1529	1546	1543	1544

L4-M15

1557	1572	1555	1558	1573
1556	1562	1567	1560	1570
1575	1561	1563	1565	1551
1574	1566	1559	1564	1552
1553	1554	1571	1568	1569

L4-M16

1582	1597	1580	1583	1598
1581	1587	1592	1585	1595
1600	1586	1588	1590	1576
1599	1591	1584	1589	1577
1578	1579	1596	1593	1594

L5-M1

1607	1622	1605	1608	1623
1606	1612	1617	1610	1620
1625	1611	1613	1615	1601
1624	1616	1609	1614	1602
1603	1604	1621	1618	1619

L5-M2

1632	1647	1630	1633	1648
1631	1637	1642	1635	1645
1650	1636	1638	1640	1626
1649	1641	1634	1639	1627
1628	1629	1646	1643	1644

L5-M3

1657	1672	1655	1658	1673
1656	1662	1667	1660	1670
1675	1661	1663	1665	1651
1674	1666	1659	1664	1652
1653	1654	1671	1668	1669

L5-M4

1682	1697	1680	1683	1698
1681	1687	1692	1685	1695
1700	1686	1688	1690	1676
1699	1691	1684	1689	1677
1678	1679	1696	1693	1694

L5-M5

1707	1722	1705	1708	1723
1706	1712	1717	1710	1720
1725	1711	1713	1715	1701
1724	1716	1709	1714	1702
1703	1704	1721	1718	1719

L5-M6

1732	1747	1730	1733	1748
1731	1737	1742	1735	1745
1750	1736	1738	1740	1726
1749	1741	1734	1739	1727
1728	1729	1746	1743	1744

L5-M7

1757	1772	1755	1758	1773
1756	1762	1767	1760	1770
1775	1761	1763	1765	1751
1774	1766	1759	1764	1752
1753	1754	1771	1768	1769

L5-M8

1782	1797	1780	1783	1798
1781	1787	1792	1785	1795
1800	1786	1788	1790	1776
1799	1791	1784	1789	1777
1778	1779	1796	1793	1794

L5-M9

1807	1822	1805	1808	1823
1806	1812	1817	1810	1820
1825	1811	1813	1815	1801
1824	1816	1809	1814	1802
1803	1804	1821	1818	1819

L5-M10

1832	1847	1830	1833	1848
1831	1837	1842	1835	1845
1850	1836	1838	1840	1826
1849	1841	1834	1839	1827
1828	1829	1846	1843	1844

L5-M11

1857	1872	1855	1858	1873
1856	1862	1867	1860	1870
1875	1861	1863	1865	1851
1874	1866	1859	1864	1852
1853	1854	1871	1868	1869

L5-M12

1882	1897	1880	1883	1898
1881	1887	1892	1885	1895
1900	1886	1888	1890	1876
1899	1891	1884	1889	1877
1878	1879	1896	1893	1894

L5-M13

1907	1922	1905	1908	1923
1906	1912	1917	1910	1920
1925	1911	1913	1915	1901
1924	1916	1909	1914	1902
1903	1904	1921	1918	1919

L5-M14

1932	1947	1930	1933	1948
1931	1937	1942	1935	1945
1950	1936	1938	1940	1926
1949	1941	1934	1939	1927
1928	1929	1946	1943	1944

L5-M15

1957	1972	1955	1958	1973
1956	1962	1967	1960	1970
1975	1961	1963	1965	1951
1974	1966	1959	1964	1952
1953	1954	1971	1968	1969

L5-M16

1982	1997	1980	1983	1998
1981	1987	1992	1985	1995
2000	1986	1988	1990	1976
1999	1991	1984	1989	1977
1978	1979	1996	1993	1994

L6-M1

2007	2022	2005	2008	2023
2006	2012	2017	2010	2020
2025	2011	2013	2015	2001
2024	2016	2009	2014	2002
2003	2004	2021	2018	2019

L6-M2

2032	2047	2030	2033	2048
2031	2037	2042	2035	2045
2050	2036	2038	2040	2026
2049	2041	2034	2039	2027
2028	2029	2046	2043	2044

L6-M3

2057	2072	2055	2058	2073
2056	2062	2067	2060	2070
2075	2061	2063	2065	2051
2074	2066	2059	2064	2052
2053	2054	2071	2068	2069

L6-M4

2082	2097	2080	2083	2098
2081	2087	2092	2085	2095
2100	2086	2088	2090	2076
2099	2091	2084	2089	2077
2078	2079	2096	2093	2094

L6-M5

2107	2122	2105	2108	2123
2106	2112	2117	2110	2120
2125	2111	2113	2115	2101
2124	2116	2109	2114	2102
2103	2104	2121	2118	2119

L6-M6

2132	2147	2130	2133	2148
2131	2137	2142	2135	2145
2150	2136	2138	2140	2126
2149	2141	2134	2139	2127
2128	2129	2146	2143	2144

L6-M7

2157	2172	2155	2158	2173
2156	2162	2167	2160	2170
2175	2161	2163	2165	2151
2174	2166	2159	2164	2152
2153	2154	2171	2168	2169

L6-M8

2182	2197	2180	2183	2198
2181	2187	2192	2185	2195
2200	2186	2188	2190	2176
2199	2191	2184	2189	2177
2178	2179	2196	2193	2194

L6-M9

2207	2222	2205	2208	2223
2206	2212	2217	2210	2220
2225	2211	2213	2215	2201
2224	2216	2209	2214	2202
2203	2204	2221	2218	2219

L6-M10

2232	2247	2230	2233	2248
2231	2237	2242	2235	2245
2250	2236	2238	2240	2226
2249	2241	2234	2239	2227
2228	2229	2246	2243	2244

L6-M11

2257	2272	2255	2258	2273
2256	2262	2267	2260	2270
2275	2261	2263	2265	2251
2274	2266	2259	2264	2252
2253	2254	2271	2268	2269

L6-M12

2282	2297	2280	2283	2298
2281	2287	2292	2285	2295
2300	2286	2288	2290	2276
2299	2291	2284	2289	2277
2278	2279	2296	2293	2294

L6-M13

2307	2322	2305	2308	2323
2306	2312	2317	2310	2320
2325	2311	2313	2315	2301
2324	2316	2309	2314	2302
2303	2304	2321	2318	2319

L6-M14

2332	2347	2330	2333	2348
2331	2337	2342	2335	2345
2350	2336	2338	2340	2326
2349	2341	2334	2339	2327
2328	2329	2346	2343	2344

L6-M15

2357	2372	2355	2358	2373
2356	2362	2367	2360	2370
2375	2361	2363	2365	2351
2374	2366	2359	2364	2352
2353	2354	2371	2368	2369

L6-M16

2382	2397	2380	2383	2398
2381	2387	2392	2385	2395
2400	2386	2388	2390	2376
2399	2391	2384	2389	2377
2378	2379	2396	2393	2394

L7-M1

2407	2422	2405	2408	2423
2406	2412	2417	2410	2420
2425	2411	2413	2415	2401
2424	2416	2409	2414	2402
2403	2404	2421	2418	2419

L7-M2

2432	2447	2430	2433	2448
2431	2437	2442	2435	2445
2450	2436	2438	2440	2426
2449	2441	2434	2439	2427
2428	2429	2446	2443	2444

L7-M3

2457	2472	2455	2458	2473
2456	2462	2467	2460	2470
2475	2461	2463	2465	2451
2474	2466	2459	2464	2452
2453	2454	2471	2468	2469

L7-M4

2482	2497	2480	2483	2498
2481	2487	2492	2485	2495
2500	2486	2488	2490	2476
2499	2491	2484	2489	2477
2478	2479	2496	2493	2494

L7-M5

2507	2522	2505	2508	2523
2506	2512	2517	2510	2520
2525	2511	2513	2515	2501
2524	2516	2509	2514	2502
2503	2504	2521	2518	2519

L7-M6

2532	2547	2530	2533	2548
2531	2537	2542	2535	2545
2550	2536	2538	2540	2526
2549	2541	2534	2539	2527
2528	2529	2546	2543	2544

L7-M7

2557	2572	2555	2558	2573
2556	2562	2567	2560	2570
2575	2561	2563	2565	2551
2574	2566	2559	2564	2552
2553	2554	2571	2568	2569

L7-M8

2582	2597	2580	2583	2598
2581	2587	2592	2585	2595
2600	2586	2588	2590	2576
2599	2591	2584	2589	2577
2578	2579	2596	2593	2594

L7-M9

2607	2622	2605	2608	2623
2606	2612	2617	2610	2620
2625	2611	2613	2615	2601
2624	2616	2609	2614	2602
2603	2604	2621	2618	2619

L7-M10

2632	2647	2630	2633	2648
2631	2637	2642	2635	2645
2650	2636	2638	2640	2626
2649	2641	2634	2639	2627
2628	2629	2646	2643	2644

L7-M11

2657	2672	2655	2658	2673
2656	2662	2667	2660	2670
2675	2661	2663	2665	2651
2674	2666	2659	2664	2652
2653	2654	2671	2668	2669

L7-M12

2682	2697	2680	2683	2698
2681	2687	2692	2685	2695
2700	2686	2688	2690	2676
2699	2691	2684	2689	2677
2678	2679	2696	2693	2694

L7-M13

2707	2722	2705	2708	2723
2706	2712	2717	2710	2720
2725	2711	2713	2715	2701
2724	2716	2709	2714	2702
2703	2704	2721	2718	2719

L7-M14

2732	2747	2730	2733	2748
2731	2737	2742	2735	2745
2750	2736	2738	2740	2726
2749	2741	2734	2739	2727
2728	2729	2746	2743	2744

L7-M15

2757	2772	2755	2758	2773
2756	2762	2767	2760	2770
2775	2761	2763	2765	2751
2774	2766	2759	2764	2752
2753	2754	2771	2768	2769

L7-M16

2782	2797	2780	2783	2798
2781	2787	2792	2785	2795
2800	2786	2788	2790	2776
2799	2791	2784	2789	2777
2778	2779	2796	2793	2794

L8M1

2807	2822	2805	2808	2823
2806	2812	2817	2810	2820
2825	2811	2813	2815	2801
2824	2816	2809	2814	2802
2803	2804	2821	2818	2819

L8-M2

2832	2847	2830	2833	2848
2831	2837	2842	2835	2845
2850	2836	2838	2840	2826
2849	2841	2834	2839	2827
2828	2829	2846	2843	2844

L8-M3

2857	2872	2855	2858	2873
2856	2862	2867	2860	2870
2875	2861	2863	2865	2851
2874	2866	2859	2864	2852
2853	2854	2871	2868	2869

L8-M4

2882	2897	2880	2883	2898
2881	2887	2892	2885	2895
2900	2886	2888	2890	2876
2899	2891	2884	2889	2877
2878	2879	2896	2893	2894

L8-M5

2907	2922	2905	2908	2923
2906	2912	2917	2910	2920
2925	2911	2913	2915	2901
2924	2916	2909	2914	2902
2903	2904	2921	2918	2919

L8-M6

2932	2947	2930	2933	2948
2931	2937	2942	2935	2945
2950	2936	2938	2940	2926
2949	2941	2934	2939	2927
2928	2929	2946	2943	2944

L8-M7

2957	2972	2955	2958	2973
2956	2962	2967	2960	2970
2975	2961	2963	2965	2951
2974	2966	2959	2964	2952
2953	2954	2971	2968	2969

L8-M8

2982	2997	2980	2983	2998
2981	2987	2992	2985	2995
3000	2986	2988	2990	2976
2999	2991	2984	2989	2977
2978	2979	2996	2993	2994

L8-M9

3007	3022	3005	3008	3023
3006	3012	3017	3010	3020
3025	3011	3013	3015	3001
3024	3016	3009	3014	3002
3003	3004	3021	3018	3019

L8-M10

3032	3047	3030	3033	3048
3031	3037	3042	3035	3045
3050	3036	3038	3040	3026
3049	3041	3034	3039	3027
3028	3029	3046	3043	3044

L8-M11

3057	3072	3055	3058	3073
3056	3062	3067	3060	3070
3075	3061	3063	3065	3051
3074	3066	3059	3064	3052
3053	3054	3071	3068	3069

L8-M12

3082	3097	3080	3083	3098
3081	3087	3092	3085	3095
3100	3086	3088	3090	3076
3099	3091	3084	3089	3077
3078	3079	3096	3093	3094

L8-M13

3107	3122	3105	3108	3123
3106	3112	3117	3110	3120
3125	3111	3113	3115	3101
3124	3116	3109	3114	3102
3103	3104	3121	3118	3119

L8-M14

3132	3147	3130	3133	3148
3131	3137	3142	3135	3145
3150	3136	3138	3140	3126
3149	3141	3134	3139	3127
3128	3129	3146	3143	3144

L8-M15

3157	3172	3155	3158	3173
3156	3162	3167	3160	3170
3175	3161	3163	3165	3151
3174	3166	3159	3164	3152
3153	3154	3171	3168	3169

L8-M16

3182	3197	3180	3183	3198
3181	3187	3192	3185	3195
3200	3186	3188	3190	3176
3199	3191	3184	3189	3177
3178	3179	3196	3193	3194

L9-M1

3207	3222	3205	3208	3223
3206	3212	3217	3210	3220
3225	3211	3213	3215	3201
3224	3216	3209	3214	3202
3203	3204	3221	3218	3219

L9-M2

3232	3247	3230	3233	3248
3231	3237	3242	3235	3245
3250	3236	3238	3240	3226
3249	3241	3234	3239	3227
3228	3229	3246	3243	3244

L9-M3

3257	3272	3255	3258	3273
3256	3262	3267	3260	3270
3275	3261	3263	3265	3251
3274	3266	3259	3264	3252
3253	3254	3271	3268	3269

L9-M4

3282	3297	3280	3283	3298
3281	3287	3292	3285	3295
3300	3286	3288	3290	3276
3299	3291	3284	3289	3277
3278	3279	3296	3293	3294

L9-M5

3307	3322	3305	3308	3323
3306	3312	3317	3310	3320
3325	3311	3313	3315	3301
3324	3316	3309	3314	3302
3303	3304	3321	3318	3319

L9-M6

3332	3347	3330	3333	3348
3331	3337	3342	3335	3345
3350	3336	3338	3340	3326
3349	3341	3334	3339	3327
3328	3329	3346	3343	3344

L9-M7

3357	3372	3355	3358	3373
3356	3362	3367	3360	3370
3375	3361	3363	3365	3351
3374	3366	3359	3364	3352
3353	3354	3371	3368	3369

L9-M8

3382	3397	3380	3383	3398
3381	3387	3392	3385	3395
3400	3386	3388	3390	3376
3399	3391	3384	3389	3377
3378	3379	3396	3393	3394

L9-M9

3407	3422	3405	3408	3423
3406	3412	3417	3410	3420
3425	3411	3413	3415	3401
3424	3416	3409	3414	3402
3403	3404	3421	3418	3419

L9-M10

3432	3447	3430	3433	3448
3431	3437	3442	3435	3445
3450	3436	3438	3440	3426
3449	3441	3434	3439	3427
3428	3429	3446	3443	3444

L9-M11

3457	3472	3455	3458	3473
3456	3462	3467	3460	3470
3475	3461	3463	3465	3451
3474	3466	3459	3464	3452
3453	3454	3471	3468	3469

L9-M12

3482	3497	3480	3483	3498
3481	3487	3492	3485	3495
3500	3486	3488	3490	3476
3499	3491	3484	3489	3477
3478	3479	3496	3493	3494

L9-M13

3507	3522	3505	3508	3523
3506	3512	3517	3510	3520
3525	3511	3513	3515	3501
3524	3516	3509	3514	3502
3503	3504	3521	3518	3519

L9-M14

3532	3547	3530	3533	3548
3531	3537	3542	3535	3545
3550	3536	3538	3540	3526
3549	3541	3534	3539	3527
3528	3529	3546	3543	3544

L9-M15

3557	3572	3555	3558	3573
3556	3562	3567	3560	3570
3575	3561	3563	3565	3551
3574	3566	3559	3564	3552
3553	3554	3571	3568	3569

L9-M16

3582	3597	3580	3583	3598
3581	3587	3592	3585	3595
3600	3586	3588	3590	3576
3599	3591	3584	3589	3577
3578	3579	3596	3593	3594

L10-M1

3607	3622	3605	3608	3623
3606	3612	3617	3610	3620
3625	3611	3613	3615	3601
3624	3616	3609	3614	3602
3603	3604	3621	3618	3619

L10-M2

3632	3647	3630	3633	3648
3631	3637	3642	3635	3645
3650	3636	3638	3640	3626
3649	3641	3634	3639	3627
3628	3629	3646	3643	3644

L10-M3

3657	3672	3655	3658	3673
3656	3662	3667	3660	3670
3675	3661	3663	3665	3651
3674	3666	3659	3664	3652
3653	3654	3671	3668	3669

L10-M4

3682	3697	3680	3683	3698
3681	3687	3692	3685	3695
3700	3686	3688	3690	3676
3699	3691	3684	3689	3677
3678	3679	3696	3693	3694

L10-M5

3707	3722	3705	3708	3723
3706	3712	3717	3710	3720
3725	3711	3713	3715	3701
3724	3716	3709	3714	3702
3703	3704	3721	3718	3719

L10-M6

3732	3747	3730	3733	3748
3731	3737	3742	3735	3745
3750	3736	3738	3740	3726
3749	3741	3734	3739	3727
3728	3729	3746	3743	3744

L10-M7

3757	3772	3755	3758	3773
3756	3762	3767	3760	3770
3775	3761	3763	3765	3751
3774	3766	3759	3764	3752
3753	3754	3771	3768	3769

L10-M8

3782	3797	3780	3783	3798
3781	3787	3792	3785	3795
3800	3786	3788	3790	3776
3799	3791	3784	3789	3777
3778	3779	3796	3793	3794

L10-M9

3807	3822	3805	3808	3823
3806	3812	3817	3810	3820
3825	3811	3813	3815	3801
3824	3816	3809	3814	3802
3803	3804	3821	3818	3819

L10-M10

3832	3847	3830	3833	3848
3831	3837	3842	3835	3845
3850	3836	3838	3840	3826
3849	3841	3834	3839	3827
3828	3829	3846	3843	3844

L10-M11

3857	3872	3855	3858	3873
3856	3862	3867	3860	3870
3875	3861	3863	3865	3851
3874	3866	3859	3864	3852
3853	3854	3871	3868	3869

L10-M12

3882	3897	3880	3883	3898
3881	3887	3892	3885	3895
3900	3886	3888	3890	3876
3899	3891	3884	3889	3877
3878	3879	3896	3893	3894

L10-M13

3907	3922	3905	3908	3923
3906	3912	3917	3910	3920
3925	3911	3913	3915	3901
3924	3916	3909	3914	3902
3903	3904	3921	3918	3919

L10-M14

3932	3947	3930	3933	3948
3931	3937	3942	3935	3945
3950	3936	3938	3940	3926
3949	3941	3934	3939	3927
3928	3929	3946	3943	3944

L10-M15

3957	3972	3955	3958	3973
3956	3962	3967	3960	3970
3975	3961	3963	3965	3951
3974	3966	3959	3964	3952
3953	3954	3971	3968	3969

L10-M16

3982	3997	3980	3983	3998
3981	3987	3992	3985	3995
4000	3986	3988	3990	3976
3999	3991	3984	3989	3977
3978	3979	3996	3993	3994

L11-M1

4007	4022	4005	4008	4023
4006	4012	4017	4010	4020
4025	4011	4013	4015	4001
4024	4016	4009	4014	4002
4003	4004	4021	4018	4019

L11-M2

4032	4047	4030	4033	4048
4031	4037	4042	4035	4045
4050	4036	4038	4040	4026
4049	4041	4034	4039	4027
4028	4029	4046	4043	4044

L11-M3

4057	4072	4055	4058	4073
4056	4062	4067	4060	4070
4075	4061	4063	4065	4051
4074	4066	4059	4064	4052
4053	4054	4071	4068	4069

L11-M4

4082	4097	4080	4083	4098
4081	4087	4092	4085	4095
4100	4086	4088	4090	4076
4099	4091	4084	4089	4077
4078	4079	4096	4093	4094

L11-M5

4107	4122	4105	4108	4123
4106	4112	4117	4110	4120
4125	4111	4113	4115	4101
4124	4116	4109	4114	4102
4103	4104	4121	4118	4119

L11-M6

4132	4147	4130	4133	4148
4131	4137	4142	4135	4145
4150	4136	4138	4140	4126
4149	4141	4134	4139	4127
4128	4129	4146	4143	4144

L11-M7

4157	4172	4155	4158	4173
4156	4162	4167	4160	4170
4175	4161	4163	4165	4151
4174	4166	4159	4164	4152
4153	4154	4171	4168	4169

L11-M8

4182	4197	4180	4183	4198
4181	4187	4192	4185	4195
4200	4186	4188	4190	4176
4199	4191	4184	4189	4177
4178	4179	4196	4193	4194

L11-M9

4207	4222	4205	4208	4223
4206	4212	4217	4210	4220
4225	4211	4213	4215	4201
4224	4216	4209	4214	4202
4203	4204	4221	4218	4219

L11-M10

4232	4247	4230	4233	4248
4231	4237	4242	4235	4245
4250	4236	4238	4240	4226
4249	4241	4234	4239	4227
4228	4229	4246	4243	4244

L11-M11

4257	4272	4255	4258	4273
4256	4262	4267	4260	4270
4275	4261	4263	4265	4251
4274	4266	4259	4264	4252
4253	4254	4271	4268	4269

L11-M12

4282	4297	4280	4283	4298
4281	4287	4292	4285	4295
4300	4286	4288	4290	4276
4299	4291	4284	4289	4277
4278	4279	4296	4293	4294

L11-M13

4307	4322	4305	4308	4323
4306	4312	4317	4310	4320
4325	4311	4313	4315	4301
4324	4316	4309	4314	4302
4303	4304	4321	4318	4319

L11-M14

4332	4347	4330	4333	4348
4331	4337	4342	4335	4345
4350	4336	4338	4340	4326
4349	4341	4334	4339	4327
4328	4329	4346	4343	4344

L11-M15

4357	4372	4355	4358	4373
4356	4362	4367	4360	4370
4375	4361	4363	4365	4351
4374	4366	4359	4364	4352
4353	4354	4371	4368	4369

L11-M16

4382	4397	4380	4383	4398
4381	4387	4392	4385	4395
4400	4386	4388	4390	4376
4399	4391	4384	4389	4377
4378	4379	4396	4393	4394

L12-M1

4407	4422	4405	4408	4423
4406	4412	4417	4410	4420
4425	4411	4413	4415	4401
4424	4416	4409	4414	4402
4403	4404	4421	4418	4419

L12-M2

4432	4447	4430	4433	4448
4431	4437	4442	4435	4445
4450	4436	4438	4440	4426
4449	4441	4434	4439	4427
4428	4429	4446	4443	4444

L12-M3

4457	4472	4455	4458	4473
4456	4462	4467	4460	4470
4475	4461	4463	4465	4451
4474	4466	4459	4464	4452
4453	4454	4471	4468	4469

L12-M4

4482	4497	4480	4483	4498
4481	4487	4492	4485	4495
4500	4486	4488	4490	4476
4499	4491	4484	4489	4477
4478	4479	4496	4493	4494

L12-M5

4507	4522	4505	4508	4523
4506	4512	4517	4510	4520
4525	4511	4513	4515	4501
4524	4516	4509	4514	4502
4503	4504	4521	4518	4519

L12-M6

4532	4547	4530	4533	4548
4531	4537	4542	4535	4545
4550	4536	4538	4540	4526
4549	4541	4534	4539	4527
4528	4529	4546	4543	4544

L12-M7

4557	4572	4555	4558	4573
4556	4562	4567	4560	4570
4575	4561	4563	4565	4551
4574	4566	4559	4564	4552
4553	4554	4571	4568	4569

L12-M8

4582	4597	4580	4583	4598
4581	4587	4592	4585	4595
4600	4586	4588	4590	4576
4599	4591	4584	4589	4577
4578	4579	4596	4593	4594

L12-M9

4607	4622	4605	4608	4623
4606	4612	4617	4610	4620
4625	4611	4613	4615	4601
4624	4616	4609	4614	4602
4603	4604	4621	4618	4619

L12-M10

4632	4647	4630	4633	4648
4631	4637	4642	4635	4645
4650	4636	4638	4640	4626
4649	4641	4634	4639	4627
4628	4629	4646	4643	4644

L12-M11

4657	4672	4655	4658	4673
4656	4662	4667	4660	4670
4675	4661	4663	4665	4651
4674	4666	4659	4664	4652
4653	4654	4671	4668	4669

L12-M12

4682	4697	4680	4683	4698
4681	4687	4692	4685	4695
4700	4686	4688	4690	4676
4699	4691	4684	4689	4677
4678	4679	4696	4693	4694

L12-M13

4707	4722	4705	4708	4723
4706	4712	4717	4710	4720
4725	4711	4713	4715	4701
4724	4716	4709	4714	4702
4703	4704	4721	4718	4719

L12-M14

4732	4747	4730	4733	4748
4731	4737	4742	4735	4745
4750	4736	4738	4740	4726
4749	4741	4734	4739	4727
4728	4729	4746	4743	4744

L12-M15

4757	4772	4755	4758	4773
4756	4762	4767	4760	4770
4775	4761	4763	4765	4751
4774	4766	4759	4764	4752
4753	4754	4771	4768	4769

L12-M16

4782	4797	4780	4783	4798
4781	4787	4792	4785	4795
4800	4786	4788	4790	4776
4799	4791	4784	4789	4777
4778	4779	4796	4793	4794

L13-M1

4807	4822	4805	4808	4823
4806	4812	4817	4810	4820
4825	4811	4813	4815	4801
4824	4816	4809	4814	4802
4803	4804	4821	4818	4819

L13-M2

4832	4847	4830	4833	4848
4831	4837	4842	4835	4845
4850	4836	4838	4840	4826
4849	4841	4834	4839	4827
4828	4829	4846	4843	4844

L13-M3

4857	4872	4855	4858	4873
4856	4862	4867	4860	4870
4875	4861	4863	4865	4851
4874	4866	4859	4864	4852
4853	4854	4871	4868	4869

L13-M4

4882	4897	4880	4883	4898
4881	4887	4892	4885	4895
4900	4886	4888	4890	4876
4899	4891	4884	4889	4877
4878	4879	4896	4893	4894

L13-M5

4907	4922	4905	4908	4923
4906	4912	4917	4910	4920
4925	4911	4913	4915	4901
4924	4916	4909	4914	4902
4903	4904	4921	4918	4919

L13-M6

4932	4947	4930	4933	4948
4931	4937	4942	4935	4945
4950	4936	4938	4940	4926
4949	4941	4934	4939	4927
4928	4929	4946	4943	4944

L13-M7

4957	4972	4955	4958	4973
4956	4962	4967	4960	4970
4975	4961	4963	4965	4951
4974	4966	4959	4964	4952
4953	4954	4971	4968	4969

L13-M8

4982	4997	4980	4983	4998
4981	4987	4992	4985	4995
5000	4986	4988	4990	4976
4999	4991	4984	4989	4977
4978	4979	4996	4993	4994

L13-M9

5007	5022	5005	5008	5023
5006	5012	5017	5010	5020
5025	5011	5013	5015	5001
5024	5016	5009	5014	5002
5003	5004	5021	5018	5019

L13-M10

5032	5047	5030	5033	5048
5031	5037	5042	5035	5045
5050	5036	5038	5040	5026
5049	5041	5034	5039	5027
5028	5029	5046	5043	5044

L13-M11

5057	5072	5055	5058	5073
5056	5062	5067	5060	5070
5075	5061	5063	5065	5051
5074	5066	5059	5064	5052
5053	5054	5071	5068	5069

L13-M12

5082	5097	5080	5083	5098
5081	5087	5092	5085	5095
5100	5086	5088	5090	5076
5099	5091	5084	5089	5077
5078	5079	5096	5093	5094

L13-M13

5107	5122	5105	5108	5123
5106	5112	5117	5110	5120
5125	5111	5113	5115	5101
5124	5116	5109	5114	5102
5103	5104	5121	5118	5119

L13-M14

5132	5147	5130	5133	5148
5131	5137	5142	5135	5145
5150	5136	5138	5140	5126
5149	5141	5134	5139	5127
5128	5129	5146	5143	5144

L13-M15

5157	5172	5155	5158	5173
5156	5162	5167	5160	5170
5175	5161	5163	5165	5151
5174	5166	5159	5164	5152
5153	5154	5171	5168	5169

L13-M16

5182	5197	5180	5183	5198
5181	5187	5192	5185	5195
5200	5186	5188	5190	5176
5199	5191	5184	5189	5177
5178	5179	5196	5193	5194

L14-M1

5207	5222	5205	5208	5223
5206	5212	5217	5210	5220
5225	5211	5213	5215	5201
5224	5216	5209	5214	5202
5203	5204	5221	5218	5219

L14-M2

5232	5247	5230	5233	5248
5231	5237	5242	5235	5245
5250	5236	5238	5240	5226
5249	5241	5234	5239	5227
5228	5229	5246	5243	5244

L14-M3

5257	5272	5255	5258	5273
5256	5262	5267	5260	5270
5275	5261	5263	5265	5251
5274	5266	5259	5264	5252
5253	5254	5271	5268	5269

L14-M4

5282	5297	5280	5283	5298
5281	5287	5292	5285	5295
5300	5286	5288	5290	5276
5299	5291	5284	5289	5277
5278	5279	5296	5293	5294

L14-M5

5307	5322	5305	5308	5323
5306	5312	5317	5310	5320
5325	5311	5313	5315	5301
5324	5316	5309	5314	5302
5303	5304	5321	5318	5319

L14-M6

5332	5347	5330	5333	5348
5331	5337	5342	5335	5345
5350	5336	5338	5340	5326
5349	5341	5334	5339	5327
5328	5329	5346	5343	5344

L14-M7

5357	5372	5355	5358	5373
5356	5362	5367	5360	5370
5375	5361	5363	5365	5351
5374	5366	5359	5364	5352
5353	5354	5371	5368	5369

L14-M8

5382	5397	5380	5383	5398
5381	5387	5392	5385	5395
5400	5386	5388	5390	5376
5399	5391	5384	5389	5377
5378	5379	5396	5393	5394

L14-M9

5407	5422	5405	5408	5423
5406	5412	5417	5410	5420
5425	5411	5413	5415	5401
5424	5416	5409	5414	5402
5403	5404	5421	5418	5419

L14-M10

5432	5447	5430	5433	5448
5431	5437	5442	5435	5445
5450	5436	5438	5440	5426
5449	5441	5434	5439	5427
5428	5429	5446	5443	5444

L14-M11

5457	5472	5455	5458	5473
5456	5462	5467	5460	5470
5475	5461	5463	5465	5451
5474	5466	5459	5464	5452
5453	5454	5471	5468	5469

L14-M12

5482	5497	5480	5483	5498
5481	5487	5492	5485	5495
5500	5486	5488	5490	5476
5499	5491	5484	5489	5477
5478	5479	5496	5493	5494

L14-M13

5507	5522	5505	5508	5523
5506	5512	5517	5510	5520
5525	5511	5513	5515	5501
5524	5516	5509	5514	5502
5503	5504	5521	5518	5519

L14-M14

5532	5547	5530	5533	5548
5531	5537	5542	5535	5545
5550	5536	5538	5540	5526
5549	5541	5534	5539	5527
5528	5529	5546	5543	5544

L14-M15

5557	5572	5555	5558	5573
5556	5562	5567	5560	5570
5575	5561	5563	5565	5551
5574	5566	5559	5564	5552
5553	5554	5571	5568	5569

L14-M16

5582	5597	5580	5583	5598
5581	5587	5592	5585	5595
5600	5586	5588	5590	5576
5599	5591	5584	5589	5577
5578	5579	5596	5593	5594

L15-M1

5607	5622	5605	5608	5623
5606	5612	5617	5610	5620
5625	5611	5613	5615	5601
5624	5616	5609	5614	5602
5603	5604	5621	5618	5619

L15-M2

5632	5647	5630	5633	5648
5631	5637	5642	5635	5645
5650	5636	5638	5640	5626
5649	5641	5634	5639	5627
5628	5629	5646	5643	5644

L15-M3

5657	5672	5655	5658	5673
5656	5662	5667	5660	5670
5675	5661	5663	5665	5651
5674	5666	5659	5664	5652
5653	5654	5671	5668	5669

L15-M4

5682	5697	5680	5683	5698
5681	5687	5692	5685	5695
5700	5686	5688	5690	5676
5699	5691	5684	5689	5677
5678	5679	5696	5693	5694

L15-M5

5707	5722	5705	5708	5723
5706	5712	5717	5710	5720
5725	5711	5713	5715	5701
5724	5716	5709	5714	5702
5703	5704	5721	5718	5719

L15-M6

5732	5747	5730	5733	5748
5731	5737	5742	5735	5745
5750	5736	5738	5740	5726
5749	5741	5734	5739	5727
5728	5729	5746	5743	5744

L15-M7

5757	5772	5755	5758	5773
5756	5762	5767	5760	5770
5775	5761	5763	5765	5751
5774	5766	5759	5764	5752
5753	5754	5771	5768	5769

L15-M8

5782	5797	5780	5783	5798
5781	5787	5792	5785	5795
5800	5786	5788	5790	5776
5799	5791	5784	5789	5777
5778	5779	5796	5793	5794

L15-M9

5807	5822	5805	5808	5823
5806	5812	5817	5810	5820
5825	5811	5813	5815	5801
5824	5816	5809	5814	5802
5803	5804	5821	5818	5819

L15-M10

5832	5847	5830	5833	5848
5831	5837	5842	5835	5845
5850	5836	5838	5840	5826
5849	5841	5834	5839	5827
5828	5829	5846	5843	5844

L15-M11

5857	5872	5855	5858	5873
5856	5862	5867	5860	5870
5875	5861	5863	5865	5851
5874	5866	5859	5864	5852
5853	5854	5871	5868	5869

L15-M12

5882	5897	5880	5883	5898
5881	5887	5892	5885	5895
5900	5886	5888	5890	5876
5899	5891	5884	5889	5877
5878	5879	5896	5893	5894

L15-M13

5907	5922	5905	5908	5923
5906	5912	5917	5910	5920
5925	5911	5913	5915	5901
5924	5916	5909	5914	5902
5903	5904	5921	5918	5919

L15-M14

5932	5947	5930	5933	5948
5931	5937	5942	5935	5945
5950	5936	5938	5940	5926
5949	5941	5934	5939	5927
5928	5929	5946	5943	5944

L15-M15

5957	5972	5955	5958	5973
5956	5962	5967	5960	5970
5975	5961	5963	5965	5951
5974	5966	5959	5964	5952
5953	5954	5971	5968	5969

L15-M16

5982	5997	5980	5983	5998
5981	5987	5992	5985	5995
6000	5986	5988	5990	5976
5999	5991	5984	5989	5977
5978	5979	5996	5993	5994

L16-M1

6007	6022	6005	6008	6023
6006	6012	6017	6010	6020
6025	6011	6013	6015	6001
6024	6016	6009	6014	6002
6003	6004	6021	6018	6019

L16-M2

6032	6047	6030	6033	6048
6031	6037	6042	6035	6045
6050	6036	6038	6040	6026
6049	6041	6034	6039	6027
6028	6029	6046	6043	6044

L16-M3

6057	6072	6055	6058	6073
6056	6062	6067	6060	6070
6075	6061	6063	6065	6051
6074	6066	6059	6064	6052
6053	6054	6071	6068	6069

L16-M4

6082	6097	6080	6083	6098
6081	6087	6092	6085	6095
6100	6086	6088	6090	6076
6099	6091	6084	6089	6077
6078	6079	6096	6093	6094

L16-M5

6107	6122	6105	6108	6123
6106	6112	6117	6110	6120
6125	6111	6113	6115	6101
6124	6116	6109	6114	6102
6103	6104	6121	6118	6119

L16-M6

6132	6147	6130	6133	6148
6131	6137	6142	6135	6145
6150	6136	6138	6140	6126
6149	6141	6134	6139	6127
6128	6129	6146	6143	6144

L16-M7

6157	6172	6155	6158	6173
6156	6162	6167	6160	6170
6175	6161	6163	6165	6151
6174	6166	6159	6164	6152
6153	6154	6171	6168	6169

L16-M8

6182	6197	6180	6183	6198
6181	6187	6192	6185	6195
6200	6186	6188	6190	6176
6199	6191	6184	6189	6177
6178	6179	6196	6193	6194

L16-M9

6207	6222	6205	6208	6223
6206	6212	6217	6210	6220
6225	6211	6213	6215	6201
6224	6216	6209	6214	6202
6203	6204	6221	6218	6219

L16-M10

6232	6247	6230	6233	6248
6231	6237	6242	6235	6245
6250	6236	6238	6240	6226
6249	6241	6234	6239	6227
6228	6229	6246	6243	6244

L16-M11

6257	6272	6255	6258	6273
6256	6262	6267	6260	6270
6275	6261	6263	6265	6251
6274	6266	6259	6264	6252
6253	6254	6271	6268	6269

L16-M12

6282	6297	6280	6283	6298
6281	6287	6292	6285	6295
6300	6286	6288	6290	6276
6299	6291	6284	6289	6277
6278	6279	6296	6293	6294

L16-M13

6307	6322	6305	6308	6323
6306	6312	6317	6310	6320
6325	6311	6313	6315	6301
6324	6316	6309	6314	6302
6303	6304	6321	6318	6319

L16-M14

6332	6347	6330	6333	6348
6331	6337	6342	6335	6345
6350	6336	6338	6340	6326
6349	6341	6334	6339	6327
6328	6329	6346	6343	6344

L16-M15

6357	6372	6355	6358	6373
6356	6362	6367	6360	6370
6375	6361	6363	6365	6351
6374	6366	6359	6364	6352
6353	6354	6371	6368	6369

L16M16

6382	6397	6380	6383	6398
6381	6387	6392	6385	6395
6400	6386	6388	6390	6376
6399	6391	6384	6389	6377
6378	6379	6396	6393	6394

L17-M1

6407	6422	6405	6408	6423
6406	6412	6417	6410	6420
6425	6411	6413	6415	6401
6424	6416	6409	6414	6402
6403	6404	6421	6418	6419

L17-M2

6432	6447	6430	6433	6448
6431	6437	6442	6435	6445
6450	6436	6438	6440	6426
6449	6441	6434	6439	6427
6428	6429	6446	6443	6444

L17-M3

6457	6472	6455	6458	6473
6456	6462	6467	6460	6470
6475	6461	6463	6465	6451
6474	6466	6459	6464	6452
6453	6454	6471	6468	6469

L17-M4

6482	6497	6480	6483	6498
6481	6487	6492	6485	6495
6500	6486	6488	6490	6476
6499	6491	6484	6489	6477
6478	6479	6496	6493	6494

L17-M5

6507	6522	6505	6508	6523
6506	6512	6517	6510	6520
6525	6511	6513	6515	6501
6524	6516	6509	6514	6502
6503	6504	6521	6518	6519

L17-M6

6532	6547	6530	6533	6548
6531	6537	6542	6535	6545
6550	6536	6538	6540	6526
6549	6541	6534	6539	6527
6528	6529	6546	6543	6544

L17-M7

6557	6572	6555	6558	6573
6556	6562	6567	6560	6570
6575	6561	6563	6565	6551
6574	6566	6559	6564	6552
6553	6554	6571	6568	6569

L17-M8

6582	6597	6580	6583	6598
6581	6587	6592	6585	6595
6600	6586	6588	6590	6576
6599	6591	6584	6589	6577
6578	6579	6596	6593	6594

L17-M9

6607	6622	6605	6608	6623
6606	6612	6617	6610	6620
6625	6611	6613	6615	6601
6624	6616	6609	6614	6602
6603	6604	6621	6618	6619

L17-M10

6632	6647	6630	6633	6648
6631	6637	6642	6635	6645
6650	6636	6638	6640	6626
6649	6641	6634	6639	6627
6628	6629	6646	6643	6644

L17-M11

6657	6672	6655	6658	6673
6656	6662	6667	6660	6670
6675	6661	6663	6665	6651
6674	6666	6659	6664	6652
6653	6654	6671	6668	6669

L17-M12

6682	6697	6680	6683	6698
6681	6687	6692	6685	6695
6700	6686	6688	6690	6676
6699	6691	6684	6689	6677
6678	6679	6696	6693	6694

L17-M13

6707	6722	6705	6708	6723
6706	6712	6717	6710	6720
6725	6711	6713	6715	6701
6724	6716	6709	6714	6702
6703	6704	6721	6718	6719

L17-M14

6732	6747	6730	6733	6748
6731	6737	6742	6735	6745
6750	6736	6738	6740	6726
6749	6741	6734	6739	6727
6728	6729	6746	6743	6744

L17-M15

6757	6772	6755	6758	6773
6756	6762	6767	6760	6770
6775	6761	6763	6765	6751
6774	6766	6759	6764	6752
6753	6754	6771	6768	6769

L18-M8

6982	6997	6980	6983	6998
6981	6987	6992	6985	6995
7000	6986	6988	6990	6976
6999	6991	6984	6989	6977
6978	6979	6996	6993	6994

L17-M16

6782	6797	6780	6783	6798
6781	6787	6792	6785	6795
6800	6786	6788	6790	6776
6799	6791	6784	6789	6777
6778	6779	6796	6793	6794

L18-M9

7007	7022	7005	7008	7023
7006	7012	7017	7010	7020
7025	7011	7013	7015	7001
7024	7016	7009	7014	7002
7003	7004	7021	7018	7019

L18-M1

6807	6822	6805	6808	6823
6806	6812	6817	6810	6820
6825	6811	6813	6815	6801
6824	6816	6809	6814	6802
6803	6804	6821	6818	6819

L18-M10

7032	7047	7030	7033	7048
7031	7037	7042	7035	7045
7050	7036	7038	7040	7026
7049	7041	7034	7039	7027
7028	7029	7046	7043	7044

L18-M2

6832	6847	6830	6833	6848
6831	6837	6842	6835	6845
6850	6836	6838	6840	6826
6849	6841	6834	6839	6827
6828	6829	6846	6843	6844

L18-M11

7057	7072	7055	7058	7073
7056	7062	7067	7060	7070
7075	7061	7063	7065	7051
7074	7066	7059	7064	7052
7053	7054	7071	7068	7069

L18-M3

6857	6872	6855	6858	6873
6856	6862	6867	6860	6870
6875	6861	6863	6865	6851
6874	6866	6859	6864	6852
6853	6854	6871	6868	6869

L18-M12

7082	7097	7080	7083	7098
7081	7087	7092	7085	7095
7100	7086	7088	7090	7076
7099	7091	7084	7089	7077
7078	7079	7096	7093	7094

L18-M4

6882	6897	6880	6883	6898
6881	6887	6892	6885	6895
6900	6886	6888	6890	6876
6899	6891	6884	6889	6877
6878	6879	6896	6893	6894

L18-M13

7107	7122	7105	7108	7123
7106	7112	7117	7110	7120
7125	7111	7113	7115	7101
7124	7116	7109	7114	7102
7103	7104	7121	7118	7119

L18-M5

6907	6922	6905	6908	6923
6906	6912	6917	6910	6920
6925	6911	6913	6915	6901
6924	6916	6909	6914	6902
6903	6904	6921	6918	6919

L18-M14

7132	7147	7130	7133	7148
7131	7137	7142	7135	7145
7150	7136	7138	7140	7126
7149	7141	7134	7139	7127
7128	7129	7146	7143	7144

L18-M6

6932	6947	6930	6933	6948
6931	6937	6942	6935	6945
6950	6936	6938	6940	6926
6949	6941	6934	6939	6927
6928	6929	6946	6943	6944

L18-M15

7157	7172	7155	7158	7173
7156	7162	7167	7160	7170
7175	7161	7163	7165	7151
7174	7166	7159	7164	7152
7153	7154	7171	7168	7169

L18-M7

6957	6972	6955	6958	6973
6956	6962	6967	6960	6970
6975	6961	6963	6965	6951
6974	6966	6959	6964	6952
6953	6954	6971	6968	6969

L18-M16

7182	7197	7180	7183	7198
7181	7187	7192	7185	7195
7200	7186	7188	7190	7176
7199	7191	7184	7189	7177
7178	7179	7196	7193	7194

L19-M1

7207	7222	7205	7208	7223
7206	7212	7217	7210	7220
7225	7211	7213	7215	7201
7224	7216	7209	7214	7202
7203	7204	7221	7218	7219

L19-M2

7232	7247	7230	7233	7248
7231	7237	7242	7235	7245
7250	7236	7238	7240	7226
7249	7241	7234	7239	7227
7228	7229	7246	7243	7244

L19-M3

7257	7272	7255	7258	7273
7256	7262	7267	7260	7270
7275	7261	7263	7265	7251
7274	7266	7259	7264	7252
7253	7254	7271	7268	7269

L19-M4

7282	7297	7280	7283	7298
7281	7287	7292	7285	7295
7300	7286	7288	7290	7276
7299	7291	7284	7289	7277
7278	7279	7296	7293	7294

L19-M5

7307	7322	7305	7308	7323
7306	7312	7317	7310	7320
7325	7311	7313	7315	7301
7324	7316	7309	7314	7302
7303	7304	7321	7318	7319

L19-M6

7332	7347	7330	7333	7348
7331	7337	7342	7335	7345
7350	7336	7338	7340	7326
7349	7341	7334	7339	7327
7328	7329	7346	7343	7344

L19-M7

7357	7372	7355	7358	7373
7356	7362	7367	7360	7370
7375	7361	7363	7365	7351
7374	7366	7359	7364	7352
7353	7354	7371	7368	7369

L19-M8

7382	7397	7380	7383	7398
7381	7387	7392	7385	7395
7400	7386	7388	7390	7376
7399	7391	7384	7389	7377
7378	7379	7396	7393	7394

L19-M9

7407	7422	7405	7408	7423
7406	7412	7417	7410	7420
7425	7411	7413	7415	7401
7424	7416	7409	7414	7402
7403	7404	7421	7418	7419

L19-M10

7432	7447	7430	7433	7448
7431	7437	7442	7435	7445
7450	7436	7438	7440	7426
7449	7441	7434	7439	7427
7428	7429	7446	7443	7444

L19-M11

7457	7472	7455	7458	7473
7456	7462	7467	7460	7470
7475	7461	7463	7465	7451
7474	7466	7459	7464	7452
7453	7454	7471	7468	7469

L19-M12

7482	7497	7480	7483	7498
7481	7487	7492	7485	7495
7500	7486	7488	7490	7476
7499	7491	7484	7489	7477
7478	7479	7496	7493	7494

L19-M13

7507	7522	7505	7508	7523
7506	7512	7517	7510	7520
7525	7511	7513	7515	7501
7524	7516	7509	7514	7502
7503	7504	7521	7518	7519

L19-M14

7532	7547	7530	7533	7548
7531	7537	7542	7535	7545
7550	7536	7538	7540	7526
7549	7541	7534	7539	7527
7528	7529	7546	7543	7544

L19-M15

7557	7572	7555	7558	7573
7556	7562	7567	7560	7570
7575	7561	7563	7565	7551
7574	7566	7559	7564	7552
7553	7554	7571	7568	7569

L19-M16

7582	7597	7580	7583	7598
7581	7587	7592	7585	7595
7600	7586	7588	7590	7576
7599	7591	7584	7589	7577
7578	7579	7596	7593	7594

L20-M1

7607	7622	7605	7608	7623
7606	7612	7617	7610	7620
7625	7611	7613	7615	7601
7624	7616	7609	7614	7602
7603	7604	7621	7618	7619

L20-M2

7632	7647	7630	7633	7648
7631	7637	7642	7635	7645
7650	7636	7638	7640	7626
7649	7641	7634	7639	7627
7628	7629	7646	7643	7644

L20-M3

7657	7672	7655	7658	7673
7656	7662	7667	7660	7670
7675	7661	7663	7665	7651
7674	7666	7659	7664	7652
7653	7654	7671	7668	7669

L20-M4

7682	7697	7680	7683	7698
7681	7687	7692	7685	7695
7700	7686	7688	7690	7676
7699	7691	7684	7689	7677
7678	7679	7696	7693	7694

L20-M5

7707	7722	7705	7708	7723
7706	7712	7717	7710	7720
7725	7711	7713	7715	7701
7724	7716	7709	7714	7702
7703	7704	7721	7718	7719

L20-M6

7732	7747	7730	7733	7748
7731	7737	7742	7735	7745
7750	7736	7738	7740	7726
7749	7741	7734	7739	7727
7728	7729	7746	7743	7744

L20-M7

7757	7772	7755	7758	7773
7756	7762	7767	7760	7770
7775	7761	7763	7765	7751
7774	7766	7759	7764	7752
7753	7754	7771	7768	7769

L20-M8

7782	7797	7780	7783	7798
7781	7787	7792	7785	7795
7800	7786	7788	7790	7776
7799	7791	7784	7789	7777
7778	7779	7796	7793	7794

L20-M9

7807	7822	7805	7808	7823
7806	7812	7817	7810	7820
7825	7811	7813	7815	7801
7824	7816	7809	7814	7802
7803	7804	7821	7818	7819

L20-M10

7832	7847	7830	7833	7848
7831	7837	7842	7835	7845
7850	7836	7838	7840	7826
7849	7841	7834	7839	7827
7828	7829	7846	7843	7844

L20-M11

7857	7872	7855	7858	7873
7856	7862	7867	7860	7870
7875	7861	7863	7865	7851
7874	7866	7859	7864	7852
7853	7854	7871	7868	7869

L20-M12

7882	7897	7880	7883	7898
7881	7887	7892	7885	7895
7900	7886	7888	7890	7876
7899	7891	7884	7889	7877
7878	7879	7896	7893	7894

L20-M13

7907	7922	7905	7908	7923
7906	7912	7917	7910	7920
7925	7911	7913	7915	7901
7924	7916	7909	7914	7902
7903	7904	7921	7918	7919

L20-M14

7932	7947	7930	7933	7948
7931	7937	7942	7935	7945
7950	7936	7938	7940	7926
7949	7941	7934	7939	7927
7928	7929	7946	7943	7944

L20-M15

7957	7972	7955	7958	7973
7956	7962	7967	7960	7970
7975	7961	7963	7965	7951
7974	7966	7959	7964	7952
7953	7954	7971	7968	7969

L20-M16

7982	7997	7980	7983	7998
7981	7987	7992	7985	7995
8000	7986	7988	7990	7976
7999	7991	7984	7989	7977
7978	7979	7996	7993	7994

L21-M1

8007	8022	8005	8008	8023
8006	8012	8017	8010	8020
8025	8011	8013	8015	8001
8024	8016	8009	8014	8002
8003	8004	8021	8018	8019

L21-M2

8032	8047	8030	8033	8048
8031	8037	8042	8035	8045
8050	8036	8038	8040	8026
8049	8041	8034	8039	8027
8028	8029	8046	8043	8044

L21-M3

8057	8072	8055	8058	8073
8056	8062	8067	8060	8070
8075	8061	8063	8065	8051
8074	8066	8059	8064	8052
8053	8054	8071	8068	8069

L21-M4

8082	8097	8080	8083	8098
8081	8087	8092	8085	8095
8100	8086	8088	8090	8076
8099	8091	8084	8089	8077
8078	8079	8096	8093	8094

L21-M5

8107	8122	8105	8108	8123
8106	8112	8117	8110	8120
8125	8111	8113	8115	8101
8124	8116	8109	8114	8102
8103	8104	8121	8118	8119

L21-M6

8132	8147	8130	8133	8148
8131	8137	8142	8135	8145
8150	8136	8138	8140	8126
8149	8141	8134	8139	8127
8128	8129	8146	8143	8144

L21-M7

8157	8172	8155	8158	8173
8156	8162	8167	8160	8170
8175	8161	8163	8165	8151
8174	8166	8159	8164	8152
8153	8154	8171	8168	8169

L21-M8

8182	8197	8180	8183	8198
8181	8187	8192	8185	8195
8200	8186	8188	8190	8176
8199	8191	8184	8189	8177
8178	8179	8196	8193	8194

L21-M9

8207	8222	8205	8208	8223
8206	8212	8217	8210	8220
8225	8211	8213	8215	8201
8224	8216	8209	8214	8202
8203	8204	8221	8218	8219

L21-M10

8232	8247	8230	8233	8248
8231	8237	8242	8235	8245
8250	8236	8238	8240	8226
8249	8241	8234	8239	8227
8228	8229	8246	8243	8244

L21-M11

8257	8272	8255	8258	8273
8256	8262	8267	8260	8270
8275	8261	8263	8265	8251
8274	8266	8259	8264	8252
8253	8254	8271	8268	8269

L21-M12

8282	8297	8280	8283	8298
8281	8287	8292	8285	8295
8300	8286	8288	8290	8276
8299	8291	8284	8289	8277
8278	8279	8296	8293	8294

L21-M13

8307	8322	8305	8308	8323
8306	8312	8317	8310	8320
8325	8311	8313	8315	8301
8324	8316	8309	8314	8302
8303	8304	8321	8318	8319

L21-M14

8332	8347	8330	8333	8348
8331	8337	8342	8335	8345
8350	8336	8338	8340	8326
8349	8341	8334	8339	8327
8328	8329	8346	8343	8344

L21-M15

8357	8372	8355	8358	8373
8356	8362	8367	8360	8370
8375	8361	8363	8365	8351
8374	8366	8359	8364	8352
8353	8354	8371	8368	8369

L21-M16

8382	8397	8380	8383	8398
8381	8387	8392	8385	8395
8400	8386	8388	8390	8376
8399	8391	8384	8389	8377
8378	8379	8396	8393	8394

L22-M1

8407	8422	8405	8408	8423
8406	8412	8417	8410	8420
8425	8411	8413	8415	8401
8424	8416	8409	8414	8402
8403	8404	8421	8418	8419

L22-M2

8432	8447	8430	8433	8448
8431	8437	8442	8435	8445
8450	8436	8438	8440	8426
8449	8441	8434	8439	8427
8428	8429	8446	8443	8444

L22-M3

8457	8472	8455	8458	8473
8456	8462	8467	8460	8470
8475	8461	8463	8465	8451
8474	8466	8459	8464	8452
8453	8454	8471	8468	8469

L22-M4

8482	8497	8480	8483	8498
8481	8487	8492	8485	8495
8500	8486	8488	8490	8476
8499	8491	8484	8489	8477
8478	8479	8496	8493	8494

L22-M5

8507	8522	8505	8508	8523
8506	8512	8517	8510	8520
8525	8511	8513	8515	8501
8524	8516	8509	8514	8502
8503	8504	8521	8518	8519

L22-M6

8532	8547	8530	8533	8548
8531	8537	8542	8535	8545
8550	8536	8538	8540	8526
8549	8541	8534	8539	8527
8528	8529	8546	8543	8544

L22-M7

8557	8572	8555	8558	8573
8556	8562	8567	8560	8570
8575	8561	8563	8565	8551
8574	8566	8559	8564	8552
8553	8554	8571	8568	8569

L22-M8

8582	8597	8580	8583	8598
8581	8587	8592	8585	8595
8600	8586	8588	8590	8576
8599	8591	8584	8589	8577
8578	8579	8596	8593	8594

L22-M9

8607	8622	8605	8608	8623
8606	8612	8617	8610	8620
8625	8611	8613	8615	8601
8624	8616	8609	8614	8602
8603	8604	8621	8618	8619

L22-M10

8632	8647	8630	8633	8648
8631	8637	8642	8635	8645
8650	8636	8638	8640	8626
8649	8641	8634	8639	8627
8628	8629	8646	8643	8644

L22-M11

8657	8672	8655	8658	8673
8656	8662	8667	8660	8670
8675	8661	8663	8665	8651
8674	8666	8659	8664	8652
8653	8654	8671	8668	8669

L22-M12

8682	8697	8680	8683	8698
8681	8687	8692	8685	8695
8700	8686	8688	8690	8676
8699	8691	8684	8689	8677
8678	8679	8696	8693	8694

L22-M13

8707	8722	8705	8708	8723
8706	8712	8717	8710	8720
8725	8711	8713	8715	8701
8724	8716	8709	8714	8702
8703	8704	8721	8718	8719

L22-M14

8732	8747	8730	8733	8748
8731	8737	8742	8735	8745
8750	8736	8738	8740	8726
8749	8741	8734	8739	8727
8728	8729	8746	8743	8744

L22-M15

8757	8772	8755	8758	8773
8756	8762	8767	8760	8770
8775	8761	8763	8765	8751
8774	8766	8759	8764	8752
8753	8754	8771	8768	8769

L22-M16

8782	8797	8780	8783	8798
8781	8787	8792	8785	8795
8800	8786	8788	8790	8776
8799	8791	8784	8789	8777
8778	8779	8796	8793	8794

L23-M1

8807	8822	8805	8808	8823
8806	8812	8817	8810	8820
8825	8811	8813	8815	8801
8824	8816	8809	8814	8802
8803	8804	8821	8818	8819

L23-M2

8832	8847	8830	8833	8848
8831	8837	8842	8835	8845
8850	8836	8838	8840	8826
8849	8841	8834	8839	8827
8828	8829	8846	8843	8844

L23-M3

8857	8872	8855	8858	8873
8856	8862	8867	8860	8870
8875	8861	8863	8865	8851
8874	8866	8859	8864	8852
8853	8854	8871	8868	8869

L23-M4

8882	8897	8880	8883	8898
8881	8887	8892	8885	8895
8900	8886	8888	8890	8876
8899	8891	8884	8889	8877
8878	8879	8896	8893	8894

L23-M5

8907	8922	8905	8908	8923
8906	8912	8917	8910	8920
8925	8911	8913	8915	8901
8924	8916	8909	8914	8902
8903	8904	8921	8918	8919

L23-M6

8932	8947	8930	8933	8948
8931	8937	8942	8935	8945
8950	8936	8938	8940	8926
8949	8941	8934	8939	8927
8928	8929	8946	8943	8944

L23-M7

8957	8972	8955	8958	8973
8956	8962	8967	8960	8970
8975	8961	8963	8965	8951
8974	8966	8959	8964	8952
8953	8954	8971	8968	8969

L23-M8

8982	8997	8980	8983	8998
8981	8987	8992	8985	8995
9000	8986	8988	8990	8976
8999	8991	8984	8989	8977
8978	8979	8996	8993	8994

L23-M9

9007	9022	9005	9008	9023
9006	9012	9017	9010	9020
9025	9011	9013	9015	9001
9024	9016	9009	9014	9002
9003	9004	9021	9018	9019

L23-M10

9032	9047	9030	9033	9048
9031	9037	9042	9035	9045
9050	9036	9038	9040	9026
9049	9041	9034	9039	9027
9028	9029	9046	9043	9044

L23-M11

9057	9072	9055	9058	9073
9056	9062	9067	9060	9070
9075	9061	9063	9065	9051
9074	9066	9059	9064	9052
9053	9054	9071	9068	9069

L23-M12

9082	9097	9080	9083	9098
9081	9087	9092	9085	9095
9100	9086	9088	9090	9076
9099	9091	9084	9089	9077
9078	9079	9096	9093	9094

L23-M13

9107	9122	9105	9108	9123
9106	9112	9117	9110	9120
9125	9111	9113	9115	9101
9124	9116	9109	9114	9102
9103	9104	9121	9118	9119

L23-M14

9132	9147	9130	9133	9148
9131	9137	9142	9135	9145
9150	9136	9138	9140	9126
9149	9141	9134	9139	9127
9128	9129	9146	9143	9144

L23-M15

9157	9172	9155	9158	9173
9156	9162	9167	9160	9170
9175	9161	9163	9165	9151
9174	9166	9159	9164	9152
9153	9154	9171	9168	9169

L23-M16

9182	9197	9180	9183	9198
9181	9187	9192	9185	9195
9200	9186	9188	9190	9176
9199	9191	9184	9189	9177
9178	9179	9196	9193	9194

L24-M1

9207	9222	9205	9208	9223
9206	9212	9217	9210	9220
9225	9211	9213	9215	9201
9224	9216	9209	9214	9202
9203	9204	9221	9218	9219

L24-M2

9232	9247	9230	9233	9248
9231	9237	9242	9235	9245
9250	9236	9238	9240	9226
9249	9241	9234	9239	9227
9228	9229	9246	9243	9244

L24-M3

9257	9272	9255	9258	9273
9256	9262	9267	9260	9270
9275	9261	9263	9265	9251
9274	9266	9259	9264	9252
9253	9254	9271	9268	9269

L24-M4

9282	9297	9280	9283	9298
9281	9287	9292	9285	9295
9300	9286	9288	9290	9276
9299	9291	9284	9289	9277
9278	9279	9296	9293	9294

L24-M5

9307	9322	9305	9308	9323
9306	9312	9317	9310	9320
9325	9311	9313	9315	9301
9324	9316	9309	9314	9302
9303	9304	9321	9318	9319

L24-M6

9332	9347	9330	9333	9348
9331	9337	9342	9335	9345
9350	9336	9338	9340	9326
9349	9341	9334	9339	9327
9328	9329	9346	9343	9344

L24-M7

9357	9372	9355	9358	9373
9356	9362	9367	9360	9370
9375	9361	9363	9365	9351
9374	9366	9359	9364	9352
9353	9354	9371	9368	9369

L24-M8

9382	9397	9380	9383	9398
9381	9387	9392	9385	9395
9400	9386	9388	9390	9376
9399	9391	9384	9389	9377
9378	9379	9396	9393	9394

L24-M9

9407	9422	9405	9408	9423
9406	9412	9417	9410	9420
9425	9411	9413	9415	9401
9424	9416	9409	9414	9402
9403	9404	9421	9418	9419

L24-M10

9432	9447	9430	9433	9448
9431	9437	9442	9435	9445
9450	9436	9438	9440	9426
9449	9441	9434	9439	9427
9428	9429	9446	9443	9444

L24-M11

9457	9472	9455	9458	9473
9456	9462	9467	9460	9470
9475	9461	9463	9465	9451
9474	9466	9459	9464	9452
9453	9454	9471	9468	9469

L24-M12

9482	9497	9480	9483	9498
9481	9487	9492	9485	9495
9500	9486	9488	9490	9476
9499	9491	9484	9489	9477
9478	9479	9496	9493	9494

L24-M13

9507	9522	9505	9508	9523
9506	9512	9517	9510	9520
9525	9511	9513	9515	9501
9524	9516	9509	9514	9502
9503	9504	9521	9518	9519

L24-M14

9532	9547	9530	9533	9548
9531	9537	9542	9535	9545
9550	9536	9538	9540	9526
9549	9541	9534	9539	9527
9528	9529	9546	9543	9544

L24-M15

9557	9572	9555	9558	9573
9556	9562	9567	9560	9570
9575	9561	9563	9565	9551
9574	9566	9559	9564	9552
9553	9554	9571	9568	9569

L24-M16

9582	9597	9580	9583	9598
9581	9587	9592	9585	9595
9600	9586	9588	9590	9576
9599	9591	9584	9589	9577
9578	9579	9596	9593	9594

L25-M1

9607	9622	9605	9608	9623
9606	9612	9617	9610	9620
9625	9611	9613	9615	9601
9624	9616	9609	9614	9602
9603	9604	9621	9618	9619

L25-M2

9632	9647	9630	9633	9648
9631	9637	9642	9635	9645
9650	9636	9638	9640	9626
9649	9641	9634	9639	9627
9628	9629	9646	9643	9644

L25-M3

9657	9672	9655	9658	9673
9656	9662	9667	9660	9670
9675	9661	9663	9665	9651
9674	9666	9659	9664	9652
9653	9654	9671	9668	9669

L25-M4

9682	9697	9680	9683	9698
9681	9687	9692	9685	9695
9700	9686	9688	9690	9676
9699	9691	9684	9689	9677
9678	9679	9696	9693	9694

L25-M5

9707	9722	9705	9708	9723
9706	9712	9717	9710	9720
9725	9711	9713	9715	9701
9724	9716	9709	9714	9702
9703	9704	9721	9718	9719

L25-M6

9732	9747	9730	9733	9748
9731	9737	9742	9735	9745
9750	9736	9738	9740	9726
9749	9741	9734	9739	9727
9728	9729	9746	9743	9744

L25-M7

9757	9772	9755	9758	9773
9756	9762	9767	9760	9770
9775	9761	9763	9765	9751
9774	9766	9759	9764	9752
9753	9754	9771	9768	9769

L25-M8

9782	9797	9780	9783	9798
9781	9787	9792	9785	9795
9800	9786	9788	9790	9776
9799	9791	9784	9789	9777
9778	9779	9796	9793	9794

L25-M9

9807	9822	9805	9808	9823
9806	9812	9817	9810	9820
9825	9811	9813	9815	9801
9824	9816	9809	9814	9802
9803	9804	9821	9818	9819

L25-M10

9832	9847	9830	9833	9848
9831	9837	9842	9835	9845
9850	9836	9838	9840	9826
9849	9841	9834	9839	9827
9828	9829	9846	9843	9844

L25-M11

9857	9872	9855	9858	9873
9856	9862	9867	9860	9870
9875	9861	9863	9865	9851
9874	9866	9859	9864	9852
9853	9854	9871	9868	9869

L25-M12

9882	9897	9880	9883	9898
9881	9887	9892	9885	9895
9900	9886	9888	9890	9876
9899	9891	9884	9889	9877
9878	9879	9896	9893	9894

L25-M13

9907	9922	9905	9908	9923
9906	9912	9917	9910	9920
9925	9911	9913	9915	9901
9924	9916	9909	9914	9902
9903	9904	9921	9918	9919

L25-M14

9932	9947	9930	9933	9948
9931	9937	9942	9935	9945
9950	9936	9938	9940	9926
9949	9941	9934	9939	9927
9928	9929	9946	9943	9944

L25-M15

9957	9972	9955	9958	9973
9956	9962	9967	9960	9970
9975	9961	9963	9965	9951
9974	9966	9959	9964	9952
9953	9954	9971	9968	9969

L25-M16

9982	9997	9980	9983	9998
9981	9987	9992	9985	9995
10000	9986	9988	9990	9976
9999	9991	9984	9989	9977
9978	9979	9996	9993	9994

KETHER

L1-M1

7009	24529	4673	8177	25697
5841	12849	18689	10513	22193
28033	11681	14017	16353	1
26865	17521	9345	15185	1169
2337	3505	23361	19857	21025

L1-M2

36209	53729	33873	37377	54897
35041	42049	47889	39713	51393
57233	40881	43217	45553	29201
56065	46721	38545	44385	30369
31537	32705	52561	49057	50225

L1-M3

65409	82929	63073	66577	84097
64241	71249	77089	68913	80593
86433	70081	72417	74753	58401
85265	75921	67745	73585	59569
60737	61905	81761	78257	79425

L1-M4

94609	112129	92273	95777	113297
93441	100449	106289	98113	109793
115633	99281	101617	103953	87601
114465	105121	96945	102785	88769
89937	91105	110961	107457	108625

L1-M5

123809	141329	121473	124977	142497
122641	129649	135489	127313	138993
144833	128481	130817	133153	116801
143665	134321	126145	131985	117969
119137	120305	140161	136657	137825

L1-M6

153009	170529	150673	154177	171697
151841	158849	164689	156513	168193
174033	157681	160017	162353	146001
172865	163521	155345	161185	147169
148337	149505	169361	165857	167025

L1-M7

182209	199729	179873	183377	200897
181041	188049	193889	185713	197393
203233	186881	189217	191553	175201
202065	192721	184545	190385	176369
177537	178705	198561	195057	196225

L1-M8

211409	228929	209073	212577	230097
210241	217249	223089	214913	226593
232433	216081	218417	220753	204401
231265	221921	213745	219585	205569
206737	207905	227761	224257	225425

L1-M9

240609	258129	238273	241777	259297
239441	246449	252289	244113	255793
261633	245281	247617	249953	233601
260465	251121	242945	248785	234769
235937	237105	256961	253457	254625

L1-M10

269809	287329	267473	270977	288497
268641	275649	281489	273313	284993
290833	274481	276817	279153	262801
289665	280321	272145	277985	263969
265137	266305	286161	282657	283825

L1-M11

299009	316529	296673	300177	317697
297841	304849	310689	302513	314193
320033	303681	306017	308353	292001
318865	309521	301345	307185	293169
294337	295505	315361	311857	313025

L1-M12

328209	345729	325873	329377	346897
327041	334049	339889	331713	343393
349233	332881	335217	337553	321201
348065	338721	330545	336385	322369
323537	324705	344561	341057	342225

L1-M13

357409	374929	355073	358577	376097
356241	363249	369089	360913	372593
378433	362081	364417	366753	350401
377265	367921	359745	365585	351569
352737	353905	373761	370257	371425

L1-M14

386609	404129	384273	387777	405297
385441	392449	398289	390113	401793
407633	391281	393617	395953	379601
406465	397121	388945	394785	380769
381937	383105	402961	399457	400625

L1-M15

415809	433329	413473	416977	434497
414641	421649	427489	419313	430993
436833	420481	422817	425153	408801
435665	426321	418145	423985	409969
411137	412305	432161	428657	429825

L1-M16

445009	462529	442673	446177	463697
443841	450849	456689	448513	460193
466033	449681	452017	454353	438001
464865	455521	447345	453185	439169
440337	441505	461361	457857	459025

L2-M1

474209	491729	471873	475377	492897
473041	480049	485889	477713	489393
495233	478881	481217	483553	467201
494065	484721	476545	482385	468369
469537	470705	490561	487057	488225

L2-M2

503409	520929	501073	504577	522097
502241	509249	515089	506913	518593
524433	508081	510417	512753	496401
523265	513921	505745	511585	497569
498737	499905	519761	516257	517425

L2-M3

532609	550129	530273	533777	551297
531441	538449	544289	536113	547793
553633	537281	539617	541953	525601
552465	543121	534945	540785	526769
527937	529105	548961	545457	546625

L2-M4

561809	579329	559473	562977	580497
560641	567649	573489	565313	576993
582833	566481	568817	571153	554801
581665	572321	564145	569985	555969
557137	558305	578161	574657	575825

L2-M5

591009	608529	588673	592177	609697
589841	596849	602689	594513	606193
612033	595681	598017	600353	584001
610865	601521	593345	599185	585169
586337	587505	607361	603857	605025

L2-M6

620209	637729	617873	621377	638897
619041	626049	631889	623713	635393
641233	624881	627217	629553	613201
640065	630721	622545	628385	614369
615537	616705	636561	633057	634225

L2-M7

649409	666929	647073	650577	668097
648241	655249	661089	652913	664593
670433	654081	656417	658753	642401
669265	659921	651745	657585	643569
644737	645905	665761	662257	663425

L2-M8

678609	696129	676273	679777	697297
677441	684449	690289	682113	693793
699633	683281	685617	687953	671601
698465	689121	680945	686785	672769
673937	675105	694961	691457	692625

L2-M9

707809	725329	705473	708977	726497
706641	713649	719489	711313	722993
728833	712481	714817	717153	700801
727665	718321	710145	715985	701969
703137	704305	724161	720657	721825

L2-M10

737009	754529	734673	738177	755697
735841	742849	748689	740513	752193
758033	741681	744017	746353	730001
756865	747521	739345	745185	731169
732337	733505	753361	749857	751025

L2-M11

766209	783729	763873	767377	784897
765041	772049	777889	769713	781393
787233	770881	773217	775553	759201
786065	776721	768545	774385	760369
761537	762705	782561	779057	780225

L2-M12

795409	812929	793073	796577	814097
794241	801249	807089	798913	810593
816433	800081	802417	804753	788401
815265	805921	797745	803585	789569
790737	791905	811761	808257	809425

L2-M13

824609	842129	822273	825777	843297
823441	830449	836289	828113	839793
845633	829281	831617	833953	817601
844465	835121	826945	832785	818769
819937	821105	840961	837457	838625

L2-M14

853809	871329	851473	854977	872497
852641	859649	865489	857313	868993
874833	858481	860817	863153	846801
873665	864321	856145	861985	847969
849137	850305	870161	866657	867825

L2-M15

883009	900529	880673	884177	901697
881841	888849	894689	886513	898193
904033	887681	890017	892353	876001
902865	893521	885345	891185	877169
878337	879505	899361	895857	897025

L2-M16

912209	929729	909873	913377	930897
911041	918049	923889	915713	927393
933233	916881	919217	921553	905201
932065	922721	914545	920385	906369
907537	908705	928561	925057	926225

L3-M1

941409	958929	939073	942577	960097
940241	947249	953089	944913	956593
962433	946081	948417	950753	934401
961265	951921	943745	949585	935569
936737	937905	957761	954257	955425

L3-M2

970609	988129	968273	971777	989297
969441	976449	982289	974113	985793
991633	975281	977617	979953	963601
990465	981121	972945	978785	964769
965937	967105	986961	983457	984625

L3-M3

999809	1017329	997473	1000977	1018497
998641	1005649	1011489	1003313	1014993
1020833	1004481	1006817	1009153	992801
1019665	1010321	1002145	1007985	993969
995137	996305	1016161	1012657	1013825

L3-M4

1029009	1046529	1026673	1030177	1047697
1027841	1034849	1040689	1032513	1044193
1050033	1033681	1036017	1038353	1022001
1048865	1039521	1031345	1037185	1023169
1024337	1025505	1045361	1041857	1043025

L3-M5

1058209	1075729	1055873	1059377	1076897
1057041	1064049	1069889	1061713	1073393
1079233	1062881	1065217	1067553	1051201
1078065	1068721	1060545	1066385	1052369
1053537	1054705	1074561	1071057	1072225

L3-M6

1087409	1104929	1085073	1088577	1106097
1086241	1093249	1099089	1090913	1102593
1108433	1092081	1094417	1096753	1080401
1107265	1097921	1089745	1095585	1081569
1082737	1083905	1103761	1100257	1101425

L3-M7

1116609	1134129	1114273	1117777	1135297
1115441	1122449	1128289	1120113	1131793
1137633	1121281	1123617	1125953	1109601
1136465	1127121	1118945	1124785	1110769
1111937	1113105	1132961	1129457	1130625

L3-M8

1145809	1163329	1143473	1146977	1164497
1144641	1151649	1157489	1149313	1160993
1166833	1150481	1152817	1155153	1138801
1165665	1156321	1148145	1153985	1139969
1141137	1142305	1162161	1158657	1159825

L3-M9

1175009	1192529	1172673	1176177	1193697
1173841	1180849	1186689	1178513	1190193
1196033	1179681	1182017	1184353	1168001
1194865	1185521	1177345	1183185	1169169
1170337	1171505	1191361	1187857	1189025

L3-M10

1204209	1221729	1201873	1205377	1222897
1203041	1210049	1215889	1207713	1219393
1225233	1208881	1211217	1213553	1197201
1224065	1214721	1206545	1212385	1198369
1199537	1200705	1220561	1217057	1218225

L3-M11

1233409	1250929	1231073	1234577	1252097
1232241	1239249	1245089	1236913	1248593
1254433	1238081	1240417	1242753	1226401
1253265	1243921	1235745	1241585	1227569
1228737	1229905	1249761	1246257	1247425

L3-M12

1262609	1280129	1260273	1263777	1281297
1261441	1268449	1274289	1266113	1277793
1283633	1267281	1269617	1271953	1255601
1282465	1273121	1264945	1270785	1256769
1257937	1259105	1278961	1275457	1276625

L3-M13

1291809	1309329	1289473	1292977	1310497
1290641	1297649	1303489	1295313	1306993
1312833	1296481	1298817	1301153	1284801
1311665	1302321	1294145	1299985	1285969
1287137	1288305	1308161	1304657	1305825

L3-M14

1321009	1338529	1318673	1322177	1339697
1319841	1326849	1332689	1324513	1336193
1342033	1325681	1328017	1330353	1314001
1340865	1331521	1323345	1329185	1315169
1316337	1317505	1337361	1333857	1335025

L3-M15

1350209	1367729	1347873	1351377	1368897
1349041	1356049	1361889	1353713	1365393
1371233	1354881	1357217	1359553	1343201
1370065	1360721	1352545	1358385	1344369
1345537	1346705	1366561	1363057	1364225

L3-M16

1379409	1396929	1377073	1380577	1398097
1378241	1385249	1391089	1382913	1394593
1400433	1384081	1386417	1388753	1372401
1399265	1389921	1381745	1387585	1373569
1374737	1375905	1395761	1392257	1393425

L4-M1

1408609	1426129	1406273	1409777	1427297
1407441	1414449	1420289	1412113	1423793
1429633	1413281	1415617	1417953	1401601
1428465	1419121	1410945	1416785	1402769
1403937	1405105	1424961	1421457	1422625

L4-M2

1437809	1455329	1435473	1438977	1456497
1436641	1443649	1449489	1441313	1452993
1458833	1442481	1444817	1447153	1430801
1457665	1448321	1440145	1445985	1431969
1433137	1434305	1454161	1450657	1451825

L4-M3

1467009	1484529	1464673	1468177	1485697
1465841	1472849	1478689	1470513	1482193
1488033	1471681	1474017	1476353	1460001
1486865	1477521	1469345	1475185	1461169
1462337	1463505	1483361	1479857	1481025

L4-M4

1496209	1513729	1493873	1497377	1514897
1495041	1502049	1507889	1499713	1511393
1517233	1500881	1503217	1505553	1489201
1516065	1506721	1498545	1504385	1490369
1491537	1492705	1512561	1509057	1510225

L4-M5

1525409	1542929	1523073	1526577	1544097
1524241	1531249	1537089	1528913	1540593
1546433	1530081	1532417	1534753	1518401
1545265	1535921	1527745	1533585	1519569
1520737	1521905	1541761	1538257	1539425

L4-M6

1554609	1572129	1552273	1555777	1573297
1553441	1560449	1566289	1558113	1569793
1575633	1559281	1561617	1563953	1547601
1574465	1565121	1556945	1562785	1548769
1549937	1551105	1570961	1567457	1568625

L4-M7

1583809	1601329	1581473	1584977	1602497
1582641	1589649	1595489	1587313	1598993
1604833	1588481	1590817	1593153	1576801
1603665	1594321	1586145	1591985	1577969
1579137	1580305	1600161	1596657	1597825

L4-M8

1613009	1630529	1610673	1614177	1631697
1611841	1618849	1624689	1616513	1628193
1634033	1617681	1620017	1622353	1606001
1632865	1623521	1615345	1621185	1607169
1608337	1609505	1629361	1625857	1627025

L4-M9

1642209	1659729	1639873	1643377	1660897
1641041	1648049	1653889	1645713	1657393
1663233	1646881	1649217	1651553	1635201
1662065	1652721	1644545	1650385	1636369
1637537	1638705	1658561	1655057	1656225

L4-M10

1671409	1688929	1669073	1672577	1690097
1670241	1677249	1683089	1674913	1686593
1692433	1676081	1678417	1680753	1664401
1691265	1681921	1673745	1679585	1665569
1666737	1667905	1687761	1684257	1685425

L4-M11

1700609	1718129	1698273	1701777	1719297
1699441	1706449	1712289	1704113	1715793
1721633	1705281	1707617	1709953	1693601
1720465	1711121	1702945	1708785	1694769
1695937	1697105	1716961	1713457	1714625

L4-M12

1729809	1747329	1727473	1730977	1748497
1728641	1735649	1741489	1733313	1744993
1750833	1734481	1736817	1739153	1722801
1749665	1740321	1732145	1737985	1723969
1725137	1726305	1746161	1742657	1743825

L4-M13

1759009	1776529	1756673	1760177	1777697
1757841	1764849	1770689	1762513	1774193
1780033	1763681	1766017	1768353	1752001
1778865	1769521	1761345	1767185	1753169
1754337	1755505	1775361	1771857	1773025

L4-M14

1788209	1805729	1785873	1789377	1806897
1787041	1794049	1799889	1791713	1803393
1809233	1792881	1795217	1797553	1781201
1808065	1798721	1790545	1796385	1782369
1783537	1784705	1804561	1801057	1802225

L4-M15

1817409	1834929	1815073	1818577	1836097
1816241	1823249	1829089	1820913	1832593
1838433	1822081	1824417	1826753	1810401
1837265	1827921	1819745	1825585	1811569
1812737	1813905	1833761	1830257	1831425

L4-M16

1846609	1864129	1844273	1847777	1865297
1845441	1852449	1858289	1850113	1861793
1867633	1851281	1853617	1855953	1839601
1866465	1857121	1848945	1854785	1840769
1841937	1843105	1862961	1859457	1860625

L5-M1

1875809	1893329	1873473	1876977	1894497
1874641	1881649	1887489	1879313	1890993
1896833	1880481	1882817	1885153	1868801
1895665	1886321	1878145	1883985	1869969
1871137	1872305	1892161	1888657	1889825

L5-M2

1905009	1922529	1902673	1906177	1923697
1903841	1910849	1916689	1908513	1920193
1926033	1909681	1912017	1914353	1898001
1924865	1915521	1907345	1913185	1899169
1900337	1901505	1921361	1917857	1919025

L5-M3

1934209	1951729	1931873	1935377	1952897
1933041	1940049	1945889	1937713	1949393
1955233	1938881	1941217	1943553	1927201
1954065	1944721	1936545	1942385	1928369
1929537	1930705	1950561	1947057	1948225

L5-M4

1963409	1980929	1961073	1964577	1982097
1962241	1969249	1975089	1966913	1978593
1984433	1968081	1970417	1972753	1956401
1983265	1973921	1965745	1971585	1957569
1958737	1959905	1979761	1976257	1977425

L5-M5

1992609	2010129	1990273	1993777	2011297
1991441	1998449	2004289	1996113	2007793
2013633	1997281	1999617	2001953	1985601
2012465	2003121	1994945	2000785	1986769
1987937	1989105	2008961	2005457	2006625

L5-M6

2021809	2039329	2019473	2022977	2040497
2020641	2027649	2033489	2025313	2036993
2042833	2026481	2028817	2031153	2014801
2041665	2032321	2024145	2029985	2015969
2017137	2018305	2038161	2034657	2035825

L5-M7

2051009	2068529	2048673	2052177	2069697
2049841	2056849	2062689	2054513	2066193
2072033	2055681	2058017	2060353	2044001
2070865	2061521	2053345	2059185	2045169
2046337	2047505	2067361	2063857	2065025

L5-M8

2080209	2097729	2077873	2081377	2098897
2079041	2086049	2091889	2083713	2095393
2101233	2084881	2087217	2089553	2073201
2100065	2090721	2082545	2088385	2074369
2075537	2076705	2096561	2093057	2094225

L5-M9

2109409	2126929	2107073	2110577	2128097
2108241	2115249	2121089	2112913	2124593
2130433	2114081	2116417	2118753	2102401
2129265	2119921	2111745	2117585	2103569
2104737	2105905	2125761	2122257	2123425

L6-M2

2372209	2389729	2369873	2373377	2390897
2371041	2378049	2383889	2375713	2387393
2393233	2376881	2379217	2381553	2365201
2392065	2382721	2374545	2380385	2366369
2367537	2368705	2388561	2385057	2386225

L5-M10

2138609	2156129	2136273	2139777	2157297
2137441	2144449	2150289	2142113	2153793
2159633	2143281	2145617	2147953	2131601
2158465	2149121	2140945	2146785	2132769
2133937	2135105	2154961	2151457	2152625

L6-M3

2401409	2418929	2399073	2402577	2420097
2400241	2407249	2413089	2404913	2416593
2422433	2406081	2408417	2410753	2394401
2421265	2411921	2403745	2409585	2395569
2396737	2397905	2417761	2414257	2415425

L5-M11

2167809	2185329	2165473	2168977	2186497
2166641	2173649	2179489	2171313	2182993
2188833	2172481	2174817	2177153	2160801
2187665	2178321	2170145	2175985	2161969
2163137	2164305	2184161	2180657	2181825

L6-M4

2430609	2448129	2428273	2431777	2449297
2429441	2436449	2442289	2434113	2445793
2451633	2435281	2437617	2439953	2423601
2450465	2441121	2432945	2438785	2424769
2425937	2427105	2446961	2443457	2444625

L5-M12

2197009	2214529	2194673	2198177	2215697
2195841	2202849	2208689	2200513	2212193
2218033	2201681	2204017	2206353	2190001
2216865	2207521	2199345	2205185	2191169
2192337	2193505	2213361	2209857	2211025

L6-M5

2459809	2477329	2457473	2460977	2478497
2458641	2465649	2471489	2463313	2474993
2480833	2464481	2466817	2469153	2452801
2479665	2470321	2462145	2467985	2453969
2455137	2456305	2476161	2472657	2473825

L5-M13

2226209	2243729	2223873	2227377	2244897
2225041	2232049	2237889	2229713	2241393
2247233	2230881	2233217	2235553	2219201
2246065	2236721	2228545	2234385	2220369
2221537	2222705	2242561	2239057	2240225

L6-M6

2489009	2506529	2486673	2490177	2507697
2487841	2494849	2500689	2492513	2504193
2510033	2493681	2496017	2498353	2482001
2508865	2499521	2491345	2497185	2483169
2484337	2485505	2505361	2501857	2503025

L5-M14

2255409	2272929	2253073	2256577	2274097
2254241	2261249	2267089	2258913	2270593
2276433	2260081	2262417	2264753	2248401
2275265	2265921	2257745	2263585	2249569
2250737	2251905	2271761	2268257	2269425

L6-M7

2518209	2535729	2515873	2519377	2536897
2517041	2524049	2529889	2521713	2533393
2539233	2522881	2525217	2527553	2511201
2538065	2528721	2520545	2526385	2512369
2513537	2514705	2534561	2531057	2532225

L5-M15

2284609	2302129	2282273	2285777	2303297
2283441	2290449	2296289	2288113	2299793
2305633	2289281	2291617	2293953	2277601
2304465	2295121	2286945	2292785	2278769
2279937	2281105	2300961	2297457	2298625

L6-M8

2547409	2564929	2545073	2548577	2566097
2546241	2553249	2559089	2550913	2562593
2568433	2552081	2554417	2556753	2540401
2567265	2557921	2549745	2555585	2541569
2542737	2543905	2563761	2560257	2561425

L5-M16

2313809	2331329	2311473	2314977	2332497
2312641	2319649	2325489	2317313	2328993
2334833	2318481	2320817	2323153	2306801
2333665	2324321	2316145	2321985	2307969
2309137	2310305	2330161	2326657	2327825

L6-M9

2576609	2594129	2574273	2577777	2595297
2575441	2582449	2588289	2580113	2591793
2597633	2581281	2583617	2585953	2569601
2596465	2587121	2578945	2584785	2570769
2571937	2573105	2592961	2589457	2590625

L6-M1

2343009	2360529	2340673	2344177	2361697
2341841	2348849	2354689	2346513	2358193
2364033	2347681	2350017	2352353	2336001
2362865	2353521	2345345	2351185	2337169
2338337	2339505	2359361	2355857	2357025

L6-M10

2605809	2623329	2603473	2606977	2624497
2604641	2611649	2617489	2609313	2620993
2626833	2610481	2612817	2615153	2598801
2625665	2616321	2608145	2613985	2599969
2601137	2602305	2622161	2618657	2619825

L6-M11

2635009	2652529	2632673	2636177	2653697
2633841	2640849	2646689	2638513	2650193
2656033	2639681	2642017	2644353	2628001
2654865	2645521	2637345	2643185	2629169
2630337	2631505	2651361	2647857	2649025

L6-M12

2664209	2681729	2661873	2665377	2682897
2663041	2670049	2675889	2667713	2679393
2685233	2668881	2671217	2673553	2657201
2684065	2674721	2666545	2672385	2658369
2659537	2660705	2680561	2677057	2678225

L6-M13

2693409	2710929	2691073	2694577	2712097
2692241	2699249	2705089	2696913	2708593
2714433	2698081	2700417	2702753	2686401
2713265	2703921	2695745	2701585	2687569
2688737	2689905	2709761	2706257	2707425

L6-M14

2722609	2740129	2720273	2723777	2741297
2721441	2728449	2734289	2726113	2737793
2743633	2727281	2729617	2731953	2715601
2742465	2733121	2724945	2730785	2716769
2717937	2719105	2738961	2735457	2736625

L6-M15

2751809	2769329	2749473	2752977	2770497
2750641	2757649	2763489	2755313	2766993
2772833	2756481	2758817	2761153	2744801
2771665	2762321	2754145	2759985	2745969
2747137	2748305	2768161	2764657	2765825

L6-M16

2781009	2798529	2778673	2782177	2799697
2779841	2786849	2792689	2784513	2796193
2802033	2785681	2788017	2790353	2774001
2800865	2791521	2783345	2789185	2775169
2776337	2777505	2797361	2793857	2795025

L7-M1

2810209	2827729	2807873	2811377	2828897
2809041	2816049	2821889	2813713	2825393
2831233	2814881	2817217	2819553	2803201
2830065	2820721	2812545	2818385	2804369
2805537	2806705	2826561	2823057	2824225

L7-M2

2839409	2856929	2837073	2840577	2858097
2838241	2845249	2851089	2842913	2854593
2860433	2844081	2846417	2848753	2832401
2859265	2849921	2841745	2847585	2833569
2834737	2835905	2855761	2852257	2853425

L7-M3

2868609	2886129	2866273	2869777	2887297
2867441	2874449	2880289	2872113	2883793
2889633	2873281	2875617	2877953	2861601
2888465	2879121	2870945	2876785	2862769
2863937	2865105	2884961	2881457	2882625

L7-M4

2897809	2915329	2895473	2898977	2916497
2896641	2903649	2909489	2901313	2912993
2918833	2902481	2904817	2907153	2890801
2917665	2908321	2900145	2905985	2891969
2893137	2894305	2914161	2910657	2911825

L7-M5

2927009	2944529	2924673	2928177	2945697
2925841	2932849	2938689	2930513	2942193
2948033	2931681	2934017	2936353	2920001
2946865	2937521	2929345	2935185	2921169
2922337	2923505	2943361	2939857	2941025

L7-M6

2956209	2973729	2953873	2957377	2974897
2955041	2962049	2967889	2959713	2971393
2977233	2960881	2963217	2965553	2949201
2976065	2966721	2958545	2964385	2950369
2951537	2952705	2972561	2969057	2970225

L7-M7

2985409	3002929	2983073	2986577	3004097
2984241	2991249	2997089	2988913	3000593
3006433	2990081	2992417	2994753	2978401
3005265	2995921	2987745	2993585	2979569
2980737	2981905	3001761	2998257	2999425

L7-M8

3014609	3032129	3012273	3015777	3033297
3013441	3020449	3026289	3018113	3029793
3035633	3019281	3021617	3023953	3007601
3034465	3025121	3016945	3022785	3008769
3009937	3011105	3030961	3027457	3028625

L7-M9

3043809	3061329	3041473	3044977	3062497
3042641	3049649	3055489	3047313	3058993
3064833	3048481	3050817	3053153	3036801
3063665	3054321	3046145	3051985	3037969
3039137	3040305	3060161	3056657	3057825

L7-M10

3073009	3090529	3070673	3074177	3091697
3071841	3078849	3084689	3076513	3088193
3094033	3077681	3080017	3082353	3066001
3092865	3083521	3075345	3081185	3067169
3068337	3069505	3089361	3085857	3087025

L7-M11

3102209	3119729	3099873	3103377	3120897
3101041	3108049	3113889	3105713	3117393
3123233	3106881	3109217	3111553	3095201
3122065	3112721	3104545	3110385	3096369
3097537	3098705	3118561	3115057	3116225

L7-M12

3131409	3148929	3129073	3132577	3150097
3130241	3137249	3143089	3134913	3146593
3152433	3136081	3138417	3140753	3124401
3151265	3141921	3133745	3139585	3125569
3126737	3127905	3147761	3144257	3145425

L7-M13

3160609	3178129	3158273	3161777	3179297
3159441	3166449	3172289	3164113	3175793
3181633	3165281	3167617	3169953	3153601
3180465	3171121	3162945	3168785	3154769
3155937	3157105	3176961	3173457	3174625

L8-M6

3423409	3440929	3421073	3424577	3442097
3422241	3429249	3435089	3426913	3438593
3444433	3428081	3430417	3432753	3416401
3443265	3433921	3425745	3431585	3417569
3418737	3419905	3439761	3436257	3437425

L7-M14

3189809	3207329	3187473	3190977	3208497
3188641	3195649	3201489	3193313	3204993
3210833	3194481	3196817	3199153	3182801
3209665	3200321	3192145	3197985	3183969
3185137	3186305	3206161	3202657	3203825

L8-M7

3452609	3470129	3450273	3453777	3471297
3451441	3458449	3464289	3456113	3467793
3473633	3457281	3459617	3461953	3445601
3472465	3463121	3454945	3460785	3446769
3447937	3449105	3468961	3465457	3466625

L7-M15

3219009	3236529	3216673	3220177	3237697
3217841	3224849	3230689	3222513	3234193
3240033	3223681	3226017	3228353	3212001
3238865	3229521	3221345	3227185	3213169
3214337	3215505	3235361	3231857	3233025

L8-M8

3481809	3499329	3479473	3482977	3500497
3480641	3487649	3493489	3485313	3496993
3502833	3486481	3488817	3491153	3474801
3501665	3492321	3484145	3489985	3475969
3477137	3478305	3498161	3494657	3495825

L7-M16

3248209	3265729	3245873	3249377	3266897
3247041	3254049	3259889	3251713	3263393
3269233	3252881	3255217	3257553	3241201
3268065	3258721	3250545	3256385	3242369
3243537	3244705	3264561	3261057	3262225

L8-M9

3511009	3528529	3508673	3512177	3529697
3509841	3516849	3522689	3514513	3526193
3532033	3515681	3518017	3520353	3504001
3530865	3521521	3513345	3519185	3505169
3506337	3507505	3527361	3523857	3525025

L8M1

3277409	3294929	3275073	3278577	3296097
3276241	3283249	3289089	3280913	3292593
3298433	3282081	3284417	3286753	3270401
3297265	3287921	3279745	3285585	3271569
3272737	3273905	3293761	3290257	3291425

L8-M10

3540209	3557729	3537873	3541377	3558897
3539041	3546049	3551889	3543713	3555393
3561233	3544881	3547217	3549553	3533201
3560065	3550721	3542545	3548385	3534369
3535537	3536705	3556561	3553057	3554225

L8-M2

3306609	3324129	3304273	3307777	3325297
3305441	3312449	3318289	3310113	3321793
3327633	3311281	3313617	3315953	3299601
3326465	3317121	3308945	3314785	3300769
3301937	3303105	3322961	3319457	3320625

L8-M11

3569409	3586929	3567073	3570577	3588097
3568241	3575249	3581089	3572913	3584593
3590433	3574081	3576417	3578753	3562401
3589265	3579921	3571745	3577585	3563569
3564737	3565905	3585761	3582257	3583425

L8-M3

3335809	3353329	3333473	3336977	3354497
3334641	3341649	3347489	3339313	3350993
3356833	3340481	3342817	3345153	3328801
3355665	3346321	3338145	3343985	3329969
3331137	3332305	3352161	3348657	3349825

L8-M12

3598609	3616129	3596273	3599777	3617297
3597441	3604449	3610289	3602113	3613793
3619633	3603281	3605617	3607953	3591601
3618465	3609121	3600945	3606785	3592769
3593937	3595105	3614961	3611457	3612625

L8-M4

3365009	3382529	3362673	3366177	3383697
3363841	3370849	3376689	3368513	3380193
3386033	3369681	3372017	3374353	3358001
3384865	3375521	3367345	3373185	3359169
3360337	3361505	3381361	3377857	3379025

L8-M13

3627809	3645329	3625473	3628977	3646497
3626641	3633649	3639489	3631313	3642993
3648833	3632481	3634817	3637153	3620801
3647665	3638321	3630145	3635985	3621969
3623137	3624305	3644161	3640657	3641825

L8-M5

3394209	3411729	3391873	3395377	3412897
3393041	3400049	3405889	3397713	3409393
3415233	3398881	3401217	3403553	3387201
3414065	3404721	3396545	3402385	3388369
3389537	3390705	3410561	3407057	3408225

L8-M14

3657009	3674529	3654673	3658177	3675697
3655841	3662849	3668689	3660513	3672193
3678033	3661681	3664017	3666353	3650001
3676865	3667521	3659345	3665185	3651169
3652337	3653505	3673361	3669857	3671025

L8-M15

3686209	3703729	3683873	3687377	3704897
3685041	3692049	3697889	3689713	3701393
3707233	3690881	3693217	3695553	3679201
3706065	3696721	3688545	3694385	3680369
3681537	3682705	3702561	3699057	3700225

L8-M16

3715409	3732929	3713073	3716577	3734097
3714241	3721249	3727089	3718913	3730593
3736433	3720081	3722417	3724753	3708401
3735265	3725921	3717745	3723585	3709569
3710737	3711905	3731761	3728257	3729425

L9-M1

3744609	3762129	3742273	3745777	3763297
3743441	3750449	3756289	3748113	3759793
3765633	3749281	3751617	3753953	3737601
3764465	3755121	3746945	3752785	3738769
3739937	3741105	3760961	3757457	3758625

L9-M2

3773809	3791329	3771473	3774977	3792497
3772641	3779649	3785489	3777313	3788993
3794833	3778481	3780817	3783153	3766801
3793665	3784321	3776145	3781985	3767969
3769137	3770305	3790161	3786657	3787825

L9-M3

3803009	3820529	3800673	3804177	3821697
3801841	3808849	3814689	3806513	3818193
3824033	3807681	3810017	3812353	3796001
3822865	3813521	3805345	3811185	3797169
3798337	3799505	3819361	3815857	3817025

L9-M4

3832209	3849729	3829873	3833377	3850897
3831041	3838049	3843889	3835713	3847393
3853233	3836881	3839217	3841553	3825201
3852065	3842721	3834545	3840385	3826369
3827537	3828705	3848561	3845057	3846225

L9-M5

3861409	3878929	3859073	3862577	3880097
3860241	3867249	3873089	3864913	3876593
3882433	3866081	3868417	3870753	3854401
3881265	3871921	3863745	3869585	3855569
3856737	3857905	3877761	3874257	3875425

L9-M6

3890609	3908129	3888273	3891777	3909297
3889441	3896449	3902289	3894113	3905793
3911633	3895281	3897617	3899953	3883601
3910465	3901121	3892945	3898785	3884769
3885937	3887105	3906961	3903457	3904625

L9-M7

3919809	3937329	3917473	3920977	3938497
3918641	3925649	3931489	3923313	3934993
3940833	3924481	3926817	3929153	3912801
3939665	3930321	3922145	3927985	3913969
3915137	3916305	3936161	3932657	3933825

L9-M8

3949009	3966529	3946673	3950177	3967697
3947841	3954849	3960689	3952513	3964193
3970033	3953681	3956017	3958353	3942001
3968865	3959521	3951345	3957185	3943169
3944337	3945505	3965361	3961857	3963025

L9-M9

3978209	3995729	3975873	3979377	3996897
3977041	3984049	3989889	3981713	3993393
3999233	3982881	3985217	3987553	3971201
3998065	3988721	3980545	3986385	3972369
3973537	3974705	3994561	3991057	3992225

L9-M10

4007409	4024929	4005073	4008577	4026097
4006241	4013249	4019089	4010913	4022593
4028433	4012081	4014417	4016753	4000401
4027265	4017921	4009745	4015585	4001569
4002737	4003905	4023761	4020257	4021425

L9-M11

4036609	4054129	4034273	4037777	4055297
4035441	4042449	4048289	4040113	4051793
4057633	4041281	4043617	4045953	4029601
4056465	4047121	4038945	4044785	4030769
4031937	4033105	4052961	4049457	4050625

L9-M12

4065809	4083329	4063473	4066977	4084497
4064641	4071649	4077489	4069313	4080993
4086833	4070481	4072817	4075153	4058801
4085665	4076321	4068145	4073985	4059969
4061137	4062305	4082161	4078657	4079825

L9-M13

4095009	4112529	4092673	4096177	4113697
4093841	4100849	4106689	4098513	4110193
4116033	4099681	4102017	4104353	4088001
4114865	4105521	4097345	4103185	4089169
4090337	4091505	4111361	4107857	4109025

L9-M14

4124209	4141729	4121873	4125377	4142897
4123041	4130049	4135889	4127713	4139393
4145233	4128881	4131217	4133553	4117201
4144065	4134721	4126545	4132385	4118369
4119537	4120705	4140561	4137057	4138225

L9-M15

4153409	4170929	4151073	4154577	4172097
4152241	4159249	4165089	4156913	4168593
4174433	4158081	4160417	4162753	4146401
4173265	4163921	4155745	4161585	4147569
4148737	4149905	4169761	4166257	4167425

L9-M16

4182609	4200129	4180273	4183777	4201297
4181441	4188449	4194289	4186113	4197793
4203633	4187281	4189617	4191953	4175601
4202465	4193121	4184945	4190785	4176769
4177937	4179105	4198961	4195457	4196625

L10-M1

4211809	4229329	4209473	4212977	4230497
4210641	4217649	4223489	4215313	4226993
4232833	4216481	4218817	4221153	4204801
4231665	4222321	4214145	4219985	4205969
4207137	4208305	4228161	4224657	4225825

L10-M2

4241009	4258529	4238673	4242177	4259697
4239841	4246849	4252689	4244513	4256193
4262033	4245681	4248017	4250353	4234001
4260865	4251521	4243345	4249185	4235169
4236337	4237505	4257361	4253857	4255025

L10-M3

4270209	4287729	4267873	4271377	4288897
4269041	4276049	4281889	4273713	4285393
4291233	4274881	4277217	4279553	4263201
4290065	4280721	4272545	4278385	4264369
4265537	4266705	4286561	4283057	4284225

L10-M4

4299409	4316929	4297073	4300577	4318097
4298241	4305249	4311089	4302913	4314593
4320433	4304081	4306417	4308753	4292401
4319265	4309921	4301745	4307585	4293569
4294737	4295905	4315761	4312257	4313425

L10-M5

4328609	4346129	4326273	4329777	4347297
4327441	4334449	4340289	4332113	4343793
4349633	4333281	4335617	4337953	4321601
4348465	4339121	4330945	4336785	4322769
4323937	4325105	4344961	4341457	4342625

L10-M6

4357809	4375329	4355473	4358977	4376497
4356641	4363649	4369489	4361313	4372993
4378833	4362481	4364817	4367153	4350801
4377665	4368321	4360145	4365985	4351969
4353137	4354305	4374161	4370657	4371825

L10-M7

4387009	4404529	4384673	4388177	4405697
4385841	4392849	4398689	4390513	4402193
4408033	4391681	4394017	4396353	4380001
4406865	4397521	4389345	4395185	4381169
4382337	4383505	4403361	4399857	4401025

L10-M8

4416209	4433729	4413873	4417377	4434897
4415041	4422049	4427889	4419713	4431393
4437233	4420881	4423217	4425553	4409201
4436065	4426721	4418545	4424385	4410369
4411537	4412705	4432561	4429057	4430225

L10-M9

4445409	4462929	4443073	4446577	4464097
4444241	4451249	4457089	4448913	4460593
4466433	4450081	4452417	4454753	4438401
4465265	4455921	4447745	4453585	4439569
4440737	4441905	4461761	4458257	4459425

L10-M10

4474609	4492129	4472273	4475777	4493297
4473441	4480449	4486289	4478113	4489793
4495633	4479281	4481617	4483953	4467601
4494465	4485121	4476945	4482785	4468769
4469937	4471105	4490961	4487457	4488625

L10-M11

4503809	4521329	4501473	4504977	4522497
4502641	4509649	4515489	4507313	4518993
4524833	4508481	4510817	4513153	4496801
4523665	4514321	4506145	4511985	4497969
4499137	4500305	4520161	4516657	4517825

L10-M12

4533009	4550529	4530673	4534177	4551697
4531841	4538849	4544689	4536513	4548193
4554033	4537681	4540017	4542353	4526001
4552865	4543521	4535345	4541185	4527169
4528337	4529505	4549361	4545857	4547025

L10-M13

4562209	4579729	4559873	4563377	4580897
4561041	4568049	4573889	4565713	4577393
4583233	4566881	4569217	4571553	4555201
4582065	4572721	4564545	4570385	4556369
4557537	4558705	4578561	4575057	4576225

L10-M14

4591409	4608929	4589073	4592577	4610097
4590241	4597249	4603089	4594913	4606593
4612433	4596081	4598417	4600753	4584401
4611265	4601921	4593745	4599585	4585569
4586737	4587905	4607761	4604257	4605425

L10-M15

4620609	4638129	4618273	4621777	4639297
4619441	4626449	4632289	4624113	4635793
4641633	4625281	4627617	4629953	4613601
4640465	4631121	4622945	4628785	4614769
4615937	4617105	4636961	4633457	4634625

L10-M16

4649809	4667329	4647473	4650977	4668497
4648641	4655649	4661489	4653313	4664993
4670833	4654481	4656817	4659153	4642801
4669665	4660321	4652145	4657985	4643969
4645137	4646305	4666161	4662657	4663825

L11-M1

4679009	4696529	4676673	4680177	4697697
4677841	4684849	4690689	4682513	4694193
4700033	4683681	4686017	4688353	4672001
4698865	4689521	4681345	4687185	4673169
4674337	4675505	4695361	4691857	4693025

L11-M2

4708209	4725729	4705873	4709377	4726897
4707041	4714049	4719889	4711713	4723393
4729233	4712881	4715217	4717553	4701201
4728065	4718721	4710545	4716385	4702369
4703537	4704705	4724561	4721057	4722225

L11-M3

4737409	4754929	4735073	4738577	4756097
4736241	4743249	4749089	4740913	4752593
4758433	4742081	4744417	4746753	4730401
4757265	4747921	4739745	4745585	4731569
4732737	4733905	4753761	4750257	4751425

L11-M4

4766609	4784129	4764273	4767777	4785297
4765441	4772449	4778289	4770113	4781793
4787633	4771281	4773617	4775953	4759601
4786465	4777121	4768945	4774785	4760769
4761937	4763105	4782961	4779457	4780625

L11-M5

4795809	4813329	4793473	4796977	4814497
4794641	4801649	4807489	4799313	4810993
4816833	4800481	4802817	4805153	4788801
4815665	4806321	4798145	4803985	4789969
4791137	4792305	4812161	4808657	4809825

L11-M6

4825009	4842529	4822673	4826177	4843697
4823841	4830849	4836689	4828513	4840193
4846033	4829681	4832017	4834353	4818001
4844865	4835521	4827345	4833185	4819169
4820337	4821505	4841361	4837857	4839025

L11-M7

4854209	4871729	4851873	4855377	4872897
4853041	4860049	4865889	4857713	4869393
4875233	4858881	4861217	4863553	4847201
4874065	4864721	4856545	4862385	4848369
4849537	4850705	4870561	4867057	4868225

L11-M8

4883409	4900929	4881073	4884577	4902097
4882241	4889249	4895089	4886913	4898593
4904433	4888081	4890417	4892753	4876401
4903265	4893921	4885745	4891585	4877569
4878737	4879905	4899761	4896257	4897425

L11-M9

4912609	4930129	4910273	4913777	4931297
4911441	4918449	4924289	4916113	4927793
4933633	4917281	4919617	4921953	4905601
4932465	4923121	4914945	4920785	4906769
4907937	4909105	4928961	4925457	4926625

L11-M10

4941809	4959329	4939473	4942977	4960497
4940641	4947649	4953489	4945313	4956993
4962833	4946481	4948817	4951153	4934801
4961665	4952321	4944145	4949985	4935969
4937137	4938305	4958161	4954657	4955825

L11-M11

4971009	4988529	4968673	4972177	4989697
4969841	4976849	4982689	4974513	4986193
4992033	4975681	4978017	4980353	4964001
4990865	4981521	4973345	4979185	4965169
4966337	4967505	4987361	4983857	4985025

L11-M12

5000209	5017729	4997873	5001377	5018897
4999041	5006049	5011889	5003713	5015393
5021233	5004881	5007217	5009553	4993201
5020065	5010721	5002545	5008385	4994369
4995537	4996705	5016561	5013057	5014225

L11-M13

5029409	5046929	5027073	5030577	5048097
5028241	5035249	5041089	5032913	5044593
5050433	5034081	5036417	5038753	5022401
5049265	5039921	5031745	5037585	5023569
5024737	5025905	5045761	5042257	5043425

L11-M14

5058609	5076129	5056273	5059777	5077297
5057441	5064449	5070289	5062113	5073793
5079633	5063281	5065617	5067953	5051601
5078465	5069121	5060945	5066785	5052769
5053937	5055105	5074961	5071457	5072625

L11-M15

5087809	5105329	5085473	5088977	5106497
5086641	5093649	5099489	5091313	5102993
5108833	5092481	5094817	5097153	5080801
5107665	5098321	5090145	5095985	5081969
5083137	5084305	5104161	5100657	5101825

L11-M16

5117009	5134529	5114673	5118177	5135697
5115841	5122849	5128689	5120513	5132193
5138033	5121681	5124017	5126353	5110001
5136865	5127521	5119345	5125185	5111169
5112337	5113505	5133361	5129857	5131025

L12-M1

5146209	5163729	5143873	5147377	5164897
5145041	5152049	5157889	5149713	5161393
5167233	5150881	5153217	5155553	5139201
5166065	5156721	5148545	5154385	5140369
5141537	5142705	5162561	5159057	5160225

L12-M2

5175409	5192929	5173073	5176577	5194097
5174241	5181249	5187089	5178913	5190593
5196433	5180081	5182417	5184753	5168401
5195265	5185921	5177745	5183585	5169569
5170737	5171905	5191761	5188257	5189425

L12-M3

5204609	5222129	5202273	5205777	5223297
5203441	5210449	5216289	5208113	5219793
5225633	5209281	5211617	5213953	5197601
5224465	5215121	5206945	5212785	5198769
5199937	5201105	5220961	5217457	5218625

L12-M4

5233809	5251329	5231473	5234977	5252497
5232641	5239649	5245489	5237313	5248993
5254833	5238481	5240817	5243153	5226801
5253665	5244321	5236145	5241985	5227969
5229137	5230305	5250161	5246657	5247825

L12-M5

5263009	5280529	5260673	5264177	5281697
5261841	5268849	5274689	5266513	5278193
5284033	5267681	5270017	5272353	5256001
5282865	5273521	5265345	5271185	5257169
5258337	5259505	5279361	5275857	5277025

L12-M6

5292209	5309729	5289873	5293377	5310897
5291041	5298049	5303889	5295713	5307393
5313233	5296881	5299217	5301553	5285201
5312065	5302721	5294545	5300385	5286369
5287537	5288705	5308561	5305057	5306225

L12-M7

5321409	5338929	5319073	5322577	5340097
5320241	5327249	5333089	5324913	5336593
5342433	5326081	5328417	5330753	5314401
5341265	5331921	5323745	5329585	5315569
5316737	5317905	5337761	5334257	5335425

L12-M8

5350609	5368129	5348273	5351777	5369297
5349441	5356449	5362289	5354113	5365793
5371633	5355281	5357617	5359953	5343601
5370465	5361121	5352945	5358785	5344769
5345937	5347105	5366961	5363457	5364625

L12-M9

5379809	5397329	5377473	5380977	5398497
5378641	5385649	5391489	5383313	5394993
5400833	5384481	5386817	5389153	5372801
5399665	5390321	5382145	5387985	5373969
5375137	5376305	5396161	5392657	5393825

L12-M10

5409009	5426529	5406673	5410177	5427697
5407841	5414849	5420689	5412513	5424193
5430033	5413681	5416017	5418353	5402001
5428865	5419521	5411345	5417185	5403169
5404337	5405505	5425361	5421857	5423025

L12-M11

5438209	5455729	5435873	5439377	5456897
5437041	5444049	5449889	5441713	5453393
5459233	5442881	5445217	5447553	5431201
5458065	5448721	5440545	5446385	5432369
5433537	5434705	5454561	5451057	5452225

L12-M12

5467409	5484929	5465073	5468577	5486097
5466241	5473249	5479089	5470913	5482593
5488433	5472081	5474417	5476753	5460401
5487265	5477921	5469745	5475585	5461569
5462737	5463905	5483761	5480257	5481425

L12-M13

5496609	5514129	5494273	5497777	5515297
5495441	5502449	5508289	5500113	5511793
5517633	5501281	5503617	5505953	5489601
5516465	5507121	5498945	5504785	5490769
5491937	5493105	5512961	5509457	5510625

L12-M14

5525809	5543329	5523473	5526977	5544497
5524641	5531649	5537489	5529313	5540993
5546833	5530481	5532817	5535153	5518801
5545665	5536321	5528145	5533985	5519969
5521137	5522305	5542161	5538657	5539825

L12-M15

5555009	5572529	5552673	5556177	5573697
5553841	5560849	5566689	5558513	5570193
5576033	5559681	5562017	5564353	5548001
5574865	5565521	5557345	5563185	5549169
5550337	5551505	5571361	5567857	5569025

L12-M16

5584209	5601729	5581873	5585377	5602897
5583041	5590049	5595889	5587713	5599393
5605233	5588881	5591217	5593553	5577201
5604065	5594721	5586545	5592385	5578369
5579537	5580705	5600561	5597057	5598225

L13-M1

5613409	5630929	5611073	5614577	5632097
5612241	5619249	5625089	5616913	5628593
5634433	5618081	5620417	5622753	5606401
5633265	5623921	5615745	5621585	5607569
5608737	5609905	5629761	5626257	5627425

L13-M2

5642609	5660129	5640273	5643777	5661297
5641441	5648449	5654289	5646113	5657793
5663633	5647281	5649617	5651953	5635601
5662465	5653121	5644945	5650785	5636769
5637937	5639105	5658961	5655457	5656625

L13-M3

5671809	5689329	5669473	5672977	5690497
5670641	5677649	5683489	5675313	5686993
5692833	5676481	5678817	5681153	5664801
5691665	5682321	5674145	5679985	5665969
5667137	5668305	5688161	5684657	5685825

L13-M4

5701009	5718529	5698673	5702177	5719697
5699841	5706849	5712689	5704513	5716193
5722033	5705681	5708017	5710353	5694001
5720865	5711521	5703345	5709185	5695169
5696337	5697505	5717361	5713857	5715025

L13-M5

5730209	5747729	5727873	5731377	5748897
5729041	5736049	5741889	5733713	5745393
5751233	5734881	5737217	5739553	5723201
5750065	5740721	5732545	5738385	5724369
5725537	5726705	5746561	5743057	5744225

L13-M6

5759409	5776929	5757073	5760577	5778097
5758241	5765249	5771089	5762913	5774593
5780433	5764081	5766417	5768753	5752401
5779265	5769921	5761745	5767585	5753569
5754737	5755905	5775761	5772257	5773425

L13-M7

5788609	5806129	5786273	5789777	5807297
5787441	5794449	5800289	5792113	5803793
5809633	5793281	5795617	5797953	5781601
5808465	5799121	5790945	5796785	5782769
5783937	5785105	5804961	5801457	5802625

L13-M8

5817809	5835329	5815473	5818977	5836497
5816641	5823649	5829489	5821313	5832993
5838833	5822481	5824817	5827153	5810801
5837665	5828321	5820145	5825985	5811969
5813137	5814305	5834161	5830657	5831825

L13-M9

5847009	5864529	5844673	5848177	5865697
5845841	5852849	5858689	5850513	5862193
5868033	5851681	5854017	5856353	5840001
5866865	5857521	5849345	5855185	5841169
5842337	5843505	5863361	5859857	5861025

L13-M10

5876209	5893729	5873873	5877377	5894897
5875041	5882049	5887889	5879713	5891393
5897233	5880881	5883217	5885553	5869201
5896065	5886721	5878545	5884385	5870369
5871537	5872705	5892561	5889057	5890225

L13-M11

5905409	5922929	5903073	5906577	5924097
5904241	5911249	5917089	5908913	5920593
5926433	5910081	5912417	5914753	5898401
5925265	5915921	5907745	5913585	5899569
5900737	5901905	5921761	5918257	5919425

L13-M12

5934609	5952129	5932273	5935777	5953297
5933441	5940449	5946289	5938113	5949793
5955633	5939281	5941617	5943953	5927601
5954465	5945121	5936945	5942785	5928769
5929937	5931105	5950961	5947457	5948625

L13-M13

5963809	5981329	5961473	5964977	5982497
5962641	5969649	5975489	5967313	5978993
5984833	5968481	5970817	5973153	5956801
5983665	5974321	5966145	5971985	5957969
5959137	5960305	5980161	5976657	5977825

L13-M14

5993009	6010529	5990673	5994177	6011697
5991841	5998849	6004689	5996513	6008193
6014033	5997681	6000017	6002353	5986001
6012865	6003521	5995345	6001185	5987169
5988337	5989505	6009361	6005857	6007025

L13-M15

6022209	6039729	6019873	6023377	6040897
6021041	6028049	6033889	6025713	6037393
6043233	6026881	6029217	6031553	6015201
6042065	6032721	6024545	6030385	6016369
6017537	6018705	6038561	6035057	6036225

L13-M16

6051409	6068929	6049073	6052577	6070097
6050241	6057249	6063089	6054913	6066593
6072433	6056081	6058417	6060753	6044401
6071265	6061921	6053745	6059585	6045569
6046737	6047905	6067761	6064257	6065425

L14-M1

6080609	6098129	6078273	6081777	6099297
6079441	6086449	6092289	6084113	6095793
6101633	6085281	6087617	6089953	6073601
6100465	6091121	6082945	6088785	6074769
6075937	6077105	6096961	6093457	6094625

L14-M2

6109809	6127329	6107473	6110977	6128497
6108641	6115649	6121489	6113313	6124993
6130833	6114481	6116817	6119153	6102801
6129665	6120321	6112145	6117985	6103969
6105137	6106305	6126161	6122657	6123825

L14-M3

6139009	6156529	6136673	6140177	6157697
6137841	6144849	6150689	6142513	6154193
6160033	6143681	6146017	6148353	6132001
6158865	6149521	6141345	6147185	6133169
6134337	6135505	6155361	6151857	6153025

L14-M4

6168209	6185729	6165873	6169377	6186897
6167041	6174049	6179889	6171713	6183393
6189233	6172881	6175217	6177553	6161201
6188065	6178721	6170545	6176385	6162369
6163537	6164705	6184561	6181057	6182225

L14-M5

6197409	6214929	6195073	6198577	6216097
6196241	6203249	6209089	6200913	6212593
6218433	6202081	6204417	6206753	6190401
6217265	6207921	6199745	6205585	6191569
6192737	6193905	6213761	6210257	6211425

L14-M6

6226609	6244129	6224273	6227777	6245297
6225441	6232449	6238289	6230113	6241793
6247633	6231281	6233617	6235953	6219601
6246465	6237121	6228945	6234785	6220769
6221937	6223105	6242961	6239457	6240625

L14-M7

6255809	6273329	6253473	6256977	6274497
6254641	6261649	6267489	6259313	6270993
6276833	6260481	6262817	6265153	6248801
6275665	6266321	6258145	6263985	6249969
6251137	6252305	6272161	6268657	6269825

L14-M8

6285009	6302529	6282673	6286177	6303697
6283841	6290849	6296689	6288513	6300193
6306033	6289681	6292017	6294353	6278001
6304865	6295521	6287345	6293185	6279169
6280337	6281505	6301361	6297857	6299025

L14-M9

6314209	6331729	6311873	6315377	6332897
6313041	6320049	6325889	6317713	6329393
6335233	6318881	6321217	6323553	6307201
6334065	6324721	6316545	6322385	6308369
6309537	6310705	6330561	6327057	6328225

L14-M10

6343409	6360929	6341073	6344577	6362097
6342241	6349249	6355089	6346913	6358593
6364433	6348081	6350417	6352753	6336401
6363265	6353921	6345745	6351585	6337569
6338737	6339905	6359761	6356257	6357425

L14-M11

6372609	6390129	6370273	6373777	6391297
6371441	6378449	6384289	6376113	6387793
6393633	6377281	6379617	6381953	6365601
6392465	6383121	6374945	6380785	6366769
6367937	6369105	6388961	6385457	6386625

L14-M12

6401809	6419329	6399473	6402977	6420497
6400641	6407649	6413489	6405313	6416993
6422833	6406481	6408817	6411153	6394801
6421665	6412321	6404145	6409985	6395969
6397137	6398305	6418161	6414657	6415825

L14-M13

6431009	6448529	6428673	6432177	6449697
6429841	6436849	6442689	6434513	6446193
6452033	6435681	6438017	6440353	6424001
6450865	6441521	6433345	6439185	6425169
6426337	6427505	6447361	6443857	6445025

L14-M14

6460209	6477729	6457873	6461377	6478897
6459041	6466049	6471889	6463713	6475393
6481233	6464881	6467217	6469553	6453201
6480065	6470721	6462545	6468385	6454369
6455537	6456705	6476561	6473057	6474225

L14-M15

6489409	6506929	6487073	6490577	6508097
6488241	6495249	6501089	6492913	6504593
6510433	6494081	6496417	6498753	6482401
6509265	6499921	6491745	6497585	6483569
6484737	6485905	6505761	6502257	6503425

L14-M16

6518609	6536129	6516273	6519777	6537297
6517441	6524449	6530289	6522113	6533793
6539633	6523281	6525617	6527953	6511601
6538465	6529121	6520945	6526785	6512769
6513937	6515105	6534961	6531457	6532625

L15-M1

6547809	6565329	6545473	6548977	6566497
6546641	6553649	6559489	6551313	6562993
6568833	6552481	6554817	6557153	6540801
6567665	6558321	6550145	6555985	6541969
6543137	6544305	6564161	6560657	6561825

L15-M2

6577009	6594529	6574673	6578177	6595697
6575841	6582849	6588689	6580513	6592193
6598033	6581681	6584017	6586353	6570001
6596865	6587521	6579345	6585185	6571169
6572337	6573505	6593361	6589857	6591025

L15-M3

6606209	6623729	6603873	6607377	6624897
6605041	6612049	6617889	6609713	6621393
6627233	6610881	6613217	6615553	6599201
6626065	6616721	6608545	6614385	6600369
6601537	6602705	6622561	6619057	6620225

L15-M4

6635409	6652929	6633073	6636577	6654097
6634241	6641249	6647089	6638913	6650593
6656433	6640081	6642417	6644753	6628401
6655265	6645921	6637745	6643585	6629569
6630737	6631905	6651761	6648257	6649425

L15-M5

6664609	6682129	6662273	6665777	6683297
6663441	6670449	6676289	6668113	6679793
6685633	6669281	6671617	6673953	6657601
6684465	6675121	6666945	6672785	6658769
6659937	6661105	6680961	6677457	6678625

L15-M6

6693809	6711329	6691473	6694977	6712497
6692641	6699649	6705489	6697313	6708993
6714833	6698481	6700817	6703153	6686801
6713665	6704321	6696145	6701985	6687969
6689137	6690305	6710161	6706657	6707825

L15-M7

6723009	6740529	6720673	6724177	6741697
6721841	6728849	6734689	6726513	6738193
6744033	6727681	6730017	6732353	6716001
6742865	6733521	6725345	6731185	6717169
6718337	6719505	6739361	6735857	6737025

L15-M8

6752209	6769729	6749873	6753377	6770897
6751041	6758049	6763889	6755713	6767393
6773233	6756881	6759217	6761553	6745201
6772065	6762721	6754545	6760385	6746369
6747537	6748705	6768561	6765057	6766225

L15-M9

6781409	6798929	6779073	6782577	6800097
6780241	6787249	6793089	6784913	6796593
6802433	6786081	6788417	6790753	6774401
6801265	6791921	6783745	6789585	6775569
6776737	6777905	6797761	6794257	6795425

L15-M10

6810609	6828129	6808273	6811777	6829297
6809441	6816449	6822289	6814113	6825793
6831633	6815281	6817617	6819953	6803601
6830465	6821121	6812945	6818785	6804769
6805937	6807105	6826961	6823457	6824625

L15-M11

6839809	6857329	6837473	6840977	6858497
6838641	6845649	6851489	6843313	6854993
6860833	6844481	6846817	6849153	6832801
6859665	6850321	6842145	6847985	6833969
6835137	6836305	6856161	6852657	6853825

L15-M12

6869009	6886529	6866673	6870177	6887697
6867841	6874849	6880689	6872513	6884193
6890033	6873681	6876017	6878353	6862001
6888865	6879521	6871345	6877185	6863169
6864337	6865505	6885361	6881857	6883025

L15-M13

6898209	6915729	6895873	6899377	6916897
6897041	6904049	6909889	6901713	6913393
6919233	6902881	6905217	6907553	6891201
6918065	6908721	6900545	6906385	6892369
6893537	6894705	6914561	6911057	6912225

L15-M14

6927409	6944929	6925073	6928577	6946097
6926241	6933249	6939089	6930913	6942593
6948433	6932081	6934417	6936753	6920401
6947265	6937921	6929745	6935585	6921569
6922737	6923905	6943761	6940257	6941425

L15-M15

6956609	6974129	6954273	6957777	6975297
6955441	6962449	6968289	6960113	6971793
6977633	6961281	6963617	6965953	6949601
6976465	6967121	6958945	6964785	6950769
6951937	6953105	6972961	6969457	6970625

L15-M16

6985809	7003329	6983473	6986977	7004497
6984641	6991649	6997489	6989313	7000993
7006833	6990481	6992817	6995153	6978801
7005665	6996321	6988145	6993985	6979969
6981137	6982305	7002161	6998657	6999825

L16-M1

7015009	7032529	7012673	7016177	7033697
7013841	7020849	7026689	7018513	7030193
7036033	7019681	7022017	7024353	7008001
7034865	7025521	7017345	7023185	7009169
7010337	7011505	7031361	7027857	7029025

L16-M2

7044209	7061729	7041873	7045377	7062897
7043041	7050049	7055889	7047713	7059393
7065233	7048881	7051217	7053553	7037201
7064065	7054721	7046545	7052385	7038369
7039537	7040705	7060561	7057057	7058225

L16-M3

7073409	7090929	7071073	7074577	7092097
7072241	7079249	7085089	7076913	7088593
7094433	7078081	7080417	7082753	7066401
7093265	7083921	7075745	7081585	7067569
7068737	7069905	7089761	7086257	7087425

L16-M4

7102609	7120129	7100273	7103777	7121297
7101441	7108449	7114289	7106113	7117793
7123633	7107281	7109617	7111953	7095601
7122465	7113121	7104945	7110785	7096769
7097937	7099105	7118961	7115457	7116625

L16-M5

7131809	7149329	7129473	7132977	7150497
7130641	7137649	7143489	7135313	7146993
7152833	7136481	7138817	7141153	7124801
7151665	7142321	7134145	7139985	7125969
7127137	7128305	7148161	7144657	7145825

L16-M6

7161009	7178529	7158673	7162177	7179697
7159841	7166849	7172689	7164513	7176193
7182033	7165681	7168017	7170353	7154001
7180865	7171521	7163345	7169185	7155169
7156337	7157505	7177361	7173857	7175025

L16-M7

7190209	7207729	7187873	7191377	7208897
7189041	7196049	7201889	7193713	7205393
7211233	7194881	7197217	7199553	7183201
7210065	7200721	7192545	7198385	7184369
7185537	7186705	7206561	7203057	7204225

L16-M8

7219409	7236929	7217073	7220577	7238097
7218241	7225249	7231089	7222913	7234593
7240433	7224081	7226417	7228753	7212401
7239265	7229921	7221745	7227585	7213569
7214737	7215905	7235761	7232257	7233425

L16-M9

7248609	7266129	7246273	7249777	7267297
7247441	7254449	7260289	7252113	7263793
7269633	7253281	7255617	7257953	7241601
7268465	7259121	7250945	7256785	7242769
7243937	7245105	7264961	7261457	7262625

L16-M10

7277809	7295329	7275473	7278977	7296497
7276641	7283649	7289489	7281313	7292993
7298833	7282481	7284817	7287153	7270801
7297665	7288321	7280145	7285985	7271969
7273137	7274305	7294161	7290657	7291825

L16-M11

7307009	7324529	7304673	7308177	7325697
7305841	7312849	7318689	7310513	7322193
7328033	7311681	7314017	7316353	7300001
7326865	7317521	7309345	7315185	7301169
7302337	7303505	7323361	7319857	7321025

L16-M12

7336209	7353729	7333873	7337377	7354897
7335041	7342049	7347889	7339713	7351393
7357233	7340881	7343217	7345553	7329201
7356065	7346721	7338545	7344385	7330369
7331537	7332705	7352561	7349057	7350225

L16-M13

7365409	7382929	7363073	7366577	7384097
7364241	7371249	7377089	7368913	7380593
7386433	7370081	7372417	7374753	7358401
7385265	7375921	7367745	7373585	7359569
7360737	7361905	7381761	7378257	7379425

L16-M14

7394609	7412129	7392273	7395777	7413297
7393441	7400449	7406289	7398113	7409793
7415633	7399281	7401617	7403953	7387601
7414465	7405121	7396945	7402785	7388769
7389937	7391105	7410961	7407457	7408625

L16-M15

7423809	7441329	7421473	7424977	7442497
7422641	7429649	7435489	7427313	7438993
7444833	7428481	7430817	7433153	7416801
7443665	7434321	7426145	7431985	7417969
7419137	7420305	7440161	7436657	7437825

L16M16

7453009	7470529	7450673	7454177	7471697
7451841	7458849	7464689	7456513	7468193
7474033	7457681	7460017	7462353	7446001
7472865	7463521	7455345	7461185	7447169
7448337	7449505	7469361	7465857	7467025

L17-M1

7482209	7499729	7479873	7483377	7500897
7481041	7488049	7493889	7485713	7497393
7503233	7486881	7489217	7491553	7475201
7502065	7492721	7484545	7490385	7476369
7477537	7478705	7498561	7495057	7496225

L17-M2

7511409	7528929	7509073	7512577	7530097
7510241	7517249	7523089	7514913	7526593
7532433	7516081	7518417	7520753	7504401
7531265	7521921	7513745	7519585	7505569
7506737	7507905	7527761	7524257	7525425

L17-M3

7540609	7558129	7538273	7541777	7559297
7539441	7546449	7552289	7544113	7555793
7561633	7545281	7547617	7549953	7533601
7560465	7551121	7542945	7548785	7534769
7535937	7537105	7556961	7553457	7554625

L17-M4

7569809	7587329	7567473	7570977	7588497
7568641	7575649	7581489	7573313	7584993
7590833	7574481	7576817	7579153	7562801
7589665	7580321	7572145	7577985	7563969
7565137	7566305	7586161	7582657	7583825

L17-M5

7599009	7616529	7596673	7600177	7617697
7597841	7604849	7610689	7602513	7614193
7620033	7603681	7606017	7608353	7592001
7618865	7609521	7601345	7607185	7593169
7594337	7595505	7615361	7611857	7613025

L17-M6

7628209	7645729	7625873	7629377	7646897
7627041	7634049	7639889	7631713	7643393
7649233	7632881	7635217	7637553	7621201
7648065	7638721	7630545	7636385	7622369
7623537	7624705	7644561	7641057	7642225

L17-M7

7657409	7674929	7655073	7658577	7676097
7656241	7663249	7669089	7660913	7672593
7678433	7662081	7664417	7666753	7650401
7677265	7667921	7659745	7665585	7651569
7652737	7653905	7673761	7670257	7671425

L17-M8

7686609	7704129	7684273	7687777	7705297
7685441	7692449	7698289	7690113	7701793
7707633	7691281	7693617	7695953	7679601
7706465	7697121	7688945	7694785	7680769
7681937	7683105	7702961	7699457	7700625

L17-M9

7715809	7733329	7713473	7716977	7734497
7714641	7721649	7727489	7719313	7730993
7736833	7720481	7722817	7725153	7708801
7735665	7726321	7718145	7723985	7709969
7711137	7712305	7732161	7728657	7729825

L17-M10

7745009	7762529	7742673	7746177	7763697
7743841	7750849	7756689	7748513	7760193
7766033	7749681	7752017	7754353	7738001
7764865	7755521	7747345	7753185	7739169
7740337	7741505	7761361	7757857	7759025

L17-M11

7774209	7791729	7771873	7775377	7792897
7773041	7780049	7785889	7777713	7789393
7795233	7778881	7781217	7783553	7767201
7794065	7784721	7776545	7782385	7768369
7769537	7770705	7790561	7787057	7788225

L17-M12

7803409	7820929	7801073	7804577	7822097
7802241	7809249	7815089	7806913	7818593
7824433	7808081	7810417	7812753	7796401
7823265	7813921	7805745	7811585	7797569
7798737	7799905	7819761	7816257	7817425

L17-M13

7832609	7850129	7830273	7833777	7851297
7831441	7838449	7844289	7836113	7847793
7853633	7837281	7839617	7841953	7825601
7852465	7843121	7834945	7840785	7826769
7827937	7829105	7848961	7845457	7846625

L17-M14

7861809	7879329	7859473	7862977	7880497
7860641	7867649	7873489	7865313	7876993
7882833	7866481	7868817	7871153	7854801
7881665	7872321	7864145	7869985	7855969
7857137	7858305	7878161	7874657	7875825

L17-M15

7891009	7908529	7888673	7892177	7909697
7889841	7896849	7902689	7894513	7906193
7912033	7895681	7898017	7900353	7884001
7910865	7901521	7893345	7899185	7885169
7886337	7887505	7907361	7903857	7905025

L17-M16

7920209	7937729	7917873	7921377	7938897
7919041	7926049	7931889	7923713	7935393
7941233	7924881	7927217	7929553	7913201
7940065	7930721	7922545	7928385	7914369
7915537	7916705	7936561	7933057	7934225

L18-M1

7949409	7966929	7947073	7950577	7968097
7948241	7955249	7961089	7952913	7964593
7970433	7954081	7956417	7958753	7942401
7969265	7959921	7951745	7957585	7943569
7944737	7945905	7965761	7962257	7963425

L18-M2

7978609	7996129	7976273	7979777	7997297
7977441	7984449	7990289	7982113	7993793
7999633	7983281	7985617	7987953	7971601
7998465	7989121	7980945	7986785	7972769
7973937	7975105	7994961	7991457	7992625

L18-M3

8007809	8025329	8005473	8008977	8026497
8006641	8013649	8019489	8011313	8022993
8028833	8012481	8014817	8017153	8000801
8027665	8018321	8010145	8015985	8001969
8003137	8004305	8024161	8020657	8021825

L18-M4

8037009	8054529	8034673	8038177	8055697
8035841	8042849	8048689	8040513	8052193
8058033	8041681	8044017	8046353	8030001
8056865	8047521	8039345	8045185	8031169
8032337	8033505	8053361	8049857	8051025

L18-M5

8066209	8083729	8063873	8067377	8084897
8065041	8072049	8077889	8069713	8081393
8087233	8070881	8073217	8075553	8059201
8086065	8076721	8068545	8074385	8060369
8061537	8062705	8082561	8079057	8080225

L18-M6

8095409	8112929	8093073	8096577	8114097
8094241	8101249	8107089	8098913	8110593
8116433	8100081	8102417	8104753	8088401
8115265	8105921	8097745	8103585	8089569
8090737	8091905	8111761	8108257	8109425

L18-M7

8124609	8142129	8122273	8125777	8143297
8123441	8130449	8136289	8128113	8139793
8145633	8129281	8131617	8133953	8117601
8144465	8135121	8126945	8132785	8118769
8119937	8121105	8140961	8137457	8138625

L18-M8

8153809	8171329	8151473	8154977	8172497
8152641	8159649	8165489	8157313	8168993
8174833	8158481	8160817	8163153	8146801
8173665	8164321	8156145	8161985	8147969
8149137	8150305	8170161	8166657	8167825

L18-M9

8183009	8200529	8180673	8184177	8201697
8181841	8188849	8194689	8186513	8198193
8204033	8187681	8190017	8192353	8176001
8202865	8193521	8185345	8191185	8177169
8178337	8179505	8199361	8195857	8197025

L18-M10

8212209	8229729	8209873	8213377	8230897
8211041	8218049	8223889	8215713	8227393
8233233	8216881	8219217	8221553	8205201
8232065	8222721	8214545	8220385	8206369
8207537	8208705	8228561	8225057	8226225

L18-M11

8241409	8258929	8239073	8242577	8260097
8240241	8247249	8253089	8244913	8256593
8262433	8246081	8248417	8250753	8234401
8261265	8251921	8243745	8249585	8235569
8236737	8237905	8257761	8254257	8255425

L18-M12

8270609	8288129	8268273	8271777	8289297
8269441	8276449	8282289	8274113	8285793
8291633	8275281	8277617	8279953	8263601
8290465	8281121	8272945	8278785	8264769
8265937	8267105	8286961	8283457	8284625

L18-M13

8299809	8317329	8297473	8300977	8318497
8298641	8305649	8311489	8303313	8314993
8320833	8304481	8306817	8309153	8292801
8319665	8310321	8302145	8307985	8293969
8295137	8296305	8316161	8312657	8313825

L18-M14

8329009	8346529	8326673	8330177	8347697
8327841	8334849	8340689	8332513	8344193
8350033	8333681	8336017	8338353	8322001
8348865	8339521	8331345	8337185	8323169
8324337	8325505	8345361	8341857	8343025

L18-M15

8358209	8375729	8355873	8359377	8376897
8357041	8364049	8369889	8361713	8373393
8379233	8362881	8365217	8367553	8351201
8378065	8368721	8360545	8366385	8352369
8353537	8354705	8374561	8371057	8372225

L18-M16

8387409	8404929	8385073	8388577	8406097
8386241	8393249	8399089	8390913	8402593
8408433	8392081	8394417	8396753	8380401
8407265	8397921	8389745	8395585	8381569
8382737	8383905	8403761	8400257	8401425

L19-M1

8416609	8434129	8414273	8417777	8435297
8415441	8422449	8428289	8420113	8431793
8437633	8421281	8423617	8425953	8409601
8436465	8427121	8418945	8424785	8410769
8411937	8413105	8432961	8429457	8430625

L19-M2

8445809	8463329	8443473	8446977	8464497
8444641	8451649	8457489	8449313	8460993
8466833	8450481	8452817	8455153	8438801
8465665	8456321	8448145	8453985	8439969
8441137	8442305	8462161	8458657	8459825

L19-M3

8475009	8492529	8472673	8476177	8493697
8473841	8480849	8486689	8478513	8490193
8496033	8479681	8482017	8484353	8468001
8494865	8485521	8477345	8483185	8469169
8470337	8471505	8491361	8487857	8489025

L19-M4

8504209	8521729	8501873	8505377	8522897
8503041	8510049	8515889	8507713	8519393
8525233	8508881	8511217	8513553	8497201
8524065	8514721	8506545	8512385	8498369
8499537	8500705	8520561	8517057	8518225

L19-M5

8533409	8550929	8531073	8534577	8552097
8532241	8539249	8545089	8536913	8548593
8554433	8538081	8540417	8542753	8526401
8553265	8543921	8535745	8541585	8527569
8528737	8529905	8549761	8546257	8547425

L19-M6

8562609	8580129	8560273	8563777	8581297
8561441	8568449	8574289	8566113	8577793
8583633	8567281	8569617	8571953	8555601
8582465	8573121	8564945	8570785	8556769
8557937	8559105	8578961	8575457	8576625

L19-M7

8591809	8609329	8589473	8592977	8610497
8590641	8597649	8603489	8595313	8606993
8612833	8596481	8598817	8601153	8584801
8611665	8602321	8594145	8599985	8585969
8587137	8588305	8608161	8604657	8605825

L19-M8

8621009	8638529	8618673	8622177	8639697
8619841	8626849	8632689	8624513	8636193
8642033	8625681	8628017	8630353	8614001
8640865	8631521	8623345	8629185	8615169
8616337	8617505	8637361	8633857	8635025

L19-M9

8650209	8667729	8647873	8651377	8668897
8649041	8656049	8661889	8653713	8665393
8671233	8654881	8657217	8659553	8643201
8670065	8660721	8652545	8658385	8644369
8645537	8646705	8666561	8663057	8664225

L19-M10

8679409	8696929	8677073	8680577	8698097
8678241	8685249	8691089	8682913	8694593
8700433	8684081	8686417	8688753	8672401
8699265	8689921	8681745	8687585	8673569
8674737	8675905	8695761	8692257	8693425

L19-M11

8708609	8726129	8706273	8709777	8727297
8707441	8714449	8720289	8712113	8723793
8729633	8713281	8715617	8717953	8701601
8728465	8719121	8710945	8716785	8702769
8703937	8705105	8724961	8721457	8722625

L19-M12

8737809	8755329	8735473	8738977	8756497
8736641	8743649	8749489	8741313	8752993
8758833	8742481	8744817	8747153	8730801
8757665	8748321	8740145	8745985	8731969
8733137	8734305	8754161	8750657	8751825

L19-M13

8767009	8784529	8764673	8768177	8785697
8765841	8772849	8778689	8770513	8782193
8788033	8771681	8774017	8776353	8760001
8786865	8777521	8769345	8775185	8761169
8762337	8763505	8783361	8779857	8781025

L19-M14

8796209	8813729	8793873	8797377	8814897
8795041	8802049	8807889	8799713	8811393
8817233	8800881	8803217	8805553	8789201
8816065	8806721	8798545	8804385	8790369
8791537	8792705	8812561	8809057	8810225

L19-M15

8825409	8842929	8823073	8826577	8844097
8824241	8831249	8837089	8828913	8840593
8846433	8830081	8832417	8834753	8818401
8845265	8835921	8827745	8833585	8819569
8820737	8821905	8841761	8838257	8839425

L19-M16

8854609	8872129	8852273	8855777	8873297
8853441	8860449	8866289	8858113	8869793
8875633	8859281	8861617	8863953	8847601
8874465	8865121	8856945	8862785	8848769
8849937	8851105	8870961	8867457	8868625

L20-M1

8883809	8901329	8881473	8884977	8902497
8882641	8889649	8895489	8887313	8898993
8904833	8888481	8890817	8893153	8876801
8903665	8894321	8886145	8891985	8877969
8879137	8880305	8900161	8896657	8897825

L20-M2

8913009	8930529	8910673	8914177	8931697
8911841	8918849	8924689	8916513	8928193
8934033	8917681	8920017	8922353	8906001
8932865	8923521	8915345	8921185	8907169
8908337	8909505	8929361	8925857	8927025

L20-M3

8942209	8959729	8939873	8943377	8960897
8941041	8948049	8953889	8945713	8957393
8963233	8946881	8949217	8951553	8935201
8962065	8952721	8944545	8950385	8936369
8937537	8938705	8958561	8955057	8956225

L20-M12

9205009	9222529	9202673	9206177	9223697
9203841	9210849	9216689	9208513	9220193
9226033	9209681	9212017	9214353	9198001
9224865	9215521	9207345	9213185	9199169
9200337	9201505	9221361	9217857	9219025

L20-M4

8971409	8988929	8969073	8972577	8990097
8970241	8977249	8983089	8974913	8986593
8992433	8976081	8978417	8980753	8964401
8991265	8981921	8973745	8979585	8965569
8966737	8967905	8987761	8984257	8985425

L20-M13

9234209	9251729	9231873	9235377	9252897
9233041	9240049	9245889	9237713	9249393
9255233	9238881	9241217	9243553	9227201
9254065	9244721	9236545	9242385	9228369
9229537	9230705	9250561	9247057	9248225

L20-M5

9000609	9018129	8998273	9001777	9019297
8999441	9006449	9012289	9004113	9015793
9021633	9005281	9007617	9009953	8993601
9020465	9011121	9002945	9008785	8994769
8995937	8997105	9016961	9013457	9014625

L20-M14

9263409	9280929	9261073	9264577	9282097
9262241	9269249	9275089	9266913	9278593
9284433	9268081	9270417	9272753	9256401
9283265	9273921	9265745	9271585	9257569
9258737	9259905	9279761	9276257	9277425

L20-M6

9029809	9047329	9027473	9030977	9048497
9028641	9035649	9041489	9033313	9044993
9050833	9034481	9036817	9039153	9022801
9049665	9040321	9032145	9037985	9023969
9025137	9026305	9046161	9042657	9043825

L20-M15

9292609	9310129	9290273	9293777	9311297
9291441	9298449	9304289	9296113	9307793
9313633	9297281	9299617	9301953	9285601
9312465	9303121	9294945	9300785	9286769
9287937	9289105	9308961	9305457	9306625

L20-M7

9059009	9076529	9056673	9060177	9077697
9057841	9064849	9070689	9062513	9074193
9080033	9063681	9066017	9068353	9052001
9078865	9069521	9061345	9067185	9053169
9054337	9055505	9075361	9071857	9073025

L20-M16

9321809	9339329	9319473	9322977	9340497
9320641	9327649	9333489	9325313	9336993
9342833	9326481	9328817	9331153	9314801
9341665	9332321	9324145	9329985	9315969
9317137	9318305	9338161	9334657	9335825

L20-M8

9088209	9105729	9085873	9089377	9106897
9087041	9094049	9099889	9091713	9103393
9109233	9092881	9095217	9097553	9081201
9108065	9098721	9090545	9096385	9082369
9083537	9084705	9104561	9101057	9102225

L21-M1

9351009	9368529	9348673	9352177	9369697
9349841	9356849	9362689	9354513	9366193
9372033	9355681	9358017	9360353	9344001
9370865	9361521	9353345	9359185	9345169
9346337	9347505	9367361	9363857	9365025

L20-M9

9117409	9134929	9115073	9118577	9136097
9116241	9123249	9129089	9120913	9132593
9138433	9122081	9124417	9126753	9110401
9137265	9127921	9119745	9125585	9111569
9112737	9113905	9133761	9130257	9131425

L21-M2

9380209	9397729	9377873	9381377	9398897
9379041	9386049	9391889	9383713	9395393
9401233	9384881	9387217	9389553	9373201
9400065	9390721	9382545	9388385	9374369
9375537	9376705	9396561	9393057	9394225

L20-M10

9146609	9164129	9144273	9147777	9165297
9145441	9152449	9158289	9150113	9161793
9167633	9151281	9153617	9155953	9139601
9166465	9157121	9148945	9154785	9140769
9141937	9143105	9162961	9159457	9160625

L21-M3

9409409	9426929	9407073	9410577	9428097
9408241	9415249	9421089	9412913	9424593
9430433	9414081	9416417	9418753	9402401
9429265	9419921	9411745	9417585	9403569
9404737	9405905	9425761	9422257	9423425

L20-M11

9175809	9193329	9173473	9176977	9194497
9174641	9181649	9187489	9179313	9190993
9196833	9180481	9182817	9185153	9168801
9195665	9186321	9178145	9183985	9169969
9171137	9172305	9192161	9188657	9189825

L21-M4

9438609	9456129	9436273	9439777	9457297
9437441	9444449	9450289	9442113	9453793
9459633	9443281	9445617	9447953	9431601
9458465	9449121	9440945	9446785	9432769
9433937	9435105	9454961	9451457	9452625

L21-M5

9467809	9485329	9465473	9468977	9486497
9466641	9473649	9479489	9471313	9482993
9488833	9472481	9474817	9477153	9460801
9487665	9478321	9470145	9475985	9461969
9463137	9464305	9484161	9480657	9481825

L21-M14

9730609	9748129	9728273	9731777	9749297
9729441	9736449	9742289	9734113	9745793
9751633	9735281	9737617	9739953	9723601
9750465	9741121	9732945	9738785	9724769
9725937	9727105	9746961	9743457	9744625

L21-M6

9497009	9514529	9494673	9498177	9515697
9495841	9502849	9508689	9500513	9512193
9518033	9501681	9504017	9506353	9490001
9516865	9507521	9499345	9505185	9491169
9492337	9493505	9513361	9509857	9511025

L21-M15

9759809	9777329	9757473	9760977	9778497
9758641	9765649	9771489	9763313	9774993
9780833	9764481	9766817	9769153	9752801
9779665	9770321	9762145	9767985	9753969
9755137	9756305	9776161	9772657	9773825

L21-M7

9526209	9543729	9523873	9527377	9544897
9525041	9532049	9537889	9529713	9541393
9547233	9530881	9533217	9535553	9519201
9546065	9536721	9528545	9534385	9520369
9521537	9522705	9542561	9539057	9540225

L21-M16

9789009	9806529	9786673	9790177	9807697
9787841	9794849	9800689	9792513	9804193
9810033	9793681	9796017	9798353	9782001
9808865	9799521	9791345	9797185	9783169
9784337	9785505	9805361	9801857	9803025

L21-M8

9555409	9572929	9553073	9556577	9574097
9554241	9561249	9567089	9558913	9570593
9576433	9560081	9562417	9564753	9548401
9575265	9565921	9557745	9563585	9549569
9550737	9551905	9571761	9568257	9569425

L22-M1

9818209	9835729	9815873	9819377	9836897
9817041	9824049	9829889	9821713	9833393
9839233	9822881	9825217	9827553	9811201
9838065	9828721	9820545	9826385	9812369
9813537	9814705	9834561	9831057	9832225

L21-M9

9584609	9602129	9582273	9585777	9603297
9583441	9590449	9596289	9588113	9599793
9605633	9589281	9591617	9593953	9577601
9604465	9595121	9586945	9592785	9578769
9579937	9581105	9600961	9597457	9598625

L22-M2

9847409	9864929	9845073	9848577	9866097
9846241	9853249	9859089	9850913	9862593
9868433	9852081	9854417	9856753	9840401
9867265	9857921	9849745	9855585	9841569
9842737	9843905	9863761	9860257	9861425

L21-M10

9613809	9631329	9611473	9614977	9632497
9612641	9619649	9625489	9617313	9628993
9634833	9618481	9620817	9623153	9606801
9633665	9624321	9616145	9621985	9607969
9609137	9610305	9630161	9626657	9627825

L22-M3

9876609	9894129	9874273	9877777	9895297
9875441	9882449	9888289	9880113	9891793
9897633	9881281	9883617	9885953	9869601
9896465	9887121	9878945	9884785	9870769
9871937	9873105	9892961	9889457	9890625

L21-M11

9643009	9660529	9640673	9644177	9661697
9641841	9648849	9654689	9646513	9658193
9664033	9647681	9650017	9652353	9636001
9662865	9653521	9645345	9651185	9637169
9638337	9639505	9659361	9655857	9657025

L22-M4

9905809	9923329	9903473	9906977	9924497
9904641	9911649	9917489	9909313	9920993
9926833	9910481	9912817	9915153	9898801
9925665	9916321	9908145	9913985	9899969
9901137	9902305	9922161	9918657	9919825

L21-M12

9672209	9689729	9669873	9673377	9690897
9671041	9678049	9683889	9675713	9687393
9693233	9676881	9679217	9681553	9665201
9692065	9682721	9674545	9680385	9666369
9667537	9668705	9688561	9685057	9686225

L22-M5

9935009	9952529	9932673	9936177	9953697
9933841	9940849	9946689	9938513	9950193
9956033	9939681	9942017	9944353	9928001
9954865	9945521	9937345	9943185	9929169
9930337	9931505	9951361	9947857	9949025

L21-M13

9701409	9718929	9699073	9702577	9720097
9700241	9707249	9713089	9704913	9716593
9722433	9706081	9708417	9710753	9694401
9721265	9711921	9703745	9709585	9695569
9696737	9697905	9717761	9714257	9715425

L22-M6

9964209	9981729	9961873	9965377	9982897
9963041	9970049	9975889	9967713	9979393
9985233	9968881	9971217	9973553	9957201
9984065	9974721	9966545	9972385	9958369
9959537	9960705	9980561	9977057	9978225

L22-M7

9993409	10010929	9991073	9994577	10012097
9992241	9999249	10005089	9996913	10008593
10014433	9998081	10000417	10002753	9986401
10013265	10003921	9995745	10001585	9987569
9988737	9989905	10009761	10006257	10007425

L22-M16

10256209	10273729	10253873	10257377	10274897
10255041	10262049	10267889	10259713	10271393
10277233	10260881	10263217	10265553	10249201
10276065	10266721	10258545	10264385	10250369
10251537	10252705	10272561	10269057	10270225

L22-M8

10022609	10040129	10020273	10023777	10041297
10021441	10028449	10034289	10026113	10037793
10043633	10027281	10029617	10031953	10015601
10042465	10033121	10024945	10030785	10016769
10017937	10019105	10038961	10035457	10036625

L23-M1

10285409	10302929	10283073	10286577	10304097
10284241	10291249	10297089	10288913	10300593
10306433	10290081	10292417	10294753	10278401
10305265	10295921	10287745	10293585	10279569
10280737	10281905	10301761	10298257	10299425

L22-M9

10051809	10069329	10049473	10052977	10070497
10050641	10057649	10063489	10055313	10066993
10072833	10056481	10058817	10061153	10044801
10071665	10062321	10054145	10059985	10045969
10047137	10048305	10068161	10064657	10065825

L23-M2

10314609	10332129	10312273	10315777	10333297
10313441	10320449	10326289	10318113	10329793
10335633	10319281	10321617	10323953	10307601
10334465	10325121	10316945	10322785	10308769
10309937	10311105	10330961	10327457	10328625

L22-M10

10081009	10098529	10078673	10082177	10099697
10079841	10086849	10092689	10084513	10096193
10102033	10085681	10088017	10090353	10074001
10100865	10091521	10083345	10089185	10075169
10076337	10077505	10097361	10093857	10095025

L23-M3

10343809	10361329	10341473	10344977	10362497
10342641	10349649	10355489	10347313	10358993
10364833	10348481	10350817	10353153	10336801
10363665	10354321	10346145	10351985	10337969
10339137	10340305	10360161	10356657	10357825

L22-M11

10110209	10127729	10107873	10111377	10128897
10109041	10116049	10121889	10113713	10125393
10131233	10114881	10117217	10119553	10103201
10130065	10120721	10112545	10118385	10104369
10105537	10106705	10126561	10123057	10124225

L23-M4

10373009	10390529	10370673	10374177	10391697
10371841	10378849	10384689	10376513	10388193
10394033	10377681	10380017	10382353	10366001
10392865	10383521	10375345	10381185	10367169
10368337	10369505	10389361	10385857	10387025

L22-M12

10139409	10156929	10137073	10140577	10158097
10138241	10145249	10151089	10142913	10154593
10160433	10144081	10146417	10148753	10132401
10159265	10149921	10141745	10147585	10133569
10134737	10135905	10155761	10152257	10153425

L23-M5

10402209	10419729	10399873	10403377	10420897
10401041	10408049	10413889	10405713	10417393
10423233	10406881	10409217	10411553	10395201
10422065	10412721	10404545	10410385	10396369
10397537	10398705	10418561	10415057	10416225

L22-M13

10168609	10186129	10166273	10169777	10187297
10167441	10174449	10180289	10172113	10183793
10189633	10173281	10175617	10177953	10161601
10188465	10179121	10170945	10176785	10162769
10163937	10165105	10184961	10181457	10182625

L23-M6

10431409	10448929	10429073	10432577	10450097
10430241	10437249	10443089	10434913	10446593
10452433	10436081	10438417	10440753	10424401
10451265	10441921	10433745	10439585	10425569
10426737	10427905	10447761	10444257	10445425

L22-M14

10197809	10215329	10195473	10198977	10216497
10196641	10203649	10209489	10201313	10212993
10218833	10202481	10204817	10207153	10190801
10217665	10208321	10200145	10205985	10191969
10193137	10194305	10214161	10210657	10211825

L23-M7

10460609	10478129	10458273	10461777	10479297
10459441	10466449	10472289	10464113	10475793
10481633	10465281	10467617	10469953	10453601
10480465	10471121	10462945	10468785	10454769
10455937	10457105	10476961	10473457	10474625

L22-M15

10227009	10244529	10224673	10228177	10245697
10225841	10232849	10238689	10230513	10242193
10248033	10231681	10234017	10236353	10220001
10246865	10237521	10229345	10235185	10221169
10222337	10223505	10243361	10239857	10241025

L23-M8

10489809	10507329	10487473	10490977	10508497
10488641	10495649	10501489	10493313	10504993
10510833	10494481	10496817	10499153	10482801
10509665	10500321	10492145	10497985	10483969
10485137	10486305	10506161	10502657	10503825

L23-M9

10519009	10536529	10516673	10520177	10537697
10517841	10524849	10530689	10522513	10534193
10540033	10523681	10526017	10528353	10512001
10538865	10529521	10521345	10527185	10513169
10514337	10515505	10535361	10531857	10533025

L24-M2

10781809	10799329	10779473	10782977	10800497
10780641	10787649	10793489	10785313	10796993
10802833	10786481	10788817	10791153	10774801
10801665	10792321	10784145	10789985	10775969
10777137	10778305	10798161	10794657	10795825

L23-M10

10548209	10565729	10545873	10549377	10566897
10547041	10554049	10559889	10551713	10563393
10569233	10552881	10555217	10557553	10541201
10568065	10558721	10550545	10556385	10542369
10543537	10544705	10564561	10561057	10562225

L24-M3

10811009	10828529	10808673	10812177	10829697
10809841	10816849	10822689	10814513	10826193
10832033	10815681	10818017	10820353	10804001
10830865	10821521	10813345	10819185	10805169
10806337	10807505	10827361	10823857	10825025

L23-M11

10577409	10594929	10575073	10578577	10596097
10576241	10583249	10589089	10580913	10592593
10598433	10582081	10584417	10586753	10570401
10597265	10587921	10579745	10585585	10571569
10572737	10573905	10593761	10590257	10591425

L24-M4

10840209	10857729	10837873	10841377	10858897
10839041	10846049	10851889	10843713	10855393
10861233	10844881	10847217	10849553	10833201
10860065	10850721	10842545	10848385	10834369
10835537	10836705	10856561	10853057	10854225

L23-M12

10606609	10624129	10604273	10607777	10625297
10605441	10612449	10618289	10610113	10621793
10627633	10611281	10613617	10615953	10599601
10626465	10617121	10608945	10614785	10600769
10601937	10603105	10622961	10619457	10620625

L24-M5

10869409	10886929	10867073	10870577	10888097
10868241	10875249	10881089	10872913	10884593
10890433	10874081	10876417	10878753	10862401
10889265	10879921	10871745	10877585	10863569
10864737	10865905	10885761	10882257	10883425

L23-M13

10635809	10653329	10633473	10636977	10654497
10634641	10641649	10647489	10639313	10650993
10656833	10640481	10642817	10645153	10628801
10655665	10646321	10638145	10643985	10629969
10631137	10632305	10652161	10648657	10649825

L24-M6

10898609	10916129	10896273	10899777	10917297
10897441	10904449	10910289	10902113	10913793
10919633	10903281	10905617	10907953	10891601
10918465	10909121	10900945	10906785	10892769
10893937	10895105	10914961	10911457	10912625

L23-M14

10665009	10682529	10662673	10666177	10683697
10663841	10670849	10676689	10668513	10680193
10686033	10669681	10672017	10674353	10658001
10684865	10675521	10667345	10673185	10659169
10660337	10661505	10681361	10677857	10679025

L24-M7

10927809	10945329	10925473	10928977	10946497
10926641	10933649	10939489	10931313	10942993
10948833	10932481	10934817	10937153	10920801
10947665	10938321	10930145	10935985	10921969
10923137	10924305	10944161	10940657	10941825

L23-M15

10694209	10711729	10691873	10695377	10712897
10693041	10700049	10705889	10697713	10709393
10715233	10698881	10701217	10703553	10687201
10714065	10704721	10696545	10702385	10688369
10689537	10690705	10710561	10707057	10708225

L24-M8

10957009	10974529	10954673	10958177	10975697
10955841	10962849	10968689	10960513	10972193
10978033	10961681	10964017	10966353	10950001
10976865	10967521	10959345	10965185	10951169
10952337	10953505	10973361	10969857	10971025

L23-M16

10723409	10740929	10721073	10724577	10742097
10722241	10729249	10735089	10726913	10738593
10744433	10728081	10730417	10732753	10716401
10743265	10733921	10725745	10731585	10717569
10718737	10719905	10739761	10736257	10737425

L24-M9

10986209	11003729	10983873	10987377	11004897
10985041	10992049	10997889	10989713	11001393
11007233	10990881	10993217	10995553	10979201
11006065	10996721	10988545	10994385	10980369
10981537	10982705	11002561	10999057	11000225

L24-M1

10752609	10770129	10750273	10753777	10771297
10751441	10758449	10764289	10756113	10767793
10773633	10757281	10759617	10761953	10745601
10772465	10763121	10754945	10760785	10746769
10747937	10749105	10768961	10765457	10766625

L24-M10

11015409	11032929	11013073	11016577	11034097
11014241	11021249	11027089	11018913	11030593
11036433	11020081	11022417	11024753	11008401
11035265	11025921	11017745	11023585	11009569
11010737	11011905	11031761	11028257	11029425

L24-M11

11044609	11062129	11042273	11045777	11063297
11043441	11050449	11056289	11048113	11059793
11065633	11049281	11051617	11053953	11037601
11064465	11055121	11046945	11052785	11038769
11039937	11041105	11060961	11057457	11058625

L24-M12

11073809	11091329	11071473	11074977	11092497
11072641	11079649	11085489	11077313	11088993
11094833	11078481	11080817	11083153	11066801
11093665	11084321	11076145	11081985	11067969
11069137	11070305	11090161	11086657	11087825

L24-M13

11103009	11120529	11100673	11104177	11121697
11101841	11108849	11114689	11106513	11118193
11124033	11107681	11110017	11112353	11096001
11122865	11113521	11105345	11111185	11097169
11098337	11099505	11119361	11115857	11117025

L24-M14

11132209	11149729	11129873	11133377	11150897
11131041	11138049	11143889	11135713	11147393
11153233	11136881	11139217	11141553	11125201
11152065	11142721	11134545	11140385	11126369
11127537	11128705	11148561	11145057	11146225

L24-M15

11161409	11178929	11159073	11162577	11180097
11160241	11167249	11173089	11164913	11176593
11182433	11166081	11168417	11170753	11154401
11181265	11171921	11163745	11169585	11155569
11156737	11157905	11177761	11174257	11175425

L24-M16

11190609	11208129	11188273	11191777	11209297
11189441	11196449	11202289	11194113	11205793
11211633	11195281	11197617	11199953	11183601
11210465	11201121	11192945	11198785	11184769
11185937	11187105	11206961	11203457	11204625

L25-M1

11219809	11237329	11217473	11220977	11238497
11218641	11225649	11231489	11223313	11234993
11240833	11224481	11226817	11229153	11212801
11239665	11230321	11222145	11227985	11213969
11215137	11216305	11236161	11232657	11233825

L25-M2

11249009	11266529	11246673	11250177	11267697
11247841	11254849	11260689	11252513	11264193
11270033	11253681	11256017	11258353	11242001
11268865	11259521	11251345	11257185	11243169
11244337	11245505	11265361	11261857	11263025

L25-M3

11278209	11295729	11275873	11279377	11296897
11277041	11284049	11289889	11281713	11293393
11299233	11282881	11285217	11287553	11271201
11298065	11288721	11280545	11286385	11272369
11273537	11274705	11294561	11291057	11292225

L25-M4

11307409	11324929	11305073	11308577	11326097
11306241	11313249	11319089	11310913	11322593
11328433	11312081	11314417	11316753	11300401
11327265	11317921	11309745	11315585	11301569
11302737	11303905	11323761	11320257	11321425

L25-M5

11336609	11354129	11334273	11337777	11355297
11335441	11342449	11348289	11340113	11351793
11357633	11341281	11343617	11345953	11329601
11356465	11347121	11338945	11344785	11330769
11331937	11333105	11352961	11349457	11350625

L25-M6

11365809	11383329	11363473	11366977	11384497
11364641	11371649	11377489	11369313	11380993
11386833	11370481	11372817	11375153	11358801
11385665	11376321	11368145	11373985	11359969
11361137	11362305	11382161	11378657	11379825

L25-M7

11395009	11412529	11392673	11396177	11413697
11393841	11400849	11406689	11398513	11410193
11416033	11399681	11402017	11404353	11388001
11414865	11405521	11397345	11403185	11389169
11390337	11391505	11411361	11407857	11409025

L25-M8

11424209	11441729	11421873	11425377	11442897
11423041	11430049	11435889	11427713	11439393
11445233	11428881	11431217	11433553	11417201
11444065	11434721	11426545	11432385	11418369
11419537	11420705	11440561	11437057	11438225

L25-M9

11453409	11470929	11451073	11454577	11472097
11452241	11459249	11465089	11456913	11468593
11474433	11458081	11460417	11462753	11446401
11473265	11463921	11455745	11461585	11447569
11448737	11449905	11469761	11466257	11467425

L25-M10

11482609	11500129	11480273	11483777	11501297
11481441	11488449	11494289	11486113	11497793
11503633	11487281	11489617	11491953	11475601
11502465	11493121	11484945	11490785	11476769
11477937	11479105	11498961	11495457	11496625

L25-M11

11511809	11529329	11509473	11512977	11530497
11510641	11517649	11523489	11515313	11526993
11532833	11516481	11518817	11521153	11504801
11531665	11522321	11514145	11519985	11505969
11507137	11508305	11528161	11524657	11525825

L25-M12

11541009	11558529	11538673	11542177	11559697
11539841	11546849	11552689	11544513	11556193
11562033	11545681	11548017	11550353	11534001
11560865	11551521	11543345	11549185	11535169
11536337	11537505	11557361	11553857	11555025

L25-M13

11570209	11587729	11567873	11571377	11588897
11569041	11576049	11581889	11573713	11585393
11591233	11574881	11577217	11579553	11563201
11590065	11580721	11572545	11578385	11564369
11565537	11566705	11586561	11583057	11584225

L25-M14

11599409	11616929	11597073	11600577	11618097
11598241	11605249	11611089	11602913	11614593
11620433	11604081	11606417	11608753	11592401
11619265	11609921	11601745	11607585	11593569
11594737	11595905	11615761	11612257	11613425

L25-M15

11628609	11646129	11626273	11629777	11647297
11627441	11634449	11640289	11632113	11643793
11649633	11633281	11635617	11637953	11621601
11648465	11639121	11630945	11636785	11622769
11623937	11625105	11644961	11641457	11642625

L25-M16

11657809	11675329	11655473	11658977	11676497
11656641	11663649	11669489	11661313	11672993
11678833	11662481	11664817	11667153	11650801
11677665	11668321	11660145	11665985	11651969
11653137	11654305	11674161	11670657	11671825

Chokmah

L1-M1

559	1954	373	652	2047
466	1024	1489	838	1768
2233	931	1117	1303	1
2140	1396	745	1210	94
187	280	1861	1582	1675

L1-M2

2884	4279	2698	2977	4372
2791	3349	3814	3163	4093
4558	3256	3442	3628	2326
4465	3721	3070	3535	2419
2512	2605	4186	3907	4000

L1-M3

5209	6604	5023	5302	6697
5116	5674	6139	5488	6418
6883	5581	5767	5953	4651
6790	6046	5395	5860	4744
4837	4930	6511	6232	6325

L1-M4

7534	8929	7348	7627	9022
7441	7999	8464	7813	8743
9208	7906	8092	8278	6976
9115	8371	7720	8185	7069
7162	7255	8836	8557	8650

L1-M5

9859	11254	9673	9952	11347
9766	10324	10789	10138	11068
11533	10231	10417	10603	9301
11440	10696	10045	10510	9394
9487	9580	11161	10882	10975

L1-M6

12184	13579	11998	12277	13672
12091	12649	13114	12463	13393
13858	12556	12742	12928	11626
13765	13021	12370	12835	11719
11812	11905	13486	13207	13300

L1-M7

14509	15904	14323	14602	15997
14416	14974	15439	14788	15718
16183	14881	15067	15253	13951
16090	15346	14695	15160	14044
14137	14230	15811	15532	15625

L1-M8

16834	18229	16648	16927	18322
16741	17299	17764	17113	18043
18508	17206	17392	17578	16276
18415	17671	17020	17485	16369
16462	16555	18136	17857	17950

L1-M9

19159	20554	18973	19252	20647
19066	19624	20089	19438	20368
20833	19531	19717	19903	18601
20740	19996	19345	19810	18694
18787	18880	20461	20182	20275

L1-M10

21484	22879	21298	21577	22972
21391	21949	22414	21763	22693
23158	21856	22042	22228	20926
23065	22321	21670	22135	21019
21112	21205	22786	22507	22600

L1-M11

23809	25204	23623	23902	25297
23716	24274	24739	24088	25018
25483	24181	24367	24553	23251
25390	24646	23995	24460	23344
23437	23530	25111	24832	24925

L1-M12

26134	27529	25948	26227	27622
26041	26599	27064	26413	27343
27808	26506	26692	26878	25576
27715	26971	26320	26785	25669
25762	25855	27436	27157	27250

L1-M13

28459	29854	28273	28552	29947
28366	28924	29389	28738	29668
30133	28831	29017	29203	27901
30040	29296	28645	29110	27994
28087	28180	29761	29482	29575

L1-M14

30784	32179	30598	30877	32272
30691	31249	31714	31063	31993
32458	31156	31342	31528	30226
32365	31621	30970	31435	30319
30412	30505	32086	31807	31900

L1-M15

33109	34504	32923	33202	34597
33016	33574	34039	33388	34318
34783	33481	33667	33853	32551
34690	33946	33295	33760	32644
32737	32830	34411	34132	34225

L1-M16

35434	36829	35248	35527	36922
35341	35899	36364	35713	36643
37108	35806	35992	36178	34876
37015	36271	35620	36085	34969
35062	35155	36736	36457	36550

L2-M1

37759	39154	37573	37852	39247
37666	38224	38689	38038	38968
39433	38131	38317	38503	37201
39340	38596	37945	38410	37294
37387	37480	39061	38782	38875

L2-M2

40084	41479	39898	40177	41572
39991	40549	41014	40363	41293
41758	40456	40642	40828	39526
41665	40921	40270	40735	39619
39712	39805	41386	41107	41200

L2-M3

42409	43804	42223	42502	43897
42316	42874	43339	42688	43618
44083	42781	42967	43153	41851
43990	43246	42595	43060	41944
42037	42130	43711	43432	43525

L2-M4

44734	46129	44548	44827	46222
44641	45199	45664	45013	45943
46408	45106	45292	45478	44176
46315	45571	44920	45385	44269
44362	44455	46036	45757	45850

L2-M5

47059	48454	46873	47152	48547
46966	47524	47989	47338	48268
48733	47431	47617	47803	46501
48640	47896	47245	47710	46594
46687	46780	48361	48082	48175

L2-M6

49384	50779	49198	49477	50872
49291	49849	50314	49663	50593
51058	49756	49942	50128	48826
50965	50221	49570	50035	48919
49012	49105	50686	50407	50500

L2-M7

51709	53104	51523	51802	53197
51616	52174	52639	51988	52918
53383	52081	52267	52453	51151
53290	52546	51895	52360	51244
51337	51430	53011	52732	52825

L2-M8

54034	55429	53848	54127	55522
53941	54499	54964	54313	55243
55708	54406	54592	54778	53476
55615	54871	54220	54685	53569
53662	53755	55336	55057	55150

L2-M9

56359	57754	56173	56452	57847
56266	56824	57289	56638	57568
58033	56731	56917	57103	55801
57940	57196	56545	57010	55894
55987	56080	57661	57382	57475

L2-M10

58684	60079	58498	58777	60172
58591	59149	59614	58963	59893
60358	59056	59242	59428	58126
60265	59521	58870	59335	58219
58312	58405	59986	59707	59800

L2-M11

61009	62404	60823	61102	62497
60916	61474	61939	61288	62218
62683	61381	61567	61753	60451
62590	61846	61195	61660	60544
60637	60730	62311	62032	62125

L2-M12

63334	64729	63148	63427	64822
63241	63799	64264	63613	64543
65008	63706	63892	64078	62776
64915	64171	63520	63985	62869
62962	63055	64636	64357	64450

L2-M13

65659	67054	65473	65752	67147
65566	66124	66589	65938	66868
67333	66031	66217	66403	65101
67240	66496	65845	66310	65194
65287	65380	66961	66682	66775

L2-M14

67984	69379	67798	68077	69472
67891	68449	68914	68263	69193
69658	68356	68542	68728	67426
69565	68821	68170	68635	67519
67612	67705	69286	69007	69100

L2-M15

70309	71704	70123	70402	71797
70216	70774	71239	70588	71518
71983	70681	70867	71053	69751
71890	71146	70495	70960	69844
69937	70030	71611	71332	71425

L2-M16

72634	74029	72448	72727	74122
72541	73099	73564	72913	73843
74308	73006	73192	73378	72076
74215	73471	72820	73285	72169
72262	72355	73936	73657	73750

L3-M1

74959	76354	74773	75052	76447
74866	75424	75889	75238	76168
76633	75331	75517	75703	74401
76540	75796	75145	75610	74494
74587	74680	76261	75982	76075

L3-M2

77284	78679	77098	77377	78772
77191	77749	78214	77563	78493
78958	77656	77842	78028	76726
78865	78121	77470	77935	76819
76912	77005	78586	78307	78400

L3-M3

79609	81004	79423	79702	81097
79516	80074	80539	79888	80818
81283	79981	80167	80353	79051
81190	80446	79795	80260	79144
79237	79330	80911	80632	80725

L3-M4

81934	83329	81748	82027	83422
81841	82399	82864	82213	83143
83608	82306	82492	82678	81376
83515	82771	82120	82585	81469
81562	81655	83236	82957	83050

L3-M5

84259	85654	84073	84352	85747
84166	84724	85189	84538	85468
85933	84631	84817	85003	83701
85840	85096	84445	84910	83794
83887	83980	85561	85282	85375

L3-M14

105184	106579	104998	105277	106672
105091	105649	106114	105463	106393
106858	105556	105742	105928	104626
106765	106021	105370	105835	104719
104812	104905	106486	106207	106300

L3-M6

86584	87979	86398	86677	88072
86491	87049	87514	86863	87793
88258	86956	87142	87328	86026
88165	87421	86770	87235	86119
86212	86305	87886	87607	87700

L3-M15

107509	108904	107323	107602	108997
107416	107974	108439	107788	108718
109183	107881	108067	108253	106951
109090	108346	107695	108160	107044
107137	107230	108811	108532	108625

L3-M7

88909	90304	88723	89002	90397
88816	89374	89839	89188	90118
90583	89281	89467	89653	88351
90490	89746	89095	89560	88444
88537	88630	90211	89932	90025

L3-M16

109834	111229	109648	109927	111322
109741	110299	110764	110113	111043
111508	110206	110392	110578	109276
111415	110671	110020	110485	109369
109462	109555	111136	110857	110950

L3-M8

91234	92629	91048	91327	92722
91141	91699	92164	91513	92443
92908	91606	91792	91978	90676
92815	92071	91420	91885	90769
90862	90955	92536	92257	92350

L4-M1

112159	113554	111973	112252	113647
112066	112624	113089	112438	113368
113833	112531	112717	112903	111601
113740	112996	112345	112810	111694
111787	111880	113461	113182	113275

L3-M9

93559	94954	93373	93652	95047
93466	94024	94489	93838	94768
95233	93931	94117	94303	93001
95140	94396	93745	94210	93094
93187	93280	94861	94582	94675

L4-M2

114484	115879	114298	114577	115972
114391	114949	115414	114763	115693
116158	114856	115042	115228	113926
116065	115321	114670	115135	114019
114112	114205	115786	115507	115600

L3-M10

95884	97279	95698	95977	97372
95791	96349	96814	96163	97093
97558	96256	96442	96628	95326
97465	96721	96070	96535	95419
95512	95605	97186	96907	97000

L4-M3

116809	118204	116623	116902	118297
116716	117274	117739	117088	118018
118483	117181	117367	117553	116251
118390	117646	116995	117460	116344
116437	116530	118111	117832	117925

L3-M11

98209	99604	98023	98302	99697
98116	98674	99139	98488	99418
99883	98581	98767	98953	97651
99790	99046	98395	98860	97744
97837	97930	99511	99232	99325

L4-M4

119134	120529	118948	119227	120622
119041	119599	120064	119413	120343
120808	119506	119692	119878	118576
120715	119971	119320	119785	118669
118762	118855	120436	120157	120250

L3-M12

100534	101929	100348	100627	102022
100441	100999	101464	100813	101743
102208	100906	101092	101278	99976
102115	101371	100720	101185	100069
100162	100255	101836	101557	101650

L4-M5

121459	122854	121273	121552	122947
121366	121924	122389	121738	122668
123133	121831	122017	122203	120901
123040	122296	121645	122110	120994
121087	121180	122761	122482	122575

L3-M13

102859	104254	102673	102952	104347
102766	103324	103789	103138	104068
104533	103231	103417	103603	102301
104440	103696	103045	103510	102394
102487	102580	104161	103882	103975

L4-M6

123784	125179	123598	123877	125272
123691	124249	124714	124063	124993
125458	124156	124342	124528	123226
125365	124621	123970	124435	123319
123412	123505	125086	124807	124900

L4-M7

126109	127504	125923	126202	127597
126016	126574	127039	126388	127318
127783	126481	126667	126853	125551
127690	126946	126295	126760	125644
125737	125830	127411	127132	127225

L4-M8

128434	129829	128248	128527	129922
128341	128899	129364	128713	129643
130108	128806	128992	129178	127876
130015	129271	128620	129085	127969
128062	128155	129736	129457	129550

L4-M9

130759	132154	130573	130852	132247
130666	131224	131689	131038	131968
132433	131131	131317	131503	130201
132340	131596	130945	131410	130294
130387	130480	132061	131782	131875

L4-M10

133084	134479	132898	133177	134572
132991	133549	134014	133363	134293
134758	133456	133642	133828	132526
134665	133921	133270	133735	132619
132712	132805	134386	134107	134200

L4-M11

135409	136804	135223	135502	136897
135316	135874	136339	135688	136618
137083	135781	135967	136153	134851
136990	136246	135595	136060	134944
135037	135130	136711	136432	136525

L4-M12

137734	139129	137548	137827	139222
137641	138199	138664	138013	138943
139408	138106	138292	138478	137176
139315	138571	137920	138385	137269
137362	137455	139036	138757	138850

L4-M13

140059	141454	139873	140152	141547
139966	140524	140989	140338	141268
141733	140431	140617	140803	139501
141640	140896	140245	140710	139594
139687	139780	141361	141082	141175

L4-M14

142384	143779	142198	142477	143872
142291	142849	143314	142663	143593
144058	142756	142942	143128	141826
143965	143221	142570	143035	141919
142012	142105	143686	143407	143500

L4-M15

144709	146104	144523	144802	146197
144616	145174	145639	144988	145918
146383	145081	145267	145453	144151
146290	145546	144895	145360	144244
144337	144430	146011	145732	145825

L4-M16

147034	148429	146848	147127	148522
146941	147499	147964	147313	148243
148708	147406	147592	147778	146476
148615	147871	147220	147685	146569
146662	146755	148336	148057	148150

L5-M1

149359	150754	149173	149452	150847
149266	149824	150289	149638	150568
151033	149731	149917	150103	148801
150940	150196	149545	150010	148894
148987	149080	150661	150382	150475

L5-M2

151684	153079	151498	151777	153172
151591	152149	152614	151963	152893
153358	152056	152242	152428	151126
153265	152521	151870	152335	151219
151312	151405	152986	152707	152800

L5-M3

154009	155404	153823	154102	155497
153916	154474	154939	154288	155218
155683	154381	154567	154753	153451
155590	154846	154195	154660	153544
153637	153730	155311	155032	155125

L5-M4

156334	157729	156148	156427	157822
156241	156799	157264	156613	157543
158008	156706	156892	157078	155776
157915	157171	156520	156985	155869
155962	156055	157636	157357	157450

L5-M5

158659	160054	158473	158752	160147
158566	159124	159589	158938	159868
160333	159031	159217	159403	158101
160240	159496	158845	159310	158194
158287	158380	159961	159682	159775

L5-M6

160984	162379	160798	161077	162472
160891	161449	161914	161263	162193
162658	161356	161542	161728	160426
162565	161821	161170	161635	160519
160612	160705	162286	162007	162100

L5-M7

163309	164704	163123	163402	164797
163216	163774	164239	163588	164518
164983	163681	163867	164053	162751
164890	164146	163495	163960	162844
162937	163030	164611	164332	164425

L5-M8

165634	167029	165448	165727	167122
165541	166099	166564	165913	166843
167308	166006	166192	166378	165076
167215	166471	165820	166285	165169
165262	165355	166936	166657	166750

L5-M9

167959	169354	167773	168052	169447
167866	168424	168889	168238	169168
169633	168331	168517	168703	167401
169540	168796	168145	168610	167494
167587	167680	169261	168982	169075

L5-M10

170284	171679	170098	170377	171772
170191	170749	171214	170563	171493
171958	170656	170842	171028	169726
171865	171121	170470	170935	169819
169912	170005	171586	171307	171400

L5-M11

172609	174004	172423	172702	174097
172516	173074	173539	172888	173818
174283	172981	173167	173353	172051
174190	173446	172795	173260	172144
172237	172330	173911	173632	173725

L5-M12

174934	176329	174748	175027	176422
174841	175399	175864	175213	176143
176608	175306	175492	175678	174376
176515	175771	175120	175585	174469
174562	174655	176236	175957	176050

L5-M13

177259	178654	177073	177352	178747
177166	177724	178189	177538	178468
178933	177631	177817	178003	176701
178840	178096	177445	177910	176794
176887	176980	178561	178282	178375

L5-M14

179584	180979	179398	179677	181072
179491	180049	180514	179863	180793
181258	179956	180142	180328	179026
181165	180421	179770	180235	179119
179212	179305	180886	180607	180700

L5-M15

181909	183304	181723	182002	183397
181816	182374	182839	182188	183118
183583	182281	182467	182653	181351
183490	182746	182095	182560	181444
181537	181630	183211	182932	183025

L5-M16

184234	185629	184048	184327	185722
184141	184699	185164	184513	185443
185908	184606	184792	184978	183676
185815	185071	184420	184885	183769
183862	183955	185536	185257	185350

L6-M1

186559	187954	186373	186652	188047
186466	187024	187489	186838	187768
188233	186931	187117	187303	186001
188140	187396	186745	187210	186094
186187	186280	187861	187582	187675

L6-M2

188884	190279	188698	188977	190372
188791	189349	189814	189163	190093
190558	189256	189442	189628	188326
190465	189721	189070	189535	188419
188512	188605	190186	189907	190000

L6-M3

191209	192604	191023	191302	192697
191116	191674	192139	191488	192418
192883	191581	191767	191953	190651
192790	192046	191395	191860	190744
190837	190930	192511	192232	192325

L6-M4

193534	194929	193348	193627	195022
193441	193999	194464	193813	194743
195208	193906	194092	194278	192976
195115	194371	193720	194185	193069
193162	193255	194836	194557	194650

L6-M5

195859	197254	195673	195952	197347
195766	196324	196789	196138	197068
197533	196231	196417	196603	195301
197440	196696	196045	196510	195394
195487	195580	197161	196882	196975

L6-M6

198184	199579	197998	198277	199672
198091	198649	199114	198463	199393
199858	198556	198742	198928	197626
199765	199021	198370	198835	197719
197812	197905	199486	199207	199300

L6-M7

200509	201904	200323	200602	201997
200416	200974	201439	200788	201718
202183	200881	201067	201253	199951
202090	201346	200695	201160	200044
200137	200230	201811	201532	201625

L6-M8

202834	204229	202648	202927	204322
202741	203299	203764	203113	204043
204508	203206	203392	203578	202276
204415	203671	203020	203485	202369
202462	202555	204136	203857	203950

L6-M9

205159	206554	204973	205252	206647
205066	205624	206089	205438	206368
206833	205531	205717	205903	204601
206740	205996	205345	205810	204694
204787	204880	206461	206182	206275

L6-M10

207484	208879	207298	207577	208972
207391	207949	208414	207763	208693
209158	207856	208042	208228	206926
209065	208321	207670	208135	207019
207112	207205	208786	208507	208600

L6-M11

209809	211204	209623	209902	211297
209716	210274	210739	210088	211018
211483	210181	210367	210553	209251
211390	210646	209995	210460	209344
209437	209530	211111	210832	210925

L6-M12

212134	213529	211948	212227	213622
212041	212599	213064	212413	213343
213808	212506	212692	212878	211576
213715	212971	212320	212785	211669
211762	211855	213436	213157	213250

L6-M13

214459	215854	214273	214552	215947
214366	214924	215389	214738	215668
216133	214831	215017	215203	213901
216040	215296	214645	215110	213994
214087	214180	215761	215482	215575

L6-M14

216784	218179	216598	216877	218272
216691	217249	217714	217063	217993
218458	217156	217342	217528	216226
218365	217621	216970	217435	216319
216412	216505	218086	217807	217900

L6-M15

219109	220504	218923	219202	220597
219016	219574	220039	219388	220318
220783	219481	219667	219853	218551
220690	219946	219295	219760	218644
218737	218830	220411	220132	220225

L6-M16

221434	222829	221248	221527	222922
221341	221899	222364	221713	222643
223108	221806	221992	222178	220876
223015	222271	221620	222085	220969
221062	221155	222736	222457	222550

L7-M1

223759	225154	223573	223852	225247
223666	224224	224689	224038	224968
225433	224131	224317	224503	223201
225340	224596	223945	224410	223294
223387	223480	225061	224782	224875

L7-M2

226084	227479	225898	226177	227572
225991	226549	227014	226363	227293
227758	226456	226642	226828	225526
227665	226921	226270	226735	225619
225712	225805	227386	227107	227200

L7-M3

228409	229804	228223	228502	229897
228316	228874	229339	228688	229618
230083	228781	228967	229153	227851
229990	229246	228595	229060	227944
228037	228130	229711	229432	229525

L7-M4

230734	232129	230548	230827	232222
230641	231199	231664	231013	231943
232408	231106	231292	231478	230176
232315	231571	230920	231385	230269
230362	230455	232036	231757	231850

L7-M5

233059	234454	232873	233152	234547
232966	233524	233989	233338	234268
234733	233431	233617	233803	232501
234640	233896	233245	233710	232594
232687	232780	234361	234082	234175

L7-M6

235384	236779	235198	235477	236872
235291	235849	236314	235663	236593
237058	235756	235942	236128	234826
236965	236221	235570	236035	234919
235012	235105	236686	236407	236500

L7-M7

237709	239104	237523	237802	239197
237616	238174	238639	237988	238918
239383	238081	238267	238453	237151
239290	238546	237895	238360	237244
237337	237430	239011	238732	238825

L7-M8

240034	241429	239848	240127	241522
239941	240499	240964	240313	241243
241708	240406	240592	240778	239476
241615	240871	240220	240685	239569
239662	239755	241336	241057	241150

L7-M9

242359	243754	242173	242452	243847
242266	242824	243289	242638	243568
244033	242731	242917	243103	241801
243940	243196	242545	243010	241894
241987	242080	243661	243382	243475

L7-M10

244684	246079	244498	244777	246172
244591	245149	245614	244963	245893
246358	245056	245242	245428	244126
246265	245521	244870	245335	244219
244312	244405	245986	245707	245800

L7-M11

247009	248404	246823	247102	248497
246916	247474	247939	247288	248218
248683	247381	247567	247753	246451
248590	247846	247195	247660	246544
246637	246730	248311	248032	248125

L7-M12

249334	250729	249148	249427	250822
249241	249799	250264	249613	250543
251008	249706	249892	250078	248776
250915	250171	249520	249985	248869
248962	249055	250636	250357	250450

L7-M13

251659	253054	251473	251752	253147
251566	252124	252589	251938	252868
253333	252031	252217	252403	251101
253240	252496	251845	252310	251194
251287	251380	252961	252682	252775

L7-M14

253984	255379	253798	254077	255472
253891	254449	254914	254263	255193
255658	254356	254542	254728	253426
255565	254821	254170	254635	253519
253612	253705	255286	255007	255100

L7-M15

256309	257704	256123	256402	257797
256216	256774	257239	256588	257518
257983	256681	256867	257053	255751
257890	257146	256495	256960	255844
255937	256030	257611	257332	257425

L7-M16

258634	260029	258448	258727	260122
258541	259099	259564	258913	259843
260308	259006	259192	259378	258076
260215	259471	258820	259285	258169
258262	258355	259936	259657	259750

L8M1

260959	262354	260773	261052	262447
260866	261424	261889	261238	262168
262633	261331	261517	261703	260401
262540	261796	261145	261610	260494
260587	260680	262261	261982	262075

L8-M2

263284	264679	263098	263377	264772
263191	263749	264214	263563	264493
264958	263656	263842	264028	262726
264865	264121	263470	263935	262819
262912	263005	264586	264307	264400

L8-M3

265609	267004	265423	265702	267097
265516	266074	266539	265888	266818
267283	265981	266167	266353	265051
267190	266446	265795	266260	265144
265237	265330	266911	266632	266725

L8-M4

267934	269329	267748	268027	269422
267841	268399	268864	268213	269143
269608	268306	268492	268678	267376
269515	268771	268120	268585	267469
267562	267655	269236	268957	269050

L8-M5

270259	271654	270073	270352	271747
270166	270724	271189	270538	271468
271933	270631	270817	271003	269701
271840	271096	270445	270910	269794
269887	269980	271561	271282	271375

L8-M6

272584	273979	272398	272677	274072
272491	273049	273514	272863	273793
274258	272956	273142	273328	272026
274165	273421	272770	273235	272119
272212	272305	273886	273607	273700

L8-M7

274909	276304	274723	275002	276397
274816	275374	275839	275188	276118
276583	275281	275467	275653	274351
276490	275746	275095	275560	274444
274537	274630	276211	275932	276025

L8-M8

277234	278629	277048	277327	278722
277141	277699	278164	277513	278443
278908	277606	277792	277978	276676
278815	278071	277420	277885	276769
276862	276955	278536	278257	278350

L8-M9

279559	280954	279373	279652	281047
279466	280024	280489	279838	280768
281233	279931	280117	280303	279001
281140	280396	279745	280210	279094
279187	279280	280861	280582	280675

L8-M10

281884	283279	281698	281977	283372
281791	282349	282814	282163	283093
283558	282256	282442	282628	281326
283465	282721	282070	282535	281419
281512	281605	283186	282907	283000

L8-M11

284209	285604	284023	284302	285697
284116	284674	285139	284488	285418
285883	284581	284767	284953	283651
285790	285046	284395	284860	283744
283837	283930	285511	285232	285325

L8-M12

286534	287929	286348	286627	288022
286441	286999	287464	286813	287743
288208	286906	287092	287278	285976
288115	287371	286720	287185	286069
286162	286255	287836	287557	287650

L8-M13

288859	290254	288673	288952	290347
288766	289324	289789	289138	290068
290533	289231	289417	289603	288301
290440	289696	289045	289510	288394
288487	288580	290161	289882	289975

L8-M14

291184	292579	290998	291277	292672
291091	291649	292114	291463	292393
292858	291556	291742	291928	290626
292765	292021	291370	291835	290719
290812	290905	292486	292207	292300

L8-M15

293509	294904	293323	293602	294997
293416	293974	294439	293788	294718
295183	293881	294067	294253	292951
295090	294346	293695	294160	293044
293137	293230	294811	294532	294625

L9-M8

314434	315829	314248	314527	315922
314341	314899	315364	314713	315643
316108	314806	314992	315178	313876
316015	315271	314620	315085	313969
314062	314155	315736	315457	315550

L8-M16

295834	297229	295648	295927	297322
295741	296299	296764	296113	297043
297508	296206	296392	296578	295276
297415	296671	296020	296485	295369
295462	295555	297136	296857	296950

L9-M9

316759	318154	316573	316852	318247
316666	317224	317689	317038	317968
318433	317131	317317	317503	316201
318340	317596	316945	317410	316294
316387	316480	318061	317782	317875

L9-M1

298159	299554	297973	298252	299647
298066	298624	299089	298438	299368
299833	298531	298717	298903	297601
299740	298996	298345	298810	297694
297787	297880	299461	299182	299275

L9-M10

319084	320479	318898	319177	320572
318991	319549	320014	319363	320293
320758	319456	319642	319828	318526
320665	319921	319270	319735	318619
318712	318805	320386	320107	320200

L9-M2

300484	301879	300298	300577	301972
300391	300949	301414	300763	301693
302158	300856	301042	301228	299926
302065	301321	300670	301135	300019
300112	300205	301786	301507	301600

L9-M11

321409	322804	321223	321502	322897
321316	321874	322339	321688	322618
323083	321781	321967	322153	320851
322990	322246	321595	322060	320944
321037	321130	322711	322432	322525

L9-M3

302809	304204	302623	302902	304297
302716	303274	303739	303088	304018
304483	303181	303367	303553	302251
304390	303646	302995	303460	302344
302437	302530	304111	303832	303925

L9-M12

323734	325129	323548	323827	325222
323641	324199	324664	324013	324943
325408	324106	324292	324478	323176
325315	324571	323920	324385	323269
323362	323455	325036	324757	324850

L9-M4

305134	306529	304948	305227	306622
305041	305599	306064	305413	306343
306808	305506	305692	305878	304576
306715	305971	305320	305785	304669
304762	304855	306436	306157	306250

L9-M13

326059	327454	325873	326152	327547
325966	326524	326989	326338	327268
327733	326431	326617	326803	325501
327640	326896	326245	326710	325594
325687	325780	327361	327082	327175

L9-M5

307459	308854	307273	307552	308947
307366	307924	308389	307738	308668
309133	307831	308017	308203	306901
309040	308296	307645	308110	306994
307087	307180	308761	308482	308575

L9-M14

328384	329779	328198	328477	329872
328291	328849	329314	328663	329593
330058	328756	328942	329128	327826
329965	329221	328570	329035	327919
328012	328105	329686	329407	329500

L9-M6

309784	311179	309598	309877	311272
309691	310249	310714	310063	310993
311458	310156	310342	310528	309226
311365	310621	309970	310435	309319
309412	309505	311086	310807	310900

L9-M15

330709	332104	330523	330802	332197
330616	331174	331639	330988	331918
332383	331081	331267	331453	330151
332290	331546	330895	331360	330244
330337	330430	332011	331732	331825

L9-M7

312109	313504	311923	312202	313597
312016	312574	313039	312388	313318
313783	312481	312667	312853	311551
313690	312946	312295	312760	311644
311737	311830	313411	313132	313225

L9-M16

333034	334429	332848	333127	334522
332941	333499	333964	333313	334243
334708	333406	333592	333778	332476
334615	333871	333220	333685	332569
332662	332755	334336	334057	334150

L10-M1

335359	336754	335173	335452	336847
335266	335824	336289	335638	336568
337033	335731	335917	336103	334801
336940	336196	335545	336010	334894
334987	335080	336661	336382	336475

L10-M10

356284	357679	356098	356377	357772
356191	356749	357214	356563	357493
357958	356656	356842	357028	355726
357865	357121	356470	356935	355819
355912	356005	357586	357307	357400

L10-M2

337684	339079	337498	337777	339172
337591	338149	338614	337963	338893
339358	338056	338242	338428	337126
339265	338521	337870	338335	337219
337312	337405	338986	338707	338800

L10-M11

358609	360004	358423	358702	360097
358516	359074	359539	358888	359818
360283	358981	359167	359353	358051
360190	359446	358795	359260	358144
358237	358330	359911	359632	359725

L10-M3

340009	341404	339823	340102	341497
339916	340474	340939	340288	341218
341683	340381	340567	340753	339451
341590	340846	340195	340660	339544
339637	339730	341311	341032	341125

L10-M12

360934	362329	360748	361027	362422
360841	361399	361864	361213	362143
362608	361306	361492	361678	360376
362515	361771	361120	361585	360469
360562	360655	362236	361957	362050

L10-M4

342334	343729	342148	342427	343822
342241	342799	343264	342613	343543
344008	342706	342892	343078	341776
343915	343171	342520	342985	341869
341962	342055	343636	343357	343450

L10-M13

363259	364654	363073	363352	364747
363166	363724	364189	363538	364468
364933	363631	363817	364003	362701
364840	364096	363445	363910	362794
362887	362980	364561	364282	364375

L10-M5

344659	346054	344473	344752	346147
344566	345124	345589	344938	345868
346333	345031	345217	345403	344101
346240	345496	344845	345310	344194
344287	344380	345961	345682	345775

L10-M14

365584	366979	365398	365677	367072
365491	366049	366514	365863	366793
367258	365956	366142	366328	365026
367165	366421	365770	366235	365119
365212	365305	366886	366607	366700

L10-M6

346984	348379	346798	347077	348472
346891	347449	347914	347263	348193
348658	347356	347542	347728	346426
348565	347821	347170	347635	346519
346612	346705	348286	348007	348100

L10-M15

367909	369304	367723	368002	369397
367816	368374	368839	368188	369118
369583	368281	368467	368653	367351
369490	368746	368095	368560	367444
367537	367630	369211	368932	369025

L10-M7

349309	350704	349123	349402	350797
349216	349774	350239	349588	350518
350983	349681	349867	350053	348751
350890	350146	349495	349960	348844
348937	349030	350611	350332	350425

L10-M16

370234	371629	370048	370327	371722
370141	370699	371164	370513	371443
371908	370606	370792	370978	369676
371815	371071	370420	370885	369769
369862	369955	371536	371257	371350

L10-M8

351634	353029	351448	351727	353122
351541	352099	352564	351913	352843
353308	352006	352192	352378	351076
353215	352471	351820	352285	351169
351262	351355	352936	352657	352750

L11-M1

372559	373954	372373	372652	374047
372466	373024	373489	372838	373768
374233	372931	373117	373303	372001
374140	373396	372745	373210	372094
372187	372280	373861	373582	373675

L10-M9

353959	355354	353773	354052	355447
353866	354424	354889	354238	355168
355633	354331	354517	354703	353401
355540	354796	354145	354610	353494
353587	353680	355261	354982	355075

L11-M2

374884	376279	374698	374977	376372
374791	375349	375814	375163	376093
376558	375256	375442	375628	374326
376465	375721	375070	375535	374419
374512	374605	376186	375907	376000

L11-M3

377209	378604	377023	377302	378697
377116	377674	378139	377488	378418
378883	377581	377767	377953	376651
378790	378046	377395	377860	376744
376837	376930	378511	378232	378325

L11-M12

398134	399529	397948	398227	399622
398041	398599	399064	398413	399343
399808	398506	398692	398878	397576
399715	398971	398320	398785	397669
397762	397855	399436	399157	399250

L11-M4

379534	380929	379348	379627	381022
379441	379999	380464	379813	380743
381208	379906	380092	380278	378976
381115	380371	379720	380185	379069
379162	379255	380836	380557	380650

L11-M13

400459	401854	400273	400552	401947
400366	400924	401389	400738	401668
402133	400831	401017	401203	399901
402040	401296	400645	401110	399994
400087	400180	401761	401482	401575

L11-M5

381859	383254	381673	381952	383347
381766	382324	382789	382138	383068
383533	382231	382417	382603	381301
383440	382696	382045	382510	381394
381487	381580	383161	382882	382975

L11-M14

402784	404179	402598	402877	404272
402691	403249	403714	403063	403993
404458	403156	403342	403528	402226
404365	403621	402970	403435	402319
402412	402505	404086	403807	403900

L11-M6

384184	385579	383998	384277	385672
384091	384649	385114	384463	385393
385858	384556	384742	384928	383626
385765	385021	384370	384835	383719
383812	383905	385486	385207	385300

L11-M15

405109	406504	404923	405202	406597
405016	405574	406039	405388	406318
406783	405481	405667	405853	404551
406690	405946	405295	405760	404644
404737	404830	406411	406132	406225

L11-M7

386509	387904	386323	386602	387997
386416	386974	387439	386788	387718
388183	386881	387067	387253	385951
388090	387346	386695	387160	386044
386137	386230	387811	387532	387625

L11-M16

407434	408829	407248	407527	408922
407341	407899	408364	407713	408643
409108	407806	407992	408178	406876
409015	408271	407620	408085	406969
407062	407155	408736	408457	408550

L11-M8

388834	390229	388648	388927	390322
388741	389299	389764	389113	390043
390508	389206	389392	389578	388276
390415	389671	389020	389485	388369
388462	388555	390136	389857	389950

L12-M1

409759	411154	409573	409852	411247
409666	410224	410689	410038	410968
411433	410131	410317	410503	409201
411340	410596	409945	410410	409294
409387	409480	411061	410782	410875

L11-M9

391159	392554	390973	391252	392647
391066	391624	392089	391438	392368
392833	391531	391717	391903	390601
392740	391996	391345	391810	390694
390787	390880	392461	392182	392275

L12-M2

412084	413479	411898	412177	413572
411991	412549	413014	412363	413293
413758	412456	412642	412828	411526
413665	412921	412270	412735	411619
411712	411805	413386	413107	413200

L11-M10

393484	394879	393298	393577	394972
393391	393949	394414	393763	394693
395158	393856	394042	394228	392926
395065	394321	393670	394135	393019
393112	393205	394786	394507	394600

L12-M3

414409	415804	414223	414502	415897
414316	414874	415339	414688	415618
416083	414781	414967	415153	413851
415990	415246	414595	415060	413944
414037	414130	415711	415432	415525

L11-M11

395809	397204	395623	395902	397297
395716	396274	396739	396088	397018
397483	396181	396367	396553	395251
397390	396646	395995	396460	395344
395437	395530	397111	396832	396925

L12-M4

416734	418129	416548	416827	418222
416641	417199	417664	417013	417943
418408	417106	417292	417478	416176
418315	417571	416920	417385	416269
416362	416455	418036	417757	417850

L12-M5

419059	420454	418873	419152	420547
418966	419524	419989	419338	420268
420733	419431	419617	419803	418501
420640	419896	419245	419710	418594
418687	418780	420361	420082	420175

L12-M6

421384	422779	421198	421477	422872
421291	421849	422314	421663	422593
423058	421756	421942	422128	420826
422965	422221	421570	422035	420919
421012	421105	422686	422407	422500

L12-M7

423709	425104	423523	423802	425197
423616	424174	424639	423988	424918
425383	424081	424267	424453	423151
425290	424546	423895	424360	423244
423337	423430	425011	424732	424825

L12-M8

426034	427429	425848	426127	427522
425941	426499	426964	426313	427243
427708	426406	426592	426778	425476
427615	426871	426220	426685	425569
425662	425755	427336	427057	427150

L12-M9

428359	429754	428173	428452	429847
428266	428824	429289	428638	429568
430033	428731	428917	429103	427801
429940	429196	428545	429010	427894
427987	428080	429661	429382	429475

L12-M10

430684	432079	430498	430777	432172
430591	431149	431614	430963	431893
432358	431056	431242	431428	430126
432265	431521	430870	431335	430219
430312	430405	431986	431707	431800

L12-M11

433009	434404	432823	433102	434497
432916	433474	433939	433288	434218
434683	433381	433567	433753	432451
434590	433846	433195	433660	432544
432637	432730	434311	434032	434125

L12-M12

435334	436729	435148	435427	436822
435241	435799	436264	435613	436543
437008	435706	435892	436078	434776
436915	436171	435520	435985	434869
434962	435055	436636	436357	436450

L12-M13

437659	439054	437473	437752	439147
437566	438124	438589	437938	438868
439333	438031	438217	438403	437101
439240	438496	437845	438310	437194
437287	437380	438961	438682	438775

L12-M14

439984	441379	439798	440077	441472
439891	440449	440914	440263	441193
441658	440356	440542	440728	439426
441565	440821	440170	440635	439519
439612	439705	441286	441007	441100

L12-M15

442309	443704	442123	442402	443797
442216	442774	443239	442588	443518
443983	442681	442867	443053	441751
443890	443146	442495	442960	441844
441937	442030	443611	443332	443425

L12-M16

444634	446029	444448	444727	446122
444541	445099	445564	444913	445843
446308	445006	445192	445378	444076
446215	445471	444820	445285	444169
444262	444355	445936	445657	445750

L13-M1

446959	448354	446773	447052	448447
446866	447424	447889	447238	448168
448633	447331	447517	447703	446401
448540	447796	447145	447610	446494
446587	446680	448261	447982	448075

L13-M2

449284	450679	449098	449377	450772
449191	449749	450214	449563	450493
450958	449656	449842	450028	448726
450865	450121	449470	449935	448819
448912	449005	450586	450307	450400

L13-M3

451609	453004	451423	451702	453097
451516	452074	452539	451888	452818
453283	451981	452167	452353	451051
453190	452446	451795	452260	451144
451237	451330	452911	452632	452725

L13-M4

453934	455329	453748	454027	455422
453841	454399	454864	454213	455143
455608	454306	454492	454678	453376
455515	454771	454120	454585	453469
453562	453655	455236	454957	455050

L13-M5

456259	457654	456073	456352	457747
456166	456724	457189	456538	457468
457933	456631	456817	457003	455701
457840	457096	456445	456910	455794
455887	455980	457561	457282	457375

L13-M6

458584	459979	458398	458677	460072
458491	459049	459514	458863	459793
460258	458956	459142	459328	458026
460165	459421	458770	459235	458119
458212	458305	459886	459607	459700

L13-M7

460909	462304	460723	461002	462397
460816	461374	461839	461188	462118
462583	461281	461467	461653	460351
462490	461746	461095	461560	460444
460537	460630	462211	461932	462025

L13-M8

463234	464629	463048	463327	464722
463141	463699	464164	463513	464443
464908	463606	463792	463978	462676
464815	464071	463420	463885	462769
462862	462955	464536	464257	464350

L13-M9

465559	466954	465373	465652	467047
465466	466024	466489	465838	466768
467233	465931	466117	466303	465001
467140	466396	465745	466210	465094
465187	465280	466861	466582	466675

L13-M10

467884	469279	467698	467977	469372
467791	468349	468814	468163	469093
469558	468256	468442	468628	467326
469465	468721	468070	468535	467419
467512	467605	469186	468907	469000

L13-M11

470209	471604	470023	470302	471697
470116	470674	471139	470488	471418
471883	470581	470767	470953	469651
471790	471046	470395	470860	469744
469837	469930	471511	471232	471325

L13-M12

472534	473929	472348	472627	474022
472441	472999	473464	472813	473743
474208	472906	473092	473278	471976
474115	473371	472720	473185	472069
472162	472255	473836	473557	473650

L13-M13

474859	476254	474673	474952	476347
474766	475324	475789	475138	476068
476533	475231	475417	475603	474301
476440	475696	475045	475510	474394
474487	474580	476161	475882	475975

L13-M14

477184	478579	476998	477277	478672
477091	477649	478114	477463	478393
478858	477556	477742	477928	476626
478765	478021	477370	477835	476719
476812	476905	478486	478207	478300

L13-M15

479509	480904	479323	479602	480997
479416	479974	480439	479788	480718
481183	479881	480067	480253	478951
481090	480346	479695	480160	479044
479137	479230	480811	480532	480625

L13-M16

481834	483229	481648	481927	483322
481741	482299	482764	482113	483043
483508	482206	482392	482578	481276
483415	482671	482020	482485	481369
481462	481555	483136	482857	482950

L14-M1

484159	485554	483973	484252	485647
484066	484624	485089	484438	485368
485833	484531	484717	484903	483601
485740	484996	484345	484810	483694
483787	483880	485461	485182	485275

L14-M2

486484	487879	486298	486577	487972
486391	486949	487414	486763	487693
488158	486856	487042	487228	485926
488065	487321	486670	487135	486019
486112	486205	487786	487507	487600

L14-M3

488809	490204	488623	488902	490297
488716	489274	489739	489088	490018
490483	489181	489367	489553	488251
490390	489646	488995	489460	488344
488437	488530	490111	489832	489925

L14-M4

491134	492529	490948	491227	492622
491041	491599	492064	491413	492343
492808	491506	491692	491878	490576
492715	491971	491320	491785	490669
490762	490855	492436	492157	492250

L14-M5

493459	494854	493273	493552	494947
493366	493924	494389	493738	494668
495133	493831	494017	494203	492901
495040	494296	493645	494110	492994
493087	493180	494761	494482	494575

L14-M6

495784	497179	495598	495877	497272
495691	496249	496714	496063	496993
497458	496156	496342	496528	495226
497365	496621	495970	496435	495319
495412	495505	497086	496807	496900

L14-M7

498109	499504	497923	498202	499597
498016	498574	499039	498388	499318
499783	498481	498667	498853	497551
499690	498946	498295	498760	497644
497737	497830	499411	499132	499225

L14-M8

500434	501829	500248	500527	501922
500341	500899	501364	500713	501643
502108	500806	500992	501178	499876
502015	501271	500620	501085	499969
500062	500155	501736	501457	501550

L14-M9

502759	504154	502573	502852	504247
502666	503224	503689	503038	503968
504433	503131	503317	503503	502201
504340	503596	502945	503410	502294
502387	502480	504061	503782	503875

L14-M10

505084	506479	504898	505177	506572
504991	505549	506014	505363	506293
506758	505456	505642	505828	504526
506665	505921	505270	505735	504619
504712	504805	506386	506107	506200

L14-M11

507409	508804	507223	507502	508897
507316	507874	508339	507688	508618
509083	507781	507967	508153	506851
508990	508246	507595	508060	506944
507037	507130	508711	508432	508525

L14-M12

509734	511129	509548	509827	511222
509641	510199	510664	510013	510943
511408	510106	510292	510478	509176
511315	510571	509920	510385	509269
509362	509455	511036	510757	510850

L14-M13

512059	513454	511873	512152	513547
511966	512524	512989	512338	513268
513733	512431	512617	512803	511501
513640	512896	512245	512710	511594
511687	511780	513361	513082	513175

L14-M14

514384	515779	514198	514477	515872
514291	514849	515314	514663	515593
516058	514756	514942	515128	513826
515965	515221	514570	515035	513919
514012	514105	515686	515407	515500

L14-M15

516709	518104	516523	516802	518197
516616	517174	517639	516988	517918
518383	517081	517267	517453	516151
518290	517546	516895	517360	516244
516337	516430	518011	517732	517825

L14-M16

519034	520429	518848	519127	520522
518941	519499	519964	519313	520243
520708	519406	519592	519778	518476
520615	519871	519220	519685	518569
518662	518755	520336	520057	520150

L15-M1

521359	522754	521173	521452	522847
521266	521824	522289	521638	522568
523033	521731	521917	522103	520801
522940	522196	521545	522010	520894
520987	521080	522661	522382	522475

L15-M2

523684	525079	523498	523777	525172
523591	524149	524614	523963	524893
525358	524056	524242	524428	523126
525265	524521	523870	524335	523219
523312	523405	524986	524707	524800

L15-M3

526009	527404	525823	526102	527497
525916	526474	526939	526288	527218
527683	526381	526567	526753	525451
527590	526846	526195	526660	525544
525637	525730	527311	527032	527125

L15-M4

528334	529729	528148	528427	529822
528241	528799	529264	528613	529543
530008	528706	528892	529078	527776
529915	529171	528520	528985	527869
527962	528055	529636	529357	529450

L15-M5

530659	532054	530473	530752	532147
530566	531124	531589	530938	531868
532333	531031	531217	531403	530101
532240	531496	530845	531310	530194
530287	530380	531961	531682	531775

L15-M6

532984	534379	532798	533077	534472
532891	533449	533914	533263	534193
534658	533356	533542	533728	532426
534565	533821	533170	533635	532519
532612	532705	534286	534007	534100

L15-M7

535309	536704	535123	535402	536797
535216	535774	536239	535588	536518
536983	535681	535867	536053	534751
536890	536146	535495	535960	534844
534937	535030	536611	536332	536425

L15-M8

537634	539029	537448	537727	539122
537541	538099	538564	537913	538843
539308	538006	538192	538378	537076
539215	538471	537820	538285	537169
537262	537355	538936	538657	538750

L15-M9

539959	541354	539773	540052	541447
539866	540424	540889	540238	541168
541633	540331	540517	540703	539401
541540	540796	540145	540610	539494
539587	539680	541261	540982	541075

L15-M10

542284	543679	542098	542377	543772
542191	542749	543214	542563	543493
543958	542656	542842	543028	541726
543865	543121	542470	542935	541819
541912	542005	543586	543307	543400

L15-M11

544609	546004	544423	544702	546097
544516	545074	545539	544888	545818
546283	544981	545167	545353	544051
546190	545446	544795	545260	544144
544237	544330	545911	545632	545725

L16-M4

565534	566929	565348	565627	567022
565441	565999	566464	565813	566743
567208	565906	566092	566278	564976
567115	566371	565720	566185	565069
565162	565255	566836	566557	566650

L15-M12

546934	548329	546748	547027	548422
546841	547399	547864	547213	548143
548608	547306	547492	547678	546376
548515	547771	547120	547585	546469
546562	546655	548236	547957	548050

L16-M5

567859	569254	567673	567952	569347
567766	568324	568789	568138	569068
569533	568231	568417	568603	567301
569440	568696	568045	568510	567394
567487	567580	569161	568882	568975

L15-M13

549259	550654	549073	549352	550747
549166	549724	550189	549538	550468
550933	549631	549817	550003	548701
550840	550096	549445	549910	548794
548887	548980	550561	550282	550375

L16-M6

570184	571579	569998	570277	571672
570091	570649	571114	570463	571393
571858	570556	570742	570928	569626
571765	571021	570370	570835	569719
569812	569905	571486	571207	571300

L15-M14

551584	552979	551398	551677	553072
551491	552049	552514	551863	552793
553258	551956	552142	552328	551026
553165	552421	551770	552235	551119
551212	551305	552886	552607	552700

L16-M7

572509	573904	572323	572602	573997
572416	572974	573439	572788	573718
574183	572881	573067	573253	571951
574090	573346	572695	573160	572044
572137	572230	573811	573532	573625

L15-M15

553909	555304	553723	554002	555397
553816	554374	554839	554188	555118
555583	554281	554467	554653	553351
555490	554746	554095	554560	553444
553537	553630	555211	554932	555025

L16-M8

574834	576229	574648	574927	576322
574741	575299	575764	575113	576043
576508	575206	575392	575578	574276
576415	575671	575020	575485	574369
574462	574555	576136	575857	575950

L15-M16

556234	557629	556048	556327	557722
556141	556699	557164	556513	557443
557908	556606	556792	556978	555676
557815	557071	556420	556885	555769
555862	555955	557536	557257	557350

L16-M9

577159	578554	576973	577252	578647
577066	577624	578089	577438	578368
578833	577531	577717	577903	576601
578740	577996	577345	577810	576694
576787	576880	578461	578182	578275

L16-M1

558559	559954	558373	558652	560047
558466	559024	559489	558838	559768
560233	558931	559117	559303	558001
560140	559396	558745	559210	558094
558187	558280	559861	559582	559675

L16-M10

579484	580879	579298	579577	580972
579391	579949	580414	579763	580693
581158	579856	580042	580228	578926
581065	580321	579670	580135	579019
579112	579205	580786	580507	580600

L16-M2

560884	562279	560698	560977	562372
560791	561349	561814	561163	562093
562558	561256	561442	561628	560326
562465	561721	561070	561535	560419
560512	560605	562186	561907	562000

L16-M11

581809	583204	581623	581902	583297
581716	582274	582739	582088	583018
583483	582181	582367	582553	581251
583390	582646	581995	582460	581344
581437	581530	583111	582832	582925

L16-M3

563209	564604	563023	563302	564697
563116	563674	564139	563488	564418
564883	563581	563767	563953	562651
564790	564046	563395	563860	562744
562837	562930	564511	564232	564325

L16-M12

584134	585529	583948	584227	585622
584041	584599	585064	584413	585343
585808	584506	584692	584878	583576
585715	584971	584320	584785	583669
583762	583855	585436	585157	585250

L16-M13

586459	587854	586273	586552	587947
586366	586924	587389	586738	587668
588133	586831	587017	587203	585901
588040	587296	586645	587110	585994
586087	586180	587761	587482	587575

L17-M6

607384	608779	607198	607477	608872
607291	607849	608314	607663	608593
609058	607756	607942	608128	606826
608965	608221	607570	608035	606919
607012	607105	608686	608407	608500

L16-M14

588784	590179	588598	588877	590272
588691	589249	589714	589063	589993
590458	589156	589342	589528	588226
590365	589621	588970	589435	588319
588412	588505	590086	589807	589900

L17-M7

609709	611104	609523	609802	611197
609616	610174	610639	609988	610918
611383	610081	610267	610453	609151
611290	610546	609895	610360	609244
609337	609430	611011	610732	610825

L16-M15

591109	592504	590923	591202	592597
591016	591574	592039	591388	592318
592783	591481	591667	591853	590551
592690	591946	591295	591760	590644
590737	590830	592411	592132	592225

L17-M8

612034	613429	611848	612127	613522
611941	612499	612964	612313	613243
613708	612406	612592	612778	611476
613615	612871	612220	612685	611569
611662	611755	613336	613057	613150

L16M16

593434	594829	593248	593527	594922
593341	593899	594364	593713	594643
595108	593806	593992	594178	592876
595015	594271	593620	594085	592969
593062	593155	594736	594457	594550

L17-M9

614359	615754	614173	614452	615847
614266	614824	615289	614638	615568
616033	614731	614917	615103	613801
615940	615196	614545	615010	613894
613987	614080	615661	615382	615475

L17-M1

595759	597154	595573	595852	597247
595666	596224	596689	596038	596968
597433	596131	596317	596503	595201
597340	596596	595945	596410	595294
595387	595480	597061	596782	596875

L17-M10

616684	618079	616498	616777	618172
616591	617149	617614	616963	617893
618358	617056	617242	617428	616126
618265	617521	616870	617335	616219
616312	616405	617986	617707	617800

L17-M2

598084	599479	597898	598177	599572
597991	598549	599014	598363	599293
599758	598456	598642	598828	597526
599665	598921	598270	598735	597619
597712	597805	599386	599107	599200

L17-M11

619009	620404	618823	619102	620497
618916	619474	619939	619288	620218
620683	619381	619567	619753	618451
620590	619846	619195	619660	618544
618637	618730	620311	620032	620125

L17-M3

600409	601804	600223	600502	601897
600316	600874	601339	600688	601618
602083	600781	600967	601153	599851
601990	601246	600595	601060	599944
600037	600130	601711	601432	601525

L17-M12

621334	622729	621148	621427	622822
621241	621799	622264	621613	622543
623008	621706	621892	622078	620776
622915	622171	621520	621985	620869
620962	621055	622636	622357	622450

L17-M4

602734	604129	602548	602827	604222
602641	603199	603664	603013	603943
604408	603106	603292	603478	602176
604315	603571	602920	603385	602269
602362	602455	604036	603757	603850

L17-M13

623659	625054	623473	623752	625147
623566	624124	624589	623938	624868
625333	624031	624217	624403	623101
625240	624496	623845	624310	623194
623287	623380	624961	624682	624775

L17-M5

605059	606454	604873	605152	606547
604966	605524	605989	605338	606268
606733	605431	605617	605803	604501
606640	605896	605245	605710	604594
604687	604780	606361	606082	606175

L17-M14

625984	627379	625798	626077	627472
625891	626449	626914	626263	627193
627658	626356	626542	626728	625426
627565	626821	626170	626635	625519
625612	625705	627286	627007	627100

L17-M15

628309	629704	628123	628402	629797
628216	628774	629239	628588	629518
629983	628681	628867	629053	627751
629890	629146	628495	628960	627844
627937	628030	629611	629332	629425

L17-M16

630634	632029	630448	630727	632122
630541	631099	631564	630913	631843
632308	631006	631192	631378	630076
632215	631471	630820	631285	630169
630262	630355	631936	631657	631750

L18-M1

632959	634354	632773	633052	634447
632866	633424	633889	633238	634168
634633	633331	633517	633703	632401
634540	633796	633145	633610	632494
632587	632680	634261	633982	634075

L18-M2

635284	636679	635098	635377	636772
635191	635749	636214	635563	636493
636958	635656	635842	636028	634726
636865	636121	635470	635935	634819
634912	635005	636586	636307	636400

L18-M3

637609	639004	637423	637702	639097
637516	638074	638539	637888	638818
639283	637981	638167	638353	637051
639190	638446	637795	638260	637144
637237	637330	638911	638632	638725

L18-M4

639934	641329	639748	640027	641422
639841	640399	640864	640213	641143
641608	640306	640492	640678	639376
641515	640771	640120	640585	639469
639562	639655	641236	640957	641050

L18-M5

642259	643654	642073	642352	643747
642166	642724	643189	642538	643468
643933	642631	642817	643003	641701
643840	643096	642445	642910	641794
641887	641980	643561	643282	643375

L18-M6

644584	645979	644398	644677	646072
644491	645049	645514	644863	645793
646258	644956	645142	645328	644026
646165	645421	644770	645235	644119
644212	644305	645886	645607	645700

L18-M7

646909	648304	646723	647002	648397
646816	647374	647839	647188	648118
648583	647281	647467	647653	646351
648490	647746	647095	647560	646444
646537	646630	648211	647932	648025

L18-M8

649234	650629	649048	649327	650722
649141	649699	650164	649513	650443
650908	649606	649792	649978	648676
650815	650071	649420	649885	648769
648862	648955	650536	650257	650350

L18-M9

651559	652954	651373	651652	653047
651466	652024	652489	651838	652768
653233	651931	652117	652303	651001
653140	652396	651745	652210	651094
651187	651280	652861	652582	652675

L18-M10

653884	655279	653698	653977	655372
653791	654349	654814	654163	655093
655558	654256	654442	654628	653326
655465	654721	654070	654535	653419
653512	653605	655186	654907	655000

L18-M11

656209	657604	656023	656302	657697
656116	656674	657139	656488	657418
657883	656581	656767	656953	655651
657790	657046	656395	656860	655744
655837	655930	657511	657232	657325

L18-M12

658534	659929	658348	658627	660022
658441	658999	659464	658813	659743
660208	658906	659092	659278	657976
660115	659371	658720	659185	658069
658162	658255	659836	659557	659650

L18-M13

660859	662254	660673	660952	662347
660766	661324	661789	661138	662068
662533	661231	661417	661603	660301
662440	661696	661045	661510	660394
660487	660580	662161	661882	661975

L18-M14

663184	664579	662998	663277	664672
663091	663649	664114	663463	664393
664858	663556	663742	663928	662626
664765	664021	663370	663835	662719
662812	662905	664486	664207	664300

L18-M15

665509	666904	665323	665602	666997
665416	665974	666439	665788	666718
667183	665881	666067	666253	664951
667090	666346	665695	666160	665044
665137	665230	666811	666532	666625

L18-M16

667834	669229	667648	667927	669322
667741	668299	668764	668113	669043
669508	668206	668392	668578	667276
669415	668671	668020	668485	667369
667462	667555	669136	668857	668950

L19-M1

670159	671554	669973	670252	671647
670066	670624	671089	670438	671368
671833	670531	670717	670903	669601
671740	670996	670345	670810	669694
669787	669880	671461	671182	671275

L19-M2

672484	673879	672298	672577	673972
672391	672949	673414	672763	673693
674158	672856	673042	673228	671926
674065	673321	672670	673135	672019
672112	672205	673786	673507	673600

L19-M3

674809	676204	674623	674902	676297
674716	675274	675739	675088	676018
676483	675181	675367	675553	674251
676390	675646	674995	675460	674344
674437	674530	676111	675832	675925

L19-M4

677134	678529	676948	677227	678622
677041	677599	678064	677413	678343
678808	677506	677692	677878	676576
678715	677971	677320	677785	676669
676762	676855	678436	678157	678250

L19-M5

679459	680854	679273	679552	680947
679366	679924	680389	679738	680668
681133	679831	680017	680203	678901
681040	680296	679645	680110	678994
679087	679180	680761	680482	680575

L19-M6

681784	683179	681598	681877	683272
681691	682249	682714	682063	682993
683458	682156	682342	682528	681226
683365	682621	681970	682435	681319
681412	681505	683086	682807	682900

L19-M7

684109	685504	683923	684202	685597
684016	684574	685039	684388	685318
685783	684481	684667	684853	683551
685690	684946	684295	684760	683644
683737	683830	685411	685132	685225

L19-M8

686434	687829	686248	686527	687922
686341	686899	687364	686713	687643
688108	686806	686992	687178	685876
688015	687271	686620	687085	685969
686062	686155	687736	687457	687550

L19-M9

688759	690154	688573	688852	690247
688666	689224	689689	689038	689968
690433	689131	689317	689503	688201
690340	689596	688945	689410	688294
688387	688480	690061	689782	689875

L19-M10

691084	692479	690898	691177	692572
690991	691549	692014	691363	692293
692758	691456	691642	691828	690526
692665	691921	691270	691735	690619
690712	690805	692386	692107	692200

L19-M11

693409	694804	693223	693502	694897
693316	693874	694339	693688	694618
695083	693781	693967	694153	692851
694990	694246	693595	694060	692944
693037	693130	694711	694432	694525

L19-M12

695734	697129	695548	695827	697222
695641	696199	696664	696013	696943
697408	696106	696292	696478	695176
697315	696571	695920	696385	695269
695362	695455	697036	696757	696850

L19-M13

698059	699454	697873	698152	699547
697966	698524	698989	698338	699268
699733	698431	698617	698803	697501
699640	698896	698245	698710	697594
697687	697780	699361	699082	699175

L19-M14

700384	701779	700198	700477	701872
700291	700849	701314	700663	701593
702058	700756	700942	701128	699826
701965	701221	700570	701035	699919
700012	700105	701686	701407	701500

L19-M15

702709	704104	702523	702802	704197
702616	703174	703639	702988	703918
704383	703081	703267	703453	702151
704290	703546	702895	703360	702244
702337	702430	704011	703732	703825

L19-M16

705034	706429	704848	705127	706522
704941	705499	705964	705313	706243
706708	705406	705592	705778	704476
706615	705871	705220	705685	704569
704662	704755	706336	706057	706150

L20-M1

707359	708754	707173	707452	708847
707266	707824	708289	707638	708568
709033	707731	707917	708103	706801
708940	708196	707545	708010	706894
706987	707080	708661	708382	708475

L20-M2

709684	711079	709498	709777	711172
709591	710149	710614	709963	710893
711358	710056	710242	710428	709126
711265	710521	709870	710335	709219
709312	709405	710986	710707	710800

L20-M3

712009	713404	711823	712102	713497
711916	712474	712939	712288	713218
713683	712381	712567	712753	711451
713590	712846	712195	712660	711544
711637	711730	713311	713032	713125

L20-M12

732934	734329	732748	733027	734422
732841	733399	733864	733213	734143
734608	733306	733492	733678	732376
734515	733771	733120	733585	732469
732562	732655	734236	733957	734050

L20-M4

714334	715729	714148	714427	715822
714241	714799	715264	714613	715543
716008	714706	714892	715078	713776
715915	715171	714520	714985	713869
713962	714055	715636	715357	715450

L20-M13

735259	736654	735073	735352	736747
735166	735724	736189	735538	736468
736933	735631	735817	736003	734701
736840	736096	735445	735910	734794
734887	734980	736561	736282	736375

L20-M5

716659	718054	716473	716752	718147
716566	717124	717589	716938	717868
718333	717031	717217	717403	716101
718240	717496	716845	717310	716194
716287	716380	717961	717682	717775

L20-M14

737584	738979	737398	737677	739072
737491	738049	738514	737863	738793
739258	737956	738142	738328	737026
739165	738421	737770	738235	737119
737212	737305	738886	738607	738700

L20-M6

718984	720379	718798	719077	720472
718891	719449	719914	719263	720193
720658	719356	719542	719728	718426
720565	719821	719170	719635	718519
718612	718705	720286	720007	720100

L20-M15

739909	741304	739723	740002	741397
739816	740374	740839	740188	741118
741583	740281	740467	740653	739351
741490	740746	740095	740560	739444
739537	739630	741211	740932	741025

L20-M7

721309	722704	721123	721402	722797
721216	721774	722239	721588	722518
722983	721681	721867	722053	720751
722890	722146	721495	721960	720844
720937	721030	722611	722332	722425

L20-M16

742234	743629	742048	742327	743722
742141	742699	743164	742513	743443
743908	742606	742792	742978	741676
743815	743071	742420	742885	741769
741862	741955	743536	743257	743350

L20-M8

723634	725029	723448	723727	725122
723541	724099	724564	723913	724843
725308	724006	724192	724378	723076
725215	724471	723820	724285	723169
723262	723355	724936	724657	724750

L21-M1

744559	745954	744373	744652	746047
744466	745024	745489	744838	745768
746233	744931	745117	745303	744001
746140	745396	744745	745210	744094
744187	744280	745861	745582	745675

L20-M9

725959	727354	725773	726052	727447
725866	726424	726889	726238	727168
727633	726331	726517	726703	725401
727540	726796	726145	726610	725494
725587	725680	727261	726982	727075

L21-M2

746884	748279	746698	746977	748372
746791	747349	747814	747163	748093
748558	747256	747442	747628	746326
748465	747721	747070	747535	746419
746512	746605	748186	747907	748000

L20-M10

728284	729679	728098	728377	729772
728191	728749	729214	728563	729493
729958	728656	728842	729028	727726
729865	729121	728470	728935	727819
727912	728005	729586	729307	729400

L21-M3

749209	750604	749023	749302	750697
749116	749674	750139	749488	750418
750883	749581	749767	749953	748651
750790	750046	749395	749860	748744
748837	748930	750511	750232	750325

L20-M11

730609	732004	730423	730702	732097
730516	731074	731539	730888	731818
732283	730981	731167	731353	730051
732190	731446	730795	731260	730144
730237	730330	731911	731632	731725

L21-M4

751534	752929	751348	751627	753022
751441	751999	752464	751813	752743
753208	751906	752092	752278	750976
753115	752371	751720	752185	751069
751162	751255	752836	752557	752650

L21-M5

753859	755254	753673	753952	755347
753766	754324	754789	754138	755068
755533	754231	754417	754603	753301
755440	754696	754045	754510	753394
753487	753580	755161	754882	754975

L21-M6

756184	757579	755998	756277	757672
756091	756649	757114	756463	757393
757858	756556	756742	756928	755626
757765	757021	756370	756835	755719
755812	755905	757486	757207	757300

L21-M7

758509	759904	758323	758602	759997
758416	758974	759439	758788	759718
760183	758881	759067	759253	757951
760090	759346	758695	759160	758044
758137	758230	759811	759532	759625

L21-M8

760834	762229	760648	760927	762322
760741	761299	761764	761113	762043
762508	761206	761392	761578	760276
762415	761671	761020	761485	760369
760462	760555	762136	761857	761950

L21-M9

763159	764554	762973	763252	764647
763066	763624	764089	763438	764368
764833	763531	763717	763903	762601
764740	763996	763345	763810	762694
762787	762880	764461	764182	764275

L21-M10

765484	766879	765298	765577	766972
765391	765949	766414	765763	766693
767158	765856	766042	766228	764926
767065	766321	765670	766135	765019
765112	765205	766786	766507	766600

L21-M11

767809	769204	767623	767902	769297
767716	768274	768739	768088	769018
769483	768181	768367	768553	767251
769390	768646	767995	768460	767344
767437	767530	769111	768832	768925

L21-M12

770134	771529	769948	770227	771622
770041	770599	771064	770413	771343
771808	770506	770692	770878	769576
771715	770971	770320	770785	769669
769762	769855	771436	771157	771250

L21-M13

772459	773854	772273	772552	773947
772366	772924	773389	772738	773668
774133	772831	773017	773203	771901
774040	773296	772645	773110	771994
772087	772180	773761	773482	773575

L21-M14

774784	776179	774598	774877	776272
774691	775249	775714	775063	775993
776458	775156	775342	775528	774226
776365	775621	774970	775435	774319
774412	774505	776086	775807	775900

L21-M15

777109	778504	776923	777202	778597
777016	777574	778039	777388	778318
778783	777481	777667	777853	776551
778690	777946	777295	777760	776644
776737	776830	778411	778132	778225

L21-M16

779434	780829	779248	779527	780922
779341	779899	780364	779713	780643
781108	779806	779992	780178	778876
781015	780271	779620	780085	778969
779062	779155	780736	780457	780550

L22-M1

781759	783154	781573	781852	783247
781666	782224	782689	782038	782968
783433	782131	782317	782503	781201
783340	782596	781945	782410	781294
781387	781480	783061	782782	782875

L22-M2

784084	785479	783898	784177	785572
783991	784549	785014	784363	785293
785758	784456	784642	784828	783526
785665	784921	784270	784735	783619
783712	783805	785386	785107	785200

L22-M3

786409	787804	786223	786502	787897
786316	786874	787339	786688	787618
788083	786781	786967	787153	785851
787990	787246	786595	787060	785944
786037	786130	787711	787432	787525

L22-M4

788734	790129	788548	788827	790222
788641	789199	789664	789013	789943
790408	789106	789292	789478	788176
790315	789571	788920	789385	788269
788362	788455	790036	789757	789850

L22-M5

791059	792454	790873	791152	792547
790966	791524	791989	791338	792268
792733	791431	791617	791803	790501
792640	791896	791245	791710	790594
790687	790780	792361	792082	792175

L22-M6

793384	794779	793198	793477	794872
793291	793849	794314	793663	794593
795058	793756	793942	794128	792826
794965	794221	793570	794035	792919
793012	793105	794686	794407	794500

L22-M7

795709	797104	795523	795802	797197
795616	796174	796639	795988	796918
797383	796081	796267	796453	795151
797290	796546	795895	796360	795244
795337	795430	797011	796732	796825

L22-M8

798034	799429	797848	798127	799522
797941	798499	798964	798313	799243
799708	798406	798592	798778	797476
799615	798871	798220	798685	797569
797662	797755	799336	799057	799150

L22-M9

800359	801754	800173	800452	801847
800266	800824	801289	800638	801568
802033	800731	800917	801103	799801
801940	801196	800545	801010	799894
799987	800080	801661	801382	801475

L22-M10

802684	804079	802498	802777	804172
802591	803149	803614	802963	803893
804358	803056	803242	803428	802126
804265	803521	802870	803335	802219
802312	802405	803986	803707	803800

L22-M11

805009	806404	804823	805102	806497
804916	805474	805939	805288	806218
806683	805381	805567	805753	804451
806590	805846	805195	805660	804544
804637	804730	806311	806032	806125

L22-M12

807334	808729	807148	807427	808822
807241	807799	808264	807613	808543
809008	807706	807892	808078	806776
808915	808171	807520	807985	806869
806962	807055	808636	808357	808450

L22-M13

809659	811054	809473	809752	811147
809566	810124	810589	809938	810868
811333	810031	810217	810403	809101
811240	810496	809845	810310	809194
809287	809380	810961	810682	810775

L22-M14

811984	813379	811798	812077	813472
811891	812449	812914	812263	813193
813658	812356	812542	812728	811426
813565	812821	812170	812635	811519
811612	811705	813286	813007	813100

L22-M15

814309	815704	814123	814402	815797
814216	814774	815239	814588	815518
815983	814681	814867	815053	813751
815890	815146	814495	814960	813844
813937	814030	815611	815332	815425

L22-M16

816634	818029	816448	816727	818122
816541	817099	817564	816913	817843
818308	817006	817192	817378	816076
818215	817471	816820	817285	816169
816262	816355	817936	817657	817750

L23-M1

818959	820354	818773	819052	820447
818866	819424	819889	819238	820168
820633	819331	819517	819703	818401
820540	819796	819145	819610	818494
818587	818680	820261	819982	820075

L23-M2

821284	822679	821098	821377	822772
821191	821749	822214	821563	822493
822958	821656	821842	822028	820726
822865	822121	821470	821935	820819
820912	821005	822586	822307	822400

L23-M3

823609	825004	823423	823702	825097
823516	824074	824539	823888	824818
825283	823981	824167	824353	823051
825190	824446	823795	824260	823144
823237	823330	824911	824632	824725

L23-M4

825934	827329	825748	826027	827422
825841	826399	826864	826213	827143
827608	826306	826492	826678	825376
827515	826771	826120	826585	825469
825562	825655	827236	826957	827050

L23-M5

828259	829654	828073	828352	829747
828166	828724	829189	828538	829468
829933	828631	828817	829003	827701
829840	829096	828445	828910	827794
827887	827980	829561	829282	829375

L23-M6

830584	831979	830398	830677	832072
830491	831049	831514	830863	831793
832258	830956	831142	831328	830026
832165	831421	830770	831235	830119
830212	830305	831886	831607	831700

L23-M7

832909	834304	832723	833002	834397
832816	833374	833839	833188	834118
834583	833281	833467	833653	832351
834490	833746	833095	833560	832444
832537	832630	834211	833932	834025

L23-M8

835234	836629	835048	835327	836722
835141	835699	836164	835513	836443
836908	835606	835792	835978	834676
836815	836071	835420	835885	834769
834862	834955	836536	836257	836350

L23-M9

837559	838954	837373	837652	839047
837466	838024	838489	837838	838768
839233	837931	838117	838303	837001
839140	838396	837745	838210	837094
837187	837280	838861	838582	838675

L23-M10

839884	841279	839698	839977	841372
839791	840349	840814	840163	841093
841558	840256	840442	840628	839326
841465	840721	840070	840535	839419
839512	839605	841186	840907	841000

L23-M11

842209	843604	842023	842302	843697
842116	842674	843139	842488	843418
843883	842581	842767	842953	841651
843790	843046	842395	842860	841744
841837	841930	843511	843232	843325

L23-M12

844534	845929	844348	844627	846022
844441	844999	845464	844813	845743
846208	844906	845092	845278	843976
846115	845371	844720	845185	844069
844162	844255	845836	845557	845650

L23-M13

846859	848254	846673	846952	848347
846766	847324	847789	847138	848068
848533	847231	847417	847603	846301
848440	847696	847045	847510	846394
846487	846580	848161	847882	847975

L23-M14

849184	850579	848998	849277	850672
849091	849649	850114	849463	850393
850858	849556	849742	849928	848626
850765	850021	849370	849835	848719
848812	848905	850486	850207	850300

L23-M15

851509	852904	851323	851602	852997
851416	851974	852439	851788	852718
853183	851881	852067	852253	850951
853090	852346	851695	852160	851044
851137	851230	852811	852532	852625

L23-M16

853834	855229	853648	853927	855322
853741	854299	854764	854113	855043
855508	854206	854392	854578	853276
855415	854671	854020	854485	853369
853462	853555	855136	854857	854950

L24-M1

856159	857554	855973	856252	857647
856066	856624	857089	856438	857368
857833	856531	856717	856903	855601
857740	856996	856345	856810	855694
855787	855880	857461	857182	857275

L24-M2

858484	859879	858298	858577	859972
858391	858949	859414	858763	859693
860158	858856	859042	859228	857926
860065	859321	858670	859135	858019
858112	858205	859786	859507	859600

L24-M3

860809	862204	860623	860902	862297
860716	861274	861739	861088	862018
862483	861181	861367	861553	860251
862390	861646	860995	861460	860344
860437	860530	862111	861832	861925

L24-M4

863134	864529	862948	863227	864622
863041	863599	864064	863413	864343
864808	863506	863692	863878	862576
864715	863971	863320	863785	862669
862762	862855	864436	864157	864250

L24-M5

865459	866854	865273	865552	866947
865366	865924	866389	865738	866668
867133	865831	866017	866203	864901
867040	866296	865645	866110	864994
865087	865180	866761	866482	866575

L24-M6

867784	869179	867598	867877	869272
867691	868249	868714	868063	868993
869458	868156	868342	868528	867226
869365	868621	867970	868435	867319
867412	867505	869086	868807	868900

L24-M7

870109	871504	869923	870202	871597
870016	870574	871039	870388	871318
871783	870481	870667	870853	869551
871690	870946	870295	870760	869644
869737	869830	871411	871132	871225

L24-M8

872434	873829	872248	872527	873922
872341	872899	873364	872713	873643
874108	872806	872992	873178	871876
874015	873271	872620	873085	871969
872062	872155	873736	873457	873550

L24-M9

874759	876154	874573	874852	876247
874666	875224	875689	875038	875968
876433	875131	875317	875503	874201
876340	875596	874945	875410	874294
874387	874480	876061	875782	875875

L24-M10

877084	878479	876898	877177	878572
876991	877549	878014	877363	878293
878758	877456	877642	877828	876526
878665	877921	877270	877735	876619
876712	876805	878386	878107	878200

L24-M11

879409	880804	879223	879502	880897
879316	879874	880339	879688	880618
881083	879781	879967	880153	878851
880990	880246	879595	880060	878944
879037	879130	880711	880432	880525

L24-M12

881734	883129	881548	881827	883222
881641	882199	882664	882013	882943
883408	882106	882292	882478	881176
883315	882571	881920	882385	881269
881362	881455	883036	882757	882850

L24-M13

884059	885454	883873	884152	885547
883966	884524	884989	884338	885268
885733	884431	884617	884803	883501
885640	884896	884245	884710	883594
883687	883780	885361	885082	885175

L24-M14

886384	887779	886198	886477	887872
886291	886849	887314	886663	887593
888058	886756	886942	887128	885826
887965	887221	886570	887035	885919
886012	886105	887686	887407	887500

L24-M15

888709	890104	888523	888802	890197
888616	889174	889639	888988	889918
890383	889081	889267	889453	888151
890290	889546	888895	889360	888244
888337	888430	890011	889732	889825

L24-M16

891034	892429	890848	891127	892522
890941	891499	891964	891313	892243
892708	891406	891592	891778	890476
892615	891871	891220	891685	890569
890662	890755	892336	892057	892150

L25-M1

893359	894754	893173	893452	894847
893266	893824	894289	893638	894568
895033	893731	893917	894103	892801
894940	894196	893545	894010	892894
892987	893080	894661	894382	894475

L25-M2

895684	897079	895498	895777	897172
895591	896149	896614	895963	896893
897358	896056	896242	896428	895126
897265	896521	895870	896335	895219
895312	895405	896986	896707	896800

L25-M3

898009	899404	897823	898102	899497
897916	898474	898939	898288	899218
899683	898381	898567	898753	897451
899590	898846	898195	898660	897544
897637	897730	899311	899032	899125

L25-M4

900334	901729	900148	900427	901822
900241	900799	901264	900613	901543
902008	900706	900892	901078	899776
901915	901171	900520	900985	899869
899962	900055	901636	901357	901450

L25-M5

902659	904054	902473	902752	904147
902566	903124	903589	902938	903868
904333	903031	903217	903403	902101
904240	903496	902845	903310	902194
902287	902380	903961	903682	903775

L25-M6

904984	906379	904798	905077	906472
904891	905449	905914	905263	906193
906658	905356	905542	905728	904426
906565	905821	905170	905635	904519
904612	904705	906286	906007	906100

L25-M7

907309	908704	907123	907402	908797
907216	907774	908239	907588	908518
908983	907681	907867	908053	906751
908890	908146	907495	907960	906844
906937	907030	908611	908332	908425

L25-M8

909634	911029	909448	909727	911122
909541	910099	910564	909913	910843
911308	910006	910192	910378	909076
911215	910471	909820	910285	909169
909262	909355	910936	910657	910750

L25-M9

911959	913354	911773	912052	913447
911866	912424	912889	912238	913168
913633	912331	912517	912703	911401
913540	912796	912145	912610	911494
911587	911680	913261	912982	913075

L25-M10

914284	915679	914098	914377	915772
914191	914749	915214	914563	915493
915958	914656	914842	915028	913726
915865	915121	914470	914935	913819
913912	914005	915586	915307	915400

L25-M11

916609	918004	916423	916702	918097
916516	917074	917539	916888	917818
918283	916981	917167	917353	916051
918190	917446	916795	917260	916144
916237	916330	917911	917632	917725

L25-M12

918934	920329	918748	919027	920422
918841	919399	919864	919213	920143
920608	919306	919492	919678	918376
920515	919771	919120	919585	918469
918562	918655	920236	919957	920050

L25-M13

921259	922654	921073	921352	922747
921166	921724	922189	921538	922468
922933	921631	921817	922003	920701
922840	922096	921445	921910	920794
920887	920980	922561	922282	922375

L25-M14

923584	924979	923398	923677	925072
923491	924049	924514	923863	924793
925258	923956	924142	924328	923026
925165	924421	923770	924235	923119
923212	923305	924886	924607	924700

L25-M15

925909	927304	925723	926002	927397
925816	926374	926839	926188	927118
927583	926281	926467	926653	925351
927490	926746	926095	926560	925444
925537	925630	927211	926932	927025

L25-M16

928234	929629	928048	928327	929722
928141	928699	929164	928513	929443
929908	928606	928792	928978	927676
929815	929071	928420	928885	927769
927862	927955	929536	929257	929350

BINAH

L1-M1

1105	3865	737	1289	4049
921	2025	2945	1657	3497
4417	1841	2209	2577	1
4233	2761	1473	2393	185
369	553	3681	3129	3313

L1-M2

5705	8465	5337	5889	8649
5521	6625	7545	6257	8097
9017	6441	6809	7177	4601
8833	7361	6073	6993	4785
4969	5153	8281	7729	7913

L1-M3

10305	13065	9937	10489	13249
10121	11225	12145	10857	12697
13617	11041	11409	11777	9201
13433	11961	10673	11593	9385
9569	9753	12881	12329	12513

L1-M4

14905	17665	14537	15089	17849
14721	15825	16745	15457	17297
18217	15641	16009	16377	13801
18033	16561	15273	16193	13985
14169	14353	17481	16929	17113

L1-M5

19505	22265	19137	19689	22449
19321	20425	21345	20057	21897
22817	20241	20609	20977	18401
22633	21161	19873	20793	18585
18769	18953	22081	21529	21713

L1-M6

24105	26865	23737	24289	27049
23921	25025	25945	24657	26497
27417	24841	25209	25577	23001
27233	25761	24473	25393	23185
23369	23553	26681	26129	26313

L1-M7

28705	31465	28337	28889	31649
28521	29625	30545	29257	31097
32017	29441	29809	30177	27601
31833	30361	29073	29993	27785
27969	28153	31281	30729	30913

L1-M8

33305	36065	32937	33489	36249
33121	34225	35145	33857	35697
36617	34041	34409	34777	32201
36433	34961	33673	34593	32385
32569	32753	35881	35329	35513

L1-M9

37905	40665	37537	38089	40849
37721	38825	39745	38457	40297
41217	38641	39009	39377	36801
41033	39561	38273	39193	36985
37169	37353	40481	39929	40113

L1-M10

42505	45265	42137	42689	45449
42321	43425	44345	43057	44897
45817	43241	43609	43977	41401
45633	44161	42873	43793	41585
41769	41953	45081	44529	44713

L1-M11

47105	49865	46737	47289	50049
46921	48025	48945	47657	49497
50417	47841	48209	48577	46001
50233	48761	47473	48393	46185
46369	46553	49681	49129	49313

L1-M12

51705	54465	51337	51889	54649
51521	52625	53545	52257	54097
55017	52441	52809	53177	50601
54833	53361	52073	52993	50785
50969	51153	54281	53729	53913

L1-M13

56305	59065	55937	56489	59249
56121	57225	58145	56857	58697
59617	57041	57409	57777	55201
59433	57961	56673	57593	55385
55569	55753	58881	58329	58513

L1-M14

60905	63665	60537	61089	63849
60721	61825	62745	61457	63297
64217	61641	62009	62377	59801
64033	62561	61273	62193	59985
60169	60353	63481	62929	63113

L1-M15

65505	68265	65137	65689	68449
65321	66425	67345	66057	67897
68817	66241	66609	66977	64401
68633	67161	65873	66793	64585
64769	64953	68081	67529	67713

L1-M16

70105	72865	69737	70289	73049
69921	71025	71945	70657	72497
73417	70841	71209	71577	69001
73233	71761	70473	71393	69185
69369	69553	72681	72129	72313

L2-M1

74705	77465	74337	74889	77649
74521	75625	76545	75257	77097
78017	75441	75809	76177	73601
77833	76361	75073	75993	73785
73969	74153	77281	76729	76913

L2-M2

79305	82065	78937	79489	82249
79121	80225	81145	79857	81697
82617	80041	80409	80777	78201
82433	80961	79673	80593	78385
78569	78753	81881	81329	81513

L2-M3

83905	86665	83537	84089	86849
83721	84825	85745	84457	86297
87217	84641	85009	85377	82801
87033	85561	84273	85193	82985
83169	83353	86481	85929	86113

L2-M12

125305	128065	124937	125489	128249
125121	126225	127145	125857	127697
128617	126041	126409	126777	124201
128433	126961	125673	126593	124385
124569	124753	127881	127329	127513

L2-M4

88505	91265	88137	88689	91449
88321	89425	90345	89057	90897
91817	89241	89609	89977	87401
91633	90161	88873	89793	87585
87769	87953	91081	90529	90713

L2-M13

129905	132665	129537	130089	132849
129721	130825	131745	130457	132297
133217	130641	131009	131377	128801
133033	131561	130273	131193	128985
129169	129353	132481	131929	132113

L2-M5

93105	95865	92737	93289	96049
92921	94025	94945	93657	95497
96417	93841	94209	94577	92001
96233	94761	93473	94393	92185
92369	92553	95681	95129	95313

L2-M14

134505	137265	134137	134689	137449
134321	135425	136345	135057	136897
137817	135241	135609	135977	133401
137633	136161	134873	135793	133585
133769	133953	137081	136529	136713

L2-M6

97705	100465	97337	97889	100649
97521	98625	99545	98257	100097
101017	98441	98809	99177	96601
100833	99361	98073	98993	96785
96969	97153	100281	99729	99913

L2-M15

139105	141865	138737	139289	142049
138921	140025	140945	139657	141497
142417	139841	140209	140577	138001
142233	140761	139473	140393	138185
138369	138553	141681	141129	141313

L2-M7

102305	105065	101937	102489	105249
102121	103225	104145	102857	104697
105617	103041	103409	103777	101201
105433	103961	102673	103593	101385
101569	101753	104881	104329	104513

L2-M16

143705	146465	143337	143889	146649
143521	144625	145545	144257	146097
147017	144441	144809	145177	142601
146833	145361	144073	144993	142785
142969	143153	146281	145729	145913

L2-M8

106905	109665	106537	107089	109849
106721	107825	108745	107457	109297
110217	107641	108009	108377	105801
110033	108561	107273	108193	105985
106169	106353	109481	108929	109113

L3-M1

148305	151065	147937	148489	151249
148121	149225	150145	148857	150697
151617	149041	149409	149777	147201
151433	149961	148673	149593	147385
147569	147753	150881	150329	150513

L2-M9

111505	114265	111137	111689	114449
111321	112425	113345	112057	113897
114817	112241	112609	112977	110401
114633	113161	111873	112793	110585
110769	110953	114081	113529	113713

L3-M2

152905	155665	152537	153089	155849
152721	153825	154745	153457	155297
156217	153641	154009	154377	151801
156033	154561	153273	154193	151985
152169	152353	155481	154929	155113

L2-M10

116105	118865	115737	116289	119049
115921	117025	117945	116657	118497
119417	116841	117209	117577	115001
119233	117761	116473	117393	115185
115369	115553	118681	118129	118313

L3-M3

157505	160265	157137	157689	160449
157321	158425	159345	158057	159897
160817	158241	158609	158977	156401
160633	159161	157873	158793	156585
156769	156953	160081	159529	159713

L2-M11

120705	123465	120337	120889	123649
120521	121625	122545	121257	123097
124017	121441	121809	122177	119601
123833	122361	121073	121993	119785
119969	120153	123281	122729	122913

L3-M4

162105	164865	161737	162289	165049
161921	163025	163945	162657	164497
165417	162841	163209	163577	161001
165233	163761	162473	163393	161185
161369	161553	164681	164129	164313

L3-M5

166705	169465	166337	166889	169649
166521	167625	168545	167257	169097
170017	167441	167809	168177	165601
169833	168361	167073	167993	165785
165969	166153	169281	168729	168913

L3-M14

208105	210865	207737	208289	211049
207921	209025	209945	208657	210497
211417	208841	209209	209577	207001
211233	209761	208473	209393	207185
207369	207553	210681	210129	210313

L3-M6

171305	174065	170937	171489	174249
171121	172225	173145	171857	173697
174617	172041	172409	172777	170201
174433	172961	171673	172593	170385
170569	170753	173881	173329	173513

L3-M15

212705	215465	212337	212889	215649
212521	213625	214545	213257	215097
216017	213441	213809	214177	211601
215833	214361	213073	213993	211785
211969	212153	215281	214729	214913

L3-M7

175905	178665	175537	176089	178849
175721	176825	177745	176457	178297
179217	176641	177009	177377	174801
179033	177561	176273	177193	174985
175169	175353	178481	177929	178113

L3-M16

217305	220065	216937	217489	220249
217121	218225	219145	217857	219697
220617	218041	218409	218777	216201
220433	218961	217673	218593	216385
216569	216753	219881	219329	219513

L3-M8

180505	183265	180137	180689	183449
180321	181425	182345	181057	182897
183817	181241	181609	181977	179401
183633	182161	180873	181793	179585
179769	179953	183081	182529	182713

L4-M1

221905	224665	221537	222089	224849
221721	222825	223745	222457	224297
225217	222641	223009	223377	220801
225033	223561	222273	223193	220985
221169	221353	224481	223929	224113

L3-M9

185105	187865	184737	185289	188049
184921	186025	186945	185657	187497
188417	185841	186209	186577	184001
188233	186761	185473	186393	184185
184369	184553	187681	187129	187313

L4-M2

226505	229265	226137	226689	229449
226321	227425	228345	227057	228897
229817	227241	227609	227977	225401
229633	228161	226873	227793	225585
225769	225953	229081	228529	228713

L3-M10

189705	192465	189337	189889	192649
189521	190625	191545	190257	192097
193017	190441	190809	191177	188601
192833	191361	190073	190993	188785
188969	189153	192281	191729	191913

L4-M3

231105	233865	230737	231289	234049
230921	232025	232945	231657	233497
234417	231841	232209	232577	230001
234233	232761	231473	232393	230185
230369	230553	233681	233129	233313

L3-M11

194305	197065	193937	194489	197249
194121	195225	196145	194857	196697
197617	195041	195409	195777	193201
197433	195961	194673	195593	193385
193569	193753	196881	196329	196513

L4-M4

235705	238465	235337	235889	238649
235521	236625	237545	236257	238097
239017	236441	236809	237177	234601
238833	237361	236073	236993	234785
234969	235153	238281	237729	237913

L3-M12

198905	201665	198537	199089	201849
198721	199825	200745	199457	201297
202217	199641	200009	200377	197801
202033	200561	199273	200193	197985
198169	198353	201481	200929	201113

L4-M5

240305	243065	239937	240489	243249
240121	241225	242145	240857	242697
243617	241041	241409	241777	239201
243433	241961	240673	241593	239385
239569	239753	242881	242329	242513

L3-M13

203505	206265	203137	203689	206449
203321	204425	205345	204057	205897
206817	204241	204609	204977	202401
206633	205161	203873	204793	202585
202769	202953	206081	205529	205713

L4-M6

244905	247665	244537	245089	247849
244721	245825	246745	245457	247297
248217	245641	246009	246377	243801
248033	246561	245273	246193	243985
244169	244353	247481	246929	247113

L4-M7

249505	252265	249137	249689	252449
249321	250425	251345	250057	251897
252817	250241	250609	250977	248401
252633	251161	249873	250793	248585
248769	248953	252081	251529	251713

L4-M16

290905	293665	290537	291089	293849
290721	291825	292745	291457	293297
294217	291641	292009	292377	289801
294033	292561	291273	292193	289985
290169	290353	293481	292929	293113

L4-M8

254105	256865	253737	254289	257049
253921	255025	255945	254657	256497
257417	254841	255209	255577	253001
257233	255761	254473	255393	253185
253369	253553	256681	256129	256313

L5-M1

295505	298265	295137	295689	298449
295321	296425	297345	296057	297897
298817	296241	296609	296977	294401
298633	297161	295873	296793	294585
294769	294953	298081	297529	297713

L4-M9

258705	261465	258337	258889	261649
258521	259625	260545	259257	261097
262017	259441	259809	260177	257601
261833	260361	259073	259993	257785
257969	258153	261281	260729	260913

L5-M2

300105	302865	299737	300289	303049
299921	301025	301945	300657	302497
303417	300841	301209	301577	299001
303233	301761	300473	301393	299185
299369	299553	302681	302129	302313

L4-M10

263305	266065	262937	263489	266249
263121	264225	265145	263857	265697
266617	264041	264409	264777	262201
266433	264961	263673	264593	262385
262569	262753	265881	265329	265513

L5-M3

304705	307465	304337	304889	307649
304521	305625	306545	305257	307097
308017	305441	305809	306177	303601
307833	306361	305073	305993	303785
303969	304153	307281	306729	306913

L4-M11

267905	270665	267537	268089	270849
267721	268825	269745	268457	270297
271217	268641	269009	269377	266801
271033	269561	268273	269193	266985
267169	267353	270481	269929	270113

L5-M4

309305	312065	308937	309489	312249
309121	310225	311145	309857	311697
312617	310041	310409	310777	308201
312433	310961	309673	310593	308385
308569	308753	311881	311329	311513

L4-M12

272505	275265	272137	272689	275449
272321	273425	274345	273057	274897
275817	273241	273609	273977	271401
275633	274161	272873	273793	271585
271769	271953	275081	274529	274713

L5-M5

313905	316665	313537	314089	316849
313721	314825	315745	314457	316297
317217	314641	315009	315377	312801
317033	315561	314273	315193	312985
313169	313353	316481	315929	316113

L4-M13

277105	279865	276737	277289	280049
276921	278025	278945	277657	279497
280417	277841	278209	278577	276001
280233	278761	277473	278393	276185
276369	276553	279681	279129	279313

L5-M6

318505	321265	318137	318689	321449
318321	319425	320345	319057	320897
321817	319241	319609	319977	317401
321633	320161	318873	319793	317585
317769	317953	321081	320529	320713

L4-M14

281705	284465	281337	281889	284649
281521	282625	283545	282257	284097
285017	282441	282809	283177	280601
284833	283361	282073	282993	280785
280969	281153	284281	283729	283913

L5-M7

323105	325865	322737	323289	326049
322921	324025	324945	323657	325497
326417	323841	324209	324577	322001
326233	324761	323473	324393	322185
322369	322553	325681	325129	325313

L4-M15

286305	289065	285937	286489	289249
286121	287225	288145	286857	288697
289617	287041	287409	287777	285201
289433	287961	286673	287593	285385
285569	285753	288881	288329	288513

L5-M8

327705	330465	327337	327889	330649
327521	328625	329545	328257	330097
331017	328441	328809	329177	326601
330833	329361	328073	328993	326785
326969	327153	330281	329729	329913

L5-M9

332305	335065	331937	332489	335249
332121	333225	334145	332857	334697
335617	333041	333409	333777	331201
335433	333961	332673	333593	331385
331569	331753	334881	334329	334513

L5-M10

336905	339665	336537	337089	339849
336721	337825	338745	337457	339297
340217	337641	338009	338377	335801
340033	338561	337273	338193	335985
336169	336353	339481	338929	339113

L5-M11

341505	344265	341137	341689	344449
341321	342425	343345	342057	343897
344817	342241	342609	342977	340401
344633	343161	341873	342793	340585
340769	340953	344081	343529	343713

L5-M12

346105	348865	345737	346289	349049
345921	347025	347945	346657	348497
349417	346841	347209	347577	345001
349233	347761	346473	347393	345185
345369	345553	348681	348129	348313

L5-M13

350705	353465	350337	350889	353649
350521	351625	352545	351257	353097
354017	351441	351809	352177	349601
353833	352361	351073	351993	349785
349969	350153	353281	352729	352913

L5-M14

355305	358065	354937	355489	358249
355121	356225	357145	355857	357697
358617	356041	356409	356777	354201
358433	356961	355673	356593	354385
354569	354753	357881	357329	357513

L5-M15

359905	362665	359537	360089	362849
359721	360825	361745	360457	362297
363217	360641	361009	361377	358801
363033	361561	360273	361193	358985
359169	359353	362481	361929	362113

L5-M16

364505	367265	364137	364689	367449
364321	365425	366345	365057	366897
367817	365241	365609	365977	363401
367633	366161	364873	365793	363585
363769	363953	367081	366529	366713

L6-M1

369105	371865	368737	369289	372049
368921	370025	370945	369657	371497
372417	369841	370209	370577	368001
372233	370761	369473	370393	368185
368369	368553	371681	371129	371313

L6-M2

373705	376465	373337	373889	376649
373521	374625	375545	374257	376097
377017	374441	374809	375177	372601
376833	375361	374073	374993	372785
372969	373153	376281	375729	375913

L6-M3

378305	381065	377937	378489	381249
378121	379225	380145	378857	380697
381617	379041	379409	379777	377201
381433	379961	378673	379593	377385
377569	377753	380881	380329	380513

L6-M4

382905	385665	382537	383089	385849
382721	383825	384745	383457	385297
386217	383641	384009	384377	381801
386033	384561	383273	384193	381985
382169	382353	385481	384929	385113

L6-M5

387505	390265	387137	387689	390449
387321	388425	389345	388057	389897
390817	388241	388609	388977	386401
390633	389161	387873	388793	386585
386769	386953	390081	389529	389713

L6-M6

392105	394865	391737	392289	395049
391921	393025	393945	392657	394497
395417	392841	393209	393577	391001
395233	393761	392473	393393	391185
391369	391553	394681	394129	394313

L6-M7

396705	399465	396337	396889	399649
396521	397625	398545	397257	399097
400017	397441	397809	398177	395601
399833	398361	397073	397993	395785
395969	396153	399281	398729	398913

L6-M8

401305	404065	400937	401489	404249
401121	402225	403145	401857	403697
404617	402041	402409	402777	400201
404433	402961	401673	402593	400385
400569	400753	403881	403329	403513

L6-M9

405905	408665	405537	406089	408849
405721	406825	407745	406457	408297
409217	406641	407009	407377	404801
409033	407561	406273	407193	404985
405169	405353	408481	407929	408113

L6-M10

410505	413265	410137	410689	413449
410321	411425	412345	411057	412897
413817	411241	411609	411977	409401
413633	412161	410873	411793	409585
409769	409953	413081	412529	412713

L6-M11

415105	417865	414737	415289	418049
414921	416025	416945	415657	417497
418417	415841	416209	416577	414001
418233	416761	415473	416393	414185
414369	414553	417681	417129	417313

L6-M12

419705	422465	419337	419889	422649
419521	420625	421545	420257	422097
423017	420441	420809	421177	418601
422833	421361	420073	420993	418785
418969	419153	422281	421729	421913

L6-M13

424305	427065	423937	424489	427249
424121	425225	426145	424857	426697
427617	425041	425409	425777	423201
427433	425961	424673	425593	423385
423569	423753	426881	426329	426513

L6-M14

428905	431665	428537	429089	431849
428721	429825	430745	429457	431297
432217	429641	430009	430377	427801
432033	430561	429273	430193	427985
428169	428353	431481	430929	431113

L6-M15

433505	436265	433137	433689	436449
433321	434425	435345	434057	435897
436817	434241	434609	434977	432401
436633	435161	433873	434793	432585
432769	432953	436081	435529	435713

L6-M16

438105	440865	437737	438289	441049
437921	439025	439945	438657	440497
441417	438841	439209	439577	437001
441233	439761	438473	439393	437185
437369	437553	440681	440129	440313

L7-M1

442705	445465	442337	442889	445649
442521	443625	444545	443257	445097
446017	443441	443809	444177	441601
445833	444361	443073	443993	441785
441969	442153	445281	444729	444913

L7-M2

447305	450065	446937	447489	450249
447121	448225	449145	447857	449697
450617	448041	448409	448777	446201
450433	448961	447673	448593	446385
446569	446753	449881	449329	449513

L7-M3

451905	454665	451537	452089	454849
451721	452825	453745	452457	454297
455217	452641	453009	453377	450801
455033	453561	452273	453193	450985
451169	451353	454481	453929	454113

L7-M4

456505	459265	456137	456689	459449
456321	457425	458345	457057	458897
459817	457241	457609	457977	455401
459633	458161	456873	457793	455585
455769	455953	459081	458529	458713

L7-M5

461105	463865	460737	461289	464049
460921	462025	462945	461657	463497
464417	461841	462209	462577	460001
464233	462761	461473	462393	460185
460369	460553	463681	463129	463313

L7-M6

465705	468465	465337	465889	468649
465521	466625	467545	466257	468097
469017	466441	466809	467177	464601
468833	467361	466073	466993	464785
464969	465153	468281	467729	467913

L7-M7

470305	473065	469937	470489	473249
470121	471225	472145	470857	472697
473617	471041	471409	471777	469201
473433	471961	470673	471593	469385
469569	469753	472881	472329	472513

L7-M8

474905	477665	474537	475089	477849
474721	475825	476745	475457	477297
478217	475641	476009	476377	473801
478033	476561	475273	476193	473985
474169	474353	477481	476929	477113

L7-M9

479505	482265	479137	479689	482449
479321	480425	481345	480057	481897
482817	480241	480609	480977	478401
482633	481161	479873	480793	478585
478769	478953	482081	481529	481713

L7-M10

484105	486865	483737	484289	487049
483921	485025	485945	484657	486497
487417	484841	485209	485577	483001
487233	485761	484473	485393	483185
483369	483553	486681	486129	486313

L7-M11

488705	491465	488337	488889	491649
488521	489625	490545	489257	491097
492017	489441	489809	490177	487601
491833	490361	489073	489993	487785
487969	488153	491281	490729	490913

L7-M12

493305	496065	492937	493489	496249
493121	494225	495145	493857	495697
496617	494041	494409	494777	492201
496433	494961	493673	494593	492385
492569	492753	495881	495329	495513

L7-M13

497905	500665	497537	498089	500849
497721	498825	499745	498457	500297
501217	498641	499009	499377	496801
501033	499561	498273	499193	496985
497169	497353	500481	499929	500113

L7-M14

502505	505265	502137	502689	505449
502321	503425	504345	503057	504897
505817	503241	503609	503977	501401
505633	504161	502873	503793	501585
501769	501953	505081	504529	504713

L7-M15

507105	509865	506737	507289	510049
506921	508025	508945	507657	509497
510417	507841	508209	508577	506001
510233	508761	507473	508393	506185
506369	506553	509681	509129	509313

L7-M16

511705	514465	511337	511889	514649
511521	512625	513545	512257	514097
515017	512441	512809	513177	510601
514833	513361	512073	512993	510785
510969	511153	514281	513729	513913

L8M1

516305	519065	515937	516489	519249
516121	517225	518145	516857	518697
519617	517041	517409	517777	515201
519433	517961	516673	517593	515385
515569	515753	518881	518329	518513

L8-M2

520905	523665	520537	521089	523849
520721	521825	522745	521457	523297
524217	521641	522009	522377	519801
524033	522561	521273	522193	519985
520169	520353	523481	522929	523113

L8-M3

525505	528265	525137	525689	528449
525321	526425	527345	526057	527897
528817	526241	526609	526977	524401
528633	527161	525873	526793	524585
524769	524953	528081	527529	527713

L8-M4

530105	532865	529737	530289	533049
529921	531025	531945	530657	532497
533417	530841	531209	531577	529001
533233	531761	530473	531393	529185
529369	529553	532681	532129	532313

L8-M5

534705	537465	534337	534889	537649
534521	535625	536545	535257	537097
538017	535441	535809	536177	533601
537833	536361	535073	535993	533785
533969	534153	537281	536729	536913

L8-M6

539305	542065	538937	539489	542249
539121	540225	541145	539857	541697
542617	540041	540409	540777	538201
542433	540961	539673	540593	538385
538569	538753	541881	541329	541513

L8-M7

543905	546665	543537	544089	546849
543721	544825	545745	544457	546297
547217	544641	545009	545377	542801
547033	545561	544273	545193	542985
543169	543353	546481	545929	546113

L8-M8

548505	551265	548137	548689	551449
548321	549425	550345	549057	550897
551817	549241	549609	549977	547401
551633	550161	548873	549793	547585
547769	547953	551081	550529	550713

L8-M9

553105	555865	552737	553289	556049
552921	554025	554945	553657	555497
556417	553841	554209	554577	552001
556233	554761	553473	554393	552185
552369	552553	555681	555129	555313

L8-M10

557705	560465	557337	557889	560649
557521	558625	559545	558257	560097
561017	558441	558809	559177	556601
560833	559361	558073	558993	556785
556969	557153	560281	559729	559913

L8-M11

562305	565065	561937	562489	565249
562121	563225	564145	562857	564697
565617	563041	563409	563777	561201
565433	563961	562673	563593	561385
561569	561753	564881	564329	564513

L8-M12

566905	569665	566537	567089	569849
566721	567825	568745	567457	569297
570217	567641	568009	568377	565801
570033	568561	567273	568193	565985
566169	566353	569481	568929	569113

L8-M13

571505	574265	571137	571689	574449
571321	572425	573345	572057	573897
574817	572241	572609	572977	570401
574633	573161	571873	572793	570585
570769	570953	574081	573529	573713

L8-M14

576105	578865	575737	576289	579049
575921	577025	577945	576657	578497
579417	576841	577209	577577	575001
579233	577761	576473	577393	575185
575369	575553	578681	578129	578313

L8-M15

580705	583465	580337	580889	583649
580521	581625	582545	581257	583097
584017	581441	581809	582177	579601
583833	582361	581073	581993	579785
579969	580153	583281	582729	582913

L8-M16

585305	588065	584937	585489	588249
585121	586225	587145	585857	587697
588617	586041	586409	586777	584201
588433	586961	585673	586593	584385
584569	584753	587881	587329	587513

L9-M1

589905	592665	589537	590089	592849
589721	590825	591745	590457	592297
593217	590641	591009	591377	588801
593033	591561	590273	591193	588985
589169	589353	592481	591929	592113

L9-M2

594505	597265	594137	594689	597449
594321	595425	596345	595057	596897
597817	595241	595609	595977	593401
597633	596161	594873	595793	593585
593769	593953	597081	596529	596713

L9-M3

599105	601865	598737	599289	602049
598921	600025	600945	599657	601497
602417	599841	600209	600577	598001
602233	600761	599473	600393	598185
598369	598553	601681	601129	601313

L9-M4

603705	606465	603337	603889	606649
603521	604625	605545	604257	606097
607017	604441	604809	605177	602601
606833	605361	604073	604993	602785
602969	603153	606281	605729	605913

L9-M5

608305	611065	607937	608489	611249
608121	609225	610145	608857	610697
611617	609041	609409	609777	607201
611433	609961	608673	609593	607385
607569	607753	610881	610329	610513

L9-M6

612905	615665	612537	613089	615849
612721	613825	614745	613457	615297
616217	613641	614009	614377	611801
616033	614561	613273	614193	611985
612169	612353	615481	614929	615113

L9-M7

617505	620265	617137	617689	620449
617321	618425	619345	618057	619897
620817	618241	618609	618977	616401
620633	619161	617873	618793	616585
616769	616953	620081	619529	619713

L9-M8

622105	624865	621737	622289	625049
621921	623025	623945	622657	624497
625417	622841	623209	623577	621001
625233	623761	622473	623393	621185
621369	621553	624681	624129	624313

L9-M9

626705	629465	626337	626889	629649
626521	627625	628545	627257	629097
630017	627441	627809	628177	625601
629833	628361	627073	627993	625785
625969	626153	629281	628729	628913

L9-M10

631305	634065	630937	631489	634249
631121	632225	633145	631857	633697
634617	632041	632409	632777	630201
634433	632961	631673	632593	630385
630569	630753	633881	633329	633513

L9-M11

635905	638665	635537	636089	638849
635721	636825	637745	636457	638297
639217	636641	637009	637377	634801
639033	637561	636273	637193	634985
635169	635353	638481	637929	638113

L9-M12

640505	643265	640137	640689	643449
640321	641425	642345	641057	642897
643817	641241	641609	641977	639401
643633	642161	640873	641793	639585
639769	639953	643081	642529	642713

L9-M13

645105	647865	644737	645289	648049
644921	646025	646945	645657	647497
648417	645841	646209	646577	644001
648233	646761	645473	646393	644185
644369	644553	647681	647129	647313

L9-M14

649705	652465	649337	649889	652649
649521	650625	651545	650257	652097
653017	650441	650809	651177	648601
652833	651361	650073	650993	648785
648969	649153	652281	651729	651913

L9-M15

654305	657065	653937	654489	657249
654121	655225	656145	654857	656697
657617	655041	655409	655777	653201
657433	655961	654673	655593	653385
653569	653753	656881	656329	656513

L9-M16

658905	661665	658537	659089	661849
658721	659825	660745	659457	661297
662217	659641	660009	660377	657801
662033	660561	659273	660193	657985
658169	658353	661481	660929	661113

L10-M1

663505	666265	663137	663689	666449
663321	664425	665345	664057	665897
666817	664241	664609	664977	662401
666633	665161	663873	664793	662585
662769	662953	666081	665529	665713

L10-M2

668105	670865	667737	668289	671049
667921	669025	669945	668657	670497
671417	668841	669209	669577	667001
671233	669761	668473	669393	667185
667369	667553	670681	670129	670313

L10-M3

672705	675465	672337	672889	675649
672521	673625	674545	673257	675097
676017	673441	673809	674177	671601
675833	674361	673073	673993	671785
671969	672153	675281	674729	674913

L10-M4

677305	680065	676937	677489	680249
677121	678225	679145	677857	679697
680617	678041	678409	678777	676201
680433	678961	677673	678593	676385
676569	676753	679881	679329	679513

L10-M5

681905	684665	681537	682089	684849
681721	682825	683745	682457	684297
685217	682641	683009	683377	680801
685033	683561	682273	683193	680985
681169	681353	684481	683929	684113

L10-M6

686505	689265	686137	686689	689449
686321	687425	688345	687057	688897
689817	687241	687609	687977	685401
689633	688161	686873	687793	685585
685769	685953	689081	688529	688713

L10-M7

691105	693865	690737	691289	694049
690921	692025	692945	691657	693497
694417	691841	692209	692577	690001
694233	692761	691473	692393	690185
690369	690553	693681	693129	693313

L10-M8

695705	698465	695337	695889	698649
695521	696625	697545	696257	698097
699017	696441	696809	697177	694601
698833	697361	696073	696993	694785
694969	695153	698281	697729	697913

L10-M9

700305	703065	699937	700489	703249
700121	701225	702145	700857	702697
703617	701041	701409	701777	699201
703433	701961	700673	701593	699385
699569	699753	702881	702329	702513

L10-M10

704905	707665	704537	705089	707849
704721	705825	706745	705457	707297
708217	705641	706009	706377	703801
708033	706561	705273	706193	703985
704169	704353	707481	706929	707113

L10-M11

709505	712265	709137	709689	712449
709321	710425	711345	710057	711897
712817	710241	710609	710977	708401
712633	711161	709873	710793	708585
708769	708953	712081	711529	711713

L10-M12

714105	716865	713737	714289	717049
713921	715025	715945	714657	716497
717417	714841	715209	715577	713001
717233	715761	714473	715393	713185
713369	713553	716681	716129	716313

L10-M13

718705	721465	718337	718889	721649
718521	719625	720545	719257	721097
722017	719441	719809	720177	717601
721833	720361	719073	719993	717785
717969	718153	721281	720729	720913

L10-M14

723305	726065	722937	723489	726249
723121	724225	725145	723857	725697
726617	724041	724409	724777	722201
726433	724961	723673	724593	722385
722569	722753	725881	725329	725513

L10-M15

727905	730665	727537	728089	730849
727721	728825	729745	728457	730297
731217	728641	729009	729377	726801
731033	729561	728273	729193	726985
727169	727353	730481	729929	730113

L10-M16

732505	735265	732137	732689	735449
732321	733425	734345	733057	734897
735817	733241	733609	733977	731401
735633	734161	732873	733793	731585
731769	731953	735081	734529	734713

L11-M1

737105	739865	736737	737289	740049
736921	738025	738945	737657	739497
740417	737841	738209	738577	736001
740233	738761	737473	738393	736185
736369	736553	739681	739129	739313

L11-M2

741705	744465	741337	741889	744649
741521	742625	743545	742257	744097
745017	742441	742809	743177	740601
744833	743361	742073	742993	740785
740969	741153	744281	743729	743913

L11-M3

746305	749065	745937	746489	749249
746121	747225	748145	746857	748697
749617	747041	747409	747777	745201
749433	747961	746673	747593	745385
745569	745753	748881	748329	748513

L11-M4

750905	753665	750537	751089	753849
750721	751825	752745	751457	753297
754217	751641	752009	752377	749801
754033	752561	751273	752193	749985
750169	750353	753481	752929	753113

L11-M5

755505	758265	755137	755689	758449
755321	756425	757345	756057	757897
758817	756241	756609	756977	754401
758633	757161	755873	756793	754585
754769	754953	758081	757529	757713

L11-M6

760105	762865	759737	760289	763049
759921	761025	761945	760657	762497
763417	760841	761209	761577	759001
763233	761761	760473	761393	759185
759369	759553	762681	762129	762313

L11-M7

764705	767465	764337	764889	767649
764521	765625	766545	765257	767097
768017	765441	765809	766177	763601
767833	766361	765073	765993	763785
763969	764153	767281	766729	766913

L11-M8

769305	772065	768937	769489	772249
769121	770225	771145	769857	771697
772617	770041	770409	770777	768201
772433	770961	769673	770593	768385
768569	768753	771881	771329	771513

L11-M9

773905	776665	773537	774089	776849
773721	774825	775745	774457	776297
777217	774641	775009	775377	772801
777033	775561	774273	775193	772985
773169	773353	776481	775929	776113

L11-M10

778505	781265	778137	778689	781449
778321	779425	780345	779057	780897
781817	779241	779609	779977	777401
781633	780161	778873	779793	777585
777769	777953	781081	780529	780713

L11-M11

783105	785865	782737	783289	786049
782921	784025	784945	783657	785497
786417	783841	784209	784577	782001
786233	784761	783473	784393	782185
782369	782553	785681	785129	785313

L11-M12

787705	790465	787337	787889	790649
787521	788625	789545	788257	790097
791017	788441	788809	789177	786601
790833	789361	788073	788993	786785
786969	787153	790281	789729	789913

L11-M13

792305	795065	791937	792489	795249
792121	793225	794145	792857	794697
795617	793041	793409	793777	791201
795433	793961	792673	793593	791385
791569	791753	794881	794329	794513

L11-M14

796905	799665	796537	797089	799849
796721	797825	798745	797457	799297
800217	797641	798009	798377	795801
800033	798561	797273	798193	795985
796169	796353	799481	798929	799113

L11-M15

801505	804265	801137	801689	804449
801321	802425	803345	802057	803897
804817	802241	802609	802977	800401
804633	803161	801873	802793	800585
800769	800953	804081	803529	803713

L11-M16

806105	808865	805737	806289	809049
805921	807025	807945	806657	808497
809417	806841	807209	807577	805001
809233	807761	806473	807393	805185
805369	805553	808681	808129	808313

L12-M1

810705	813465	810337	810889	813649
810521	811625	812545	811257	813097
814017	811441	811809	812177	809601
813833	812361	811073	811993	809785
809969	810153	813281	812729	812913

L12-M2

815305	818065	814937	815489	818249
815121	816225	817145	815857	817697
818617	816041	816409	816777	814201
818433	816961	815673	816593	814385
814569	814753	817881	817329	817513

L12-M3

819905	822665	819537	820089	822849
819721	820825	821745	820457	822297
823217	820641	821009	821377	818801
823033	821561	820273	821193	818985
819169	819353	822481	821929	822113

L12-M4

824505	827265	824137	824689	827449
824321	825425	826345	825057	826897
827817	825241	825609	825977	823401
827633	826161	824873	825793	823585
823769	823953	827081	826529	826713

L12-M5

829105	831865	828737	829289	832049
828921	830025	830945	829657	831497
832417	829841	830209	830577	828001
832233	830761	829473	830393	828185
828369	828553	831681	831129	831313

L12-M14

870505	873265	870137	870689	873449
870321	871425	872345	871057	872897
873817	871241	871609	871977	869401
873633	872161	870873	871793	869585
869769	869953	873081	872529	872713

L12-M6

833705	836465	833337	833889	836649
833521	834625	835545	834257	836097
837017	834441	834809	835177	832601
836833	835361	834073	834993	832785
832969	833153	836281	835729	835913

L12-M15

875105	877865	874737	875289	878049
874921	876025	876945	875657	877497
878417	875841	876209	876577	874001
878233	876761	875473	876393	874185
874369	874553	877681	877129	877313

L12-M7

838305	841065	837937	838489	841249
838121	839225	840145	838857	840697
841617	839041	839409	839777	837201
841433	839961	838673	839593	837385
837569	837753	840881	840329	840513

L12-M16

879705	882465	879337	879889	882649
879521	880625	881545	880257	882097
883017	880441	880809	881177	878601
882833	881361	880073	880993	878785
878969	879153	882281	881729	881913

L12-M8

842905	845665	842537	843089	845849
842721	843825	844745	843457	845297
846217	843641	844009	844377	841801
846033	844561	843273	844193	841985
842169	842353	845481	844929	845113

L13-M1

884305	887065	883937	884489	887249
884121	885225	886145	884857	886697
887617	885041	885409	885777	883201
887433	885961	884673	885593	883385
883569	883753	886881	886329	886513

L12-M9

847505	850265	847137	847689	850449
847321	848425	849345	848057	849897
850817	848241	848609	848977	846401
850633	849161	847873	848793	846585
846769	846953	850081	849529	849713

L13-M2

888905	891665	888537	889089	891849
888721	889825	890745	889457	891297
892217	889641	890009	890377	887801
892033	890561	889273	890193	887985
888169	888353	891481	890929	891113

L12-M10

852105	854865	851737	852289	855049
851921	853025	853945	852657	854497
855417	852841	853209	853577	851001
855233	853761	852473	853393	851185
851369	851553	854681	854129	854313

L13-M3

893505	896265	893137	893689	896449
893321	894425	895345	894057	895897
896817	894241	894609	894977	892401
896633	895161	893873	894793	892585
892769	892953	896081	895529	895713

L12-M11

856705	859465	856337	856889	859649
856521	857625	858545	857257	859097
860017	857441	857809	858177	855601
859833	858361	857073	857993	855785
855969	856153	859281	858729	858913

L13-M4

898105	900865	897737	898289	901049
897921	899025	899945	898657	900497
901417	898841	899209	899577	897001
901233	899761	898473	899393	897185
897369	897553	900681	900129	900313

L12-M12

861305	864065	860937	861489	864249
861121	862225	863145	861857	863697
864617	862041	862409	862777	860201
864433	862961	861673	862593	860385
860569	860753	863881	863329	863513

L13-M5

902705	905465	902337	902889	905649
902521	903625	904545	903257	905097
906017	903441	903809	904177	901601
905833	904361	903073	903993	901785
901969	902153	905281	904729	904913

L12-M13

865905	868665	865537	866089	868849
865721	866825	867745	866457	868297
869217	866641	867009	867377	864801
869033	867561	866273	867193	864985
865169	865353	868481	867929	868113

L13-M6

907305	910065	906937	907489	910249
907121	908225	909145	907857	909697
910617	908041	908409	908777	906201
910433	908961	907673	908593	906385
906569	906753	909881	909329	909513

L13-M7

911905	914665	911537	912089	914849
911721	912825	913745	912457	914297
915217	912641	913009	913377	910801
915033	913561	912273	913193	910985
911169	911353	914481	913929	914113

L13-M8

916505	919265	916137	916689	919449
916321	917425	918345	917057	918897
919817	917241	917609	917977	915401
919633	918161	916873	917793	915585
915769	915953	919081	918529	918713

L13-M9

921105	923865	920737	921289	924049
920921	922025	922945	921657	923497
924417	921841	922209	922577	920001
924233	922761	921473	922393	920185
920369	920553	923681	923129	923313

L13-M10

925705	928465	925337	925889	928649
925521	926625	927545	926257	928097
929017	926441	926809	927177	924601
928833	927361	926073	926993	924785
924969	925153	928281	927729	927913

L13-M11

930305	933065	929937	930489	933249
930121	931225	932145	930857	932697
933617	931041	931409	931777	929201
933433	931961	930673	931593	929385
929569	929753	932881	932329	932513

L13-M12

934905	937665	934537	935089	937849
934721	935825	936745	935457	937297
938217	935641	936009	936377	933801
938033	936561	935273	936193	933985
934169	934353	937481	936929	937113

L13-M13

939505	942265	939137	939689	942449
939321	940425	941345	940057	941897
942817	940241	940609	940977	938401
942633	941161	939873	940793	938585
938769	938953	942081	941529	941713

L13-M14

944105	946865	943737	944289	947049
943921	945025	945945	944657	946497
947417	944841	945209	945577	943001
947233	945761	944473	945393	943185
943369	943553	946681	946129	946313

L13-M15

948705	951465	948337	948889	951649
948521	949625	950545	949257	951097
952017	949441	949809	950177	947601
951833	950361	949073	949993	947785
947969	948153	951281	950729	950913

L13-M16

953305	956065	952937	953489	956249
953121	954225	955145	953857	955697
956617	954041	954409	954777	952201
956433	954961	953673	954593	952385
952569	952753	955881	955329	955513

L14-M1

957905	960665	957537	958089	960849
957721	958825	959745	958457	960297
961217	958641	959009	959377	956801
961033	959561	958273	959193	956985
957169	957353	960481	959929	960113

L14-M2

962505	965265	962137	962689	965449
962321	963425	964345	963057	964897
965817	963241	963609	963977	961401
965633	964161	962873	963793	961585
961769	961953	965081	964529	964713

L14-M3

967105	969865	966737	967289	970049
966921	968025	968945	967657	969497
970417	967841	968209	968577	966001
970233	968761	967473	968393	966185
966369	966553	969681	969129	969313

L14-M4

971705	974465	971337	971889	974649
971521	972625	973545	972257	974097
975017	972441	972809	973177	970601
974833	973361	972073	972993	970785
970969	971153	974281	973729	973913

L14-M5

976305	979065	975937	976489	979249
976121	977225	978145	976857	978697
979617	977041	977409	977777	975201
979433	977961	976673	977593	975385
975569	975753	978881	978329	978513

L14-M6

980905	983665	980537	981089	983849
980721	981825	982745	981457	983297
984217	981641	982009	982377	979801
984033	982561	981273	982193	979985
980169	980353	983481	982929	983113

L14-M7

985505	988265	985137	985689	988449
985321	986425	987345	986057	987897
988817	986241	986609	986977	984401
988633	987161	985873	986793	984585
984769	984953	988081	987529	987713

L14-M8

990105	992865	989737	990289	993049
989921	991025	991945	990657	992497
993417	990841	991209	991577	989001
993233	991761	990473	991393	989185
989369	989553	992681	992129	992313

L14-M9

994705	997465	994337	994889	997649
994521	995625	996545	995257	997097
998017	995441	995809	996177	993601
997833	996361	995073	995993	993785
993969	994153	997281	996729	996913

L15-M2

1036105	1038865	1035737	1036289	1039049
1035921	1037025	1037945	1036657	1038497
1039417	1036841	1037209	1037577	1035001
1039233	1037761	1036473	1037393	1035185
1035369	1035553	1038681	1038129	1038313

L14-M10

999305	1002065	998937	999489	1002249
999121	1000225	1001145	999857	1001697
1002617	1000041	1000409	1000777	998201
1002433	1000961	999673	1000593	998385
998569	998753	1001881	1001329	1001513

L15-M3

1040705	1043465	1040337	1040889	1043649
1040521	1041625	1042545	1041257	1043097
1044017	1041441	1041809	1042177	1039601
1043833	1042361	1041073	1041993	1039785
1039969	1040153	1043281	1042729	1042913

L14-M11

1003905	1006665	1003537	1004089	1006849
1003721	1004825	1005745	1004457	1006297
1007217	1004641	1005009	1005377	1002801
1007033	1005561	1004273	1005193	1002985
1003169	1003353	1006481	1005929	1006113

L15-M4

1045305	1048065	1044937	1045489	1048249
1045121	1046225	1047145	1045857	1047697
1048617	1046041	1046409	1046777	1044201
1048433	1046961	1045673	1046593	1044385
1044569	1044753	1047881	1047329	1047513

L14-M12

1008505	1011265	1008137	1008689	1011449
1008321	1009425	1010345	1009057	1010897
1011817	1009241	1009609	1009977	1007401
1011633	1010161	1008873	1009793	1007585
1007769	1007953	1011081	1010529	1010713

L15-M5

1049905	1052665	1049537	1050089	1052849
1049721	1050825	1051745	1050457	1052297
1053217	1050641	1051009	1051377	1048801
1053033	1051561	1050273	1051193	1048985
1049169	1049353	1052481	1051929	1052113

L14-M13

1013105	1015865	1012737	1013289	1016049
1012921	1014025	1014945	1013657	1015497
1016417	1013841	1014209	1014577	1012001
1016233	1014761	1013473	1014393	1012185
1012369	1012553	1015681	1015129	1015313

L15-M6

1054505	1057265	1054137	1054689	1057449
1054321	1055425	1056345	1055057	1056897
1057817	1055241	1055609	1055977	1053401
1057633	1056161	1054873	1055793	1053585
1053769	1053953	1057081	1056529	1056713

L14-M14

1017705	1020465	1017337	1017889	1020649
1017521	1018625	1019545	1018257	1020097
1021017	1018441	1018809	1019177	1016601
1020833	1019361	1018073	1018993	1016785
1016969	1017153	1020281	1019729	1019913

L15-M7

1059105	1061865	1058737	1059289	1062049
1058921	1060025	1060945	1059657	1061497
1062417	1059841	1060209	1060577	1058001
1062233	1060761	1059473	1060393	1058185
1058369	1058553	1061681	1061129	1061313

L14-M15

1022305	1025065	1021937	1022489	1025249
1022121	1023225	1024145	1022857	1024697
1025617	1023041	1023409	1023777	1021201
1025433	1023961	1022673	1023593	1021385
1021569	1021753	1024881	1024329	1024513

L15-M8

1063705	1066465	1063337	1063889	1066649
1063521	1064625	1065545	1064257	1066097
1067017	1064441	1064809	1065177	1062601
1066833	1065361	1064073	1064993	1062785
1062969	1063153	1066281	1065729	1065913

L14-M16

1026905	1029665	1026537	1027089	1029849
1026721	1027825	1028745	1027457	1029297
1030217	1027641	1028009	1028377	1025801
1030033	1028561	1027273	1028193	1025985
1026169	1026353	1029481	1028929	1029113

L15-M9

1068305	1071065	1067937	1068489	1071249
1068121	1069225	1070145	1068857	1070697
1071617	1069041	1069409	1069777	1067201
1071433	1069961	1068673	1069593	1067385
1067569	1067753	1070881	1070329	1070513

L15-M1

1031505	1034265	1031137	1031689	1034449
1031321	1032425	1033345	1032057	1033897
1034817	1032241	1032609	1032977	1030401
1034633	1033161	1031873	1032793	1030585
1030769	1030953	1034081	1033529	1033713

L15-M10

1072905	1075665	1072537	1073089	1075849
1072721	1073825	1074745	1073457	1075297
1076217	1073641	1074009	1074377	1071801
1076033	1074561	1073273	1074193	1071985
1072169	1072353	1075481	1074929	1075113

L15-M11

1077505	1080265	1077137	1077689	1080449
1077321	1078425	1079345	1078057	1079897
1080817	1078241	1078609	1078977	1076401
1080633	1079161	1077873	1078793	1076585
1076769	1076953	1080081	1079529	1079713

L15-M12

1082105	1084865	1081737	1082289	1085049
1081921	1083025	1083945	1082657	1084497
1085417	1082841	1083209	1083577	1081001
1085233	1083761	1082473	1083393	1081185
1081369	1081553	1084681	1084129	1084313

L15-M13

1086705	1089465	1086337	1086889	1089649
1086521	1087625	1088545	1087257	1089097
1090017	1087441	1087809	1088177	1085601
1089833	1088361	1087073	1087993	1085785
1085969	1086153	1089281	1088729	1088913

L15-M14

1091305	1094065	1090937	1091489	1094249
1091121	1092225	1093145	1091857	1093697
1094617	1092041	1092409	1092777	1090201
1094433	1092961	1091673	1092593	1090385
1090569	1090753	1093881	1093329	1093513

L15-M15

1095905	1098665	1095537	1096089	1098849
1095721	1096825	1097745	1096457	1098297
1099217	1096641	1097009	1097377	1094801
1099033	1097561	1096273	1097193	1094985
1095169	1095353	1098481	1097929	1098113

L15-M16

1100505	1103265	1100137	1100689	1103449
1100321	1101425	1102345	1101057	1102897
1103817	1101241	1101609	1101977	1099401
1103633	1102161	1100873	1101793	1099585
1099769	1099953	1103081	1102529	1102713

L16-M1

1105105	1107865	1104737	1105289	1108049
1104921	1106025	1106945	1105657	1107497
1108417	1105841	1106209	1106577	1104001
1108233	1106761	1105473	1106393	1104185
1104369	1104553	1107681	1107129	1107313

L16-M2

1109705	1112465	1109337	1109889	1112649
1109521	1110625	1111545	1110257	1112097
1113017	1110441	1110809	1111177	1108601
1112833	1111361	1110073	1110993	1108785
1108969	1109153	1112281	1111729	1111913

L16-M3

1114305	1117065	1113937	1114489	1117249
1114121	1115225	1116145	1114857	1116697
1117617	1115041	1115409	1115777	1113201
1117433	1115961	1114673	1115593	1113385
1113569	1113753	1116881	1116329	1116513

L16-M4

1118905	1121665	1118537	1119089	1121849
1118721	1119825	1120745	1119457	1121297
1122217	1119641	1120009	1120377	1117801
1122033	1120561	1119273	1120193	1117985
1118169	1118353	1121481	1120929	1121113

L16-M5

1123505	1126265	1123137	1123689	1126449
1123321	1124425	1125345	1124057	1125897
1126817	1124241	1124609	1124977	1122401
1126633	1125161	1123873	1124793	1122585
1122769	1122953	1126081	1125529	1125713

L16-M6

1128105	1130865	1127737	1128289	1131049
1127921	1129025	1129945	1128657	1130497
1131417	1128841	1129209	1129577	1127001
1131233	1129761	1128473	1129393	1127185
1127369	1127553	1130681	1130129	1130313

L16-M7

1132705	1135465	1132337	1132889	1135649
1132521	1133625	1134545	1133257	1135097
1136017	1133441	1133809	1134177	1131601
1135833	1134361	1133073	1133993	1131785
1131969	1132153	1135281	1134729	1134913

L16-M8

1137305	1140065	1136937	1137489	1140249
1137121	1138225	1139145	1137857	1139697
1140617	1138041	1138409	1138777	1136201
1140433	1138961	1137673	1138593	1136385
1136569	1136753	1139881	1139329	1139513

L16-M9

1141905	1144665	1141537	1142089	1144849
1141721	1142825	1143745	1142457	1144297
1145217	1142641	1143009	1143377	1140801
1145033	1143561	1142273	1143193	1140985
1141169	1141353	1144481	1143929	1144113

L16-M10

1146505	1149265	1146137	1146689	1149449
1146321	1147425	1148345	1147057	1148897
1149817	1147241	1147609	1147977	1145401
1149633	1148161	1146873	1147793	1145585
1145769	1145953	1149081	1148529	1148713

L16-M11

1151105	1153865	1150737	1151289	1154049
1150921	1152025	1152945	1151657	1153497
1154417	1151841	1152209	1152577	1150001
1154233	1152761	1151473	1152393	1150185
1150369	1150553	1153681	1153129	1153313

L16-M12

1155705	1158465	1155337	1155889	1158649
1155521	1156625	1157545	1156257	1158097
1159017	1156441	1156809	1157177	1154601
1158833	1157361	1156073	1156993	1154785
1154969	1155153	1158281	1157729	1157913

L16-M13

1160305	1163065	1159937	1160489	1163249
1160121	1161225	1162145	1160857	1162697
1163617	1161041	1161409	1161777	1159201
1163433	1161961	1160673	1161593	1159385
1159569	1159753	1162881	1162329	1162513

L16-M14

1164905	1167665	1164537	1165089	1167849
1164721	1165825	1166745	1165457	1167297
1168217	1165641	1166009	1166377	1163801
1168033	1166561	1165273	1166193	1163985
1164169	1164353	1167481	1166929	1167113

L16-M15

1169505	1172265	1169137	1169689	1172449
1169321	1170425	1171345	1170057	1171897
1172817	1170241	1170609	1170977	1168401
1172633	1171161	1169873	1170793	1168585
1168769	1168953	1172081	1171529	1171713

L16M16

1174105	1176865	1173737	1174289	1177049
1173921	1175025	1175945	1174657	1176497
1177417	1174841	1175209	1175577	1173001
1177233	1175761	1174473	1175393	1173185
1173369	1173553	1176681	1176129	1176313

L17-M1

1178705	1181465	1178337	1178889	1181649
1178521	1179625	1180545	1179257	1181097
1182017	1179441	1179809	1180177	1177601
1181833	1180361	1179073	1179993	1177785
1177969	1178153	1181281	1180729	1180913

L17-M2

1183305	1186065	1182937	1183489	1186249
1183121	1184225	1185145	1183857	1185697
1186617	1184041	1184409	1184777	1182201
1186433	1184961	1183673	1184593	1182385
1182569	1182753	1185881	1185329	1185513

L17-M3

1187905	1190665	1187537	1188089	1190849
1187721	1188825	1189745	1188457	1190297
1191217	1188641	1189009	1189377	1186801
1191033	1189561	1188273	1189193	1186985
1187169	1187353	1190481	1189929	1190113

L17-M4

1192505	1195265	1192137	1192689	1195449
1192321	1193425	1194345	1193057	1194897
1195817	1193241	1193609	1193977	1191401
1195633	1194161	1192873	1193793	1191585
1191769	1191953	1195081	1194529	1194713

L17-M5

1197105	1199865	1196737	1197289	1200049
1196921	1198025	1198945	1197657	1199497
1200417	1197841	1198209	1198577	1196001
1200233	1198761	1197473	1198393	1196185
1196369	1196553	1199681	1199129	1199313

L17-M6

1201705	1204465	1201337	1201889	1204649
1201521	1202625	1203545	1202257	1204097
1205017	1202441	1202809	1203177	1200601
1204833	1203361	1202073	1202993	1200785
1200969	1201153	1204281	1203729	1203913

L17-M7

1206305	1209065	1205937	1206489	1209249
1206121	1207225	1208145	1206857	1208697
1209617	1207041	1207409	1207777	1205201
1209433	1207961	1206673	1207593	1205385
1205569	1205753	1208881	1208329	1208513

L17-M8

1210905	1213665	1210537	1211089	1213849
1210721	1211825	1212745	1211457	1213297
1214217	1211641	1212009	1212377	1209801
1214033	1212561	1211273	1212193	1209985
1210169	1210353	1213481	1212929	1213113

L17-M9

1215505	1218265	1215137	1215689	1218449
1215321	1216425	1217345	1216057	1217897
1218817	1216241	1216609	1216977	1214401
1218633	1217161	1215873	1216793	1214585
1214769	1214953	1218081	1217529	1217713

L17-M10

1220105	1222865	1219737	1220289	1223049
1219921	1221025	1221945	1220657	1222497
1223417	1220841	1221209	1221577	1219001
1223233	1221761	1220473	1221393	1219185
1219369	1219553	1222681	1222129	1222313

L17-M11

1224705	1227465	1224337	1224889	1227649
1224521	1225625	1226545	1225257	1227097
1228017	1225441	1225809	1226177	1223601
1227833	1226361	1225073	1225993	1223785
1223969	1224153	1227281	1226729	1226913

L17-M12

1229305	1232065	1228937	1229489	1232249
1229121	1230225	1231145	1229857	1231697
1232617	1230041	1230409	1230777	1228201
1232433	1230961	1229673	1230593	1228385
1228569	1228753	1231881	1231329	1231513

L17-M13

1233905	1236665	1233537	1234089	1236849
1233721	1234825	1235745	1234457	1236297
1237217	1234641	1235009	1235377	1232801
1237033	1235561	1234273	1235193	1232985
1233169	1233353	1236481	1235929	1236113

L17-M14

1238505	1241265	1238137	1238689	1241449
1238321	1239425	1240345	1239057	1240897
1241817	1239241	1239609	1239977	1237401
1241633	1240161	1238873	1239793	1237585
1237769	1237953	1241081	1240529	1240713

L17-M15

1243105	1245865	1242737	1243289	1246049
1242921	1244025	1244945	1243657	1245497
1246417	1243841	1244209	1244577	1242001
1246233	1244761	1243473	1244393	1242185
1242369	1242553	1245681	1245129	1245313

L17-M16

1247705	1250465	1247337	1247889	1250649
1247521	1248625	1249545	1248257	1250097
1251017	1248441	1248809	1249177	1246601
1250833	1249361	1248073	1248993	1246785
1246969	1247153	1250281	1249729	1249913

L18-M1

1252305	1255065	1251937	1252489	1255249
1252121	1253225	1254145	1252857	1254697
1255617	1253041	1253409	1253777	1251201
1255433	1253961	1252673	1253593	1251385
1251569	1251753	1254881	1254329	1254513

L18-M2

1256905	1259665	1256537	1257089	1259849
1256721	1257825	1258745	1257457	1259297
1260217	1257641	1258009	1258377	1255801
1260033	1258561	1257273	1258193	1255985
1256169	1256353	1259481	1258929	1259113

L18-M3

1261505	1264265	1261137	1261689	1264449
1261321	1262425	1263345	1262057	1263897
1264817	1262241	1262609	1262977	1260401
1264633	1263161	1261873	1262793	1260585
1260769	1260953	1264081	1263529	1263713

L18-M4

1266105	1268865	1265737	1266289	1269049
1265921	1267025	1267945	1266657	1268497
1269417	1266841	1267209	1267577	1265001
1269233	1267761	1266473	1267393	1265185
1265369	1265553	1268681	1268129	1268313

L18-M5

1270705	1273465	1270337	1270889	1273649
1270521	1271625	1272545	1271257	1273097
1274017	1271441	1271809	1272177	1269601
1273833	1272361	1271073	1271993	1269785
1269969	1270153	1273281	1272729	1272913

L18-M6

1275305	1278065	1274937	1275489	1278249
1275121	1276225	1277145	1275857	1277697
1278617	1276041	1276409	1276777	1274201
1278433	1276961	1275673	1276593	1274385
1274569	1274753	1277881	1277329	1277513

L18-M7

1279905	1282665	1279537	1280089	1282849
1279721	1280825	1281745	1280457	1282297
1283217	1280641	1281009	1281377	1278801
1283033	1281561	1280273	1281193	1278985
1279169	1279353	1282481	1281929	1282113

L18-M8

1284505	1287265	1284137	1284689	1287449
1284321	1285425	1286345	1285057	1286897
1287817	1285241	1285609	1285977	1283401
1287633	1286161	1284873	1285793	1283585
1283769	1283953	1287081	1286529	1286713

L18-M9

1289105	1291865	1288737	1289289	1292049
1288921	1290025	1290945	1289657	1291497
1292417	1289841	1290209	1290577	1288001
1292233	1290761	1289473	1290393	1288185
1288369	1288553	1291681	1291129	1291313

L18-M10

1293705	1296465	1293337	1293889	1296649
1293521	1294625	1295545	1294257	1296097
1297017	1294441	1294809	1295177	1292601
1296833	1295361	1294073	1294993	1292785
1292969	1293153	1296281	1295729	1295913

L18-M11

1298305	1301065	1297937	1298489	1301249
1298121	1299225	1300145	1298857	1300697
1301617	1299041	1299409	1299777	1297201
1301433	1299961	1298673	1299593	1297385
1297569	1297753	1300881	1300329	1300513

L18-M12

1302905	1305665	1302537	1303089	1305849
1302721	1303825	1304745	1303457	1305297
1306217	1303641	1304009	1304377	1301801
1306033	1304561	1303273	1304193	1301985
1302169	1302353	1305481	1304929	1305113

L18-M13

1307505	1310265	1307137	1307689	1310449
1307321	1308425	1309345	1308057	1309897
1310817	1308241	1308609	1308977	1306401
1310633	1309161	1307873	1308793	1306585
1306769	1306953	1310081	1309529	1309713

L18-M14

1312105	1314865	1311737	1312289	1315049
1311921	1313025	1313945	1312657	1314497
1315417	1312841	1313209	1313577	1311001
1315233	1313761	1312473	1313393	1311185
1311369	1311553	1314681	1314129	1314313

L18-M15

1316705	1319465	1316337	1316889	1319649
1316521	1317625	1318545	1317257	1319097
1320017	1317441	1317809	1318177	1315601
1319833	1318361	1317073	1317993	1315785
1315969	1316153	1319281	1318729	1318913

L18-M16

1321305	1324065	1320937	1321489	1324249
1321121	1322225	1323145	1321857	1323697
1324617	1322041	1322409	1322777	1320201
1324433	1322961	1321673	1322593	1320385
1320569	1320753	1323881	1323329	1323513

L19-M1

1325905	1328665	1325537	1326089	1328849
1325721	1326825	1327745	1326457	1328297
1329217	1326641	1327009	1327377	1324801
1329033	1327561	1326273	1327193	1324985
1325169	1325353	1328481	1327929	1328113

L19-M2

1330505	1333265	1330137	1330689	1333449
1330321	1331425	1332345	1331057	1332897
1333817	1331241	1331609	1331977	1329401
1333633	1332161	1330873	1331793	1329585
1329769	1329953	1333081	1332529	1332713

L19-M3

1335105	1337865	1334737	1335289	1338049
1334921	1336025	1336945	1335657	1337497
1338417	1335841	1336209	1336577	1334001
1338233	1336761	1335473	1336393	1334185
1334369	1334553	1337681	1337129	1337313

L19-M4

1339705	1342465	1339337	1339889	1342649
1339521	1340625	1341545	1340257	1342097
1343017	1340441	1340809	1341177	1338601
1342833	1341361	1340073	1340993	1338785
1338969	1339153	1342281	1341729	1341913

L19-M5

1344305	1347065	1343937	1344489	1347249
1344121	1345225	1346145	1344857	1346697
1347617	1345041	1345409	1345777	1343201
1347433	1345961	1344673	1345593	1343385
1343569	1343753	1346881	1346329	1346513

L19-M6

1348905	1351665	1348537	1349089	1351849
1348721	1349825	1350745	1349457	1351297
1352217	1349641	1350009	1350377	1347801
1352033	1350561	1349273	1350193	1347985
1348169	1348353	1351481	1350929	1351113

L19-M7

1353505	1356265	1353137	1353689	1356449
1353321	1354425	1355345	1354057	1355897
1356817	1354241	1354609	1354977	1352401
1356633	1355161	1353873	1354793	1352585
1352769	1352953	1356081	1355529	1355713

L19-M8

1358105	1360865	1357737	1358289	1361049
1357921	1359025	1359945	1358657	1360497
1361417	1358841	1359209	1359577	1357001
1361233	1359761	1358473	1359393	1357185
1357369	1357553	1360681	1360129	1360313

L19-M9

1362705	1365465	1362337	1362889	1365649
1362521	1363625	1364545	1363257	1365097
1366017	1363441	1363809	1364177	1361601
1365833	1364361	1363073	1363993	1361785
1361969	1362153	1365281	1364729	1364913

L19-M10

1367305	1370065	1366937	1367489	1370249
1367121	1368225	1369145	1367857	1369697
1370617	1368041	1368409	1368777	1366201
1370433	1368961	1367673	1368593	1366385
1366569	1366753	1369881	1369329	1369513

L19-M11

1371905	1374665	1371537	1372089	1374849
1371721	1372825	1373745	1372457	1374297
1375217	1372641	1373009	1373377	1370801
1375033	1373561	1372273	1373193	1370985
1371169	1371353	1374481	1373929	1374113

L19-M12

1376505	1379265	1376137	1376689	1379449
1376321	1377425	1378345	1377057	1378897
1379817	1377241	1377609	1377977	1375401
1379633	1378161	1376873	1377793	1375585
1375769	1375953	1379081	1378529	1378713

L19-M13

1381105	1383865	1380737	1381289	1384049
1380921	1382025	1382945	1381657	1383497
1384417	1381841	1382209	1382577	1380001
1384233	1382761	1381473	1382393	1380185
1380369	1380553	1383681	1383129	1383313

L19-M14

1385705	1388465	1385337	1385889	1388649
1385521	1386625	1387545	1386257	1388097
1389017	1386441	1386809	1387177	1384601
1388833	1387361	1386073	1386993	1384785
1384969	1385153	1388281	1387729	1387913

L19-M15

1390305	1393065	1389937	1390489	1393249
1390121	1391225	1392145	1390857	1392697
1393617	1391041	1391409	1391777	1389201
1393433	1391961	1390673	1391593	1389385
1389569	1389753	1392881	1392329	1392513

L19-M16

1394905	1397665	1394537	1395089	1397849
1394721	1395825	1396745	1395457	1397297
1398217	1395641	1396009	1396377	1393801
1398033	1396561	1395273	1396193	1393985
1394169	1394353	1397481	1396929	1397113

L20-M1

1399505	1402265	1399137	1399689	1402449
1399321	1400425	1401345	1400057	1401897
1402817	1400241	1400609	1400977	1398401
1402633	1401161	1399873	1400793	1398585
1398769	1398953	1402081	1401529	1401713

L20-M2

1404105	1406865	1403737	1404289	1407049
1403921	1405025	1405945	1404657	1406497
1407417	1404841	1405209	1405577	1403001
1407233	1405761	1404473	1405393	1403185
1403369	1403553	1406681	1406129	1406313

L20-M3

1408705	1411465	1408337	1408889	1411649
1408521	1409625	1410545	1409257	1411097
1412017	1409441	1409809	1410177	1407601
1411833	1410361	1409073	1409993	1407785
1407969	1408153	1411281	1410729	1410913

L20-M4

1413305	1416065	1412937	1413489	1416249
1413121	1414225	1415145	1413857	1415697
1416617	1414041	1414409	1414777	1412201
1416433	1414961	1413673	1414593	1412385
1412569	1412753	1415881	1415329	1415513

L20-M5

1417905	1420665	1417537	1418089	1420849
1417721	1418825	1419745	1418457	1420297
1421217	1418641	1419009	1419377	1416801
1421033	1419561	1418273	1419193	1416985
1417169	1417353	1420481	1419929	1420113

L20-M6

1422505	1425265	1422137	1422689	1425449
1422321	1423425	1424345	1423057	1424897
1425817	1423241	1423609	1423977	1421401
1425633	1424161	1422873	1423793	1421585
1421769	1421953	1425081	1424529	1424713

L20-M7

1427105	1429865	1426737	1427289	1430049
1426921	1428025	1428945	1427657	1429497
1430417	1427841	1428209	1428577	1426001
1430233	1428761	1427473	1428393	1426185
1426369	1426553	1429681	1429129	1429313

L20-M8

1431705	1434465	1431337	1431889	1434649
1431521	1432625	1433545	1432257	1434097
1435017	1432441	1432809	1433177	1430601
1434833	1433361	1432073	1432993	1430785
1430969	1431153	1434281	1433729	1433913

L20-M9

1436305	1439065	1435937	1436489	1439249
1436121	1437225	1438145	1436857	1438697
1439617	1437041	1437409	1437777	1435201
1439433	1437961	1436673	1437593	1435385
1435569	1435753	1438881	1438329	1438513

L20-M10

1440905	1443665	1440537	1441089	1443849
1440721	1441825	1442745	1441457	1443297
1444217	1441641	1442009	1442377	1439801
1444033	1442561	1441273	1442193	1439985
1440169	1440353	1443481	1442929	1443113

L20-M11

1445505	1448265	1445137	1445689	1448449
1445321	1446425	1447345	1446057	1447897
1448817	1446241	1446609	1446977	1444401
1448633	1447161	1445873	1446793	1444585
1444769	1444953	1448081	1447529	1447713

L20-M12

1450105	1452865	1449737	1450289	1453049
1449921	1451025	1451945	1450657	1452497
1453417	1450841	1451209	1451577	1449001
1453233	1451761	1450473	1451393	1449185
1449369	1449553	1452681	1452129	1452313

L20-M13

1454705	1457465	1454337	1454889	1457649
1454521	1455625	1456545	1455257	1457097
1458017	1455441	1455809	1456177	1453601
1457833	1456361	1455073	1455993	1453785
1453969	1454153	1457281	1456729	1456913

L20-M14

1459305	1462065	1458937	1459489	1462249
1459121	1460225	1461145	1459857	1461697
1462617	1460041	1460409	1460777	1458201
1462433	1460961	1459673	1460593	1458385
1458569	1458753	1461881	1461329	1461513

L20-M15

1463905	1466665	1463537	1464089	1466849
1463721	1464825	1465745	1464457	1466297
1467217	1464641	1465009	1465377	1462801
1467033	1465561	1464273	1465193	1462985
1463169	1463353	1466481	1465929	1466113

L20-M16

1468505	1471265	1468137	1468689	1471449
1468321	1469425	1470345	1469057	1470897
1471817	1469241	1469609	1469977	1467401
1471633	1470161	1468873	1469793	1467585
1467769	1467953	1471081	1470529	1470713

L21-M1

1473105	1475865	1472737	1473289	1476049
1472921	1474025	1474945	1473657	1475497
1476417	1473841	1474209	1474577	1472001
1476233	1474761	1473473	1474393	1472185
1472369	1472553	1475681	1475129	1475313

L21-M2

1477705	1480465	1477337	1477889	1480649
1477521	1478625	1479545	1478257	1480097
1481017	1478441	1478809	1479177	1476601
1480833	1479361	1478073	1478993	1476785
1476969	1477153	1480281	1479729	1479913

L21-M3

1482305	1485065	1481937	1482489	1485249
1482121	1483225	1484145	1482857	1484697
1485617	1483041	1483409	1483777	1481201
1485433	1483961	1482673	1483593	1481385
1481569	1481753	1484881	1484329	1484513

L21-M4

1486905	1489665	1486537	1487089	1489849
1486721	1487825	1488745	1487457	1489297
1490217	1487641	1488009	1488377	1485801
1490033	1488561	1487273	1488193	1485985
1486169	1486353	1489481	1488929	1489113

L21-M5

1491505	1494265	1491137	1491689	1494449
1491321	1492425	1493345	1492057	1493897
1494817	1492241	1492609	1492977	1490401
1494633	1493161	1491873	1492793	1490585
1490769	1490953	1494081	1493529	1493713

L21-M6

1496105	1498865	1495737	1496289	1499049
1495921	1497025	1497945	1496657	1498497
1499417	1496841	1497209	1497577	1495001
1499233	1497761	1496473	1497393	1495185
1495369	1495553	1498681	1498129	1498313

L21-M7

1500705	1503465	1500337	1500889	1503649
1500521	1501625	1502545	1501257	1503097
1504017	1501441	1501809	1502177	1499601
1503833	1502361	1501073	1501993	1499785
1499969	1500153	1503281	1502729	1502913

L21-M8

1505305	1508065	1504937	1505489	1508249
1505121	1506225	1507145	1505857	1507697
1508617	1506041	1506409	1506777	1504201
1508433	1506961	1505673	1506593	1504385
1504569	1504753	1507881	1507329	1507513

L21-M9

1509905	1512665	1509537	1510089	1512849
1509721	1510825	1511745	1510457	1512297
1513217	1510641	1511009	1511377	1508801
1513033	1511561	1510273	1511193	1508985
1509169	1509353	1512481	1511929	1512113

L21-M10

1514505	1517265	1514137	1514689	1517449
1514321	1515425	1516345	1515057	1516897
1517817	1515241	1515609	1515977	1513401
1517633	1516161	1514873	1515793	1513585
1513769	1513953	1517081	1516529	1516713

L21-M11

1519105	1521865	1518737	1519289	1522049
1518921	1520025	1520945	1519657	1521497
1522417	1519841	1520209	1520577	1518001
1522233	1520761	1519473	1520393	1518185
1518369	1518553	1521681	1521129	1521313

L21-M12

1523705	1526465	1523337	1523889	1526649
1523521	1524625	1525545	1524257	1526097
1527017	1524441	1524809	1525177	1522601
1526833	1525361	1524073	1524993	1522785
1522969	1523153	1526281	1525729	1525913

L21-M13

1528305	1531065	1527937	1528489	1531249
1528121	1529225	1530145	1528857	1530697
1531617	1529041	1529409	1529777	1527201
1531433	1529961	1528673	1529593	1527385
1527569	1527753	1530881	1530329	1530513

L21-M14

1532905	1535665	1532537	1533089	1535849
1532721	1533825	1534745	1533457	1535297
1536217	1533641	1534009	1534377	1531801
1536033	1534561	1533273	1534193	1531985
1532169	1532353	1535481	1534929	1535113

L21-M15

1537505	1540265	1537137	1537689	1540449
1537321	1538425	1539345	1538057	1539897
1540817	1538241	1538609	1538977	1536401
1540633	1539161	1537873	1538793	1536585
1536769	1536953	1540081	1539529	1539713

L21-M16

1542105	1544865	1541737	1542289	1545049
1541921	1543025	1543945	1542657	1544497
1545417	1542841	1543209	1543577	1541001
1545233	1543761	1542473	1543393	1541185
1541369	1541553	1544681	1544129	1544313

L22-M1

1546705	1549465	1546337	1546889	1549649
1546521	1547625	1548545	1547257	1549097
1550017	1547441	1547809	1548177	1545601
1549833	1548361	1547073	1547993	1545785
1545969	1546153	1549281	1548729	1548913

L22-M2

1551305	1554065	1550937	1551489	1554249
1551121	1552225	1553145	1551857	1553697
1554617	1552041	1552409	1552777	1550201
1554433	1552961	1551673	1552593	1550385
1550569	1550753	1553881	1553329	1553513

L22-M3

1555905	1558665	1555537	1556089	1558849
1555721	1556825	1557745	1556457	1558297
1559217	1556641	1557009	1557377	1554801
1559033	1557561	1556273	1557193	1554985
1555169	1555353	1558481	1557929	1558113

L22-M4

1560505	1563265	1560137	1560689	1563449
1560321	1561425	1562345	1561057	1562897
1563817	1561241	1561609	1561977	1559401
1563633	1562161	1560873	1561793	1559585
1559769	1559953	1563081	1562529	1562713

L22-M5

1565105	1567865	1564737	1565289	1568049
1564921	1566025	1566945	1565657	1567497
1568417	1565841	1566209	1566577	1564001
1568233	1566761	1565473	1566393	1564185
1564369	1564553	1567681	1567129	1567313

L22-M6

1569705	1572465	1569337	1569889	1572649
1569521	1570625	1571545	1570257	1572097
1573017	1570441	1570809	1571177	1568601
1572833	1571361	1570073	1570993	1568785
1568969	1569153	1572281	1571729	1571913

L22-M7

1574305	1577065	1573937	1574489	1577249
1574121	1575225	1576145	1574857	1576697
1577617	1575041	1575409	1575777	1573201
1577433	1575961	1574673	1575593	1573385
1573569	1573753	1576881	1576329	1576513

L22-M8

1578905	1581665	1578537	1579089	1581849
1578721	1579825	1580745	1579457	1581297
1582217	1579641	1580009	1580377	1577801
1582033	1580561	1579273	1580193	1577985
1578169	1578353	1581481	1580929	1581113

L22-M9

1583505	1586265	1583137	1583689	1586449
1583321	1584425	1585345	1584057	1585897
1586817	1584241	1584609	1584977	1582401
1586633	1585161	1583873	1584793	1582585
1582769	1582953	1586081	1585529	1585713

L22-M10

1588105	1590865	1587737	1588289	1591049
1587921	1589025	1589945	1588657	1590497
1591417	1588841	1589209	1589577	1587001
1591233	1589761	1588473	1589393	1587185
1587369	1587553	1590681	1590129	1590313

L22-M11

1592705	1595465	1592337	1592889	1595649
1592521	1593625	1594545	1593257	1595097
1596017	1593441	1593809	1594177	1591601
1595833	1594361	1593073	1593993	1591785
1591969	1592153	1595281	1594729	1594913

L22-M12

1597305	1600065	1596937	1597489	1600249
1597121	1598225	1599145	1597857	1599697
1600617	1598041	1598409	1598777	1596201
1600433	1598961	1597673	1598593	1596385
1596569	1596753	1599881	1599329	1599513

L22-M13

1601905	1604665	1601537	1602089	1604849
1601721	1602825	1603745	1602457	1604297
1605217	1602641	1603009	1603377	1600801
1605033	1603561	1602273	1603193	1600985
1601169	1601353	1604481	1603929	1604113

L22-M14

1606505	1609265	1606137	1606689	1609449
1606321	1607425	1608345	1607057	1608897
1609817	1607241	1607609	1607977	1605401
1609633	1608161	1606873	1607793	1605585
1605769	1605953	1609081	1608529	1608713

L22-M15

1611105	1613865	1610737	1611289	1614049
1610921	1612025	1612945	1611657	1613497
1614417	1611841	1612209	1612577	1610001
1614233	1612761	1611473	1612393	1610185
1610369	1610553	1613681	1613129	1613313

L22-M16

1615705	1618465	1615337	1615889	1618649
1615521	1616625	1617545	1616257	1618097
1619017	1616441	1616809	1617177	1614601
1618833	1617361	1616073	1616993	1614785
1614969	1615153	1618281	1617729	1617913

L23-M1

1620305	1623065	1619937	1620489	1623249
1620121	1621225	1622145	1620857	1622697
1623617	1621041	1621409	1621777	1619201
1623433	1621961	1620673	1621593	1619385
1619569	1619753	1622881	1622329	1622513

L23-M2

1624905	1627665	1624537	1625089	1627849
1624721	1625825	1626745	1625457	1627297
1628217	1625641	1626009	1626377	1623801
1628033	1626561	1625273	1626193	1623985
1624169	1624353	1627481	1626929	1627113

L23-M3

1629505	1632265	1629137	1629689	1632449
1629321	1630425	1631345	1630057	1631897
1632817	1630241	1630609	1630977	1628401
1632633	1631161	1629873	1630793	1628585
1628769	1628953	1632081	1631529	1631713

L23-M4

1634105	1636865	1633737	1634289	1637049
1633921	1635025	1635945	1634657	1636497
1637417	1634841	1635209	1635577	1633001
1637233	1635761	1634473	1635393	1633185
1633369	1633553	1636681	1636129	1636313

L23-M5

1638705	1641465	1638337	1638889	1641649
1638521	1639625	1640545	1639257	1641097
1642017	1639441	1639809	1640177	1637601
1641833	1640361	1639073	1639993	1637785
1637969	1638153	1641281	1640729	1640913

L23-M6

1643305	1646065	1642937	1643489	1646249
1643121	1644225	1645145	1643857	1645697
1646617	1644041	1644409	1644777	1642201
1646433	1644961	1643673	1644593	1642385
1642569	1642753	1645881	1645329	1645513

L23-M7

1647905	1650665	1647537	1648089	1650849
1647721	1648825	1649745	1648457	1650297
1651217	1648641	1649009	1649377	1646801
1651033	1649561	1648273	1649193	1646985
1647169	1647353	1650481	1649929	1650113

L23-M8

1652505	1655265	1652137	1652689	1655449
1652321	1653425	1654345	1653057	1654897
1655817	1653241	1653609	1653977	1651401
1655633	1654161	1652873	1653793	1651585
1651769	1651953	1655081	1654529	1654713

L23-M9

1657105	1659865	1656737	1657289	1660049
1656921	1658025	1658945	1657657	1659497
1660417	1657841	1658209	1658577	1656001
1660233	1658761	1657473	1658393	1656185
1656369	1656553	1659681	1659129	1659313

L23-M10

1661705	1664465	1661337	1661889	1664649
1661521	1662625	1663545	1662257	1664097
1665017	1662441	1662809	1663177	1660601
1664833	1663361	1662073	1662993	1660785
1660969	1661153	1664281	1663729	1663913

L23-M11

1666305	1669065	1665937	1666489	1669249
1666121	1667225	1668145	1666857	1668697
1669617	1667041	1667409	1667777	1665201
1669433	1667961	1666673	1667593	1665385
1665569	1665753	1668881	1668329	1668513

L23-M12

1670905	1673665	1670537	1671089	1673849
1670721	1671825	1672745	1671457	1673297
1674217	1671641	1672009	1672377	1669801
1674033	1672561	1671273	1672193	1669985
1670169	1670353	1673481	1672929	1673113

L23-M13

1675505	1678265	1675137	1675689	1678449
1675321	1676425	1677345	1676057	1677897
1678817	1676241	1676609	1676977	1674401
1678633	1677161	1675873	1676793	1674585
1674769	1674953	1678081	1677529	1677713

L23-M14

1680105	1682865	1679737	1680289	1683049
1679921	1681025	1681945	1680657	1682497
1683417	1680841	1681209	1681577	1679001
1683233	1681761	1680473	1681393	1679185
1679369	1679553	1682681	1682129	1682313

L23-M15

1684705	1687465	1684337	1684889	1687649
1684521	1685625	1686545	1685257	1687097
1688017	1685441	1685809	1686177	1683601
1687833	1686361	1685073	1685993	1683785
1683969	1684153	1687281	1686729	1686913

L23-M16

1689305	1692065	1688937	1689489	1692249
1689121	1690225	1691145	1689857	1691697
1692617	1690041	1690409	1690777	1688201
1692433	1690961	1689673	1690593	1688385
1688569	1688753	1691881	1691329	1691513

L24-M1

1693905	1696665	1693537	1694089	1696849
1693721	1694825	1695745	1694457	1696297
1697217	1694641	1695009	1695377	1692801
1697033	1695561	1694273	1695193	1692985
1693169	1693353	1696481	1695929	1696113

L24-M2

1698505	1701265	1698137	1698689	1701449
1698321	1699425	1700345	1699057	1700897
1701817	1699241	1699609	1699977	1697401
1701633	1700161	1698873	1699793	1697585
1697769	1697953	1701081	1700529	1700713

L24-M3

1703105	1705865	1702737	1703289	1706049
1702921	1704025	1704945	1703657	1705497
1706417	1703841	1704209	1704577	1702001
1706233	1704761	1703473	1704393	1702185
1702369	1702553	1705681	1705129	1705313

L24-M4

1707705	1710465	1707337	1707889	1710649
1707521	1708625	1709545	1708257	1710097
1711017	1708441	1708809	1709177	1706601
1710833	1709361	1708073	1708993	1706785
1706969	1707153	1710281	1709729	1709913

L24-M5

1712305	1715065	1711937	1712489	1715249
1712121	1713225	1714145	1712857	1714697
1715617	1713041	1713409	1713777	1711201
1715433	1713961	1712673	1713593	1711385
1711569	1711753	1714881	1714329	1714513

L24-M6

1716905	1719665	1716537	1717089	1719849
1716721	1717825	1718745	1717457	1719297
1720217	1717641	1718009	1718377	1715801
1720033	1718561	1717273	1718193	1715985
1716169	1716353	1719481	1718929	1719113

L24-M7

1721505	1724265	1721137	1721689	1724449
1721321	1722425	1723345	1722057	1723897
1724817	1722241	1722609	1722977	1720401
1724633	1723161	1721873	1722793	1720585
1720769	1720953	1724081	1723529	1723713

L24-M8

1726105	1728865	1725737	1726289	1729049
1725921	1727025	1727945	1726657	1728497
1729417	1726841	1727209	1727577	1725001
1729233	1727761	1726473	1727393	1725185
1725369	1725553	1728681	1728129	1728313

L24-M9

1730705	1733465	1730337	1730889	1733649
1730521	1731625	1732545	1731257	1733097
1734017	1731441	1731809	1732177	1729601
1733833	1732361	1731073	1731993	1729785
1729969	1730153	1733281	1732729	1732913

L24-M10

1735305	1738065	1734937	1735489	1738249
1735121	1736225	1737145	1735857	1737697
1738617	1736041	1736409	1736777	1734201
1738433	1736961	1735673	1736593	1734385
1734569	1734753	1737881	1737329	1737513

L24-M11

1739905	1742665	1739537	1740089	1742849
1739721	1740825	1741745	1740457	1742297
1743217	1740641	1741009	1741377	1738801
1743033	1741561	1740273	1741193	1738985
1739169	1739353	1742481	1741929	1742113

L24-M12

1744505	1747265	1744137	1744689	1747449
1744321	1745425	1746345	1745057	1746897
1747817	1745241	1745609	1745977	1743401
1747633	1746161	1744873	1745793	1743585
1743769	1743953	1747081	1746529	1746713

L24-M13

1749105	1751865	1748737	1749289	1752049
1748921	1750025	1750945	1749657	1751497
1752417	1749841	1750209	1750577	1748001
1752233	1750761	1749473	1750393	1748185
1748369	1748553	1751681	1751129	1751313

L24-M14

1753705	1756465	1753337	1753889	1756649
1753521	1754625	1755545	1754257	1756097
1757017	1754441	1754809	1755177	1752601
1756833	1755361	1754073	1754993	1752785
1752969	1753153	1756281	1755729	1755913

L24-M15

1758305	1761065	1757937	1758489	1761249
1758121	1759225	1760145	1758857	1760697
1761617	1759041	1759409	1759777	1757201
1761433	1759961	1758673	1759593	1757385
1757569	1757753	1760881	1760329	1760513

L24-M16

1762905	1765665	1762537	1763089	1765849
1762721	1763825	1764745	1763457	1765297
1766217	1763641	1764009	1764377	1761801
1766033	1764561	1763273	1764193	1761985
1762169	1762353	1765481	1764929	1765113

L25-M1

1767505	1770265	1767137	1767689	1770449
1767321	1768425	1769345	1768057	1769897
1770817	1768241	1768609	1768977	1766401
1770633	1769161	1767873	1768793	1766585
1766769	1766953	1770081	1769529	1769713

L25-M2

1772105	1774865	1771737	1772289	1775049
1771921	1773025	1773945	1772657	1774497
1775417	1772841	1773209	1773577	1771001
1775233	1773761	1772473	1773393	1771185
1771369	1771553	1774681	1774129	1774313

L25-M3

1776705	1779465	1776337	1776889	1779649
1776521	1777625	1778545	1777257	1779097
1780017	1777441	1777809	1778177	1775601
1779833	1778361	1777073	1777993	1775785
1775969	1776153	1779281	1778729	1778913

L25-M4

1781305	1784065	1780937	1781489	1784249
1781121	1782225	1783145	1781857	1783697
1784617	1782041	1782409	1782777	1780201
1784433	1782961	1781673	1782593	1780385
1780569	1780753	1783881	1783329	1783513

L25-M5

1785905	1788665	1785537	1786089	1788849
1785721	1786825	1787745	1786457	1788297
1789217	1786641	1787009	1787377	1784801
1789033	1787561	1786273	1787193	1784985
1785169	1785353	1788481	1787929	1788113

L25-M6

1790505	1793265	1790137	1790689	1793449
1790321	1791425	1792345	1791057	1792897
1793817	1791241	1791609	1791977	1789401
1793633	1792161	1790873	1791793	1789585
1789769	1789953	1793081	1792529	1792713

L25-M7

1795105	1797865	1794737	1795289	1798049
1794921	1796025	1796945	1795657	1797497
1798417	1795841	1796209	1796577	1794001
1798233	1796761	1795473	1796393	1794185
1794369	1794553	1797681	1797129	1797313

L25-M8

1799705	1802465	1799337	1799889	1802649
1799521	1800625	1801545	1800257	1802097
1803017	1800441	1800809	1801177	1798601
1802833	1801361	1800073	1800993	1798785
1798969	1799153	1802281	1801729	1801913

L25-M9

1804305	1807065	1803937	1804489	1807249
1804121	1805225	1806145	1804857	1806697
1807617	1805041	1805409	1805777	1803201
1807433	1805961	1804673	1805593	1803385
1803569	1803753	1806881	1806329	1806513

L25-M10

1808905	1811665	1808537	1809089	1811849
1808721	1809825	1810745	1809457	1811297
1812217	1809641	1810009	1810377	1807801
1812033	1810561	1809273	1810193	1807985
1808169	1808353	1811481	1810929	1811113

L25-M11

1813505	1816265	1813137	1813689	1816449
1813321	1814425	1815345	1814057	1815897
1816817	1814241	1814609	1814977	1812401
1816633	1815161	1813873	1814793	1812585
1812769	1812953	1816081	1815529	1815713

L25-M12

1818105	1820865	1817737	1818289	1821049
1817921	1819025	1819945	1818657	1820497
1821417	1818841	1819209	1819577	1817001
1821233	1819761	1818473	1819393	1817185
1817369	1817553	1820681	1820129	1820313

L25-M13

1822705	1825465	1822337	1822889	1825649
1822521	1823625	1824545	1823257	1825097
1826017	1823441	1823809	1824177	1821601
1825833	1824361	1823073	1823993	1821785
1821969	1822153	1825281	1824729	1824913

L25-M14

1827305	1830065	1826937	1827489	1830249
1827121	1828225	1829145	1827857	1829697
1830617	1828041	1828409	1828777	1826201
1830433	1828961	1827673	1828593	1826385
1826569	1826753	1829881	1829329	1829513

L25-M15

1831905	1834665	1831537	1832089	1834849
1831721	1832825	1833745	1832457	1834297
1835217	1832641	1833009	1833377	1830801
1835033	1833561	1832273	1833193	1830985
1831169	1831353	1834481	1833929	1834113

L25-M16

1836505	1839265	1836137	1836689	1839449
1836321	1837425	1838345	1837057	1838897
1839817	1837241	1837609	1837977	1835401
1839633	1838161	1836873	1837793	1835585
1835769	1835953	1839081	1838529	1838713

CHESED

L1-M1

649	2269	433	757	2377
541	1189	1729	973	2053
2593	1081	1297	1513	1
2485	1621	865	1405	109
217	325	2161	1837	1945

L1-M2

3349	4969	3133	3457	5077
3241	3889	4429	3673	4753
5293	3781	3997	4213	2701
5185	4321	3565	4105	2809
2917	3025	4861	4537	4645

L1-M3

6049	7669	5833	6157	7777
5941	6589	7129	6373	7453
7993	6481	6697	6913	5401
7885	7021	6265	6805	5509
5617	5725	7561	7237	7345

L1-M4

8749	10369	8533	8857	10477
8641	9289	9829	9073	10153
10693	9181	9397	9613	8101
10585	9721	8965	9505	8209
8317	8425	10261	9937	10045

L1-M5

11449	13069	11233	11557	13177
11341	11989	12529	11773	12853
13393	11881	12097	12313	10801
13285	12421	11665	12205	10909
11017	11125	12961	12637	12745

L1-M6

14149	15769	13933	14257	15877
14041	14689	15229	14473	15553
16093	14581	14797	15013	13501
15985	15121	14365	14905	13609
13717	13825	15661	15337	15445

L1-M7

16849	18469	16633	16957	18577
16741	17389	17929	17173	18253
18793	17281	17497	17713	16201
18685	17821	17065	17605	16309
16417	16525	18361	18037	18145

L1-M8

19549	21169	19333	19657	21277
19441	20089	20629	19873	20953
21493	19981	20197	20413	18901
21385	20521	19765	20305	19009
19117	19225	21061	20737	20845

L1-M9

22249	23869	22033	22357	23977
22141	22789	23329	22573	23653
24193	22681	22897	23113	21601
24085	23221	22465	23005	21709
21817	21925	23761	23437	23545

L1-M10

24949	26569	24733	25057	26677
24841	25489	26029	25273	26353
26893	25381	25597	25813	24301
26785	25921	25165	25705	24409
24517	24625	26461	26137	26245

L1-M11

27649	29269	27433	27757	29377
27541	28189	28729	27973	29053
29593	28081	28297	28513	27001
29485	28621	27865	28405	27109
27217	27325	29161	28837	28945

L1-M12

30349	31969	30133	30457	32077
30241	30889	31429	30673	31753
32293	30781	30997	31213	29701
32185	31321	30565	31105	29809
29917	30025	31861	31537	31645

L1-M13

33049	34669	32833	33157	34777
32941	33589	34129	33373	34453
34993	33481	33697	33913	32401
34885	34021	33265	33805	32509
32617	32725	34561	34237	34345

L1-M14

35749	37369	35533	35857	37477
35641	36289	36829	36073	37153
37693	36181	36397	36613	35101
37585	36721	35965	36505	35209
35317	35425	37261	36937	37045

L1-M15

38449	40069	38233	38557	40177
38341	38989	39529	38773	39853
40393	38881	39097	39313	37801
40285	39421	38665	39205	37909
38017	38125	39961	39637	39745

L1-M16

41149	42769	40933	41257	42877
41041	41689	42229	41473	42553
43093	41581	41797	42013	40501
42985	42121	41365	41905	40609
40717	40825	42661	42337	42445

L2-M1

43849	45469	43633	43957	45577
43741	44389	44929	44173	45253
45793	44281	44497	44713	43201
45685	44821	44065	44605	43309
43417	43525	45361	45037	45145

L2-M2

46549	48169	46333	46657	48277
46441	47089	47629	46873	47953
48493	46981	47197	47413	45901
48385	47521	46765	47305	46009
46117	46225	48061	47737	47845

L2-M3

49249	50869	49033	49357	50977
49141	49789	50329	49573	50653
51193	49681	49897	50113	48601
51085	50221	49465	50005	48709
48817	48925	50761	50437	50545

L2-M12

73549	75169	73333	73657	75277
73441	74089	74629	73873	74953
75493	73981	74197	74413	72901
75385	74521	73765	74305	73009
73117	73225	75061	74737	74845

L2-M4

51949	53569	51733	52057	53677
51841	52489	53029	52273	53353
53893	52381	52597	52813	51301
53785	52921	52165	52705	51409
51517	51625	53461	53137	53245

L2-M13

76249	77869	76033	76357	77977
76141	76789	77329	76573	77653
78193	76681	76897	77113	75601
78085	77221	76465	77005	75709
75817	75925	77761	77437	77545

L2-M5

54649	56269	54433	54757	56377
54541	55189	55729	54973	56053
56593	55081	55297	55513	54001
56485	55621	54865	55405	54109
54217	54325	56161	55837	55945

L2-M14

78949	80569	78733	79057	80677
78841	79489	80029	79273	80353
80893	79381	79597	79813	78301
80785	79921	79165	79705	78409
78517	78625	80461	80137	80245

L2-M6

57349	58969	57133	57457	59077
57241	57889	58429	57673	58753
59293	57781	57997	58213	56701
59185	58321	57565	58105	56809
56917	57025	58861	58537	58645

L2-M15

81649	83269	81433	81757	83377
81541	82189	82729	81973	83053
83593	82081	82297	82513	81001
83485	82621	81865	82405	81109
81217	81325	83161	82837	82945

L2-M7

60049	61669	59833	60157	61777
59941	60589	61129	60373	61453
61993	60481	60697	60913	59401
61885	61021	60265	60805	59509
59617	59725	61561	61237	61345

L2-M16

84349	85969	84133	84457	86077
84241	84889	85429	84673	85753
86293	84781	84997	85213	83701
86185	85321	84565	85105	83809
83917	84025	85861	85537	85645

L2-M8

62749	64369	62533	62857	64477
62641	63289	63829	63073	64153
64693	63181	63397	63613	62101
64585	63721	62965	63505	62209
62317	62425	64261	63937	64045

L3-M1

87049	88669	86833	87157	88777
86941	87589	88129	87373	88453
88993	87481	87697	87913	86401
88885	88021	87265	87805	86509
86617	86725	88561	88237	88345

L2-M9

65449	67069	65233	65557	67177
65341	65989	66529	65773	66853
67393	65881	66097	66313	64801
67285	66421	65665	66205	64909
65017	65125	66961	66637	66745

L3-M2

89749	91369	89533	89857	91477
89641	90289	90829	90073	91153
91693	90181	90397	90613	89101
91585	90721	89965	90505	89209
89317	89425	91261	90937	91045

L2-M10

68149	69769	67933	68257	69877
68041	68689	69229	68473	69553
70093	68581	68797	69013	67501
69985	69121	68365	68905	67609
67717	67825	69661	69337	69445

L3-M3

92449	94069	92233	92557	94177
92341	92989	93529	92773	93853
94393	92881	93097	93313	91801
94285	93421	92665	93205	91909
92017	92125	93961	93637	93745

L2-M11

70849	72469	70633	70957	72577
70741	71389	71929	71173	72253
72793	71281	71497	71713	70201
72685	71821	71065	71605	70309
70417	70525	72361	72037	72145

L3-M4

95149	96769	94933	95257	96877
95041	95689	96229	95473	96553
97093	95581	95797	96013	94501
96985	96121	95365	95905	94609
94717	94825	96661	96337	96445

L3-M5

97849	99469	97633	97957	99577
97741	98389	98929	98173	99253
99793	98281	98497	98713	97201
99685	98821	98065	98605	97309
97417	97525	99361	99037	99145

L3-M6

100549	102169	100333	100657	102277
100441	101089	101629	100873	101953
102493	100981	101197	101413	99901
102385	101521	100765	101305	100009
100117	100225	102061	101737	101845

L3-M7

103249	104869	103033	103357	104977
103141	103789	104329	103573	104653
105193	103681	103897	104113	102601
105085	104221	103465	104005	102709
102817	102925	104761	104437	104545

L3-M8

105949	107569	105733	106057	107677
105841	106489	107029	106273	107353
107893	106381	106597	106813	105301
107785	106921	106165	106705	105409
105517	105625	107461	107137	107245

L3-M9

108649	110269	108433	108757	110377
108541	109189	109729	108973	110053
110593	109081	109297	109513	108001
110485	109621	108865	109405	108109
108217	108325	110161	109837	109945

L3-M10

111349	112969	111133	111457	113077
111241	111889	112429	111673	112753
113293	111781	111997	112213	110701
113185	112321	111565	112105	110809
110917	111025	112861	112537	112645

L3-M11

114049	115669	113833	114157	115777
113941	114589	115129	114373	115453
115993	114481	114697	114913	113401
115885	115021	114265	114805	113509
113617	113725	115561	115237	115345

L3-M12

116749	118369	116533	116857	118477
116641	117289	117829	117073	118153
118693	117181	117397	117613	116101
118585	117721	116965	117505	116209
116317	116425	118261	117937	118045

L3-M13

119449	121069	119233	119557	121177
119341	119989	120529	119773	120853
121393	119881	120097	120313	118801
121285	120421	119665	120205	118909
119017	119125	120961	120637	120745

L3-M14

122149	123769	121933	122257	123877
122041	122689	123229	122473	123553
124093	122581	122797	123013	121501
123985	123121	122365	122905	121609
121717	121825	123661	123337	123445

L3-M15

124849	126469	124633	124957	126577
124741	125389	125929	125173	126253
126793	125281	125497	125713	124201
126685	125821	125065	125605	124309
124417	124525	126361	126037	126145

L3-M16

127549	129169	127333	127657	129277
127441	128089	128629	127873	128953
129493	127981	128197	128413	126901
129385	128521	127765	128305	127009
127117	127225	129061	128737	128845

L4-M1

130249	131869	130033	130357	131977
130141	130789	131329	130573	131653
132193	130681	130897	131113	129601
132085	131221	130465	131005	129709
129817	129925	131761	131437	131545

L4-M2

132949	134569	132733	133057	134677
132841	133489	134029	133273	134353
134893	133381	133597	133813	132301
134785	133921	133165	133705	132409
132517	132625	134461	134137	134245

L4-M3

135649	137269	135433	135757	137377
135541	136189	136729	135973	137053
137593	136081	136297	136513	135001
137485	136621	135865	136405	135109
135217	135325	137161	136837	136945

L4-M4

138349	139969	138133	138457	140077
138241	138889	139429	138673	139753
140293	138781	138997	139213	137701
140185	139321	138565	139105	137809
137917	138025	139861	139537	139645

L4-M5

141049	142669	140833	141157	142777
140941	141589	142129	141373	142453
142993	141481	141697	141913	140401
142885	142021	141265	141805	140509
140617	140725	142561	142237	142345

L4-M6

143749	145369	143533	143857	145477
143641	144289	144829	144073	145153
145693	144181	144397	144613	143101
145585	144721	143965	144505	143209
143317	143425	145261	144937	145045

L4-M7

146449	148069	146233	146557	148177
146341	146989	147529	146773	147853
148393	146881	147097	147313	145801
148285	147421	146665	147205	145909
146017	146125	147961	147637	147745

L4-M16

170749	172369	170533	170857	172477
170641	171289	171829	171073	172153
172693	171181	171397	171613	170101
172585	171721	170965	171505	170209
170317	170425	172261	171937	172045

L4-M8

149149	150769	148933	149257	150877
149041	149689	150229	149473	150553
151093	149581	149797	150013	148501
150985	150121	149365	149905	148609
148717	148825	150661	150337	150445

L5-M1

173449	175069	173233	173557	175177
173341	173989	174529	173773	174853
175393	173881	174097	174313	172801
175285	174421	173665	174205	172909
173017	173125	174961	174637	174745

L4-M9

151849	153469	151633	151957	153577
151741	152389	152929	152173	153253
153793	152281	152497	152713	151201
153685	152821	152065	152605	151309
151417	151525	153361	153037	153145

L5-M2

176149	177769	175933	176257	177877
176041	176689	177229	176473	177553
178093	176581	176797	177013	175501
177985	177121	176365	176905	175609
175717	175825	177661	177337	177445

L4-M10

154549	156169	154333	154657	156277
154441	155089	155629	154873	155953
156493	154981	155197	155413	153901
156385	155521	154765	155305	154009
154117	154225	156061	155737	155845

L5-M3

178849	180469	178633	178957	180577
178741	179389	179929	179173	180253
180793	179281	179497	179713	178201
180685	179821	179065	179605	178309
178417	178525	180361	180037	180145

L4-M11

157249	158869	157033	157357	158977
157141	157789	158329	157573	158653
159193	157681	157897	158113	156601
159085	158221	157465	158005	156709
156817	156925	158761	158437	158545

L5-M4

181549	183169	181333	181657	183277
181441	182089	182629	181873	182953
183493	181981	182197	182413	180901
183385	182521	181765	182305	181009
181117	181225	183061	182737	182845

L4-M12

159949	161569	159733	160057	161677
159841	160489	161029	160273	161353
161893	160381	160597	160813	159301
161785	160921	160165	160705	159409
159517	159625	161461	161137	161245

L5-M5

184249	185869	184033	184357	185977
184141	184789	185329	184573	185653
186193	184681	184897	185113	183601
186085	185221	184465	185005	183709
183817	183925	185761	185437	185545

L4-M13

162649	164269	162433	162757	164377
162541	163189	163729	162973	164053
164593	163081	163297	163513	162001
164485	163621	162865	163405	162109
162217	162325	164161	163837	163945

L5-M6

186949	188569	186733	187057	188677
186841	187489	188029	187273	188353
188893	187381	187597	187813	186301
188785	187921	187165	187705	186409
186517	186625	188461	188137	188245

L4-M14

165349	166969	165133	165457	167077
165241	165889	166429	165673	166753
167293	165781	165997	166213	164701
167185	166321	165565	166105	164809
164917	165025	166861	166537	166645

L5-M7

189649	191269	189433	189757	191377
189541	190189	190729	189973	191053
191593	190081	190297	190513	189001
191485	190621	189865	190405	189109
189217	189325	191161	190837	190945

L4-M15

168049	169669	167833	168157	169777
167941	168589	169129	168373	169453
169993	168481	168697	168913	167401
169885	169021	168265	168805	167509
167617	167725	169561	169237	169345

L5-M8

192349	193969	192133	192457	194077
192241	192889	193429	192673	193753
194293	192781	192997	193213	191701
194185	193321	192565	193105	191809
191917	192025	193861	193537	193645

L5-M9

195049	196669	194833	195157	196777
194941	195589	196129	195373	196453
196993	195481	195697	195913	194401
196885	196021	195265	195805	194509
194617	194725	196561	196237	196345

L5-M10

197749	199369	197533	197857	199477
197641	198289	198829	198073	199153
199693	198181	198397	198613	197101
199585	198721	197965	198505	197209
197317	197425	199261	198937	199045

L5-M11

200449	202069	200233	200557	202177
200341	200989	201529	200773	201853
202393	200881	201097	201313	199801
202285	201421	200665	201205	199909
200017	200125	201961	201637	201745

L5-M12

203149	204769	202933	203257	204877
203041	203689	204229	203473	204553
205093	203581	203797	204013	202501
204985	204121	203365	203905	202609
202717	202825	204661	204337	204445

L5-M13

205849	207469	205633	205957	207577
205741	206389	206929	206173	207253
207793	206281	206497	206713	205201
207685	206821	206065	206605	205309
205417	205525	207361	207037	207145

L5-M14

208549	210169	208333	208657	210277
208441	209089	209629	208873	209953
210493	208981	209197	209413	207901
210385	209521	208765	209305	208009
208117	208225	210061	209737	209845

L5-M15

211249	212869	211033	211357	212977
211141	211789	212329	211573	212653
213193	211681	211897	212113	210601
213085	212221	211465	212005	210709
210817	210925	212761	212437	212545

L5-M16

213949	215569	213733	214057	215677
213841	214489	215029	214273	215353
215893	214381	214597	214813	213301
215785	214921	214165	214705	213409
213517	213625	215461	215137	215245

L6-M1

216649	218269	216433	216757	218377
216541	217189	217729	216973	218053
218593	217081	217297	217513	216001
218485	217621	216865	217405	216109
216217	216325	218161	217837	217945

L6-M2

219349	220969	219133	219457	221077
219241	219889	220429	219673	220753
221293	219781	219997	220213	218701
221185	220321	219565	220105	218809
218917	219025	220861	220537	220645

L6-M3

222049	223669	221833	222157	223777
221941	222589	223129	222373	223453
223993	222481	222697	222913	221401
223885	223021	222265	222805	221509
221617	221725	223561	223237	223345

L6-M4

224749	226369	224533	224857	226477
224641	225289	225829	225073	226153
226693	225181	225397	225613	224101
226585	225721	224965	225505	224209
224317	224425	226261	225937	226045

L6-M5

227449	229069	227233	227557	229177
227341	227989	228529	227773	228853
229393	227881	228097	228313	226801
229285	228421	227665	228205	226909
227017	227125	228961	228637	228745

L6-M6

230149	231769	229933	230257	231877
230041	230689	231229	230473	231553
232093	230581	230797	231013	229501
231985	231121	230365	230905	229609
229717	229825	231661	231337	231445

L6-M7

232849	234469	232633	232957	234577
232741	233389	233929	233173	234253
234793	233281	233497	233713	232201
234685	233821	233065	233605	232309
232417	232525	234361	234037	234145

L6-M8

235549	237169	235333	235657	237277
235441	236089	236629	235873	236953
237493	235981	236197	236413	234901
237385	236521	235765	236305	235009
235117	235225	237061	236737	236845

L6-M9

238249	239869	238033	238357	239977
238141	238789	239329	238573	239653
240193	238681	238897	239113	237601
240085	239221	238465	239005	237709
237817	237925	239761	239437	239545

L6-M10

240949	242569	240733	241057	242677
240841	241489	242029	241273	242353
242893	241381	241597	241813	240301
242785	241921	241165	241705	240409
240517	240625	242461	242137	242245

L6-M11

243649	245269	243433	243757	245377
243541	244189	244729	243973	245053
245593	244081	244297	244513	243001
245485	244621	243865	244405	243109
243217	243325	245161	244837	244945

L7-M4

267949	269569	267733	268057	269677
267841	268489	269029	268273	269353
269893	268381	268597	268813	267301
269785	268921	268165	268705	267409
267517	267625	269461	269137	269245

L6-M12

246349	247969	246133	246457	248077
246241	246889	247429	246673	247753
248293	246781	246997	247213	245701
248185	247321	246565	247105	245809
245917	246025	247861	247537	247645

L7-M5

270649	272269	270433	270757	272377
270541	271189	271729	270973	272053
272593	271081	271297	271513	270001
272485	271621	270865	271405	270109
270217	270325	272161	271837	271945

L6-M13

249049	250669	248833	249157	250777
248941	249589	250129	249373	250453
250993	249481	249697	249913	248401
250885	250021	249265	249805	248509
248617	248725	250561	250237	250345

L7-M6

273349	274969	273133	273457	275077
273241	273889	274429	273673	274753
275293	273781	273997	274213	272701
275185	274321	273565	274105	272809
272917	273025	274861	274537	274645

L6-M14

251749	253369	251533	251857	253477
251641	252289	252829	252073	253153
253693	252181	252397	252613	251101
253585	252721	251965	252505	251209
251317	251425	253261	252937	253045

L7-M7

276049	277669	275833	276157	277777
275941	276589	277129	276373	277453
277993	276481	276697	276913	275401
277885	277021	276265	276805	275509
275617	275725	277561	277237	277345

L6-M15

254449	256069	254233	254557	256177
254341	254989	255529	254773	255853
256393	254881	255097	255313	253801
256285	255421	254665	255205	253909
254017	254125	255961	255637	255745

L7-M8

278749	280369	278533	278857	280477
278641	279289	279829	279073	280153
280693	279181	279397	279613	278101
280585	279721	278965	279505	278209
278317	278425	280261	279937	280045

L6-M16

257149	258769	256933	257257	258877
257041	257689	258229	257473	258553
259093	257581	257797	258013	256501
258985	258121	257365	257905	256609
256717	256825	258661	258337	258445

L7-M9

281449	283069	281233	281557	283177
281341	281989	282529	281773	282853
283393	281881	282097	282313	280801
283285	282421	281665	282205	280909
281017	281125	282961	282637	282745

L7-M1

259849	261469	259633	259957	261577
259741	260389	260929	260173	261253
261793	260281	260497	260713	259201
261685	260821	260065	260605	259309
259417	259525	261361	261037	261145

L7-M10

284149	285769	283933	284257	285877
284041	284689	285229	284473	285553
286093	284581	284797	285013	283501
285985	285121	284365	284905	283609
283717	283825	285661	285337	285445

L7-M2

262549	264169	262333	262657	264277
262441	263089	263629	262873	263953
264493	262981	263197	263413	261901
264385	263521	262765	263305	262009
262117	262225	264061	263737	263845

L7-M11

286849	288469	286633	286957	288577
286741	287389	287929	287173	288253
288793	287281	287497	287713	286201
288685	287821	287065	287605	286309
286417	286525	288361	288037	288145

L7-M3

265249	266869	265033	265357	266977
265141	265789	266329	265573	266653
267193	265681	265897	266113	264601
267085	266221	265465	266005	264709
264817	264925	266761	266437	266545

L7-M12

289549	291169	289333	289657	291277
289441	290089	290629	289873	290953
291493	289981	290197	290413	288901
291385	290521	289765	290305	289009
289117	289225	291061	290737	290845

L7-M13

292249	293869	292033	292357	293977
292141	292789	293329	292573	293653
294193	292681	292897	293113	291601
294085	293221	292465	293005	291709
291817	291925	293761	293437	293545

L7-M14

294949	296569	294733	295057	296677
294841	295489	296029	295273	296353
296893	295381	295597	295813	294301
296785	295921	295165	295705	294409
294517	294625	296461	296137	296245

L7-M15

297649	299269	297433	297757	299377
297541	298189	298729	297973	299053
299593	298081	298297	298513	297001
299485	298621	297865	298405	297109
297217	297325	299161	298837	298945

L7-M16

300349	301969	300133	300457	302077
300241	300889	301429	300673	301753
302293	300781	300997	301213	299701
302185	301321	300565	301105	299809
299917	300025	301861	301537	301645

L8M1

303049	304669	302833	303157	304777
302941	303589	304129	303373	304453
304993	303481	303697	303913	302401
304885	304021	303265	303805	302509
302617	302725	304561	304237	304345

L8-M2

305749	307369	305533	305857	307477
305641	306289	306829	306073	307153
307693	306181	306397	306613	305101
307585	306721	305965	306505	305209
305317	305425	307261	306937	307045

L8-M3

308449	310069	308233	308557	310177
308341	308989	309529	308773	309853
310393	308881	309097	309313	307801
310285	309421	308665	309205	307909
308017	308125	309961	309637	309745

L8-M4

311149	312769	310933	311257	312877
311041	311689	312229	311473	312553
313093	311581	311797	312013	310501
312985	312121	311365	311905	310609
310717	310825	312661	312337	312445

L8-M5

313849	315469	313633	313957	315577
313741	314389	314929	314173	315253
315793	314281	314497	314713	313201
315685	314821	314065	314605	313309
313417	313525	315361	315037	315145

L8-M6

316549	318169	316333	316657	318277
316441	317089	317629	316873	317953
318493	316981	317197	317413	315901
318385	317521	316765	317305	316009
316117	316225	318061	317737	317845

L8-M7

319249	320869	319033	319357	320977
319141	319789	320329	319573	320653
321193	319681	319897	320113	318601
321085	320221	319465	320005	318709
318817	318925	320761	320437	320545

L8-M8

321949	323569	321733	322057	323677
321841	322489	323029	322273	323353
323893	322381	322597	322813	321301
323785	322921	322165	322705	321409
321517	321625	323461	323137	323245

L8-M9

324649	326269	324433	324757	326377
324541	325189	325729	324973	326053
326593	325081	325297	325513	324001
326485	325621	324865	325405	324109
324217	324325	326161	325837	325945

L8-M10

327349	328969	327133	327457	329077
327241	327889	328429	327673	328753
329293	327781	327997	328213	326701
329185	328321	327565	328105	326809
326917	327025	328861	328537	328645

L8-M11

330049	331669	329833	330157	331777
329941	330589	331129	330373	331453
331993	330481	330697	330913	329401
331885	331021	330265	330805	329509
329617	329725	331561	331237	331345

L8-M12

332749	334369	332533	332857	334477
332641	333289	333829	333073	334153
334693	333181	333397	333613	332101
334585	333721	332965	333505	332209
332317	332425	334261	333937	334045

L8-M13

335449	337069	335233	335557	337177
335341	335989	336529	335773	336853
337393	335881	336097	336313	334801
337285	336421	335665	336205	334909
335017	335125	336961	336637	336745

L8-M14

338149	339769	337933	338257	339877
338041	338689	339229	338473	339553
340093	338581	338797	339013	337501
339985	339121	338365	338905	337609
337717	337825	339661	339337	339445

L8-M15

340849	342469	340633	340957	342577
340741	341389	341929	341173	342253
342793	341281	341497	341713	340201
342685	341821	341065	341605	340309
340417	340525	342361	342037	342145

L8-M16

343549	345169	343333	343657	345277
343441	344089	344629	343873	344953
345493	343981	344197	344413	342901
345385	344521	343765	344305	343009
343117	343225	345061	344737	344845

L9-M1

346249	347869	346033	346357	347977
346141	346789	347329	346573	347653
348193	346681	346897	347113	345601
348085	347221	346465	347005	345709
345817	345925	347761	347437	347545

L9-M2

348949	350569	348733	349057	350677
348841	349489	350029	349273	350353
350893	349381	349597	349813	348301
350785	349921	349165	349705	348409
348517	348625	350461	350137	350245

L9-M3

351649	353269	351433	351757	353377
351541	352189	352729	351973	353053
353593	352081	352297	352513	351001
353485	352621	351865	352405	351109
351217	351325	353161	352837	352945

L9-M4

354349	355969	354133	354457	356077
354241	354889	355429	354673	355753
356293	354781	354997	355213	353701
356185	355321	354565	355105	353809
353917	354025	355861	355537	355645

L9-M5

357049	358669	356833	357157	358777
356941	357589	358129	357373	358453
358993	357481	357697	357913	356401
358885	358021	357265	357805	356509
356617	356725	358561	358237	358345

L9-M6

359749	361369	359533	359857	361477
359641	360289	360829	360073	361153
361693	360181	360397	360613	359101
361585	360721	359965	360505	359209
359317	359425	361261	360937	361045

L9-M7

362449	364069	362233	362557	364177
362341	362989	363529	362773	363853
364393	362881	363097	363313	361801
364285	363421	362665	363205	361909
362017	362125	363961	363637	363745

L9-M8

365149	366769	364933	365257	366877
365041	365689	366229	365473	366553
367093	365581	365797	366013	364501
366985	366121	365365	365905	364609
364717	364825	366661	366337	366445

L9-M9

367849	369469	367633	367957	369577
367741	368389	368929	368173	369253
369793	368281	368497	368713	367201
369685	368821	368065	368605	367309
367417	367525	369361	369037	369145

L9-M10

370549	372169	370333	370657	372277
370441	371089	371629	370873	371953
372493	370981	371197	371413	369901
372385	371521	370765	371305	370009
370117	370225	372061	371737	371845

L9-M11

373249	374869	373033	373357	374977
373141	373789	374329	373573	374653
375193	373681	373897	374113	372601
375085	374221	373465	374005	372709
372817	372925	374761	374437	374545

L9-M12

375949	377569	375733	376057	377677
375841	376489	377029	376273	377353
377893	376381	376597	376813	375301
377785	376921	376165	376705	375409
375517	375625	377461	377137	377245

L9-M13

378649	380269	378433	378757	380377
378541	379189	379729	378973	380053
380593	379081	379297	379513	378001
380485	379621	378865	379405	378109
378217	378325	380161	379837	379945

L9-M14

381349	382969	381133	381457	383077
381241	381889	382429	381673	382753
383293	381781	381997	382213	380701
383185	382321	381565	382105	380809
380917	381025	382861	382537	382645

L9-M15

384049	385669	383833	384157	385777
383941	384589	385129	384373	385453
385993	384481	384697	384913	383401
385885	385021	384265	384805	383509
383617	383725	385561	385237	385345

L9-M16

386749	388369	386533	386857	388477
386641	387289	387829	387073	388153
388693	387181	387397	387613	386101
388585	387721	386965	387505	386209
386317	386425	388261	387937	388045

L10-M1

389449	391069	389233	389557	391177
389341	389989	390529	389773	390853
391393	389881	390097	390313	388801
391285	390421	389665	390205	388909
389017	389125	390961	390637	390745

L10-M2

392149	393769	391933	392257	393877
392041	392689	393229	392473	393553
394093	392581	392797	393013	391501
393985	393121	392365	392905	391609
391717	391825	393661	393337	393445

L10-M3

394849	396469	394633	394957	396577
394741	395389	395929	395173	396253
396793	395281	395497	395713	394201
396685	395821	395065	395605	394309
394417	394525	396361	396037	396145

L10-M4

397549	399169	397333	397657	399277
397441	398089	398629	397873	398953
399493	397981	398197	398413	396901
399385	398521	397765	398305	397009
397117	397225	399061	398737	398845

L10-M5

400249	401869	400033	400357	401977
400141	400789	401329	400573	401653
402193	400681	400897	401113	399601
402085	401221	400465	401005	399709
399817	399925	401761	401437	401545

L10-M6

402949	404569	402733	403057	404677
402841	403489	404029	403273	404353
404893	403381	403597	403813	402301
404785	403921	403165	403705	402409
402517	402625	404461	404137	404245

L10-M7

405649	407269	405433	405757	407377
405541	406189	406729	405973	407053
407593	406081	406297	406513	405001
407485	406621	405865	406405	405109
405217	405325	407161	406837	406945

L10-M8

408349	409969	408133	408457	410077
408241	408889	409429	408673	409753
410293	408781	408997	409213	407701
410185	409321	408565	409105	407809
407917	408025	409861	409537	409645

L10-M9

411049	412669	410833	411157	412777
410941	411589	412129	411373	412453
412993	411481	411697	411913	410401
412885	412021	411265	411805	410509
410617	410725	412561	412237	412345

L10-M10

413749	415369	413533	413857	415477
413641	414289	414829	414073	415153
415693	414181	414397	414613	413101
415585	414721	413965	414505	413209
413317	413425	415261	414937	415045

L10-M11

416449	418069	416233	416557	418177
416341	416989	417529	416773	417853
418393	416881	417097	417313	415801
418285	417421	416665	417205	415909
416017	416125	417961	417637	417745

L10-M12

419149	420769	418933	419257	420877
419041	419689	420229	419473	420553
421093	419581	419797	420013	418501
420985	420121	419365	419905	418609
418717	418825	420661	420337	420445

L10-M13

421849	423469	421633	421957	423577
421741	422389	422929	422173	423253
423793	422281	422497	422713	421201
423685	422821	422065	422605	421309
421417	421525	423361	423037	423145

L10-M14

424549	426169	424333	424657	426277
424441	425089	425629	424873	425953
426493	424981	425197	425413	423901
426385	425521	424765	425305	424009
424117	424225	426061	425737	425845

L10-M15

427249	428869	427033	427357	428977
427141	427789	428329	427573	428653
429193	427681	427897	428113	426601
429085	428221	427465	428005	426709
426817	426925	428761	428437	428545

L10-M16

429949	431569	429733	430057	431677
429841	430489	431029	430273	431353
431893	430381	430597	430813	429301
431785	430921	430165	430705	429409
429517	429625	431461	431137	431245

L11-M1

432649	434269	432433	432757	434377
432541	433189	433729	432973	434053
434593	433081	433297	433513	432001
434485	433621	432865	433405	432109
432217	432325	434161	433837	433945

L11-M2

435349	436969	435133	435457	437077
435241	435889	436429	435673	436753
437293	435781	435997	436213	434701
437185	436321	435565	436105	434809
434917	435025	436861	436537	436645

Magic Squares And The Tree of Life

L11-M3

438049	439669	437833	438157	439777
437941	438589	439129	438373	439453
439993	438481	438697	438913	437401
439885	439021	438265	438805	437509
437617	437725	439561	439237	439345

L11-M4

440749	442369	440533	440857	442477
440641	441289	441829	441073	442153
442693	441181	441397	441613	440101
442585	441721	440965	441505	440209
440317	440425	442261	441937	442045

L11-M5

443449	445069	443233	443557	445177
443341	443989	444529	443773	444853
445393	443881	444097	444313	442801
445285	444421	443665	444205	442909
443017	443125	444961	444637	444745

L11-M6

446149	447769	445933	446257	447877
446041	446689	447229	446473	447553
448093	446581	446797	447013	445501
447985	447121	446365	446905	445609
445717	445825	447661	447337	447445

L11-M7

448849	450469	448633	448957	450577
448741	449389	449929	449173	450253
450793	449281	449497	449713	448201
450685	449821	449065	449605	448309
448417	448525	450361	450037	450145

L11-M8

451549	453169	451333	451657	453277
451441	452089	452629	451873	452953
453493	451981	452197	452413	450901
453385	452521	451765	452305	451009
451117	451225	453061	452737	452845

L11-M9

454249	455869	454033	454357	455977
454141	454789	455329	454573	455653
456193	454681	454897	455113	453601
456085	455221	454465	455005	453709
453817	453925	455761	455437	455545

L11-M10

456949	458569	456733	457057	458677
456841	457489	458029	457273	458353
458893	457381	457597	457813	456301
458785	457921	457165	457705	456409
456517	456625	458461	458137	458245

L11-M11

459649	461269	459433	459757	461377
459541	460189	460729	459973	461053
461593	460081	460297	460513	459001
461485	460621	459865	460405	459109
459217	459325	461161	460837	460945

L11-M12

462349	463969	462133	462457	464077
462241	462889	463429	462673	463753
464293	462781	462997	463213	461701
464185	463321	462565	463105	461809
461917	462025	463861	463537	463645

L11-M13

465049	466669	464833	465157	466777
464941	465589	466129	465373	466453
466993	465481	465697	465913	464401
466885	466021	465265	465805	464509
464617	464725	466561	466237	466345

L11-M14

467749	469369	467533	467857	469477
467641	468289	468829	468073	469153
469693	468181	468397	468613	467101
469585	468721	467965	468505	467209
467317	467425	469261	468937	469045

L11-M15

470449	472069	470233	470557	472177
470341	470989	471529	470773	471853
472393	470881	471097	471313	469801
472285	471421	470665	471205	469909
470017	470125	471961	471637	471745

L11-M16

473149	474769	472933	473257	474877
473041	473689	474229	473473	474553
475093	473581	473797	474013	472501
474985	474121	473365	473905	472609
472717	472825	474661	474337	474445

L12-M1

475849	477469	475633	475957	477577
475741	476389	476929	476173	477253
477793	476281	476497	476713	475201
477685	476821	476065	476605	475309
475417	475525	477361	477037	477145

L12-M2

478549	480169	478333	478657	480277
478441	479089	479629	478873	479953
480493	478981	479197	479413	477901
480385	479521	478765	479305	478009
478117	478225	480061	479737	479845

L12-M3

481249	482869	481033	481357	482977
481141	481789	482329	481573	482653
483193	481681	481897	482113	480601
483085	482221	481465	482005	480709
480817	480925	482761	482437	482545

L12-M4

483949	485569	483733	484057	485677
483841	484489	485029	484273	485353
485893	484381	484597	484813	483301
485785	484921	484165	484705	483409
483517	483625	485461	485137	485245

L12-M5

486649	488269	486433	486757	488377
486541	487189	487729	486973	488053
488593	487081	487297	487513	486001
488485	487621	486865	487405	486109
486217	486325	488161	487837	487945

L12-M6

489349	490969	489133	489457	491077
489241	489889	490429	489673	490753
491293	489781	489997	490213	488701
491185	490321	489565	490105	488809
488917	489025	490861	490537	490645

L12-M7

492049	493669	491833	492157	493777
491941	492589	493129	492373	493453
493993	492481	492697	492913	491401
493885	493021	492265	492805	491509
491617	491725	493561	493237	493345

L12-M8

494749	496369	494533	494857	496477
494641	495289	495829	495073	496153
496693	495181	495397	495613	494101
496585	495721	494965	495505	494209
494317	494425	496261	495937	496045

L12-M9

497449	499069	497233	497557	499177
497341	497989	498529	497773	498853
499393	497881	498097	498313	496801
499285	498421	497665	498205	496909
497017	497125	498961	498637	498745

L12-M10

500149	501769	499933	500257	501877
500041	500689	501229	500473	501553
502093	500581	500797	501013	499501
501985	501121	500365	500905	499609
499717	499825	501661	501337	501445

L12-M11

502849	504469	502633	502957	504577
502741	503389	503929	503173	504253
504793	503281	503497	503713	502201
504685	503821	503065	503605	502309
502417	502525	504361	504037	504145

L12-M12

505549	507169	505333	505657	507277
505441	506089	506629	505873	506953
507493	505981	506197	506413	504901
507385	506521	505765	506305	505009
505117	505225	507061	506737	506845

L12-M13

508249	509869	508033	508357	509977
508141	508789	509329	508573	509653
510193	508681	508897	509113	507601
510085	509221	508465	509005	507709
507817	507925	509761	509437	509545

L12-M14

510949	512569	510733	511057	512677
510841	511489	512029	511273	512353
512893	511381	511597	511813	510301
512785	511921	511165	511705	510409
510517	510625	512461	512137	512245

L12-M15

513649	515269	513433	513757	515377
513541	514189	514729	513973	515053
515593	514081	514297	514513	513001
515485	514621	513865	514405	513109
513217	513325	515161	514837	514945

L12-M16

516349	517969	516133	516457	518077
516241	516889	517429	516673	517753
518293	516781	516997	517213	515701
518185	517321	516565	517105	515809
515917	516025	517861	517537	517645

L13-M1

519049	520669	518833	519157	520777
518941	519589	520129	519373	520453
520993	519481	519697	519913	518401
520885	520021	519265	519805	518509
518617	518725	520561	520237	520345

L13-M2

521749	523369	521533	521857	523477
521641	522289	522829	522073	523153
523693	522181	522397	522613	521101
523585	522721	521965	522505	521209
521317	521425	523261	522937	523045

L13-M3

524449	526069	524233	524557	526177
524341	524989	525529	524773	525853
526393	524881	525097	525313	523801
526285	525421	524665	525205	523909
524017	524125	525961	525637	525745

L13-M4

527149	528769	526933	527257	528877
527041	527689	528229	527473	528553
529093	527581	527797	528013	526501
528985	528121	527365	527905	526609
526717	526825	528661	528337	528445

L13-M5

529849	531469	529633	529957	531577
529741	530389	530929	530173	531253
531793	530281	530497	530713	529201
531685	530821	530065	530605	529309
529417	529525	531361	531037	531145

L13-M6

532549	534169	532333	532657	534277
532441	533089	533629	532873	533953
534493	532981	533197	533413	531901
534385	533521	532765	533305	532009
532117	532225	534061	533737	533845

L13-M7

535249	536869	535033	535357	536977
535141	535789	536329	535573	536653
537193	535681	535897	536113	534601
537085	536221	535465	536005	534709
534817	534925	536761	536437	536545

L13-M8

537949	539569	537733	538057	539677
537841	538489	539029	538273	539353
539893	538381	538597	538813	537301
539785	538921	538165	538705	537409
537517	537625	539461	539137	539245

L13-M9

540649	542269	540433	540757	542377
540541	541189	541729	540973	542053
542593	541081	541297	541513	540001
542485	541621	540865	541405	540109
540217	540325	542161	541837	541945

L13-M10

543349	544969	543133	543457	545077
543241	543889	544429	543673	544753
545293	543781	543997	544213	542701
545185	544321	543565	544105	542809
542917	543025	544861	544537	544645

L13-M11

546049	547669	545833	546157	547777
545941	546589	547129	546373	547453
547993	546481	546697	546913	545401
547885	547021	546265	546805	545509
545617	545725	547561	547237	547345

L13-M12

548749	550369	548533	548857	550477
548641	549289	549829	549073	550153
550693	549181	549397	549613	548101
550585	549721	548965	549505	548209
548317	548425	550261	549937	550045

L13-M13

551449	553069	551233	551557	553177
551341	551989	552529	551773	552853
553393	551881	552097	552313	550801
553285	552421	551665	552205	550909
551017	551125	552961	552637	552745

L13-M14

554149	555769	553933	554257	555877
554041	554689	555229	554473	555553
556093	554581	554797	555013	553501
555985	555121	554365	554905	553609
553717	553825	555661	555337	555445

L13-M15

556849	558469	556633	556957	558577
556741	557389	557929	557173	558253
558793	557281	557497	557713	556201
558685	557821	557065	557605	556309
556417	556525	558361	558037	558145

L13-M16

559549	561169	559333	559657	561277
559441	560089	560629	559873	560953
561493	559981	560197	560413	558901
561385	560521	559765	560305	559009
559117	559225	561061	560737	560845

L14-M1

562249	563869	562033	562357	563977
562141	562789	563329	562573	563653
564193	562681	562897	563113	561601
564085	563221	562465	563005	561709
561817	561925	563761	563437	563545

L14-M2

564949	566569	564733	565057	566677
564841	565489	566029	565273	566353
566893	565381	565597	565813	564301
566785	565921	565165	565705	564409
564517	564625	566461	566137	566245

L14-M3

567649	569269	567433	567757	569377
567541	568189	568729	567973	569053
569593	568081	568297	568513	567001
569485	568621	567865	568405	567109
567217	567325	569161	568837	568945

L14-M4

570349	571969	570133	570457	572077
570241	570889	571429	570673	571753
572293	570781	570997	571213	569701
572185	571321	570565	571105	569809
569917	570025	571861	571537	571645

L14-M5

573049	574669	572833	573157	574777
572941	573589	574129	573373	574453
574993	573481	573697	573913	572401
574885	574021	573265	573805	572509
572617	572725	574561	574237	574345

L14-M6

575749	577369	575533	575857	577477
575641	576289	576829	576073	577153
577693	576181	576397	576613	575101
577585	576721	575965	576505	575209
575317	575425	577261	576937	577045

L14-M7

578449	580069	578233	578557	580177
578341	578989	579529	578773	579853
580393	578881	579097	579313	577801
580285	579421	578665	579205	577909
578017	578125	579961	579637	579745

L14-M8

581149	582769	580933	581257	582877
581041	581689	582229	581473	582553
583093	581581	581797	582013	580501
582985	582121	581365	581905	580609
580717	580825	582661	582337	582445

L14-M9

583849	585469	583633	583957	585577
583741	584389	584929	584173	585253
585793	584281	584497	584713	583201
585685	584821	584065	584605	583309
583417	583525	585361	585037	585145

L14-M10

586549	588169	586333	586657	588277
586441	587089	587629	586873	587953
588493	586981	587197	587413	585901
588385	587521	586765	587305	586009
586117	586225	588061	587737	587845

L14-M11

589249	590869	589033	589357	590977
589141	589789	590329	589573	590653
591193	589681	589897	590113	588601
591085	590221	589465	590005	588709
588817	588925	590761	590437	590545

L14-M12

591949	593569	591733	592057	593677
591841	592489	593029	592273	593353
593893	592381	592597	592813	591301
593785	592921	592165	592705	591409
591517	591625	593461	593137	593245

L14-M13

594649	596269	594433	594757	596377
594541	595189	595729	594973	596053
596593	595081	595297	595513	594001
596485	595621	594865	595405	594109
594217	594325	596161	595837	595945

L14-M14

597349	598969	597133	597457	599077
597241	597889	598429	597673	598753
599293	597781	597997	598213	596701
599185	598321	597565	598105	596809
596917	597025	598861	598537	598645

L14-M15

600049	601669	599833	600157	601777
599941	600589	601129	600373	601453
601993	600481	600697	600913	599401
601885	601021	600265	600805	599509
599617	599725	601561	601237	601345

L14-M16

602749	604369	602533	602857	604477
602641	603289	603829	603073	604153
604693	603181	603397	603613	602101
604585	603721	602965	603505	602209
602317	602425	604261	603937	604045

L15-M1

605449	607069	605233	605557	607177
605341	605989	606529	605773	606853
607393	605881	606097	606313	604801
607285	606421	605665	606205	604909
605017	605125	606961	606637	606745

L15-M2

608149	609769	607933	608257	609877
608041	608689	609229	608473	609553
610093	608581	608797	609013	607501
609985	609121	608365	608905	607609
607717	607825	609661	609337	609445

L15-M3

610849	612469	610633	610957	612577
610741	611389	611929	611173	612253
612793	611281	611497	611713	610201
612685	611821	611065	611605	610309
610417	610525	612361	612037	612145

L15-M4

613549	615169	613333	613657	615277
613441	614089	614629	613873	614953
615493	613981	614197	614413	612901
615385	614521	613765	614305	613009
613117	613225	615061	614737	614845

L15-M5

616249	617869	616033	616357	617977
616141	616789	617329	616573	617653
618193	616681	616897	617113	615601
618085	617221	616465	617005	615709
615817	615925	617761	617437	617545

L15-M6

618949	620569	618733	619057	620677
618841	619489	620029	619273	620353
620893	619381	619597	619813	618301
620785	619921	619165	619705	618409
618517	618625	620461	620137	620245

L15-M7

621649	623269	621433	621757	623377
621541	622189	622729	621973	623053
623593	622081	622297	622513	621001
623485	622621	621865	622405	621109
621217	621325	623161	622837	622945

L15-M8

624349	625969	624133	624457	626077
624241	624889	625429	624673	625753
626293	624781	624997	625213	623701
626185	625321	624565	625105	623809
623917	624025	625861	625537	625645

L15-M9

627049	628669	626833	627157	628777
626941	627589	628129	627373	628453
628993	627481	627697	627913	626401
628885	628021	627265	627805	626509
626617	626725	628561	628237	628345

L15-M10

629749	631369	629533	629857	631477
629641	630289	630829	630073	631153
631693	630181	630397	630613	629101
631585	630721	629965	630505	629209
629317	629425	631261	630937	631045

L15-M11

632449	634069	632233	632557	634177
632341	632989	633529	632773	633853
634393	632881	633097	633313	631801
634285	633421	632665	633205	631909
632017	632125	633961	633637	633745

L16-M4

656749	658369	656533	656857	658477
656641	657289	657829	657073	658153
658693	657181	657397	657613	656101
658585	657721	656965	657505	656209
656317	656425	658261	657937	658045

L15-M12

635149	636769	634933	635257	636877
635041	635689	636229	635473	636553
637093	635581	635797	636013	634501
636985	636121	635365	635905	634609
634717	634825	636661	636337	636445

L16-M5

659449	661069	659233	659557	661177
659341	659989	660529	659773	660853
661393	659881	660097	660313	658801
661285	660421	659665	660205	658909
659017	659125	660961	660637	660745

L15-M13

637849	639469	637633	637957	639577
637741	638389	638929	638173	639253
639793	638281	638497	638713	637201
639685	638821	638065	638605	637309
637417	637525	639361	639037	639145

L16-M6

662149	663769	661933	662257	663877
662041	662689	663229	662473	663553
664093	662581	662797	663013	661501
663985	663121	662365	662905	661609
661717	661825	663661	663337	663445

L15-M14

640549	642169	640333	640657	642277
640441	641089	641629	640873	641953
642493	640981	641197	641413	639901
642385	641521	640765	641305	640009
640117	640225	642061	641737	641845

L16-M7

664849	666469	664633	664957	666577
664741	665389	665929	665173	666253
666793	665281	665497	665713	664201
666685	665821	665065	665605	664309
664417	664525	666361	666037	666145

L15-M15

643249	644869	643033	643357	644977
643141	643789	644329	643573	644653
645193	643681	643897	644113	642601
645085	644221	643465	644005	642709
642817	642925	644761	644437	644545

L16-M8

667549	669169	667333	667657	669277
667441	668089	668629	667873	668953
669493	667981	668197	668413	666901
669385	668521	667765	668305	667009
667117	667225	669061	668737	668845

L15-M16

645949	647569	645733	646057	647677
645841	646489	647029	646273	647353
647893	646381	646597	646813	645301
647785	646921	646165	646705	645409
645517	645625	647461	647137	647245

L16-M9

670249	671869	670033	670357	671977
670141	670789	671329	670573	671653
672193	670681	670897	671113	669601
672085	671221	670465	671005	669709
669817	669925	671761	671437	671545

L16-M1

648649	650269	648433	648757	650377
648541	649189	649729	648973	650053
650593	649081	649297	649513	648001
650485	649621	648865	649405	648109
648217	648325	650161	649837	649945

L16-M10

672949	674569	672733	673057	674677
672841	673489	674029	673273	674353
674893	673381	673597	673813	672301
674785	673921	673165	673705	672409
672517	672625	674461	674137	674245

L16-M2

651349	652969	651133	651457	653077
651241	651889	652429	651673	652753
653293	651781	651997	652213	650701
653185	652321	651565	652105	650809
650917	651025	652861	652537	652645

L16-M11

675649	677269	675433	675757	677377
675541	676189	676729	675973	677053
677593	676081	676297	676513	675001
677485	676621	675865	676405	675109
675217	675325	677161	676837	676945

L16-M3

654049	655669	653833	654157	655777
653941	654589	655129	654373	655453
655993	654481	654697	654913	653401
655885	655021	654265	654805	653509
653617	653725	655561	655237	655345

L16-M12

678349	679969	678133	678457	680077
678241	678889	679429	678673	679753
680293	678781	678997	679213	677701
680185	679321	678565	679105	677809
677917	678025	679861	679537	679645

L16-M13

681049	682669	680833	681157	682777
680941	681589	682129	681373	682453
682993	681481	681697	681913	680401
682885	682021	681265	681805	680509
680617	680725	682561	682237	682345

L16-M14

683749	685369	683533	683857	685477
683641	684289	684829	684073	685153
685693	684181	684397	684613	683101
685585	684721	683965	684505	683209
683317	683425	685261	684937	685045

L16-M15

686449	688069	686233	686557	688177
686341	686989	687529	686773	687853
688393	686881	687097	687313	685801
688285	687421	686665	687205	685909
686017	686125	687961	687637	687745

L16M16

689149	690769	688933	689257	690877
689041	689689	690229	689473	690553
691093	689581	689797	690013	688501
690985	690121	689365	689905	688609
688717	688825	690661	690337	690445

L17-M1

691849	693469	691633	691957	693577
691741	692389	692929	692173	693253
693793	692281	692497	692713	691201
693685	692821	692065	692605	691309
691417	691525	693361	693037	693145

L17-M2

694549	696169	694333	694657	696277
694441	695089	695629	694873	695953
696493	694981	695197	695413	693901
696385	695521	694765	695305	694009
694117	694225	696061	695737	695845

L17-M3

697249	698869	697033	697357	698977
697141	697789	698329	697573	698653
699193	697681	697897	698113	696601
699085	698221	697465	698005	696709
696817	696925	698761	698437	698545

L17-M4

699949	701569	699733	700057	701677
699841	700489	701029	700273	701353
701893	700381	700597	700813	699301
701785	700921	700165	700705	699409
699517	699625	701461	701137	701245

L17-M5

702649	704269	702433	702757	704377
702541	703189	703729	702973	704053
704593	703081	703297	703513	702001
704485	703621	702865	703405	702109
702217	702325	704161	703837	703945

L17-M6

705349	706969	705133	705457	707077
705241	705889	706429	705673	706753
707293	705781	705997	706213	704701
707185	706321	705565	706105	704809
704917	705025	706861	706537	706645

L17-M7

708049	709669	707833	708157	709777
707941	708589	709129	708373	709453
709993	708481	708697	708913	707401
709885	709021	708265	708805	707509
707617	707725	709561	709237	709345

L17-M8

710749	712369	710533	710857	712477
710641	711289	711829	711073	712153
712693	711181	711397	711613	710101
712585	711721	710965	711505	710209
710317	710425	712261	711937	712045

L17-M9

713449	715069	713233	713557	715177
713341	713989	714529	713773	714853
715393	713881	714097	714313	712801
715285	714421	713665	714205	712909
713017	713125	714961	714637	714745

L17-M10

716149	717769	715933	716257	717877
716041	716689	717229	716473	717553
718093	716581	716797	717013	715501
717985	717121	716365	716905	715609
715717	715825	717661	717337	717445

L17-M11

718849	720469	718633	718957	720577
718741	719389	719929	719173	720253
720793	719281	719497	719713	718201
720685	719821	719065	719605	718309
718417	718525	720361	720037	720145

L17-M12

721549	723169	721333	721657	723277
721441	722089	722629	721873	722953
723493	721981	722197	722413	720901
723385	722521	721765	722305	721009
721117	721225	723061	722737	722845

L17-M13

724249	725869	724033	724357	725977
724141	724789	725329	724573	725653
726193	724681	724897	725113	723601
726085	725221	724465	725005	723709
723817	723925	725761	725437	725545

L17-M14

726949	728569	726733	727057	728677
726841	727489	728029	727273	728353
728893	727381	727597	727813	726301
728785	727921	727165	727705	726409
726517	726625	728461	728137	728245

L17-M15

729649	731269	729433	729757	731377
729541	730189	730729	729973	731053
731593	730081	730297	730513	729001
731485	730621	729865	730405	729109
729217	729325	731161	730837	730945

L18-M8

753949	755569	753733	754057	755677
753841	754489	755029	754273	755353
755893	754381	754597	754813	753301
755785	754921	754165	754705	753409
753517	753625	755461	755137	755245

L17-M16

732349	733969	732133	732457	734077
732241	732889	733429	732673	733753
734293	732781	732997	733213	731701
734185	733321	732565	733105	731809
731917	732025	733861	733537	733645

L18-M9

756649	758269	756433	756757	758377
756541	757189	757729	756973	758053
758593	757081	757297	757513	756001
758485	757621	756865	757405	756109
756217	756325	758161	757837	757945

L18-M1

735049	736669	734833	735157	736777
734941	735589	736129	735373	736453
736993	735481	735697	735913	734401
736885	736021	735265	735805	734509
734617	734725	736561	736237	736345

L18-M10

759349	760969	759133	759457	761077
759241	759889	760429	759673	760753
761293	759781	759997	760213	758701
761185	760321	759565	760105	758809
758917	759025	760861	760537	760645

L18-M2

737749	739369	737533	737857	739477
737641	738289	738829	738073	739153
739693	738181	738397	738613	737101
739585	738721	737965	738505	737209
737317	737425	739261	738937	739045

L18-M11

762049	763669	761833	762157	763777
761941	762589	763129	762373	763453
763993	762481	762697	762913	761401
763885	763021	762265	762805	761509
761617	761725	763561	763237	763345

L18-M3

740449	742069	740233	740557	742177
740341	740989	741529	740773	741853
742393	740881	741097	741313	739801
742285	741421	740665	741205	739909
740017	740125	741961	741637	741745

L18-M12

764749	766369	764533	764857	766477
764641	765289	765829	765073	766153
766693	765181	765397	765613	764101
766585	765721	764965	765505	764209
764317	764425	766261	765937	766045

L18-M4

743149	744769	742933	743257	744877
743041	743689	744229	743473	744553
745093	743581	743797	744013	742501
744985	744121	743365	743905	742609
742717	742825	744661	744337	744445

L18-M13

767449	769069	767233	767557	769177
767341	767989	768529	767773	768853
769393	767881	768097	768313	766801
769285	768421	767665	768205	766909
767017	767125	768961	768637	768745

L18-M5

745849	747469	745633	745957	747577
745741	746389	746929	746173	747253
747793	746281	746497	746713	745201
747685	746821	746065	746605	745309
745417	745525	747361	747037	747145

L18-M14

770149	771769	769933	770257	771877
770041	770689	771229	770473	771553
772093	770581	770797	771013	769501
771985	771121	770365	770905	769609
769717	769825	771661	771337	771445

L18-M6

748549	750169	748333	748657	750277
748441	749089	749629	748873	749953
750493	748981	749197	749413	747901
750385	749521	748765	749305	748009
748117	748225	750061	749737	749845

L18-M15

772849	774469	772633	772957	774577
772741	773389	773929	773173	774253
774793	773281	773497	773713	772201
774685	773821	773065	773605	772309
772417	772525	774361	774037	774145

L18-M7

751249	752869	751033	751357	752977
751141	751789	752329	751573	752653
753193	751681	751897	752113	750601
753085	752221	751465	752005	750709
750817	750925	752761	752437	752545

L18-M16

775549	777169	775333	775657	777277
775441	776089	776629	775873	776953
777493	775981	776197	776413	774901
777385	776521	775765	776305	775009
775117	775225	777061	776737	776845

L19-M1

778249	779869	778033	778357	779977
778141	778789	779329	778573	779653
780193	778681	778897	779113	777601
780085	779221	778465	779005	777709
777817	777925	779761	779437	779545

L19-M10

802549	804169	802333	802657	804277
802441	803089	803629	802873	803953
804493	802981	803197	803413	801901
804385	803521	802765	803305	802009
802117	802225	804061	803737	803845

L19-M2

780949	782569	780733	781057	782677
780841	781489	782029	781273	782353
782893	781381	781597	781813	780301
782785	781921	781165	781705	780409
780517	780625	782461	782137	782245

L19-M11

805249	806869	805033	805357	806977
805141	805789	806329	805573	806653
807193	805681	805897	806113	804601
807085	806221	805465	806005	804709
804817	804925	806761	806437	806545

L19-M3

783649	785269	783433	783757	785377
783541	784189	784729	783973	785053
785593	784081	784297	784513	783001
785485	784621	783865	784405	783109
783217	783325	785161	784837	784945

L19-M12

807949	809569	807733	808057	809677
807841	808489	809029	808273	809353
809893	808381	808597	808813	807301
809785	808921	808165	808705	807409
807517	807625	809461	809137	809245

L19-M4

786349	787969	786133	786457	788077
786241	786889	787429	786673	787753
788293	786781	786997	787213	785701
788185	787321	786565	787105	785809
785917	786025	787861	787537	787645

L19-M13

810649	812269	810433	810757	812377
810541	811189	811729	810973	812053
812593	811081	811297	811513	810001
812485	811621	810865	811405	810109
810217	810325	812161	811837	811945

L19-M5

789049	790669	788833	789157	790777
788941	789589	790129	789373	790453
790993	789481	789697	789913	788401
790885	790021	789265	789805	788509
788617	788725	790561	790237	790345

L19-M14

813349	814969	813133	813457	815077
813241	813889	814429	813673	814753
815293	813781	813997	814213	812701
815185	814321	813565	814105	812809
812917	813025	814861	814537	814645

L19-M6

791749	793369	791533	791857	793477
791641	792289	792829	792073	793153
793693	792181	792397	792613	791101
793585	792721	791965	792505	791209
791317	791425	793261	792937	793045

L19-M15

816049	817669	815833	816157	817777
815941	816589	817129	816373	817453
817993	816481	816697	816913	815401
817885	817021	816265	816805	815509
815617	815725	817561	817237	817345

L19-M7

794449	796069	794233	794557	796177
794341	794989	795529	794773	795853
796393	794881	795097	795313	793801
796285	795421	794665	795205	793909
794017	794125	795961	795637	795745

L19-M16

818749	820369	818533	818857	820477
818641	819289	819829	819073	820153
820693	819181	819397	819613	818101
820585	819721	818965	819505	818209
818317	818425	820261	819937	820045

L19-M8

797149	798769	796933	797257	798877
797041	797689	798229	797473	798553
799093	797581	797797	798013	796501
798985	798121	797365	797905	796609
796717	796825	798661	798337	798445

L20-M1

821449	823069	821233	821557	823177
821341	821989	822529	821773	822853
823393	821881	822097	822313	820801
823285	822421	821665	822205	820909
821017	821125	822961	822637	822745

L19-M9

799849	801469	799633	799957	801577
799741	800389	800929	800173	801253
801793	800281	800497	800713	799201
801685	800821	800065	800605	799309
799417	799525	801361	801037	801145

L20-M2

824149	825769	823933	824257	825877
824041	824689	825229	824473	825553
826093	824581	824797	825013	823501
825985	825121	824365	824905	823609
823717	823825	825661	825337	825445

L20-M3

826849	828469	826633	826957	828577
826741	827389	827929	827173	828253
828793	827281	827497	827713	826201
828685	827821	827065	827605	826309
826417	826525	828361	828037	828145

L20-M4

829549	831169	829333	829657	831277
829441	830089	830629	829873	830953
831493	829981	830197	830413	828901
831385	830521	829765	830305	829009
829117	829225	831061	830737	830845

L20-M5

832249	833869	832033	832357	833977
832141	832789	833329	832573	833653
834193	832681	832897	833113	831601
834085	833221	832465	833005	831709
831817	831925	833761	833437	833545

L20-M6

834949	836569	834733	835057	836677
834841	835489	836029	835273	836353
836893	835381	835597	835813	834301
836785	835921	835165	835705	834409
834517	834625	836461	836137	836245

L20-M7

837649	839269	837433	837757	839377
837541	838189	838729	837973	839053
839593	838081	838297	838513	837001
839485	838621	837865	838405	837109
837217	837325	839161	838837	838945

L20-M8

840349	841969	840133	840457	842077
840241	840889	841429	840673	841753
842293	840781	840997	841213	839701
842185	841321	840565	841105	839809
839917	840025	841861	841537	841645

L20-M9

843049	844669	842833	843157	844777
842941	843589	844129	843373	844453
844993	843481	843697	843913	842401
844885	844021	843265	843805	842509
842617	842725	844561	844237	844345

L20-M10

845749	847369	845533	845857	847477
845641	846289	846829	846073	847153
847693	846181	846397	846613	845101
847585	846721	845965	846505	845209
845317	845425	847261	846937	847045

L20-M11

848449	850069	848233	848557	850177
848341	848989	849529	848773	849853
850393	848881	849097	849313	847801
850285	849421	848665	849205	847909
848017	848125	849961	849637	849745

L20-M12

851149	852769	850933	851257	852877
851041	851689	852229	851473	852553
853093	851581	851797	852013	850501
852985	852121	851365	851905	850609
850717	850825	852661	852337	852445

L20-M13

853849	855469	853633	853957	855577
853741	854389	854929	854173	855253
855793	854281	854497	854713	853201
855685	854821	854065	854605	853309
853417	853525	855361	855037	855145

L20-M14

856549	858169	856333	856657	858277
856441	857089	857629	856873	857953
858493	856981	857197	857413	855901
858385	857521	856765	857305	856009
856117	856225	858061	857737	857845

L20-M15

859249	860869	859033	859357	860977
859141	859789	860329	859573	860653
861193	859681	859897	860113	858601
861085	860221	859465	860005	858709
858817	858925	860761	860437	860545

L20-M16

861949	863569	861733	862057	863677
861841	862489	863029	862273	863353
863893	862381	862597	862813	861301
863785	862921	862165	862705	861409
861517	861625	863461	863137	863245

L21-M1

864649	866269	864433	864757	866377
864541	865189	865729	864973	866053
866593	865081	865297	865513	864001
866485	865621	864865	865405	864109
864217	864325	866161	865837	865945

L21-M2

867349	868969	867133	867457	869077
867241	867889	868429	867673	868753
869293	867781	867997	868213	866701
869185	868321	867565	868105	866809
866917	867025	868861	868537	868645

L21-M3

870049	871669	869833	870157	871777
869941	870589	871129	870373	871453
871993	870481	870697	870913	869401
871885	871021	870265	870805	869509
869617	869725	871561	871237	871345

L21-M4

872749	874369	872533	872857	874477
872641	873289	873829	873073	874153
874693	873181	873397	873613	872101
874585	873721	872965	873505	872209
872317	872425	874261	873937	874045

L21-M5

875449	877069	875233	875557	877177
875341	875989	876529	875773	876853
877393	875881	876097	876313	874801
877285	876421	875665	876205	874909
875017	875125	876961	876637	876745

L21-M6

878149	879769	877933	878257	879877
878041	878689	879229	878473	879553
880093	878581	878797	879013	877501
879985	879121	878365	878905	877609
877717	877825	879661	879337	879445

L21-M7

880849	882469	880633	880957	882577
880741	881389	881929	881173	882253
882793	881281	881497	881713	880201
882685	881821	881065	881605	880309
880417	880525	882361	882037	882145

L21-M8

883549	885169	883333	883657	885277
883441	884089	884629	883873	884953
885493	883981	884197	884413	882901
885385	884521	883765	884305	883009
883117	883225	885061	884737	884845

L21-M9

886249	887869	886033	886357	887977
886141	886789	887329	886573	887653
888193	886681	886897	887113	885601
888085	887221	886465	887005	885709
885817	885925	887761	887437	887545

L21-M10

888949	890569	888733	889057	890677
888841	889489	890029	889273	890353
890893	889381	889597	889813	888301
890785	889921	889165	889705	888409
888517	888625	890461	890137	890245

L21-M11

891649	893269	891433	891757	893377
891541	892189	892729	891973	893053
893593	892081	892297	892513	891001
893485	892621	891865	892405	891109
891217	891325	893161	892837	892945

L21-M12

894349	895969	894133	894457	896077
894241	894889	895429	894673	895753
896293	894781	894997	895213	893701
896185	895321	894565	895105	893809
893917	894025	895861	895537	895645

L21-M13

897049	898669	896833	897157	898777
896941	897589	898129	897373	898453
898993	897481	897697	897913	896401
898885	898021	897265	897805	896509
896617	896725	898561	898237	898345

L21-M14

899749	901369	899533	899857	901477
899641	900289	900829	900073	901153
901693	900181	900397	900613	899101
901585	900721	899965	900505	899209
899317	899425	901261	900937	901045

L21-M15

902449	904069	902233	902557	904177
902341	902989	903529	902773	903853
904393	902881	903097	903313	901801
904285	903421	902665	903205	901909
902017	902125	903961	903637	903745

L21-M16

905149	906769	904933	905257	906877
905041	905689	906229	905473	906553
907093	905581	905797	906013	904501
906985	906121	905365	905905	904609
904717	904825	906661	906337	906445

L22-M1

907849	909469	907633	907957	909577
907741	908389	908929	908173	909253
909793	908281	908497	908713	907201
909685	908821	908065	908605	907309
907417	907525	909361	909037	909145

L22-M2

910549	912169	910333	910657	912277
910441	911089	911629	910873	911953
912493	910981	911197	911413	909901
912385	911521	910765	911305	910009
910117	910225	912061	911737	911845

L22-M3

913249	914869	913033	913357	914977
913141	913789	914329	913573	914653
915193	913681	913897	914113	912601
915085	914221	913465	914005	912709
912817	912925	914761	914437	914545

L22-M4

915949	917569	915733	916057	917677
915841	916489	917029	916273	917353
917893	916381	916597	916813	915301
917785	916921	916165	916705	915409
915517	915625	917461	917137	917245

L22-M5

918649	920269	918433	918757	920377
918541	919189	919729	918973	920053
920593	919081	919297	919513	918001
920485	919621	918865	919405	918109
918217	918325	920161	919837	919945

L22-M6

921349	922969	921133	921457	923077
921241	921889	922429	921673	922753
923293	921781	921997	922213	920701
923185	922321	921565	922105	920809
920917	921025	922861	922537	922645

L22-M7

924049	925669	923833	924157	925777
923941	924589	925129	924373	925453
925993	924481	924697	924913	923401
925885	925021	924265	924805	923509
923617	923725	925561	925237	925345

L22-M8

926749	928369	926533	926857	928477
926641	927289	927829	927073	928153
928693	927181	927397	927613	926101
928585	927721	926965	927505	926209
926317	926425	928261	927937	928045

L22-M9

929449	931069	929233	929557	931177
929341	929989	930529	929773	930853
931393	929881	930097	930313	928801
931285	930421	929665	930205	928909
929017	929125	930961	930637	930745

L22-M10

932149	933769	931933	932257	933877
932041	932689	933229	932473	933553
934093	932581	932797	933013	931501
933985	933121	932365	932905	931609
931717	931825	933661	933337	933445

L22-M11

934849	936469	934633	934957	936577
934741	935389	935929	935173	936253
936793	935281	935497	935713	934201
936685	935821	935065	935605	934309
934417	934525	936361	936037	936145

L22-M12

937549	939169	937333	937657	939277
937441	938089	938629	937873	938953
939493	937981	938197	938413	936901
939385	938521	937765	938305	937009
937117	937225	939061	938737	938845

L22-M13

940249	941869	940033	940357	941977
940141	940789	941329	940573	941653
942193	940681	940897	941113	939601
942085	941221	940465	941005	939709
939817	939925	941761	941437	941545

L22-M14

942949	944569	942733	943057	944677
942841	943489	944029	943273	944353
944893	943381	943597	943813	942301
944785	943921	943165	943705	942409
942517	942625	944461	944137	944245

L22-M15

945649	947269	945433	945757	947377
945541	946189	946729	945973	947053
947593	946081	946297	946513	945001
947485	946621	945865	946405	945109
945217	945325	947161	946837	946945

L22-M16

948349	949969	948133	948457	950077
948241	948889	949429	948673	949753
950293	948781	948997	949213	947701
950185	949321	948565	949105	947809
947917	948025	949861	949537	949645

L23-M1

951049	952669	950833	951157	952777
950941	951589	952129	951373	952453
952993	951481	951697	951913	950401
952885	952021	951265	951805	950509
950617	950725	952561	952237	952345

L23-M2

953749	955369	953533	953857	955477
953641	954289	954829	954073	955153
955693	954181	954397	954613	953101
955585	954721	953965	954505	953209
953317	953425	955261	954937	955045

L23-M3

956449	958069	956233	956557	958177
956341	956989	957529	956773	957853
958393	956881	957097	957313	955801
958285	957421	956665	957205	955909
956017	956125	957961	957637	957745

L23-M4

959149	960769	958933	959257	960877
959041	959689	960229	959473	960553
961093	959581	959797	960013	958501
960985	960121	959365	959905	958609
958717	958825	960661	960337	960445

L23-M5

961849	963469	961633	961957	963577
961741	962389	962929	962173	963253
963793	962281	962497	962713	961201
963685	962821	962065	962605	961309
961417	961525	963361	963037	963145

L23-M6

964549	966169	964333	964657	966277
964441	965089	965629	964873	965953
966493	964981	965197	965413	963901
966385	965521	964765	965305	964009
964117	964225	966061	965737	965845

L23-M7

967249	968869	967033	967357	968977
967141	967789	968329	967573	968653
969193	967681	967897	968113	966601
969085	968221	967465	968005	966709
966817	966925	968761	968437	968545

L23-M8

969949	971569	969733	970057	971677
969841	970489	971029	970273	971353
971893	970381	970597	970813	969301
971785	970921	970165	970705	969409
969517	969625	971461	971137	971245

L23-M9

972649	974269	972433	972757	974377
972541	973189	973729	972973	974053
974593	973081	973297	973513	972001
974485	973621	972865	973405	972109
972217	972325	974161	973837	973945

L23-M10

975349	976969	975133	975457	977077
975241	975889	976429	975673	976753
977293	975781	975997	976213	974701
977185	976321	975565	976105	974809
974917	975025	976861	976537	976645

L23-M11

978049	979669	977833	978157	979777
977941	978589	979129	978373	979453
979993	978481	978697	978913	977401
979885	979021	978265	978805	977509
977617	977725	979561	979237	979345

L23-M12

980749	982369	980533	980857	982477
980641	981289	981829	981073	982153
982693	981181	981397	981613	980101
982585	981721	980965	981505	980209
980317	980425	982261	981937	982045

L23-M13

983449	985069	983233	983557	985177
983341	983989	984529	983773	984853
985393	983881	984097	984313	982801
985285	984421	983665	984205	982909
983017	983125	984961	984637	984745

L23-M14

986149	987769	985933	986257	987877
986041	986689	987229	986473	987553
988093	986581	986797	987013	985501
987985	987121	986365	986905	985609
985717	985825	987661	987337	987445

L23-M15

988849	990469	988633	988957	990577
988741	989389	989929	989173	990253
990793	989281	989497	989713	988201
990685	989821	989065	989605	988309
988417	988525	990361	990037	990145

L23-M16

991549	993169	991333	991657	993277
991441	992089	992629	991873	992953
993493	991981	992197	992413	990901
993385	992521	991765	992305	991009
991117	991225	993061	992737	992845

L24-M1

994249	995869	994033	994357	995977
994141	994789	995329	994573	995653
996193	994681	994897	995113	993601
996085	995221	994465	995005	993709
993817	993925	995761	995437	995545

L24-M2

996949	998569	996733	997057	998677
996841	997489	998029	997273	998353
998893	997381	997597	997813	996301
998785	997921	997165	997705	996409
996517	996625	998461	998137	998245

L24-M3

999649	1001269	999433	999757	1001377
999541	1000189	1000729	999973	1001053
1001593	1000081	1000297	1000513	999001
1001485	1000621	999865	1000405	999109
999217	999325	1001161	1000837	1000945

L24-M4

1002349	1003969	1002133	1002457	1004077
1002241	1002889	1003429	1002673	1003753
1004293	1002781	1002997	1003213	1001701
1004185	1003321	1002565	1003105	1001809
1001917	1002025	1003861	1003537	1003645

L24-M5

1005049	1006669	1004833	1005157	1006777
1004941	1005589	1006129	1005373	1006453
1006993	1005481	1005697	1005913	1004401
1006885	1006021	1005265	1005805	1004509
1004617	1004725	1006561	1006237	1006345

L24-M6

1007749	1009369	1007533	1007857	1009477
1007641	1008289	1008829	1008073	1009153
1009693	1008181	1008397	1008613	1007101
1009585	1008721	1007965	1008505	1007209
1007317	1007425	1009261	1008937	1009045

L24-M7

1010449	1012069	1010233	1010557	1012177
1010341	1010989	1011529	1010773	1011853
1012393	1010881	1011097	1011313	1009801
1012285	1011421	1010665	1011205	1009909
1010017	1010125	1011961	1011637	1011745

L24-M8

1013149	1014769	1012933	1013257	1014877
1013041	1013689	1014229	1013473	1014553
1015093	1013581	1013797	1014013	1012501
1014985	1014121	1013365	1013905	1012609
1012717	1012825	1014661	1014337	1014445

L24-M9

1015849	1017469	1015633	1015957	1017577
1015741	1016389	1016929	1016173	1017253
1017793	1016281	1016497	1016713	1015201
1017685	1016821	1016065	1016605	1015309
1015417	1015525	1017361	1017037	1017145

L24-M10

1018549	1020169	1018333	1018657	1020277
1018441	1019089	1019629	1018873	1019953
1020493	1018981	1019197	1019413	1017901
1020385	1019521	1018765	1019305	1018009
1018117	1018225	1020061	1019737	1019845

L24-M11

1021249	1022869	1021033	1021357	1022977
1021141	1021789	1022329	1021573	1022653
1023193	1021681	1021897	1022113	1020601
1023085	1022221	1021465	1022005	1020709
1020817	1020925	1022761	1022437	1022545

L24-M12

1023949	1025569	1023733	1024057	1025677
1023841	1024489	1025029	1024273	1025353
1025893	1024381	1024597	1024813	1023301
1025785	1024921	1024165	1024705	1023409
1023517	1023625	1025461	1025137	1025245

L24-M13

1026649	1028269	1026433	1026757	1028377
1026541	1027189	1027729	1026973	1028053
1028593	1027081	1027297	1027513	1026001
1028485	1027621	1026865	1027405	1026109
1026217	1026325	1028161	1027837	1027945

L24-M14

1029349	1030969	1029133	1029457	1031077
1029241	1029889	1030429	1029673	1030753
1031293	1029781	1029997	1030213	1028701
1031185	1030321	1029565	1030105	1028809
1028917	1029025	1030861	1030537	1030645

L24-M15

1032049	1033669	1031833	1032157	1033777
1031941	1032589	1033129	1032373	1033453
1033993	1032481	1032697	1032913	1031401
1033885	1033021	1032265	1032805	1031509
1031617	1031725	1033561	1033237	1033345

L24-M16

1034749	1036369	1034533	1034857	1036477
1034641	1035289	1035829	1035073	1036153
1036693	1035181	1035397	1035613	1034101
1036585	1035721	1034965	1035505	1034209
1034317	1034425	1036261	1035937	1036045

L25-M1

1037449	1039069	1037233	1037557	1039177
1037341	1037989	1038529	1037773	1038853
1039393	1037881	1038097	1038313	1036801
1039285	1038421	1037665	1038205	1036909
1037017	1037125	1038961	1038637	1038745

L25-M2

1040149	1041769	1039933	1040257	1041877
1040041	1040689	1041229	1040473	1041553
1042093	1040581	1040797	1041013	1039501
1041985	1041121	1040365	1040905	1039609
1039717	1039825	1041661	1041337	1041445

L25-M3

1042849	1044469	1042633	1042957	1044577
1042741	1043389	1043929	1043173	1044253
1044793	1043281	1043497	1043713	1042201
1044685	1043821	1043065	1043605	1042309
1042417	1042525	1044361	1044037	1044145

L25-M4

1045549	1047169	1045333	1045657	1047277
1045441	1046089	1046629	1045873	1046953
1047493	1045981	1046197	1046413	1044901
1047385	1046521	1045765	1046305	1045009
1045117	1045225	1047061	1046737	1046845

L25-M5

1048249	1049869	1048033	1048357	1049977
1048141	1048789	1049329	1048573	1049653
1050193	1048681	1048897	1049113	1047601
1050085	1049221	1048465	1049005	1047709
1047817	1047925	1049761	1049437	1049545

L25-M6

1050949	1052569	1050733	1051057	1052677
1050841	1051489	1052029	1051273	1052353
1052893	1051381	1051597	1051813	1050301
1052785	1051921	1051165	1051705	1050409
1050517	1050625	1052461	1052137	1052245

L25-M7

1053649	1055269	1053433	1053757	1055377
1053541	1054189	1054729	1053973	1055053
1055593	1054081	1054297	1054513	1053001
1055485	1054621	1053865	1054405	1053109
1053217	1053325	1055161	1054837	1054945

L25-M8

1056349	1057969	1056133	1056457	1058077
1056241	1056889	1057429	1056673	1057753
1058293	1056781	1056997	1057213	1055701
1058185	1057321	1056565	1057105	1055809
1055917	1056025	1057861	1057537	1057645

L25-M9

1059049	1060669	1058833	1059157	1060777
1058941	1059589	1060129	1059373	1060453
1060993	1059481	1059697	1059913	1058401
1060885	1060021	1059265	1059805	1058509
1058617	1058725	1060561	1060237	1060345

L25-M10

1061749	1063369	1061533	1061857	1063477
1061641	1062289	1062829	1062073	1063153
1063693	1062181	1062397	1062613	1061101
1063585	1062721	1061965	1062505	1061209
1061317	1061425	1063261	1062937	1063045

L25-M11

1064449	1066069	1064233	1064557	1066177
1064341	1064989	1065529	1064773	1065853
1066393	1064881	1065097	1065313	1063801
1066285	1065421	1064665	1065205	1063909
1064017	1064125	1065961	1065637	1065745

L25-M12

1067149	1068769	1066933	1067257	1068877
1067041	1067689	1068229	1067473	1068553
1069093	1067581	1067797	1068013	1066501
1068985	1068121	1067365	1067905	1066609
1066717	1066825	1068661	1068337	1068445

L25-M13

1069849	1071469	1069633	1069957	1071577
1069741	1070389	1070929	1070173	1071253
1071793	1070281	1070497	1070713	1069201
1071685	1070821	1070065	1070605	1069309
1069417	1069525	1071361	1071037	1071145

L25-M14

1072549	1074169	1072333	1072657	1074277
1072441	1073089	1073629	1072873	1073953
1074493	1072981	1073197	1073413	1071901
1074385	1073521	1072765	1073305	1072009
1072117	1072225	1074061	1073737	1073845

L25-M15

1075249	1076869	1075033	1075357	1076977
1075141	1075789	1076329	1075573	1076653
1077193	1075681	1075897	1076113	1074601
1077085	1076221	1075465	1076005	1074709
1074817	1074925	1076761	1076437	1076545

L25-M16

1077949	1079569	1077733	1078057	1079677
1077841	1078489	1079029	1078273	1079353
1079893	1078381	1078597	1078813	1077301
1079785	1078921	1078165	1078705	1077409
1077517	1077625	1079461	1079137	1079245

GEBURAH

L1-M1

3109	10879	2073	3627	11397
2591	5699	8289	4663	9843
12433	5181	6217	7253	1
11915	7771	4145	6735	519
1037	1555	10361	8807	9325

L1-M2

16059	23829	15023	16577	24347
15541	18649	21239	17613	22793
25383	18131	19167	20203	12951
24865	20721	17095	19685	13469
13987	14505	23311	21757	22275

L1-M3

29009	36779	27973	29527	37297
28491	31599	34189	30563	35743
38333	31081	32117	33153	25901
37815	33671	30045	32635	26419
26937	27455	36261	34707	35225

L1-M4

41959	49729	40923	42477	50247
41441	44549	47139	43513	48693
51283	44031	45067	46103	38851
50765	46621	42995	45585	39369
39887	40405	49211	47657	48175

L1-M5

54909	62679	53873	55427	63197
54391	57499	60089	56463	61643
64233	56981	58017	59053	51801
63715	59571	55945	58535	52319
52837	53355	62161	60607	61125

L1-M6

67859	75629	66823	68377	76147
67341	70449	73039	69413	74593
77183	69931	70967	72003	64751
76665	72521	68895	71485	65269
65787	66305	75111	73557	74075

L1-M7

80809	88579	79773	81327	89097
80291	83399	85989	82363	87543
90133	82881	83917	84953	77701
89615	85471	81845	84435	78219
78737	79255	88061	86507	87025

L1-M8

93759	101529	92723	94277	102047
93241	96349	98939	95313	100493
103083	95831	96867	97903	90651
102565	98421	94795	97385	91169
91687	92205	101011	99457	99975

L1-M9

106709	114479	105673	107227	114997
106191	109299	111889	108263	113443
116033	108781	109817	110853	103601
115515	111371	107745	110335	104119
104637	105155	113961	112407	112925

L1-M10

119659	127429	118623	120177	127947
119141	122249	124839	121213	126393
128983	121731	122767	123803	116551
128465	124321	120695	123285	117069
117587	118105	126911	125357	125875

L1-M11

132609	140379	131573	133127	140897
132091	135199	137789	134163	139343
141933	134681	135717	136753	129501
141415	137271	133645	136235	130019
130537	131055	139861	138307	138825

L1-M12

145559	153329	144523	146077	153847
145041	148149	150739	147113	152293
154883	147631	148667	149703	142451
154365	150221	146595	149185	142969
143487	144005	152811	151257	151775

L1-M13

158509	166279	157473	159027	166797
157991	161099	163689	160063	165243
167833	160581	161617	162653	155401
167315	163171	159545	162135	155919
156437	156955	165761	164207	164725

L1-M14

171459	179229	170423	171977	179747
170941	174049	176639	173013	178193
180783	173531	174567	175603	168351
180265	176121	172495	175085	168869
169387	169905	178711	177157	177675

L1-M15

184409	192179	183373	184927	192697
183891	186999	189589	185963	191143
193733	186481	187517	188553	181301
193215	189071	185445	188035	181819
182337	182855	191661	190107	190625

L1-M16

197359	205129	196323	197877	205647
196841	199949	202539	198913	204093
206683	199431	200467	201503	194251
206165	202021	198395	200985	194769
195287	195805	204611	203057	203575

L2-M1

210309	218079	209273	210827	218597
209791	212899	215489	211863	217043
219633	212381	213417	214453	207201
219115	214971	211345	213935	207719
208237	208755	217561	216007	216525

L2-M2

223259	231029	222223	223777	231547
222741	225849	228439	224813	229993
232583	225331	226367	227403	220151
232065	227921	224295	226885	220669
221187	221705	230511	228957	229475

L2-M3

236209	243979	235173	236727	244497
235691	238799	241389	237763	242943
245533	238281	239317	240353	233101
245015	240871	237245	239835	233619
234137	234655	243461	241907	242425

L2-M4

249159	256929	248123	249677	257447
248641	251749	254339	250713	255893
258483	251231	252267	253303	246051
257965	253821	250195	252785	246569
247087	247605	256411	254857	255375

L2-M5

262109	269879	261073	262627	270397
261591	264699	267289	263663	268843
271433	264181	265217	266253	259001
270915	266771	263145	265735	259519
260037	260555	269361	267807	268325

L2-M6

275059	282829	274023	275577	283347
274541	277649	280239	276613	281793
284383	277131	278167	279203	271951
283865	279721	276095	278685	272469
272987	273505	282311	280757	281275

L2-M7

288009	295779	286973	288527	296297
287491	290599	293189	289563	294743
297333	290081	291117	292153	284901
296815	292671	289045	291635	285419
285937	286455	295261	293707	294225

L2-M8

300959	308729	299923	301477	309247
300441	303549	306139	302513	307693
310283	303031	304067	305103	297851
309765	305621	301995	304585	298369
298887	299405	308211	306657	307175

L2-M9

313909	321679	312873	314427	322197
313391	316499	319089	315463	320643
323233	315981	317017	318053	310801
322715	318571	314945	317535	311319
311837	312355	321161	319607	320125

L2-M10

326859	334629	325823	327377	335147
326341	329449	332039	328413	333593
336183	328931	329967	331003	323751
335665	331521	327895	330485	324269
324787	325305	334111	332557	333075

L2-M11

339809	347579	338773	340327	348097
339291	342399	344989	341363	346543
349133	341881	342917	343953	336701
348615	344471	340845	343435	337219
337737	338255	347061	345507	346025

L2-M12

352759	360529	351723	353277	361047
352241	355349	357939	354313	359493
362083	354831	355867	356903	349651
361565	357421	353795	356385	350169
350687	351205	360011	358457	358975

L2-M13

365709	373479	364673	366227	373997
365191	368299	370889	367263	372443
375033	367781	368817	369853	362601
374515	370371	366745	369335	363119
363637	364155	372961	371407	371925

L2-M14

378659	386429	377623	379177	386947
378141	381249	383839	380213	385393
387983	380731	381767	382803	375551
387465	383321	379695	382285	376069
376587	377105	385911	384357	384875

L2-M15

391609	399379	390573	392127	399897
391091	394199	396789	393163	398343
400933	393681	394717	395753	388501
400415	396271	392645	395235	389019
389537	390055	398861	397307	397825

L2-M16

404559	412329	403523	405077	412847
404041	407149	409739	406113	411293
413883	406631	407667	408703	401451
413365	409221	405595	408185	401969
402487	403005	411811	410257	410775

L3-M1

417509	425279	416473	418027	425797
416991	420099	422689	419063	424243
426833	419581	420617	421653	414401
426315	422171	418545	421135	414919
415437	415955	424761	423207	423725

L3-M2

430459	438229	429423	430977	438747
429941	433049	435639	432013	437193
439783	432531	433567	434603	427351
439265	435121	431495	434085	427869
428387	428905	437711	436157	436675

L3-M3

443409	451179	442373	443927	451697
442891	445999	448589	444963	450143
452733	445481	446517	447553	440301
452215	448071	444445	447035	440819
441337	441855	450661	449107	449625

L3-M4

456359	464129	455323	456877	464647
455841	458949	461539	457913	463093
465683	458431	459467	460503	453251
465165	461021	457395	459985	453769
454287	454805	463611	462057	462575

L3-M5

469309	477079	468273	469827	477597
468791	471899	474489	470863	476043
478633	471381	472417	473453	466201
478115	473971	470345	472935	466719
467237	467755	476561	475007	475525

L3-M14

585859	593629	584823	586377	594147
585341	588449	591039	587413	592593
595183	587931	588967	590003	582751
594665	590521	586895	589485	583269
583787	584305	593111	591557	592075

L3-M6

482259	490029	481223	482777	490547
481741	484849	487439	483813	488993
491583	484331	485367	486403	479151
491065	486921	483295	485885	479669
480187	480705	489511	487957	488475

L3-M15

598809	606579	597773	599327	607097
598291	601399	603989	600363	605543
608133	600881	601917	602953	595701
607615	603471	599845	602435	596219
596737	597255	606061	604507	605025

L3-M7

495209	502979	494173	495727	503497
494691	497799	500389	496763	501943
504533	497281	498317	499353	492101
504015	499871	496245	498835	492619
493137	493655	502461	500907	501425

L3-M16

611759	619529	610723	612277	620047
611241	614349	616939	613313	618493
621083	613831	614867	615903	608651
620565	616421	612795	615385	609169
609687	610205	619011	617457	617975

L3-M8

508159	515929	507123	508677	516447
507641	510749	513339	509713	514893
517483	510231	511267	512303	505051
516965	512821	509195	511785	505569
506087	506605	515411	513857	514375

L4-M1

624709	632479	623673	625227	632997
624191	627299	629889	626263	631443
634033	626781	627817	628853	621601
633515	629371	625745	628335	622119
622637	623155	631961	630407	630925

L3-M9

521109	528879	520073	521627	529397
520591	523699	526289	522663	527843
530433	523181	524217	525253	518001
529915	525771	522145	524735	518519
519037	519555	528361	526807	527325

L4-M2

637659	645429	636623	638177	645947
637141	640249	642839	639213	644393
646983	639731	640767	641803	634551
646465	642321	638695	641285	635069
635587	636105	644911	643357	643875

L3-M10

534059	541829	533023	534577	542347
533541	536649	539239	535613	540793
543383	536131	537167	538203	530951
542865	538721	535095	537685	531469
531987	532505	541311	539757	540275

L4-M3

650609	658379	649573	651127	658897
650091	653199	655789	652163	657343
659933	652681	653717	654753	647501
659415	655271	651645	654235	648019
648537	649055	657861	656307	656825

L3-M11

547009	554779	545973	547527	555297
546491	549599	552189	548563	553743
556333	549081	550117	551153	543901
555815	551671	548045	550635	544419
544937	545455	554261	552707	553225

L4-M4

663559	671329	662523	664077	671847
663041	666149	668739	665113	670293
672883	665631	666667	667703	660451
672365	668221	664595	667185	660969
661487	662005	670811	669257	669775

L3-M12

559959	567729	558923	560477	568247
559441	562549	565139	561513	566693
569283	562031	563067	564103	556851
568765	564621	560995	563585	557369
557887	558405	567211	565657	566175

L4-M5

676509	684279	675473	677027	684797
675991	679099	681689	678063	683243
685833	678581	679617	680653	673401
685315	681171	677545	680135	673919
674437	674955	683761	682207	682725

L3-M13

572909	580679	571873	573427	581197
572391	575499	578089	574463	579643
582233	574981	576017	577053	569801
581715	577571	573945	576535	570319
570837	571355	580161	578607	579125

L4-M6

689459	697229	688423	689977	697747
688941	692049	694639	691013	696193
698783	691531	692567	693603	686351
698265	694121	690495	693085	686869
687387	687905	696711	695157	695675

L4-M7

702409	710179	701373	702927	710697
701891	704999	707589	703963	709143
711733	704481	705517	706553	699301
711215	707071	703445	706035	699819
700337	700855	709661	708107	708625

L4-M8

715359	723129	714323	715877	723647
714841	717949	720539	716913	722093
724683	717431	718467	719503	712251
724165	720021	716395	718985	712769
713287	713805	722611	721057	721575

L4-M9

728309	736079	727273	728827	736597
727791	730899	733489	729863	735043
737633	730381	731417	732453	725201
737115	732971	729345	731935	725719
726237	726755	735561	734007	734525

L4-M10

741259	749029	740223	741777	749547
740741	743849	746439	742813	747993
750583	743331	744367	745403	738151
750065	745921	742295	744885	738669
739187	739705	748511	746957	747475

L4-M11

754209	761979	753173	754727	762497
753691	756799	759389	755763	760943
763533	756281	757317	758353	751101
763015	758871	755245	757835	751619
752137	752655	761461	759907	760425

L4-M12

767159	774929	766123	767677	775447
766641	769749	772339	768713	773893
776483	769231	770267	771303	764051
775965	771821	768195	770785	764569
765087	765605	774411	772857	773375

L4-M13

780109	787879	779073	780627	788397
779591	782699	785289	781663	786843
789433	782181	783217	784253	777001
788915	784771	781145	783735	777519
778037	778555	787361	785807	786325

L4-M14

793059	800829	792023	793577	801347
792541	795649	798239	794613	799793
802383	795131	796167	797203	789951
801865	797721	794095	796685	790469
790987	791505	800311	798757	799275

L4-M15

806009	813779	804973	806527	814297
805491	808599	811189	807563	812743
815333	808081	809117	810153	802901
814815	810671	807045	809635	803419
803937	804455	813261	811707	812225

L4-M16

818959	826729	817923	819477	827247
818441	821549	824139	820513	825693
828283	821031	822067	823103	815851
827765	823621	819995	822585	816369
816887	817405	826211	824657	825175

L5-M1

831909	839679	830873	832427	840197
831391	834499	837089	833463	838643
841233	833981	835017	836053	828801
840715	836571	832945	835535	829319
829837	830355	839161	837607	838125

L5-M2

844859	852629	843823	845377	853147
844341	847449	850039	846413	851593
854183	846931	847967	849003	841751
853665	849521	845895	848485	842269
842787	843305	852111	850557	851075

L5-M3

857809	865579	856773	858327	866097
857291	860399	862989	859363	864543
867133	859881	860917	861953	854701
866615	862471	858845	861435	855219
855737	856255	865061	863507	864025

L5-M4

870759	878529	869723	871277	879047
870241	873349	875939	872313	877493
880083	872831	873867	874903	867651
879565	875421	871795	874385	868169
868687	869205	878011	876457	876975

L5-M5

883709	891479	882673	884227	891997
883191	886299	888889	885263	890443
893033	885781	886817	887853	880601
892515	888371	884745	887335	881119
881637	882155	890961	889407	889925

L5-M6

896659	904429	895623	897177	904947
896141	899249	901839	898213	903393
905983	898731	899767	900803	893551
905465	901321	897695	900285	894069
894587	895105	903911	902357	902875

L5-M7

909609	917379	908573	910127	917897
909091	912199	914789	911163	916343
918933	911681	912717	913753	906501
918415	914271	910645	913235	907019
907537	908055	916861	915307	915825

L5-M8

922559	930329	921523	923077	930847
922041	925149	927739	924113	929293
931883	924631	925667	926703	919451
931365	927221	923595	926185	919969
920487	921005	929811	928257	928775

L5-M9

935509	943279	934473	936027	943797
934991	938099	940689	937063	942243
944833	937581	938617	939653	932401
944315	940171	936545	939135	932919
933437	933955	942761	941207	941725

L5-M10

948459	956229	947423	948977	956747
947941	951049	953639	950013	955193
957783	950531	951567	952603	945351
957265	953121	949495	952085	945869
946387	946905	955711	954157	954675

L5-M11

961409	969179	960373	961927	969697
960891	963999	966589	962963	968143
970733	963481	964517	965553	958301
970215	966071	962445	965035	958819
959337	959855	968661	967107	967625

L5-M12

974359	982129	973323	974877	982647
973841	976949	979539	975913	981093
983683	976431	977467	978503	971251
983165	979021	975395	977985	971769
972287	972805	981611	980057	980575

L5-M13

987309	995079	986273	987827	995597
986791	989899	992489	988863	994043
996633	989381	990417	991453	984201
996115	991971	988345	990935	984719
985237	985755	994561	993007	993525

L5-M14

1000259	1008029	999223	1000777	1008547
999741	1002849	1005439	1001813	1006993
1009583	1002331	1003367	1004403	997151
1009065	1004921	1001295	1003885	997669
998187	998705	1007511	1005957	1006475

L5-M15

1013209	1020979	1012173	1013727	1021497
1012691	1015799	1018389	1014763	1019943
1022533	1015281	1016317	1017353	1010101
1022015	1017871	1014245	1016835	1010619
1011137	1011655	1020461	1018907	1019425

L5-M16

1026159	1033929	1025123	1026677	1034447
1025641	1028749	1031339	1027713	1032893
1035483	1028231	1029267	1030303	1023051
1034965	1030821	1027195	1029785	1023569
1024087	1024605	1033411	1031857	1032375

L6-M1

1039109	1046879	1038073	1039627	1047397
1038591	1041699	1044289	1040663	1045843
1048433	1041181	1042217	1043253	1036001
1047915	1043771	1040145	1042735	1036519
1037037	1037555	1046361	1044807	1045325

L6-M2

1052059	1059829	1051023	1052577	1060347
1051541	1054649	1057239	1053613	1058793
1061383	1054131	1055167	1056203	1048951
1060865	1056721	1053095	1055685	1049469
1049987	1050505	1059311	1057757	1058275

L6-M3

1065009	1072779	1063973	1065527	1073297
1064491	1067599	1070189	1066563	1071743
1074333	1067081	1068117	1069153	1061901
1073815	1069671	1066045	1068635	1062419
1062937	1063455	1072261	1070707	1071225

L6-M4

1077959	1085729	1076923	1078477	1086247
1077441	1080549	1083139	1079513	1084693
1087283	1080031	1081067	1082103	1074851
1086765	1082621	1078995	1081585	1075369
1075887	1076405	1085211	1083657	1084175

L6-M5

1090909	1098679	1089873	1091427	1099197
1090391	1093499	1096089	1092463	1097643
1100233	1092981	1094017	1095053	1087801
1099715	1095571	1091945	1094535	1088319
1088837	1089355	1098161	1096607	1097125

L6-M6

1103859	1111629	1102823	1104377	1112147
1103341	1106449	1109039	1105413	1110593
1113183	1105931	1106967	1108003	1100751
1112665	1108521	1104895	1107485	1101269
1101787	1102305	1111111	1109557	1110075

L6-M7

1116809	1124579	1115773	1117327	1125097
1116291	1119399	1121989	1118363	1123543
1126133	1118881	1119917	1120953	1113701
1125615	1121471	1117845	1120435	1114219
1114737	1115255	1124061	1122507	1123025

L6-M8

1129759	1137529	1128723	1130277	1138047
1129241	1132349	1134939	1131313	1136493
1139083	1131831	1132867	1133903	1126651
1138565	1134421	1130795	1133385	1127169
1127687	1128205	1137011	1135457	1135975

L6-M9

1142709	1150479	1141673	1143227	1150997
1142191	1145299	1147889	1144263	1149443
1152033	1144781	1145817	1146853	1139601
1151515	1147371	1143745	1146335	1140119
1140637	1141155	1149961	1148407	1148925

L6-M10

1155659	1163429	1154623	1156177	1163947
1155141	1158249	1160839	1157213	1162393
1164983	1157731	1158767	1159803	1152551
1164465	1160321	1156695	1159285	1153069
1153587	1154105	1162911	1161357	1161875

L6-M11

1168609	1176379	1167573	1169127	1176897
1168091	1171199	1173789	1170163	1175343
1177933	1170681	1171717	1172753	1165501
1177415	1173271	1169645	1172235	1166019
1166537	1167055	1175861	1174307	1174825

L6-M12

1181559	1189329	1180523	1182077	1189847
1181041	1184149	1186739	1183113	1188293
1190883	1183631	1184667	1185703	1178451
1190365	1186221	1182595	1185185	1178969
1179487	1180005	1188811	1187257	1187775

L6-M13

1194509	1202279	1193473	1195027	1202797
1193991	1197099	1199689	1196063	1201243
1203833	1196581	1197617	1198653	1191401
1203315	1199171	1195545	1198135	1191919
1192437	1192955	1201761	1200207	1200725

L6-M14

1207459	1215229	1206423	1207977	1215747
1206941	1210049	1212639	1209013	1214193
1216783	1209531	1210567	1211603	1204351
1216265	1212121	1208495	1211085	1204869
1205387	1205905	1214711	1213157	1213675

L6-M15

1220409	1228179	1219373	1220927	1228697
1219891	1222999	1225589	1221963	1227143
1229733	1222481	1223517	1224553	1217301
1229215	1225071	1221445	1224035	1217819
1218337	1218855	1227661	1226107	1226625

L6-M16

1233359	1241129	1232323	1233877	1241647
1232841	1235949	1238539	1234913	1240093
1242683	1235431	1236467	1237503	1230251
1242165	1238021	1234395	1236985	1230769
1231287	1231805	1240611	1239057	1239575

L7-M1

1246309	1254079	1245273	1246827	1254597
1245791	1248899	1251489	1247863	1253043
1255633	1248381	1249417	1250453	1243201
1255115	1250971	1247345	1249935	1243719
1244237	1244755	1253561	1252007	1252525

L7-M2

1259259	1267029	1258223	1259777	1267547
1258741	1261849	1264439	1260813	1265993
1268583	1261331	1262367	1263403	1256151
1268065	1263921	1260295	1262885	1256669
1257187	1257705	1266511	1264957	1265475

L7-M3

1272209	1279979	1271173	1272727	1280497
1271691	1274799	1277389	1273763	1278943
1281533	1274281	1275317	1276353	1269101
1281015	1276871	1273245	1275835	1269619
1270137	1270655	1279461	1277907	1278425

L7-M4

1285159	1292929	1284123	1285677	1293447
1284641	1287749	1290339	1286713	1291893
1294483	1287231	1288267	1289303	1282051
1293965	1289821	1286195	1288785	1282569
1283087	1283605	1292411	1290857	1291375

L7-M5

1298109	1305879	1297073	1298627	1306397
1297591	1300699	1303289	1299663	1304843
1307433	1300181	1301217	1302253	1295001
1306915	1302771	1299145	1301735	1295519
1296037	1296555	1305361	1303807	1304325

L7-M6

1311059	1318829	1310023	1311577	1319347
1310541	1313649	1316239	1312613	1317793
1320383	1313131	1314167	1315203	1307951
1319865	1315721	1312095	1314685	1308469
1308987	1309505	1318311	1316757	1317275

L7-M7

1324009	1331779	1322973	1324527	1332297
1323491	1326599	1329189	1325563	1330743
1333333	1326081	1327117	1328153	1320901
1332815	1328671	1325045	1327635	1321419
1321937	1322455	1331261	1329707	1330225

L7-M8

1336959	1344729	1335923	1337477	1345247
1336441	1339549	1342139	1338513	1343693
1346283	1339031	1340067	1341103	1333851
1345765	1341621	1337995	1340585	1334369
1334887	1335405	1344211	1342657	1343175

L7-M9

1349909	1357679	1348873	1350427	1358197
1349391	1352499	1355089	1351463	1356643
1359233	1351981	1353017	1354053	1346801
1358715	1354571	1350945	1353535	1347319
1347837	1348355	1357161	1355607	1356125

L7-M10

1362859	1370629	1361823	1363377	1371147
1362341	1365449	1368039	1364413	1369593
1372183	1364931	1365967	1367003	1359751
1371665	1367521	1363895	1366485	1360269
1360787	1361305	1370111	1368557	1369075

L7-M11

1375809	1383579	1374773	1376327	1384097
1375291	1378399	1380989	1377363	1382543
1385133	1377881	1378917	1379953	1372701
1384615	1380471	1376845	1379435	1373219
1373737	1374255	1383061	1381507	1382025

L7-M12

1388759	1396529	1387723	1389277	1397047
1388241	1391349	1393939	1390313	1395493
1398083	1390831	1391867	1392903	1385651
1397565	1393421	1389795	1392385	1386169
1386687	1387205	1396011	1394457	1394975

L7-M13

1401709	1409479	1400673	1402227	1409997
1401191	1404299	1406889	1403263	1408443
1411033	1403781	1404817	1405853	1398601
1410515	1406371	1402745	1405335	1399119
1399637	1400155	1408961	1407407	1407925

L7-M14

1414659	1422429	1413623	1415177	1422947
1414141	1417249	1419839	1416213	1421393
1423983	1416731	1417767	1418803	1411551
1423465	1419321	1415695	1418285	1412069
1412587	1413105	1421911	1420357	1420875

L7-M15

1427609	1435379	1426573	1428127	1435897
1427091	1430199	1432789	1429163	1434343
1436933	1429681	1430717	1431753	1424501
1436415	1432271	1428645	1431235	1425019
1425537	1426055	1434861	1433307	1433825

L7-M16

1440559	1448329	1439523	1441077	1448847
1440041	1443149	1445739	1442113	1447293
1449883	1442631	1443667	1444703	1437451
1449365	1445221	1441595	1444185	1437969
1438487	1439005	1447811	1446257	1446775

L8M1

1453509	1461279	1452473	1454027	1461797
1452991	1456099	1458689	1455063	1460243
1462833	1455581	1456617	1457653	1450401
1462315	1458171	1454545	1457135	1450919
1451437	1451955	1460761	1459207	1459725

L8-M2

1466459	1474229	1465423	1466977	1474747
1465941	1469049	1471639	1468013	1473193
1475783	1468531	1469567	1470603	1463351
1475265	1471121	1467495	1470085	1463869
1464387	1464905	1473711	1472157	1472675

L8-M3

1479409	1487179	1478373	1479927	1487697
1478891	1481999	1484589	1480963	1486143
1488733	1481481	1482517	1483553	1476301
1488215	1484071	1480445	1483035	1476819
1477337	1477855	1486661	1485107	1485625

L8-M4

1492359	1500129	1491323	1492877	1500647
1491841	1494949	1497539	1493913	1499093
1501683	1494431	1495467	1496503	1489251
1501165	1497021	1493395	1495985	1489769
1490287	1490805	1499611	1498057	1498575

L8-M5

1505309	1513079	1504273	1505827	1513597
1504791	1507899	1510489	1506863	1512043
1514633	1507381	1508417	1509453	1502201
1514115	1509971	1506345	1508935	1502719
1503237	1503755	1512561	1511007	1511525

L8-M6

1518259	1526029	1517223	1518777	1526547
1517741	1520849	1523439	1519813	1524993
1527583	1520331	1521367	1522403	1515151
1527065	1522921	1519295	1521885	1515669
1516187	1516705	1525511	1523957	1524475

L8-M7

1531209	1538979	1530173	1531727	1539497
1530691	1533799	1536389	1532763	1537943
1540533	1533281	1534317	1535353	1528101
1540015	1535871	1532245	1534835	1528619
1529137	1529655	1538461	1536907	1537425

L8-M8

1544159	1551929	1543123	1544677	1552447
1543641	1546749	1549339	1545713	1550893
1553483	1546231	1547267	1548303	1541051
1552965	1548821	1545195	1547785	1541569
1542087	1542605	1551411	1549857	1550375

L8-M9

1557109	1564879	1556073	1557627	1565397
1556591	1559699	1562289	1558663	1563843
1566433	1559181	1560217	1561253	1554001
1565915	1561771	1558145	1560735	1554519
1555037	1555555	1564361	1562807	1563325

L8-M10

1570059	1577829	1569023	1570577	1578347
1569541	1572649	1575239	1571613	1576793
1579383	1572131	1573167	1574203	1566951
1578865	1574721	1571095	1573685	1567469
1567987	1568505	1577311	1575757	1576275

L8-M11

1583009	1590779	1581973	1583527	1591297
1582491	1585599	1588189	1584563	1589743
1592333	1585081	1586117	1587153	1579901
1591815	1587671	1584045	1586635	1580419
1580937	1581455	1590261	1588707	1589225

L8-M12

1595959	1603729	1594923	1596477	1604247
1595441	1598549	1601139	1597513	1602693
1605283	1598031	1599067	1600103	1592851
1604765	1600621	1596995	1599585	1593369
1593887	1594405	1603211	1601657	1602175

L8-M13

1608909	1616679	1607873	1609427	1617197
1608391	1611499	1614089	1610463	1615643
1618233	1610981	1612017	1613053	1605801
1617715	1613571	1609945	1612535	1606319
1606837	1607355	1616161	1614607	1615125

L8-M14

1621859	1629629	1620823	1622377	1630147
1621341	1624449	1627039	1623413	1628593
1631183	1623931	1624967	1626003	1618751
1630665	1626521	1622895	1625485	1619269
1619787	1620305	1629111	1627557	1628075

L8-M15

1634809	1642579	1633773	1635327	1643097
1634291	1637399	1639989	1636363	1641543
1644133	1636881	1637917	1638953	1631701
1643615	1639471	1635845	1638435	1632219
1632737	1633255	1642061	1640507	1641025

L8-M16

1647759	1655529	1646723	1648277	1656047
1647241	1650349	1652939	1649313	1654493
1657083	1649831	1650867	1651903	1644651
1656565	1652421	1648795	1651385	1645169
1645687	1646205	1655011	1653457	1653975

L9-M1

1660709	1668479	1659673	1661227	1668997
1660191	1663299	1665889	1662263	1667443
1670033	1662781	1663817	1664853	1657601
1669515	1665371	1661745	1664335	1658119
1658637	1659155	1667961	1666407	1666925

L9-M2

1673659	1681429	1672623	1674177	1681947
1673141	1676249	1678839	1675213	1680393
1682983	1675731	1676767	1677803	1670551
1682465	1678321	1674695	1677285	1671069
1671587	1672105	1680911	1679357	1679875

L9-M3

1686609	1694379	1685573	1687127	1694897
1686091	1689199	1691789	1688163	1693343
1695933	1688681	1689717	1690753	1683501
1695415	1691271	1687645	1690235	1684019
1684537	1685055	1693861	1692307	1692825

L9-M4

1699559	1707329	1698523	1700077	1707847
1699041	1702149	1704739	1701113	1706293
1708883	1701631	1702667	1703703	1696451
1708365	1704221	1700595	1703185	1696969
1697487	1698005	1706811	1705257	1705775

L9-M5

1712509	1720279	1711473	1713027	1720797
1711991	1715099	1717689	1714063	1719243
1721833	1714581	1715617	1716653	1709401
1721315	1717171	1713545	1716135	1709919
1710437	1710955	1719761	1718207	1718725

L9-M6

1725459	1733229	1724423	1725977	1733747
1724941	1728049	1730639	1727013	1732193
1734783	1727531	1728567	1729603	1722351
1734265	1730121	1726495	1729085	1722869
1723387	1723905	1732711	1731157	1731675

L9-M7

1738409	1746179	1737373	1738927	1746697
1737891	1740999	1743589	1739963	1745143
1747733	1740481	1741517	1742553	1735301
1747215	1743071	1739445	1742035	1735819
1736337	1736855	1745661	1744107	1744625

L9-M8

1751359	1759129	1750323	1751877	1759647
1750841	1753949	1756539	1752913	1758093
1760683	1753431	1754467	1755503	1748251
1760165	1756021	1752395	1754985	1748769
1749287	1749805	1758611	1757057	1757575

L9-M9

1764309	1772079	1763273	1764827	1772597
1763791	1766899	1769489	1765863	1771043
1773633	1766381	1767417	1768453	1761201
1773115	1768971	1765345	1767935	1761719
1762237	1762755	1771561	1770007	1770525

L9-M10

1777259	1785029	1776223	1777777	1785547
1776741	1779849	1782439	1778813	1783993
1786583	1779331	1780367	1781403	1774151
1786065	1781921	1778295	1780885	1774669
1775187	1775705	1784511	1782957	1783475

L9-M11

1790209	1797979	1789173	1790727	1798497
1789691	1792799	1795389	1791763	1796943
1799533	1792281	1793317	1794353	1787101
1799015	1794871	1791245	1793835	1787619
1788137	1788655	1797461	1795907	1796425

L9-M12

1803159	1810929	1802123	1803677	1811447
1802641	1805749	1808339	1804713	1809893
1812483	1805231	1806267	1807303	1800051
1811965	1807821	1804195	1806785	1800569
1801087	1801605	1810411	1808857	1809375

L9-M13

1816109	1823879	1815073	1816627	1824397
1815591	1818699	1821289	1817663	1822843
1825433	1818181	1819217	1820253	1813001
1824915	1820771	1817145	1819735	1813519
1814037	1814555	1823361	1821807	1822325

L9-M14

1829059	1836829	1828023	1829577	1837347
1828541	1831649	1834239	1830613	1835793
1838383	1831131	1832167	1833203	1825951
1837865	1833721	1830095	1832685	1826469
1826987	1827505	1836311	1834757	1835275

L9-M15

1842009	1849779	1840973	1842527	1850297
1841491	1844599	1847189	1843563	1848743
1851333	1844081	1845117	1846153	1838901
1850815	1846671	1843045	1845635	1839419
1839937	1840455	1849261	1847707	1848225

L9-M16

1854959	1862729	1853923	1855477	1863247
1854441	1857549	1860139	1856513	1861693
1864283	1857031	1858067	1859103	1851851
1863765	1859621	1855995	1858585	1852369
1852887	1853405	1862211	1860657	1861175

L10-M1

1867909	1875679	1866873	1868427	1876197
1867391	1870499	1873089	1869463	1874643
1877233	1869981	1871017	1872053	1864801
1876715	1872571	1868945	1871535	1865319
1865837	1866355	1875161	1873607	1874125

L10-M10

1984459	1992229	1983423	1984977	1992747
1983941	1987049	1989639	1986013	1991193
1993783	1986531	1987567	1988603	1981351
1993265	1989121	1985495	1988085	1981869
1982387	1982905	1991711	1990157	1990675

L10-M2

1880859	1888629	1879823	1881377	1889147
1880341	1883449	1886039	1882413	1887593
1890183	1882931	1883967	1885003	1877751
1889665	1885521	1881895	1884485	1878269
1878787	1879305	1888111	1886557	1887075

L10-M11

1997409	2005179	1996373	1997927	2005697
1996891	1999999	2002589	1998963	2004143
2006733	1999481	2000517	2001553	1994301
2006215	2002071	1998445	2001035	1994819
1995337	1995855	2004661	2003107	2003625

L10-M3

1893809	1901579	1892773	1894327	1902097
1893291	1896399	1898989	1895363	1900543
1903133	1895881	1896917	1897953	1890701
1902615	1898471	1894845	1897435	1891219
1891737	1892255	1901061	1899507	1900025

L10-M12

2010359	2018129	2009323	2010877	2018647
2009841	2012949	2015539	2011913	2017093
2019683	2012431	2013467	2014503	2007251
2019165	2015021	2011395	2013985	2007769
2008287	2008805	2017611	2016057	2016575

L10-M4

1906759	1914529	1905723	1907277	1915047
1906241	1909349	1911939	1908313	1913493
1916083	1908831	1909867	1910903	1903651
1915565	1911421	1907795	1910385	1904169
1904687	1905205	1914011	1912457	1912975

L10-M13

2023309	2031079	2022273	2023827	2031597
2022791	2025899	2028489	2024863	2030043
2032633	2025381	2026417	2027453	2020201
2032115	2027971	2024345	2026935	2020719
2021237	2021755	2030561	2029007	2029525

L10-M5

1919709	1927479	1918673	1920227	1927997
1919191	1922299	1924889	1921263	1926443
1929033	1921781	1922817	1923853	1916601
1928515	1924371	1920745	1923335	1917119
1917637	1918155	1926961	1925407	1925925

L10-M14

2036259	2044029	2035223	2036777	2044547
2035741	2038849	2041439	2037813	2042993
2045583	2038331	2039367	2040403	2033151
2045065	2040921	2037295	2039885	2033669
2034187	2034705	2043511	2041957	2042475

L10-M6

1932659	1940429	1931623	1933177	1940947
1932141	1935249	1937839	1934213	1939393
1941983	1934731	1935767	1936803	1929551
1941465	1937321	1933695	1936285	1930069
1930587	1931105	1939911	1938357	1938875

L10-M15

2049209	2056979	2048173	2049727	2057497
2048691	2051799	2054389	2050763	2055943
2058533	2051281	2052317	2053353	2046101
2058015	2053871	2050245	2052835	2046619
2047137	2047655	2056461	2054907	2055425

L10-M7

1945609	1953379	1944573	1946127	1953897
1945091	1948199	1950789	1947163	1952343
1954933	1947681	1948717	1949753	1942501
1954415	1950271	1946645	1949235	1943019
1943537	1944055	1952861	1951307	1951825

L10-M16

2062159	2069929	2061123	2062677	2070447
2061641	2064749	2067339	2063713	2068893
2071483	2064231	2065267	2066303	2059051
2070965	2066821	2063195	2065785	2059569
2060087	2060605	2069411	2067857	2068375

L10-M8

1958559	1966329	1957523	1959077	1966847
1958041	1961149	1963739	1960113	1965293
1967883	1960631	1961667	1962703	1955451
1967365	1963221	1959595	1962185	1955969
1956487	1957005	1965811	1964257	1964775

L11-M1

2075109	2082879	2074073	2075627	2083397
2074591	2077699	2080289	2076663	2081843
2084433	2077181	2078217	2079253	2072001
2083915	2079771	2076145	2078735	2072519
2073037	2073555	2082361	2080807	2081325

L10-M9

1971509	1979279	1970473	1972027	1979797
1970991	1974099	1976689	1973063	1978243
1980833	1973581	1974617	1975653	1968401
1980315	1976171	1972545	1975135	1968919
1969437	1969955	1978761	1977207	1977725

L11-M2

2088059	2095829	2087023	2088577	2096347
2087541	2090649	2093239	2089613	2094793
2097383	2090131	2091167	2092203	2084951
2096865	2092721	2089095	2091685	2085469
2085987	2086505	2095311	2093757	2094275

L11-M3

2101009	2108779	2099973	2101527	2109297
2100491	2103599	2106189	2102563	2107743
2110333	2103081	2104117	2105153	2097901
2109815	2105671	2102045	2104635	2098419
2098937	2099455	2108261	2106707	2107225

L11-M4

2113959	2121729	2112923	2114477	2122247
2113441	2116549	2119139	2115513	2120693
2123283	2116031	2117067	2118103	2110851
2122765	2118621	2114995	2117585	2111369
2111887	2112405	2121211	2119657	2120175

L11-M5

2126909	2134679	2125873	2127427	2135197
2126391	2129499	2132089	2128463	2133643
2136233	2128981	2130017	2131053	2123801
2135715	2131571	2127945	2130535	2124319
2124837	2125355	2134161	2132607	2133125

L11-M6

2139859	2147629	2138823	2140377	2148147
2139341	2142449	2145039	2141413	2146593
2149183	2141931	2142967	2144003	2136751
2148665	2144521	2140895	2143485	2137269
2137787	2138305	2147111	2145557	2146075

L11-M7

2152809	2160579	2151773	2153327	2161097
2152291	2155399	2157989	2154363	2159543
2162133	2154881	2155917	2156953	2149701
2161615	2157471	2153845	2156435	2150219
2150737	2151255	2160061	2158507	2159025

L11-M8

2165759	2173529	2164723	2166277	2174047
2165241	2168349	2170939	2167313	2172493
2175083	2167831	2168867	2169903	2162651
2174565	2170421	2166795	2169385	2163169
2163687	2164205	2173011	2171457	2171975

L11-M9

2178709	2186479	2177673	2179227	2186997
2178191	2181299	2183889	2180263	2185443
2188033	2180781	2181817	2182853	2175601
2187515	2183371	2179745	2182335	2176119
2176637	2177155	2185961	2184407	2184925

L11-M10

2191659	2199429	2190623	2192177	2199947
2191141	2194249	2196839	2193213	2198393
2200983	2193731	2194767	2195803	2188551
2200465	2196321	2192695	2195285	2189069
2189587	2190105	2198911	2197357	2197875

L11-M11

2204609	2212379	2203573	2205127	2212897
2204091	2207199	2209789	2206163	2211343
2213933	2206681	2207717	2208753	2201501
2213415	2209271	2205645	2208235	2202019
2202537	2203055	2211861	2210307	2210825

L11-M12

2217559	2225329	2216523	2218077	2225847
2217041	2220149	2222739	2219113	2224293
2226883	2219631	2220667	2221703	2214451
2226365	2222221	2218595	2221185	2214969
2215487	2216005	2224811	2223257	2223775

L11-M13

2230509	2238279	2229473	2231027	2238797
2229991	2233099	2235689	2232063	2237243
2239833	2232581	2233617	2234653	2227401
2239315	2235171	2231545	2234135	2227919
2228437	2228955	2237761	2236207	2236725

L11-M14

2243459	2251229	2242423	2243977	2251747
2242941	2246049	2248639	2245013	2250193
2252783	2245531	2246567	2247603	2240351
2252265	2248121	2244495	2247085	2240869
2241387	2241905	2250711	2249157	2249675

L11-M15

2256409	2264179	2255373	2256927	2264697
2255891	2258999	2261589	2257963	2263143
2265733	2258481	2259517	2260553	2253301
2265215	2261071	2257445	2260035	2253819
2254337	2254855	2263661	2262107	2262625

L11-M16

2269359	2277129	2268323	2269877	2277647
2268841	2271949	2274539	2270913	2276093
2278683	2271431	2272467	2273503	2266251
2278165	2274021	2270395	2272985	2266769
2267287	2267805	2276611	2275057	2275575

L12-M1

2282309	2290079	2281273	2282827	2290597
2281791	2284899	2287489	2283863	2289043
2291633	2284381	2285417	2286453	2279201
2291115	2286971	2283345	2285935	2279719
2280237	2280755	2289561	2288007	2288525

L12-M2

2295259	2303029	2294223	2295777	2303547
2294741	2297849	2300439	2296813	2301993
2304583	2297331	2298367	2299403	2292151
2304065	2299921	2296295	2298885	2292669
2293187	2293705	2302511	2300957	2301475

L12-M3

2308209	2315979	2307173	2308727	2316497
2307691	2310799	2313389	2309763	2314943
2317533	2310281	2311317	2312353	2305101
2317015	2312871	2309245	2311835	2305619
2306137	2306655	2315461	2313907	2314425

L12-M4

2321159	2328929	2320123	2321677	2329447
2320641	2323749	2326339	2322713	2327893
2330483	2323231	2324267	2325303	2318051
2329965	2325821	2322195	2324785	2318569
2319087	2319605	2328411	2326857	2327375

L12-M5

2334109	2341879	2333073	2334627	2342397
2333591	2336699	2339289	2335663	2340843
2343433	2336181	2337217	2338253	2331001
2342915	2338771	2335145	2337735	2331519
2332037	2332555	2341361	2339807	2340325

L12-M14

2450659	2458429	2449623	2451177	2458947
2450141	2453249	2455839	2452213	2457393
2459983	2452731	2453767	2454803	2447551
2459465	2455321	2451695	2454285	2448069
2448587	2449105	2457911	2456357	2456875

L12-M6

2347059	2354829	2346023	2347577	2355347
2346541	2349649	2352239	2348613	2353793
2356383	2349131	2350167	2351203	2343951
2355865	2351721	2348095	2350685	2344469
2344987	2345505	2354311	2352757	2353275

L12-M15

2463609	2471379	2462573	2464127	2471897
2463091	2466199	2468789	2465163	2470343
2472933	2465681	2466717	2467753	2460501
2472415	2468271	2464645	2467235	2461019
2461537	2462055	2470861	2469307	2469825

L12-M7

2360009	2367779	2358973	2360527	2368297
2359491	2362599	2365189	2361563	2366743
2369333	2362081	2363117	2364153	2356901
2368815	2364671	2361045	2363635	2357419
2357937	2358455	2367261	2365707	2366225

L12-M16

2476559	2484329	2475523	2477077	2484847
2476041	2479149	2481739	2478113	2483293
2485883	2478631	2479667	2480703	2473451
2485365	2481221	2477595	2480185	2473969
2474487	2475005	2483811	2482257	2482775

L12-M8

2372959	2380729	2371923	2373477	2381247
2372441	2375549	2378139	2374513	2379693
2382283	2375031	2376067	2377103	2369851
2381765	2377621	2373995	2376585	2370369
2370887	2371405	2380211	2378657	2379175

L13-M1

2489509	2497279	2488473	2490027	2497797
2488991	2492099	2494689	2491063	2496243
2498833	2491581	2492617	2493653	2486401
2498315	2494171	2490545	2493135	2486919
2487437	2487955	2496761	2495207	2495725

L12-M9

2385909	2393679	2384873	2386427	2394197
2385391	2388499	2391089	2387463	2392643
2395233	2387981	2389017	2390053	2382801
2394715	2390571	2386945	2389535	2383319
2383837	2384355	2393161	2391607	2392125

L13-M2

2502459	2510229	2501423	2502977	2510747
2501941	2505049	2507639	2504013	2509193
2511783	2504531	2505567	2506603	2499351
2511265	2507121	2503495	2506085	2499869
2500387	2500905	2509711	2508157	2508675

L12-M10

2398859	2406629	2397823	2399377	2407147
2398341	2401449	2404039	2400413	2405593
2408183	2400931	2401967	2403003	2395751
2407665	2403521	2399895	2402485	2396269
2396787	2397305	2406111	2404557	2405075

L13-M3

2515409	2523179	2514373	2515927	2523697
2514891	2517999	2520589	2516963	2522143
2524733	2517481	2518517	2519553	2512301
2524215	2520071	2516445	2519035	2512819
2513337	2513855	2522661	2521107	2521625

L12-M11

2411809	2419579	2410773	2412327	2420097
2411291	2414399	2416989	2413363	2418543
2421133	2413881	2414917	2415953	2408701
2420615	2416471	2412845	2415435	2409219
2409737	2410255	2419061	2417507	2418025

L13-M4

2528359	2536129	2527323	2528877	2536647
2527841	2530949	2533539	2529913	2535093
2537683	2530431	2531467	2532503	2525251
2537165	2533021	2529395	2531985	2525769
2526287	2526805	2535611	2534057	2534575

L12-M12

2424759	2432529	2423723	2425277	2433047
2424241	2427349	2429939	2426313	2431493
2434083	2426831	2427867	2428903	2421651
2433565	2429421	2425795	2428385	2422169
2422687	2423205	2432011	2430457	2430975

L13-M5

2541309	2549079	2540273	2541827	2549597
2540791	2543899	2546489	2542863	2548043
2550633	2543381	2544417	2545453	2538201
2550115	2545971	2542345	2544935	2538719
2539237	2539755	2548561	2547007	2547525

L12-M13

2437709	2445479	2436673	2438227	2445997
2437191	2440299	2442889	2439263	2444443
2447033	2439781	2440817	2441853	2434601
2446515	2442371	2438745	2441335	2435119
2435637	2436155	2444961	2443407	2443925

L13-M6

2554259	2562029	2553223	2554777	2562547
2553741	2556849	2559439	2555813	2560993
2563583	2556331	2557367	2558403	2551151
2563065	2558921	2555295	2557885	2551669
2552187	2552705	2561511	2559957	2560475

L13-M7

2567209	2574979	2566173	2567727	2575497
2566691	2569799	2572389	2568763	2573943
2576533	2569281	2570317	2571353	2564101
2576015	2571871	2568245	2570835	2564619
2565137	2565655	2574461	2572907	2573425

L13-M8

2580159	2587929	2579123	2580677	2588447
2579641	2582749	2585339	2581713	2586893
2589483	2582231	2583267	2584303	2577051
2588965	2584821	2581195	2583785	2577569
2578087	2578605	2587411	2585857	2586375

L13-M9

2593109	2600879	2592073	2593627	2601397
2592591	2595699	2598289	2594663	2599843
2602433	2595181	2596217	2597253	2590001
2601915	2597771	2594145	2596735	2590519
2591037	2591555	2600361	2598807	2599325

L13-M10

2606059	2613829	2605023	2606577	2614347
2605541	2608649	2611239	2607613	2612793
2615383	2608131	2609167	2610203	2602951
2614865	2610721	2607095	2609685	2603469
2603987	2604505	2613311	2611757	2612275

L13-M11

2619009	2626779	2617973	2619527	2627297
2618491	2621599	2624189	2620563	2625743
2628333	2621081	2622117	2623153	2615901
2627815	2623671	2620045	2622635	2616419
2616937	2617455	2626261	2624707	2625225

L13-M12

2631959	2639729	2630923	2632477	2640247
2631441	2634549	2637139	2633513	2638693
2641283	2634031	2635067	2636103	2628851
2640765	2636621	2632995	2635585	2629369
2629887	2630405	2639211	2637657	2638175

L13-M13

2644909	2652679	2643873	2645427	2653197
2644391	2647499	2650089	2646463	2651643
2654233	2646981	2648017	2649053	2641801
2653715	2649571	2645945	2648535	2642319
2642837	2643355	2652161	2650607	2651125

L13-M14

2657859	2665629	2656823	2658377	2666147
2657341	2660449	2663039	2659413	2664593
2667183	2659931	2660967	2662003	2654751
2666665	2662521	2658895	2661485	2655269
2655787	2656305	2665111	2663557	2664075

L13-M15

2670809	2678579	2669773	2671327	2679097
2670291	2673399	2675989	2672363	2677543
2680133	2672881	2673917	2674953	2667701
2679615	2675471	2671845	2674435	2668219
2668737	2669255	2678061	2676507	2677025

L13-M16

2683759	2691529	2682723	2684277	2692047
2683241	2686349	2688939	2685313	2690493
2693083	2685831	2686867	2687903	2680651
2692565	2688421	2684795	2687385	2681169
2681687	2682205	2691011	2689457	2689975

L14-M1

2696709	2704479	2695673	2697227	2704997
2696191	2699299	2701889	2698263	2703443
2706033	2698781	2699817	2700853	2693601
2705515	2701371	2697745	2700335	2694119
2694637	2695155	2703961	2702407	2702925

L14-M2

2709659	2717429	2708623	2710177	2717947
2709141	2712249	2714839	2711213	2716393
2718983	2711731	2712767	2713803	2706551
2718465	2714321	2710695	2713285	2707069
2707587	2708105	2716911	2715357	2715875

L14-M3

2722609	2730379	2721573	2723127	2730897
2722091	2725199	2727789	2724163	2729343
2731933	2724681	2725717	2726753	2719501
2731415	2727271	2723645	2726235	2720019
2720537	2721055	2729861	2728307	2728825

L14-M4

2735559	2743329	2734523	2736077	2743847
2735041	2738149	2740739	2737113	2742293
2744883	2737631	2738667	2739703	2732451
2744365	2740221	2736595	2739185	2732969
2733487	2734005	2742811	2741257	2741775

L14-M5

2748509	2756279	2747473	2749027	2756797
2747991	2751099	2753689	2750063	2755243
2757833	2750581	2751617	2752653	2745401
2757315	2753171	2749545	2752135	2745919
2746437	2746955	2755761	2754207	2754725

L14-M6

2761459	2769229	2760423	2761977	2769747
2760941	2764049	2766639	2763013	2768193
2770783	2763531	2764567	2765603	2758351
2770265	2766121	2762495	2765085	2758869
2759387	2759905	2768711	2767157	2767675

L14-M7

2774409	2782179	2773373	2774927	2782697
2773891	2776999	2779589	2775963	2781143
2783733	2776481	2777517	2778553	2771301
2783215	2779071	2775445	2778035	2771819
2772337	2772855	2781661	2780107	2780625

L14-M8

2787359	2795129	2786323	2787877	2795647
2786841	2789949	2792539	2788913	2794093
2796683	2789431	2790467	2791503	2784251
2796165	2792021	2788395	2790985	2784769
2785287	2785805	2794611	2793057	2793575

L14-M9

2800309	2808079	2799273	2800827	2808597
2799791	2802899	2805489	2801863	2807043
2809633	2802381	2803417	2804453	2797201
2809115	2804971	2801345	2803935	2797719
2798237	2798755	2807561	2806007	2806525

L14-M10

2813259	2821029	2812223	2813777	2821547
2812741	2815849	2818439	2814813	2819993
2822583	2815331	2816367	2817403	2810151
2822065	2817921	2814295	2816885	2810669
2811187	2811705	2820511	2818957	2819475

L14-M11

2826209	2833979	2825173	2826727	2834497
2825691	2828799	2831389	2827763	2832943
2835533	2828281	2829317	2830353	2823101
2835015	2830871	2827245	2829835	2823619
2824137	2824655	2833461	2831907	2832425

L14-M12

2839159	2846929	2838123	2839677	2847447
2838641	2841749	2844339	2840713	2845893
2848483	2841231	2842267	2843303	2836051
2847965	2843821	2840195	2842785	2836569
2837087	2837605	2846411	2844857	2845375

L14-M13

2852109	2859879	2851073	2852627	2860397
2851591	2854699	2857289	2853663	2858843
2861433	2854181	2855217	2856253	2849001
2860915	2856771	2853145	2855735	2849519
2850037	2850555	2859361	2857807	2858325

L14-M14

2865059	2872829	2864023	2865577	2873347
2864541	2867649	2870239	2866613	2871793
2874383	2867131	2868167	2869203	2861951
2873865	2869721	2866095	2868685	2862469
2862987	2863505	2872311	2870757	2871275

L14-M15

2878009	2885779	2876973	2878527	2886297
2877491	2880599	2883189	2879563	2884743
2887333	2880081	2881117	2882153	2874901
2886815	2882671	2879045	2881635	2875419
2875937	2876455	2885261	2883707	2884225

L14-M16

2890959	2898729	2889923	2891477	2899247
2890441	2893549	2896139	2892513	2897693
2900283	2893031	2894067	2895103	2887851
2899765	2895621	2891995	2894585	2888369
2888887	2889405	2898211	2896657	2897175

L15-M1

2903909	2911679	2902873	2904427	2912197
2903391	2906499	2909089	2905463	2910643
2913233	2905981	2907017	2908053	2900801
2912715	2908571	2904945	2907535	2901319
2901837	2902355	2911161	2909607	2910125

L15-M2

2916859	2924629	2915823	2917377	2925147
2916341	2919449	2922039	2918413	2923593
2926183	2918931	2919967	2921003	2913751
2925665	2921521	2917895	2920485	2914269
2914787	2915305	2924111	2922557	2923075

L15-M3

2929809	2937579	2928773	2930327	2938097
2929291	2932399	2934989	2931363	2936543
2939133	2931881	2932917	2933953	2926701
2938615	2934471	2930845	2933435	2927219
2927737	2928255	2937061	2935507	2936025

L15-M4

2942759	2950529	2941723	2943277	2951047
2942241	2945349	2947939	2944313	2949493
2952083	2944831	2945867	2946903	2939651
2951565	2947421	2943795	2946385	2940169
2940687	2941205	2950011	2948457	2948975

L15-M5

2955709	2963479	2954673	2956227	2963997
2955191	2958299	2960889	2957263	2962443
2965033	2957781	2958817	2959853	2952601
2964515	2960371	2956745	2959335	2953119
2953637	2954155	2962961	2961407	2961925

L15-M6

2968659	2976429	2967623	2969177	2976947
2968141	2971249	2973839	2970213	2975393
2977983	2970731	2971767	2972803	2965551
2977465	2973321	2969695	2972285	2966069
2966587	2967105	2975911	2974357	2974875

L15-M7

2981609	2989379	2980573	2982127	2989897
2981091	2984199	2986789	2983163	2988343
2990933	2983681	2984717	2985753	2978501
2990415	2986271	2982645	2985235	2979019
2979537	2980055	2988861	2987307	2987825

L15-M8

2994559	3002329	2993523	2995077	3002847
2994041	2997149	2999739	2996113	3001293
3003883	2996631	2997667	2998703	2991451
3003365	2999221	2995595	2998185	2991969
2992487	2993005	3001811	3000257	3000775

L15-M9

3007509	3015279	3006473	3008027	3015797
3006991	3010099	3012689	3009063	3014243
3016833	3009581	3010617	3011653	3004401
3016315	3012171	3008545	3011135	3004919
3005437	3005955	3014761	3013207	3013725

L15-M10

3020459	3028229	3019423	3020977	3028747
3019941	3023049	3025639	3022013	3027193
3029783	3022531	3023567	3024603	3017351
3029265	3025121	3021495	3024085	3017869
3018387	3018905	3027711	3026157	3026675

L15-M11

3033409	3041179	3032373	3033927	3041697
3032891	3035999	3038589	3034963	3040143
3042733	3035481	3036517	3037553	3030301
3042215	3038071	3034445	3037035	3030819
3031337	3031855	3040661	3039107	3039625

L15-M12

3046359	3054129	3045323	3046877	3054647
3045841	3048949	3051539	3047913	3053093
3055683	3048431	3049467	3050503	3043251
3055165	3051021	3047395	3049985	3043769
3044287	3044805	3053611	3052057	3052575

L15-M13

3059309	3067079	3058273	3059827	3067597
3058791	3061899	3064489	3060863	3066043
3068633	3061381	3062417	3063453	3056201
3068115	3063971	3060345	3062935	3056719
3057237	3057755	3066561	3065007	3065525

L15-M14

3072259	3080029	3071223	3072777	3080547
3071741	3074849	3077439	3073813	3078993
3081583	3074331	3075367	3076403	3069151
3081065	3076921	3073295	3075885	3069669
3070187	3070705	3079511	3077957	3078475

L15-M15

3085209	3092979	3084173	3085727	3093497
3084691	3087799	3090389	3086763	3091943
3094533	3087281	3088317	3089353	3082101
3094015	3089871	3086245	3088835	3082619
3083137	3083655	3092461	3090907	3091425

L15-M16

3098159	3105929	3097123	3098677	3106447
3097641	3100749	3103339	3099713	3104893
3107483	3100231	3101267	3102303	3095051
3106965	3102821	3099195	3101785	3095569
3096087	3096605	3105411	3103857	3104375

L16-M1

3111109	3118879	3110073	3111627	3119397
3110591	3113699	3116289	3112663	3117843
3120433	3113181	3114217	3115253	3108001
3119915	3115771	3112145	3114735	3108519
3109037	3109555	3118361	3116807	3117325

L16-M2

3124059	3131829	3123023	3124577	3132347
3123541	3126649	3129239	3125613	3130793
3133383	3126131	3127167	3128203	3120951
3132865	3128721	3125095	3127685	3121469
3121987	3122505	3131311	3129757	3130275

L16-M3

3137009	3144779	3135973	3137527	3145297
3136491	3139599	3142189	3138563	3143743
3146333	3139081	3140117	3141153	3133901
3145815	3141671	3138045	3140635	3134419
3134937	3135455	3144261	3142707	3143225

L16-M4

3149959	3157729	3148923	3150477	3158247
3149441	3152549	3155139	3151513	3156693
3159283	3152031	3153067	3154103	3146851
3158765	3154621	3150995	3153585	3147369
3147887	3148405	3157211	3155657	3156175

L16-M5

3162909	3170679	3161873	3163427	3171197
3162391	3165499	3168089	3164463	3169643
3172233	3164981	3166017	3167053	3159801
3171715	3167571	3163945	3166535	3160319
3160837	3161355	3170161	3168607	3169125

L16-M6

3175859	3183629	3174823	3176377	3184147
3175341	3178449	3181039	3177413	3182593
3185183	3177931	3178967	3180003	3172751
3184665	3180521	3176895	3179485	3173269
3173787	3174305	3183111	3181557	3182075

L16-M7

3188809	3196579	3187773	3189327	3197097
3188291	3191399	3193989	3190363	3195543
3198133	3190881	3191917	3192953	3185701
3197615	3193471	3189845	3192435	3186219
3186737	3187255	3196061	3194507	3195025

L16-M8

3201759	3209529	3200723	3202277	3210047
3201241	3204349	3206939	3203313	3208493
3211083	3203831	3204867	3205903	3198651
3210565	3206421	3202795	3205385	3199169
3199687	3200205	3209011	3207457	3207975

L16-M9

3214709	3222479	3213673	3215227	3222997
3214191	3217299	3219889	3216263	3221443
3224033	3216781	3217817	3218853	3211601
3223515	3219371	3215745	3218335	3212119
3212637	3213155	3221961	3220407	3220925

L16-M10

3227659	3235429	3226623	3228177	3235947
3227141	3230249	3232839	3229213	3234393
3236983	3229731	3230767	3231803	3224551
3236465	3232321	3228695	3231285	3225069
3225587	3226105	3234911	3233357	3233875

L16-M11

3240609	3248379	3239573	3241127	3248897
3240091	3243199	3245789	3242163	3247343
3249933	3242681	3243717	3244753	3237501
3249415	3245271	3241645	3244235	3238019
3238537	3239055	3247861	3246307	3246825

L16-M12

3253559	3261329	3252523	3254077	3261847
3253041	3256149	3258739	3255113	3260293
3262883	3255631	3256667	3257703	3250451
3262365	3258221	3254595	3257185	3250969
3251487	3252005	3260811	3259257	3259775

L16-M13

3266509	3274279	3265473	3267027	3274797
3265991	3269099	3271689	3268063	3273243
3275833	3268581	3269617	3270653	3263401
3275315	3271171	3267545	3270135	3263919
3264437	3264955	3273761	3272207	3272725

L16-M14

3279459	3287229	3278423	3279977	3287747
3278941	3282049	3284639	3281013	3286193
3288783	3281531	3282567	3283603	3276351
3288265	3284121	3280495	3283085	3276869
3277387	3277905	3286711	3285157	3285675

L16-M15

3292409	3300179	3291373	3292927	3300697
3291891	3294999	3297589	3293963	3299143
3301733	3294481	3295517	3296553	3289301
3301215	3297071	3293445	3296035	3289819
3290337	3290855	3299661	3298107	3298625

L16M16

3305359	3313129	3304323	3305877	3313647
3304841	3307949	3310539	3306913	3312093
3314683	3307431	3308467	3309503	3302251
3314165	3310021	3306395	3308985	3302769
3303287	3303805	3312611	3311057	3311575

L17-M1

3318309	3326079	3317273	3318827	3326597
3317791	3320899	3323489	3319863	3325043
3327633	3320381	3321417	3322453	3315201
3327115	3322971	3319345	3321935	3315719
3316237	3316755	3325561	3324007	3324525

L17-M2

3331259	3339029	3330223	3331777	3339547
3330741	3333849	3336439	3332813	3337993
3340583	3333331	3334367	3335403	3328151
3340065	3335921	3332295	3334885	3328669
3329187	3329705	3338511	3336957	3337475

L17-M3

3344209	3351979	3343173	3344727	3352497
3343691	3346799	3349389	3345763	3350943
3353533	3346281	3347317	3348353	3341101
3353015	3348871	3345245	3347835	3341619
3342137	3342655	3351461	3349907	3350425

L17-M4

3357159	3364929	3356123	3357677	3365447
3356641	3359749	3362339	3358713	3363893
3366483	3359231	3360267	3361303	3354051
3365965	3361821	3358195	3360785	3354569
3355087	3355605	3364411	3362857	3363375

L17-M5

3370109	3377879	3369073	3370627	3378397
3369591	3372699	3375289	3371663	3376843
3379433	3372181	3373217	3374253	3367001
3378915	3374771	3371145	3373735	3367519
3368037	3368555	3377361	3375807	3376325

L17-M6

3383059	3390829	3382023	3383577	3391347
3382541	3385649	3388239	3384613	3389793
3392383	3385131	3386167	3387203	3379951
3391865	3387721	3384095	3386685	3380469
3380987	3381505	3390311	3388757	3389275

L17-M7

3396009	3403779	3394973	3396527	3404297
3395491	3398599	3401189	3397563	3402743
3405333	3398081	3399117	3400153	3392901
3404815	3400671	3397045	3399635	3393419
3393937	3394455	3403261	3401707	3402225

L17-M8

3408959	3416729	3407923	3409477	3417247
3408441	3411549	3414139	3410513	3415693
3418283	3411031	3412067	3413103	3405851
3417765	3413621	3409995	3412585	3406369
3406887	3407405	3416211	3414657	3415175

L17-M9

3421909	3429679	3420873	3422427	3430197
3421391	3424499	3427089	3423463	3428643
3431233	3423981	3425017	3426053	3418801
3430715	3426571	3422945	3425535	3419319
3419837	3420355	3429161	3427607	3428125

L17-M10

3434859	3442629	3433823	3435377	3443147
3434341	3437449	3440039	3436413	3441593
3444183	3436931	3437967	3439003	3431751
3443665	3439521	3435895	3438485	3432269
3432787	3433305	3442111	3440557	3441075

L17-M11

3447809	3455579	3446773	3448327	3456097
3447291	3450399	3452989	3449363	3454543
3457133	3449881	3450917	3451953	3444701
3456615	3452471	3448845	3451435	3445219
3445737	3446255	3455061	3453507	3454025

L17-M12

3460759	3468529	3459723	3461277	3469047
3460241	3463349	3465939	3462313	3467493
3470083	3462831	3463867	3464903	3457651
3469565	3465421	3461795	3464385	3458169
3458687	3459205	3468011	3466457	3466975

L17-M13

3473709	3481479	3472673	3474227	3481997
3473191	3476299	3478889	3475263	3480443
3483033	3475781	3476817	3477853	3470601
3482515	3478371	3474745	3477335	3471119
3471637	3472155	3480961	3479407	3479925

L17-M14

3486659	3494429	3485623	3487177	3494947
3486141	3489249	3491839	3488213	3493393
3495983	3488731	3489767	3490803	3483551
3495465	3491321	3487695	3490285	3484069
3484587	3485105	3493911	3492357	3492875

L17-M15

3499609	3507379	3498573	3500127	3507897
3499091	3502199	3504789	3501163	3506343
3508933	3501681	3502717	3503753	3496501
3508415	3504271	3500645	3503235	3497019
3497537	3498055	3506861	3505307	3505825

L17-M16

3512559	3520329	3511523	3513077	3520847
3512041	3515149	3517739	3514113	3519293
3521883	3514631	3515667	3516703	3509451
3521365	3517221	3513595	3516185	3509969
3510487	3511005	3519811	3518257	3518775

L18-M1

3525509	3533279	3524473	3526027	3533797
3524991	3528099	3530689	3527063	3532243
3534833	3527581	3528617	3529653	3522401
3534315	3530171	3526545	3529135	3522919
3523437	3523955	3532761	3531207	3531725

L18-M2

3538459	3546229	3537423	3538977	3546747
3537941	3541049	3543639	3540013	3545193
3547783	3540531	3541567	3542603	3535351
3547265	3543121	3539495	3542085	3535869
3536387	3536905	3545711	3544157	3544675

L18-M3

3551409	3559179	3550373	3551927	3559697
3550891	3553999	3556589	3552963	3558143
3560733	3553481	3554517	3555553	3548301
3560215	3556071	3552445	3555035	3548819
3549337	3549855	3558661	3557107	3557625

L18-M4

3564359	3572129	3563323	3564877	3572647
3563841	3566949	3569539	3565913	3571093
3573683	3566431	3567467	3568503	3561251
3573165	3569021	3565395	3567985	3561769
3562287	3562805	3571611	3570057	3570575

L18-M5

3577309	3585079	3576273	3577827	3585597
3576791	3579899	3582489	3578863	3584043
3586633	3579381	3580417	3581453	3574201
3586115	3581971	3578345	3580935	3574719
3575237	3575755	3584561	3583007	3583525

L18-M6

3590259	3598029	3589223	3590777	3598547
3589741	3592849	3595439	3591813	3596993
3599583	3592331	3593367	3594403	3587151
3599065	3594921	3591295	3593885	3587669
3588187	3588705	3597511	3595957	3596475

L18-M7

3603209	3610979	3602173	3603727	3611497
3602691	3605799	3608389	3604763	3609943
3612533	3605281	3606317	3607353	3600101
3612015	3607871	3604245	3606835	3600619
3601137	3601655	3610461	3608907	3609425

L18-M8

3616159	3623929	3615123	3616677	3624447
3615641	3618749	3621339	3617713	3622893
3625483	3618231	3619267	3620303	3613051
3624965	3620821	3617195	3619785	3613569
3614087	3614605	3623411	3621857	3622375

L18-M9

3629109	3636879	3628073	3629627	3637397
3628591	3631699	3634289	3630663	3635843
3638433	3631181	3632217	3633253	3626001
3637915	3633771	3630145	3632735	3626519
3627037	3627555	3636361	3634807	3635325

L18-M10

3642059	3649829	3641023	3642577	3650347
3641541	3644649	3647239	3643613	3648793
3651383	3644131	3645167	3646203	3638951
3650865	3646721	3643095	3645685	3639469
3639987	3640505	3649311	3647757	3648275

L18-M11

3655009	3662779	3653973	3655527	3663297
3654491	3657599	3660189	3656563	3661743
3664333	3657081	3658117	3659153	3651901
3663815	3659671	3656045	3658635	3652419
3652937	3653455	3662261	3660707	3661225

L18-M12

3667959	3675729	3666923	3668477	3676247
3667441	3670549	3673139	3669513	3674693
3677283	3670031	3671067	3672103	3664851
3676765	3672621	3668995	3671585	3665369
3665887	3666405	3675211	3673657	3674175

L18-M13

3680909	3688679	3679873	3681427	3689197
3680391	3683499	3686089	3682463	3687643
3690233	3682981	3684017	3685053	3677801
3689715	3685571	3681945	3684535	3678319
3678837	3679355	3688161	3686607	3687125

L18-M14

3693859	3701629	3692823	3694377	3702147
3693341	3696449	3699039	3695413	3700593
3703183	3695931	3696967	3698003	3690751
3702665	3698521	3694895	3697485	3691269
3691787	3692305	3701111	3699557	3700075

L18-M15

3706809	3714579	3705773	3707327	3715097
3706291	3709399	3711989	3708363	3713543
3716133	3708881	3709917	3710953	3703701
3715615	3711471	3707845	3710435	3704219
3704737	3705255	3714061	3712507	3713025

L18-M16

3719759	3727529	3718723	3720277	3728047
3719241	3722349	3724939	3721313	3726493
3729083	3721831	3722867	3723903	3716651
3728565	3724421	3720795	3723385	3717169
3717687	3718205	3727011	3725457	3725975

L19-M1

3732709	3740479	3731673	3733227	3740997
3732191	3735299	3737889	3734263	3739443
3742033	3734781	3735817	3736853	3729601
3741515	3737371	3733745	3736335	3730119
3730637	3731155	3739961	3738407	3738925

L19-M10

3849259	3857029	3848223	3849777	3857547
3848741	3851849	3854439	3850813	3855993
3858583	3851331	3852367	3853403	3846151
3858065	3853921	3850295	3852885	3846669
3847187	3847705	3856511	3854957	3855475

L19-M2

3745659	3753429	3744623	3746177	3753947
3745141	3748249	3750839	3747213	3752393
3754983	3747731	3748767	3749803	3742551
3754465	3750321	3746695	3749285	3743069
3743587	3744105	3752911	3751357	3751875

L19-M11

3862209	3869979	3861173	3862727	3870497
3861691	3864799	3867389	3863763	3868943
3871533	3864281	3865317	3866353	3859101
3871015	3866871	3863245	3865835	3859619
3860137	3860655	3869461	3867907	3868425

L19-M3

3758609	3766379	3757573	3759127	3766897
3758091	3761199	3763789	3760163	3765343
3767933	3760681	3761717	3762753	3755501
3767415	3763271	3759645	3762235	3756019
3756537	3757055	3765861	3764307	3764825

L19-M12

3875159	3882929	3874123	3875677	3883447
3874641	3877749	3880339	3876713	3881893
3884483	3877231	3878267	3879303	3872051
3883965	3879821	3876195	3878785	3872569
3873087	3873605	3882411	3880857	3881375

L19-M4

3771559	3779329	3770523	3772077	3779847
3771041	3774149	3776739	3773113	3778293
3780883	3773631	3774667	3775703	3768451
3780365	3776221	3772595	3775185	3768969
3769487	3770005	3778811	3777257	3777775

L19-M13

3888109	3895879	3887073	3888627	3896397
3887591	3890699	3893289	3889663	3894843
3897433	3890181	3891217	3892253	3885001
3896915	3892771	3889145	3891735	3885519
3886037	3886555	3895361	3893807	3894325

L19-M5

3784509	3792279	3783473	3785027	3792797
3783991	3787099	3789689	3786063	3791243
3793833	3786581	3787617	3788653	3781401
3793315	3789171	3785545	3788135	3781919
3782437	3782955	3791761	3790207	3790725

L19-M14

3901059	3908829	3900023	3901577	3909347
3900541	3903649	3906239	3902613	3907793
3910383	3903131	3904167	3905203	3897951
3909865	3905721	3902095	3904685	3898469
3898987	3899505	3908311	3906757	3907275

L19-M6

3797459	3805229	3796423	3797977	3805747
3796941	3800049	3802639	3799013	3804193
3806783	3799531	3800567	3801603	3794351
3806265	3802121	3798495	3801085	3794869
3795387	3795905	3804711	3803157	3803675

L19-M15

3914009	3921779	3912973	3914527	3922297
3913491	3916599	3919189	3915563	3920743
3923333	3916081	3917117	3918153	3910901
3922815	3918671	3915045	3917635	3911419
3911937	3912455	3921261	3919707	3920225

L19-M7

3810409	3818179	3809373	3810927	3818697
3809891	3812999	3815589	3811963	3817143
3819733	3812481	3813517	3814553	3807301
3819215	3815071	3811445	3814035	3807819
3808337	3808855	3817661	3816107	3816625

L19-M16

3926959	3934729	3925923	3927477	3935247
3926441	3929549	3932139	3928513	3933693
3936283	3929031	3930067	3931103	3923851
3935765	3931621	3927995	3930585	3924369
3924887	3925405	3934211	3932657	3933175

L19-M8

3823359	3831129	3822323	3823877	3831647
3822841	3825949	3828539	3824913	3830093
3832683	3825431	3826467	3827503	3820251
3832165	3828021	3824395	3826985	3820769
3821287	3821805	3830611	3829057	3829575

L20-M1

3939909	3947679	3938873	3940427	3948197
3939391	3942499	3945089	3941463	3946643
3949233	3941981	3943017	3944053	3936801
3948715	3944571	3940945	3943535	3937319
3937837	3938355	3947161	3945607	3946125

L19-M9

3836309	3844079	3835273	3836827	3844597
3835791	3838899	3841489	3837863	3843043
3845633	3838381	3839417	3840453	3833201
3845115	3840971	3837345	3839935	3833719
3834237	3834755	3843561	3842007	3842525

L20-M2

3952859	3960629	3951823	3953377	3961147
3952341	3955449	3958039	3954413	3959593
3962183	3954931	3955967	3957003	3949751
3961665	3957521	3953895	3956485	3950269
3950787	3951305	3960111	3958557	3959075

L20-M3

3965809	3973579	3964773	3966327	3974097
3965291	3968399	3970989	3967363	3972543
3975133	3967881	3968917	3969953	3962701
3974615	3970471	3966845	3969435	3963219
3963737	3964255	3973061	3971507	3972025

L20-M4

3978759	3986529	3977723	3979277	3987047
3978241	3981349	3983939	3980313	3985493
3988083	3980831	3981867	3982903	3975651
3987565	3983421	3979795	3982385	3976169
3976687	3977205	3986011	3984457	3984975

L20-M5

3991709	3999479	3990673	3992227	3999997
3991191	3994299	3996889	3993263	3998443
4001033	3993781	3994817	3995853	3988601
4000515	3996371	3992745	3995335	3989119
3989637	3990155	3998961	3997407	3997925

L20-M6

4004659	4012429	4003623	4005177	4012947
4004141	4007249	4009839	4006213	4011393
4013983	4006731	4007767	4008803	4001551
4013465	4009321	4005695	4008285	4002069
4002587	4003105	4011911	4010357	4010875

L20-M7

4017609	4025379	4016573	4018127	4025897
4017091	4020199	4022789	4019163	4024343
4026933	4019681	4020717	4021753	4014501
4026415	4022271	4018645	4021235	4015019
4015537	4016055	4024861	4023307	4023825

L20-M8

4030559	4038329	4029523	4031077	4038847
4030041	4033149	4035739	4032113	4037293
4039883	4032631	4033667	4034703	4027451
4039365	4035221	4031595	4034185	4027969
4028487	4029005	4037811	4036257	4036775

L20-M9

4043509	4051279	4042473	4044027	4051797
4042991	4046099	4048689	4045063	4050243
4052833	4045581	4046617	4047653	4040401
4052315	4048171	4044545	4047135	4040919
4041437	4041955	4050761	4049207	4049725

L20-M10

4056459	4064229	4055423	4056977	4064747
4055941	4059049	4061639	4058013	4063193
4065783	4058531	4059567	4060603	4053351
4065265	4061121	4057495	4060085	4053869
4054387	4054905	4063711	4062157	4062675

L20-M11

4069409	4077179	4068373	4069927	4077697
4068891	4071999	4074589	4070963	4076143
4078733	4071481	4072517	4073553	4066301
4078215	4074071	4070445	4073035	4066819
4067337	4067855	4076661	4075107	4075625

L20-M12

4082359	4090129	4081323	4082877	4090647
4081841	4084949	4087539	4083913	4089093
4091683	4084431	4085467	4086503	4079251
4091165	4087021	4083395	4085985	4079769
4080287	4080805	4089611	4088057	4088575

L20-M13

4095309	4103079	4094273	4095827	4103597
4094791	4097899	4100489	4096863	4102043
4104633	4097381	4098417	4099453	4092201
4104115	4099971	4096345	4098935	4092719
4093237	4093755	4102561	4101007	4101525

L20-M14

4108259	4116029	4107223	4108777	4116547
4107741	4110849	4113439	4109813	4114993
4117583	4110331	4111367	4112403	4105151
4117065	4112921	4109295	4111885	4105669
4106187	4106705	4115511	4113957	4114475

L20-M15

4121209	4128979	4120173	4121727	4129497
4120691	4123799	4126389	4122763	4127943
4130533	4123281	4124317	4125353	4118101
4130015	4125871	4122245	4124835	4118619
4119137	4119655	4128461	4126907	4127425

L20-M16

4134159	4141929	4133123	4134677	4142447
4133641	4136749	4139339	4135713	4140893
4143483	4136231	4137267	4138303	4131051
4142965	4138821	4135195	4137785	4131569
4132087	4132605	4141411	4139857	4140375

L21-M1

4147109	4154879	4146073	4147627	4155397
4146591	4149699	4152289	4148663	4153843
4156433	4149181	4150217	4151253	4144001
4155915	4151771	4148145	4150735	4144519
4145037	4145555	4154361	4152807	4153325

L21-M2

4160059	4167829	4159023	4160577	4168347
4159541	4162649	4165239	4161613	4166793
4169383	4162131	4163167	4164203	4156951
4168865	4164721	4161095	4163685	4157469
4157987	4158505	4167311	4165757	4166275

L21-M3

4173009	4180779	4171973	4173527	4181297
4172491	4175599	4178189	4174563	4179743
4182333	4175081	4176117	4177153	4169901
4181815	4177671	4174045	4176635	4170419
4170937	4171455	4180261	4178707	4179225

L21-M4

4185959	4193729	4184923	4186477	4194247
4185441	4188549	4191139	4187513	4192693
4195283	4188031	4189067	4190103	4182851
4194765	4190621	4186995	4189585	4183369
4183887	4184405	4193211	4191657	4192175

L21-M5

4198909	4206679	4197873	4199427	4207197
4198391	4201499	4204089	4200463	4205643
4208233	4200981	4202017	4203053	4195801
4207715	4203571	4199945	4202535	4196319
4196837	4197355	4206161	4204607	4205125

L21-M14

4315459	4323229	4314423	4315977	4323747
4314941	4318049	4320639	4317013	4322193
4324783	4317531	4318567	4319603	4312351
4324265	4320121	4316495	4319085	4312869
4313387	4313905	4322711	4321157	4321675

L21-M6

4211859	4219629	4210823	4212377	4220147
4211341	4214449	4217039	4213413	4218593
4221183	4213931	4214967	4216003	4208751
4220665	4216521	4212895	4215485	4209269
4209787	4210305	4219111	4217557	4218075

L21-M15

4328409	4336179	4327373	4328927	4336697
4327891	4330999	4333589	4329963	4335143
4337733	4330481	4331517	4332553	4325301
4337215	4333071	4329445	4332035	4325819
4326337	4326855	4335661	4334107	4334625

L21-M7

4224809	4232579	4223773	4225327	4233097
4224291	4227399	4229989	4226363	4231543
4234133	4226881	4227917	4228953	4221701
4233615	4229471	4225845	4228435	4222219
4222737	4223255	4232061	4230507	4231025

L21-M16

4341359	4349129	4340323	4341877	4349647
4340841	4343949	4346539	4342913	4348093
4350683	4343431	4344467	4345503	4338251
4350165	4346021	4342395	4344985	4338769
4339287	4339805	4348611	4347057	4347575

L21-M8

4237759	4245529	4236723	4238277	4246047
4237241	4240349	4242939	4239313	4244493
4247083	4239831	4240867	4241903	4234651
4246565	4242421	4238795	4241385	4235169
4235687	4236205	4245011	4243457	4243975

L22-M1

4354309	4362079	4353273	4354827	4362597
4353791	4356899	4359489	4355863	4361043
4363633	4356381	4357417	4358453	4351201
4363115	4358971	4355345	4357935	4351719
4352237	4352755	4361561	4360007	4360525

L21-M9

4250709	4258479	4249673	4251227	4258997
4250191	4253299	4255889	4252263	4257443
4260033	4252781	4253817	4254853	4247601
4259515	4255371	4251745	4254335	4248119
4248637	4249155	4257961	4256407	4256925

L22-M2

4367259	4375029	4366223	4367777	4375547
4366741	4369849	4372439	4368813	4373993
4376583	4369331	4370367	4371403	4364151
4376065	4371921	4368295	4370885	4364669
4365187	4365705	4374511	4372957	4373475

L21-M10

4263659	4271429	4262623	4264177	4271947
4263141	4266249	4268839	4265213	4270393
4272983	4265731	4266767	4267803	4260551
4272465	4268321	4264695	4267285	4261069
4261587	4262105	4270911	4269357	4269875

L22-M3

4380209	4387979	4379173	4380727	4388497
4379691	4382799	4385389	4381763	4386943
4389533	4382281	4383317	4384353	4377101
4389015	4384871	4381245	4383835	4377619
4378137	4378655	4387461	4385907	4386425

L21-M11

4276609	4284379	4275573	4277127	4284897
4276091	4279199	4281789	4278163	4283343
4285933	4278681	4279717	4280753	4273501
4285415	4281271	4277645	4280235	4274019
4274537	4275055	4283861	4282307	4282825

L22-M4

4393159	4400929	4392123	4393677	4401447
4392641	4395749	4398339	4394713	4399893
4402483	4395231	4396267	4397303	4390051
4401965	4397821	4394195	4396785	4390569
4391087	4391605	4400411	4398857	4399375

L21-M12

4289559	4297329	4288523	4290077	4297847
4289041	4292149	4294739	4291113	4296293
4298883	4291631	4292667	4293703	4286451
4298365	4294221	4290595	4293185	4286969
4287487	4288005	4296811	4295257	4295775

L22-M5

4406109	4413879	4405073	4406627	4414397
4405591	4408699	4411289	4407663	4412843
4415433	4408181	4409217	4410253	4403001
4414915	4410771	4407145	4409735	4403519
4404037	4404555	4413361	4411807	4412325

L21-M13

4302509	4310279	4301473	4303027	4310797
4301991	4305099	4307689	4304063	4309243
4311833	4304581	4305617	4306653	4299401
4311315	4307171	4303545	4306135	4299919
4300437	4300955	4309761	4308207	4308725

L22-M6

4419059	4426829	4418023	4419577	4427347
4418541	4421649	4424239	4420613	4425793
4428383	4421131	4422167	4423203	4415951
4427865	4423721	4420095	4422685	4416469
4416987	4417505	4426311	4424757	4425275

L22-M7

4432009	4439779	4430973	4432527	4440297
4431491	4434599	4437189	4433563	4438743
4441333	4434081	4435117	4436153	4428901
4440815	4436671	4433045	4435635	4429419
4429937	4430455	4439261	4437707	4438225

L22-M8

4444959	4452729	4443923	4445477	4453247
4444441	4447549	4450139	4446513	4451693
4454283	4447031	4448067	4449103	4441851
4453765	4449621	4445995	4448585	4442369
4442887	4443405	4452211	4450657	4451175

L22-M9

4457909	4465679	4456873	4458427	4466197
4457391	4460499	4463089	4459463	4464643
4467233	4459981	4461017	4462053	4454801
4466715	4462571	4458945	4461535	4455319
4455837	4456355	4465161	4463607	4464125

L22-M10

4470859	4478629	4469823	4471377	4479147
4470341	4473449	4476039	4472413	4477593
4480183	4472931	4473967	4475003	4467751
4479665	4475521	4471895	4474485	4468269
4468787	4469305	4478111	4476557	4477075

L22-M11

4483809	4491579	4482773	4484327	4492097
4483291	4486399	4488989	4485363	4490543
4493133	4485881	4486917	4487953	4480701
4492615	4488471	4484845	4487435	4481219
4481737	4482255	4491061	4489507	4490025

L22-M12

4496759	4504529	4495723	4497277	4505047
4496241	4499349	4501939	4498313	4503493
4506083	4498831	4499867	4500903	4493651
4505565	4501421	4497795	4500385	4494169
4494687	4495205	4504011	4502457	4502975

L22-M13

4509709	4517479	4508673	4510227	4517997
4509191	4512299	4514889	4511263	4516443
4519033	4511781	4512817	4513853	4506601
4518515	4514371	4510745	4513335	4507119
4507637	4508155	4516961	4515407	4515925

L22-M14

4522659	4530429	4521623	4523177	4530947
4522141	4525249	4527839	4524213	4529393
4531983	4524731	4525767	4526803	4519551
4531465	4527321	4523695	4526285	4520069
4520587	4521105	4529911	4528357	4528875

L22-M15

4535609	4543379	4534573	4536127	4543897
4535091	4538199	4540789	4537163	4542343
4544933	4537681	4538717	4539753	4532501
4544415	4540271	4536645	4539235	4533019
4533537	4534055	4542861	4541307	4541825

L22-M16

4548559	4556329	4547523	4549077	4556847
4548041	4551149	4553739	4550113	4555293
4557883	4550631	4551667	4552703	4545451
4557365	4553221	4549595	4552185	4545969
4546487	4547005	4555811	4554257	4554775

L23-M1

4561509	4569279	4560473	4562027	4569797
4560991	4564099	4566689	4563063	4568243
4570833	4563581	4564617	4565653	4558401
4570315	4566171	4562545	4565135	4558919
4559437	4559955	4568761	4567207	4567725

L23-M2

4574459	4582229	4573423	4574977	4582747
4573941	4577049	4579639	4576013	4581193
4583783	4576531	4577567	4578603	4571351
4583265	4579121	4575495	4578085	4571869
4572387	4572905	4581711	4580157	4580675

L23-M3

4587409	4595179	4586373	4587927	4595697
4586891	4589999	4592589	4588963	4594143
4596733	4589481	4590517	4591553	4584301
4596215	4592071	4588445	4591035	4584819
4585337	4585855	4594661	4593107	4593625

L23-M4

4600359	4608129	4599323	4600877	4608647
4599841	4602949	4605539	4601913	4607093
4609683	4602431	4603467	4604503	4597251
4609165	4605021	4601395	4603985	4597769
4598287	4598805	4607611	4606057	4606575

L23-M5

4613309	4621079	4612273	4613827	4621597
4612791	4615899	4618489	4614863	4620043
4622633	4615381	4616417	4617453	4610201
4622115	4617971	4614345	4616935	4610719
4611237	4611755	4620561	4619007	4619525

L23-M6

4626259	4634029	4625223	4626777	4634547
4625741	4628849	4631439	4627813	4632993
4635583	4628331	4629367	4630403	4623151
4635065	4630921	4627295	4629885	4623669
4624187	4624705	4633511	4631957	4632475

L23-M7

4639209	4646979	4638173	4639727	4647497
4638691	4641799	4644389	4640763	4645943
4648533	4641281	4642317	4643353	4636101
4648015	4643871	4640245	4642835	4636619
4637137	4637655	4646461	4644907	4645425

L23-M8

4652159	4659929	4651123	4652677	4660447
4651641	4654749	4657339	4653713	4658893
4661483	4654231	4655267	4656303	4649051
4660965	4656821	4653195	4655785	4649569
4650087	4650605	4659411	4657857	4658375

L23-M9

4665109	4672879	4664073	4665627	4673397
4664591	4667699	4670289	4666663	4671843
4674433	4667181	4668217	4669253	4662001
4673915	4669771	4666145	4668735	4662519
4663037	4663555	4672361	4670807	4671325

L23-M10

4678059	4685829	4677023	4678577	4686347
4677541	4680649	4683239	4679613	4684793
4687383	4680131	4681167	4682203	4674951
4686865	4682721	4679095	4681685	4675469
4675987	4676505	4685311	4683757	4684275

L23-M11

4691009	4698779	4689973	4691527	4699297
4690491	4693599	4696189	4692563	4697743
4700333	4693081	4694117	4695153	4687901
4699815	4695671	4692045	4694635	4688419
4688937	4689455	4698261	4696707	4697225

L23-M12

4703959	4711729	4702923	4704477	4712247
4703441	4706549	4709139	4705513	4710693
4713283	4706031	4707067	4708103	4700851
4712765	4708621	4704995	4707585	4701369
4701887	4702405	4711211	4709657	4710175

L23-M13

4716909	4724679	4715873	4717427	4725197
4716391	4719499	4722089	4718463	4723643
4726233	4718981	4720017	4721053	4713801
4725715	4721571	4717945	4720535	4714319
4714837	4715355	4724161	4722607	4723125

L23-M14

4729859	4737629	4728823	4730377	4738147
4729341	4732449	4735039	4731413	4736593
4739183	4731931	4732967	4734003	4726751
4738665	4734521	4730895	4733485	4727269
4727787	4728305	4737111	4735557	4736075

L23-M15

4742809	4750579	4741773	4743327	4751097
4742291	4745399	4747989	4744363	4749543
4752133	4744881	4745917	4746953	4739701
4751615	4747471	4743845	4746435	4740219
4740737	4741255	4750061	4748507	4749025

L23-M16

4755759	4763529	4754723	4756277	4764047
4755241	4758349	4760939	4757313	4762493
4765083	4757831	4758867	4759903	4752651
4764565	4760421	4756795	4759385	4753169
4753687	4754205	4763011	4761457	4761975

L24-M1

4768709	4776479	4767673	4769227	4776997
4768191	4771299	4773889	4770263	4775443
4778033	4770781	4771817	4772853	4765601
4777515	4773371	4769745	4772335	4766119
4766637	4767155	4775961	4774407	4774925

L24-M2

4781659	4789429	4780623	4782177	4789947
4781141	4784249	4786839	4783213	4788393
4790983	4783731	4784767	4785803	4778551
4790465	4786321	4782695	4785285	4779069
4779587	4780105	4788911	4787357	4787875

L24-M3

4794609	4802379	4793573	4795127	4802897
4794091	4797199	4799789	4796163	4801343
4803933	4796681	4797717	4798753	4791501
4803415	4799271	4795645	4798235	4792019
4792537	4793055	4801861	4800307	4800825

L24-M4

4807559	4815329	4806523	4808077	4815847
4807041	4810149	4812739	4809113	4814293
4816883	4809631	4810667	4811703	4804451
4816365	4812221	4808595	4811185	4804969
4805487	4806005	4814811	4813257	4813775

L24-M5

4820509	4828279	4819473	4821027	4828797
4819991	4823099	4825689	4822063	4827243
4829833	4822581	4823617	4824653	4817401
4829315	4825171	4821545	4824135	4817919
4818437	4818955	4827761	4826207	4826725

L24-M6

4833459	4841229	4832423	4833977	4841747
4832941	4836049	4838639	4835013	4840193
4842783	4835531	4836567	4837603	4830351
4842265	4838121	4834495	4837085	4830869
4831387	4831905	4840711	4839157	4839675

L24-M7

4846409	4854179	4845373	4846927	4854697
4845891	4848999	4851589	4847963	4853143
4855733	4848481	4849517	4850553	4843301
4855215	4851071	4847445	4850035	4843819
4844337	4844855	4853661	4852107	4852625

L24-M8

4859359	4867129	4858323	4859877	4867647
4858841	4861949	4864539	4860913	4866093
4868683	4861431	4862467	4863503	4856251
4868165	4864021	4860395	4862985	4856769
4857287	4857805	4866611	4865057	4865575

L24-M9

4872309	4880079	4871273	4872827	4880597
4871791	4874899	4877489	4873863	4879043
4881633	4874381	4875417	4876453	4869201
4881115	4876971	4873345	4875935	4869719
4870237	4870755	4879561	4878007	4878525

L24-M10

4885259	4893029	4884223	4885777	4893547
4884741	4887849	4890439	4886813	4891993
4894583	4887331	4888367	4889403	4882151
4894065	4889921	4886295	4888885	4882669
4883187	4883705	4892511	4890957	4891475

L24-M11

4898209	4905979	4897173	4898727	4906497
4897691	4900799	4903389	4899763	4904943
4907533	4900281	4901317	4902353	4895101
4907015	4902871	4899245	4901835	4895619
4896137	4896655	4905461	4903907	4904425

L24-M12

4911159	4918929	4910123	4911677	4919447
4910641	4913749	4916339	4912713	4917893
4920483	4913231	4914267	4915303	4908051
4919965	4915821	4912195	4914785	4908569
4909087	4909605	4918411	4916857	4917375

L24-M13

4924109	4931879	4923073	4924627	4932397
4923591	4926699	4929289	4925663	4930843
4933433	4926181	4927217	4928253	4921001
4932915	4928771	4925145	4927735	4921519
4922037	4922555	4931361	4929807	4930325

L24-M14

4937059	4944829	4936023	4937577	4945347
4936541	4939649	4942239	4938613	4943793
4946383	4939131	4940167	4941203	4933951
4945865	4941721	4938095	4940685	4934469
4934987	4935505	4944311	4942757	4943275

L24-M15

4950009	4957779	4948973	4950527	4958297
4949491	4952599	4955189	4951563	4956743
4959333	4952081	4953117	4954153	4946901
4958815	4954671	4951045	4953635	4947419
4947937	4948455	4957261	4955707	4956225

L24-M16

4962959	4970729	4961923	4963477	4971247
4962441	4965549	4968139	4964513	4969693
4972283	4965031	4966067	4967103	4959851
4971765	4967621	4963995	4966585	4960369
4960887	4961405	4970211	4968657	4969175

L25-M1

4975909	4983679	4974873	4976427	4984197
4975391	4978499	4981089	4977463	4982643
4985233	4977981	4979017	4980053	4972801
4984715	4980571	4976945	4979535	4973319
4973837	4974355	4983161	4981607	4982125

L25-M2

4988859	4996629	4987823	4989377	4997147
4988341	4991449	4994039	4990413	4995593
4998183	4990931	4991967	4993003	4985751
4997665	4993521	4989895	4992485	4986269
4986787	4987305	4996111	4994557	4995075

L25-M3

5001809	5009579	5000773	5002327	5010097
5001291	5004399	5006989	5003363	5008543
5011133	5003881	5004917	5005953	4998701
5010615	5006471	5002845	5005435	4999219
4999737	5000255	5009061	5007507	5008025

L25-M4

5014759	5022529	5013723	5015277	5023047
5014241	5017349	5019939	5016313	5021493
5024083	5016831	5017867	5018903	5011651
5023565	5019421	5015795	5018385	5012169
5012687	5013205	5022011	5020457	5020975

L25-M5

5027709	5035479	5026673	5028227	5035997
5027191	5030299	5032889	5029263	5034443
5037033	5029781	5030817	5031853	5024601
5036515	5032371	5028745	5031335	5025119
5025637	5026155	5034961	5033407	5033925

L25-M6

5040659	5048429	5039623	5041177	5048947
5040141	5043249	5045839	5042213	5047393
5049983	5042731	5043767	5044803	5037551
5049465	5045321	5041695	5044285	5038069
5038587	5039105	5047911	5046357	5046875

L25-M7

5053609	5061379	5052573	5054127	5061897
5053091	5056199	5058789	5055163	5060343
5062933	5055681	5056717	5057753	5050501
5062415	5058271	5054645	5057235	5051019
5051537	5052055	5060861	5059307	5059825

L25-M8

5066559	5074329	5065523	5067077	5074847
5066041	5069149	5071739	5068113	5073293
5075883	5068631	5069667	5070703	5063451
5075365	5071221	5067595	5070185	5063969
5064487	5065005	5073811	5072257	5072775

L25-M9

5079509	5087279	5078473	5080027	5087797
5078991	5082099	5084689	5081063	5086243
5088833	5081581	5082617	5083653	5076401
5088315	5084171	5080545	5083135	5076919
5077437	5077955	5086761	5085207	5085725

L25-M10

5092459	5100229	5091423	5092977	5100747
5091941	5095049	5097639	5094013	5099193
5101783	5094531	5095567	5096603	5089351
5101265	5097121	5093495	5096085	5089869
5090387	5090905	5099711	5098157	5098675

L25-M11

5105409	5113179	5104373	5105927	5113697
5104891	5107999	5110589	5106963	5112143
5114733	5107481	5108517	5109553	5102301
5114215	5110071	5106445	5109035	5102819
5103337	5103855	5112661	5111107	5111625

L25-M12

5118359	5126129	5117323	5118877	5126647
5117841	5120949	5123539	5119913	5125093
5127683	5120431	5121467	5122503	5115251
5127165	5123021	5119395	5121985	5115769
5116287	5116805	5125611	5124057	5124575

L25-M13

5131309	5139079	5130273	5131827	5139597
5130791	5133899	5136489	5132863	5138043
5140633	5133381	5134417	5135453	5128201
5140115	5135971	5132345	5134935	5128719
5129237	5129755	5138561	5137007	5137525

L25-M14

5144259	5152029	5143223	5144777	5152547
5143741	5146849	5149439	5145813	5150993
5153583	5146331	5147367	5148403	5141151
5153065	5148921	5145295	5147885	5141669
5142187	5142705	5151511	5149957	5150475

L25-M15

5157209	5164979	5156173	5157727	5165497
5156691	5159799	5162389	5158763	5163943
5166533	5159281	5160317	5161353	5154101
5166015	5161871	5158245	5160835	5154619
5155137	5155655	5164461	5162907	5163425

L25-M16

5170159	5177929	5169123	5170677	5178447
5169641	5172749	5175339	5171713	5176893
5179483	5172231	5173267	5174303	5167051
5178965	5174821	5171195	5173785	5167569
5168087	5168605	5177411	5175857	5176375

L1-M1

9805	34315	6537	11439	35949
8171	17975	26145	14707	31047
39217	16341	19609	22877	1
37583	24511	13073	21243	1635
3269	4903	32681	27779	29413

L1-M10

377455	401965	374187	379089	403599
375821	385625	393795	382357	398697
406867	383991	387259	390527	367651
405233	392161	380723	388893	369285
370919	372553	400331	395429	397063

L1-M2

50655	75165	47387	52289	76799
49021	58825	66995	55557	71897
80067	57191	60459	63727	40851
78433	65361	53923	62093	42485
44119	45753	73531	68629	70263

L1-M11

418305	442815	415037	419939	444449
416671	426475	434645	423207	439547
447717	424841	428109	431377	408501
446083	433011	421573	429743	410135
411769	413403	441181	436279	437913

L1-M3

91505	116015	88237	93139	117649
89871	99675	107845	96407	112747
120917	98041	101309	104577	81701
119283	106211	94773	102943	83335
84969	86603	114381	109479	111113

L1-M12

459155	483665	455887	460789	485299
457521	467325	475495	464057	480397
488567	465691	468959	472227	449351
486933	473861	462423	470593	450985
452619	454253	482031	477129	478763

L1-M4

132355	156865	129087	133989	158499
130721	140525	148695	137257	153597
161767	138891	142159	145427	122551
160133	147061	135623	143793	124185
125819	127453	155231	150329	151963

L1-M13

500005	524515	496737	501639	526149
498371	508175	516345	504907	521247
529417	506541	509809	513077	490201
527783	514711	503273	511443	491835
493469	495103	522881	517979	519613

L1-M5

173205	197715	169937	174839	199349
171571	181375	189545	178107	194447
202617	179741	183009	186277	163401
200983	187911	176473	184643	165035
166669	168303	196081	191179	192813

L1-M14

540855	565365	537587	542489	566999
539221	549025	557195	545757	562097
570267	547391	550659	553927	531051
568633	555561	544123	552293	532685
534319	535953	563731	558829	560463

L1-M6

214055	238565	210787	215689	240199
212421	222225	230395	218957	235297
243467	220591	223859	227127	204251
241833	228761	217323	225493	205885
207519	209153	236931	232029	233663

L1-M15

581705	606215	578437	583339	607849
580071	589875	598045	586607	602947
611117	588241	591509	594777	571901
609483	596411	584973	593143	573535
575169	576803	604581	599679	601313

L1-M7

254905	279415	251637	256539	281049
253271	263075	271245	259807	276147
284317	261441	264709	267977	245101
282683	269611	258173	266343	246735
248369	250003	277781	272879	274513

L1-M16

622555	647065	619287	624189	648699
620921	630725	638895	627457	643797
651967	629091	632359	635627	612751
650333	637261	625823	633993	614385
616019	617653	645431	640529	642163

L1-M8

295755	320265	292487	297389	321899
294121	303925	312095	300657	316997
325167	302291	305559	308827	285951
323533	310461	299023	307193	287585
289219	290853	318631	313729	315363

L2-M1

663405	687915	660137	665039	689549
661771	671575	679745	668307	684647
692817	669941	673209	676477	653601
691183	678111	666673	674843	655235
656869	658503	686281	681379	683013

L1-M9

336605	361115	333337	338239	362749
334971	344775	352945	341507	357847
366017	343141	346409	349677	326801
364383	351311	339873	348043	328435
330069	331703	359481	354579	356213

L2-M2

704255	728765	700987	705889	730399
702621	712425	720595	709157	725497
733667	710791	714059	717327	694451
732033	718961	707523	715693	696085
697719	699353	727131	722229	723863

L2-M3

745105	769615	741837	746739	771249
743471	753275	761445	750007	766347
774517	751641	754909	758177	735301
772883	759811	748373	756543	736935
738569	740203	767981	763079	764713

L2-M12

1112755	1137265	1109487	1114389	1138899
1111121	1120925	1129095	1117657	1133997
1142167	1119291	1122559	1125827	1102951
1140533	1127461	1116023	1124193	1104585
1106219	1107853	1135631	1130729	1132363

L2-M4

785955	810465	782687	787589	812099
784321	794125	802295	790857	807197
815367	792491	795759	799027	776151
813733	800661	789223	797393	777785
779419	781053	808831	803929	805563

L2-M13

1153605	1178115	1150337	1155239	1179749
1151971	1161775	1169945	1158507	1174847
1183017	1160141	1163409	1166677	1143801
1181383	1168311	1156873	1165043	1145435
1147069	1148703	1176481	1171579	1173213

L2-M5

826805	851315	823537	828439	852949
825171	834975	843145	831707	848047
856217	833341	836609	839877	817001
854583	841511	830073	838243	818635
820269	821903	849681	844779	846413

L2-M14

1194455	1218965	1191187	1196089	1220599
1192821	1202625	1210795	1199357	1215697
1223867	1200991	1204259	1207527	1184651
1222233	1209161	1197723	1205893	1186285
1187919	1189553	1217331	1212429	1214063

L2-M6

867655	892165	864387	869289	893799
866021	875825	883995	872557	888897
897067	874191	877459	880727	857851
895433	882361	870923	879093	859485
861119	862753	890531	885629	887263

L2-M15

1235305	1259815	1232037	1236939	1261449
1233671	1243475	1251645	1240207	1256547
1264717	1241841	1245109	1248377	1225501
1263083	1250011	1238573	1246743	1227135
1228769	1230403	1258181	1253279	1254913

L2-M7

908505	933015	905237	910139	934649
906871	916675	924845	913407	929747
937917	915041	918309	921577	898701
936283	923211	911773	919943	900335
901969	903603	931381	926479	928113

L2-M16

1276155	1300665	1272887	1277789	1302299
1274521	1284325	1292495	1281057	1297397
1305567	1282691	1285959	1289227	1266351
1303933	1290861	1279423	1287593	1267985
1269619	1271253	1299031	1294129	1295763

L2-M8

949355	973865	946087	950989	975499
947721	957525	965695	954257	970597
978767	955891	959159	962427	939551
977133	964061	952623	960793	941185
942819	944453	972231	967329	968963

L3-M1

1317005	1341515	1313737	1318639	1343149
1315371	1325175	1333345	1321907	1338247
1346417	1323541	1326809	1330077	1307201
1344783	1331711	1320273	1328443	1308835
1310469	1312103	1339881	1334979	1336613

L2-M9

990205	1014715	986937	991839	1016349
988571	998375	1006545	995107	1011447
1019617	996741	1000009	1003277	980401
1017983	1004911	993473	1001643	982035
983669	985303	1013081	1008179	1009813

L3-M2

1357855	1382365	1354587	1359489	1383999
1356221	1366025	1374195	1362757	1379097
1387267	1364391	1367659	1370927	1348051
1385633	1372561	1361123	1369293	1349685
1351319	1352953	1380731	1375829	1377463

L2-M10

1031055	1055565	1027787	1032689	1057199
1029421	1039225	1047395	1035957	1052297
1060467	1037591	1040859	1044127	1021251
1058833	1045761	1034323	1042493	1022885
1024519	1026153	1053931	1049029	1050663

L3-M3

1398705	1423215	1395437	1400339	1424849
1397071	1406875	1415045	1403607	1419947
1428117	1405241	1408509	1411777	1388901
1426483	1413411	1401973	1410143	1390535
1392169	1393803	1421581	1416679	1418313

L2-M11

1071905	1096415	1068637	1073539	1098049
1070271	1080075	1088245	1076807	1093147
1101317	1078441	1081709	1084977	1062101
1099683	1086611	1075173	1083343	1063735
1065369	1067003	1094781	1089879	1091513

L3-M4

1439555	1464065	1436287	1441189	1465699
1437921	1447725	1455895	1444457	1460797
1468967	1446091	1449359	1452627	1429751
1467333	1454261	1442823	1450993	1431385
1433019	1434653	1462431	1457529	1459163

L3-M5

1480405	1504915	1477137	1482039	1506549
1478771	1488575	1496745	1485307	1501647
1509817	1486941	1490209	1493477	1470601
1508183	1495111	1483673	1491843	1472235
1473869	1475503	1503281	1498379	1500013

L3-M6

1521255	1545765	1517987	1522889	1547399
1519621	1529425	1537595	1526157	1542497
1550667	1527791	1531059	1534327	1511451
1549033	1535961	1524523	1532693	1513085
1514719	1516353	1544131	1539229	1540863

L3-M7

1562105	1586615	1558837	1563739	1588249
1560471	1570275	1578445	1567007	1583347
1591517	1568641	1571909	1575177	1552301
1589883	1576811	1565373	1573543	1553935
1555569	1557203	1584981	1580079	1581713

L3-M8

1602955	1627465	1599687	1604589	1629099
1601321	1611125	1619295	1607857	1624197
1632367	1609491	1612759	1616027	1593151
1630733	1617661	1606223	1614393	1594785
1596419	1598053	1625831	1620929	1622563

L3-M9

1643805	1668315	1640537	1645439	1669949
1642171	1651975	1660145	1648707	1665047
1673217	1650341	1653609	1656877	1634001
1671583	1658511	1647073	1655243	1635635
1637269	1638903	1666681	1661779	1663413

L3-M10

1684655	1709165	1681387	1686289	1710799
1683021	1692825	1700995	1689557	1705897
1714067	1691191	1694459	1697727	1674851
1712433	1699361	1687923	1696093	1676485
1678119	1679753	1707531	1702629	1704263

L3-M11

1725505	1750015	1722237	1727139	1751649
1723871	1733675	1741845	1730407	1746747
1754917	1732041	1735309	1738577	1715701
1753283	1740211	1728773	1736943	1717335
1718969	1720603	1748381	1743479	1745113

L3-M12

1766355	1790865	1763087	1767989	1792499
1764721	1774525	1782695	1771257	1787597
1795767	1772891	1776159	1779427	1756551
1794133	1781061	1769623	1777793	1758185
1759819	1761453	1789231	1784329	1785963

L3-M13

1807205	1831715	1803937	1808839	1833349
1805571	1815375	1823545	1812107	1828447
1836617	1813741	1817009	1820277	1797401
1834983	1821911	1810473	1818643	1799035
1800669	1802303	1830081	1825179	1826813

L3-M14

1848055	1872565	1844787	1849689	1874199
1846421	1856225	1864395	1852957	1869297
1877467	1854591	1857859	1861127	1838251
1875833	1862761	1851323	1859493	1839885
1841519	1843153	1870931	1866029	1867663

L3-M15

1888905	1913415	1885637	1890539	1915049
1887271	1897075	1905245	1893807	1910147
1918317	1895441	1898709	1901977	1879101
1916683	1903611	1892173	1900343	1880735
1882369	1884003	1911781	1906879	1908513

L3-M16

1929755	1954265	1926487	1931389	1955899
1928121	1937925	1946095	1934657	1950997
1959167	1936291	1939559	1942827	1919951
1957533	1944461	1933023	1941193	1921585
1923219	1924853	1952631	1947729	1949363

L4-M1

1970605	1995115	1967337	1972239	1996749
1968971	1978775	1986945	1975507	1991847
2000017	1977141	1980409	1983677	1960801
1998383	1985311	1973873	1982043	1962435
1964069	1965703	1993481	1988579	1990213

L4-M2

2011455	2035965	2008187	2013089	2037599
2009821	2019625	2027795	2016357	2032697
2040867	2017991	2021259	2024527	2001651
2039233	2026161	2014723	2022893	2003285
2004919	2006553	2034331	2029429	2031063

L4-M3

2052305	2076815	2049037	2053939	2078449
2050671	2060475	2068645	2057207	2073547
2081717	2058841	2062109	2065377	2042501
2080083	2067011	2055573	2063743	2044135
2045769	2047403	2075181	2070279	2071913

L4-M4

2093155	2117665	2089887	2094789	2119299
2091521	2101325	2109495	2098057	2114397
2122567	2099691	2102959	2106227	2083351
2120933	2107861	2096423	2104593	2084985
2086619	2088253	2116031	2111129	2112763

L4-M5

2134005	2158515	2130737	2135639	2160149
2132371	2142175	2150345	2138907	2155247
2163417	2140541	2143809	2147077	2124201
2161783	2148711	2137273	2145443	2125835
2127469	2129103	2156881	2151979	2153613

L4-M6

2174855	2199365	2171587	2176489	2200999
2173221	2183025	2191195	2179757	2196097
2204267	2181391	2184659	2187927	2165051
2202633	2189561	2178123	2186293	2166685
2168319	2169953	2197731	2192829	2194463

L4-M7

2215705	2240215	2212437	2217339	2241849
2214071	2223875	2232045	2220607	2236947
2245117	2222241	2225509	2228777	2205901
2243483	2230411	2218973	2227143	2207535
2209169	2210803	2238581	2233679	2235313

L4-M8

2256555	2281065	2253287	2258189	2282699
2254921	2264725	2272895	2261457	2277797
2285967	2263091	2266359	2269627	2246751
2284333	2271261	2259823	2267993	2248385
2250019	2251653	2279431	2274529	2276163

L4-M9

2297405	2321915	2294137	2299039	2323549
2295771	2305575	2313745	2302307	2318647
2326817	2303941	2307209	2310477	2287601
2325183	2312111	2300673	2308843	2289235
2290869	2292503	2320281	2315379	2317013

L4-M10

2338255	2362765	2334987	2339889	2364399
2336621	2346425	2354595	2343157	2359497
2367667	2344791	2348059	2351327	2328451
2366033	2352961	2341523	2349693	2330085
2331719	2333353	2361131	2356229	2357863

L4-M11

2379105	2403615	2375837	2380739	2405249
2377471	2387275	2395445	2384007	2400347
2408517	2385641	2388909	2392177	2369301
2406883	2393811	2382373	2390543	2370935
2372569	2374203	2401981	2397079	2398713

L4-M12

2419955	2444465	2416687	2421589	2446099
2418321	2428125	2436295	2424857	2441197
2449367	2426491	2429759	2433027	2410151
2447733	2434661	2423223	2431393	2411785
2413419	2415053	2442831	2437929	2439563

L4-M13

2460805	2485315	2457537	2462439	2486949
2459171	2468975	2477145	2465707	2482047
2490217	2467341	2470609	2473877	2451001
2488583	2475511	2464073	2472243	2452635
2454269	2455903	2483681	2478779	2480413

L4-M14

2501655	2526165	2498387	2503289	2527799
2500021	2509825	2517995	2506557	2522897
2531067	2508191	2511459	2514727	2491851
2529433	2516361	2504923	2513093	2493485
2495119	2496753	2524531	2519629	2521263

L4-M15

2542505	2567015	2539237	2544139	2568649
2540871	2550675	2558845	2547407	2563747
2571917	2549041	2552309	2555577	2532701
2570283	2557211	2545773	2553943	2534335
2535969	2537603	2565381	2560479	2562113

L4-M16

2583355	2607865	2580087	2584989	2609499
2581721	2591525	2599695	2588257	2604597
2612767	2589891	2593159	2596427	2573551
2611133	2598061	2586623	2594793	2575185
2576819	2578453	2606231	2601329	2602963

L5-M1

2624205	2648715	2620937	2625839	2650349
2622571	2632375	2640545	2629107	2645447
2653617	2630741	2634009	2637277	2614401
2651983	2638911	2627473	2635643	2616035
2617669	2619303	2647081	2642179	2643813

L5-M2

2665055	2689565	2661787	2666689	2691199
2663421	2673225	2681395	2669957	2686297
2694467	2671591	2674859	2678127	2655251
2692833	2679761	2668323	2676493	2656885
2658519	2660153	2687931	2683029	2684663

L5-M3

2705905	2730415	2702637	2707539	2732049
2704271	2714075	2722245	2710807	2727147
2735317	2712441	2715709	2718977	2696101
2733683	2720611	2709173	2717343	2697735
2699369	2701003	2728781	2723879	2725513

L5-M4

2746755	2771265	2743487	2748389	2772899
2745121	2754925	2763095	2751657	2767997
2776167	2753291	2756559	2759827	2736951
2774533	2761461	2750023	2758193	2738585
2740219	2741853	2769631	2764729	2766363

L5-M5

2787605	2812115	2784337	2789239	2813749
2785971	2795775	2803945	2792507	2808847
2817017	2794141	2797409	2800677	2777801
2815383	2802311	2790873	2799043	2779435
2781069	2782703	2810481	2805579	2807213

L5-M6

2828455	2852965	2825187	2830089	2854599
2826821	2836625	2844795	2833357	2849697
2857867	2834991	2838259	2841527	2818651
2856233	2843161	2831723	2839893	2820285
2821919	2823553	2851331	2846429	2848063

L5-M7

2869305	2893815	2866037	2870939	2895449
2867671	2877475	2885645	2874207	2890547
2898717	2875841	2879109	2882377	2859501
2897083	2884011	2872573	2880743	2861135
2862769	2864403	2892181	2887279	2888913

L5-M8

2910155	2934665	2906887	2911789	2936299
2908521	2918325	2926495	2915057	2931397
2939567	2916691	2919959	2923227	2900351
2937933	2924861	2913423	2921593	2901985
2903619	2905253	2933031	2928129	2929763

L5-M9

2951005	2975515	2947737	2952639	2977149
2949371	2959175	2967345	2955907	2972247
2980417	2957541	2960809	2964077	2941201
2978783	2965711	2954273	2962443	2942835
2944469	2946103	2973881	2968979	2970613

L5-M10

2991855	3016365	2988587	2993489	3017999
2990221	3000025	3008195	2996757	3013097
3021267	2998391	3001659	3004927	2982051
3019633	3006561	2995123	3003293	2983685
2985319	2986953	3014731	3009829	3011463

L5-M11

3032705	3057215	3029437	3034339	3058849
3031071	3040875	3049045	3037607	3053947
3062117	3039241	3042509	3045777	3022901
3060483	3047411	3035973	3044143	3024535
3026169	3027803	3055581	3050679	3052313

L5-M12

3073555	3098065	3070287	3075189	3099699
3071921	3081725	3089895	3078457	3094797
3102967	3080091	3083359	3086627	3063751
3101333	3088261	3076823	3084993	3065385
3067019	3068653	3096431	3091529	3093163

L5-M13

3114405	3138915	3111137	3116039	3140549
3112771	3122575	3130745	3119307	3135647
3143817	3120941	3124209	3127477	3104601
3142183	3129111	3117673	3125843	3106235
3107869	3109503	3137281	3132379	3134013

L5-M14

3155255	3179765	3151987	3156889	3181399
3153621	3163425	3171595	3160157	3176497
3184667	3161791	3165059	3168327	3145451
3183033	3169961	3158523	3166693	3147085
3148719	3150353	3178131	3173229	3174863

L5-M15

3196105	3220615	3192837	3197739	3222249
3194471	3204275	3212445	3201007	3217347
3225517	3202641	3205909	3209177	3186301
3223883	3210811	3199373	3207543	3187935
3189569	3191203	3218981	3214079	3215713

L5-M16

3236955	3261465	3233687	3238589	3263099
3235321	3245125	3253295	3241857	3258197
3266367	3243491	3246759	3250027	3227151
3264733	3251661	3240223	3248393	3228785
3230419	3232053	3259831	3254929	3256563

L6-M1

3277805	3302315	3274537	3279439	3303949
3276171	3285975	3294145	3282707	3299047
3307217	3284341	3287609	3290877	3268001
3305583	3292511	3281073	3289243	3269635
3271269	3272903	3300681	3295779	3297413

L6-M2

3318655	3343165	3315387	3320289	3344799
3317021	3326825	3334995	3323557	3339897
3348067	3325191	3328459	3331727	3308851
3346433	3333361	3321923	3330093	3310485
3312119	3313753	3341531	3336629	3338263

L6-M3

3359505	3384015	3356237	3361139	3385649
3357871	3367675	3375845	3364407	3380747
3388917	3366041	3369309	3372577	3349701
3387283	3374211	3362773	3370943	3351335
3352969	3354603	3382381	3377479	3379113

L6-M4

3400355	3424865	3397087	3401989	3426499
3398721	3408525	3416695	3405257	3421597
3429767	3406891	3410159	3413427	3390551
3428133	3415061	3403623	3411793	3392185
3393819	3395453	3423231	3418329	3419963

L6-M5

3441205	3465715	3437937	3442839	3467349
3439571	3449375	3457545	3446107	3462447
3470617	3447741	3451009	3454277	3431401
3468983	3455911	3444473	3452643	3433035
3434669	3436303	3464081	3459179	3460813

L6-M6

3482055	3506565	3478787	3483689	3508199
3480421	3490225	3498395	3486957	3503297
3511467	3488591	3491859	3495127	3472251
3509833	3496761	3485323	3493493	3473885
3475519	3477153	3504931	3500029	3501663

L6-M7

3522905	3547415	3519637	3524539	3549049
3521271	3531075	3539245	3527807	3544147
3552317	3529441	3532709	3535977	3513101
3550683	3537611	3526173	3534343	3514735
3516369	3518003	3545781	3540879	3542513

L6-M8

3563755	3588265	3560487	3565389	3589899
3562121	3571925	3580095	3568657	3584997
3593167	3570291	3573559	3576827	3553951
3591533	3578461	3567023	3575193	3555585
3557219	3558853	3586631	3581729	3583363

L6-M9

3604605	3629115	3601337	3606239	3630749
3602971	3612775	3620945	3609507	3625847
3634017	3611141	3614409	3617677	3594801
3632383	3619311	3607873	3616043	3596435
3598069	3599703	3627481	3622579	3624213

L6-M10

3645455	3669965	3642187	3647089	3671599
3643821	3653625	3661795	3650357	3666697
3674867	3651991	3655259	3658527	3635651
3673233	3660161	3648723	3656893	3637285
3638919	3640553	3668331	3663429	3665063

L6-M11

3686305	3710815	3683037	3687939	3712449
3684671	3694475	3702645	3691207	3707547
3715717	3692841	3696109	3699377	3676501
3714083	3701011	3689573	3697743	3678135
3679769	3681403	3709181	3704279	3705913

L6-M12

3727155	3751665	3723887	3728789	3753299
3725521	3735325	3743495	3732057	3748397
3756567	3733691	3736959	3740227	3717351
3754933	3741861	3730423	3738593	3718985
3720619	3722253	3750031	3745129	3746763

L6-M13

3768005	3792515	3764737	3769639	3794149
3766371	3776175	3784345	3772907	3789247
3797417	3774541	3777809	3781077	3758201
3795783	3782711	3771273	3779443	3759835
3761469	3763103	3790881	3785979	3787613

L6-M14

3808855	3833365	3805587	3810489	3834999
3807221	3817025	3825195	3813757	3830097
3838267	3815391	3818659	3821927	3799051
3836633	3823561	3812123	3820293	3800685
3802319	3803953	3831731	3826829	3828463

L6-M15

3849705	3874215	3846437	3851339	3875849
3848071	3857875	3866045	3854607	3870947
3879117	3856241	3859509	3862777	3839901
3877483	3864411	3852973	3861143	3841535
3843169	3844803	3872581	3867679	3869313

L6-M16

3890555	3915065	3887287	3892189	3916699
3888921	3898725	3906895	3895457	3911797
3919967	3897091	3900359	3903627	3880751
3918333	3905261	3893823	3901993	3882385
3884019	3885653	3913431	3908529	3910163

L7-M1

3931405	3955915	3928137	3933039	3957549
3929771	3939575	3947745	3936307	3952647
3960817	3937941	3941209	3944477	3921601
3959183	3946111	3934673	3942843	3923235
3924869	3926503	3954281	3949379	3951013

L7-M2

3972255	3996765	3968987	3973889	3998399
3970621	3980425	3988595	3977157	3993497
4001667	3978791	3982059	3985327	3962451
4000033	3986961	3975523	3983693	3964085
3965719	3967353	3995131	3990229	3991863

L7-M3

4013105	4037615	4009837	4014739	4039249
4011471	4021275	4029445	4018007	4034347
4042517	4019641	4022909	4026177	4003301
4040883	4027811	4016373	4024543	4004935
4006569	4008203	4035981	4031079	4032713

L7-M4

4053955	4078465	4050687	4055589	4080099
4052321	4062125	4070295	4058857	4075197
4083367	4060491	4063759	4067027	4044151
4081733	4068661	4057223	4065393	4045785
4047419	4049053	4076831	4071929	4073563

L7-M5

4094805	4119315	4091537	4096439	4120949
4093171	4102975	4111145	4099707	4116047
4124217	4101341	4104609	4107877	4085001
4122583	4109511	4098073	4106243	4086635
4088269	4089903	4117681	4112779	4114413

L7-M6

4135655	4160165	4132387	4137289	4161799
4134021	4143825	4151995	4140557	4156897
4165067	4142191	4145459	4148727	4125851
4163433	4150361	4138923	4147093	4127485
4129119	4130753	4158531	4153629	4155263

L7-M7

4176505	4201015	4173237	4178139	4202649
4174871	4184675	4192845	4181407	4197747
4205917	4183041	4186309	4189577	4166701
4204283	4191211	4179773	4187943	4168335
4169969	4171603	4199381	4194479	4196113

L7-M8

4217355	4241865	4214087	4218989	4243499
4215721	4225525	4233695	4222257	4238597
4246767	4223891	4227159	4230427	4207551
4245133	4232061	4220623	4228793	4209185
4210819	4212453	4240231	4235329	4236963

L7-M9

4258205	4282715	4254937	4259839	4284349
4256571	4266375	4274545	4263107	4279447
4287617	4264741	4268009	4271277	4248401
4285983	4272911	4261473	4269643	4250035
4251669	4253303	4281081	4276179	4277813

L7-M10

4299055	4323565	4295787	4300689	4325199
4297421	4307225	4315395	4303957	4320297
4328467	4305591	4308859	4312127	4289251
4326833	4313761	4302323	4310493	4290885
4292519	4294153	4321931	4317029	4318663

L7-M11

4339905	4364415	4336637	4341539	4366049
4338271	4348075	4356245	4344807	4361147
4369317	4346441	4349709	4352977	4330101
4367683	4354611	4343173	4351343	4331735
4333369	4335003	4362781	4357879	4359513

L7-M12

4380755	4405265	4377487	4382389	4406899
4379121	4388925	4397095	4385657	4401997
4410167	4387291	4390559	4393827	4370951
4408533	4395461	4384023	4392193	4372585
4374219	4375853	4403631	4398729	4400363

L7-M13

4421605	4446115	4418337	4423239	4447749
4419971	4429775	4437945	4426507	4442847
4451017	4428141	4431409	4434677	4411801
4449383	4436311	4424873	4433043	4413435
4415069	4416703	4444481	4439579	4441213

L7-M14

4462455	4486965	4459187	4464089	4488599
4460821	4470625	4478795	4467357	4483697
4491867	4468991	4472259	4475527	4452651
4490233	4477161	4465723	4473893	4454285
4455919	4457553	4485331	4480429	4482063

L7-M15

4503305	4527815	4500037	4504939	4529449
4501671	4511475	4519645	4508207	4524547
4532717	4509841	4513109	4516377	4493501
4531083	4518011	4506573	4514743	4495135
4496769	4498403	4526181	4521279	4522913

L7-M16

4544155	4568665	4540887	4545789	4570299
4542521	4552325	4560495	4549057	4565397
4573567	4550691	4553959	4557227	4534351
4571933	4558861	4547423	4555593	4535985
4537619	4539253	4567031	4562129	4563763

L8M1

4585005	4609515	4581737	4586639	4611149
4583371	4593175	4601345	4589907	4606247
4614417	4591541	4594809	4598077	4575201
4612783	4599711	4588273	4596443	4576835
4578469	4580103	4607881	4602979	4604613

L8-M2

4625855	4650365	4622587	4627489	4651999
4624221	4634025	4642195	4630757	4647097
4655267	4632391	4635659	4638927	4616051
4653633	4640561	4629123	4637293	4617685
4619319	4620953	4648731	4643829	4645463

L8-M3

4666705	4691215	4663437	4668339	4692849
4665071	4674875	4683045	4671607	4687947
4696117	4673241	4676509	4679777	4656901
4694483	4681411	4669973	4678143	4658535
4660169	4661803	4689581	4684679	4686313

L8-M4

4707555	4732065	4704287	4709189	4733699
4705921	4715725	4723895	4712457	4728797
4736967	4714091	4717359	4720627	4697751
4735333	4722261	4710823	4718993	4699385
4701019	4702653	4730431	4725529	4727163

L8-M5

4748405	4772915	4745137	4750039	4774549
4746771	4756575	4764745	4753307	4769647
4777817	4754941	4758209	4761477	4738601
4776183	4763111	4751673	4759843	4740235
4741869	4743503	4771281	4766379	4768013

L8-M6

4789255	4813765	4785987	4790889	4815399
4787621	4797425	4805595	4794157	4810497
4818667	4795791	4799059	4802327	4779451
4817033	4803961	4792523	4800693	4781085
4782719	4784353	4812131	4807229	4808863

L8-M7

4830105	4854615	4826837	4831739	4856249
4828471	4838275	4846445	4835007	4851347
4859517	4836641	4839909	4843177	4820301
4857883	4844811	4833373	4841543	4821935
4823569	4825203	4852981	4848079	4849713

L8-M8

4870955	4895465	4867687	4872589	4897099
4869321	4879125	4887295	4875857	4892197
4900367	4877491	4880759	4884027	4861151
4898733	4885661	4874223	4882393	4862785
4864419	4866053	4893831	4888929	4890563

L8-M9

4911805	4936315	4908537	4913439	4937949
4910171	4919975	4928145	4916707	4933047
4941217	4918341	4921609	4924877	4902001
4939583	4926511	4915073	4923243	4903635
4905269	4906903	4934681	4929779	4931413

L8-M10

4952655	4977165	4949387	4954289	4978799
4951021	4960825	4968995	4957557	4973897
4982067	4959191	4962459	4965727	4942851
4980433	4967361	4955923	4964093	4944485
4946119	4947753	4975531	4970629	4972263

L8-M11

4993505	5018015	4990237	4995139	5019649
4991871	5001675	5009845	4998407	5014747
5022917	5000041	5003309	5006577	4983701
5021283	5008211	4996773	5004943	4985335
4986969	4988603	5016381	5011479	5013113

L8-M12

5034355	5058865	5031087	5035989	5060499
5032721	5042525	5050695	5039257	5055597
5063767	5040891	5044159	5047427	5024551
5062133	5049061	5037623	5045793	5026185
5027819	5029453	5057231	5052329	5053963

L8-M13

5075205	5099715	5071937	5076839	5101349
5073571	5083375	5091545	5080107	5096447
5104617	5081741	5085009	5088277	5065401
5102983	5089911	5078473	5086643	5067035
5068669	5070303	5098081	5093179	5094813

L8-M14

5116055	5140565	5112787	5117689	5142199
5114421	5124225	5132395	5120957	5137297
5145467	5122591	5125859	5129127	5106251
5143833	5130761	5119323	5127493	5107885
5109519	5111153	5138931	5134029	5135663

L8-M15

5156905	5181415	5153637	5158539	5183049
5155271	5165075	5173245	5161807	5178147
5186317	5163441	5166709	5169977	5147101
5184683	5171611	5160173	5168343	5148735
5150369	5152003	5179781	5174879	5176513

L8-M16

5197755	5222265	5194487	5199389	5223899
5196121	5205925	5214095	5202657	5218997
5227167	5204291	5207559	5210827	5187951
5225533	5212461	5201023	5209193	5189585
5191219	5192853	5220631	5215729	5217363

L9-M1

5238605	5263115	5235337	5240239	5264749
5236971	5246775	5254945	5243507	5259847
5268017	5245141	5248409	5251677	5228801
5266383	5253311	5241873	5250043	5230435
5232069	5233703	5261481	5256579	5258213

L9-M2

5279455	5303965	5276187	5281089	5305599
5277821	5287625	5295795	5284357	5300697
5308867	5285991	5289259	5292527	5269651
5307233	5294161	5282723	5290893	5271285
5272919	5274553	5302331	5297429	5299063

L9-M3

5320305	5344815	5317037	5321939	5346449
5318671	5328475	5336645	5325207	5341547
5349717	5326841	5330109	5333377	5310501
5348083	5335011	5323573	5331743	5312135
5313769	5315403	5343181	5338279	5339913

L9-M4

5361155	5385665	5357887	5362789	5387299
5359521	5369325	5377495	5366057	5382397
5390567	5367691	5370959	5374227	5351351
5388933	5375861	5364423	5372593	5352985
5354619	5356253	5384031	5379129	5380763

L9-M5

5402005	5426515	5398737	5403639	5428149
5400371	5410175	5418345	5406907	5423247
5431417	5408541	5411809	5415077	5392201
5429783	5416711	5405273	5413443	5393835
5395469	5397103	5424881	5419979	5421613

L9-M6

5442855	5467365	5439587	5444489	5468999
5441221	5451025	5459195	5447757	5464097
5472267	5449391	5452659	5455927	5433051
5470633	5457561	5446123	5454293	5434685
5436319	5437953	5465731	5460829	5462463

L9-M7

5483705	5508215	5480437	5485339	5509849
5482071	5491875	5500045	5488607	5504947
5513117	5490241	5493509	5496777	5473901
5511483	5498411	5486973	5495143	5475535
5477169	5478803	5506581	5501679	5503313

L9-M8

5524555	5549065	5521287	5526189	5550699
5522921	5532725	5540895	5529457	5545797
5553967	5531091	5534359	5537627	5514751
5552333	5539261	5527823	5535993	5516385
5518019	5519653	5547431	5542529	5544163

L9-M9

5565405	5589915	5562137	5567039	5591549
5563771	5573575	5581745	5570307	5586647
5594817	5571941	5575209	5578477	5555601
5593183	5580111	5568673	5576843	5557235
5558869	5560503	5588281	5583379	5585013

L9-M10

5606255	5630765	5602987	5607889	5632399
5604621	5614425	5622595	5611157	5627497
5635667	5612791	5616059	5619327	5596451
5634033	5620961	5609523	5617693	5598085
5599719	5601353	5629131	5624229	5625863

L9-M11

5647105	5671615	5643837	5648739	5673249
5645471	5655275	5663445	5652007	5668347
5676517	5653641	5656909	5660177	5637301
5674883	5661811	5650373	5658543	5638935
5640569	5642203	5669981	5665079	5666713

L9-M12

5687955	5712465	5684687	5689589	5714099
5686321	5696125	5704295	5692857	5709197
5717367	5694491	5697759	5701027	5678151
5715733	5702661	5691223	5699393	5679785
5681419	5683053	5710831	5705929	5707563

L9-M13

5728805	5753315	5725537	5730439	5754949
5727171	5736975	5745145	5733707	5750047
5758217	5735341	5738609	5741877	5719001
5756583	5743511	5732073	5740243	5720635
5722269	5723903	5751681	5746779	5748413

L9-M14

5769655	5794165	5766387	5771289	5795799
5768021	5777825	5785995	5774557	5790897
5799067	5776191	5779459	5782727	5759851
5797433	5784361	5772923	5781093	5761485
5763119	5764753	5792531	5787629	5789263

L9-M15

5810505	5835015	5807237	5812139	5836649
5808871	5818675	5826845	5815407	5831747
5839917	5817041	5820309	5823577	5800701
5838283	5825211	5813773	5821943	5802335
5803969	5805603	5833381	5828479	5830113

L9-M16

5851355	5875865	5848087	5852989	5877499
5849721	5859525	5867695	5856257	5872597
5880767	5857891	5861159	5864427	5841551
5879133	5866061	5854623	5862793	5843185
5844819	5846453	5874231	5869329	5870963

L10-M1

5892205	5916715	5888937	5893839	5918349
5890571	5900375	5908545	5897107	5913447
5921617	5898741	5902009	5905277	5882401
5919983	5906911	5895473	5903643	5884035
5885669	5887303	5915081	5910179	5911813

L10-M10

6259855	6284365	6256587	6261489	6285999
6258221	6268025	6276195	6264757	6281097
6289267	6266391	6269659	6272927	6250051
6287633	6274561	6263123	6271293	6251685
6253319	6254953	6282731	6277829	6279463

L10-M2

5933055	5957565	5929787	5934689	5959199
5931421	5941225	5949395	5937957	5954297
5962467	5939591	5942859	5946127	5923251
5960833	5947761	5936323	5944493	5924885
5926519	5928153	5955931	5951029	5952663

L10-M11

6300705	6325215	6297437	6302339	6326849
6299071	6308875	6317045	6305607	6321947
6330117	6307241	6310509	6313777	6290901
6328483	6315411	6303973	6312143	6292535
6294169	6295803	6323581	6318679	6320313

L10-M3

5973905	5998415	5970637	5975539	6000049
5972271	5982075	5990245	5978807	5995147
6003317	5980441	5983709	5986977	5964101
6001683	5988611	5977173	5985343	5965735
5967369	5969003	5996781	5991879	5993513

L10-M12

6341555	6366065	6338287	6343189	6367699
6339921	6349725	6357895	6346457	6362797
6370967	6348091	6351359	6354627	6331751
6369333	6356261	6344823	6352993	6333385
6335019	6336653	6364431	6359529	6361163

L10-M4

6014755	6039265	6011487	6016389	6040899
6013121	6022925	6031095	6019657	6035997
6044167	6021291	6024559	6027827	6004951
6042533	6029461	6018023	6026193	6006585
6008219	6009853	6037631	6032729	6034363

L10-M13

6382405	6406915	6379137	6384039	6408549
6380771	6390575	6398745	6387307	6403647
6411817	6388941	6392209	6395477	6372601
6410183	6397111	6385673	6393843	6374235
6375869	6377503	6405281	6400379	6402013

L10-M5

6055605	6080115	6052337	6057239	6081749
6053971	6063775	6071945	6060507	6076847
6085017	6062141	6065409	6068677	6045801
6083383	6070311	6058873	6067043	6047435
6049069	6050703	6078481	6073579	6075213

L10-M14

6423255	6447765	6419987	6424889	6449399
6421621	6431425	6439595	6428157	6444497
6452667	6429791	6433059	6436327	6413451
6451033	6437961	6426523	6434693	6415085
6416719	6418353	6446131	6441229	6442863

L10-M6

6096455	6120965	6093187	6098089	6122599
6094821	6104625	6112795	6101357	6117697
6125867	6102991	6106259	6109527	6086651
6124233	6111161	6099723	6107893	6088285
6089919	6091553	6119331	6114429	6116063

L10-M15

6464105	6488615	6460837	6465739	6490249
6462471	6472275	6480445	6469007	6485347
6493517	6470641	6473909	6477177	6454301
6491883	6478811	6467373	6475543	6455935
6457569	6459203	6486981	6482079	6483713

L10-M7

6137305	6161815	6134037	6138939	6163449
6135671	6145475	6153645	6142207	6158547
6166717	6143841	6147109	6150377	6127501
6165083	6152011	6140573	6148743	6129135
6130769	6132403	6160181	6155279	6156913

L10-M16

6504955	6529465	6501687	6506589	6531099
6503321	6513125	6521295	6509857	6526197
6534367	6511491	6514759	6518027	6495151
6532733	6519661	6508223	6516393	6496785
6498419	6500053	6527831	6522929	6524563

L10-M8

6178155	6202665	6174887	6179789	6204299
6176521	6186325	6194495	6183057	6199397
6207567	6184691	6187959	6191227	6168351
6205933	6192861	6181423	6189593	6169985
6171619	6173253	6201031	6196129	6197763

L11-M1

6545805	6570315	6542537	6547439	6571949
6544171	6553975	6562145	6550707	6567047
6575217	6552341	6555609	6558877	6536001
6573583	6560511	6549073	6557243	6537635
6539269	6540903	6568681	6563779	6565413

L10-M9

6219005	6243515	6215737	6220639	6245149
6217371	6227175	6235345	6223907	6240247
6248417	6225541	6228809	6232077	6209201
6246783	6233711	6222273	6230443	6210835
6212469	6214103	6241881	6236979	6238613

L11-M2

6586655	6611165	6583387	6588289	6612799
6585021	6594825	6602995	6591557	6607897
6616067	6593191	6596459	6599727	6576851
6614433	6601361	6589923	6598093	6578485
6580119	6581753	6609531	6604629	6606263

L11-M3

6627505	6652015	6624237	6629139	6653649
6625871	6635675	6643845	6632407	6648747
6656917	6634041	6637309	6640577	6617701
6655283	6642211	6630773	6638943	6619335
6620969	6622603	6650381	6645479	6647113

L11-M4

6668355	6692865	6665087	6669989	6694499
6666721	6676525	6684695	6673257	6689597
6697767	6674891	6678159	6681427	6658551
6696133	6683061	6671623	6679793	6660185
6661819	6663453	6691231	6686329	6687963

L11-M5

6709205	6733715	6705937	6710839	6735349
6707571	6717375	6725545	6714107	6730447
6738617	6715741	6719009	6722277	6699401
6736983	6723911	6712473	6720643	6701035
6702669	6704303	6732081	6727179	6728813

L11-M6

6750055	6774565	6746787	6751689	6776199
6748421	6758225	6766395	6754957	6771297
6779467	6756591	6759859	6763127	6740251
6777833	6764761	6753323	6761493	6741885
6743519	6745153	6772931	6768029	6769663

L11-M7

6790905	6815415	6787637	6792539	6817049
6789271	6799075	6807245	6795807	6812147
6820317	6797441	6800709	6803977	6781101
6818683	6805611	6794173	6802343	6782735
6784369	6786003	6813781	6808879	6810513

L11-M8

6831755	6856265	6828487	6833389	6857899
6830121	6839925	6848095	6836657	6852997
6861167	6838291	6841559	6844827	6821951
6859533	6846461	6835023	6843193	6823585
6825219	6826853	6854631	6849729	6851363

L11-M9

6872605	6897115	6869337	6874239	6898749
6870971	6880775	6888945	6877507	6893847
6902017	6879141	6882409	6885677	6862801
6900383	6887311	6875873	6884043	6864435
6866069	6867703	6895481	6890579	6892213

L11-M10

6913455	6937965	6910187	6915089	6939599
6911821	6921625	6929795	6918357	6934697
6942867	6919991	6923259	6926527	6903651
6941233	6928161	6916723	6924893	6905285
6906919	6908553	6936331	6931429	6933063

L11-M11

6954305	6978815	6951037	6955939	6980449
6952671	6962475	6970645	6959207	6975547
6983717	6960841	6964109	6967377	6944501
6982083	6969011	6957573	6965743	6946135
6947769	6949403	6977181	6972279	6973913

L11-M12

6995155	7019665	6991887	6996789	7021299
6993521	7003325	7011495	7000057	7016397
7024567	7001691	7004959	7008227	6985351
7022933	7009861	6998423	7006593	6986985
6988619	6990253	7018031	7013129	7014763

L11-M13

7036005	7060515	7032737	7037639	7062149
7034371	7044175	7052345	7040907	7057247
7065417	7042541	7045809	7049077	7026201
7063783	7050711	7039273	7047443	7027835
7029469	7031103	7058881	7053979	7055613

L11-M14

7076855	7101365	7073587	7078489	7102999
7075221	7085025	7093195	7081757	7098097
7106267	7083391	7086659	7089927	7067051
7104633	7091561	7080123	7088293	7068685
7070319	7071953	7099731	7094829	7096463

L11-M15

7117705	7142215	7114437	7119339	7143849
7116071	7125875	7134045	7122607	7138947
7147117	7124241	7127509	7130777	7107901
7145483	7132411	7120973	7129143	7109535
7111169	7112803	7140581	7135679	7137313

L11-M16

7158555	7183065	7155287	7160189	7184699
7156921	7166725	7174895	7163457	7179797
7187967	7165091	7168359	7171627	7148751
7186333	7173261	7161823	7169993	7150385
7152019	7153653	7181431	7176529	7178163

L12-M1

7199405	7223915	7196137	7201039	7225549
7197771	7207575	7215745	7204307	7220647
7228817	7205941	7209209	7212477	7189601
7227183	7214111	7202673	7210843	7191235
7192869	7194503	7222281	7217379	7219013

L12-M2

7240255	7264765	7236987	7241889	7266399
7238621	7248425	7256595	7245157	7261497
7269667	7246791	7250059	7253327	7230451
7268033	7254961	7243523	7251693	7232085
7233719	7235353	7263131	7258229	7259863

L12-M3

7281105	7305615	7277837	7282739	7307249
7279471	7289275	7297445	7286007	7302347
7310517	7287641	7290909	7294177	7271301
7308883	7295811	7284373	7292543	7272935
7274569	7276203	7303981	7299079	7300713

L12-M4

7321955	7346465	7318687	7323589	7348099
7320321	7330125	7338295	7326857	7343197
7351367	7328491	7331759	7335027	7312151
7349733	7336661	7325223	7333393	7313785
7315419	7317053	7344831	7339929	7341563

L12-M5

7362805	7387315	7359537	7364439	7388949
7361171	7370975	7379145	7367707	7384047
7392217	7369341	7372609	7375877	7353001
7390583	7377511	7366073	7374243	7354635
7356269	7357903	7385681	7380779	7382413

L12-M6

7403655	7428165	7400387	7405289	7429799
7402021	7411825	7419995	7408557	7424897
7433067	7410191	7413459	7416727	7393851
7431433	7418361	7406923	7415093	7395485
7397119	7398753	7426531	7421629	7423263

L12-M7

7444505	7469015	7441237	7446139	7470649
7442871	7452675	7460845	7449407	7465747
7473917	7451041	7454309	7457577	7434701
7472283	7459211	7447773	7455943	7436335
7437969	7439603	7467381	7462479	7464113

L12-M8

7485355	7509865	7482087	7486989	7511499
7483721	7493525	7501695	7490257	7506597
7514767	7491891	7495159	7498427	7475551
7513133	7500061	7488623	7496793	7477185
7478819	7480453	7508231	7503329	7504963

L12-M9

7526205	7550715	7522937	7527839	7552349
7524571	7534375	7542545	7531107	7547447
7555617	7532741	7536009	7539277	7516401
7553983	7540911	7529473	7537643	7518035
7519669	7521303	7549081	7544179	7545813

L12-M10

7567055	7591565	7563787	7568689	7593199
7565421	7575225	7583395	7571957	7588297
7596467	7573591	7576859	7580127	7557251
7594833	7581761	7570323	7578493	7558885
7560519	7562153	7589931	7585029	7586663

L12-M11

7607905	7632415	7604637	7609539	7634049
7606271	7616075	7624245	7612807	7629147
7637317	7614441	7617709	7620977	7598101
7635683	7622611	7611173	7619343	7599735
7601369	7603003	7630781	7625879	7627513

L12-M12

7648755	7673265	7645487	7650389	7674899
7647121	7656925	7665095	7653657	7669997
7678167	7655291	7658559	7661827	7638951
7676533	7663461	7652023	7660193	7640585
7642219	7643853	7671631	7666729	7668363

L12-M13

7689605	7714115	7686337	7691239	7715749
7687971	7697775	7705945	7694507	7710847
7719017	7696141	7699409	7702677	7679801
7717383	7704311	7692873	7701043	7681435
7683069	7684703	7712481	7707579	7709213

L12-M14

7730455	7754965	7727187	7732089	7756599
7728821	7738625	7746795	7735357	7751697
7759867	7736991	7740259	7743527	7720651
7758233	7745161	7733723	7741893	7722285
7723919	7725553	7753331	7748429	7750063

L12-M15

7771305	7795815	7768037	7772939	7797449
7769671	7779475	7787645	7776207	7792547
7800717	7777841	7781109	7784377	7761501
7799083	7786011	7774573	7782743	7763135
7764769	7766403	7794181	7789279	7790913

L12-M16

7812155	7836665	7808887	7813789	7838299
7810521	7820325	7828495	7817057	7833397
7841567	7818691	7821959	7825227	7802351
7839933	7826861	7815423	7823593	7803985
7805619	7807253	7835031	7830129	7831763

L13-M1

7853005	7877515	7849737	7854639	7879149
7851371	7861175	7869345	7857907	7874247
7882417	7859541	7862809	7866077	7843201
7880783	7867711	7856273	7864443	7844835
7846469	7848103	7875881	7870979	7872613

L13-M2

7893855	7918365	7890587	7895489	7919999
7892221	7902025	7910195	7898757	7915097
7923267	7900391	7903659	7906927	7884051
7921633	7908561	7897123	7905293	7885685
7887319	7888953	7916731	7911829	7913463

L13-M3

7934705	7959215	7931437	7936339	7960849
7933071	7942875	7951045	7939607	7955947
7964117	7941241	7944509	7947777	7924901
7962483	7949411	7937973	7946143	7926535
7928169	7929803	7957581	7952679	7954313

L13-M4

7975555	8000065	7972287	7977189	8001699
7973921	7983725	7991895	7980457	7996797
8004967	7982091	7985359	7988627	7965751
8003333	7990261	7978823	7986993	7967385
7969019	7970653	7998431	7993529	7995163

L13-M5

8016405	8040915	8013137	8018039	8042549
8014771	8024575	8032745	8021307	8037647
8045817	8022941	8026209	8029477	8006601
8044183	8031111	8019673	8027843	8008235
8009869	8011503	8039281	8034379	8036013

L13-M6

8057255	8081765	8053987	8058889	8083399
8055621	8065425	8073595	8062157	8078497
8086667	8063791	8067059	8070327	8047451
8085033	8071961	8060523	8068693	8049085
8050719	8052353	8080131	8075229	8076863

L13-M7

8098105	8122615	8094837	8099739	8124249
8096471	8106275	8114445	8103007	8119347
8127517	8104641	8107909	8111177	8088301
8125883	8112811	8101373	8109543	8089935
8091569	8093203	8120981	8116079	8117713

L13-M16

8465755	8490265	8462487	8467389	8491899
8464121	8473925	8482095	8470657	8486997
8495167	8472291	8475559	8478827	8455951
8493533	8480461	8469023	8477193	8457585
8459219	8460853	8488631	8483729	8485363

L13-M8

8138955	8163465	8135687	8140589	8165099
8137321	8147125	8155295	8143857	8160197
8168367	8145491	8148759	8152027	8129151
8166733	8153661	8142223	8150393	8130785
8132419	8134053	8161831	8156929	8158563

L14-M1

8506605	8531115	8503337	8508239	8532749
8504971	8514775	8522945	8511507	8527847
8536017	8513141	8516409	8519677	8496801
8534383	8521311	8509873	8518043	8498435
8500069	8501703	8529481	8524579	8526213

L13-M9

8179805	8204315	8176537	8181439	8205949
8178171	8187975	8196145	8184707	8201047
8209217	8186341	8189609	8192877	8170001
8207583	8194511	8183073	8191243	8171635
8173269	8174903	8202681	8197779	8199413

L14-M2

8547455	8571965	8544187	8549089	8573599
8545821	8555625	8563795	8552357	8568697
8576867	8553991	8557259	8560527	8537651
8575233	8562161	8550723	8558893	8539285
8540919	8542553	8570331	8565429	8567063

L13-M10

8220655	8245165	8217387	8222289	8246799
8219021	8228825	8236995	8225557	8241897
8250067	8227191	8230459	8233727	8210851
8248433	8235361	8223923	8232093	8212485
8214119	8215753	8243531	8238629	8240263

L14-M3

8588305	8612815	8585037	8589939	8614449
8586671	8596475	8604645	8593207	8609547
8617717	8594841	8598109	8601377	8578501
8616083	8603011	8591573	8599743	8580135
8581769	8583403	8611181	8606279	8607913

L13-M11

8261505	8286015	8258237	8263139	8287649
8259871	8269675	8277845	8266407	8282747
8290917	8268041	8271309	8274577	8251701
8289283	8276211	8264773	8272943	8253335
8254969	8256603	8284381	8279479	8281113

L14-M4

8629155	8653665	8625887	8630789	8655299
8627521	8637325	8645495	8634057	8650397
8658567	8635691	8638959	8642227	8619351
8656933	8643861	8632423	8640593	8620985
8622619	8624253	8652031	8647129	8648763

L13-M12

8302355	8326865	8299087	8303989	8328499
8300721	8310525	8318695	8307257	8323597
8331767	8308891	8312159	8315427	8292551
8330133	8317061	8305623	8313793	8294185
8295819	8297453	8325231	8320329	8321963

L14-M5

8670005	8694515	8666737	8671639	8696149
8668371	8678175	8686345	8674907	8691247
8699417	8676541	8679809	8683077	8660201
8697783	8684711	8673273	8681443	8661835
8663469	8665103	8692881	8687979	8689613

L13-M13

8343205	8367715	8339937	8344839	8369349
8341571	8351375	8359545	8348107	8364447
8372617	8349741	8353009	8356277	8333401
8370983	8357911	8346473	8354643	8335035
8336669	8338303	8366081	8361179	8362813

L14-M6

8710855	8735365	8707587	8712489	8736999
8709221	8719025	8727195	8715757	8732097
8740267	8717391	8720659	8723927	8701051
8738633	8725561	8714123	8722293	8702685
8704319	8705953	8733731	8728829	8730463

L13-M14

8384055	8408565	8380787	8385689	8410199
8382421	8392225	8400395	8388957	8405297
8413467	8390591	8393859	8397127	8374251
8411833	8398761	8387323	8395493	8375885
8377519	8379153	8406931	8402029	8403663

L14-M7

8751705	8776215	8748437	8753339	8777849
8750071	8759875	8768045	8756607	8772947
8781117	8758241	8761509	8764777	8741901
8779483	8766411	8754973	8763143	8743535
8745169	8746803	8774581	8769679	8771313

L13-M15

8424905	8449415	8421637	8426539	8451049
8423271	8433075	8441245	8429807	8446147
8454317	8431441	8434709	8437977	8415101
8452683	8439611	8428173	8436343	8416735
8418369	8420003	8447781	8442879	8444513

L14-M8

8792555	8817065	8789287	8794189	8818699
8790921	8800725	8808895	8797457	8813797
8821967	8799091	8802359	8805627	8782751
8820333	8807261	8795823	8803993	8784385
8786019	8787653	8815431	8810529	8812163

L14-M9

8833405	8857915	8830137	8835039	8859549
8831771	8841575	8849745	8838307	8854647
8862817	8839941	8843209	8846477	8823601
8861183	8848111	8836673	8844843	8825235
8826869	8828503	8856281	8851379	8853013

L14-M10

8874255	8898765	8870987	8875889	8900399
8872621	8882425	8890595	8879157	8895497
8903667	8880791	8884059	8887327	8864451
8902033	8888961	8877523	8885693	8866085
8867719	8869353	8897131	8892229	8893863

L14-M11

8915105	8939615	8911837	8916739	8941249
8913471	8923275	8931445	8920007	8936347
8944517	8921641	8924909	8928177	8905301
8942883	8929811	8918373	8926543	8906935
8908569	8910203	8937981	8933079	8934713

L14-M12

8955955	8980465	8952687	8957589	8982099
8954321	8964125	8972295	8960857	8977197
8985367	8962491	8965759	8969027	8946151
8983733	8970661	8959223	8967393	8947785
8949419	8951053	8978831	8973929	8975563

L14-M13

8996805	9021315	8993537	8998439	9022949
8995171	9004975	9013145	9001707	9018047
9026217	9003341	9006609	9009877	8987001
9024583	9011511	9000073	9008243	8988635
8990269	8991903	9019681	9014779	9016413

L14-M14

9037655	9062165	9034387	9039289	9063799
9036021	9045825	9053995	9042557	9058897
9067067	9044191	9047459	9050727	9027851
9065433	9052361	9040923	9049093	9029485
9031119	9032753	9060531	9055629	9057263

L14-M15

9078505	9103015	9075237	9080139	9104649
9076871	9086675	9094845	9083407	9099747
9107917	9085041	9088309	9091577	9068701
9106283	9093211	9081773	9089943	9070335
9071969	9073603	9101381	9096479	9098113

L14-M16

9119355	9143865	9116087	9120989	9145499
9117721	9127525	9135695	9124257	9140597
9148767	9125891	9129159	9132427	9109551
9147133	9134061	9122623	9130793	9111185
9112819	9114453	9142231	9137329	9138963

L15-M1

9160205	9184715	9156937	9161839	9186349
9158571	9168375	9176545	9165107	9181447
9189617	9166741	9170009	9173277	9150401
9187983	9174911	9163473	9171643	9152035
9153669	9155303	9183081	9178179	9179813

L15-M2

9201055	9225565	9197787	9202689	9227199
9199421	9209225	9217395	9205957	9222297
9230467	9207591	9210859	9214127	9191251
9228833	9215761	9204323	9212493	9192885
9194519	9196153	9223931	9219029	9220663

L15-M3

9241905	9266415	9238637	9243539	9268049
9240271	9250075	9258245	9246807	9263147
9271317	9248441	9251709	9254977	9232101
9269683	9256611	9245173	9253343	9233735
9235369	9237003	9264781	9259879	9261513

L15-M4

9282755	9307265	9279487	9284389	9308899
9281121	9290925	9299095	9287657	9303997
9312167	9289291	9292559	9295827	9272951
9310533	9297461	9286023	9294193	9274585
9276219	9277853	9305631	9300729	9302363

L15-M5

9323605	9348115	9320337	9325239	9349749
9321971	9331775	9339945	9328507	9344847
9353017	9330141	9333409	9336677	9313801
9351383	9338311	9326873	9335043	9315435
9317069	9318703	9346481	9341579	9343213

L15-M6

9364455	9388965	9361187	9366089	9390599
9362821	9372625	9380795	9369357	9385697
9393867	9370991	9374259	9377527	9354651
9392233	9379161	9367723	9375893	9356285
9357919	9359553	9387331	9382429	9384063

L15-M7

9405305	9429815	9402037	9406939	9431449
9403671	9413475	9421645	9410207	9426547
9434717	9411841	9415109	9418377	9395501
9433083	9420011	9408573	9416743	9397135
9398769	9400403	9428181	9423279	9424913

L15-M8

9446155	9470665	9442887	9447789	9472299
9444521	9454325	9462495	9451057	9467397
9475567	9452691	9455959	9459227	9436351
9473933	9460861	9449423	9457593	9437985
9439619	9441253	9469031	9464129	9465763

L15-M9

9487005	9511515	9483737	9488639	9513149
9485371	9495175	9503345	9491907	9508247
9516417	9493541	9496809	9500077	9477201
9514783	9501711	9490273	9498443	9478835
9480469	9482103	9509881	9504979	9506613

L15-M10

9527855	9552365	9524587	9529489	9553999
9526221	9536025	9544195	9532757	9549097
9557267	9534391	9537659	9540927	9518051
9555633	9542561	9531123	9539293	9519685
9521319	9522953	9550731	9545829	9547463

L15-M11

9568705	9593215	9565437	9570339	9594849
9567071	9576875	9585045	9573607	9589947
9598117	9575241	9578509	9581777	9558901
9596483	9583411	9571973	9580143	9560535
9562169	9563803	9591581	9586679	9588313

L16-M4

9936355	9960865	9933087	9937989	9962499
9934721	9944525	9952695	9941257	9957597
9965767	9942891	9946159	9949427	9926551
9964133	9951061	9939623	9947793	9928185
9929819	9931453	9959231	9954329	9955963

L15-M12

9609555	9634065	9606287	9611189	9635699
9607921	9617725	9625895	9614457	9630797
9638967	9616091	9619359	9622627	9599751
9637333	9624261	9612823	9620993	9601385
9603019	9604653	9632431	9627529	9629163

L16-M5

9977205	10001715	9973937	9978839	10003349
9975571	9985375	9993545	9982107	9998447
10006617	9983741	9987009	9990277	9967401
10004983	9991911	9980473	9988643	9969035
9970669	9972303	10000081	9995179	9996813

L15-M13

9650405	9674915	9647137	9652039	9676549
9648771	9658575	9666745	9655307	9671647
9679817	9656941	9660209	9663477	9640601
9678183	9665111	9653673	9661843	9642235
9643869	9645503	9673281	9668379	9670013

L16-M6

10018055	10042565	10014787	10019689	10044199
10016421	10026225	10034395	10022957	10039297
10047467	10024591	10027859	10031127	10008251
10045833	10032761	10021323	10029493	10009885
10011519	10013153	10040931	10036029	10037663

L15-M14

9691255	9715765	9687987	9692889	9717399
9689621	9699425	9707595	9696157	9712497
9720667	9697791	9701059	9704327	9681451
9719033	9705961	9694523	9702693	9683085
9684719	9686353	9714131	9709229	9710863

L16-M7

10058905	10083415	10055637	10060539	10085049
10057271	10067075	10075245	10063807	10080147
10088317	10065441	10068709	10071977	10049101
10086683	10073611	10062173	10070343	10050735
10052369	10054003	10081781	10076879	10078513

L15-M15

9732105	9756615	9728837	9733739	9758249
9730471	9740275	9748445	9737007	9753347
9761517	9738641	9741909	9745177	9722301
9759883	9746811	9735373	9743543	9723935
9725569	9727203	9754981	9750079	9751713

L16-M8

10099755	10124265	10096487	10101389	10125899
10098121	10107925	10116095	10104657	10120997
10129167	10106291	10109559	10112827	10089951
10127533	10114461	10103023	10111193	10091585
10093219	10094853	10122631	10117729	10119363

L15-M16

9772955	9797465	9769687	9774589	9799099
9771321	9781125	9789295	9777857	9794197
9802367	9779491	9782759	9786027	9763151
9800733	9787661	9776223	9784393	9764785
9766419	9768053	9795831	9790929	9792563

L16-M9

10140605	10165115	10137337	10142239	10166749
10138971	10148775	10156945	10145507	10161847
10170017	10147141	10150409	10153677	10130801
10168383	10155311	10143873	10152043	10132435
10134069	10135703	10163481	10158579	10160213

L16-M1

9813805	9838315	9810537	9815439	9839949
9812171	9821975	9830145	9818707	9835047
9843217	9820341	9823609	9826877	9804001
9841583	9828511	9817073	9825243	9805635
9807269	9808903	9836681	9831779	9833413

L16-M10

10181455	10205965	10178187	10183089	10207599
10179821	10189625	10197795	10186357	10202697
10210867	10187991	10191259	10194527	10171651
10209233	10196161	10184723	10192893	10173285
10174919	10176553	10204331	10199429	10201063

L16-M2

9854655	9879165	9851387	9856289	9880799
9853021	9862825	9870995	9859557	9875897
9884067	9861191	9864459	9867727	9844851
9882433	9869361	9857923	9866093	9846485
9848119	9849753	9877531	9872629	9874263

L16-M11

10222305	10246815	10219037	10223939	10248449
10220671	10230475	10238645	10227207	10243547
10251717	10228841	10232109	10235377	10212501
10250083	10237011	10225573	10233743	10214135
10215769	10217403	10245181	10240279	10241913

L16-M3

9895505	9920015	9892237	9897139	9921649
9893871	9903675	9911845	9900407	9916747
9924917	9902041	9905309	9908577	9885701
9923283	9910211	9898773	9906943	9887335
9888969	9890603	9918381	9913479	9915113

L16-M12

10263155	10287665	10259887	10264789	10289299
10261521	10271325	10279495	10268057	10284397
10292567	10269691	10272959	10276227	10253351
10290933	10277861	10266423	10274593	10254985
10256619	10258253	10286031	10281129	10282763

L16-M13

10304005	10328515	10300737	10305639	10330149
10302371	10312175	10320345	10308907	10325247
10333417	10310541	10313809	10317077	10294201
10331783	10318711	10307273	10315443	10295835
10297469	10299103	10326881	10321979	10323613

L16-M14

10344855	10369365	10341587	10346489	10370999
10343221	10353025	10361195	10349757	10366097
10374267	10351391	10354659	10357927	10335051
10372633	10359561	10348123	10356293	10336685
10338319	10339953	10367731	10362829	10364463

L16-M15

10385705	10410215	10382437	10387339	10411849
10384071	10393875	10402045	10390607	10406947
10415117	10392241	10395509	10398777	10375901
10413483	10400411	10388973	10397143	10377535
10379169	10380803	10408581	10403679	10405313

L16M16

10426555	10451065	10423287	10428189	10452699
10424921	10434725	10442895	10431457	10447797
10455967	10433091	10436359	10439627	10416751
10454333	10441261	10429823	10437993	10418385
10420019	10421653	10449431	10444529	10446163

L17-M1

10467405	10491915	10464137	10469039	10493549
10465771	10475575	10483745	10472307	10488647
10496817	10473941	10477209	10480477	10457601
10495183	10482111	10470673	10478843	10459235
10460869	10462503	10490281	10485379	10487013

L17-M2

10508255	10532765	10504987	10509889	10534399
10506621	10516425	10524595	10513157	10529497
10537667	10514791	10518059	10521327	10498451
10536033	10522961	10511523	10519693	10500085
10501719	10503353	10531131	10526229	10527863

L17-M3

10549105	10573615	10545837	10550739	10575249
10547471	10557275	10565445	10554007	10570347
10578517	10555641	10558909	10562177	10539301
10576883	10563811	10552373	10560543	10540935
10542569	10544203	10571981	10567079	10568713

L17-M4

10589955	10614465	10586687	10591589	10616099
10588321	10598125	10606295	10594857	10611197
10619367	10596491	10599759	10603027	10580151
10617733	10604661	10593223	10601393	10581785
10583419	10585053	10612831	10607929	10609563

L17-M5

10630805	10655315	10627537	10632439	10656949
10629171	10638975	10647145	10635707	10652047
10660217	10637341	10640609	10643877	10621001
10658583	10645511	10634073	10642243	10622635
10624269	10625903	10653681	10648779	10650413

L17-M6

10671655	10696165	10668387	10673289	10697799
10670021	10679825	10687995	10676557	10692897
10701067	10678191	10681459	10684727	10661851
10699433	10686361	10674923	10683093	10663485
10665119	10666753	10694531	10689629	10691263

L17-M7

10712505	10737015	10709237	10714139	10738649
10710871	10720675	10728845	10717407	10733747
10741917	10719041	10722309	10725577	10702701
10740283	10727211	10715773	10723943	10704335
10705969	10707603	10735381	10730479	10732113

L17-M8

10753355	10777865	10750087	10754989	10779499
10751721	10761525	10769695	10758257	10774597
10782767	10759891	10763159	10766427	10743551
10781133	10768061	10756623	10764793	10745185
10746819	10748453	10776231	10771329	10772963

L17-M9

10794205	10818715	10790937	10795839	10820349
10792571	10802375	10810545	10799107	10815447
10823617	10800741	10804009	10807277	10784401
10821983	10808911	10797473	10805643	10786035
10787669	10789303	10817081	10812179	10813813

L17-M10

10835055	10859565	10831787	10836689	10861199
10833421	10843225	10851395	10839957	10856297
10864467	10841591	10844859	10848127	10825251
10862833	10849761	10838323	10846493	10826885
10828519	10830153	10857931	10853029	10854663

L17-M11

10875905	10900415	10872637	10877539	10902049
10874271	10884075	10892245	10880807	10897147
10905317	10882441	10885709	10888977	10866101
10903683	10890611	10879173	10887343	10867735
10869369	10871003	10898781	10893879	10895513

L17-M12

10916755	10941265	10913487	10918389	10942899
10915121	10924925	10933095	10921657	10937997
10946167	10923291	10926559	10929827	10906951
10944533	10931461	10920023	10928193	10908585
10910219	10911853	10939631	10934729	10936363

L17-M13

10957605	10982115	10954337	10959239	10983749
10955971	10965775	10973945	10962507	10978847
10987017	10964141	10967409	10970677	10947801
10985383	10972311	10960873	10969043	10949435
10951069	10952703	10980481	10975579	10977213

L17-M14

10998455	11022965	10995187	11000089	11024599
10996821	11006625	11014795	11003357	11019697
11027867	11004991	11008259	11011527	10988651
11026233	11013161	11001723	11009893	10990285
10991919	10993553	11021331	11016429	11018063

L17-M15

11039305	11063815	11036037	11040939	11065449
11037671	11047475	11055645	11044207	11060547
11068717	11045841	11049109	11052377	11029501
11067083	11054011	11042573	11050743	11031135
11032769	11034403	11062181	11057279	11058913

L17-M16

11080155	11104665	11076887	11081789	11106299
11078521	11088325	11096495	11085057	11101397
11109567	11086691	11089959	11093227	11070351
11107933	11094861	11083423	11091593	11071985
11073619	11075253	11103031	11098129	11099763

L18-M1

11121005	11145515	11117737	11122639	11147149
11119371	11129175	11137345	11125907	11142247
11150417	11127541	11130809	11134077	11111201
11148783	11135711	11124273	11132443	11112835
11114469	11116103	11143881	11138979	11140613

L18-M2

11161855	11186365	11158587	11163489	11187999
11160221	11170025	11178195	11166757	11183097
11191267	11168391	11171659	11174927	11152051
11189633	11176561	11165123	11173293	11153685
11155319	11156953	11184731	11179829	11181463

L18-M3

11202705	11227215	11199437	11204339	11228849
11201071	11210875	11219045	11207607	11223947
11232117	11209241	11212509	11215777	11192901
11230483	11217411	11205973	11214143	11194535
11196169	11197803	11225581	11220679	11222313

L18-M4

11243555	11268065	11240287	11245189	11269699
11241921	11251725	11259895	11248457	11264797
11272967	11250091	11253359	11256627	11233751
11271333	11258261	11246823	11254993	11235385
11237019	11238653	11266431	11261529	11263163

L18-M5

11284405	11308915	11281137	11286039	11310549
11282771	11292575	11300745	11289307	11305647
11313817	11290941	11294209	11297477	11274601
11312183	11299111	11287673	11295843	11276235
11277869	11279503	11307281	11302379	11304013

L18-M6

11325255	11349765	11321987	11326889	11351399
11323621	11333425	11341595	11330157	11346497
11354667	11331791	11335059	11338327	11315451
11353033	11339961	11328523	11336693	11317085
11318719	11320353	11348131	11343229	11344863

L18-M7

11366105	11390615	11362837	11367739	11392249
11364471	11374275	11382445	11371007	11387347
11395517	11372641	11375909	11379177	11356301
11393883	11380811	11369373	11377543	11357935
11359569	11361203	11388981	11384079	11385713

L18-M8

11406955	11431465	11403687	11408589	11433099
11405321	11415125	11423295	11411857	11428197
11436367	11413491	11416759	11420027	11397151
11434733	11421661	11410223	11418393	11398785
11400419	11402053	11429831	11424929	11426563

L18-M9

11447805	11472315	11444537	11449439	11473949
11446171	11455975	11464145	11452707	11469047
11477217	11454341	11457609	11460877	11438001
11475583	11462511	11451073	11459243	11439635
11441269	11442903	11470681	11465779	11467413

L18-M10

11488655	11513165	11485387	11490289	11514799
11487021	11496825	11504995	11493557	11509897
11518067	11495191	11498459	11501727	11478851
11516433	11503361	11491923	11500093	11480485
11482119	11483753	11511531	11506629	11508263

L18-M11

11529505	11554015	11526237	11531139	11555649
11527871	11537675	11545845	11534407	11550747
11558917	11536041	11539309	11542577	11519701
11557283	11544211	11532773	11540943	11521335
11522969	11524603	11552381	11547479	11549113

L18-M12

11570355	11594865	11567087	11571989	11596499
11568721	11578525	11586695	11575257	11591597
11599767	11576891	11580159	11583427	11560551
11598133	11585061	11573623	11581793	11562185
11563819	11565453	11593231	11588329	11589963

L18-M13

11611205	11635715	11607937	11612839	11637349
11609571	11619375	11627545	11616107	11632447
11640617	11617741	11621009	11624277	11601401
11638983	11625911	11614473	11622643	11603035
11604669	11606303	11634081	11629179	11630813

L18-M14

11652055	11676565	11648787	11653689	11678199
11650421	11660225	11668395	11656957	11673297
11681467	11658591	11661859	11665127	11642251
11679833	11666761	11655323	11663493	11643885
11645519	11647153	11674931	11670029	11671663

L18-M15

11692905	11717415	11689637	11694539	11719049
11691271	11701075	11709245	11697807	11714147
11722317	11699441	11702709	11705977	11683101
11720683	11707611	11696173	11704343	11684735
11686369	11688003	11715781	11710879	11712513

L18-M16

11733755	11758265	11730487	11735389	11759899
11732121	11741925	11750095	11738657	11754997
11763167	11740291	11743559	11746827	11723951
11761533	11748461	11737023	11745193	11725585
11727219	11728853	11756631	11751729	11753363

L19-M1

11774605	11799115	11771337	11776239	11800749
11772971	11782775	11790945	11779507	11795847
11804017	11781141	11784409	11787677	11764801
11802383	11789311	11777873	11786043	11766435
11768069	11769703	11797481	11792579	11794213

L19-M2

11815455	11839965	11812187	11817089	11841599
11813821	11823625	11831795	11820357	11836697
11844867	11821991	11825259	11828527	11805651
11843233	11830161	11818723	11826893	11807285
11808919	11810553	11838331	11833429	11835063

L19-M3

11856305	11880815	11853037	11857939	11882449
11854671	11864475	11872645	11861207	11877547
11885717	11862841	11866109	11869377	11846501
11884083	11871011	11859573	11867743	11848135
11849769	11851403	11879181	11874279	11875913

L19-M4

11897155	11921665	11893887	11898789	11923299
11895521	11905325	11913495	11902057	11918397
11926567	11903691	11906959	11910227	11887351
11924933	11911861	11900423	11908593	11888985
11890619	11892253	11920031	11915129	11916763

L19-M5

11938005	11962515	11934737	11939639	11964149
11936371	11946175	11954345	11942907	11959247
11967417	11944541	11947809	11951077	11928201
11965783	11952711	11941273	11949443	11929835
11931469	11933103	11960881	11955979	11957613

L19-M6

11978855	12003365	11975587	11980489	12004999
11977221	11987025	11995195	11983757	12000097
12008267	11985391	11988659	11991927	11969051
12006633	11993561	11982123	11990293	11970685
11972319	11973953	12001731	11996829	11998463

L19-M7

12019705	12044215	12016437	12021339	12045849
12018071	12027875	12036045	12024607	12040947
12049117	12026241	12029509	12032777	12009901
12047483	12034411	12022973	12031143	12011535
12013169	12014803	12042581	12037679	12039313

L19-M8

12060555	12085065	12057287	12062189	12086699
12058921	12068725	12076895	12065457	12081797
12089967	12067091	12070359	12073627	12050751
12088333	12075261	12063823	12071993	12052385
12054019	12055653	12083431	12078529	12080163

L19-M9

12101405	12125915	12098137	12103039	12127549
12099771	12109575	12117745	12106307	12122647
12130817	12107941	12111209	12114477	12091601
12129183	12116111	12104673	12112843	12093235
12094869	12096503	12124281	12119379	12121013

L19-M10

12142255	12166765	12138987	12143889	12168399
12140621	12150425	12158595	12147157	12163497
12171667	12148791	12152059	12155327	12132451
12170033	12156961	12145523	12153693	12134085
12135719	12137353	12165131	12160229	12161863

L19-M11

12183105	12207615	12179837	12184739	12209249
12181471	12191275	12199445	12188007	12204347
12212517	12189641	12192909	12196177	12173301
12210883	12197811	12186373	12194543	12174935
12176569	12178203	12205981	12201079	12202713

L19-M12

12223955	12248465	12220687	12225589	12250099
12222321	12232125	12240295	12228857	12245197
12253367	12230491	12233759	12237027	12214151
12251733	12238661	12227223	12235393	12215785
12217419	12219053	12246831	12241929	12243563

L19-M13

12264805	12289315	12261537	12266439	12290949
12263171	12272975	12281145	12269707	12286047
12294217	12271341	12274609	12277877	12255001
12292583	12279511	12268073	12276243	12256635
12258269	12259903	12287681	12282779	12284413

L19-M14

12305655	12330165	12302387	12307289	12331799
12304021	12313825	12321995	12310557	12326897
12335067	12312191	12315459	12318727	12295851
12333433	12320361	12308923	12317093	12297485
12299119	12300753	12328531	12323629	12325263

L19-M15

12346505	12371015	12343237	12348139	12372649
12344871	12354675	12362845	12351407	12367747
12375917	12353041	12356309	12359577	12336701
12374283	12361211	12349773	12357943	12338335
12339969	12341603	12369381	12364479	12366113

L19-M16

12387355	12411865	12384087	12388989	12413499
12385721	12395525	12403695	12392257	12408597
12416767	12393891	12397159	12400427	12377551
12415133	12402061	12390623	12398793	12379185
12380819	12382453	12410231	12405329	12406963

L20-M1

12428205	12452715	12424937	12429839	12454349
12426571	12436375	12444545	12433107	12449447
12457617	12434741	12438009	12441277	12418401
12455983	12442911	12431473	12439643	12420035
12421669	12423303	12451081	12446179	12447813

L20-M2

12469055	12493565	12465787	12470689	12495199
12467421	12477225	12485395	12473957	12490297
12498467	12475591	12478859	12482127	12459251
12496833	12483761	12472323	12480493	12460885
12462519	12464153	12491931	12487029	12488663

L20-M3

12509905	12534415	12506637	12511539	12536049
12508271	12518075	12526245	12514807	12531147
12539317	12516441	12519709	12522977	12500101
12537683	12524611	12513173	12521343	12501735
12503369	12505003	12532781	12527879	12529513

L20-M12

12877555	12902065	12874287	12879189	12903699
12875921	12885725	12893895	12882457	12898797
12906967	12884091	12887359	12890627	12867751
12905333	12892261	12880823	12888993	12869385
12871019	12872653	12900431	12895529	12897163

L20-M4

12550755	12575265	12547487	12552389	12576899
12549121	12558925	12567095	12555657	12571997
12580167	12557291	12560559	12563827	12540951
12578533	12565461	12554023	12562193	12542585
12544219	12545853	12573631	12568729	12570363

L20-M13

12918405	12942915	12915137	12920039	12944549
12916771	12926575	12934745	12923307	12939647
12947817	12924941	12928209	12931477	12908601
12946183	12933111	12921673	12929843	12910235
12911869	12913503	12941281	12936379	12938013

L20-M5

12591605	12616115	12588337	12593239	12617749
12589971	12599775	12607945	12596507	12612847
12621017	12598141	12601409	12604677	12581801
12619383	12606311	12594873	12603043	12583435
12585069	12586703	12614481	12609579	12611213

L20-M14

12959255	12983765	12955987	12960889	12985399
12957621	12967425	12975595	12964157	12980497
12988667	12965791	12969059	12972327	12949451
12987033	12973961	12962523	12970693	12951085
12952719	12954353	12982131	12977229	12978863

L20-M6

12632455	12656965	12629187	12634089	12658599
12630821	12640625	12648795	12637357	12653697
12661867	12638991	12642259	12645527	12622651
12660233	12647161	12635723	12643893	12624285
12625919	12627553	12655331	12650429	12652063

L20-M15

13000105	13024615	12996837	13001739	13026249
12998471	13008275	13016445	13005007	13021347
13029517	13006641	13009909	13013177	12990301
13027883	13014811	13003373	13011543	12991935
12993569	12995203	13022981	13018079	13019713

L20-M7

12673305	12697815	12670037	12674939	12699449
12671671	12681475	12689645	12678207	12694547
12702717	12679841	12683109	12686377	12663501
12701083	12688011	12676573	12684743	12665135
12666769	12668403	12696181	12691279	12692913

L20-M16

13040955	13065465	13037687	13042589	13067099
13039321	13049125	13057295	13045857	13062197
13070367	13047491	13050759	13054027	13031151
13068733	13055661	13044223	13052393	13032785
13034419	13036053	13063831	13058929	13060563

L20-M8

12714155	12738665	12710887	12715789	12740299
12712521	12722325	12730495	12719057	12735397
12743567	12720691	12723959	12727227	12704351
12741933	12728861	12717423	12725593	12705985
12707619	12709253	12737031	12732129	12733763

L21-M1

13081805	13106315	13078537	13083439	13107949
13080171	13089975	13098145	13086707	13103047
13111217	13088341	13091609	13094877	13072001
13109583	13096511	13085073	13093243	13073635
13075269	13076903	13104681	13099779	13101413

L20-M9

12755005	12779515	12751737	12756639	12781149
12753371	12763175	12771345	12759907	12776247
12784417	12761541	12764809	12768077	12745201
12782783	12769711	12758273	12766443	12746835
12748469	12750103	12777881	12772979	12774613

L21-M2

13122655	13147165	13119387	13124289	13148799
13121021	13130825	13138995	13127557	13143897
13152067	13129191	13132459	13135727	13112851
13150433	13137361	13125923	13134093	13114485
13116119	13117753	13145531	13140629	13142263

L20-M10

12795855	12820365	12792587	12797489	12821999
12794221	12804025	12812195	12800757	12817097
12825267	12802391	12805659	12808927	12786051
12823633	12810561	12799123	12807293	12787685
12789319	12790953	12818731	12813829	12815463

L21-M3

13163505	13188015	13160237	13165139	13189649
13161871	13171675	13179845	13168407	13184747
13192917	13170041	13173309	13176577	13153701
13191283	13178211	13166773	13174943	13155335
13156969	13158603	13186381	13181479	13183113

L20-M11

12836705	12861215	12833437	12838339	12862849
12835071	12844875	12853045	12841607	12857947
12866117	12843241	12846509	12849777	12826901
12864483	12851411	12839973	12848143	12828535
12830169	12831803	12859581	12854679	12856313

L21-M4

13204355	13228865	13201087	13205989	13230499
13202721	13212525	13220695	13209257	13225597
13233767	13210891	13214159	13217427	13194551
13232133	13219061	13207623	13215793	13196185
13197819	13199453	13227231	13222329	13223963

L21-M5

13245205	13269715	13241937	13246839	13271349
13243571	13253375	13261545	13250107	13266447
13274617	13251741	13255009	13258277	13235401
13272983	13259911	13248473	13256643	13237035
13238669	13240303	13268081	13263179	13264813

L21-M14

13612855	13637365	13609587	13614489	13638999
13611221	13621025	13629195	13617757	13634097
13642267	13619391	13622659	13625927	13603051
13640633	13627561	13616123	13624293	13604685
13606319	13607953	13635731	13630829	13632463

L21-M6

13286055	13310565	13282787	13287689	13312199
13284421	13294225	13302395	13290957	13307297
13315467	13292591	13295859	13299127	13276251
13313833	13300761	13289323	13297493	13277885
13279519	13281153	13308931	13304029	13305663

L21-M15

13653705	13678215	13650437	13655339	13679849
13652071	13661875	13670045	13658607	13674947
13683117	13660241	13663509	13666777	13643901
13681483	13668411	13656973	13665143	13645535
13647169	13648803	13676581	13671679	13673313

L21-M7

13326905	13351415	13323637	13328539	13353049
13325271	13335075	13343245	13331807	13348147
13356317	13333441	13336709	13339977	13317101
13354683	13341611	13330173	13338343	13318735
13320369	13322003	13349781	13344879	13346513

L21-M16

13694555	13719065	13691287	13696189	13720699
13692921	13702725	13710895	13699457	13715797
13723967	13701091	13704359	13707627	13684751
13722333	13709261	13697823	13705993	13686385
13688019	13689653	13717431	13712529	13714163

L21-M8

13367755	13392265	13364487	13369389	13393899
13366121	13375925	13384095	13372657	13388997
13397167	13374291	13377559	13380827	13357951
13395533	13382461	13371023	13379193	13359585
13361219	13362853	13390631	13385729	13387363

L22-M1

13735405	13759915	13732137	13737039	13761549
13733771	13743575	13751745	13740307	13756647
13764817	13741941	13745209	13748477	13725601
13763183	13750111	13738673	13746843	13727235
13728869	13730503	13758281	13753379	13755013

L21-M9

13408605	13433115	13405337	13410239	13434749
13406971	13416775	13424945	13413507	13429847
13438017	13415141	13418409	13421677	13398801
13436383	13423311	13411873	13420043	13400435
13402069	13403703	13431481	13426579	13428213

L22-M2

13776255	13800765	13772987	13777889	13802399
13774621	13784425	13792595	13781157	13797497
13805667	13782791	13786059	13789327	13766451
13804033	13790961	13779523	13787693	13768085
13769719	13771353	13799131	13794229	13795863

L21-M10

13449455	13473965	13446187	13451089	13475599
13447821	13457625	13465795	13454357	13470697
13478867	13455991	13459259	13462527	13439651
13477233	13464161	13452723	13460893	13441285
13442919	13444553	13472331	13467429	13469063

L22-M3

13817105	13841615	13813837	13818739	13843249
13815471	13825275	13833445	13822007	13838347
13846517	13823641	13826909	13830177	13807301
13844883	13831811	13820373	13828543	13808935
13810569	13812203	13839981	13835079	13836713

L21-M11

13490305	13514815	13487037	13491939	13516449
13488671	13498475	13506645	13495207	13511547
13519717	13496841	13500109	13503377	13480501
13518083	13505011	13493573	13501743	13482135
13483769	13485403	13513181	13508279	13509913

L22-M4

13857955	13882465	13854687	13859589	13884099
13856321	13866125	13874295	13862857	13879197
13887367	13864491	13867759	13871027	13848151
13885733	13872661	13861223	13869393	13849785
13851419	13853053	13880831	13875929	13877563

L21-M12

13531155	13555665	13527887	13532789	13557299
13529521	13539325	13547495	13536057	13552397
13560567	13537691	13540959	13544227	13521351
13558933	13545861	13534423	13542593	13522985
13524619	13526253	13554031	13549129	13550763

L22-M5

13898805	13923315	13895537	13900439	13924949
13897171	13906975	13915145	13903707	13920047
13928217	13905341	13908609	13911877	13889001
13926583	13913511	13902073	13910243	13890635
13892269	13893903	13921681	13916779	13918413

L21-M13

13572005	13596515	13568737	13573639	13598149
13570371	13580175	13588345	13576907	13593247
13601417	13578541	13581809	13585077	13562201
13599783	13586711	13575273	13583443	13563835
13565469	13567103	13594881	13589979	13591613

L22-M6

13939655	13964165	13936387	13941289	13965799
13938021	13947825	13955995	13944557	13960897
13969067	13946191	13949459	13952727	13929851
13967433	13954361	13942923	13951093	13931485
13933119	13934753	13962531	13957629	13959263

L22-M7

13980505	14005015	13977237	13982139	14006649
13978871	13988675	13996845	13985407	14001747
14009917	13987041	13990309	13993577	13970701
14008283	13995211	13983773	13991943	13972335
13973969	13975603	14003381	13998479	14000113

L22-M16

14348155	14372665	14344887	14349789	14374299
14346521	14356325	14364495	14353057	14369397
14377567	14354691	14357959	14361227	14338351
14375933	14362861	14351423	14359593	14339985
14341619	14343253	14371031	14366129	14367763

L22-M8

14021355	14045865	14018087	14022989	14047499
14019721	14029525	14037695	14026257	14042597
14050767	14027891	14031159	14034427	14011551
14049133	14036061	14024623	14032793	14013185
14014819	14016453	14044231	14039329	14040963

L23-M1

14389005	14413515	14385737	14390639	14415149
14387371	14397175	14405345	14393907	14410247
14418417	14395541	14398809	14402077	14379201
14416783	14403711	14392273	14400443	14380835
14382469	14384103	14411881	14406979	14408613

L22-M9

14062205	14086715	14058937	14063839	14088349
14060571	14070375	14078545	14067107	14083447
14091617	14068741	14072009	14075277	14052401
14089983	14076911	14065473	14073643	14054035
14055669	14057303	14085081	14080179	14081813

L23-M2

14429855	14454365	14426587	14431489	14455999
14428221	14438025	14446195	14434757	14451097
14459267	14436391	14439659	14442927	14420051
14457633	14444561	14433123	14441293	14421685
14423319	14424953	14452731	14447829	14449463

L22-M10

14103055	14127565	14099787	14104689	14129199
14101421	14111225	14119395	14107957	14124297
14132467	14109591	14112859	14116127	14093251
14130833	14117761	14106323	14114493	14094885
14096519	14098153	14125931	14121029	14122663

L23-M3

14470705	14495215	14467437	14472339	14496849
14469071	14478875	14487045	14475607	14491947
14500117	14477241	14480509	14483777	14460901
14498483	14485411	14473973	14482143	14462535
14464169	14465803	14493581	14488679	14490313

L22-M11

14143905	14168415	14140637	14145539	14170049
14142271	14152075	14160245	14148807	14165147
14173317	14150441	14153709	14156977	14134101
14171683	14158611	14147173	14155343	14135735
14137369	14139003	14166781	14161879	14163513

L23-M4

14511555	14536065	14508287	14513189	14537699
14509921	14519725	14527895	14516457	14532797
14540967	14518091	14521359	14524627	14501751
14539333	14526261	14514823	14522993	14503385
14505019	14506653	14534431	14529529	14531163

L22-M12

14184755	14209265	14181487	14186389	14210899
14183121	14192925	14201095	14189657	14205997
14214167	14191291	14194559	14197827	14174951
14212533	14199461	14188023	14196193	14176585
14178219	14179853	14207631	14202729	14204363

L23-M5

14552405	14576915	14549137	14554039	14578549
14550771	14560575	14568745	14557307	14573647
14581817	14558941	14562209	14565477	14542601
14580183	14567111	14555673	14563843	14544235
14545869	14547503	14575281	14570379	14572013

L22-M13

14225605	14250115	14222337	14227239	14251749
14223971	14233775	14241945	14230507	14246847
14255017	14232141	14235409	14238677	14215801
14253383	14240311	14228873	14237043	14217435
14219069	14220703	14248481	14243579	14245213

L23-M6

14593255	14617765	14589987	14594889	14619399
14591621	14601425	14609595	14598157	14614497
14622667	14599791	14603059	14606327	14583451
14621033	14607961	14596523	14604693	14585085
14586719	14588353	14616131	14611229	14612863

L22-M14

14266455	14290965	14263187	14268089	14292599
14264821	14274625	14282795	14271357	14287697
14295867	14272991	14276259	14279527	14256651
14294233	14281161	14269723	14277893	14258285
14259919	14261553	14289331	14284429	14286063

L23-M7

14634105	14658615	14630837	14635739	14660249
14632471	14642275	14650445	14639007	14655347
14663517	14640641	14643909	14647177	14624301
14661883	14648811	14637373	14645543	14625935
14627569	14629203	14656981	14652079	14653713

L22-M15

14307305	14331815	14304037	14308939	14333449
14305671	14315475	14323645	14312207	14328547
14336717	14313841	14317109	14320377	14297501
14335083	14322011	14310573	14318743	14299135
14300769	14302403	14330181	14325279	14326913

L23-M8

14674955	14699465	14671687	14676589	14701099
14673321	14683125	14691295	14679857	14696197
14704367	14681491	14684759	14688027	14665151
14702733	14689661	14678223	14686393	14666785
14668419	14670053	14697831	14692929	14694563

L23-M9

14715805	14740315	14712537	14717439	14741949
14714171	14723975	14732145	14720707	14737047
14745217	14722341	14725609	14728877	14706001
14743583	14730511	14719073	14727243	14707635
14709269	14710903	14738681	14733779	14735413

L23-M10

14756655	14781165	14753387	14758289	14782799
14755021	14764825	14772995	14761557	14777897
14786067	14763191	14766459	14769727	14746851
14784433	14771361	14759923	14768093	14748485
14750119	14751753	14779531	14774629	14776263

L23-M11

14797505	14822015	14794237	14799139	14823649
14795871	14805675	14813845	14802407	14818747
14826917	14804041	14807309	14810577	14787701
14825283	14812211	14800773	14808943	14789335
14790969	14792603	14820381	14815479	14817113

L23-M12

14838355	14862865	14835087	14839989	14864499
14836721	14846525	14854695	14843257	14859597
14867767	14844891	14848159	14851427	14828551
14866133	14853061	14841623	14849793	14830185
14831819	14833453	14861231	14856329	14857963

L23-M13

14879205	14903715	14875937	14880839	14905349
14877571	14887375	14895545	14884107	14900447
14908617	14885741	14889009	14892277	14869401
14906983	14893911	14882473	14890643	14871035
14872669	14874303	14902081	14897179	14898813

L23-M14

14920055	14944565	14916787	14921689	14946199
14918421	14928225	14936395	14924957	14941297
14949467	14926591	14929859	14933127	14910251
14947833	14934761	14923323	14931493	14911885
14913519	14915153	14942931	14938029	14939663

L23-M15

14960905	14985415	14957637	14962539	14987049
14959271	14969075	14977245	14965807	14982147
14990317	14967441	14970709	14973977	14951101
14988683	14975611	14964173	14972343	14952735
14954369	14956003	14983781	14978879	14980513

L23-M16

15001755	15026265	14998487	15003389	15027899
15000121	15009925	15018095	15006657	15022997
15031167	15008291	15011559	15014827	14991951
15029533	15016461	15005023	15013193	14993585
14995219	14996853	15024631	15019729	15021363

L24-M1

15042605	15067115	15039337	15044239	15068749
15040971	15050775	15058945	15047507	15063847
15072017	15049141	15052409	15055677	15032801
15070383	15057311	15045873	15054043	15034435
15036069	15037703	15065481	15060579	15062213

L24-M2

15083455	15107965	15080187	15085089	15109599
15081821	15091625	15099795	15088357	15104697
15112867	15089991	15093259	15096527	15073651
15111233	15098161	15086723	15094893	15075285
15076919	15078553	15106331	15101429	15103063

L24-M3

15124305	15148815	15121037	15125939	15150449
15122671	15132475	15140645	15129207	15145547
15153717	15130841	15134109	15137377	15114501
15152083	15139011	15127573	15135743	15116135
15117769	15119403	15147181	15142279	15143913

L24-M4

15165155	15189665	15161887	15166789	15191299
15163521	15173325	15181495	15170057	15186397
15194567	15171691	15174959	15178227	15155351
15192933	15179861	15168423	15176593	15156985
15158619	15160253	15188031	15183129	15184763

L24-M5

15206005	15230515	15202737	15207639	15232149
15204371	15214175	15222345	15210907	15227247
15235417	15212541	15215809	15219077	15196201
15233783	15220711	15209273	15217443	15197835
15199469	15201103	15228881	15223979	15225613

L24-M6

15246855	15271365	15243587	15248489	15272999
15245221	15255025	15263195	15251757	15268097
15276267	15253391	15256659	15259927	15237051
15274633	15261561	15250123	15258293	15238685
15240319	15241953	15269731	15264829	15266463

L24-M7

15287705	15312215	15284437	15289339	15313849
15286071	15295875	15304045	15292607	15308947
15317117	15294241	15297509	15300777	15277901
15315483	15302411	15290973	15299143	15279535
15281169	15282803	15310581	15305679	15307313

L24-M8

15328555	15353065	15325287	15330189	15354699
15326921	15336725	15344895	15333457	15349797
15357967	15335091	15338359	15341627	15318751
15356333	15343261	15331823	15339993	15320385
15322019	15323653	15351431	15346529	15348163

L24-M9

15369405	15393915	15366137	15371039	15395549
15367771	15377575	15385745	15374307	15390647
15398817	15375941	15379209	15382477	15359601
15397183	15384111	15372673	15380843	15361235
15362869	15364503	15392281	15387379	15389013

L24-M10

15410255	15434765	15406987	15411889	15436399
15408621	15418425	15426595	15415157	15431497
15439667	15416791	15420059	15423327	15400451
15438033	15424961	15413523	15421693	15402085
15403719	15405353	15433131	15428229	15429863

L24-M11

15451105	15475615	15447837	15452739	15477249
15449471	15459275	15467445	15456007	15472347
15480517	15457641	15460909	15464177	15441301
15478883	15465811	15454373	15462543	15442935
15444569	15446203	15473981	15469079	15470713

L25-M4

15818755	15843265	15815487	15820389	15844899
15817121	15826925	15835095	15823657	15839997
15848167	15825291	15828559	15831827	15808951
15846533	15833461	15822023	15830193	15810585
15812219	15813853	15841631	15836729	15838363

L24-M12

15491955	15516465	15488687	15493589	15518099
15490321	15500125	15508295	15496857	15513197
15521367	15498491	15501759	15505027	15482151
15519733	15506661	15495223	15503393	15483785
15485419	15487053	15514831	15509929	15511563

L25-M5

15859605	15884115	15856337	15861239	15885749
15857971	15867775	15875945	15864507	15880847
15889017	15866141	15869409	15872677	15849801
15887383	15874311	15862873	15871043	15851435
15853069	15854703	15882481	15877579	15879213

L24-M13

15532805	15557315	15529537	15534439	15558949
15531171	15540975	15549145	15537707	15554047
15562217	15539341	15542609	15545877	15523001
15560583	15547511	15536073	15544243	15524635
15526269	15527903	15555681	15550779	15552413

L25-M6

15900455	15924965	15897187	15902089	15926599
15898821	15908625	15916795	15905357	15921697
15929867	15906991	15910259	15913527	15890651
15928233	15915161	15903723	15911893	15892285
15893919	15895553	15923331	15918429	15920063

L24-M14

15573655	15598165	15570387	15575289	15599799
15572021	15581825	15589995	15578557	15594897
15603067	15580191	15583459	15586727	15563851
15601433	15588361	15576923	15585093	15565485
15567119	15568753	15596531	15591629	15593263

L25-M7

15941305	15965815	15938037	15942939	15967449
15939671	15949475	15957645	15946207	15962547
15970717	15947841	15951109	15954377	15931501
15969083	15956011	15944573	15952743	15933135
15934769	15936403	15964181	15959279	15960913

L24-M15

15614505	15639015	15611237	15616139	15640649
15612871	15622675	15630845	15619407	15635747
15643917	15621041	15624309	15627577	15604701
15642283	15629211	15617773	15625943	15606335
15607969	15609603	15637381	15632479	15634113

L25-M8

15982155	16006665	15978887	15983789	16008299
15980521	15990325	15998495	15987057	16003397
16011567	15988691	15991959	15995227	15972351
16009933	15996861	15985423	15993593	15973985
15975619	15977253	16005031	16000129	16001763

L24-M16

15655355	15679865	15652087	15656989	15681499
15653721	15663525	15671695	15660257	15676597
15684767	15661891	15665159	15668427	15645551
15683133	15670061	15658623	15666793	15647185
15648819	15650453	15678231	15673329	15674963

L25-M9

16023005	16047515	16019737	16024639	16049149
16021371	16031175	16039345	16027907	16044247
16052417	16029541	16032809	16036077	16013201
16050783	16037711	16026273	16034443	16014835
16016469	16018103	16045881	16040979	16042613

L25-M1

15696205	15720715	15692937	15697839	15722349
15694571	15704375	15712545	15701107	15717447
15725617	15702741	15706009	15709277	15686401
15723983	15710911	15699473	15707643	15688035
15689669	15691303	15719081	15714179	15715813

L25-M10

16063855	16088365	16060587	16065489	16089999
16062221	16072025	16080195	16068757	16085097
16093267	16070391	16073659	16076927	16054051
16091633	16078561	16067123	16075293	16055685
16057319	16058953	16086731	16081829	16083463

L25-M2

15737055	15761565	15733787	15738689	15763199
15735421	15745225	15753395	15741957	15758297
15766467	15743591	15746859	15750127	15727251
15764833	15751761	15740323	15748493	15728885
15730519	15732153	15759931	15755029	15756663

L25-M11

16104705	16129215	16101437	16106339	16130849
16103071	16112875	16121045	16109607	16125947
16134117	16111241	16114509	16117777	16094901
16132483	16119411	16107973	16116143	16096535
16098169	16099803	16127581	16122679	16124313

L25-M3

15777905	15802415	15774637	15779539	15804049
15776271	15786075	15794245	15782807	15799147
15807317	15784441	15787709	15790977	15768101
15805683	15792611	15781173	15789343	15769735
15771369	15773003	15800781	15795879	15797513

L25-M12

16145555	16170065	16142287	16147189	16171699
16143921	16153725	16161895	16150457	16166797
16174967	16152091	16155359	16158627	16135751
16173333	16160261	16148823	16156993	16137385
16139019	16140653	16168431	16163529	16165163

L25-M13

16186405	16210915	16183137	16188039	16212549
16184771	16194575	16202745	16191307	16207647
16215817	16192941	16196209	16199477	16176601
16214183	16201111	16189673	16197843	16178235
16179869	16181503	16209281	16204379	16206013

L25-M14

16227255	16251765	16223987	16228889	16253399
16225621	16235425	16243595	16232157	16248497
16256667	16233791	16237059	16240327	16217451
16255033	16241961	16230523	16238693	16219085
16220719	16222353	16250131	16245229	16246863

L25-M15

16268105	16292615	16264837	16269739	16294249
16266471	16276275	16284445	16273007	16289347
16297517	16274641	16277909	16281177	16258301
16295883	16282811	16271373	16279543	16259935
16261569	16263203	16290981	16286079	16287713

L25-M16

16308955	16333465	16305687	16310589	16335099
16307321	16317125	16325295	16313857	16330197
16338367	16315491	16318759	16322027	16299151
16336733	16323661	16312223	16320393	16300785
16302419	16304053	16331831	16326929	16328563

L1-M1

4069	14239	2713	4747	14917
3391	7459	10849	6103	12883
16273	6781	8137	9493	1
15595	10171	5425	8815	679
1357	2035	13561	11527	12205

L1-M2

21019	31189	19663	21697	31867
20341	24409	27799	23053	29833
33223	23731	25087	26443	16951
32545	27121	22375	25765	17629
18307	18985	30511	28477	29155

L1-M3

37969	48139	36613	38647	48817
37291	41359	44749	40003	46783
50173	40681	42037	43393	33901
49495	44071	39325	42715	34579
35257	35935	47461	45427	46105

L1-M4

54919	65089	53563	55597	65767
54241	58309	61699	56953	63733
67123	57631	58987	60343	50851
66445	61021	56275	59665	51529
52207	52885	64411	62377	63055

L1-M5

71869	82039	70513	72547	82717
71191	75259	78649	73903	80683
84073	74581	75937	77293	67801
83395	77971	73225	76615	68479
69157	69835	81361	79327	80005

L1-M6

88819	98989	87463	89497	99667
88141	92209	95599	90853	97633
101023	91531	92887	94243	84751
100345	94921	90175	93565	85429
86107	86785	98311	96277	96955

L1-M7

105769	115939	104413	106447	116617
105091	109159	112549	107803	114583
117973	108481	109837	111193	101701
117295	111871	107125	110515	102379
103057	103735	115261	113227	113905

L1-M8

122719	132889	121363	123397	133567
122041	126109	129499	124753	131533
134923	125431	126787	128143	118651
134245	128821	124075	127465	119329
120007	120685	132211	130177	130855

L1-M9

139669	149839	138313	140347	150517
138991	143059	146449	141703	148483
151873	142381	143737	145093	135601
151195	145771	141025	144415	136279
136957	137635	149161	147127	147805

L1-M10

156619	166789	155263	157297	167467
155941	160009	163399	158653	165433
168823	159331	160687	162043	152551
168145	162721	157975	161365	153229
153907	154585	166111	164077	164755

L1-M11

173569	183739	172213	174247	184417
172891	176959	180349	175603	182383
185773	176281	177637	178993	169501
185095	179671	174925	178315	170179
170857	171535	183061	181027	181705

L1-M12

190519	200689	189163	191197	201367
189841	193909	197299	192553	199333
202723	193231	194587	195943	186451
202045	196621	191875	195265	187129
187807	188485	200011	197977	198655

L1-M13

207469	217639	206113	208147	218317
206791	210859	214249	209503	216283
219673	210181	211537	212893	203401
218995	213571	208825	212215	204079
204757	205435	216961	214927	215605

L1-M14

224419	234589	223063	225097	235267
223741	227809	231199	226453	233233
236623	227131	228487	229843	220351
235945	230521	225775	229165	221029
221707	222385	233911	231877	232555

L1-M15

241369	251539	240013	242047	252217
240691	244759	248149	243403	250183
253573	244081	245437	246793	237301
252895	247471	242725	246115	237979
238657	239335	250861	248827	249505

L1-M16

258319	268489	256963	258997	269167
257641	261709	265099	260353	267133
270523	261031	262387	263743	254251
269845	264421	259675	263065	254929
255607	256285	267811	265777	266455

L2-M1

275269	285439	273913	275947	286117
274591	278659	282049	277303	284083
287473	277981	279337	280693	271201
286795	281371	276625	280015	271879
272557	273235	284761	282727	283405

L2-M2

292219	302389	290863	292897	303067
291541	295609	298999	294253	301033
304423	294931	296287	297643	288151
303745	298321	293575	296965	288829
289507	290185	301711	299677	300355

L2-M3

309169	319339	307813	309847	320017
308491	312559	315949	311203	317983
321373	311881	313237	314593	305101
320695	315271	310525	313915	305779
306457	307135	318661	316627	317305

L2-M4

326119	336289	324763	326797	336967
325441	329509	332899	328153	334933
338323	328831	330187	331543	322051
337645	332221	327475	330865	322729
323407	324085	335611	333577	334255

L2-M5

343069	353239	341713	343747	353917
342391	346459	349849	345103	351883
355273	345781	347137	348493	339001
354595	349171	344425	347815	339679
340357	341035	352561	350527	351205

L2-M6

360019	370189	358663	360697	370867
359341	363409	366799	362053	368833
372223	362731	364087	365443	355951
371545	366121	361375	364765	356629
357307	357985	369511	367477	368155

L2-M7

376969	387139	375613	377647	387817
376291	380359	383749	379003	385783
389173	379681	381037	382393	372901
388495	383071	378325	381715	373579
374257	374935	386461	384427	385105

L2-M8

393919	404089	392563	394597	404767
393241	397309	400699	395953	402733
406123	396631	397987	399343	389851
405445	400021	395275	398665	390529
391207	391885	403411	401377	402055

L2-M9

410869	421039	409513	411547	421717
410191	414259	417649	412903	419683
423073	413581	414937	416293	406801
422395	416971	412225	415615	407479
408157	408835	420361	418327	419005

L2-M10

427819	437989	426463	428497	438667
427141	431209	434599	429853	436633
440023	430531	431887	433243	423751
439345	433921	429175	432565	424429
425107	425785	437311	435277	435955

L2-M11

444769	454939	443413	445447	455617
444091	448159	451549	446803	453583
456973	447481	448837	450193	440701
456295	450871	446125	449515	441379
442057	442735	454261	452227	452905

L2-M12

461719	471889	460363	462397	472567
461041	465109	468499	463753	470533
473923	464431	465787	467143	457651
473245	467821	463075	466465	458329
459007	459685	471211	469177	469855

L2-M13

478669	488839	477313	479347	489517
477991	482059	485449	480703	487483
490873	481381	482737	484093	474601
490195	484771	480025	483415	475279
475957	476635	488161	486127	486805

L2-M14

495619	505789	494263	496297	506467
494941	499009	502399	497653	504433
507823	498331	499687	501043	491551
507145	501721	496975	500365	492229
492907	493585	505111	503077	503755

L2-M15

512569	522739	511213	513247	523417
511891	515959	519349	514603	521383
524773	515281	516637	517993	508501
524095	518671	513925	517315	509179
509857	510535	522061	520027	520705

L2-M16

529519	539689	528163	530197	540367
528841	532909	536299	531553	538333
541723	532231	533587	534943	525451
541045	535621	530875	534265	526129
526807	527485	539011	536977	537655

L3-M1

546469	556639	545113	547147	557317
545791	549859	553249	548503	555283
558673	549181	550537	551893	542401
557995	552571	547825	551215	543079
543757	544435	555961	553927	554605

L3-M2

563419	573589	562063	564097	574267
562741	566809	570199	565453	572233
575623	566131	567487	568843	559351
574945	569521	564775	568165	560029
560707	561385	572911	570877	571555

L3-M3

580369	590539	579013	581047	591217
579691	583759	587149	582403	589183
592573	583081	584437	585793	576301
591895	586471	581725	585115	576979
577657	578335	589861	587827	588505

L3-M4

597319	607489	595963	597997	608167
596641	600709	604099	599353	606133
609523	600031	601387	602743	593251
608845	603421	598675	602065	593929
594607	595285	606811	604777	605455

L3-M5

614269	624439	612913	614947	625117
613591	617659	621049	616303	623083
626473	616981	618337	619693	610201
625795	620371	615625	619015	610879
611557	612235	623761	621727	622405

L3-M6

631219	641389	629863	631897	642067
630541	634609	637999	633253	640033
643423	633931	635287	636643	627151
642745	637321	632575	635965	627829
628507	629185	640711	638677	639355

L3-M7

648169	658339	646813	648847	659017
647491	651559	654949	650203	656983
660373	650881	652237	653593	644101
659695	654271	649525	652915	644779
645457	646135	657661	655627	656305

L3-M8

665119	675289	663763	665797	675967
664441	668509	671899	667153	673933
677323	667831	669187	670543	661051
676645	671221	666475	669865	661729
662407	663085	674611	672577	673255

L3-M9

682069	692239	680713	682747	692917
681391	685459	688849	684103	690883
694273	684781	686137	687493	678001
693595	688171	683425	686815	678679
679357	680035	691561	689527	690205

L3-M10

699019	709189	697663	699697	709867
698341	702409	705799	701053	707833
711223	701731	703087	704443	694951
710545	705121	700375	703765	695629
696307	696985	708511	706477	707155

L3-M11

715969	726139	714613	716647	726817
715291	719359	722749	718003	724783
728173	718681	720037	721393	711901
727495	722071	717325	720715	712579
713257	713935	725461	723427	724105

L3-M12

732919	743089	731563	733597	743767
732241	736309	739699	734953	741733
745123	735631	736987	738343	728851
744445	739021	734275	737665	729529
730207	730885	742411	740377	741055

L3-M13

749869	760039	748513	750547	760717
749191	753259	756649	751903	758683
762073	752581	753937	755293	745801
761395	755971	751225	754615	746479
747157	747835	759361	757327	758005

L3-M14

766819	776989	765463	767497	777667
766141	770209	773599	768853	775633
779023	769531	770887	772243	762751
778345	772921	768175	771565	763429
764107	764785	776311	774277	774955

L3-M15

783769	793939	782413	784447	794617
783091	787159	790549	785803	792583
795973	786481	787837	789193	779701
795295	789871	785125	788515	780379
781057	781735	793261	791227	791905

L3-M16

800719	810889	799363	801397	811567
800041	804109	807499	802753	809533
812923	803431	804787	806143	796651
812245	806821	802075	805465	797329
798007	798685	810211	808177	808855

L4-M1

817669	827839	816313	818347	828517
816991	821059	824449	819703	826483
829873	820381	821737	823093	813601
829195	823771	819025	822415	814279
814957	815635	827161	825127	825805

L4-M2

834619	844789	833263	835297	845467
833941	838009	841399	836653	843433
846823	837331	838687	840043	830551
846145	840721	835975	839365	831229
831907	832585	844111	842077	842755

L4-M3

851569	861739	850213	852247	862417
850891	854959	858349	853603	860383
863773	854281	855637	856993	847501
863095	857671	852925	856315	848179
848857	849535	861061	859027	859705

L4-M4

868519	878689	867163	869197	879367
867841	871909	875299	870553	877333
880723	871231	872587	873943	864451
880045	874621	869875	873265	865129
865807	866485	878011	875977	876655

L4-M5

885469	895639	884113	886147	896317
884791	888859	892249	887503	894283
897673	888181	889537	890893	881401
896995	891571	886825	890215	882079
882757	883435	894961	892927	893605

L4-M6

902419	912589	901063	903097	913267
901741	905809	909199	904453	911233
914623	905131	906487	907843	898351
913945	908521	903775	907165	899029
899707	900385	911911	909877	910555

L4-M7

919369	929539	918013	920047	930217
918691	922759	926149	921403	928183
931573	922081	923437	924793	915301
930895	925471	920725	924115	915979
916657	917335	928861	926827	927505

L4-M8

936319	946489	934963	936997	947167
935641	939709	943099	938353	945133
948523	939031	940387	941743	932251
947845	942421	937675	941065	932929
933607	934285	945811	943777	944455

L4-M9

953269	963439	951913	953947	964117
952591	956659	960049	955303	962083
965473	955981	957337	958693	949201
964795	959371	954625	958015	949879
950557	951235	962761	960727	961405

L4-M10

970219	980389	968863	970897	981067
969541	973609	976999	972253	979033
982423	972931	974287	975643	966151
981745	976321	971575	974965	966829
967507	968185	979711	977677	978355

L4-M11

987169	997339	985813	987847	998017
986491	990559	993949	989203	995983
999373	989881	991237	992593	983101
998695	993271	988525	991915	983779
984457	985135	996661	994627	995305

L4-M12

1004119	1014289	1002763	1004797	1014967
1003441	1007509	1010899	1006153	1012933
1016323	1006831	1008187	1009543	1000051
1015645	1010221	1005475	1008865	1000729
1001407	1002085	1013611	1011577	1012255

L4-M13

1021069	1031239	1019713	1021747	1031917
1020391	1024459	1027849	1023103	1029883
1033273	1023781	1025137	1026493	1017001
1032595	1027171	1022425	1025815	1017679
1018357	1019035	1030561	1028527	1029205

L4-M14

1038019	1048189	1036663	1038697	1048867
1037341	1041409	1044799	1040053	1046833
1050223	1040731	1042087	1043443	1033951
1049545	1044121	1039375	1042765	1034629
1035307	1035985	1047511	1045477	1046155

L4-M15

1054969	1065139	1053613	1055647	1065817
1054291	1058359	1061749	1057003	1063783
1067173	1057681	1059037	1060393	1050901
1066495	1061071	1056325	1059715	1051579
1052257	1052935	1064461	1062427	1063105

L4-M16

1071919	1082089	1070563	1072597	1082767
1071241	1075309	1078699	1073953	1080733
1084123	1074631	1075987	1077343	1067851
1083445	1078021	1073275	1076665	1068529
1069207	1069885	1081411	1079377	1080055

L5-M1

1088869	1099039	1087513	1089547	1099717
1088191	1092259	1095649	1090903	1097683
1101073	1091581	1092937	1094293	1084801
1100395	1094971	1090225	1093615	1085479
1086157	1086835	1098361	1096327	1097005

L5-M2

1105819	1115989	1104463	1106497	1116667
1105141	1109209	1112599	1107853	1114633
1118023	1108531	1109887	1111243	1101751
1117345	1111921	1107175	1110565	1102429
1103107	1103785	1115311	1113277	1113955

L5-M3

1122769	1132939	1121413	1123447	1133617
1122091	1126159	1129549	1124803	1131583
1134973	1125481	1126837	1128193	1118701
1134295	1128871	1124125	1127515	1119379
1120057	1120735	1132261	1130227	1130905

L5-M4

1139719	1149889	1138363	1140397	1150567
1139041	1143109	1146499	1141753	1148533
1151923	1142431	1143787	1145143	1135651
1151245	1145821	1141075	1144465	1136329
1137007	1137685	1149211	1147177	1147855

L5-M5

1156669	1166839	1155313	1157347	1167517
1155991	1160059	1163449	1158703	1165483
1168873	1159381	1160737	1162093	1152601
1168195	1162771	1158025	1161415	1153279
1153957	1154635	1166161	1164127	1164805

L5-M6

1173619	1183789	1172263	1174297	1184467
1172941	1177009	1180399	1175653	1182433
1185823	1176331	1177687	1179043	1169551
1185145	1179721	1174975	1178365	1170229
1170907	1171585	1183111	1181077	1181755

L5-M7

1190569	1200739	1189213	1191247	1201417
1189891	1193959	1197349	1192603	1199383
1202773	1193281	1194637	1195993	1186501
1202095	1196671	1191925	1195315	1187179
1187857	1188535	1200061	1198027	1198705

L5-M8

1207519	1217689	1206163	1208197	1218367
1206841	1210909	1214299	1209553	1216333
1219723	1210231	1211587	1212943	1203451
1219045	1213621	1208875	1212265	1204129
1204807	1205485	1217011	1214977	1215655

L5-M9

1224469	1234639	1223113	1225147	1235317
1223791	1227859	1231249	1226503	1233283
1236673	1227181	1228537	1229893	1220401
1235995	1230571	1225825	1229215	1221079
1221757	1222435	1233961	1231927	1232605

L5-M10

1241419	1251589	1240063	1242097	1252267
1240741	1244809	1248199	1243453	1250233
1253623	1244131	1245487	1246843	1237351
1252945	1247521	1242775	1246165	1238029
1238707	1239385	1250911	1248877	1249555

L5-M11

1258369	1268539	1257013	1259047	1269217
1257691	1261759	1265149	1260403	1267183
1270573	1261081	1262437	1263793	1254301
1269895	1264471	1259725	1263115	1254979
1255657	1256335	1267861	1265827	1266505

L5-M12

1275319	1285489	1273963	1275997	1286167
1274641	1278709	1282099	1277353	1284133
1287523	1278031	1279387	1280743	1271251
1286845	1281421	1276675	1280065	1271929
1272607	1273285	1284811	1282777	1283455

L5-M13

1292269	1302439	1290913	1292947	1303117
1291591	1295659	1299049	1294303	1301083
1304473	1294981	1296337	1297693	1288201
1303795	1298371	1293625	1297015	1288879
1289557	1290235	1301761	1299727	1300405

L5-M14

1309219	1319389	1307863	1309897	1320067
1308541	1312609	1315999	1311253	1318033
1321423	1311931	1313287	1314643	1305151
1320745	1315321	1310575	1313965	1305829
1306507	1307185	1318711	1316677	1317355

L5-M15

1326169	1336339	1324813	1326847	1337017
1325491	1329559	1332949	1328203	1334983
1338373	1328881	1330237	1331593	1322101
1337695	1332271	1327525	1330915	1322779
1323457	1324135	1335661	1333627	1334305

L5-M16

1343119	1353289	1341763	1343797	1353967
1342441	1346509	1349899	1345153	1351933
1355323	1345831	1347187	1348543	1339051
1354645	1349221	1344475	1347865	1339729
1340407	1341085	1352611	1350577	1351255

L6-M1

1360069	1370239	1358713	1360747	1370917
1359391	1363459	1366849	1362103	1368883
1372273	1362781	1364137	1365493	1356001
1371595	1366171	1361425	1364815	1356679
1357357	1358035	1369561	1367527	1368205

L6-M2

1377019	1387189	1375663	1377697	1387867
1376341	1380409	1383799	1379053	1385833
1389223	1379731	1381087	1382443	1372951
1388545	1383121	1378375	1381765	1373629
1374307	1374985	1386511	1384477	1385155

L6-M3

1393969	1404139	1392613	1394647	1404817
1393291	1397359	1400749	1396003	1402783
1406173	1396681	1398037	1399393	1389901
1405495	1400071	1395325	1398715	1390579
1391257	1391935	1403461	1401427	1402105

L6-M4

1410919	1421089	1409563	1411597	1421767
1410241	1414309	1417699	1412953	1419733
1423123	1413631	1414987	1416343	1406851
1422445	1417021	1412275	1415665	1407529
1408207	1408885	1420411	1418377	1419055

L6-M5

1427869	1438039	1426513	1428547	1438717
1427191	1431259	1434649	1429903	1436683
1440073	1430581	1431937	1433293	1423801
1439395	1433971	1429225	1432615	1424479
1425157	1425835	1437361	1435327	1436005

L6-M6

1444819	1454989	1443463	1445497	1455667
1444141	1448209	1451599	1446853	1453633
1457023	1447531	1448887	1450243	1440751
1456345	1450921	1446175	1449565	1441429
1442107	1442785	1454311	1452277	1452955

L6-M7

1461769	1471939	1460413	1462447	1472617
1461091	1465159	1468549	1463803	1470583
1473973	1464481	1465837	1467193	1457701
1473295	1467871	1463125	1466515	1458379
1459057	1459735	1471261	1469227	1469905

L6-M8

1478719	1488889	1477363	1479397	1489567
1478041	1482109	1485499	1480753	1487533
1490923	1481431	1482787	1484143	1474651
1490245	1484821	1480075	1483465	1475329
1476007	1476685	1488211	1486177	1486855

L6-M9

1495669	1505839	1494313	1496347	1506517
1494991	1499059	1502449	1497703	1504483
1507873	1498381	1499737	1501093	1491601
1507195	1501771	1497025	1500415	1492279
1492957	1493635	1505161	1503127	1503805

L6-M10

1512619	1522789	1511263	1513297	1523467
1511941	1516009	1519399	1514653	1521433
1524823	1515331	1516687	1518043	1508551
1524145	1518721	1513975	1517365	1509229
1509907	1510585	1522111	1520077	1520755

L6-M11

1529569	1539739	1528213	1530247	1540417
1528891	1532959	1536349	1531603	1538383
1541773	1532281	1533637	1534993	1525501
1541095	1535671	1530925	1534315	1526179
1526857	1527535	1539061	1537027	1537705

L6-M12

1546519	1556689	1545163	1547197	1557367
1545841	1549909	1553299	1548553	1555333
1558723	1549231	1550587	1551943	1542451
1558045	1552621	1547875	1551265	1543129
1543807	1544485	1556011	1553977	1554655

L6-M13

1563469	1573639	1562113	1564147	1574317
1562791	1566859	1570249	1565503	1572283
1575673	1566181	1567537	1568893	1559401
1574995	1569571	1564825	1568215	1560079
1560757	1561435	1572961	1570927	1571605

L6-M14

1580419	1590589	1579063	1581097	1591267
1579741	1583809	1587199	1582453	1589233
1592623	1583131	1584487	1585843	1576351
1591945	1586521	1581775	1585165	1577029
1577707	1578385	1589911	1587877	1588555

L6-M15

1597369	1607539	1596013	1598047	1608217
1596691	1600759	1604149	1599403	1606183
1609573	1600081	1601437	1602793	1593301
1608895	1603471	1598725	1602115	1593979
1594657	1595335	1606861	1604827	1605505

L6-M16

1614319	1624489	1612963	1614997	1625167
1613641	1617709	1621099	1616353	1623133
1626523	1617031	1618387	1619743	1610251
1625845	1620421	1615675	1619065	1610929
1611607	1612285	1623811	1621777	1622455

L7-M1

1631269	1641439	1629913	1631947	1642117
1630591	1634659	1638049	1633303	1640083
1643473	1633981	1635337	1636693	1627201
1642795	1637371	1632625	1636015	1627879
1628557	1629235	1640761	1638727	1639405

L7-M2

1648219	1658389	1646863	1648897	1659067
1647541	1651609	1654999	1650253	1657033
1660423	1650931	1652287	1653643	1644151
1659745	1654321	1649575	1652965	1644829
1645507	1646185	1657711	1655677	1656355

L7-M3

1665169	1675339	1663813	1665847	1676017
1664491	1668559	1671949	1667203	1673983
1677373	1667881	1669237	1670593	1661101
1676695	1671271	1666525	1669915	1661779
1662457	1663135	1674661	1672627	1673305

L7-M4

1682119	1692289	1680763	1682797	1692967
1681441	1685509	1688899	1684153	1690933
1694323	1684831	1686187	1687543	1678051
1693645	1688221	1683475	1686865	1678729
1679407	1680085	1691611	1689577	1690255

L7-M5

1699069	1709239	1697713	1699747	1709917
1698391	1702459	1705849	1701103	1707883
1711273	1701781	1703137	1704493	1695001
1710595	1705171	1700425	1703815	1695679
1696357	1697035	1708561	1706527	1707205

L7-M6

1716019	1726189	1714663	1716697	1726867
1715341	1719409	1722799	1718053	1724833
1728223	1718731	1720087	1721443	1711951
1727545	1722121	1717375	1720765	1712629
1713307	1713985	1725511	1723477	1724155

L7-M7

1732969	1743139	1731613	1733647	1743817
1732291	1736359	1739749	1735003	1741783
1745173	1735681	1737037	1738393	1728901
1744495	1739071	1734325	1737715	1729579
1730257	1730935	1742461	1740427	1741105

L7-M8

1749919	1760089	1748563	1750597	1760767
1749241	1753309	1756699	1751953	1758733
1762123	1752631	1753987	1755343	1745851
1761445	1756021	1751275	1754665	1746529
1747207	1747885	1759411	1757377	1758055

L7-M9

1766869	1777039	1765513	1767547	1777717
1766191	1770259	1773649	1768903	1775683
1779073	1769581	1770937	1772293	1762801
1778395	1772971	1768225	1771615	1763479
1764157	1764835	1776361	1774327	1775005

L7-M10

1783819	1793989	1782463	1784497	1794667
1783141	1787209	1790599	1785853	1792633
1796023	1786531	1787887	1789243	1779751
1795345	1789921	1785175	1788565	1780429
1781107	1781785	1793311	1791277	1791955

L7-M11

1800769	1810939	1799413	1801447	1811617
1800091	1804159	1807549	1802803	1809583
1812973	1803481	1804837	1806193	1796701
1812295	1806871	1802125	1805515	1797379
1798057	1798735	1810261	1808227	1808905

L7-M12

1817719	1827889	1816363	1818397	1828567
1817041	1821109	1824499	1819753	1826533
1829923	1820431	1821787	1823143	1813651
1829245	1823821	1819075	1822465	1814329
1815007	1815685	1827211	1825177	1825855

L7-M13

1834669	1844839	1833313	1835347	1845517
1833991	1838059	1841449	1836703	1843483
1846873	1837381	1838737	1840093	1830601
1846195	1840771	1836025	1839415	1831279
1831957	1832635	1844161	1842127	1842805

L8-M6

1987219	1997389	1985863	1987897	1998067
1986541	1990609	1993999	1989253	1996033
1999423	1989931	1991287	1992643	1983151
1998745	1993321	1988575	1991965	1983829
1984507	1985185	1996711	1994677	1995355

L7-M14

1851619	1861789	1850263	1852297	1862467
1850941	1855009	1858399	1853653	1860433
1863823	1854331	1855687	1857043	1847551
1863145	1857721	1852975	1856365	1848229
1848907	1849585	1861111	1859077	1859755

L8-M7

2004169	2014339	2002813	2004847	2015017
2003491	2007559	2010949	2006203	2012983
2016373	2006881	2008237	2009593	2000101
2015695	2010271	2005525	2008915	2000779
2001457	2002135	2013661	2011627	2012305

L7-M15

1868569	1878739	1867213	1869247	1879417
1867891	1871959	1875349	1870603	1877383
1880773	1871281	1872637	1873993	1864501
1880095	1874671	1869925	1873315	1865179
1865857	1866535	1878061	1876027	1876705

L8-M8

2021119	2031289	2019763	2021797	2031967
2020441	2024509	2027899	2023153	2029933
2033323	2023831	2025187	2026543	2017051
2032645	2027221	2022475	2025865	2017729
2018407	2019085	2030611	2028577	2029255

L7-M16

1885519	1895689	1884163	1886197	1896367
1884841	1888909	1892299	1887553	1894333
1897723	1888231	1889587	1890943	1881451
1897045	1891621	1886875	1890265	1882129
1882807	1883485	1895011	1892977	1893655

L8-M9

2038069	2048239	2036713	2038747	2048917
2037391	2041459	2044849	2040103	2046883
2050273	2040781	2042137	2043493	2034001
2049595	2044171	2039425	2042815	2034679
2035357	2036035	2047561	2045527	2046205

L8M1

1902469	1912639	1901113	1903147	1913317
1901791	1905859	1909249	1904503	1911283
1914673	1905181	1906537	1907893	1898401
1913995	1908571	1903825	1907215	1899079
1899757	1900435	1911961	1909927	1910605

L8-M10

2055019	2065189	2053663	2055697	2065867
2054341	2058409	2061799	2057053	2063833
2067223	2057731	2059087	2060443	2050951
2066545	2061121	2056375	2059765	2051629
2052307	2052985	2064511	2062477	2063155

L8-M2

1919419	1929589	1918063	1920097	1930267
1918741	1922809	1926199	1921453	1928233
1931623	1922131	1923487	1924843	1915351
1930945	1925521	1920775	1924165	1916029
1916707	1917385	1928911	1926877	1927555

L8-M11

2071969	2082139	2070613	2072647	2082817
2071291	2075359	2078749	2074003	2080783
2084173	2074681	2076037	2077393	2067901
2083495	2078071	2073325	2076715	2068579
2069257	2069935	2081461	2079427	2080105

L8-M3

1936369	1946539	1935013	1937047	1947217
1935691	1939759	1943149	1938403	1945183
1948573	1939081	1940437	1941793	1932301
1947895	1942471	1937725	1941115	1932979
1933657	1934335	1945861	1943827	1944505

L8-M12

2088919	2099089	2087563	2089597	2099767
2088241	2092309	2095699	2090953	2097733
2101123	2091631	2092987	2094343	2084851
2100445	2095021	2090275	2093665	2085529
2086207	2086885	2098411	2096377	2097055

L8-M4

1953319	1963489	1951963	1953997	1964167
1952641	1956709	1960099	1955353	1962133
1965523	1956031	1957387	1958743	1949251
1964845	1959421	1954675	1958065	1949929
1950607	1951285	1962811	1960777	1961455

L8-M13

2105869	2116039	2104513	2106547	2116717
2105191	2109259	2112649	2107903	2114683
2118073	2108581	2109937	2111293	2101801
2117395	2111971	2107225	2110615	2102479
2103157	2103835	2115361	2113327	2114005

L8-M5

1970269	1980439	1968913	1970947	1981117
1969591	1973659	1977049	1972303	1979083
1982473	1972981	1974337	1975693	1966201
1981795	1976371	1971625	1975015	1966879
1967557	1968235	1979761	1977727	1978405

L8-M14

2122819	2132989	2121463	2123497	2133667
2122141	2126209	2129599	2124853	2131633
2135023	2125531	2126887	2128243	2118751
2134345	2128921	2124175	2127565	2119429
2120107	2120785	2132311	2130277	2130955

L8-M15

2139769	2149939	2138413	2140447	2150617
2139091	2143159	2146549	2141803	2148583
2151973	2142481	2143837	2145193	2135701
2151295	2145871	2141125	2144515	2136379
2137057	2137735	2149261	2147227	2147905

L8-M16

2156719	2166889	2155363	2157397	2167567
2156041	2160109	2163499	2158753	2165533
2168923	2159431	2160787	2162143	2152651
2168245	2162821	2158075	2161465	2153329
2154007	2154685	2166211	2164177	2164855

L9-M1

2173669	2183839	2172313	2174347	2184517
2172991	2177059	2180449	2175703	2182483
2185873	2176381	2177737	2179093	2169601
2185195	2179771	2175025	2178415	2170279
2170957	2171635	2183161	2181127	2181805

L9-M2

2190619	2200789	2189263	2191297	2201467
2189941	2194009	2197399	2192653	2199433
2202823	2193331	2194687	2196043	2186551
2202145	2196721	2191975	2195365	2187229
2187907	2188585	2200111	2198077	2198755

L9-M3

2207569	2217739	2206213	2208247	2218417
2206891	2210959	2214349	2209603	2216383
2219773	2210281	2211637	2212993	2203501
2219095	2213671	2208925	2212315	2204179
2204857	2205535	2217061	2215027	2215705

L9-M4

2224519	2234689	2223163	2225197	2235367
2223841	2227909	2231299	2226553	2233333
2236723	2227231	2228587	2229943	2220451
2236045	2230621	2225875	2229265	2221129
2221807	2222485	2234011	2231977	2232655

L9-M5

2241469	2251639	2240113	2242147	2252317
2240791	2244859	2248249	2243503	2250283
2253673	2244181	2245537	2246893	2237401
2252995	2247571	2242825	2246215	2238079
2238757	2239435	2250961	2248927	2249605

L9-M6

2258419	2268589	2257063	2259097	2269267
2257741	2261809	2265199	2260453	2267233
2270623	2261131	2262487	2263843	2254351
2269945	2264521	2259775	2263165	2255029
2255707	2256385	2267911	2265877	2266555

L9-M7

2275369	2285539	2274013	2276047	2286217
2274691	2278759	2282149	2277403	2284183
2287573	2278081	2279437	2280793	2271301
2286895	2281471	2276725	2280115	2271979
2272657	2273335	2284861	2282827	2283505

L9-M8

2292319	2302489	2290963	2292997	2303167
2291641	2295709	2299099	2294353	2301133
2304523	2295031	2296387	2297743	2288251
2303845	2298421	2293675	2297065	2288929
2289607	2290285	2301811	2299777	2300455

L9-M9

2309269	2319439	2307913	2309947	2320117
2308591	2312659	2316049	2311303	2318083
2321473	2311981	2313337	2314693	2305201
2320795	2315371	2310625	2314015	2305879
2306557	2307235	2318761	2316727	2317405

L9-M10

2326219	2336389	2324863	2326897	2337067
2325541	2329609	2332999	2328253	2335033
2338423	2328931	2330287	2331643	2322151
2337745	2332321	2327575	2330965	2322829
2323507	2324185	2335711	2333677	2334355

L9-M11

2343169	2353339	2341813	2343847	2354017
2342491	2346559	2349949	2345203	2351983
2355373	2345881	2347237	2348593	2339101
2354695	2349271	2344525	2347915	2339779
2340457	2341135	2352661	2350627	2351305

L9-M12

2360119	2370289	2358763	2360797	2370967
2359441	2363509	2366899	2362153	2368933
2372323	2362831	2364187	2365543	2356051
2371645	2366221	2361475	2364865	2356729
2357407	2358085	2369611	2367577	2368255

L9-M13

2377069	2387239	2375713	2377747	2387917
2376391	2380459	2383849	2379103	2385883
2389273	2379781	2381137	2382493	2373001
2388595	2383171	2378425	2381815	2373679
2374357	2375035	2386561	2384527	2385205

L9-M14

2394019	2404189	2392663	2394697	2404867
2393341	2397409	2400799	2396053	2402833
2406223	2396731	2398087	2399443	2389951
2405545	2400121	2395375	2398765	2390629
2391307	2391985	2403511	2401477	2402155

L9-M15

2410969	2421139	2409613	2411647	2421817
2410291	2414359	2417749	2413003	2419783
2423173	2413681	2415037	2416393	2406901
2422495	2417071	2412325	2415715	2407579
2408257	2408935	2420461	2418427	2419105

L9-M16

2427919	2438089	2426563	2428597	2438767
2427241	2431309	2434699	2429953	2436733
2440123	2430631	2431987	2433343	2423851
2439445	2434021	2429275	2432665	2424529
2425207	2425885	2437411	2435377	2436055

L10-M1

2444869	2455039	2443513	2445547	2455717
2444191	2448259	2451649	2446903	2453683
2457073	2447581	2448937	2450293	2440801
2456395	2450971	2446225	2449615	2441479
2442157	2442835	2454361	2452327	2453005

L10-M10

2597419	2607589	2596063	2598097	2608267
2596741	2600809	2604199	2599453	2606233
2609623	2600131	2601487	2602843	2593351
2608945	2603521	2598775	2602165	2594029
2594707	2595385	2606911	2604877	2605555

L10-M2

2461819	2471989	2460463	2462497	2472667
2461141	2465209	2468599	2463853	2470633
2474023	2464531	2465887	2467243	2457751
2473345	2467921	2463175	2466565	2458429
2459107	2459785	2471311	2469277	2469955

L10-M11

2614369	2624539	2613013	2615047	2625217
2613691	2617759	2621149	2616403	2623183
2626573	2617081	2618437	2619793	2610301
2625895	2620471	2615725	2619115	2610979
2611657	2612335	2623861	2621827	2622505

L10-M3

2478769	2488939	2477413	2479447	2489617
2478091	2482159	2485549	2480803	2487583
2490973	2481481	2482837	2484193	2474701
2490295	2484871	2480125	2483515	2475379
2476057	2476735	2488261	2486227	2486905

L10-M12

2631319	2641489	2629963	2631997	2642167
2630641	2634709	2638099	2633353	2640133
2643523	2634031	2635387	2636743	2627251
2642845	2637421	2632675	2636065	2627929
2628607	2629285	2640811	2638777	2639455

L10-M4

2495719	2505889	2494363	2496397	2506567
2495041	2499109	2502499	2497753	2504533
2507923	2498431	2499787	2501143	2491651
2507245	2501821	2497075	2500465	2492329
2493007	2493685	2505211	2503177	2503855

L10-M13

2648269	2658439	2646913	2648947	2659117
2647591	2651659	2655049	2650303	2657083
2660473	2650981	2652337	2653693	2644201
2659795	2654371	2649625	2653015	2644879
2645557	2646235	2657761	2655727	2656405

L10-M5

2512669	2522839	2511313	2513347	2523517
2511991	2516059	2519449	2514703	2521483
2524873	2515381	2516737	2518093	2508601
2524195	2518771	2514025	2517415	2509279
2509957	2510635	2522161	2520127	2520805

L10-M14

2665219	2675389	2663863	2665897	2676067
2664541	2668609	2671999	2667253	2674033
2677423	2667931	2669287	2670643	2661151
2676745	2671321	2666575	2669965	2661829
2662507	2663185	2674711	2672677	2673355

L10-M6

2529619	2539789	2528263	2530297	2540467
2528941	2533009	2536399	2531653	2538433
2541823	2532331	2533687	2535043	2525551
2541145	2535721	2530975	2534365	2526229
2526907	2527585	2539111	2537077	2537755

L10-M15

2682169	2692339	2680813	2682847	2693017
2681491	2685559	2688949	2684203	2690983
2694373	2684881	2686237	2687593	2678101
2693695	2688271	2683525	2686915	2678779
2679457	2680135	2691661	2689627	2690305

L10-M7

2546569	2556739	2545213	2547247	2557417
2545891	2549959	2553349	2548603	2555383
2558773	2549281	2550637	2551993	2542501
2558095	2552671	2547925	2551315	2543179
2543857	2544535	2556061	2554027	2554705

L10-M16

2699119	2709289	2697763	2699797	2709967
2698441	2702509	2705899	2701153	2707933
2711323	2701831	2703187	2704543	2695051
2710645	2705221	2700475	2703865	2695729
2696407	2697085	2708611	2706577	2707255

L10-M8

2563519	2573689	2562163	2564197	2574367
2562841	2566909	2570299	2565553	2572333
2575723	2566231	2567587	2568943	2559451
2575045	2569621	2564875	2568265	2560129
2560807	2561485	2573011	2570977	2571655

L11-M1

2716069	2726239	2714713	2716747	2726917
2715391	2719459	2722849	2718103	2724883
2728273	2718781	2720137	2721493	2712001
2727595	2722171	2717425	2720815	2712679
2713357	2714035	2725561	2723527	2724205

L10-M9

2580469	2590639	2579113	2581147	2591317
2579791	2583859	2587249	2582503	2589283
2592673	2583181	2584537	2585893	2576401
2591995	2586571	2581825	2585215	2577079
2577757	2578435	2589961	2587927	2588605

L11-M2

2733019	2743189	2731663	2733697	2743867
2732341	2736409	2739799	2735053	2741833
2745223	2735731	2737087	2738443	2728951
2744545	2739121	2734375	2737765	2729629
2730307	2730985	2742511	2740477	2741155

L11-M3

2749969	2760139	2748613	2750647	2760817
2749291	2753359	2756749	2752003	2758783
2762173	2752681	2754037	2755393	2745901
2761495	2756071	2751325	2754715	2746579
2747257	2747935	2759461	2757427	2758105

L11-M4

2766919	2777089	2765563	2767597	2777767
2766241	2770309	2773699	2768953	2775733
2779123	2769631	2770987	2772343	2762851
2778445	2773021	2768275	2771665	2763529
2764207	2764885	2776411	2774377	2775055

L11-M5

2783869	2794039	2782513	2784547	2794717
2783191	2787259	2790649	2785903	2792683
2796073	2786581	2787937	2789293	2779801
2795395	2789971	2785225	2788615	2780479
2781157	2781835	2793361	2791327	2792005

L11-M6

2800819	2810989	2799463	2801497	2811667
2800141	2804209	2807599	2802853	2809633
2813023	2803531	2804887	2806243	2796751
2812345	2806921	2802175	2805565	2797429
2798107	2798785	2810311	2808277	2808955

L11-M7

2817769	2827939	2816413	2818447	2828617
2817091	2821159	2824549	2819803	2826583
2829973	2820481	2821837	2823193	2813701
2829295	2823871	2819125	2822515	2814379
2815057	2815735	2827261	2825227	2825905

L11-M8

2834719	2844889	2833363	2835397	2845567
2834041	2838109	2841499	2836753	2843533
2846923	2837431	2838787	2840143	2830651
2846245	2840821	2836075	2839465	2831329
2832007	2832685	2844211	2842177	2842855

L11-M9

2851669	2861839	2850313	2852347	2862517
2850991	2855059	2858449	2853703	2860483
2863873	2854381	2855737	2857093	2847601
2863195	2857771	2853025	2856415	2848279
2848957	2849635	2861161	2859127	2859805

L11-M10

2868619	2878789	2867263	2869297	2879467
2867941	2872009	2875399	2870653	2877433
2880823	2871331	2872687	2874043	2864551
2880145	2874721	2869975	2873365	2865229
2865907	2866585	2878111	2876077	2876755

L11-M11

2885569	2895739	2884213	2886247	2896417
2884891	2888959	2892349	2887603	2894383
2897773	2888281	2889637	2890993	2881501
2897095	2891671	2886925	2890315	2882179
2882857	2883535	2895061	2893027	2893705

L11-M12

2902519	2912689	2901163	2903197	2913367
2901841	2905909	2909299	2904553	2911333
2914723	2905231	2906587	2907943	2898451
2914045	2908621	2903875	2907265	2899129
2899807	2900485	2912011	2909977	2910655

L11-M13

2919469	2929639	2918113	2920147	2930317
2918791	2922859	2926249	2921503	2928283
2931673	2922181	2923537	2924893	2915401
2930995	2925571	2920825	2924215	2916079
2916757	2917435	2928961	2926927	2927605

L11-M14

2936419	2946589	2935063	2937097	2947267
2935741	2939809	2943199	2938453	2945233
2948623	2939131	2940487	2941843	2932351
2947945	2942521	2937775	2941165	2933029
2933707	2934385	2945911	2943877	2944555

L11-M15

2953369	2963539	2952013	2954047	2964217
2952691	2956759	2960149	2955403	2962183
2965573	2956081	2957437	2958793	2949301
2964895	2959471	2954725	2958115	2949979
2950657	2951335	2962861	2960827	2961505

L11-M16

2970319	2980489	2968963	2970997	2981167
2969641	2973709	2977099	2972353	2979133
2982523	2973031	2974387	2975743	2966251
2981845	2976421	2971675	2975065	2966929
2967607	2968285	2979811	2977777	2978455

L12-M1

2987269	2997439	2985913	2987947	2998117
2986591	2990659	2994049	2989303	2996083
2999473	2989981	2991337	2992693	2983201
2998795	2993371	2988625	2992015	2983879
2984557	2985235	2996761	2994727	2995405

L12-M2

3004219	3014389	3002863	3004897	3015067
3003541	3007609	3010999	3006253	3013033
3016423	3006931	3008287	3009643	3000151
3015745	3010321	3005575	3008965	3000829
3001507	3002185	3013711	3011677	3012355

L12-M3

3021169	3031339	3019813	3021847	3032017
3020491	3024559	3027949	3023203	3029983
3033373	3023881	3025237	3026593	3017101
3032695	3027271	3022525	3025915	3017779
3018457	3019135	3030661	3028627	3029305

L12-M4

3038119	3048289	3036763	3038797	3048967
3037441	3041509	3044899	3040153	3046933
3050323	3040831	3042187	3043543	3034051
3049645	3044221	3039475	3042865	3034729
3035407	3036085	3047611	3045577	3046255

L12-M5

3055069	3065239	3053713	3055747	3065917
3054391	3058459	3061849	3057103	3063883
3067273	3057781	3059137	3060493	3051001
3066595	3061171	3056425	3059815	3051679
3052357	3053035	3064561	3062527	3063205

L12-M6

3072019	3082189	3070663	3072697	3082867
3071341	3075409	3078799	3074053	3080833
3084223	3074731	3076087	3077443	3067951
3083545	3078121	3073375	3076765	3068629
3069307	3069985	3081511	3079477	3080155

L12-M7

3088969	3099139	3087613	3089647	3099817
3088291	3092359	3095749	3091003	3097783
3101173	3091681	3093037	3094393	3084901
3100495	3095071	3090325	3093715	3085579
3086257	3086935	3098461	3096427	3097105

L12-M8

3105919	3116089	3104563	3106597	3116767
3105241	3109309	3112699	3107953	3114733
3118123	3108631	3109987	3111343	3101851
3117445	3112021	3107275	3110665	3102529
3103207	3103885	3115411	3113377	3114055

L12-M9

3122869	3133039	3121513	3123547	3133717
3122191	3126259	3129649	3124903	3131683
3135073	3125581	3126937	3128293	3118801
3134395	3128971	3124225	3127615	3119479
3120157	3120835	3132361	3130327	3131005

L12-M10

3139819	3149989	3138463	3140497	3150667
3139141	3143209	3146599	3141853	3148633
3152023	3142531	3143887	3145243	3135751
3151345	3145921	3141175	3144565	3136429
3137107	3137785	3149311	3147277	3147955

L12-M11

3156769	3166939	3155413	3157447	3167617
3156091	3160159	3163549	3158803	3165583
3168973	3159481	3160837	3162193	3152701
3168295	3162871	3158125	3161515	3153379
3154057	3154735	3166261	3164227	3164905

L12-M12

3173719	3183889	3172363	3174397	3184567
3173041	3177109	3180499	3175753	3182533
3185923	3176431	3177787	3179143	3169651
3185245	3179821	3175075	3178465	3170329
3171007	3171685	3183211	3181177	3181855

L12-M13

3190669	3200839	3189313	3191347	3201517
3189991	3194059	3197449	3192703	3199483
3202873	3193381	3194737	3196093	3186601
3202195	3196771	3192025	3195415	3187279
3187957	3188635	3200161	3198127	3198805

L12-M14

3207619	3217789	3206263	3208297	3218467
3206941	3211009	3214399	3209653	3216433
3219823	3210331	3211687	3213043	3203551
3219145	3213721	3208975	3212365	3204229
3204907	3205585	3217111	3215077	3215755

L12-M15

3224569	3234739	3223213	3225247	3235417
3223891	3227959	3231349	3226603	3233383
3236773	3227281	3228637	3229993	3220501
3236095	3230671	3225925	3229315	3221179
3221857	3222535	3234061	3232027	3232705

L12-M16

3241519	3251689	3240163	3242197	3252367
3240841	3244909	3248299	3243553	3250333
3253723	3244231	3245587	3246943	3237451
3253045	3247621	3242875	3246265	3238129
3238807	3239485	3251011	3248977	3249655

L13-M1

3258469	3268639	3257113	3259147	3269317
3257791	3261859	3265249	3260503	3267283
3270673	3261181	3262537	3263893	3254401
3269995	3264571	3259825	3263215	3255079
3255757	3256435	3267961	3265927	3266605

L13-M2

3275419	3285589	3274063	3276097	3286267
3274741	3278809	3282199	3277453	3284233
3287623	3278131	3279487	3280843	3271351
3286945	3281521	3276775	3280165	3272029
3272707	3273385	3284911	3282877	3283555

L13-M3

3292369	3302539	3291013	3293047	3303217
3291691	3295759	3299149	3294403	3301183
3304573	3295081	3296437	3297793	3288301
3303895	3298471	3293725	3297115	3288979
3289657	3290335	3301861	3299827	3300505

L13-M4

3309319	3319489	3307963	3309997	3320167
3308641	3312709	3316099	3311353	3318133
3321523	3312031	3313387	3314743	3305251
3320845	3315421	3310675	3314065	3305929
3306607	3307285	3318811	3316777	3317455

L13-M5

3326269	3336439	3324913	3326947	3337117
3325591	3329659	3333049	3328303	3335083
3338473	3328981	3330337	3331693	3322201
3337795	3332371	3327625	3331015	3322879
3323557	3324235	3335761	3333727	3334405

L13-M6

3343219	3353389	3341863	3343897	3354067
3342541	3346609	3349999	3345253	3352033
3355423	3345931	3347287	3348643	3339151
3354745	3349321	3344575	3347965	3339829
3340507	3341185	3352711	3350677	3351355

L13-M7

3360169	3370339	3358813	3360847	3371017
3359491	3363559	3366949	3362203	3368983
3372373	3362881	3364237	3365593	3356101
3371695	3366271	3361525	3364915	3356779
3357457	3358135	3369661	3367627	3368305

L13-M8

3377119	3387289	3375763	3377797	3387967
3376441	3380509	3383899	3379153	3385933
3389323	3379831	3381187	3382543	3373051
3388645	3383221	3378475	3381865	3373729
3374407	3375085	3386611	3384577	3385255

L13-M9

3394069	3404239	3392713	3394747	3404917
3393391	3397459	3400849	3396103	3402883
3406273	3396781	3398137	3399493	3390001
3405595	3400171	3395425	3398815	3390679
3391357	3392035	3403561	3401527	3402205

L13-M10

3411019	3421189	3409663	3411697	3421867
3410341	3414409	3417799	3413053	3419833
3423223	3413731	3415087	3416443	3406951
3422545	3417121	3412375	3415765	3407629
3408307	3408985	3420511	3418477	3419155

L13-M11

3427969	3438139	3426613	3428647	3438817
3427291	3431359	3434749	3430003	3436783
3440173	3430681	3432037	3433393	3423901
3439495	3434071	3429325	3432715	3424579
3425257	3425935	3437461	3435427	3436105

L13-M12

3444919	3455089	3443563	3445597	3455767
3444241	3448309	3451699	3446953	3453733
3457123	3447631	3448987	3450343	3440851
3456445	3451021	3446275	3449665	3441529
3442207	3442885	3454411	3452377	3453055

L13-M13

3461869	3472039	3460513	3462547	3472717
3461191	3465259	3468649	3463903	3470683
3474073	3464581	3465937	3467293	3457801
3473395	3467971	3463225	3466615	3458479
3459157	3459835	3471361	3469327	3470005

L13-M14

3478819	3488989	3477463	3479497	3489667
3478141	3482209	3485599	3480853	3487633
3491023	3481531	3482887	3484243	3474751
3490345	3484921	3480175	3483565	3475429
3476107	3476785	3488311	3486277	3486955

L13-M15

3495769	3505939	3494413	3496447	3506617
3495091	3499159	3502549	3497803	3504583
3507973	3498481	3499837	3501193	3491701
3507295	3501871	3497125	3500515	3492379
3493057	3493735	3505261	3503227	3503905

L13-M16

3512719	3522889	3511363	3513397	3523567
3512041	3516109	3519499	3514753	3521533
3524923	3515431	3516787	3518143	3508651
3524245	3518821	3514075	3517465	3509329
3510007	3510685	3522211	3520177	3520855

L14-M1

3529669	3539839	3528313	3530347	3540517
3528991	3533059	3536449	3531703	3538483
3541873	3532381	3533737	3535093	3525601
3541195	3535771	3531025	3534415	3526279
3526957	3527635	3539161	3537127	3537805

L14-M2

3546619	3556789	3545263	3547297	3557467
3545941	3550009	3553399	3548653	3555433
3558823	3549331	3550687	3552043	3542551
3558145	3552721	3547975	3551365	3543229
3543907	3544585	3556111	3554077	3554755

L14-M3

3563569	3573739	3562213	3564247	3574417
3562891	3566959	3570349	3565603	3572383
3575773	3566281	3567637	3568993	3559501
3575095	3569671	3564925	3568315	3560179
3560857	3561535	3573061	3571027	3571705

L14-M4

3580519	3590689	3579163	3581197	3591367
3579841	3583909	3587299	3582553	3589333
3592723	3583231	3584587	3585943	3576451
3592045	3586621	3581875	3585265	3577129
3577807	3578485	3590011	3587977	3588655

L14-M5

3597469	3607639	3596113	3598147	3608317
3596791	3600859	3604249	3599503	3606283
3609673	3600181	3601537	3602893	3593401
3608995	3603571	3598825	3602215	3594079
3594757	3595435	3606961	3604927	3605605

L14-M6

3614419	3624589	3613063	3615097	3625267
3613741	3617809	3621199	3616453	3623233
3626623	3617131	3618487	3619843	3610351
3625945	3620521	3615775	3619165	3611029
3611707	3612385	3623911	3621877	3622555

L14-M7

3631369	3641539	3630013	3632047	3642217
3630691	3634759	3638149	3633403	3640183
3643573	3634081	3635437	3636793	3627301
3642895	3637471	3632725	3636115	3627979
3628657	3629335	3640861	3638827	3639505

L14-M8

3648319	3658489	3646963	3648997	3659167
3647641	3651709	3655099	3650353	3657133
3660523	3651031	3652387	3653743	3644251
3659845	3654421	3649675	3653065	3644929
3645607	3646285	3657811	3655777	3656455

L14-M9

3665269	3675439	3663913	3665947	3676117
3664591	3668659	3672049	3667303	3674083
3677473	3667981	3669337	3670693	3661201
3676795	3671371	3666625	3670015	3661879
3662557	3663235	3674761	3672727	3673405

L14-M10

3682219	3692389	3680863	3682897	3693067
3681541	3685609	3688999	3684253	3691033
3694423	3684931	3686287	3687643	3678151
3693745	3688321	3683575	3686965	3678829
3679507	3680185	3691711	3689677	3690355

L14-M11

3699169	3709339	3697813	3699847	3710017
3698491	3702559	3705949	3701203	3707983
3711373	3701881	3703237	3704593	3695101
3710695	3705271	3700525	3703915	3695779
3696457	3697135	3708661	3706627	3707305

L14-M12

3716119	3726289	3714763	3716797	3726967
3715441	3719509	3722899	3718153	3724933
3728323	3718831	3720187	3721543	3712051
3727645	3722221	3717475	3720865	3712729
3713407	3714085	3725611	3723577	3724255

L14-M13

3733069	3743239	3731713	3733747	3743917
3732391	3736459	3739849	3735103	3741883
3745273	3735781	3737137	3738493	3729001
3744595	3739171	3734425	3737815	3729679
3730357	3731035	3742561	3740527	3741205

L14-M14

3750019	3760189	3748663	3750697	3760867
3749341	3753409	3756799	3752053	3758833
3762223	3752731	3754087	3755443	3745951
3761545	3756121	3751375	3754765	3746629
3747307	3747985	3759511	3757477	3758155

L14-M15

3766969	3777139	3765613	3767647	3777817
3766291	3770359	3773749	3769003	3775783
3779173	3769681	3771037	3772393	3762901
3778495	3773071	3768325	3771715	3763579
3764257	3764935	3776461	3774427	3775105

L14-M16

3783919	3794089	3782563	3784597	3794767
3783241	3787309	3790699	3785953	3792733
3796123	3786631	3787987	3789343	3779851
3795445	3790021	3785275	3788665	3780529
3781207	3781885	3793411	3791377	3792055

L15-M1

3800869	3811039	3799513	3801547	3811717
3800191	3804259	3807649	3802903	3809683
3813073	3803581	3804937	3806293	3796801
3812395	3806971	3802225	3805615	3797479
3798157	3798835	3810361	3808327	3809005

L15-M2

3817819	3827989	3816463	3818497	3828667
3817141	3821209	3824599	3819853	3826633
3830023	3820531	3821887	3823243	3813751
3829345	3823921	3819175	3822565	3814429
3815107	3815785	3827311	3825277	3825955

L15-M3

3834769	3844939	3833413	3835447	3845617
3834091	3838159	3841549	3836803	3843583
3846973	3837481	3838837	3840193	3830701
3846295	3840871	3836125	3839515	3831379
3832057	3832735	3844261	3842227	3842905

L15-M4

3851719	3861889	3850363	3852397	3862567
3851041	3855109	3858499	3853753	3860533
3863923	3854431	3855787	3857143	3847651
3863245	3857821	3853075	3856465	3848329
3849007	3849685	3861211	3859177	3859855

L15-M5

3868669	3878839	3867313	3869347	3879517
3867991	3872059	3875449	3870703	3877483
3880873	3871381	3872737	3874093	3864601
3880195	3874771	3870025	3873415	3865279
3865957	3866635	3878161	3876127	3876805

L15-M6

3885619	3895789	3884263	3886297	3896467
3884941	3889009	3892399	3887653	3894433
3897823	3888331	3889687	3891043	3881551
3897145	3891721	3886975	3890365	3882229
3882907	3883585	3895111	3893077	3893755

L15-M7

3902569	3912739	3901213	3903247	3913417
3901891	3905959	3909349	3904603	3911383
3914773	3905281	3906637	3907993	3898501
3914095	3908671	3903925	3907315	3899179
3899857	3900535	3912061	3910027	3910705

L15-M8

3919519	3929689	3918163	3920197	3930367
3918841	3922909	3926299	3921553	3928333
3931723	3922231	3923587	3924943	3915451
3931045	3925621	3920875	3924265	3916129
3916807	3917485	3929011	3926977	3927655

L15-M9

3936469	3946639	3935113	3937147	3947317
3935791	3939859	3943249	3938503	3945283
3948673	3939181	3940537	3941893	3932401
3947995	3942571	3937825	3941215	3933079
3933757	3934435	3945961	3943927	3944605

L15-M10

3953419	3963589	3952063	3954097	3964267
3952741	3956809	3960199	3955453	3962233
3965623	3956131	3957487	3958843	3949351
3964945	3959521	3954775	3958165	3950029
3950707	3951385	3962911	3960877	3961555

L15-M11

3970369	3980539	3969013	3971047	3981217
3969691	3973759	3977149	3972403	3979183
3982573	3973081	3974437	3975793	3966301
3981895	3976471	3971725	3975115	3966979
3967657	3968335	3979861	3977827	3978505

L15-M12

3987319	3997489	3985963	3987997	3998167
3986641	3990709	3994099	3989353	3996133
3999523	3990031	3991387	3992743	3983251
3998845	3993421	3988675	3992065	3983929
3984607	3985285	3996811	3994777	3995455

L15-M13

4004269	4014439	4002913	4004947	4015117
4003591	4007659	4011049	4006303	4013083
4016473	4006981	4008337	4009693	4000201
4015795	4010371	4005625	4009015	4000879
4001557	4002235	4013761	4011727	4012405

L15-M14

4021219	4031389	4019863	4021897	4032067
4020541	4024609	4027999	4023253	4030033
4033423	4023931	4025287	4026643	4017151
4032745	4027321	4022575	4025965	4017829
4018507	4019185	4030711	4028677	4029355

L15-M15

4038169	4048339	4036813	4038847	4049017
4037491	4041559	4044949	4040203	4046983
4050373	4040881	4042237	4043593	4034101
4049695	4044271	4039525	4042915	4034779
4035457	4036135	4047661	4045627	4046305

L15-M16

4055119	4065289	4053763	4055797	4065967
4054441	4058509	4061899	4057153	4063933
4067323	4057831	4059187	4060543	4051051
4066645	4061221	4056475	4059865	4051729
4052407	4053085	4064611	4062577	4063255

L16-M1

4072069	4082239	4070713	4072747	4082917
4071391	4075459	4078849	4074103	4080883
4084273	4074781	4076137	4077493	4068001
4083595	4078171	4073425	4076815	4068679
4069357	4070035	4081561	4079527	4080205

L16-M2

4089019	4099189	4087663	4089697	4099867
4088341	4092409	4095799	4091053	4097833
4101223	4091731	4093087	4094443	4084951
4100545	4095121	4090375	4093765	4085629
4086307	4086985	4098511	4096477	4097155

L16-M3

4105969	4116139	4104613	4106647	4116817
4105291	4109359	4112749	4108003	4114783
4118173	4108681	4110037	4111393	4101901
4117495	4112071	4107325	4110715	4102579
4103257	4103935	4115461	4113427	4114105

L16-M4

4122919	4133089	4121563	4123597	4133767
4122241	4126309	4129699	4124953	4131733
4135123	4125631	4126987	4128343	4118851
4134445	4129021	4124275	4127665	4119529
4120207	4120885	4132411	4130377	4131055

L16-M5

4139869	4150039	4138513	4140547	4150717
4139191	4143259	4146649	4141903	4148683
4152073	4142581	4143937	4145293	4135801
4151395	4145971	4141225	4144615	4136479
4137157	4137835	4149361	4147327	4148005

L16-M6

4156819	4166989	4155463	4157497	4167667
4156141	4160209	4163599	4158853	4165633
4169023	4159531	4160887	4162243	4152751
4168345	4162921	4158175	4161565	4153429
4154107	4154785	4166311	4164277	4164955

L16-M7

4173769	4183939	4172413	4174447	4184617
4173091	4177159	4180549	4175803	4182583
4185973	4176481	4177837	4179193	4169701
4185295	4179871	4175125	4178515	4170379
4171057	4171735	4183261	4181227	4181905

L16-M8

4190719	4200889	4189363	4191397	4201567
4190041	4194109	4197499	4192753	4199533
4202923	4193431	4194787	4196143	4186651
4202245	4196821	4192075	4195465	4187329
4188007	4188685	4200211	4198177	4198855

L16-M9

4207669	4217839	4206313	4208347	4218517
4206991	4211059	4214449	4209703	4216483
4219873	4210381	4211737	4213093	4203601
4219195	4213771	4209025	4212415	4204279
4204957	4205635	4217161	4215127	4215805

L16-M10

4224619	4234789	4223263	4225297	4235467
4223941	4228009	4231399	4226653	4233433
4236823	4227331	4228687	4230043	4220551
4236145	4230721	4225975	4229365	4221229
4221907	4222585	4234111	4232077	4232755

L16-M11

4241569	4251739	4240213	4242247	4252417
4240891	4244959	4248349	4243603	4250383
4253773	4244281	4245637	4246993	4237501
4253095	4247671	4242925	4246315	4238179
4238857	4239535	4251061	4249027	4249705

L16-M12

4258519	4268689	4257163	4259197	4269367
4257841	4261909	4265299	4260553	4267333
4270723	4261231	4262587	4263943	4254451
4270045	4264621	4259875	4263265	4255129
4255807	4256485	4268011	4265977	4266655

L16-M13

4275469	4285639	4274113	4276147	4286317
4274791	4278859	4282249	4277503	4284283
4287673	4278181	4279537	4280893	4271401
4286995	4281571	4276825	4280215	4272079
4272757	4273435	4284961	4282927	4283605

L16-M14

4292419	4302589	4291063	4293097	4303267
4291741	4295809	4299199	4294453	4301233
4304623	4295131	4296487	4297843	4288351
4303945	4298521	4293775	4297165	4289029
4289707	4290385	4301911	4299877	4300555

L16-M15

4309369	4319539	4308013	4310047	4320217
4308691	4312759	4316149	4311403	4318183
4321573	4312081	4313437	4314793	4305301
4320895	4315471	4310725	4314115	4305979
4306657	4307335	4318861	4316827	4317505

L16M16

4326319	4336489	4324963	4326997	4337167
4325641	4329709	4333099	4328353	4335133
4338523	4329031	4330387	4331743	4322251
4337845	4332421	4327675	4331065	4322929
4323607	4324285	4335811	4333777	4334455

L17-M1

4343269	4353439	4341913	4343947	4354117
4342591	4346659	4350049	4345303	4352083
4355473	4345981	4347337	4348693	4339201
4354795	4349371	4344625	4348015	4339879
4340557	4341235	4352761	4350727	4351405

L17-M2

4360219	4370389	4358863	4360897	4371067
4359541	4363609	4366999	4362253	4369033
4372423	4362931	4364287	4365643	4356151
4371745	4366321	4361575	4364965	4356829
4357507	4358185	4369711	4367677	4368355

L17-M3

4377169	4387339	4375813	4377847	4388017
4376491	4380559	4383949	4379203	4385983
4389373	4379881	4381237	4382593	4373101
4388695	4383271	4378525	4381915	4373779
4374457	4375135	4386661	4384627	4385305

L17-M4

4394119	4404289	4392763	4394797	4404967
4393441	4397509	4400899	4396153	4402933
4406323	4396831	4398187	4399543	4390051
4405645	4400221	4395475	4398865	4390729
4391407	4392085	4403611	4401577	4402255

L17-M5

4411069	4421239	4409713	4411747	4421917
4410391	4414459	4417849	4413103	4419883
4423273	4413781	4415137	4416493	4407001
4422595	4417171	4412425	4415815	4407679
4408357	4409035	4420561	4418527	4419205

L17-M6

4428019	4438189	4426663	4428697	4438867
4427341	4431409	4434799	4430053	4436833
4440223	4430731	4432087	4433443	4423951
4439545	4434121	4429375	4432765	4424629
4425307	4425985	4437511	4435477	4436155

L17-M7

4444969	4455139	4443613	4445647	4455817
4444291	4448359	4451749	4447003	4453783
4457173	4447681	4449037	4450393	4440901
4456495	4451071	4446325	4449715	4441579
4442257	4442935	4454461	4452427	4453105

L17-M8

4461919	4472089	4460563	4462597	4472767
4461241	4465309	4468699	4463953	4470733
4474123	4464631	4465987	4467343	4457851
4473445	4468021	4463275	4466665	4458529
4459207	4459885	4471411	4469377	4470055

L17-M9

4478869	4489039	4477513	4479547	4489717
4478191	4482259	4485649	4480903	4487683
4491073	4481581	4482937	4484293	4474801
4490395	4484971	4480225	4483615	4475479
4476157	4476835	4488361	4486327	4487005

L17-M10

4495819	4505989	4494463	4496497	4506667
4495141	4499209	4502599	4497853	4504633
4508023	4498531	4499887	4501243	4491751
4507345	4501921	4497175	4500565	4492429
4493107	4493785	4505311	4503277	4503955

L17-M11

4512769	4522939	4511413	4513447	4523617
4512091	4516159	4519549	4514803	4521583
4524973	4515481	4516837	4518193	4508701
4524295	4518871	4514125	4517515	4509379
4510057	4510735	4522261	4520227	4520905

L17-M12

4529719	4539889	4528363	4530397	4540567
4529041	4533109	4536499	4531753	4538533
4541923	4532431	4533787	4535143	4525651
4541245	4535821	4531075	4534465	4526329
4527007	4527685	4539211	4537177	4537855

L17-M13

4546669	4556839	4545313	4547347	4557517
4545991	4550059	4553449	4548703	4555483
4558873	4549381	4550737	4552093	4542601
4558195	4552771	4548025	4551415	4543279
4543957	4544635	4556161	4554127	4554805

L17-M14

4563619	4573789	4562263	4564297	4574467
4562941	4567009	4570399	4565653	4572433
4575823	4566331	4567687	4569043	4559551
4575145	4569721	4564975	4568365	4560229
4560907	4561585	4573111	4571077	4571755

L17-M15

4580569	4590739	4579213	4581247	4591417
4579891	4583959	4587349	4582603	4589383
4592773	4583281	4584637	4585993	4576501
4592095	4586671	4581925	4585315	4577179
4577857	4578535	4590061	4588027	4588705

L17-M16

4597519	4607689	4596163	4598197	4608367
4596841	4600909	4604299	4599553	4606333
4609723	4600231	4601587	4602943	4593451
4609045	4603621	4598875	4602265	4594129
4594807	4595485	4607011	4604977	4605655

L18-M1

4614469	4624639	4613113	4615147	4625317
4613791	4617859	4621249	4616503	4623283
4626673	4617181	4618537	4619893	4610401
4625995	4620571	4615825	4619215	4611079
4611757	4612435	4623961	4621927	4622605

L18-M2

4631419	4641589	4630063	4632097	4642267
4630741	4634809	4638199	4633453	4640233
4643623	4634131	4635487	4636843	4627351
4642945	4637521	4632775	4636165	4628029
4628707	4629385	4640911	4638877	4639555

L18-M3

4648369	4658539	4647013	4649047	4659217
4647691	4651759	4655149	4650403	4657183
4660573	4651081	4652437	4653793	4644301
4659895	4654471	4649725	4653115	4644979
4645657	4646335	4657861	4655827	4656505

L18-M4

4665319	4675489	4663963	4665997	4676167
4664641	4668709	4672099	4667353	4674133
4677523	4668031	4669387	4670743	4661251
4676845	4671421	4666675	4670065	4661929
4662607	4663285	4674811	4672777	4673455

L18-M5

4682269	4692439	4680913	4682947	4693117
4681591	4685659	4689049	4684303	4691083
4694473	4684981	4686337	4687693	4678201
4693795	4688371	4683625	4687015	4678879
4679557	4680235	4691761	4689727	4690405

L18-M6

4699219	4709389	4697863	4699897	4710067
4698541	4702609	4705999	4701253	4708033
4711423	4701931	4703287	4704643	4695151
4710745	4705321	4700575	4703965	4695829
4696507	4697185	4708711	4706677	4707355

L18-M7

4716169	4726339	4714813	4716847	4727017
4715491	4719559	4722949	4718203	4724983
4728373	4718881	4720237	4721593	4712101
4727695	4722271	4717525	4720915	4712779
4713457	4714135	4725661	4723627	4724305

L18-M8

4733119	4743289	4731763	4733797	4743967
4732441	4736509	4739899	4735153	4741933
4745323	4735831	4737187	4738543	4729051
4744645	4739221	4734475	4737865	4729729
4730407	4731085	4742611	4740577	4741255

L18-M9

4750069	4760239	4748713	4750747	4760917
4749391	4753459	4756849	4752103	4758883
4762273	4752781	4754137	4755493	4746001
4761595	4756171	4751425	4754815	4746679
4747357	4748035	4759561	4757527	4758205

L18-M10

4767019	4777189	4765663	4767697	4777867
4766341	4770409	4773799	4769053	4775833
4779223	4769731	4771087	4772443	4762951
4778545	4773121	4768375	4771765	4763629
4764307	4764985	4776511	4774477	4775155

L18-M11

4783969	4794139	4782613	4784647	4794817
4783291	4787359	4790749	4786003	4792783
4796173	4786681	4788037	4789393	4779901
4795495	4790071	4785325	4788715	4780579
4781257	4781935	4793461	4791427	4792105

L18-M12

4800919	4811089	4799563	4801597	4811767
4800241	4804309	4807699	4802953	4809733
4813123	4803631	4804987	4806343	4796851
4812445	4807021	4802275	4805665	4797529
4798207	4798885	4810411	4808377	4809055

L18-M13

4817869	4828039	4816513	4818547	4828717
4817191	4821259	4824649	4819903	4826683
4830073	4820581	4821937	4823293	4813801
4829395	4823971	4819225	4822615	4814479
4815157	4815835	4827361	4825327	4826005

L18-M14

4834819	4844989	4833463	4835497	4845667
4834141	4838209	4841599	4836853	4843633
4847023	4837531	4838887	4840243	4830751
4846345	4840921	4836175	4839565	4831429
4832107	4832785	4844311	4842277	4842955

L18-M15

4851769	4861939	4850413	4852447	4862617
4851091	4855159	4858549	4853803	4860583
4863973	4854481	4855837	4857193	4847701
4863295	4857871	4853125	4856515	4848379
4849057	4849735	4861261	4859227	4859905

L18-M16

4868719	4878889	4867363	4869397	4879567
4868041	4872109	4875499	4870753	4877533
4880923	4871431	4872787	4874143	4864651
4880245	4874821	4870075	4873465	4865329
4866007	4866685	4878211	4876177	4876855

L19-M1

4885669	4895839	4884313	4886347	4896517
4884991	4889059	4892449	4887703	4894483
4897873	4888381	4889737	4891093	4881601
4897195	4891771	4887025	4890415	4882279
4882957	4883635	4895161	4893127	4893805

L19-M10

5038219	5048389	5036863	5038897	5049067
5037541	5041609	5044999	5040253	5047033
5050423	5040931	5042287	5043643	5034151
5049745	5044321	5039575	5042965	5034829
5035507	5036185	5047711	5045677	5046355

L19-M2

4902619	4912789	4901263	4903297	4913467
4901941	4906009	4909399	4904653	4911433
4914823	4905331	4906687	4908043	4898551
4914145	4908721	4903975	4907365	4899229
4899907	4900585	4912111	4910077	4910755

L19-M11

5055169	5065339	5053813	5055847	5066017
5054491	5058559	5061949	5057203	5063983
5067373	5057881	5059237	5060593	5051101
5066695	5061271	5056525	5059915	5051779
5052457	5053135	5064661	5062627	5063305

L19-M3

4919569	4929739	4918213	4920247	4930417
4918891	4922959	4926349	4921603	4928383
4931773	4922281	4923637	4924993	4915501
4931095	4925671	4920925	4924315	4916179
4916857	4917535	4929061	4927027	4927705

L19-M12

5072119	5082289	5070763	5072797	5082967
5071441	5075509	5078899	5074153	5080933
5084323	5074831	5076187	5077543	5068051
5083645	5078221	5073475	5076865	5068729
5069407	5070085	5081611	5079577	5080255

L19-M4

4936519	4946689	4935163	4937197	4947367
4935841	4939909	4943299	4938553	4945333
4948723	4939231	4940587	4941943	4932451
4948045	4942621	4937875	4941265	4933129
4933807	4934485	4946011	4943977	4944655

L19-M13

5089069	5099239	5087713	5089747	5099917
5088391	5092459	5095849	5091103	5097883
5101273	5091781	5093137	5094493	5085001
5100595	5095171	5090425	5093815	5085679
5086357	5087035	5098561	5096527	5097205

L19-M5

4953469	4963639	4952113	4954147	4964317
4952791	4956859	4960249	4955503	4962283
4965673	4956181	4957537	4958893	4949401
4964995	4959571	4954825	4958215	4950079
4950757	4951435	4962961	4960927	4961605

L19-M14

5106019	5116189	5104663	5106697	5116867
5105341	5109409	5112799	5108053	5114833
5118223	5108731	5110087	5111443	5101951
5117545	5112121	5107375	5110765	5102629
5103307	5103985	5115511	5113477	5114155

L19-M6

4970419	4980589	4969063	4971097	4981267
4969741	4973809	4977199	4972453	4979233
4982623	4973131	4974487	4975843	4966351
4981945	4976521	4971775	4975165	4967029
4967707	4968385	4979911	4977877	4978555

L19-M15

5122969	5133139	5121613	5123647	5133817
5122291	5126359	5129749	5125003	5131783
5135173	5125681	5127037	5128393	5118901
5134495	5129071	5124325	5127715	5119579
5120257	5120935	5132461	5130427	5131105

L19-M7

4987369	4997539	4986013	4988047	4998217
4986691	4990759	4994149	4989403	4996183
4999573	4990081	4991437	4992793	4983301
4998895	4993471	4988725	4992115	4983979
4984657	4985335	4996861	4994827	4995505

L19-M16

5139919	5150089	5138563	5140597	5150767
5139241	5143309	5146699	5141953	5148733
5152123	5142631	5143987	5145343	5135851
5151445	5146021	5141275	5144665	5136529
5137207	5137885	5149411	5147377	5148055

L19-M8

5004319	5014489	5002963	5004997	5015167
5003641	5007709	5011099	5006353	5013133
5016523	5007031	5008387	5009743	5000251
5015845	5010421	5005675	5009065	5000929
5001607	5002285	5013811	5011777	5012455

L20-M1

5156869	5167039	5155513	5157547	5167717
5156191	5160259	5163649	5158903	5165683
5169073	5159581	5160937	5162293	5152801
5168395	5162971	5158225	5161615	5153479
5154157	5154835	5166361	5164327	5165005

L19-M9

5021269	5031439	5019913	5021947	5032117
5020591	5024659	5028049	5023303	5030083
5033473	5023981	5025337	5026693	5017201
5032795	5027371	5022625	5026015	5017879
5018557	5019235	5030761	5028727	5029405

L20-M2

5173819	5183989	5172463	5174497	5184667
5173141	5177209	5180599	5175853	5182633
5186023	5176531	5177887	5179243	5169751
5185345	5179921	5175175	5178565	5170429
5171107	5171785	5183311	5181277	5181955

L20-M3

5190769	5200939	5189413	5191447	5201617
5190091	5194159	5197549	5192803	5199583
5202973	5193481	5194837	5196193	5186701
5202295	5196871	5192125	5195515	5187379
5188057	5188735	5200261	5198227	5198905

L20-M4

5207719	5217889	5206363	5208397	5218567
5207041	5211109	5214499	5209753	5216533
5219923	5210431	5211787	5213143	5203651
5219245	5213821	5209075	5212465	5204329
5205007	5205685	5217211	5215177	5215855

L20-M5

5224669	5234839	5223313	5225347	5235517
5223991	5228059	5231449	5226703	5233483
5236873	5227381	5228737	5230093	5220601
5236195	5230771	5226025	5229415	5221279
5221957	5222635	5234161	5232127	5232805

L20-M6

5241619	5251789	5240263	5242297	5252467
5240941	5245009	5248399	5243653	5250433
5253823	5244331	5245687	5247043	5237551
5253145	5247721	5242975	5246365	5238229
5238907	5239585	5251111	5249077	5249755

L20-M7

5258569	5268739	5257213	5259247	5269417
5257891	5261959	5265349	5260603	5267383
5270773	5261281	5262637	5263993	5254501
5270095	5264671	5259925	5263315	5255179
5255857	5256535	5268061	5266027	5266705

L20-M8

5275519	5285689	5274163	5276197	5286367
5274841	5278909	5282299	5277553	5284333
5287723	5278231	5279587	5280943	5271451
5287045	5281621	5276875	5280265	5272129
5272807	5273485	5285011	5282977	5283655

L20-M9

5292469	5302639	5291113	5293147	5303317
5291791	5295859	5299249	5294503	5301283
5304673	5295181	5296537	5297893	5288401
5303995	5298571	5293825	5297215	5289079
5289757	5290435	5301961	5299927	5300605

L20-M10

5309419	5319589	5308063	5310097	5320267
5308741	5312809	5316199	5311453	5318233
5321623	5312131	5313487	5314843	5305351
5320945	5315521	5310775	5314165	5306029
5306707	5307385	5318911	5316877	5317555

L20-M11

5326369	5336539	5325013	5327047	5337217
5325691	5329759	5333149	5328403	5335183
5338573	5329081	5330437	5331793	5322301
5337895	5332471	5327725	5331115	5322979
5323657	5324335	5335861	5333827	5334505

L20-M12

5343319	5353489	5341963	5343997	5354167
5342641	5346709	5350099	5345353	5352133
5355523	5346031	5347387	5348743	5339251
5354845	5349421	5344675	5348065	5339929
5340607	5341285	5352811	5350777	5351455

L20-M13

5360269	5370439	5358913	5360947	5371117
5359591	5363659	5367049	5362303	5369083
5372473	5362981	5364337	5365693	5356201
5371795	5366371	5361625	5365015	5356879
5357557	5358235	5369761	5367727	5368405

L20-M14

5377219	5387389	5375863	5377897	5388067
5376541	5380609	5383999	5379253	5386033
5389423	5379931	5381287	5382643	5373151
5388745	5383321	5378575	5381965	5373829
5374507	5375185	5386711	5384677	5385355

L20-M15

5394169	5404339	5392813	5394847	5405017
5393491	5397559	5400949	5396203	5402983
5406373	5396881	5398237	5399593	5390101
5405695	5400271	5395525	5398915	5390779
5391457	5392135	5403661	5401627	5402305

L20-M16

5411119	5421289	5409763	5411797	5421967
5410441	5414509	5417899	5413153	5419933
5423323	5413831	5415187	5416543	5407051
5422645	5417221	5412475	5415865	5407729
5408407	5409085	5420611	5418577	5419255

L21-M1

5428069	5438239	5426713	5428747	5438917
5427391	5431459	5434849	5430103	5436883
5440273	5430781	5432137	5433493	5424001
5439595	5434171	5429425	5432815	5424679
5425357	5426035	5437561	5435527	5436205

L21-M2

5445019	5455189	5443663	5445697	5455867
5444341	5448409	5451799	5447053	5453833
5457223	5447731	5449087	5450443	5440951
5456545	5451121	5446375	5449765	5441629
5442307	5442985	5454511	5452477	5453155

L21-M3

5461969	5472139	5460613	5462647	5472817
5461291	5465359	5468749	5464003	5470783
5474173	5464681	5466037	5467393	5457901
5473495	5468071	5463325	5466715	5458579
5459257	5459935	5471461	5469427	5470105

L21-M4

5478919	5489089	5477563	5479597	5489767
5478241	5482309	5485699	5480953	5487733
5491123	5481631	5482987	5484343	5474851
5490445	5485021	5480275	5483665	5475529
5476207	5476885	5488411	5486377	5487055

L21-M5

5495869	5506039	5494513	5496547	5506717
5495191	5499259	5502649	5497903	5504683
5508073	5498581	5499937	5501293	5491801
5507395	5501971	5497225	5500615	5492479
5493157	5493835	5505361	5503327	5504005

L21-M6

5512819	5522989	5511463	5513497	5523667
5512141	5516209	5519599	5514853	5521633
5525023	5515531	5516887	5518243	5508751
5524345	5518921	5514175	5517565	5509429
5510107	5510785	5522311	5520277	5520955

L21-M7

5529769	5539939	5528413	5530447	5540617
5529091	5533159	5536549	5531803	5538583
5541973	5532481	5533837	5535193	5525701
5541295	5535871	5531125	5534515	5526379
5527057	5527735	5539261	5537227	5537905

L21-M8

5546719	5556889	5545363	5547397	5557567
5546041	5550109	5553499	5548753	5555533
5558923	5549431	5550787	5552143	5542651
5558245	5552821	5548075	5551465	5543329
5544007	5544685	5556211	5554177	5554855

L21-M9

5563669	5573839	5562313	5564347	5574517
5562991	5567059	5570449	5565703	5572483
5575873	5566381	5567737	5569093	5559601
5575195	5569771	5565025	5568415	5560279
5560957	5561635	5573161	5571127	5571805

L21-M10

5580619	5590789	5579263	5581297	5591467
5579941	5584009	5587399	5582653	5589433
5592823	5583331	5584687	5586043	5576551
5592145	5586721	5581975	5585365	5577229
5577907	5578585	5590111	5588077	5588755

L21-M11

5597569	5607739	5596213	5598247	5608417
5596891	5600959	5604349	5599603	5606383
5609773	5600281	5601637	5602993	5593501
5609095	5603671	5598925	5602315	5594179
5594857	5595535	5607061	5605027	5605705

L21-M12

5614519	5624689	5613163	5615197	5625367
5613841	5617909	5621299	5616553	5623333
5626723	5617231	5618587	5619943	5610451
5626045	5620621	5615875	5619265	5611129
5611807	5612485	5624011	5621977	5622655

L21-M13

5631469	5641639	5630113	5632147	5642317
5630791	5634859	5638249	5633503	5640283
5643673	5634181	5635537	5636893	5627401
5642995	5637571	5632825	5636215	5628079
5628757	5629435	5640961	5638927	5639605

L21-M14

5648419	5658589	5647063	5649097	5659267
5647741	5651809	5655199	5650453	5657233
5660623	5651131	5652487	5653843	5644351
5659945	5654521	5649775	5653165	5645029
5645707	5646385	5657911	5655877	5656555

L21-M15

5665369	5675539	5664013	5666047	5676217
5664691	5668759	5672149	5667403	5674183
5677573	5668081	5669437	5670793	5661301
5676895	5671471	5666725	5670115	5661979
5662657	5663335	5674861	5672827	5673505

L21-M16

5682319	5692489	5680963	5682997	5693167
5681641	5685709	5689099	5684353	5691133
5694523	5685031	5686387	5687743	5678251
5693845	5688421	5683675	5687065	5678929
5679607	5680285	5691811	5689777	5690455

L22-M1

5699269	5709439	5697913	5699947	5710117
5698591	5702659	5706049	5701303	5708083
5711473	5701981	5703337	5704693	5695201
5710795	5705371	5700625	5704015	5695879
5696557	5697235	5708761	5706727	5707405

L22-M2

5716219	5726389	5714863	5716897	5727067
5715541	5719609	5722999	5718253	5725033
5728423	5718931	5720287	5721643	5712151
5727745	5722321	5717575	5720965	5712829
5713507	5714185	5725711	5723677	5724355

L22-M3

5733169	5743339	5731813	5733847	5744017
5732491	5736559	5739949	5735203	5741983
5745373	5735881	5737237	5738593	5729101
5744695	5739271	5734525	5737915	5729779
5730457	5731135	5742661	5740627	5741305

L22-M4

5750119	5760289	5748763	5750797	5760967
5749441	5753509	5756899	5752153	5758933
5762323	5752831	5754187	5755543	5746051
5761645	5756221	5751475	5754865	5746729
5747407	5748085	5759611	5757577	5758255

L22-M5

5767069	5777239	5765713	5767747	5777917
5766391	5770459	5773849	5769103	5775883
5779273	5769781	5771137	5772493	5763001
5778595	5773171	5768425	5771815	5763679
5764357	5765035	5776561	5774527	5775205

L22-M6

5784019	5794189	5782663	5784697	5794867
5783341	5787409	5790799	5786053	5792833
5796223	5786731	5788087	5789443	5779951
5795545	5790121	5785375	5788765	5780629
5781307	5781985	5793511	5791477	5792155

L22-M7

5800969	5811139	5799613	5801647	5811817
5800291	5804359	5807749	5803003	5809783
5813173	5803681	5805037	5806393	5796901
5812495	5807071	5802325	5805715	5797579
5798257	5798935	5810461	5808427	5809105

L22-M16

5953519	5963689	5952163	5954197	5964367
5952841	5956909	5960299	5955553	5962333
5965723	5956231	5957587	5958943	5949451
5965045	5959621	5954875	5958265	5950129
5950807	5951485	5963011	5960977	5961655

L22-M8

5817919	5828089	5816563	5818597	5828767
5817241	5821309	5824699	5819953	5826733
5830123	5820631	5821987	5823343	5813851
5829445	5824021	5819275	5822665	5814529
5815207	5815885	5827411	5825377	5826055

L23-M1

5970469	5980639	5969113	5971147	5981317
5969791	5973859	5977249	5972503	5979283
5982673	5973181	5974537	5975893	5966401
5981995	5976571	5971825	5975215	5967079
5967757	5968435	5979961	5977927	5978605

L22-M9

5834869	5845039	5833513	5835547	5845717
5834191	5838259	5841649	5836903	5843683
5847073	5837581	5838937	5840293	5830801
5846395	5840971	5836225	5839615	5831479
5832157	5832835	5844361	5842327	5843005

L23-M2

5987419	5997589	5986063	5988097	5998267
5986741	5990809	5994199	5989453	5996233
5999623	5990131	5991487	5992843	5983351
5998945	5993521	5988775	5992165	5984029
5984707	5985385	5996911	5994877	5995555

L22-M10

5851819	5861989	5850463	5852497	5862667
5851141	5855209	5858599	5853853	5860633
5864023	5854531	5855887	5857243	5847751
5863345	5857921	5853175	5856565	5848429
5849107	5849785	5861311	5859277	5859955

L23-M3

6004369	6014539	6003013	6005047	6015217
6003691	6007759	6011149	6006403	6013183
6016573	6007081	6008437	6009793	6000301
6015895	6010471	6005725	6009115	6000979
6001657	6002335	6013861	6011827	6012505

L22-M11

5868769	5878939	5867413	5869447	5879617
5868091	5872159	5875549	5870803	5877583
5880973	5871481	5872837	5874193	5864701
5880295	5874871	5870125	5873515	5865379
5866057	5866735	5878261	5876227	5876905

L23-M4

6021319	6031489	6019963	6021997	6032167
6020641	6024709	6028099	6023353	6030133
6033523	6024031	6025387	6026743	6017251
6032845	6027421	6022675	6026065	6017929
6018607	6019285	6030811	6028777	6029455

L22-M12

5885719	5895889	5884363	5886397	5896567
5885041	5889109	5892499	5887753	5894533
5897923	5888431	5889787	5891143	5881651
5897245	5891821	5887075	5890465	5882329
5883007	5883685	5895211	5893177	5893855

L23-M5

6038269	6048439	6036913	6038947	6049117
6037591	6041659	6045049	6040303	6047083
6050473	6040981	6042337	6043693	6034201
6049795	6044371	6039625	6043015	6034879
6035557	6036235	6047761	6045727	6046405

L22-M13

5902669	5912839	5901313	5903347	5913517
5901991	5906059	5909449	5904703	5911483
5914873	5905381	5906737	5908093	5898601
5914195	5908771	5904025	5907415	5899279
5899957	5900635	5912161	5910127	5910805

L23-M6

6055219	6065389	6053863	6055897	6066067
6054541	6058609	6061999	6057253	6064033
6067423	6057931	6059287	6060643	6051151
6066745	6061321	6056575	6059965	6051829
6052507	6053185	6064711	6062677	6063355

L22-M14

5919619	5929789	5918263	5920297	5930467
5918941	5923009	5926399	5921653	5928433
5931823	5922331	5923687	5925043	5915551
5931145	5925721	5920975	5924365	5916229
5916907	5917585	5929111	5927077	5927755

L23-M7

6072169	6082339	6070813	6072847	6083017
6071491	6075559	6078949	6074203	6080983
6084373	6074881	6076237	6077593	6068101
6083695	6078271	6073525	6076915	6068779
6069457	6070135	6081661	6079627	6080305

L22-M15

5936569	5946739	5935213	5937247	5947417
5935891	5939959	5943349	5938603	5945383
5948773	5939281	5940637	5941993	5932501
5948095	5942671	5937925	5941315	5933179
5933857	5934535	5946061	5944027	5944705

L23-M8

6089119	6099289	6087763	6089797	6099967
6088441	6092509	6095899	6091153	6097933
6101323	6091831	6093187	6094543	6085051
6100645	6095221	6090475	6093865	6085729
6086407	6087085	6098611	6096577	6097255

L23-M9

6106069	6116239	6104713	6106747	6116917
6105391	6109459	6112849	6108103	6114883
6118273	6108781	6110137	6111493	6102001
6117595	6112171	6107425	6110815	6102679
6103357	6104035	6115561	6113527	6114205

L24-M2

6258619	6268789	6257263	6259297	6269467
6257941	6262009	6265399	6260653	6267433
6270823	6261331	6262687	6264043	6254551
6270145	6264721	6259975	6263365	6255229
6255907	6256585	6268111	6266077	6266755

L23-M10

6123019	6133189	6121663	6123697	6133867
6122341	6126409	6129799	6125053	6131833
6135223	6125731	6127087	6128443	6118951
6134545	6129121	6124375	6127765	6119629
6120307	6120985	6132511	6130477	6131155

L24-M3

6275569	6285739	6274213	6276247	6286417
6274891	6278959	6282349	6277603	6284383
6287773	6278281	6279637	6280993	6271501
6287095	6281671	6276925	6280315	6272179
6272857	6273535	6285061	6283027	6283705

L23-M11

6139969	6150139	6138613	6140647	6150817
6139291	6143359	6146749	6142003	6148783
6152173	6142681	6144037	6145393	6135901
6151495	6146071	6141325	6144715	6136579
6137257	6137935	6149461	6147427	6148105

L24-M4

6292519	6302689	6291163	6293197	6303367
6291841	6295909	6299299	6294553	6301333
6304723	6295231	6296587	6297943	6288451
6304045	6298621	6293875	6297265	6289129
6289807	6290485	6302011	6299977	6300655

L23-M12

6156919	6167089	6155563	6157597	6167767
6156241	6160309	6163699	6158953	6165733
6169123	6159631	6160987	6162343	6152851
6168445	6163021	6158275	6161665	6153529
6154207	6154885	6166411	6164377	6165055

L24-M5

6309469	6319639	6308113	6310147	6320317
6308791	6312859	6316249	6311503	6318283
6321673	6312181	6313537	6314893	6305401
6320995	6315571	6310825	6314215	6306079
6306757	6307435	6318961	6316927	6317605

L23-M13

6173869	6184039	6172513	6174547	6184717
6173191	6177259	6180649	6175903	6182683
6186073	6176581	6177937	6179293	6169801
6185395	6179971	6175225	6178615	6170479
6171157	6171835	6183361	6181327	6182005

L24-M6

6326419	6336589	6325063	6327097	6337267
6325741	6329809	6333199	6328453	6335233
6338623	6329131	6330487	6331843	6322351
6337945	6332521	6327775	6331165	6323029
6323707	6324385	6335911	6333877	6334555

L23-M14

6190819	6200989	6189463	6191497	6201667
6190141	6194209	6197599	6192853	6199633
6203023	6193531	6194887	6196243	6186751
6202345	6196921	6192175	6195565	6187429
6188107	6188785	6200311	6198277	6198955

L24-M7

6343369	6353539	6342013	6344047	6354217
6342691	6346759	6350149	6345403	6352183
6355573	6346081	6347437	6348793	6339301
6354895	6349471	6344725	6348115	6339979
6340657	6341335	6352861	6350827	6351505

L23-M15

6207769	6217939	6206413	6208447	6218617
6207091	6211159	6214549	6209803	6216583
6219973	6210481	6211837	6213193	6203701
6219295	6213871	6209125	6212515	6204379
6205057	6205735	6217261	6215227	6215905

L24-M8

6360319	6370489	6358963	6360997	6371167
6359641	6363709	6367099	6362353	6369133
6372523	6363031	6364387	6365743	6356251
6371845	6366421	6361675	6365065	6356929
6357607	6358285	6369811	6367777	6368455

L23-M16

6224719	6234889	6223363	6225397	6235567
6224041	6228109	6231499	6226753	6233533
6236923	6227431	6228787	6230143	6220651
6236245	6230821	6226075	6229465	6221329
6222007	6222685	6234211	6232177	6232855

L24-M9

6377269	6387439	6375913	6377947	6388117
6376591	6380659	6384049	6379303	6386083
6389473	6379981	6381337	6382693	6373201
6388795	6383371	6378625	6382015	6373879
6374557	6375235	6386761	6384727	6385405

L24-M1

6241669	6251839	6240313	6242347	6252517
6240991	6245059	6248449	6243703	6250483
6253873	6244381	6245737	6247093	6237601
6253195	6247771	6243025	6246415	6238279
6238957	6239635	6251161	6249127	6249805

L24-M10

6394219	6404389	6392863	6394897	6405067
6393541	6397609	6400999	6396253	6403033
6406423	6396931	6398287	6399643	6390151
6405745	6400321	6395575	6398965	6390829
6391507	6392185	6403711	6401677	6402355

L24-M11

6411169	6421339	6409813	6411847	6422017
6410491	6414559	6417949	6413203	6419983
6423373	6413881	6415237	6416593	6407101
6422695	6417271	6412525	6415915	6407779
6408457	6409135	6420661	6418627	6419305

L24-M12

6428119	6438289	6426763	6428797	6438967
6427441	6431509	6434899	6430153	6436933
6440323	6430831	6432187	6433543	6424051
6439645	6434221	6429475	6432865	6424729
6425407	6426085	6437611	6435577	6436255

L24-M13

6445069	6455239	6443713	6445747	6455917
6444391	6448459	6451849	6447103	6453883
6457273	6447781	6449137	6450493	6441001
6456595	6451171	6446425	6449815	6441679
6442357	6443035	6454561	6452527	6453205

L24-M14

6462019	6472189	6460663	6462697	6472867
6461341	6465409	6468799	6464053	6470833
6474223	6464731	6466087	6467443	6457951
6473545	6468121	6463375	6466765	6458629
6459307	6459985	6471511	6469477	6470155

L24-M15

6478969	6489139	6477613	6479647	6489817
6478291	6482359	6485749	6481003	6487783
6491173	6481681	6483037	6484393	6474901
6490495	6485071	6480325	6483715	6475579
6476257	6476935	6488461	6486427	6487105

L24-M16

6495919	6506089	6494563	6496597	6506767
6495241	6499309	6502699	6497953	6504733
6508123	6498631	6499987	6501343	6491851
6507445	6502021	6497275	6500665	6492529
6493207	6493885	6505411	6503377	6504055

L25-M1

6512869	6523039	6511513	6513547	6523717
6512191	6516259	6519649	6514903	6521683
6525073	6515581	6516937	6518293	6508801
6524395	6518971	6514225	6517615	6509479
6510157	6510835	6522361	6520327	6521005

L25-M2

6529819	6539989	6528463	6530497	6540667
6529141	6533209	6536599	6531853	6538633
6542023	6532531	6533887	6535243	6525751
6541345	6535921	6531175	6534565	6526429
6527107	6527785	6539311	6537277	6537955

L25-M3

6546769	6556939	6545413	6547447	6557617
6546091	6550159	6553549	6548803	6555583
6558973	6549481	6550837	6552193	6542701
6558295	6552871	6548125	6551515	6543379
6544057	6544735	6556261	6554227	6554905

L25-M4

6563719	6573889	6562363	6564397	6574567
6563041	6567109	6570499	6565753	6572533
6575923	6566431	6567787	6569143	6559651
6575245	6569821	6565075	6568465	6560329
6561007	6561685	6573211	6571177	6571855

L25-M5

6580669	6590839	6579313	6581347	6591517
6579991	6584059	6587449	6582703	6589483
6592873	6583381	6584737	6586093	6576601
6592195	6586771	6582025	6585415	6577279
6577957	6578635	6590161	6588127	6588805

L25-M6

6597619	6607789	6596263	6598297	6608467
6596941	6601009	6604399	6599653	6606433
6609823	6600331	6601687	6603043	6593551
6609145	6603721	6598975	6602365	6594229
6594907	6595585	6607111	6605077	6605755

L25-M7

6614569	6624739	6613213	6615247	6625417
6613891	6617959	6621349	6616603	6623383
6626773	6617281	6618637	6619993	6610501
6626095	6620671	6615925	6619315	6611179
6611857	6612535	6624061	6622027	6622705

L25-M8

6631519	6641689	6630163	6632197	6642367
6630841	6634909	6638299	6633553	6640333
6643723	6634231	6635587	6636943	6627451
6643045	6637621	6632875	6636265	6628129
6628807	6629485	6641011	6638977	6639655

L25-M9

6648469	6658639	6647113	6649147	6659317
6647791	6651859	6655249	6650503	6657283
6660673	6651181	6652537	6653893	6644401
6659995	6654571	6649825	6653215	6645079
6645757	6646435	6657961	6655927	6656605

L25-M10

6665419	6675589	6664063	6666097	6676267
6664741	6668809	6672199	6667453	6674233
6677623	6668131	6669487	6670843	6661351
6676945	6671521	6666775	6670165	6662029
6662707	6663385	6674911	6672877	6673555

L25-M11

6682369	6692539	6681013	6683047	6693217
6681691	6685759	6689149	6684403	6691183
6694573	6685081	6686437	6687793	6678301
6693895	6688471	6683725	6687115	6678979
6679657	6680335	6691861	6689827	6690505

L25-M12

6699319	6709489	6697963	6699997	6710167
6698641	6702709	6706099	6701353	6708133
6711523	6702031	6703387	6704743	6695251
6710845	6705421	6700675	6704065	6695929
6696607	6697285	6708811	6706777	6707455

L25-M13

6716269	6726439	6714913	6716947	6727117
6715591	6719659	6723049	6718303	6725083
6728473	6718981	6720337	6721693	6712201
6727795	6722371	6717625	6721015	6712879
6713557	6714235	6725761	6723727	6724405

L25-M14

6733219	6743389	6731863	6733897	6744067
6732541	6736609	6739999	6735253	6742033
6745423	6735931	6737287	6738643	6729151
6744745	6739321	6734575	6737965	6729829
6730507	6731185	6742711	6740677	6741355

L25-M15

6750169	6760339	6748813	6750847	6761017
6749491	6753559	6756949	6752203	6758983
6762373	6752881	6754237	6755593	6746101
6761695	6756271	6751525	6754915	6746779
6747457	6748135	6759661	6757627	6758305

L25-M16

6767119	6777289	6765763	6767797	6777967
6766441	6770509	6773899	6769153	6775933
6779323	6769831	6771187	6772543	6763051
6778645	6773221	6768475	6771865	6763729
6764407	6765085	6776611	6774577	6775255

HOD

L1-M1

3631	12706	2421	4236	13311
3026	6656	9681	5446	11496
14521	6051	7261	8471	1
13916	9076	4841	7866	606
1211	1816	12101	10286	10891

L1-M2

18756	27831	17546	19361	28436
18151	21781	24806	20571	26621
29646	21176	22386	23596	15126
29041	24201	19966	22991	15731
16336	16941	27226	25411	26016

L1-M3

33881	42956	32671	34486	43561
33276	36906	39931	35696	41746
44771	36301	37511	38721	30251
44166	39326	35091	38116	30856
31461	32066	42351	40536	41141

L1-M4

49006	58081	47796	49611	58686
48401	52031	55056	50821	56871
59896	51426	52636	53846	45376
59291	54451	50216	53241	45981
46586	47191	57476	55661	56266

L1-M5

64131	73206	62921	64736	73811
63526	67156	70181	65946	71996
75021	66551	67761	68971	60501
74416	69576	65341	68366	61106
61711	62316	72601	70786	71391

L1-M6

79256	88331	78046	79861	88936
78651	82281	85306	81071	87121
90146	81676	82886	84096	75626
89541	84701	80466	83491	76231
76836	77441	87726	85911	86516

L1-M7

94381	103456	93171	94986	104061
93776	97406	100431	96196	102246
105271	96801	98011	99221	90751
104666	99826	95591	98616	91356
91961	92566	102851	101036	101641

L1-M8

109506	118581	108296	110111	119186
108901	112531	115556	111321	117371
120396	111926	113136	114346	105876
119791	114951	110716	113741	106481
107086	107691	117976	116161	116766

L1-M9

124631	133706	123421	125236	134311
124026	127656	130681	126446	132496
135521	127051	128261	129471	121001
134916	130076	125841	128866	121606
122211	122816	133101	131286	131891

L1-M10

139756	148831	138546	140361	149436
139151	142781	145806	141571	147621
150646	142176	143386	144596	136126
150041	145201	140966	143991	136731
137336	137941	148226	146411	147016

L1-M11

154881	163956	153671	155486	164561
154276	157906	160931	156696	162746
165771	157301	158511	159721	151251
165166	160326	156091	159116	151856
152461	153066	163351	161536	162141

L1-M12

170006	179081	168796	170611	179686
169401	173031	176056	171821	177871
180896	172426	173636	174846	166376
180291	175451	171216	174241	166981
167586	168191	178476	176661	177266

L1-M13

185131	194206	183921	185736	194811
184526	188156	191181	186946	192996
196021	187551	188761	189971	181501
195416	190576	186341	189366	182106
182711	183316	193601	191786	192391

L1-M14

200256	209331	199046	200861	209936
199651	203281	206306	202071	208121
211146	202676	203886	205096	196626
210541	205701	201466	204491	197231
197836	198441	208726	206911	207516

L1-M15

215381	224456	214171	215986	225061
214776	218406	221431	217196	223246
226271	217801	219011	220221	211751
225666	220826	216591	219616	212356
212961	213566	223851	222036	222641

L1-M16

230506	239581	229296	231111	240186
229901	233531	236556	232321	238371
241396	232926	234136	235346	226876
240791	235951	231716	234741	227481
228086	228691	238976	237161	237766

L2-M1

245631	254706	244421	246236	255311
245026	248656	251681	247446	253496
256521	248051	249261	250471	242001
255916	251076	246841	249866	242606
243211	243816	254101	252286	252891

L2-M2

260756	269831	259546	261361	270436
260151	263781	266806	262571	268621
271646	263176	264386	265596	257126
271041	266201	261966	264991	257731
258336	258941	269226	267411	268016

L2-M3

275881	284956	274671	276486	285561
275276	278906	281931	277696	283746
286771	278301	279511	280721	272251
286166	281326	277091	280116	272856
273461	274066	284351	282536	283141

L2-M4

291006	300081	289796	291611	300686
290401	294031	297056	292821	298871
301896	293426	294636	295846	287376
301291	296451	292216	295241	287981
288586	289191	299476	297661	298266

L2-M5

306131	315206	304921	306736	315811
305526	309156	312181	307946	313996
317021	308551	309761	310971	302501
316416	311576	307341	310366	303106
303711	304316	314601	312786	313391

L2-M6

321256	330331	320046	321861	330936
320651	324281	327306	323071	329121
332146	323676	324886	326096	317626
331541	326701	322466	325491	318231
318836	319441	329726	327911	328516

L2-M7

336381	345456	335171	336986	346061
335776	339406	342431	338196	344246
347271	338801	340011	341221	332751
346666	341826	337591	340616	333356
333961	334566	344851	343036	343641

L2-M8

351506	360581	350296	352111	361186
350901	354531	357556	353321	359371
362396	353926	355136	356346	347876
361791	356951	352716	355741	348481
349086	349691	359976	358161	358766

L2-M9

366631	375706	365421	367236	376311
366026	369656	372681	368446	374496
377521	369051	370261	371471	363001
376916	372076	367841	370866	363606
364211	364816	375101	373286	373891

L2-M10

381756	390831	380546	382361	391436
381151	384781	387806	383571	389621
392646	384176	385386	386596	378126
392041	387201	382966	385991	378731
379336	379941	390226	388411	389016

L2-M11

396881	405956	395671	397486	406561
396276	399906	402931	398696	404746
407771	399301	400511	401721	393251
407166	402326	398091	401116	393856
394461	395066	405351	403536	404141

L2-M12

412006	421081	410796	412611	421686
411401	415031	418056	413821	419871
422896	414426	415636	416846	408376
422291	417451	413216	416241	408981
409586	410191	420476	418661	419266

L2-M13

427131	436206	425921	427736	436811
426526	430156	433181	428946	434996
438021	429551	430761	431971	423501
437416	432576	428341	431366	424106
424711	425316	435601	433786	434391

L2-M14

442256	451331	441046	442861	451936
441651	445281	448306	444071	450121
453146	444676	445886	447096	438626
452541	447701	443466	446491	439231
439836	440441	450726	448911	449516

L2-M15

457381	466456	456171	457986	467061
456776	460406	463431	459196	465246
468271	459801	461011	462221	453751
467666	462826	458591	461616	454356
454961	455566	465851	464036	464641

L2-M16

472506	481581	471296	473111	482186
471901	475531	478556	474321	480371
483396	474926	476136	477346	468876
482791	477951	473716	476741	469481
470086	470691	480976	479161	479766

L3-M1

487631	496706	486421	488236	497311
487026	490656	493681	489446	495496
498521	490051	491261	492471	484001
497916	493076	488841	491866	484606
485211	485816	496101	494286	494891

L3-M2

502756	511831	501546	503361	512436
502151	505781	508806	504571	510621
513646	505176	506386	507596	499126
513041	508201	503966	506991	499731
500336	500941	511226	509411	510016

L3-M3

517881	526956	516671	518486	527561
517276	520906	523931	519696	525746
528771	520301	521511	522721	514251
528166	523326	519091	522116	514856
515461	516066	526351	524536	525141

L3-M4

533006	542081	531796	533611	542686
532401	536031	539056	534821	540871
543896	535426	536636	537846	529376
543291	538451	534216	537241	529981
530586	531191	541476	539661	540266

L3-M5

548131	557206	546921	548736	557811
547526	551156	554181	549946	555996
559021	550551	551761	552971	544501
558416	553576	549341	552366	545106
545711	546316	556601	554786	555391

L3-M6

563256	572331	562046	563861	572936
562651	566281	569306	565071	571121
574146	565676	566886	568096	559626
573541	568701	564466	567491	560231
560836	561441	571726	569911	570516

L3-M7

578381	587456	577171	578986	588061
577776	581406	584431	580196	586246
589271	580801	582011	583221	574751
588666	583826	579591	582616	575356
575961	576566	586851	585036	585641

L3-M8

593506	602581	592296	594111	603186
592901	596531	599556	595321	601371
604396	595926	597136	598346	589876
603791	598951	594716	597741	590481
591086	591691	601976	600161	600766

L3-M9

608631	617706	607421	609236	618311
608026	611656	614681	610446	616496
619521	611051	612261	613471	605001
618916	614076	609841	612866	605606
606211	606816	617101	615286	615891

L3-M10

623756	632831	622546	624361	633436
623151	626781	629806	625571	631621
634646	626176	627386	628596	620126
634041	629201	624966	627991	620731
621336	621941	632226	630411	631016

L3-M11

638881	647956	637671	639486	648561
638276	641906	644931	640696	646746
649771	641301	642511	643721	635251
649166	644326	640091	643116	635856
636461	637066	647351	645536	646141

L3-M12

654006	663081	652796	654611	663686
653401	657031	660056	655821	661871
664896	656426	657636	658846	650376
664291	659451	655216	658241	650981
651586	652191	662476	660661	661266

L3-M13

669131	678206	667921	669736	678811
668526	672156	675181	670946	676996
680021	671551	672761	673971	665501
679416	674576	670341	673366	666106
666711	667316	677601	675786	676391

L3-M14

684256	693331	683046	684861	693936
683651	687281	690306	686071	692121
695146	686676	687886	689096	680626
694541	689701	685466	688491	681231
681836	682441	692726	690911	691516

L3-M15

699381	708456	698171	699986	709061
698776	702406	705431	701196	707246
710271	701801	703011	704221	695751
709666	704826	700591	703616	696356
696961	697566	707851	706036	706641

L3-M16

714506	723581	713296	715111	724186
713901	717531	720556	716321	722371
725396	716926	718136	719346	710876
724791	719951	715716	718741	711481
712086	712691	722976	721161	721766

L4-M1

729631	738706	728421	730236	739311
729026	732656	735681	731446	737496
740521	732051	733261	734471	726001
739916	735076	730841	733866	726606
727211	727816	738101	736286	736891

L4-M2

744756	753831	743546	745361	754436
744151	747781	750806	746571	752621
755646	747176	748386	749596	741126
755041	750201	745966	748991	741731
742336	742941	753226	751411	752016

L4-M3

759881	768956	758671	760486	769561
759276	762906	765931	761696	767746
770771	762301	763511	764721	756251
770166	765326	761091	764116	756856
757461	758066	768351	766536	767141

L4-M4

775006	784081	773796	775611	784686
774401	778031	781056	776821	782871
785896	777426	778636	779846	771376
785291	780451	776216	779241	771981
772586	773191	783476	781661	782266

L4-M5

790131	799206	788921	790736	799811
789526	793156	796181	791946	797996
801021	792551	793761	794971	786501
800416	795576	791341	794366	787106
787711	788316	798601	796786	797391

L4-M6

805256	814331	804046	805861	814936
804651	808281	811306	807071	813121
816146	807676	808886	810096	801626
815541	810701	806466	809491	802231
802836	803441	813726	811911	812516

L4-M7

820381	829456	819171	820986	830061
819776	823406	826431	822196	828246
831271	822801	824011	825221	816751
830666	825826	821591	824616	817356
817961	818566	828851	827036	827641

L4-M16

956506	965581	955296	957111	966186
955901	959531	962556	958321	964371
967396	958926	960136	961346	952876
966791	961951	957716	960741	953481
954086	954691	964976	963161	963766

L4-M8

835506	844581	834296	836111	845186
834901	838531	841556	837321	843371
846396	837926	839136	840346	831876
845791	840951	836716	839741	832481
833086	833691	843976	842161	842766

L5-M1

971631	980706	970421	972236	981311
971026	974656	977681	973446	979496
982521	974051	975261	976471	968001
981916	977076	972841	975866	968606
969211	969816	980101	978286	978891

L4-M9

850631	859706	849421	851236	860311
850026	853656	856681	852446	858496
861521	853051	854261	855471	847001
860916	856076	851841	854866	847606
848211	848816	859101	857286	857891

L5-M2

986756	995831	985546	987361	996436
986151	989781	992806	988571	994621
997646	989176	990386	991596	983126
997041	992201	987966	990991	983731
984336	984941	995226	993411	994016

L4-M10

865756	874831	864546	866361	875436
865151	868781	871806	867571	873621
876646	868176	869386	870596	862126
876041	871201	866966	869991	862731
863336	863941	874226	872411	873016

L5-M3

1001881	1010956	1000671	1002486	1011561
1001276	1004906	1007931	1003696	1009746
1012771	1004301	1005511	1006721	998251
1012166	1007326	1003091	1006116	998856
999461	1000066	1010351	1008536	1009141

L4-M11

880881	889956	879671	881486	890561
880276	883906	886931	882696	888746
891771	883301	884511	885721	877251
891166	886326	882091	885116	877856
878461	879066	889351	887536	888141

L5-M4

1017006	1026081	1015796	1017611	1026686
1016401	1020031	1023056	1018821	1024871
1027896	1019426	1020636	1021846	1013376
1027291	1022451	1018216	1021241	1013981
1014586	1015191	1025476	1023661	1024266

L4-M12

896006	905081	894796	896611	905686
895401	899031	902056	897821	903871
906896	898426	899636	900846	892376
906291	901451	897216	900241	892981
893586	894191	904476	902661	903266

L5-M5

1032131	1041206	1030921	1032736	1041811
1031526	1035156	1038181	1033946	1039996
1043021	1034551	1035761	1036971	1028501
1042416	1037576	1033341	1036366	1029106
1029711	1030316	1040601	1038786	1039391

L4-M13

911131	920206	909921	911736	920811
910526	914156	917181	912946	918996
922021	913551	914761	915971	907501
921416	916576	912341	915366	908106
908711	909316	919601	917786	918391

L5-M6

1047256	1056331	1046046	1047861	1056936
1046651	1050281	1053306	1049071	1055121
1058146	1049676	1050886	1052096	1043626
1057541	1052701	1048466	1051491	1044231
1044836	1045441	1055726	1053911	1054516

L4-M14

926256	935331	925046	926861	935936
925651	929281	932306	928071	934121
937146	928676	929886	931096	922626
936541	931701	927466	930491	923231
923836	924441	934726	932911	933516

L5-M7

1062381	1071456	1061171	1062986	1072061
1061776	1065406	1068431	1064196	1070246
1073271	1064801	1066011	1067221	1058751
1072666	1067826	1063591	1066616	1059356
1059961	1060566	1070851	1069036	1069641

L4-M15

941381	950456	940171	941986	951061
940776	944406	947431	943196	949246
952271	943801	945011	946221	937751
951666	946826	942591	945616	938356
938961	939566	949851	948036	948641

L5-M8

1077506	1086581	1076296	1078111	1087186
1076901	1080531	1083556	1079321	1085371
1088396	1079926	1081136	1082346	1073876
1087791	1082951	1078716	1081741	1074481
1075086	1075691	1085976	1084161	1084766

L5-M9

1092631	1101706	1091421	1093236	1102311
1092026	1095656	1098681	1094446	1100496
1103521	1095051	1096261	1097471	1089001
1102916	1098076	1093841	1096866	1089606
1090211	1090816	1101101	1099286	1099891

L5-M10

1107756	1116831	1106546	1108361	1117436
1107151	1110781	1113806	1109571	1115621
1118646	1110176	1111386	1112596	1104126
1118041	1113201	1108966	1111991	1104731
1105336	1105941	1116226	1114411	1115016

L5-M11

1122881	1131956	1121671	1123486	1132561
1122276	1125906	1128931	1124696	1130746
1133771	1125301	1126511	1127721	1119251
1133166	1128326	1124091	1127116	1119856
1120461	1121066	1131351	1129536	1130141

L5-M12

1138006	1147081	1136796	1138611	1147686
1137401	1141031	1144056	1139821	1145871
1148896	1140426	1141636	1142846	1134376
1148291	1143451	1139216	1142241	1134981
1135586	1136191	1146476	1144661	1145266

L5-M13

1153131	1162206	1151921	1153736	1162811
1152526	1156156	1159181	1154946	1160996
1164021	1155551	1156761	1157971	1149501
1163416	1158576	1154341	1157366	1150106
1150711	1151316	1161601	1159786	1160391

L5-M14

1168256	1177331	1167046	1168861	1177936
1167651	1171281	1174306	1170071	1176121
1179146	1170676	1171886	1173096	1164626
1178541	1173701	1169466	1172491	1165231
1165836	1166441	1176726	1174911	1175516

L5-M15

1183381	1192456	1182171	1183986	1193061
1182776	1186406	1189431	1185196	1191246
1194271	1185801	1187011	1188221	1179751
1193666	1188826	1184591	1187616	1180356
1180961	1181566	1191851	1190036	1190641

L5-M16

1198506	1207581	1197296	1199111	1208186
1197901	1201531	1204556	1200321	1206371
1209396	1200926	1202136	1203346	1194876
1208791	1203951	1199716	1202741	1195481
1196086	1196691	1206976	1205161	1205766

L6-M1

1213631	1222706	1212421	1214236	1223311
1213026	1216656	1219681	1215446	1221496
1224521	1216051	1217261	1218471	1210001
1223916	1219076	1214841	1217866	1210606
1211211	1211816	1222101	1220286	1220891

L6-M2

1228756	1237831	1227546	1229361	1238436
1228151	1231781	1234806	1230571	1236621
1239646	1231176	1232386	1233596	1225126
1239041	1234201	1229966	1232991	1225731
1226336	1226941	1237226	1235411	1236016

L6-M3

1243881	1252956	1242671	1244486	1253561
1243276	1246906	1249931	1245696	1251746
1254771	1246301	1247511	1248721	1240251
1254166	1249326	1245091	1248116	1240856
1241461	1242066	1252351	1250536	1251141

L6-M4

1259006	1268081	1257796	1259611	1268686
1258401	1262031	1265056	1260821	1266871
1269896	1261426	1262636	1263846	1255376
1269291	1264451	1260216	1263241	1255981
1256586	1257191	1267476	1265661	1266266

L6-M5

1274131	1283206	1272921	1274736	1283811
1273526	1277156	1280181	1275946	1281996
1285021	1276551	1277761	1278971	1270501
1284416	1279576	1275341	1278366	1271106
1271711	1272316	1282601	1280786	1281391

L6-M6

1289256	1298331	1288046	1289861	1298936
1288651	1292281	1295306	1291071	1297121
1300146	1291676	1292886	1294096	1285626
1299541	1294701	1290466	1293491	1286231
1286836	1287441	1297726	1295911	1296516

L6-M7

1304381	1313456	1303171	1304986	1314061
1303776	1307406	1310431	1306196	1312246
1315271	1306801	1308011	1309221	1300751
1314666	1309826	1305591	1308616	1301356
1301961	1302566	1312851	1311036	1311641

L6-M8

1319506	1328581	1318296	1320111	1329186
1318901	1322531	1325556	1321321	1327371
1330396	1321926	1323136	1324346	1315876
1329791	1324951	1320716	1323741	1316481
1317086	1317691	1327976	1326161	1326766

L6-M9

1334631	1343706	1333421	1335236	1344311
1334026	1337656	1340681	1336446	1342496
1345521	1337051	1338261	1339471	1331001
1344916	1340076	1335841	1338866	1331606
1332211	1332816	1343101	1341286	1341891

L6-M10

1349756	1358831	1348546	1350361	1359436
1349151	1352781	1355806	1351571	1357621
1360646	1352176	1353386	1354596	1346126
1360041	1355201	1350966	1353991	1346731
1347336	1347941	1358226	1356411	1357016

L6-M11

1364881	1373956	1363671	1365486	1374561
1364276	1367906	1370931	1366696	1372746
1375771	1367301	1368511	1369721	1361251
1375166	1370326	1366091	1369116	1361856
1362461	1363066	1373351	1371536	1372141

L7-M4

1501006	1510081	1499796	1501611	1510686
1500401	1504031	1507056	1502821	1508871
1511896	1503426	1504636	1505846	1497376
1511291	1506451	1502216	1505241	1497981
1498586	1499191	1509476	1507661	1508266

L6-M12

1380006	1389081	1378796	1380611	1389686
1379401	1383031	1386056	1381821	1387871
1390896	1382426	1383636	1384846	1376376
1390291	1385451	1381216	1384241	1376981
1377586	1378191	1388476	1386661	1387266

L7-M5

1516131	1525206	1514921	1516736	1525811
1515526	1519156	1522181	1517946	1523996
1527021	1518551	1519761	1520971	1512501
1526416	1521576	1517341	1520366	1513106
1513711	1514316	1524601	1522786	1523391

L6-M13

1395131	1404206	1393921	1395736	1404811
1394526	1398156	1401181	1396946	1402996
1406021	1397551	1398761	1399971	1391501
1405416	1400576	1396341	1399366	1392106
1392711	1393316	1403601	1401786	1402391

L7-M6

1531256	1540331	1530046	1531861	1540936
1530651	1534281	1537306	1533071	1539121
1542146	1533676	1534886	1536096	1527626
1541541	1536701	1532466	1535491	1528231
1528836	1529441	1539726	1537911	1538516

L6-M14

1410256	1419331	1409046	1410861	1419936
1409651	1413281	1416306	1412071	1418121
1421146	1412676	1413886	1415096	1406626
1420541	1415701	1411466	1414491	1407231
1407836	1408441	1418726	1416911	1417516

L7-M7

1546381	1555456	1545171	1546986	1556061
1545776	1549406	1552431	1548196	1554246
1557271	1548801	1550011	1551221	1542751
1556666	1551826	1547591	1550616	1543356
1543961	1544566	1554851	1553036	1553641

L6-M15

1425381	1434456	1424171	1425986	1435061
1424776	1428406	1431431	1427196	1433246
1436271	1427801	1429011	1430221	1421751
1435666	1430826	1426591	1429616	1422356
1422961	1423566	1433851	1432036	1432641

L7-M8

1561506	1570581	1560296	1562111	1571186
1560901	1564531	1567556	1563321	1569371
1572396	1563926	1565136	1566346	1557876
1571791	1566951	1562716	1565741	1558481
1559086	1559691	1569976	1568161	1568766

L6-M16

1440506	1449581	1439296	1441111	1450186
1439901	1443531	1446556	1442321	1448371
1451396	1442926	1444136	1445346	1436876
1450791	1445951	1441716	1444741	1437481
1438086	1438691	1448976	1447161	1447766

L7-M9

1576631	1585706	1575421	1577236	1586311
1576026	1579656	1582681	1578446	1584496
1587521	1579051	1580261	1581471	1573001
1586916	1582076	1577841	1580866	1573606
1574211	1574816	1585101	1583286	1583891

L7-M1

1455631	1464706	1454421	1456236	1465311
1455026	1458656	1461681	1457446	1463496
1466521	1458051	1459261	1460471	1452001
1465916	1461076	1456841	1459866	1452606
1453211	1453816	1464101	1462286	1462891

L7-M10

1591756	1600831	1590546	1592361	1601436
1591151	1594781	1597806	1593571	1599621
1602646	1594176	1595386	1596596	1588126
1602041	1597201	1592966	1595991	1588731
1589336	1589941	1600226	1598411	1599016

L7-M2

1470756	1479831	1469546	1471361	1480436
1470151	1473781	1476806	1472571	1478621
1481646	1473176	1474386	1475596	1467126
1481041	1476201	1471966	1474991	1467731
1468336	1468941	1479226	1477411	1478016

L7-M11

1606881	1615956	1605671	1607486	1616561
1606276	1609906	1612931	1608696	1614746
1617771	1609301	1610511	1611721	1603251
1617166	1612326	1608091	1611116	1603856
1604461	1605066	1615351	1613536	1614141

L7-M3

1485881	1494956	1484671	1486486	1495561
1485276	1488906	1491931	1487696	1493746
1496771	1488301	1489511	1490721	1482251
1496166	1491326	1487091	1490116	1482856
1483461	1484066	1494351	1492536	1493141

L7-M12

1622006	1631081	1620796	1622611	1631686
1621401	1625031	1628056	1623821	1629871
1632896	1624426	1625636	1626846	1618376
1632291	1627451	1623216	1626241	1618981
1619586	1620191	1630476	1628661	1629266

L7-M13

1637131	1646206	1635921	1637736	1646811
1636526	1640156	1643181	1638946	1644996
1648021	1639551	1640761	1641971	1633501
1647416	1642576	1638341	1641366	1634106
1634711	1635316	1645601	1643786	1644391

L7-M14

1652256	1661331	1651046	1652861	1661936
1651651	1655281	1658306	1654071	1660121
1663146	1654676	1655886	1657096	1648626
1662541	1657701	1653466	1656491	1649231
1649836	1650441	1660726	1658911	1659516

L7-M15

1667381	1676456	1666171	1667986	1677061
1666776	1670406	1673431	1669196	1675246
1678271	1669801	1671011	1672221	1663751
1677666	1672826	1668591	1671616	1664356
1664961	1665566	1675851	1674036	1674641

L7-M16

1682506	1691581	1681296	1683111	1692186
1681901	1685531	1688556	1684321	1690371
1693396	1684926	1686136	1687346	1678876
1692791	1687951	1683716	1686741	1679481
1680086	1680691	1690976	1689161	1689766

L8M1

1697631	1706706	1696421	1698236	1707311
1697026	1700656	1703681	1699446	1705496
1708521	1700051	1701261	1702471	1694001
1707916	1703076	1698841	1701866	1694606
1695211	1695816	1706101	1704286	1704891

L8-M2

1712756	1721831	1711546	1713361	1722436
1712151	1715781	1718806	1714571	1720621
1723646	1715176	1716386	1717596	1709126
1723041	1718201	1713966	1716991	1709731
1710336	1710941	1721226	1719411	1720016

L8-M3

1727881	1736956	1726671	1728486	1737561
1727276	1730906	1733931	1729696	1735746
1738771	1730301	1731511	1732721	1724251
1738166	1733326	1729091	1732116	1724856
1725461	1726066	1736351	1734536	1735141

L8-M4

1743006	1752081	1741796	1743611	1752686
1742401	1746031	1749056	1744821	1750871
1753896	1745426	1746636	1747846	1739376
1753291	1748451	1744216	1747241	1739981
1740586	1741191	1751476	1749661	1750266

L8-M5

1758131	1767206	1756921	1758736	1767811
1757526	1761156	1764181	1759946	1765996
1769021	1760551	1761761	1762971	1754501
1768416	1763576	1759341	1762366	1755106
1755711	1756316	1766601	1764786	1765391

L8-M6

1773256	1782331	1772046	1773861	1782936
1772651	1776281	1779306	1775071	1781121
1784146	1775676	1776886	1778096	1769626
1783541	1778701	1774466	1777491	1770231
1770836	1771441	1781726	1779911	1780516

L8-M7

1788381	1797456	1787171	1788986	1798061
1787776	1791406	1794431	1790196	1796246
1799271	1790801	1792011	1793221	1784751
1798666	1793826	1789591	1792616	1785356
1785961	1786566	1796851	1795036	1795641

L8-M8

1803506	1812581	1802296	1804111	1813186
1802901	1806531	1809556	1805321	1811371
1814396	1805926	1807136	1808346	1799876
1813791	1808951	1804716	1807741	1800481
1801086	1801691	1811976	1810161	1810766

L8-M9

1818631	1827706	1817421	1819236	1828311
1818026	1821656	1824681	1820446	1826496
1829521	1821051	1822261	1823471	1815001
1828916	1824076	1819841	1822866	1815606
1816211	1816816	1827101	1825286	1825891

L8-M10

1833756	1842831	1832546	1834361	1843436
1833151	1836781	1839806	1835571	1841621
1844646	1836176	1837386	1838596	1830126
1844041	1839201	1834966	1837991	1830731
1831336	1831941	1842226	1840411	1841016

L8-M11

1848881	1857956	1847671	1849486	1858561
1848276	1851906	1854931	1850696	1856746
1859771	1851301	1852511	1853721	1845251
1859166	1854326	1850091	1853116	1845856
1846461	1847066	1857351	1855536	1856141

L8-M12

1864006	1873081	1862796	1864611	1873686
1863401	1867031	1870056	1865821	1871871
1874896	1866426	1867636	1868846	1860376
1874291	1869451	1865216	1868241	1860981
1861586	1862191	1872476	1870661	1871266

L8-M13

1879131	1888206	1877921	1879736	1888811
1878526	1882156	1885181	1880946	1886996
1890021	1881551	1882761	1883971	1875501
1889416	1884576	1880341	1883366	1876106
1876711	1877316	1887601	1885786	1886391

L8-M14

1894256	1903331	1893046	1894861	1903936
1893651	1897281	1900306	1896071	1902121
1905146	1896676	1897886	1899096	1890626
1904541	1899701	1895466	1898491	1891231
1891836	1892441	1902726	1900911	1901516

L8-M15

1909381	1918456	1908171	1909986	1919061
1908776	1912406	1915431	1911196	1917246
1920271	1911801	1913011	1914221	1905751
1919666	1914826	1910591	1913616	1906356
1906961	1907566	1917851	1916036	1916641

L9-M8

2045506	2054581	2044296	2046111	2055186
2044901	2048531	2051556	2047321	2053371
2056396	2047926	2049136	2050346	2041876
2055791	2050951	2046716	2049741	2042481
2043086	2043691	2053976	2052161	2052766

L8-M16

1924506	1933581	1923296	1925111	1934186
1923901	1927531	1930556	1926321	1932371
1935396	1926926	1928136	1929346	1920876
1934791	1929951	1925716	1928741	1921481
1922086	1922691	1932976	1931161	1931766

L9-M9

2060631	2069706	2059421	2061236	2070311
2060026	2063656	2066681	2062446	2068496
2071521	2063051	2064261	2065471	2057001
2070916	2066076	2061841	2064866	2057606
2058211	2058816	2069101	2067286	2067891

L9-M1

1939631	1948706	1938421	1940236	1949311
1939026	1942656	1945681	1941446	1947496
1950521	1942051	1943261	1944471	1936001
1949916	1945076	1940841	1943866	1936606
1937211	1937816	1948101	1946286	1946891

L9-M10

2075756	2084831	2074546	2076361	2085436
2075151	2078781	2081806	2077571	2083621
2086646	2078176	2079386	2080596	2072126
2086041	2081201	2076966	2079991	2072731
2073336	2073941	2084226	2082411	2083016

L9-M2

1954756	1963831	1953546	1955361	1964436
1954151	1957781	1960806	1956571	1962621
1965646	1957176	1958386	1959596	1951126
1965041	1960201	1955966	1958991	1951731
1952336	1952941	1963226	1961411	1962016

L9-M11

2090881	2099956	2089671	2091486	2100561
2090276	2093906	2096931	2092696	2098746
2101771	2093301	2094511	2095721	2087251
2101166	2096326	2092091	2095116	2087856
2088461	2089066	2099351	2097536	2098141

L9-M3

1969881	1978956	1968671	1970486	1979561
1969276	1972906	1975931	1971696	1977746
1980771	1972301	1973511	1974721	1966251
1980166	1975326	1971091	1974116	1966856
1967461	1968066	1978351	1976536	1977141

L9-M12

2106006	2115081	2104796	2106611	2115686
2105401	2109031	2112056	2107821	2113871
2116896	2108426	2109636	2110846	2102376
2116291	2111451	2107216	2110241	2102981
2103586	2104191	2114476	2112661	2113266

L9-M4

1985006	1994081	1983796	1985611	1994686
1984401	1988031	1991056	1986821	1992871
1995896	1987426	1988636	1989846	1981376
1995291	1990451	1986216	1989241	1981981
1982586	1983191	1993476	1991661	1992266

L9-M13

2121131	2130206	2119921	2121736	2130811
2120526	2124156	2127181	2122946	2128996
2132021	2123551	2124761	2125971	2117501
2131416	2126576	2122341	2125366	2118106
2118711	2119316	2129601	2127786	2128391

L9-M5

2000131	2009206	1998921	2000736	2009811
1999526	2003156	2006181	2001946	2007996
2011021	2002551	2003761	2004971	1996501
2010416	2005576	2001341	2004366	1997106
1997711	1998316	2008601	2006786	2007391

L9-M14

2136256	2145331	2135046	2136861	2145936
2135651	2139281	2142306	2138071	2144121
2147146	2138676	2139886	2141096	2132626
2146541	2141701	2137466	2140491	2133231
2133836	2134441	2144726	2142911	2143516

L9-M6

2015256	2024331	2014046	2015861	2024936
2014651	2018281	2021306	2017071	2023121
2026146	2017676	2018886	2020096	2011626
2025541	2020701	2016466	2019491	2012231
2012836	2013441	2023726	2021911	2022516

L9-M15

2151381	2160456	2150171	2151986	2161061
2150776	2154406	2157431	2153196	2159246
2162271	2153801	2155011	2156221	2147751
2161666	2156826	2152591	2155616	2148356
2148961	2149566	2159851	2158036	2158641

L9-M7

2030381	2039456	2029171	2030986	2040061
2029776	2033406	2036431	2032196	2038246
2041271	2032801	2034011	2035221	2026751
2040666	2035826	2031591	2034616	2027356
2027961	2028566	2038851	2037036	2037641

L9-M16

2166506	2175581	2165296	2167111	2176186
2165901	2169531	2172556	2168321	2174371
2177396	2168926	2170136	2171346	2162876
2176791	2171951	2167716	2170741	2163481
2164086	2164691	2174976	2173161	2173766

L10-M1

2181631	2190706	2180421	2182236	2191311
2181026	2184656	2187681	2183446	2189496
2192521	2184051	2185261	2186471	2178001
2191916	2187076	2182841	2185866	2178606
2179211	2179816	2190101	2188286	2188891

L10-M2

2196756	2205831	2195546	2197361	2206436
2196151	2199781	2202806	2198571	2204621
2207646	2199176	2200386	2201596	2193126
2207041	2202201	2197966	2200991	2193731
2194336	2194941	2205226	2203411	2204016

L10-M3

2211881	2220956	2210671	2212486	2221561
2211276	2214906	2217931	2213696	2219746
2222771	2214301	2215511	2216721	2208251
2222166	2217326	2213091	2216116	2208856
2209461	2210066	2220351	2218536	2219141

L10-M4

2227006	2236081	2225796	2227611	2236686
2226401	2230031	2233056	2228821	2234871
2237896	2229426	2230636	2231846	2223376
2237291	2232451	2228216	2231241	2223981
2224586	2225191	2235476	2233661	2234266

L10-M5

2242131	2251206	2240921	2242736	2251811
2241526	2245156	2248181	2243946	2249996
2253021	2244551	2245761	2246971	2238501
2252416	2247576	2243341	2246366	2239106
2239711	2240316	2250601	2248786	2249391

L10-M6

2257256	2266331	2256046	2257861	2266936
2256651	2260281	2263306	2259071	2265121
2268146	2259676	2260886	2262096	2253626
2267541	2262701	2258466	2261491	2254231
2254836	2255441	2265726	2263911	2264516

L10-M7

2272381	2281456	2271171	2272986	2282061
2271776	2275406	2278431	2274196	2280246
2283271	2274801	2276011	2277221	2268751
2282666	2277826	2273591	2276616	2269356
2269961	2270566	2280851	2279036	2279641

L10-M8

2287506	2296581	2286296	2288111	2297186
2286901	2290531	2293556	2289321	2295371
2298396	2289926	2291136	2292346	2283876
2297791	2292951	2288716	2291741	2284481
2285086	2285691	2295976	2294161	2294766

L10-M9

2302631	2311706	2301421	2303236	2312311
2302026	2305656	2308681	2304446	2310496
2313521	2305051	2306261	2307471	2299001
2312916	2308076	2303841	2306866	2299606
2300211	2300816	2311101	2309286	2309891

L10-M10

2317756	2326831	2316546	2318361	2327436
2317151	2320781	2323806	2319571	2325621
2328646	2320176	2321386	2322596	2314126
2328041	2323201	2318966	2321991	2314731
2315336	2315941	2326226	2324411	2325016

L10-M11

2332881	2341956	2331671	2333486	2342561
2332276	2335906	2338931	2334696	2340746
2343771	2335301	2336511	2337721	2329251
2343166	2338326	2334091	2337116	2329856
2330461	2331066	2341351	2339536	2340141

L10-M12

2348006	2357081	2346796	2348611	2357686
2347401	2351031	2354056	2349821	2355871
2358896	2350426	2351636	2352846	2344376
2358291	2353451	2349216	2352241	2344981
2345586	2346191	2356476	2354661	2355266

L10-M13

2363131	2372206	2361921	2363736	2372811
2362526	2366156	2369181	2364946	2370996
2374021	2365551	2366761	2367971	2359501
2373416	2368576	2364341	2367366	2360106
2360711	2361316	2371601	2369786	2370391

L10-M14

2378256	2387331	2377046	2378861	2387936
2377651	2381281	2384306	2380071	2386121
2389146	2380676	2381886	2383096	2374626
2388541	2383701	2379466	2382491	2375231
2375836	2376441	2386726	2384911	2385516

L10-M15

2393381	2402456	2392171	2393986	2403061
2392776	2396406	2399431	2395196	2401246
2404271	2395801	2397011	2398221	2389751
2403666	2398826	2394591	2397616	2390356
2390961	2391566	2401851	2400036	2400641

L10-M16

2408506	2417581	2407296	2409111	2418186
2407901	2411531	2414556	2410321	2416371
2419396	2410926	2412136	2413346	2404876
2418791	2413951	2409716	2412741	2405481
2406086	2406691	2416976	2415161	2415766

L11-M1

2423631	2432706	2422421	2424236	2433311
2423026	2426656	2429681	2425446	2431496
2434521	2426051	2427261	2428471	2420001
2433916	2429076	2424841	2427866	2420606
2421211	2421816	2432101	2430286	2430891

L11-M2

2438756	2447831	2437546	2439361	2448436
2438151	2441781	2444806	2440571	2446621
2449646	2441176	2442386	2443596	2435126
2449041	2444201	2439966	2442991	2435731
2436336	2436941	2447226	2445411	2446016

L11-M3

2453881	2462956	2452671	2454486	2463561
2453276	2456906	2459931	2455696	2461746
2464771	2456301	2457511	2458721	2450251
2464166	2459326	2455091	2458116	2450856
2451461	2452066	2462351	2460536	2461141

L11-M12

2590006	2599081	2588796	2590611	2599686
2589401	2593031	2596056	2591821	2597871
2600896	2592426	2593636	2594846	2586376
2600291	2595451	2591216	2594241	2586981
2587586	2588191	2598476	2596661	2597266

L11-M4

2469006	2478081	2467796	2469611	2478686
2468401	2472031	2475056	2470821	2476871
2479896	2471426	2472636	2473846	2465376
2479291	2474451	2470216	2473241	2465981
2466586	2467191	2477476	2475661	2476266

L11-M13

2605131	2614206	2603921	2605736	2614811
2604526	2608156	2611181	2606946	2612996
2616021	2607551	2608761	2609971	2601501
2615416	2610576	2606341	2609366	2602106
2602711	2603316	2613601	2611786	2612391

L11-M5

2484131	2493206	2482921	2484736	2493811
2483526	2487156	2490181	2485946	2491996
2495021	2486551	2487761	2488971	2480501
2494416	2489576	2485341	2488366	2481106
2481711	2482316	2492601	2490786	2491391

L11-M14

2620256	2629331	2619046	2620861	2629936
2619651	2623281	2626306	2622071	2628121
2631146	2622676	2623886	2625096	2616626
2630541	2625701	2621466	2624491	2617231
2617836	2618441	2628726	2626911	2627516

L11-M6

2499256	2508331	2498046	2499861	2508936
2498651	2502281	2505306	2501071	2507121
2510146	2501676	2502886	2504096	2495626
2509541	2504701	2500466	2503491	2496231
2496836	2497441	2507726	2505911	2506516

L11-M15

2635381	2644456	2634171	2635986	2645061
2634776	2638406	2641431	2637196	2643246
2646271	2637801	2639011	2640221	2631751
2645666	2640826	2636591	2639616	2632356
2632961	2633566	2643851	2642036	2642641

L11-M7

2514381	2523456	2513171	2514986	2524061
2513776	2517406	2520431	2516196	2522246
2525271	2516801	2518011	2519221	2510751
2524666	2519826	2515591	2518616	2511356
2511961	2512566	2522851	2521036	2521641

L11-M16

2650506	2659581	2649296	2651111	2660186
2649901	2653531	2656556	2652321	2658371
2661396	2652926	2654136	2655346	2646876
2660791	2655951	2651716	2654741	2647481
2648086	2648691	2658976	2657161	2657766

L11-M8

2529506	2538581	2528296	2530111	2539186
2528901	2532531	2535556	2531321	2537371
2540396	2531926	2533136	2534346	2525876
2539791	2534951	2530716	2533741	2526481
2527086	2527691	2537976	2536161	2536766

L12-M1

2665631	2674706	2664421	2666236	2675311
2665026	2668656	2671681	2667446	2673496
2676521	2668051	2669261	2670471	2662001
2675916	2671076	2666841	2669866	2662606
2663211	2663816	2674101	2672286	2672891

L11-M9

2544631	2553706	2543421	2545236	2554311
2544026	2547656	2550681	2546446	2552496
2555521	2547051	2548261	2549471	2541001
2554916	2550076	2545841	2548866	2541606
2542211	2542816	2553101	2551286	2551891

L12-M2

2680756	2689831	2679546	2681361	2690436
2680151	2683781	2686806	2682571	2688621
2691646	2683176	2684386	2685596	2677126
2691041	2686201	2681966	2684991	2677731
2678336	2678941	2689226	2687411	2688016

L11-M10

2559756	2568831	2558546	2560361	2569436
2559151	2562781	2565806	2561571	2567621
2570646	2562176	2563386	2564596	2556126
2570041	2565201	2560966	2563991	2556731
2557336	2557941	2568226	2566411	2567016

L12-M3

2695881	2704956	2694671	2696486	2705561
2695276	2698906	2701931	2697696	2703746
2706771	2698301	2699511	2700721	2692251
2706166	2701326	2697091	2700116	2692856
2693461	2694066	2704351	2702536	2703141

L11-M11

2574881	2583956	2573671	2575486	2584561
2574276	2577906	2580931	2576696	2582746
2585771	2577301	2578511	2579721	2571251
2585166	2580326	2576091	2579116	2571856
2572461	2573066	2583351	2581536	2582141

L12-M4

2711006	2720081	2709796	2711611	2720686
2710401	2714031	2717056	2712821	2718871
2721896	2713426	2714636	2715846	2707376
2721291	2716451	2712216	2715241	2707981
2708586	2709191	2719476	2717661	2718266

L12-M5

2726131	2735206	2724921	2726736	2735811
2725526	2729156	2732181	2727946	2733996
2737021	2728551	2729761	2730971	2722501
2736416	2731576	2727341	2730366	2723106
2723711	2724316	2734601	2732786	2733391

L12-M14

2862256	2871331	2861046	2862861	2871936
2861651	2865281	2868306	2864071	2870121
2873146	2864676	2865886	2867096	2858626
2872541	2867701	2863466	2866491	2859231
2859836	2860441	2870726	2868911	2869516

L12-M6

2741256	2750331	2740046	2741861	2750936
2740651	2744281	2747306	2743071	2749121
2752146	2743676	2744886	2746096	2737626
2751541	2746701	2742466	2745491	2738231
2738836	2739441	2749726	2747911	2748516

L12-M15

2877381	2886456	2876171	2877986	2887061
2876776	2880406	2883431	2879196	2885246
2888271	2879801	2881011	2882221	2873751
2887666	2882826	2878591	2881616	2874356
2874961	2875566	2885851	2884036	2884641

L12-M7

2756381	2765456	2755171	2756986	2766061
2755776	2759406	2762431	2758196	2764246
2767271	2758801	2760011	2761221	2752751
2766666	2761826	2757591	2760616	2753356
2753961	2754566	2764851	2763036	2763641

L12-M16

2892506	2901581	2891296	2893111	2902186
2891901	2895531	2898556	2894321	2900371
2903396	2894926	2896136	2897346	2888876
2902791	2897951	2893716	2896741	2889481
2890086	2890691	2900976	2899161	2899766

L12-M8

2771506	2780581	2770296	2772111	2781186
2770901	2774531	2777556	2773321	2779371
2782396	2773926	2775136	2776346	2767876
2781791	2776951	2772716	2775741	2768481
2769086	2769691	2779976	2778161	2778766

L13-M1

2907631	2916706	2906421	2908236	2917311
2907026	2910656	2913681	2909446	2915496
2918521	2910051	2911261	2912471	2904001
2917916	2913076	2908841	2911866	2904606
2905211	2905816	2916101	2914286	2914891

L12-M9

2786631	2795706	2785421	2787236	2796311
2786026	2789656	2792681	2788446	2794496
2797521	2789051	2790261	2791471	2783001
2796916	2792076	2787841	2790866	2783606
2784211	2784816	2795101	2793286	2793891

L13-M2

2922756	2931831	2921546	2923361	2932436
2922151	2925781	2928806	2924571	2930621
2933646	2925176	2926386	2927596	2919126
2933041	2928201	2923966	2926991	2919731
2920336	2920941	2931226	2929411	2930016

L12-M10

2801756	2810831	2800546	2802361	2811436
2801151	2804781	2807806	2803571	2809621
2812646	2804176	2805386	2806596	2798126
2812041	2807201	2802966	2805991	2798731
2799336	2799941	2810226	2808411	2809016

L13-M3

2937881	2946956	2936671	2938486	2947561
2937276	2940906	2943931	2939696	2945746
2948771	2940301	2941511	2942721	2934251
2948166	2943326	2939091	2942116	2934856
2935461	2936066	2946351	2944536	2945141

L12-M11

2816881	2825956	2815671	2817486	2826561
2816276	2819906	2822931	2818696	2824746
2827771	2819301	2820511	2821721	2813251
2827166	2822326	2818091	2821116	2813856
2814461	2815066	2825351	2823536	2824141

L13-M4

2953006	2962081	2951796	2953611	2962686
2952401	2956031	2959056	2954821	2960871
2963896	2955426	2956636	2957846	2949376
2963291	2958451	2954216	2957241	2949981
2950586	2951191	2961476	2959661	2960266

L12-M12

2832006	2841081	2830796	2832611	2841686
2831401	2835031	2838056	2833821	2839871
2842896	2834426	2835636	2836846	2828376
2842291	2837451	2833216	2836241	2828981
2829586	2830191	2840476	2838661	2839266

L13-M5

2968131	2977206	2966921	2968736	2977811
2967526	2971156	2974181	2969946	2975996
2979021	2970551	2971761	2972971	2964501
2978416	2973576	2969341	2972366	2965106
2965711	2966316	2976601	2974786	2975391

L12-M13

2847131	2856206	2845921	2847736	2856811
2846526	2850156	2853181	2848946	2854996
2858021	2849551	2850761	2851971	2843501
2857416	2852576	2848341	2851366	2844106
2844711	2845316	2855601	2853786	2854391

L13-M6

2983256	2992331	2982046	2983861	2992936
2982651	2986281	2989306	2985071	2991121
2994146	2985676	2986886	2988096	2979626
2993541	2988701	2984466	2987491	2980231
2980836	2981441	2991726	2989911	2990516

L13-M7

2998381	3007456	2997171	2998986	3008061
2997776	3001406	3004431	3000196	3006246
3009271	3000801	3002011	3003221	2994751
3008666	3003826	2999591	3002616	2995356
2995961	2996566	3006851	3005036	3005641

L13-M8

3013506	3022581	3012296	3014111	3023186
3012901	3016531	3019556	3015321	3021371
3024396	3015926	3017136	3018346	3009876
3023791	3018951	3014716	3017741	3010481
3011086	3011691	3021976	3020161	3020766

L13-M9

3028631	3037706	3027421	3029236	3038311
3028026	3031656	3034681	3030446	3036496
3039521	3031051	3032261	3033471	3025001
3038916	3034076	3029841	3032866	3025606
3026211	3026816	3037101	3035286	3035891

L13-M10

3043756	3052831	3042546	3044361	3053436
3043151	3046781	3049806	3045571	3051621
3054646	3046176	3047386	3048596	3040126
3054041	3049201	3044966	3047991	3040731
3041336	3041941	3052226	3050411	3051016

L13-M11

3058881	3067956	3057671	3059486	3068561
3058276	3061906	3064931	3060696	3066746
3069771	3061301	3062511	3063721	3055251
3069166	3064326	3060091	3063116	3055856
3056461	3057066	3067351	3065536	3066141

L13-M12

3074006	3083081	3072796	3074611	3083686
3073401	3077031	3080056	3075821	3081871
3084896	3076426	3077636	3078846	3070376
3084291	3079451	3075216	3078241	3070981
3071586	3072191	3082476	3080661	3081266

L13-M13

3089131	3098206	3087921	3089736	3098811
3088526	3092156	3095181	3090946	3096996
3100021	3091551	3092761	3093971	3085501
3099416	3094576	3090341	3093366	3086106
3086711	3087316	3097601	3095786	3096391

L13-M14

3104256	3113331	3103046	3104861	3113936
3103651	3107281	3110306	3106071	3112121
3115146	3106676	3107886	3109096	3100626
3114541	3109701	3105466	3108491	3101231
3101836	3102441	3112726	3110911	3111516

L13-M15

3119381	3128456	3118171	3119986	3129061
3118776	3122406	3125431	3121196	3127246
3130271	3121801	3123011	3124221	3115751
3129666	3124826	3120591	3123616	3116356
3116961	3117566	3127851	3126036	3126641

L13-M16

3134506	3143581	3133296	3135111	3144186
3133901	3137531	3140556	3136321	3142371
3145396	3136926	3138136	3139346	3130876
3144791	3139951	3135716	3138741	3131481
3132086	3132691	3142976	3141161	3141766

L14-M1

3149631	3158706	3148421	3150236	3159311
3149026	3152656	3155681	3151446	3157496
3160521	3152051	3153261	3154471	3146001
3159916	3155076	3150841	3153866	3146606
3147211	3147816	3158101	3156286	3156891

L14-M2

3164756	3173831	3163546	3165361	3174436
3164151	3167781	3170806	3166571	3172621
3175646	3167176	3168386	3169596	3161126
3175041	3170201	3165966	3168991	3161731
3162336	3162941	3173226	3171411	3172016

L14-M3

3179881	3188956	3178671	3180486	3189561
3179276	3182906	3185931	3181696	3187746
3190771	3182301	3183511	3184721	3176251
3190166	3185326	3181091	3184116	3176856
3177461	3178066	3188351	3186536	3187141

L14-M4

3195006	3204081	3193796	3195611	3204686
3194401	3198031	3201056	3196821	3202871
3205896	3197426	3198636	3199846	3191376
3205291	3200451	3196216	3199241	3191981
3192586	3193191	3203476	3201661	3202266

L14-M5

3210131	3219206	3208921	3210736	3219811
3209526	3213156	3216181	3211946	3217996
3221021	3212551	3213761	3214971	3206501
3220416	3215576	3211341	3214366	3207106
3207711	3208316	3218601	3216786	3217391

L14-M6

3225256	3234331	3224046	3225861	3234936
3224651	3228281	3231306	3227071	3233121
3236146	3227676	3228886	3230096	3221626
3235541	3230701	3226466	3229491	3222231
3222836	3223441	3233726	3231911	3232516

L14-M7

3240381	3249456	3239171	3240986	3250061
3239776	3243406	3246431	3242196	3248246
3251271	3242801	3244011	3245221	3236751
3250666	3245826	3241591	3244616	3237356
3237961	3238566	3248851	3247036	3247641

L14-M8

3255506	3264581	3254296	3256111	3265186
3254901	3258531	3261556	3257321	3263371
3266396	3257926	3259136	3260346	3251876
3265791	3260951	3256716	3259741	3252481
3253086	3253691	3263976	3262161	3262766

L14-M9

3270631	3279706	3269421	3271236	3280311
3270026	3273656	3276681	3272446	3278496
3281521	3273051	3274261	3275471	3267001
3280916	3276076	3271841	3274866	3267606
3268211	3268816	3279101	3277286	3277891

L15-M2

3406756	3415831	3405546	3407361	3416436
3406151	3409781	3412806	3408571	3414621
3417646	3409176	3410386	3411596	3403126
3417041	3412201	3407966	3410991	3403731
3404336	3404941	3415226	3413411	3414016

L14-M10

3285756	3294831	3284546	3286361	3295436
3285151	3288781	3291806	3287571	3293621
3296646	3288176	3289386	3290596	3282126
3296041	3291201	3286966	3289991	3282731
3283336	3283941	3294226	3292411	3293016

L15-M3

3421881	3430956	3420671	3422486	3431561
3421276	3424906	3427931	3423696	3429746
3432771	3424301	3425511	3426721	3418251
3432166	3427326	3423091	3426116	3418856
3419461	3420066	3430351	3428536	3429141

L14-M11

3300881	3309956	3299671	3301486	3310561
3300276	3303906	3306931	3302696	3308746
3311771	3303301	3304511	3305721	3297251
3311166	3306326	3302091	3305116	3297856
3298461	3299066	3309351	3307536	3308141

L15-M4

3437006	3446081	3435796	3437611	3446686
3436401	3440031	3443056	3438821	3444871
3447896	3439426	3440636	3441846	3433376
3447291	3442451	3438216	3441241	3433981
3434586	3435191	3445476	3443661	3444266

L14-M12

3316006	3325081	3314796	3316611	3325686
3315401	3319031	3322056	3317821	3323871
3326896	3318426	3319636	3320846	3312376
3326291	3321451	3317216	3320241	3312981
3313586	3314191	3324476	3322661	3323266

L15-M5

3452131	3461206	3450921	3452736	3461811
3451526	3455156	3458181	3453946	3459996
3463021	3454551	3455761	3456971	3448501
3462416	3457576	3453341	3456366	3449106
3449711	3450316	3460601	3458786	3459391

L14-M13

3331131	3340206	3329921	3331736	3340811
3330526	3334156	3337181	3332946	3338996
3342021	3333551	3334761	3335971	3327501
3341416	3336576	3332341	3335366	3328106
3328711	3329316	3339601	3337786	3338391

L15-M6

3467256	3476331	3466046	3467861	3476936
3466651	3470281	3473306	3469071	3475121
3478146	3469676	3470886	3472096	3463626
3477541	3472701	3468466	3471491	3464231
3464836	3465441	3475726	3473911	3474516

L14-M14

3346256	3355331	3345046	3346861	3355936
3345651	3349281	3352306	3348071	3354121
3357146	3348676	3349886	3351096	3342626
3356541	3351701	3347466	3350491	3343231
3343836	3344441	3354726	3352911	3353516

L15-M7

3482381	3491456	3481171	3482986	3492061
3481776	3485406	3488431	3484196	3490246
3493271	3484801	3486011	3487221	3478751
3492666	3487826	3483591	3486616	3479356
3479961	3480566	3490851	3489036	3489641

L14-M15

3361381	3370456	3360171	3361986	3371061
3360776	3364406	3367431	3363196	3369246
3372271	3363801	3365011	3366221	3357751
3371666	3366826	3362591	3365616	3358356
3358961	3359566	3369851	3368036	3368641

L15-M8

3497506	3506581	3496296	3498111	3507186
3496901	3500531	3503556	3499321	3505371
3508396	3499926	3501136	3502346	3493876
3507791	3502951	3498716	3501741	3494481
3495086	3495691	3505976	3504161	3504766

L14-M16

3376506	3385581	3375296	3377111	3386186
3375901	3379531	3382556	3378321	3384371
3387396	3378926	3380136	3381346	3372876
3386791	3381951	3377716	3380741	3373481
3374086	3374691	3384976	3383161	3383766

L15-M9

3512631	3521706	3511421	3513236	3522311
3512026	3515656	3518681	3514446	3520496
3523521	3515051	3516261	3517471	3509001
3522916	3518076	3513841	3516866	3509606
3510211	3510816	3521101	3519286	3519891

L15-M1

3391631	3400706	3390421	3392236	3401311
3391026	3394656	3397681	3393446	3399496
3402521	3394051	3395261	3396471	3388001
3401916	3397076	3392841	3395866	3388606
3389211	3389816	3400101	3398286	3398891

L15-M10

3527756	3536831	3526546	3528361	3537436
3527151	3530781	3533806	3529571	3535621
3538646	3530176	3531386	3532596	3524126
3538041	3533201	3528966	3531991	3524731
3525336	3525941	3536226	3534411	3535016

L15-M11

3542881	3551956	3541671	3543486	3552561
3542276	3545906	3548931	3544696	3550746
3553771	3545301	3546511	3547721	3539251
3553166	3548326	3544091	3547116	3539856
3540461	3541066	3551351	3549536	3550141

L15-M12

3558006	3567081	3556796	3558611	3567686
3557401	3561031	3564056	3559821	3565871
3568896	3560426	3561636	3562846	3554376
3568291	3563451	3559216	3562241	3554981
3555586	3556191	3566476	3564661	3565266

L15-M13

3573131	3582206	3571921	3573736	3582811
3572526	3576156	3579181	3574946	3580996
3584021	3575551	3576761	3577971	3569501
3583416	3578576	3574341	3577366	3570106
3570711	3571316	3581601	3579786	3580391

L15-M14

3588256	3597331	3587046	3588861	3597936
3587651	3591281	3594306	3590071	3596121
3599146	3590676	3591886	3593096	3584626
3598541	3593701	3589466	3592491	3585231
3585836	3586441	3596726	3594911	3595516

L15-M15

3603381	3612456	3602171	3603986	3613061
3602776	3606406	3609431	3605196	3611246
3614271	3605801	3607011	3608221	3599751
3613666	3608826	3604591	3607616	3600356
3600961	3601566	3611851	3610036	3610641

L15-M16

3618506	3627581	3617296	3619111	3628186
3617901	3621531	3624556	3620321	3626371
3629396	3620926	3622136	3623346	3614876
3628791	3623951	3619716	3622741	3615481
3616086	3616691	3626976	3625161	3625766

L16-M1

3633631	3642706	3632421	3634236	3643311
3633026	3636656	3639681	3635446	3641496
3644521	3636051	3637261	3638471	3630001
3643916	3639076	3634841	3637866	3630606
3631211	3631816	3642101	3640286	3640891

L16-M2

3648756	3657831	3647546	3649361	3658436
3648151	3651781	3654806	3650571	3656621
3659646	3651176	3652386	3653596	3645126
3659041	3654201	3649966	3652991	3645731
3646336	3646941	3657226	3655411	3656016

L16-M3

3663881	3672956	3662671	3664486	3673561
3663276	3666906	3669931	3665696	3671746
3674771	3666301	3667511	3668721	3660251
3674166	3669326	3665091	3668116	3660856
3661461	3662066	3672351	3670536	3671141

L16-M4

3679006	3688081	3677796	3679611	3688686
3678401	3682031	3685056	3680821	3686871
3689896	3681426	3682636	3683846	3675376
3689291	3684451	3680216	3683241	3675981
3676586	3677191	3687476	3685661	3686266

L16-M5

3694131	3703206	3692921	3694736	3703811
3693526	3697156	3700181	3695946	3701996
3705021	3696551	3697761	3698971	3690501
3704416	3699576	3695341	3698366	3691106
3691711	3692316	3702601	3700786	3701391

L16-M6

3709256	3718331	3708046	3709861	3718936
3708651	3712281	3715306	3711071	3717121
3720146	3711676	3712886	3714096	3705626
3719541	3714701	3710466	3713491	3706231
3706836	3707441	3717726	3715911	3716516

L16-M7

3724381	3733456	3723171	3724986	3734061
3723776	3727406	3730431	3726196	3732246
3735271	3726801	3728011	3729221	3720751
3734666	3729826	3725591	3728616	3721356
3721961	3722566	3732851	3731036	3731641

L16-M8

3739506	3748581	3738296	3740111	3749186
3738901	3742531	3745556	3741321	3747371
3750396	3741926	3743136	3744346	3735876
3749791	3744951	3740716	3743741	3736481
3737086	3737691	3747976	3746161	3746766

L16-M9

3754631	3763706	3753421	3755236	3764311
3754026	3757656	3760681	3756446	3762496
3765521	3757051	3758261	3759471	3751001
3764916	3760076	3755841	3758866	3751606
3752211	3752816	3763101	3761286	3761891

L16-M10

3769756	3778831	3768546	3770361	3779436
3769151	3772781	3775806	3771571	3777621
3780646	3772176	3773386	3774596	3766126
3780041	3775201	3770966	3773991	3766731
3767336	3767941	3778226	3776411	3777016

L16-M11

3784881	3793956	3783671	3785486	3794561
3784276	3787906	3790931	3786696	3792746
3795771	3787301	3788511	3789721	3781251
3795166	3790326	3786091	3789116	3781856
3782461	3783066	3793351	3791536	3792141

L16-M12

3800006	3809081	3798796	3800611	3809686
3799401	3803031	3806056	3801821	3807871
3810896	3802426	3803636	3804846	3796376
3810291	3805451	3801216	3804241	3796981
3797586	3798191	3808476	3806661	3807266

L16-M13

3815131	3824206	3813921	3815736	3824811
3814526	3818156	3821181	3816946	3822996
3826021	3817551	3818761	3819971	3811501
3825416	3820576	3816341	3819366	3812106
3812711	3813316	3823601	3821786	3822391

L17-M6

3951256	3960331	3950046	3951861	3960936
3950651	3954281	3957306	3953071	3959121
3962146	3953676	3954886	3956096	3947626
3961541	3956701	3952466	3955491	3948231
3948836	3949441	3959726	3957911	3958516

L16-M14

3830256	3839331	3829046	3830861	3839936
3829651	3833281	3836306	3832071	3838121
3841146	3832676	3833886	3835096	3826626
3840541	3835701	3831466	3834491	3827231
3827836	3828441	3838726	3836911	3837516

L17-M7

3966381	3975456	3965171	3966986	3976061
3965776	3969406	3972431	3968196	3974246
3977271	3968801	3970011	3971221	3962751
3976666	3971826	3967591	3970616	3963356
3963961	3964566	3974851	3973036	3973641

L16-M15

3845381	3854456	3844171	3845986	3855061
3844776	3848406	3851431	3847196	3853246
3856271	3847801	3849011	3850221	3841751
3855666	3850826	3846591	3849616	3842356
3842961	3843566	3853851	3852036	3852641

L17-M8

3981506	3990581	3980296	3982111	3991186
3980901	3984531	3987556	3983321	3989371
3992396	3983926	3985136	3986346	3977876
3991791	3986951	3982716	3985741	3978481
3979086	3979691	3989976	3988161	3988766

L16M16

3860506	3869581	3859296	3861111	3870186
3859901	3863531	3866556	3862321	3868371
3871396	3862926	3864136	3865346	3856876
3870791	3865951	3861716	3864741	3857481
3858086	3858691	3868976	3867161	3867766

L17-M9

3996631	4005706	3995421	3997236	4006311
3996026	3999656	4002681	3998446	4004496
4007521	3999051	4000261	4001471	3993001
4006916	4002076	3997841	4000866	3993606
3994211	3994816	4005101	4003286	4003891

L17-M1

3875631	3884706	3874421	3876236	3885311
3875026	3878656	3881681	3877446	3883496
3886521	3878051	3879261	3880471	3872001
3885916	3881076	3876841	3879866	3872606
3873211	3873816	3884101	3882286	3882891

L17-M10

4011756	4020831	4010546	4012361	4021436
4011151	4014781	4017806	4013571	4019621
4022646	4014176	4015386	4016596	4008126
4022041	4017201	4012966	4015991	4008731
4009336	4009941	4020226	4018411	4019016

L17-M2

3890756	3899831	3889546	3891361	3900436
3890151	3893781	3896806	3892571	3898621
3901646	3893176	3894386	3895596	3887126
3901041	3896201	3891966	3894991	3887731
3888336	3888941	3899226	3897411	3898016

L17-M11

4026881	4035956	4025671	4027486	4036561
4026276	4029906	4032931	4028696	4034746
4037771	4029301	4030511	4031721	4023251
4037166	4032326	4028091	4031116	4023856
4024461	4025066	4035351	4033536	4034141

L17-M3

3905881	3914956	3904671	3906486	3915561
3905276	3908906	3911931	3907696	3913746
3916771	3908301	3909511	3910721	3902251
3916166	3911326	3907091	3910116	3902856
3903461	3904066	3914351	3912536	3913141

L17-M12

4042006	4051081	4040796	4042611	4051686
4041401	4045031	4048056	4043821	4049871
4052896	4044426	4045636	4046846	4038376
4052291	4047451	4043216	4046241	4038981
4039586	4040191	4050476	4048661	4049266

L17-M4

3921006	3930081	3919796	3921611	3930686
3920401	3924031	3927056	3922821	3928871
3931896	3923426	3924636	3925846	3917376
3931291	3926451	3922216	3925241	3917981
3918586	3919191	3929476	3927661	3928266

L17-M13

4057131	4066206	4055921	4057736	4066811
4056526	4060156	4063181	4058946	4064996
4068021	4059551	4060761	4061971	4053501
4067416	4062576	4058341	4061366	4054106
4054711	4055316	4065601	4063786	4064391

L17-M5

3936131	3945206	3934921	3936736	3945811
3935526	3939156	3942181	3937946	3943996
3947021	3938551	3939761	3940971	3932501
3946416	3941576	3937341	3940366	3933106
3933711	3934316	3944601	3942786	3943391

L17-M14

4072256	4081331	4071046	4072861	4081936
4071651	4075281	4078306	4074071	4080121
4083146	4074676	4075886	4077096	4068626
4082541	4077701	4073466	4076491	4069231
4069836	4070441	4080726	4078911	4079516

L17-M15

4087381	4096456	4086171	4087986	4097061
4086776	4090406	4093431	4089196	4095246
4098271	4089801	4091011	4092221	4083751
4097666	4092826	4088591	4091616	4084356
4084961	4085566	4095851	4094036	4094641

L17-M16

4102506	4111581	4101296	4103111	4112186
4101901	4105531	4108556	4104321	4110371
4113396	4104926	4106136	4107346	4098876
4112791	4107951	4103716	4106741	4099481
4100086	4100691	4110976	4109161	4109766

L18-M1

4117631	4126706	4116421	4118236	4127311
4117026	4120656	4123681	4119446	4125496
4128521	4120051	4121261	4122471	4114001
4127916	4123076	4118841	4121866	4114606
4115211	4115816	4126101	4124286	4124891

L18-M2

4132756	4141831	4131546	4133361	4142436
4132151	4135781	4138806	4134571	4140621
4143646	4135176	4136386	4137596	4129126
4143041	4138201	4133966	4136991	4129731
4130336	4130941	4141226	4139411	4140016

L18-M3

4147881	4156956	4146671	4148486	4157561
4147276	4150906	4153931	4149696	4155746
4158771	4150301	4151511	4152721	4144251
4158166	4153326	4149091	4152116	4144856
4145461	4146066	4156351	4154536	4155141

L18-M4

4163006	4172081	4161796	4163611	4172686
4162401	4166031	4169056	4164821	4170871
4173896	4165426	4166636	4167846	4159376
4173291	4168451	4164216	4167241	4159981
4160586	4161191	4171476	4169661	4170266

L18-M5

4178131	4187206	4176921	4178736	4187811
4177526	4181156	4184181	4179946	4185996
4189021	4180551	4181761	4182971	4174501
4188416	4183576	4179341	4182366	4175106
4175711	4176316	4186601	4184786	4185391

L18-M6

4193256	4202331	4192046	4193861	4202936
4192651	4196281	4199306	4195071	4201121
4204146	4195676	4196886	4198096	4189626
4203541	4198701	4194466	4197491	4190231
4190836	4191441	4201726	4199911	4200516

L18-M7

4208381	4217456	4207171	4208986	4218061
4207776	4211406	4214431	4210196	4216246
4219271	4210801	4212011	4213221	4204751
4218666	4213826	4209591	4212616	4205356
4205961	4206566	4216851	4215036	4215641

L18-M8

4223506	4232581	4222296	4224111	4233186
4222901	4226531	4229556	4225321	4231371
4234396	4225926	4227136	4228346	4219876
4233791	4228951	4224716	4227741	4220481
4221086	4221691	4231976	4230161	4230766

L18-M9

4238631	4247706	4237421	4239236	4248311
4238026	4241656	4244681	4240446	4246496
4249521	4241051	4242261	4243471	4235001
4248916	4244076	4239841	4242866	4235606
4236211	4236816	4247101	4245286	4245891

L18-M10

4253756	4262831	4252546	4254361	4263436
4253151	4256781	4259806	4255571	4261621
4264646	4256176	4257386	4258596	4250126
4264041	4259201	4254966	4257991	4250731
4251336	4251941	4262226	4260411	4261016

L18-M11

4268881	4277956	4267671	4269486	4278561
4268276	4271906	4274931	4270696	4276746
4279771	4271301	4272511	4273721	4265251
4279166	4274326	4270091	4273116	4265856
4266461	4267066	4277351	4275536	4276141

L18-M12

4284006	4293081	4282796	4284611	4293686
4283401	4287031	4290056	4285821	4291871
4294896	4286426	4287636	4288846	4280376
4294291	4289451	4285216	4288241	4280981
4281586	4282191	4292476	4290661	4291266

L18-M13

4299131	4308206	4297921	4299736	4308811
4298526	4302156	4305181	4300946	4306996
4310021	4301551	4302761	4303971	4295501
4309416	4304576	4300341	4303366	4296106
4296711	4297316	4307601	4305786	4306391

L18-M14

4314256	4323331	4313046	4314861	4323936
4313651	4317281	4320306	4316071	4322121
4325146	4316676	4317886	4319096	4310626
4324541	4319701	4315466	4318491	4311231
4311836	4312441	4322726	4320911	4321516

L18-M15

4329381	4338456	4328171	4329986	4339061
4328776	4332406	4335431	4331196	4337246
4340271	4331801	4333011	4334221	4325751
4339666	4334826	4330591	4333616	4326356
4326961	4327566	4337851	4336036	4336641

L18-M16

4344506	4353581	4343296	4345111	4354186
4343901	4347531	4350556	4346321	4352371
4355396	4346926	4348136	4349346	4340876
4354791	4349951	4345716	4348741	4341481
4342086	4342691	4352976	4351161	4351766

L19-M1

4359631	4368706	4358421	4360236	4369311
4359026	4362656	4365681	4361446	4367496
4370521	4362051	4363261	4364471	4356001
4369916	4365076	4360841	4363866	4356606
4357211	4357816	4368101	4366286	4366891

L19-M2

4374756	4383831	4373546	4375361	4384436
4374151	4377781	4380806	4376571	4382621
4385646	4377176	4378386	4379596	4371126
4385041	4380201	4375966	4378991	4371731
4372336	4372941	4383226	4381411	4382016

L19-M3

4389881	4398956	4388671	4390486	4399561
4389276	4392906	4395931	4391696	4397746
4400771	4392301	4393511	4394721	4386251
4400166	4395326	4391091	4394116	4386856
4387461	4388066	4398351	4396536	4397141

L19-M4

4405006	4414081	4403796	4405611	4414686
4404401	4408031	4411056	4406821	4412871
4415896	4407426	4408636	4409846	4401376
4415291	4410451	4406216	4409241	4401981
4402586	4403191	4413476	4411661	4412266

L19-M5

4420131	4429206	4418921	4420736	4429811
4419526	4423156	4426181	4421946	4427996
4431021	4422551	4423761	4424971	4416501
4430416	4425576	4421341	4424366	4417106
4417711	4418316	4428601	4426786	4427391

L19-M6

4435256	4444331	4434046	4435861	4444936
4434651	4438281	4441306	4437071	4443121
4446146	4437676	4438886	4440096	4431626
4445541	4440701	4436466	4439491	4432231
4432836	4433441	4443726	4441911	4442516

L19-M7

4450381	4459456	4449171	4450986	4460061
4449776	4453406	4456431	4452196	4458246
4461271	4452801	4454011	4455221	4446751
4460666	4455826	4451591	4454616	4447356
4447961	4448566	4458851	4457036	4457641

L19-M8

4465506	4474581	4464296	4466111	4475186
4464901	4468531	4471556	4467321	4473371
4476396	4467926	4469136	4470346	4461876
4475791	4470951	4466716	4469741	4462481
4463086	4463691	4473976	4472161	4472766

L19-M9

4480631	4489706	4479421	4481236	4490311
4480026	4483656	4486681	4482446	4488496
4491521	4483051	4484261	4485471	4477001
4490916	4486076	4481841	4484866	4477606
4478211	4478816	4489101	4487286	4487891

L19-M10

4495756	4504831	4494546	4496361	4505436
4495151	4498781	4501806	4497571	4503621
4506646	4498176	4499386	4500596	4492126
4506041	4501201	4496966	4499991	4492731
4493336	4493941	4504226	4502411	4503016

L19-M11

4510881	4519956	4509671	4511486	4520561
4510276	4513906	4516931	4512696	4518746
4521771	4513301	4514511	4515721	4507251
4521166	4516326	4512091	4515116	4507856
4508461	4509066	4519351	4517536	4518141

L19-M12

4526006	4535081	4524796	4526611	4535686
4525401	4529031	4532056	4527821	4533871
4536896	4528426	4529636	4530846	4522376
4536291	4531451	4527216	4530241	4522981
4523586	4524191	4534476	4532661	4533266

L19-M13

4541131	4550206	4539921	4541736	4550811
4540526	4544156	4547181	4542946	4548996
4552021	4543551	4544761	4545971	4537501
4551416	4546576	4542341	4545366	4538106
4538711	4539316	4549601	4547786	4548391

L19-M14

4556256	4565331	4555046	4556861	4565936
4555651	4559281	4562306	4558071	4564121
4567146	4558676	4559886	4561096	4552626
4566541	4561701	4557466	4560491	4553231
4553836	4554441	4564726	4562911	4563516

L19-M15

4571381	4580456	4570171	4571986	4581061
4570776	4574406	4577431	4573196	4579246
4582271	4573801	4575011	4576221	4567751
4581666	4576826	4572591	4575616	4568356
4568961	4569566	4579851	4578036	4578641

L19-M16

4586506	4595581	4585296	4587111	4596186
4585901	4589531	4592556	4588321	4594371
4597396	4588926	4590136	4591346	4582876
4596791	4591951	4587716	4590741	4583481
4584086	4584691	4594976	4593161	4593766

L20-M1

4601631	4610706	4600421	4602236	4611311
4601026	4604656	4607681	4603446	4609496
4612521	4604051	4605261	4606471	4598001
4611916	4607076	4602841	4605866	4598606
4599211	4599816	4610101	4608286	4608891

L20-M2

4616756	4625831	4615546	4617361	4626436
4616151	4619781	4622806	4618571	4624621
4627646	4619176	4620386	4621596	4613126
4627041	4622201	4617966	4620991	4613731
4614336	4614941	4625226	4623411	4624016

L20-M3

4631881	4640956	4630671	4632486	4641561
4631276	4634906	4637931	4633696	4639746
4642771	4634301	4635511	4636721	4628251
4642166	4637326	4633091	4636116	4628856
4629461	4630066	4640351	4638536	4639141

L20-M12

4768006	4777081	4766796	4768611	4777686
4767401	4771031	4774056	4769821	4775871
4778896	4770426	4771636	4772846	4764376
4778291	4773451	4769216	4772241	4764981
4765586	4766191	4776476	4774661	4775266

L20-M4

4647006	4656081	4645796	4647611	4656686
4646401	4650031	4653056	4648821	4654871
4657896	4649426	4650636	4651846	4643376
4657291	4652451	4648216	4651241	4643981
4644586	4645191	4655476	4653661	4654266

L20-M13

4783131	4792206	4781921	4783736	4792811
4782526	4786156	4789181	4784946	4790996
4794021	4785551	4786761	4787971	4779501
4793416	4788576	4784341	4787366	4780106
4780711	4781316	4791601	4789786	4790391

L20-M5

4662131	4671206	4660921	4662736	4671811
4661526	4665156	4668181	4663946	4669996
4673021	4664551	4665761	4666971	4658501
4672416	4667576	4663341	4666366	4659106
4659711	4660316	4670601	4668786	4669391

L20-M14

4798256	4807331	4797046	4798861	4807936
4797651	4801281	4804306	4800071	4806121
4809146	4800676	4801886	4803096	4794626
4808541	4803701	4799466	4802491	4795231
4795836	4796441	4806726	4804911	4805516

L20-M6

4677256	4686331	4676046	4677861	4686936
4676651	4680281	4683306	4679071	4685121
4688146	4679676	4680886	4682096	4673626
4687541	4682701	4678466	4681491	4674231
4674836	4675441	4685726	4683911	4684516

L20-M15

4813381	4822456	4812171	4813986	4823061
4812776	4816406	4819431	4815196	4821246
4824271	4815801	4817011	4818221	4809751
4823666	4818826	4814591	4817616	4810356
4810961	4811566	4821851	4820036	4820641

L20-M7

4692381	4701456	4691171	4692986	4702061
4691776	4695406	4698431	4694196	4700246
4703271	4694801	4696011	4697221	4688751
4702666	4697826	4693591	4696616	4689356
4689961	4690566	4700851	4699036	4699641

L20-M16

4828506	4837581	4827296	4829111	4838186
4827901	4831531	4834556	4830321	4836371
4839396	4830926	4832136	4833346	4824876
4838791	4833951	4829716	4832741	4825481
4826086	4826691	4836976	4835161	4835766

L20-M8

4707506	4716581	4706296	4708111	4717186
4706901	4710531	4713556	4709321	4715371
4718396	4709926	4711136	4712346	4703876
4717791	4712951	4708716	4711741	4704481
4705086	4705691	4715976	4714161	4714766

L21-M1

4843631	4852706	4842421	4844236	4853311
4843026	4846656	4849681	4845446	4851496
4854521	4846051	4847261	4848471	4840001
4853916	4849076	4844841	4847866	4840606
4841211	4841816	4852101	4850286	4850891

L20-M9

4722631	4731706	4721421	4723236	4732311
4722026	4725656	4728681	4724446	4730496
4733521	4725051	4726261	4727471	4719001
4732916	4728076	4723841	4726866	4719606
4720211	4720816	4731101	4729286	4729891

L21-M2

4858756	4867831	4857546	4859361	4868436
4858151	4861781	4864806	4860571	4866621
4869646	4861176	4862386	4863596	4855126
4869041	4864201	4859966	4862991	4855731
4856336	4856941	4867226	4865411	4866016

L20-M10

4737756	4746831	4736546	4738361	4747436
4737151	4740781	4743806	4739571	4745621
4748646	4740176	4741386	4742596	4734126
4748041	4743201	4738966	4741991	4734731
4735336	4735941	4746226	4744411	4745016

L21-M3

4873881	4882956	4872671	4874486	4883561
4873276	4876906	4879931	4875696	4881746
4884771	4876301	4877511	4878721	4870251
4884166	4879326	4875091	4878116	4870856
4871461	4872066	4882351	4880536	4881141

L20-M11

4752881	4761956	4751671	4753486	4762561
4752276	4755906	4758931	4754696	4760746
4763771	4755301	4756511	4757721	4749251
4763166	4758326	4754091	4757116	4749856
4750461	4751066	4761351	4759536	4760141

L21-M4

4889006	4898081	4887796	4889611	4898686
4888401	4892031	4895056	4890821	4896871
4899896	4891426	4892636	4893846	4885376
4899291	4894451	4890216	4893241	4885981
4886586	4887191	4897476	4895661	4896266

L21-M5

4904131	4913206	4902921	4904736	4913811
4903526	4907156	4910181	4905946	4911996
4915021	4906551	4907761	4908971	4900501
4914416	4909576	4905341	4908366	4901106
4901711	4902316	4912601	4910786	4911391

L21-M6

4919256	4928331	4918046	4919861	4928936
4918651	4922281	4925306	4921071	4927121
4930146	4921676	4922886	4924096	4915626
4929541	4924701	4920466	4923491	4916231
4916836	4917441	4927726	4925911	4926516

L21-M7

4934381	4943456	4933171	4934986	4944061
4933776	4937406	4940431	4936196	4942246
4945271	4936801	4938011	4939221	4930751
4944666	4939826	4935591	4938616	4931356
4931961	4932566	4942851	4941036	4941641

L21-M8

4949506	4958581	4948296	4950111	4959186
4948901	4952531	4955556	4951321	4957371
4960396	4951926	4953136	4954346	4945876
4959791	4954951	4950716	4953741	4946481
4947086	4947691	4957976	4956161	4956766

L21-M9

4964631	4973706	4963421	4965236	4974311
4964026	4967656	4970681	4966446	4972496
4975521	4967051	4968261	4969471	4961001
4974916	4970076	4965841	4968866	4961606
4962211	4962816	4973101	4971286	4971891

L21-M10

4979756	4988831	4978546	4980361	4989436
4979151	4982781	4985806	4981571	4987621
4990646	4982176	4983386	4984596	4976126
4990041	4985201	4980966	4983991	4976731
4977336	4977941	4988226	4986411	4987016

L21-M11

4994881	5003956	4993671	4995486	5004561
4994276	4997906	5000931	4996696	5002746
5005771	4997301	4998511	4999721	4991251
5005166	5000326	4996091	4999116	4991856
4992461	4993066	5003351	5001536	5002141

L21-M12

5010006	5019081	5008796	5010611	5019686
5009401	5013031	5016056	5011821	5017871
5020896	5012426	5013636	5014846	5006376
5020291	5015451	5011216	5014241	5006981
5007586	5008191	5018476	5016661	5017266

L21-M13

5025131	5034206	5023921	5025736	5034811
5024526	5028156	5031181	5026946	5032996
5036021	5027551	5028761	5029971	5021501
5035416	5030576	5026341	5029366	5022106
5022711	5023316	5033601	5031786	5032391

L21-M14

5040256	5049331	5039046	5040861	5049936
5039651	5043281	5046306	5042071	5048121
5051146	5042676	5043886	5045096	5036626
5050541	5045701	5041466	5044491	5037231
5037836	5038441	5048726	5046911	5047516

L21-M15

5055381	5064456	5054171	5055986	5065061
5054776	5058406	5061431	5057196	5063246
5066271	5057801	5059011	5060221	5051751
5065666	5060826	5056591	5059616	5052356
5052961	5053566	5063851	5062036	5062641

L21-M16

5070506	5079581	5069296	5071111	5080186
5069901	5073531	5076556	5072321	5078371
5081396	5072926	5074136	5075346	5066876
5080791	5075951	5071716	5074741	5067481
5068086	5068691	5078976	5077161	5077766

L22-M1

5085631	5094706	5084421	5086236	5095311
5085026	5088656	5091681	5087446	5093496
5096521	5088051	5089261	5090471	5082001
5095916	5091076	5086841	5089866	5082606
5083211	5083816	5094101	5092286	5092891

L22-M2

5100756	5109831	5099546	5101361	5110436
5100151	5103781	5106806	5102571	5108621
5111646	5103176	5104386	5105596	5097126
5111041	5106201	5101966	5104991	5097731
5098336	5098941	5109226	5107411	5108016

L22-M3

5115881	5124956	5114671	5116486	5125561
5115276	5118906	5121931	5117696	5123746
5126771	5118301	5119511	5120721	5112251
5126166	5121326	5117091	5120116	5112856
5113461	5114066	5124351	5122536	5123141

L22-M4

5131006	5140081	5129796	5131611	5140686
5130401	5134031	5137056	5132821	5138871
5141896	5133426	5134636	5135846	5127376
5141291	5136451	5132216	5135241	5127981
5128586	5129191	5139476	5137661	5138266

L22-M5

5146131	5155206	5144921	5146736	5155811
5145526	5149156	5152181	5147946	5153996
5157021	5148551	5149761	5150971	5142501
5156416	5151576	5147341	5150366	5143106
5143711	5144316	5154601	5152786	5153391

L22-M6

5161256	5170331	5160046	5161861	5170936
5160651	5164281	5167306	5163071	5169121
5172146	5163676	5164886	5166096	5157626
5171541	5166701	5162466	5165491	5158231
5158836	5159441	5169726	5167911	5168516

L22-M7

5176381	5185456	5175171	5176986	5186061
5175776	5179406	5182431	5178196	5184246
5187271	5178801	5180011	5181221	5172751
5186666	5181826	5177591	5180616	5173356
5173961	5174566	5184851	5183036	5183641

L22-M16

5312506	5321581	5311296	5313111	5322186
5311901	5315531	5318556	5314321	5320371
5323396	5314926	5316136	5317346	5308876
5322791	5317951	5313716	5316741	5309481
5310086	5310691	5320976	5319161	5319766

L22-M8

5191506	5200581	5190296	5192111	5201186
5190901	5194531	5197556	5193321	5199371
5202396	5193926	5195136	5196346	5187876
5201791	5196951	5192716	5195741	5188481
5189086	5189691	5199976	5198161	5198766

L23-M1

5327631	5336706	5326421	5328236	5337311
5327026	5330656	5333681	5329446	5335496
5338521	5330051	5331261	5332471	5324001
5337916	5333076	5328841	5331866	5324606
5325211	5325816	5336101	5334286	5334891

L22-M9

5206631	5215706	5205421	5207236	5216311
5206026	5209656	5212681	5208446	5214496
5217521	5209051	5210261	5211471	5203001
5216916	5212076	5207841	5210866	5203606
5204211	5204816	5215101	5213286	5213891

L23-M2

5342756	5351831	5341546	5343361	5352436
5342151	5345781	5348806	5344571	5350621
5353646	5345176	5346386	5347596	5339126
5353041	5348201	5343966	5346991	5339731
5340336	5340941	5351226	5349411	5350016

L22-M10

5221756	5230831	5220546	5222361	5231436
5221151	5224781	5227806	5223571	5229621
5232646	5224176	5225386	5226596	5218126
5232041	5227201	5222966	5225991	5218731
5219336	5219941	5230226	5228411	5229016

L23-M3

5357881	5366956	5356671	5358486	5367561
5357276	5360906	5363931	5359696	5365746
5368771	5360301	5361511	5362721	5354251
5368166	5363326	5359091	5362116	5354856
5355461	5356066	5366351	5364536	5365141

L22-M11

5236881	5245956	5235671	5237486	5246561
5236276	5239906	5242931	5238696	5244746
5247771	5239301	5240511	5241721	5233251
5247166	5242326	5238091	5241116	5233856
5234461	5235066	5245351	5243536	5244141

L23-M4

5373006	5382081	5371796	5373611	5382686
5372401	5376031	5379056	5374821	5380871
5383896	5375426	5376636	5377846	5369376
5383291	5378451	5374216	5377241	5369981
5370586	5371191	5381476	5379661	5380266

L22-M12

5252006	5261081	5250796	5252611	5261686
5251401	5255031	5258056	5253821	5259871
5262896	5254426	5255636	5256846	5248376
5262291	5257451	5253216	5256241	5248981
5249586	5250191	5260476	5258661	5259266

L23-M5

5388131	5397206	5386921	5388736	5397811
5387526	5391156	5394181	5389946	5395996
5399021	5390551	5391761	5392971	5384501
5398416	5393576	5389341	5392366	5385106
5385711	5386316	5396601	5394786	5395391

L22-M13

5267131	5276206	5265921	5267736	5276811
5266526	5270156	5273181	5268946	5274996
5278021	5269551	5270761	5271971	5263501
5277416	5272576	5268341	5271366	5264106
5264711	5265316	5275601	5273786	5274391

L23-M6

5403256	5412331	5402046	5403861	5412936
5402651	5406281	5409306	5405071	5411121
5414146	5405676	5406886	5408096	5399626
5413541	5408701	5404466	5407491	5400231
5400836	5401441	5411726	5409911	5410516

L22-M14

5282256	5291331	5281046	5282861	5291936
5281651	5285281	5288306	5284071	5290121
5293146	5284676	5285886	5287096	5278626
5292541	5287701	5283466	5286491	5279231
5279836	5280441	5290726	5288911	5289516

L23-M7

5418381	5427456	5417171	5418986	5428061
5417776	5421406	5424431	5420196	5426246
5429271	5420801	5422011	5423221	5414751
5428666	5423826	5419591	5422616	5415356
5415961	5416566	5426851	5425036	5425641

L22-M15

5297381	5306456	5296171	5297986	5307061
5296776	5300406	5303431	5299196	5305246
5308271	5299801	5301011	5302221	5293751
5307666	5302826	5298591	5301616	5294356
5294961	5295566	5305851	5304036	5304641

L23-M8

5433506	5442581	5432296	5434111	5443186
5432901	5436531	5439556	5435321	5441371
5444396	5435926	5437136	5438346	5429876
5443791	5438951	5434716	5437741	5430481
5431086	5431691	5441976	5440161	5440766

L23-M9

5448631	5457706	5447421	5449236	5458311
5448026	5451656	5454681	5450446	5456496
5459521	5451051	5452261	5453471	5445001
5458916	5454076	5449841	5452866	5445606
5446211	5446816	5457101	5455286	5455891

L23-M10

5463756	5472831	5462546	5464361	5473436
5463151	5466781	5469806	5465571	5471621
5474646	5466176	5467386	5468596	5460126
5474041	5469201	5464966	5467991	5460731
5461336	5461941	5472226	5470411	5471016

L23-M11

5478881	5487956	5477671	5479486	5488561
5478276	5481906	5484931	5480696	5486746
5489771	5481301	5482511	5483721	5475251
5489166	5484326	5480091	5483116	5475856
5476461	5477066	5487351	5485536	5486141

L23-M12

5494006	5503081	5492796	5494611	5503686
5493401	5497031	5500056	5495821	5501871
5504896	5496426	5497636	5498846	5490376
5504291	5499451	5495216	5498241	5490981
5491586	5492191	5502476	5500661	5501266

L23-M13

5509131	5518206	5507921	5509736	5518811
5508526	5512156	5515181	5510946	5516996
5520021	5511551	5512761	5513971	5505501
5519416	5514576	5510341	5513366	5506106
5506711	5507316	5517601	5515786	5516391

L23-M14

5524256	5533331	5523046	5524861	5533936
5523651	5527281	5530306	5526071	5532121
5535146	5526676	5527886	5529096	5520626
5534541	5529701	5525466	5528491	5521231
5521836	5522441	5532726	5530911	5531516

L23-M15

5539381	5548456	5538171	5539986	5549061
5538776	5542406	5545431	5541196	5547246
5550271	5541801	5543011	5544221	5535751
5549666	5544826	5540591	5543616	5536356
5536961	5537566	5547851	5546036	5546641

L23-M16

5554506	5563581	5553296	5555111	5564186
5553901	5557531	5560556	5556321	5562371
5565396	5556926	5558136	5559346	5550876
5564791	5559951	5555716	5558741	5551481
5552086	5552691	5562976	5561161	5561766

L24-M1

5569631	5578706	5568421	5570236	5579311
5569026	5572656	5575681	5571446	5577496
5580521	5572051	5573261	5574471	5566001
5579916	5575076	5570841	5573866	5566606
5567211	5567816	5578101	5576286	5576891

L24-M2

5584756	5593831	5583546	5585361	5594436
5584151	5587781	5590806	5586571	5592621
5595646	5587176	5588386	5589596	5581126
5595041	5590201	5585966	5588991	5581731
5582336	5582941	5593226	5591411	5592016

L24-M3

5599881	5608956	5598671	5600486	5609561
5599276	5602906	5605931	5601696	5607746
5610771	5602301	5603511	5604721	5596251
5610166	5605326	5601091	5604116	5596856
5597461	5598066	5608351	5606536	5607141

L24-M4

5615006	5624081	5613796	5615611	5624686
5614401	5618031	5621056	5616821	5622871
5625896	5617426	5618636	5619846	5611376
5625291	5620451	5616216	5619241	5611981
5612586	5613191	5623476	5621661	5622266

L24-M5

5630131	5639206	5628921	5630736	5639811
5629526	5633156	5636181	5631946	5637996
5641021	5632551	5633761	5634971	5626501
5640416	5635576	5631341	5634366	5627106
5627711	5628316	5638601	5636786	5637391

L24-M6

5645256	5654331	5644046	5645861	5654936
5644651	5648281	5651306	5647071	5653121
5656146	5647676	5648886	5650096	5641626
5655541	5650701	5646466	5649491	5642231
5642836	5643441	5653726	5651911	5652516

L24-M7

5660381	5669456	5659171	5660986	5670061
5659776	5663406	5666431	5662196	5668246
5671271	5662801	5664011	5665221	5656751
5670666	5665826	5661591	5664616	5657356
5657961	5658566	5668851	5667036	5667641

L24-M8

5675506	5684581	5674296	5676111	5685186
5674901	5678531	5681556	5677321	5683371
5686396	5677926	5679136	5680346	5671876
5685791	5680951	5676716	5679741	5672481
5673086	5673691	5683976	5682161	5682766

L24-M9

5690631	5699706	5689421	5691236	5700311
5690026	5693656	5696681	5692446	5698496
5701521	5693051	5694261	5695471	5687001
5700916	5696076	5691841	5694866	5687606
5688211	5688816	5699101	5697286	5697891

L24-M10

5705756	5714831	5704546	5706361	5715436
5705151	5708781	5711806	5707571	5713621
5716646	5708176	5709386	5710596	5702126
5716041	5711201	5706966	5709991	5702731
5703336	5703941	5714226	5712411	5713016

L24-M11

5720881	5729956	5719671	5721486	5730561
5720276	5723906	5726931	5722696	5728746
5731771	5723301	5724511	5725721	5717251
5731166	5726326	5722091	5725116	5717856
5718461	5719066	5729351	5727536	5728141

L24-M12

5736006	5745081	5734796	5736611	5745686
5735401	5739031	5742056	5737821	5743871
5746896	5738426	5739636	5740846	5732376
5746291	5741451	5737216	5740241	5732981
5733586	5734191	5744476	5742661	5743266

L24-M13

5751131	5760206	5749921	5751736	5760811
5750526	5754156	5757181	5752946	5758996
5762021	5753551	5754761	5755971	5747501
5761416	5756576	5752341	5755366	5748106
5748711	5749316	5759601	5757786	5758391

L24-M14

5766256	5775331	5765046	5766861	5775936
5765651	5769281	5772306	5768071	5774121
5777146	5768676	5769886	5771096	5762626
5776541	5771701	5767466	5770491	5763231
5763836	5764441	5774726	5772911	5773516

L24-M15

5781381	5790456	5780171	5781986	5791061
5780776	5784406	5787431	5783196	5789246
5792271	5783801	5785011	5786221	5777751
5791666	5786826	5782591	5785616	5778356
5778961	5779566	5789851	5788036	5788641

L24-M16

5796506	5805581	5795296	5797111	5806186
5795901	5799531	5802556	5798321	5804371
5807396	5798926	5800136	5801346	5792876
5806791	5801951	5797716	5800741	5793481
5794086	5794691	5804976	5803161	5803766

L25-M1

5811631	5820706	5810421	5812236	5821311
5811026	5814656	5817681	5813446	5819496
5822521	5814051	5815261	5816471	5808001
5821916	5817076	5812841	5815866	5808606
5809211	5809816	5820101	5818286	5818891

L25-M2

5826756	5835831	5825546	5827361	5836436
5826151	5829781	5832806	5828571	5834621
5837646	5829176	5830386	5831596	5823126
5837041	5832201	5827966	5830991	5823731
5824336	5824941	5835226	5833411	5834016

L25-M3

5841881	5850956	5840671	5842486	5851561
5841276	5844906	5847931	5843696	5849746
5852771	5844301	5845511	5846721	5838251
5852166	5847326	5843091	5846116	5838856
5839461	5840066	5850351	5848536	5849141

L25-M4

5857006	5866081	5855796	5857611	5866686
5856401	5860031	5863056	5858821	5864871
5867896	5859426	5860636	5861846	5853376
5867291	5862451	5858216	5861241	5853981
5854586	5855191	5865476	5863661	5864266

L25-M5

5872131	5881206	5870921	5872736	5881811
5871526	5875156	5878181	5873946	5879996
5883021	5874551	5875761	5876971	5868501
5882416	5877576	5873341	5876366	5869106
5869711	5870316	5880601	5878786	5879391

L25-M6

5887256	5896331	5886046	5887861	5896936
5886651	5890281	5893306	5889071	5895121
5898146	5889676	5890886	5892096	5883626
5897541	5892701	5888466	5891491	5884231
5884836	5885441	5895726	5893911	5894516

L25-M7

5902381	5911456	5901171	5902986	5912061
5901776	5905406	5908431	5904196	5910246
5913271	5904801	5906011	5907221	5898751
5912666	5907826	5903591	5906616	5899356
5899961	5900566	5910851	5909036	5909641

L25-M8

5917506	5926581	5916296	5918111	5927186
5916901	5920531	5923556	5919321	5925371
5928396	5919926	5921136	5922346	5913876
5927791	5922951	5918716	5921741	5914481
5915086	5915691	5925976	5924161	5924766

L25-M9

5932631	5941706	5931421	5933236	5942311
5932026	5935656	5938681	5934446	5940496
5943521	5935051	5936261	5937471	5929001
5942916	5938076	5933841	5936866	5929606
5930211	5930816	5941101	5939286	5939891

L25-M10

5947756	5956831	5946546	5948361	5957436
5947151	5950781	5953806	5949571	5955621
5958646	5950176	5951386	5952596	5944126
5958041	5953201	5948966	5951991	5944731
5945336	5945941	5956226	5954411	5955016

L25-M11

5962881	5971956	5961671	5963486	5972561
5962276	5965906	5968931	5964696	5970746
5973771	5965301	5966511	5967721	5959251
5973166	5968326	5964091	5967116	5959856
5960461	5961066	5971351	5969536	5970141

L25-M12

5978006	5987081	5976796	5978611	5987686
5977401	5981031	5984056	5979821	5985871
5988896	5980426	5981636	5982846	5974376
5988291	5983451	5979216	5982241	5974981
5975586	5976191	5986476	5984661	5985266

L25-M13

5993131	6002206	5991921	5993736	6002811
5992526	5996156	5999181	5994946	6000996
6004021	5995551	5996761	5997971	5989501
6003416	5998576	5994341	5997366	5990106
5990711	5991316	6001601	5999786	6000391

L25-M14

6008256	6017331	6007046	6008861	6017936
6007651	6011281	6014306	6010071	6016121
6019146	6010676	6011886	6013096	6004626
6018541	6013701	6009466	6012491	6005231
6005836	6006441	6016726	6014911	6015516

L25-M15

6023381	6032456	6022171	6023986	6033061
6022776	6026406	6029431	6025196	6031246
6034271	6025801	6027011	6028221	6019751
6033666	6028826	6024591	6027616	6020356
6020961	6021566	6031851	6030036	6030641

L25-M16

6038506	6047581	6037296	6039111	6048186
6037901	6041531	6044556	6040321	6046371
6049396	6040926	6042136	6043346	6034876
6048791	6043951	6039716	6042741	6035481
6036086	6036691	6046976	6045161	6045766

YESOD

L1-M1

2689	9409	1793	3137	9857
2241	4929	7169	4033	8513
10753	4481	5377	6273	1
10305	6721	3585	5825	449
897	1345	8961	7617	8065

L1-M2

13889	20609	12993	14337	21057
13441	16129	18369	15233	19713
21953	15681	16577	17473	11201
21505	17921	14785	17025	11649
12097	12545	20161	18817	19265

L1-M3

25089	31809	24193	25537	32257
24641	27329	29569	26433	30913
33153	26881	27777	28673	22401
32705	29121	25985	28225	22849
23297	23745	31361	30017	30465

L1-M4

36289	43009	35393	36737	43457
35841	38529	40769	37633	42113
44353	38081	38977	39873	33601
43905	40321	37185	39425	34049
34497	34945	42561	41217	41665

L1-M5

47489	54209	46593	47937	54657
47041	49729	51969	48833	53313
55553	49281	50177	51073	44801
55105	51521	48385	50625	45249
45697	46145	53761	52417	52865

L1-M6

58689	65409	57793	59137	65857
58241	60929	63169	60033	64513
66753	60481	61377	62273	56001
66305	62721	59585	61825	56449
56897	57345	64961	63617	64065

L1-M7

69889	76609	68993	70337	77057
69441	72129	74369	71233	75713
77953	71681	72577	73473	67201
77505	73921	70785	73025	67649
68097	68545	76161	74817	75265

L1-M8

81089	87809	80193	81537	88257
80641	83329	85569	82433	86913
89153	82881	83777	84673	78401
88705	85121	81985	84225	78849
79297	79745	87361	86017	86465

L1-M9

92289	99009	91393	92737	99457
91841	94529	96769	93633	98113
100353	94081	94977	95873	89601
99905	96321	93185	95425	90049
90497	90945	98561	97217	97665

L1-M10

103489	110209	102593	103937	110657
103041	105729	107969	104833	109313
111553	105281	106177	107073	100801
111105	107521	104385	106625	101249
101697	102145	109761	108417	108865

L1-M11

114689	121409	113793	115137	121857
114241	116929	119169	116033	120513
122753	116481	117377	118273	112001
122305	118721	115585	117825	112449
112897	113345	120961	119617	120065

L1-M12

125889	132609	124993	126337	133057
125441	128129	130369	127233	131713
133953	127681	128577	129473	123201
133505	129921	126785	129025	123649
124097	124545	132161	130817	131265

L1-M13

137089	143809	136193	137537	144257
136641	139329	141569	138433	142913
145153	138881	139777	140673	134401
144705	141121	137985	140225	134849
135297	135745	143361	142017	142465

L1-M14

148289	155009	147393	148737	155457
147841	150529	152769	149633	154113
156353	150081	150977	151873	145601
155905	152321	149185	151425	146049
146497	146945	154561	153217	153665

L1-M15

159489	166209	158593	159937	166657
159041	161729	163969	160833	165313
167553	161281	162177	163073	156801
167105	163521	160385	162625	157249
157697	158145	165761	164417	164865

L1-M16

170689	177409	169793	171137	177857
170241	172929	175169	172033	176513
178753	172481	173377	174273	168001
178305	174721	171585	173825	168449
168897	169345	176961	175617	176065

L2-M1

181889	188609	180993	182337	189057
181441	184129	186369	183233	187713
189953	183681	184577	185473	179201
189505	185921	182785	185025	179649
180097	180545	188161	186817	187265

L2-M2

193089	199809	192193	193537	200257
192641	195329	197569	194433	198913
201153	194881	195777	196673	190401
200705	197121	193985	196225	190849
191297	191745	199361	198017	198465

L2-M3

204289	211009	203393	204737	211457
203841	206529	208769	205633	210113
212353	206081	206977	207873	201601
211905	208321	205185	207425	202049
202497	202945	210561	209217	209665

L2-M4

215489	222209	214593	215937	222657
215041	217729	219969	216833	221313
223553	217281	218177	219073	212801
223105	219521	216385	218625	213249
213697	214145	221761	220417	220865

L2-M5

226689	233409	225793	227137	233857
226241	228929	231169	228033	232513
234753	228481	229377	230273	224001
234305	230721	227585	229825	224449
224897	225345	232961	231617	232065

L2-M6

237889	244609	236993	238337	245057
237441	240129	242369	239233	243713
245953	239681	240577	241473	235201
245505	241921	238785	241025	235649
236097	236545	244161	242817	243265

L2-M7

249089	255809	248193	249537	256257
248641	251329	253569	250433	254913
257153	250881	251777	252673	246401
256705	253121	249985	252225	246849
247297	247745	255361	254017	254465

L2-M8

260289	267009	259393	260737	267457
259841	262529	264769	261633	266113
268353	262081	262977	263873	257601
267905	264321	261185	263425	258049
258497	258945	266561	265217	265665

L2-M9

271489	278209	270593	271937	278657
271041	273729	275969	272833	277313
279553	273281	274177	275073	268801
279105	275521	272385	274625	269249
269697	270145	277761	276417	276865

L2-M10

282689	289409	281793	283137	289857
282241	284929	287169	284033	288513
290753	284481	285377	286273	280001
290305	286721	283585	285825	280449
280897	281345	288961	287617	288065

L2-M11

293889	300609	292993	294337	301057
293441	296129	298369	295233	299713
301953	295681	296577	297473	291201
301505	297921	294785	297025	291649
292097	292545	300161	298817	299265

L2-M12

305089	311809	304193	305537	312257
304641	307329	309569	306433	310913
313153	306881	307777	308673	302401
312705	309121	305985	308225	302849
303297	303745	311361	310017	310465

L2-M13

316289	323009	315393	316737	323457
315841	318529	320769	317633	322113
324353	318081	318977	319873	313601
323905	320321	317185	319425	314049
314497	314945	322561	321217	321665

L2-M14

327489	334209	326593	327937	334657
327041	329729	331969	328833	333313
335553	329281	330177	331073	324801
335105	331521	328385	330625	325249
325697	326145	333761	332417	332865

L2-M15

338689	345409	337793	339137	345857
338241	340929	343169	340033	344513
346753	340481	341377	342273	336001
346305	342721	339585	341825	336449
336897	337345	344961	343617	344065

L2-M16

349889	356609	348993	350337	357057
349441	352129	354369	351233	355713
357953	351681	352577	353473	347201
357505	353921	350785	353025	347649
348097	348545	356161	354817	355265

L3-M1

361089	367809	360193	361537	368257
360641	363329	365569	362433	366913
369153	362881	363777	364673	358401
368705	365121	361985	364225	358849
359297	359745	367361	366017	366465

L3-M2

372289	379009	371393	372737	379457
371841	374529	376769	373633	378113
380353	374081	374977	375873	369601
379905	376321	373185	375425	370049
370497	370945	378561	377217	377665

L3-M3

383489	390209	382593	383937	390657
383041	385729	387969	384833	389313
391553	385281	386177	387073	380801
391105	387521	384385	386625	381249
381697	382145	389761	388417	388865

L3-M4

394689	401409	393793	395137	401857
394241	396929	399169	396033	400513
402753	396481	397377	398273	392001
402305	398721	395585	397825	392449
392897	393345	400961	399617	400065

L3-M5

405889	412609	404993	406337	413057
405441	408129	410369	407233	411713
413953	407681	408577	409473	403201
413505	409921	406785	409025	403649
404097	404545	412161	410817	411265

L3-M14

506689	513409	505793	507137	513857
506241	508929	511169	508033	512513
514753	508481	509377	510273	504001
514305	510721	507585	509825	504449
504897	505345	512961	511617	512065

L3-M6

417089	423809	416193	417537	424257
416641	419329	421569	418433	422913
425153	418881	419777	420673	414401
424705	421121	417985	420225	414849
415297	415745	423361	422017	422465

L3-M15

517889	524609	516993	518337	525057
517441	520129	522369	519233	523713
525953	519681	520577	521473	515201
525505	521921	518785	521025	515649
516097	516545	524161	522817	523265

L3-M7

428289	435009	427393	428737	435457
427841	430529	432769	429633	434113
436353	430081	430977	431873	425601
435905	432321	429185	431425	426049
426497	426945	434561	433217	433665

L3-M16

529089	535809	528193	529537	536257
528641	531329	533569	530433	534913
537153	530881	531777	532673	526401
536705	533121	529985	532225	526849
527297	527745	535361	534017	534465

L3-M8

439489	446209	438593	439937	446657
439041	441729	443969	440833	445313
447553	441281	442177	443073	436801
447105	443521	440385	442625	437249
437697	438145	445761	444417	444865

L4-M1

540289	547009	539393	540737	547457
539841	542529	544769	541633	546113
548353	542081	542977	543873	537601
547905	544321	541185	543425	538049
538497	538945	546561	545217	545665

L3-M9

450689	457409	449793	451137	457857
450241	452929	455169	452033	456513
458753	452481	453377	454273	448001
458305	454721	451585	453825	448449
448897	449345	456961	455617	456065

L4-M2

551489	558209	550593	551937	558657
551041	553729	555969	552833	557313
559553	553281	554177	555073	548801
559105	555521	552385	554625	549249
549697	550145	557761	556417	556865

L3-M10

461889	468609	460993	462337	469057
461441	464129	466369	463233	467713
469953	463681	464577	465473	459201
469505	465921	462785	465025	459649
460097	460545	468161	466817	467265

L4-M3

562689	569409	561793	563137	569857
562241	564929	567169	564033	568513
570753	564481	565377	566273	560001
570305	566721	563585	565825	560449
560897	561345	568961	567617	568065

L3-M11

473089	479809	472193	473537	480257
472641	475329	477569	474433	478913
481153	474881	475777	476673	470401
480705	477121	473985	476225	470849
471297	471745	479361	478017	478465

L4-M4

573889	580609	572993	574337	581057
573441	576129	578369	575233	579713
581953	575681	576577	577473	571201
581505	577921	574785	577025	571649
572097	572545	580161	578817	579265

L3-M12

484289	491009	483393	484737	491457
483841	486529	488769	485633	490113
492353	486081	486977	487873	481601
491905	488321	485185	487425	482049
482497	482945	490561	489217	489665

L4-M5

585089	591809	584193	585537	592257
584641	587329	589569	586433	590913
593153	586881	587777	588673	582401
592705	589121	585985	588225	582849
583297	583745	591361	590017	590465

L3-M13

495489	502209	494593	495937	502657
495041	497729	499969	496833	501313
503553	497281	498177	499073	492801
503105	499521	496385	498625	493249
493697	494145	501761	500417	500865

L4-M6

596289	603009	595393	596737	603457
595841	598529	600769	597633	602113
604353	598081	598977	599873	593601
603905	600321	597185	599425	594049
594497	594945	602561	601217	601665

L4-M7

607489	614209	606593	607937	614657
607041	609729	611969	608833	613313
615553	609281	610177	611073	604801
615105	611521	608385	610625	605249
605697	606145	613761	612417	612865

L4-M8

618689	625409	617793	619137	625857
618241	620929	623169	620033	624513
626753	620481	621377	622273	616001
626305	622721	619585	621825	616449
616897	617345	624961	623617	624065

L4-M9

629889	636609	628993	630337	637057
629441	632129	634369	631233	635713
637953	631681	632577	633473	627201
637505	633921	630785	633025	627649
628097	628545	636161	634817	635265

L4-M10

641089	647809	640193	641537	648257
640641	643329	645569	642433	646913
649153	642881	643777	644673	638401
648705	645121	641985	644225	638849
639297	639745	647361	646017	646465

L4-M11

652289	659009	651393	652737	659457
651841	654529	656769	653633	658113
660353	654081	654977	655873	649601
659905	656321	653185	655425	650049
650497	650945	658561	657217	657665

L4-M12

663489	670209	662593	663937	670657
663041	665729	667969	664833	669313
671553	665281	666177	667073	660801
671105	667521	664385	666625	661249
661697	662145	669761	668417	668865

L4-M13

674689	681409	673793	675137	681857
674241	676929	679169	676033	680513
682753	676481	677377	678273	672001
682305	678721	675585	677825	672449
672897	673345	680961	679617	680065

L4-M14

685889	692609	684993	686337	693057
685441	688129	690369	687233	691713
693953	687681	688577	689473	683201
693505	689921	686785	689025	683649
684097	684545	692161	690817	691265

L4-M15

697089	703809	696193	697537	704257
696641	699329	701569	698433	702913
705153	698881	699777	700673	694401
704705	701121	697985	700225	694849
695297	695745	703361	702017	702465

L4-M16

708289	715009	707393	708737	715457
707841	710529	712769	709633	714113
716353	710081	710977	711873	705601
715905	712321	709185	711425	706049
706497	706945	714561	713217	713665

L5-M1

719489	726209	718593	719937	726657
719041	721729	723969	720833	725313
727553	721281	722177	723073	716801
727105	723521	720385	722625	717249
717697	718145	725761	724417	724865

L5-M2

730689	737409	729793	731137	737857
730241	732929	735169	732033	736513
738753	732481	733377	734273	728001
738305	734721	731585	733825	728449
728897	729345	736961	735617	736065

L5-M3

741889	748609	740993	742337	749057
741441	744129	746369	743233	747713
749953	743681	744577	745473	739201
749505	745921	742785	745025	739649
740097	740545	748161	746817	747265

L5-M4

753089	759809	752193	753537	760257
752641	755329	757569	754433	758913
761153	754881	755777	756673	750401
760705	757121	753985	756225	750849
751297	751745	759361	758017	758465

L5-M5

764289	771009	763393	764737	771457
763841	766529	768769	765633	770113
772353	766081	766977	767873	761601
771905	768321	765185	767425	762049
762497	762945	770561	769217	769665

L5-M6

775489	782209	774593	775937	782657
775041	777729	779969	776833	781313
783553	777281	778177	779073	772801
783105	779521	776385	778625	773249
773697	774145	781761	780417	780865

L5-M7

786689	793409	785793	787137	793857
786241	788929	791169	788033	792513
794753	788481	789377	790273	784001
794305	790721	787585	789825	784449
784897	785345	792961	791617	792065

L5-M8

797889	804609	796993	798337	805057
797441	800129	802369	799233	803713
805953	799681	800577	801473	795201
805505	801921	798785	801025	795649
796097	796545	804161	802817	803265

L5-M9

809089	815809	808193	809537	816257
808641	811329	813569	810433	814913
817153	810881	811777	812673	806401
816705	813121	809985	812225	806849
807297	807745	815361	814017	814465

L5-M10

820289	827009	819393	820737	827457
819841	822529	824769	821633	826113
828353	822081	822977	823873	817601
827905	824321	821185	823425	818049
818497	818945	826561	825217	825665

L5-M11

831489	838209	830593	831937	838657
831041	833729	835969	832833	837313
839553	833281	834177	835073	828801
839105	835521	832385	834625	829249
829697	830145	837761	836417	836865

L5-M12

842689	849409	841793	843137	849857
842241	844929	847169	844033	848513
850753	844481	845377	846273	840001
850305	846721	843585	845825	840449
840897	841345	848961	847617	848065

L5-M13

853889	860609	852993	854337	861057
853441	856129	858369	855233	859713
861953	855681	856577	857473	851201
861505	857921	854785	857025	851649
852097	852545	860161	858817	859265

L5-M14

865089	871809	864193	865537	872257
864641	867329	869569	866433	870913
873153	866881	867777	868673	862401
872705	869121	865985	868225	862849
863297	863745	871361	870017	870465

L5-M15

876289	883009	875393	876737	883457
875841	878529	880769	877633	882113
884353	878081	878977	879873	873601
883905	880321	877185	879425	874049
874497	874945	882561	881217	881665

L5-M16

887489	894209	886593	887937	894657
887041	889729	891969	888833	893313
895553	889281	890177	891073	884801
895105	891521	888385	890625	885249
885697	886145	893761	892417	892865

L6-M1

898689	905409	897793	899137	905857
898241	900929	903169	900033	904513
906753	900481	901377	902273	896001
906305	902721	899585	901825	896449
896897	897345	904961	903617	904065

L6-M2

909889	916609	908993	910337	917057
909441	912129	914369	911233	915713
917953	911681	912577	913473	907201
917505	913921	910785	913025	907649
908097	908545	916161	914817	915265

L6-M3

921089	927809	920193	921537	928257
920641	923329	925569	922433	926913
929153	922881	923777	924673	918401
928705	925121	921985	924225	918849
919297	919745	927361	926017	926465

L6-M4

932289	939009	931393	932737	939457
931841	934529	936769	933633	938113
940353	934081	934977	935873	929601
939905	936321	933185	935425	930049
930497	930945	938561	937217	937665

L6-M5

943489	950209	942593	943937	950657
943041	945729	947969	944833	949313
951553	945281	946177	947073	940801
951105	947521	944385	946625	941249
941697	942145	949761	948417	948865

L6-M6

954689	961409	953793	955137	961857
954241	956929	959169	956033	960513
962753	956481	957377	958273	952001
962305	958721	955585	957825	952449
952897	953345	960961	959617	960065

L6-M7

965889	972609	964993	966337	973057
965441	968129	970369	967233	971713
973953	967681	968577	969473	963201
973505	969921	966785	969025	963649
964097	964545	972161	970817	971265

L6-M8

977089	983809	976193	977537	984257
976641	979329	981569	978433	982913
985153	978881	979777	980673	974401
984705	981121	977985	980225	974849
975297	975745	983361	982017	982465

L6-M9

988289	995009	987393	988737	995457
987841	990529	992769	989633	994113
996353	990081	990977	991873	985601
995905	992321	989185	991425	986049
986497	986945	994561	993217	993665

L6-M10

999489	1006209	998593	999937	1006657
999041	1001729	1003969	1000833	1005313
1007553	1001281	1002177	1003073	996801
1007105	1003521	1000385	1002625	997249
997697	998145	1005761	1004417	1004865

L6-M11

1010689	1017409	1009793	1011137	1017857
1010241	1012929	1015169	1012033	1016513
1018753	1012481	1013377	1014273	1008001
1018305	1014721	1011585	1013825	1008449
1008897	1009345	1016961	1015617	1016065

L6-M12

1021889	1028609	1020993	1022337	1029057
1021441	1024129	1026369	1023233	1027713
1029953	1023681	1024577	1025473	1019201
1029505	1025921	1022785	1025025	1019649
1020097	1020545	1028161	1026817	1027265

L6-M13

1033089	1039809	1032193	1033537	1040257
1032641	1035329	1037569	1034433	1038913
1041153	1034881	1035777	1036673	1030401
1040705	1037121	1033985	1036225	1030849
1031297	1031745	1039361	1038017	1038465

L6-M14

1044289	1051009	1043393	1044737	1051457
1043841	1046529	1048769	1045633	1050113
1052353	1046081	1046977	1047873	1041601
1051905	1048321	1045185	1047425	1042049
1042497	1042945	1050561	1049217	1049665

L6-M15

1055489	1062209	1054593	1055937	1062657
1055041	1057729	1059969	1056833	1061313
1063553	1057281	1058177	1059073	1052801
1063105	1059521	1056385	1058625	1053249
1053697	1054145	1061761	1060417	1060865

L6-M16

1066689	1073409	1065793	1067137	1073857
1066241	1068929	1071169	1068033	1072513
1074753	1068481	1069377	1070273	1064001
1074305	1070721	1067585	1069825	1064449
1064897	1065345	1072961	1071617	1072065

L7-M1

1077889	1084609	1076993	1078337	1085057
1077441	1080129	1082369	1079233	1083713
1085953	1079681	1080577	1081473	1075201
1085505	1081921	1078785	1081025	1075649
1076097	1076545	1084161	1082817	1083265

L7-M2

1089089	1095809	1088193	1089537	1096257
1088641	1091329	1093569	1090433	1094913
1097153	1090881	1091777	1092673	1086401
1096705	1093121	1089985	1092225	1086849
1087297	1087745	1095361	1094017	1094465

L7-M3

1100289	1107009	1099393	1100737	1107457
1099841	1102529	1104769	1101633	1106113
1108353	1102081	1102977	1103873	1097601
1107905	1104321	1101185	1103425	1098049
1098497	1098945	1106561	1105217	1105665

L7-M4

1111489	1118209	1110593	1111937	1118657
1111041	1113729	1115969	1112833	1117313
1119553	1113281	1114177	1115073	1108801
1119105	1115521	1112385	1114625	1109249
1109697	1110145	1117761	1116417	1116865

L7-M5

1122689	1129409	1121793	1123137	1129857
1122241	1124929	1127169	1124033	1128513
1130753	1124481	1125377	1126273	1120001
1130305	1126721	1123585	1125825	1120449
1120897	1121345	1128961	1127617	1128065

L7-M6

1133889	1140609	1132993	1134337	1141057
1133441	1136129	1138369	1135233	1139713
1141953	1135681	1136577	1137473	1131201
1141505	1137921	1134785	1137025	1131649
1132097	1132545	1140161	1138817	1139265

L7-M7

1145089	1151809	1144193	1145537	1152257
1144641	1147329	1149569	1146433	1150913
1153153	1146881	1147777	1148673	1142401
1152705	1149121	1145985	1148225	1142849
1143297	1143745	1151361	1150017	1150465

L7-M8

1156289	1163009	1155393	1156737	1163457
1155841	1158529	1160769	1157633	1162113
1164353	1158081	1158977	1159873	1153601
1163905	1160321	1157185	1159425	1154049
1154497	1154945	1162561	1161217	1161665

L7-M9

1167489	1174209	1166593	1167937	1174657
1167041	1169729	1171969	1168833	1173313
1175553	1169281	1170177	1171073	1164801
1175105	1171521	1168385	1170625	1165249
1165697	1166145	1173761	1172417	1172865

L7-M10

1178689	1185409	1177793	1179137	1185857
1178241	1180929	1183169	1180033	1184513
1186753	1180481	1181377	1182273	1176001
1186305	1182721	1179585	1181825	1176449
1176897	1177345	1184961	1183617	1184065

L7-M11

1189889	1196609	1188993	1190337	1197057
1189441	1192129	1194369	1191233	1195713
1197953	1191681	1192577	1193473	1187201
1197505	1193921	1190785	1193025	1187649
1188097	1188545	1196161	1194817	1195265

L7-M12

1201089	1207809	1200193	1201537	1208257
1200641	1203329	1205569	1202433	1206913
1209153	1202881	1203777	1204673	1198401
1208705	1205121	1201985	1204225	1198849
1199297	1199745	1207361	1206017	1206465

L7-M13

1212289	1219009	1211393	1212737	1219457
1211841	1214529	1216769	1213633	1218113
1220353	1214081	1214977	1215873	1209601
1219905	1216321	1213185	1215425	1210049
1210497	1210945	1218561	1217217	1217665

L8-M6

1313089	1319809	1312193	1313537	1320257
1312641	1315329	1317569	1314433	1318913
1321153	1314881	1315777	1316673	1310401
1320705	1317121	1313985	1316225	1310849
1311297	1311745	1319361	1318017	1318465

L7-M14

1223489	1230209	1222593	1223937	1230657
1223041	1225729	1227969	1224833	1229313
1231553	1225281	1226177	1227073	1220801
1231105	1227521	1224385	1226625	1221249
1221697	1222145	1229761	1228417	1228865

L8-M7

1324289	1331009	1323393	1324737	1331457
1323841	1326529	1328769	1325633	1330113
1332353	1326081	1326977	1327873	1321601
1331905	1328321	1325185	1327425	1322049
1322497	1322945	1330561	1329217	1329665

L7-M15

1234689	1241409	1233793	1235137	1241857
1234241	1236929	1239169	1236033	1240513
1242753	1236481	1237377	1238273	1232001
1242305	1238721	1235585	1237825	1232449
1232897	1233345	1240961	1239617	1240065

L8-M8

1335489	1342209	1334593	1335937	1342657
1335041	1337729	1339969	1336833	1341313
1343553	1337281	1338177	1339073	1332801
1343105	1339521	1336385	1338625	1333249
1333697	1334145	1341761	1340417	1340865

L7-M16

1245889	1252609	1244993	1246337	1253057
1245441	1248129	1250369	1247233	1251713
1253953	1247681	1248577	1249473	1243201
1253505	1249921	1246785	1249025	1243649
1244097	1244545	1252161	1250817	1251265

L8-M9

1346689	1353409	1345793	1347137	1353857
1346241	1348929	1351169	1348033	1352513
1354753	1348481	1349377	1350273	1344001
1354305	1350721	1347585	1349825	1344449
1344897	1345345	1352961	1351617	1352065

L8M1

1257089	1263809	1256193	1257537	1264257
1256641	1259329	1261569	1258433	1262913
1265153	1258881	1259777	1260673	1254401
1264705	1261121	1257985	1260225	1254849
1255297	1255745	1263361	1262017	1262465

L8-M10

1357889	1364609	1356993	1358337	1365057
1357441	1360129	1362369	1359233	1363713
1365953	1359681	1360577	1361473	1355201
1365505	1361921	1358785	1361025	1355649
1356097	1356545	1364161	1362817	1363265

L8-M2

1268289	1275009	1267393	1268737	1275457
1267841	1270529	1272769	1269633	1274113
1276353	1270081	1270977	1271873	1265601
1275905	1272321	1269185	1271425	1266049
1266497	1266945	1274561	1273217	1273665

L8-M11

1369089	1375809	1368193	1369537	1376257
1368641	1371329	1373569	1370433	1374913
1377153	1370881	1371777	1372673	1366401
1376705	1373121	1369985	1372225	1366849
1367297	1367745	1375361	1374017	1374465

L8-M3

1279489	1286209	1278593	1279937	1286657
1279041	1281729	1283969	1280833	1285313
1287553	1281281	1282177	1283073	1276801
1287105	1283521	1280385	1282625	1277249
1277697	1278145	1285761	1284417	1284865

L8-M12

1380289	1387009	1379393	1380737	1387457
1379841	1382529	1384769	1381633	1386113
1388353	1382081	1382977	1383873	1377601
1387905	1384321	1381185	1383425	1378049
1378497	1378945	1386561	1385217	1385665

L8-M4

1290689	1297409	1289793	1291137	1297857
1290241	1292929	1295169	1292033	1296513
1298753	1292481	1293377	1294273	1288001
1298305	1294721	1291585	1293825	1288449
1288897	1289345	1296961	1295617	1296065

L8-M13

1391489	1398209	1390593	1391937	1398657
1391041	1393729	1395969	1392833	1397313
1399553	1393281	1394177	1395073	1388801
1399105	1395521	1392385	1394625	1389249
1389697	1390145	1397761	1396417	1396865

L8-M5

1301889	1308609	1300993	1302337	1309057
1301441	1304129	1306369	1303233	1307713
1309953	1303681	1304577	1305473	1299201
1309505	1305921	1302785	1305025	1299649
1300097	1300545	1308161	1306817	1307265

L8-M14

1402689	1409409	1401793	1403137	1409857
1402241	1404929	1407169	1404033	1408513
1410753	1404481	1405377	1406273	1400001
1410305	1406721	1403585	1405825	1400449
1400897	1401345	1408961	1407617	1408065

L8-M15

1413889	1420609	1412993	1414337	1421057
1413441	1416129	1418369	1415233	1419713
1421953	1415681	1416577	1417473	1411201
1421505	1417921	1414785	1417025	1411649
1412097	1412545	1420161	1418817	1419265

L8-M16

1425089	1431809	1424193	1425537	1432257
1424641	1427329	1429569	1426433	1430913
1433153	1426881	1427777	1428673	1422401
1432705	1429121	1425985	1428225	1422849
1423297	1423745	1431361	1430017	1430465

L9-M1

1436289	1443009	1435393	1436737	1443457
1435841	1438529	1440769	1437633	1442113
1444353	1438081	1438977	1439873	1433601
1443905	1440321	1437185	1439425	1434049
1434497	1434945	1442561	1441217	1441665

L9-M2

1447489	1454209	1446593	1447937	1454657
1447041	1449729	1451969	1448833	1453313
1455553	1449281	1450177	1451073	1444801
1455105	1451521	1448385	1450625	1445249
1445697	1446145	1453761	1452417	1452865

L9-M3

1458689	1465409	1457793	1459137	1465857
1458241	1460929	1463169	1460033	1464513
1466753	1460481	1461377	1462273	1456001
1466305	1462721	1459585	1461825	1456449
1456897	1457345	1464961	1463617	1464065

L9-M4

1469889	1476609	1468993	1470337	1477057
1469441	1472129	1474369	1471233	1475713
1477953	1471681	1472577	1473473	1467201
1477505	1473921	1470785	1473025	1467649
1468097	1468545	1476161	1474817	1475265

L9-M5

1481089	1487809	1480193	1481537	1488257
1480641	1483329	1485569	1482433	1486913
1489153	1482881	1483777	1484673	1478401
1488705	1485121	1481985	1484225	1478849
1479297	1479745	1487361	1486017	1486465

L9-M6

1492289	1499009	1491393	1492737	1499457
1491841	1494529	1496769	1493633	1498113
1500353	1494081	1494977	1495873	1489601
1499905	1496321	1493185	1495425	1490049
1490497	1490945	1498561	1497217	1497665

L9-M7

1503489	1510209	1502593	1503937	1510657
1503041	1505729	1507969	1504833	1509313
1511553	1505281	1506177	1507073	1500801
1511105	1507521	1504385	1506625	1501249
1501697	1502145	1509761	1508417	1508865

L9-M8

1514689	1521409	1513793	1515137	1521857
1514241	1516929	1519169	1516033	1520513
1522753	1516481	1517377	1518273	1512001
1522305	1518721	1515585	1517825	1512449
1512897	1513345	1520961	1519617	1520065

L9-M9

1525889	1532609	1524993	1526337	1533057
1525441	1528129	1530369	1527233	1531713
1533953	1527681	1528577	1529473	1523201
1533505	1529921	1526785	1529025	1523649
1524097	1524545	1532161	1530817	1531265

L9-M10

1537089	1543809	1536193	1537537	1544257
1536641	1539329	1541569	1538433	1542913
1545153	1538881	1539777	1540673	1534401
1544705	1541121	1537985	1540225	1534849
1535297	1535745	1543361	1542017	1542465

L9-M11

1548289	1555009	1547393	1548737	1555457
1547841	1550529	1552769	1549633	1554113
1556353	1550081	1550977	1551873	1545601
1555905	1552321	1549185	1551425	1546049
1546497	1546945	1554561	1553217	1553665

L9-M12

1559489	1566209	1558593	1559937	1566657
1559041	1561729	1563969	1560833	1565313
1567553	1561281	1562177	1563073	1556801
1567105	1563521	1560385	1562625	1557249
1557697	1558145	1565761	1564417	1564865

L9-M13

1570689	1577409	1569793	1571137	1577857
1570241	1572929	1575169	1572033	1576513
1578753	1572481	1573377	1574273	1568001
1578305	1574721	1571585	1573825	1568449
1568897	1569345	1576961	1575617	1576065

L9-M14

1581889	1588609	1580993	1582337	1589057
1581441	1584129	1586369	1583233	1587713
1589953	1583681	1584577	1585473	1579201
1589505	1585921	1582785	1585025	1579649
1580097	1580545	1588161	1586817	1587265

L9-M15

1593089	1599809	1592193	1593537	1600257
1592641	1595329	1597569	1594433	1598913
1601153	1594881	1595777	1596673	1590401
1600705	1597121	1593985	1596225	1590849
1591297	1591745	1599361	1598017	1598465

L9-M16

1604289	1611009	1603393	1604737	1611457
1603841	1606529	1608769	1605633	1610113
1612353	1606081	1606977	1607873	1601601
1611905	1608321	1605185	1607425	1602049
1602497	1602945	1610561	1609217	1609665

L10-M1

1615489	1622209	1614593	1615937	1622657
1615041	1617729	1619969	1616833	1621313
1623553	1617281	1618177	1619073	1612801
1623105	1619521	1616385	1618625	1613249
1613697	1614145	1621761	1620417	1620865

L10-M10

1716289	1723009	1715393	1716737	1723457
1715841	1718529	1720769	1717633	1722113
1724353	1718081	1718977	1719873	1713601
1723905	1720321	1717185	1719425	1714049
1714497	1714945	1722561	1721217	1721665

L10-M2

1626689	1633409	1625793	1627137	1633857
1626241	1628929	1631169	1628033	1632513
1634753	1628481	1629377	1630273	1624001
1634305	1630721	1627585	1629825	1624449
1624897	1625345	1632961	1631617	1632065

L10-M11

1727489	1734209	1726593	1727937	1734657
1727041	1729729	1731969	1728833	1733313
1735553	1729281	1730177	1731073	1724801
1735105	1731521	1728385	1730625	1725249
1725697	1726145	1733761	1732417	1732865

L10-M3

1637889	1644609	1636993	1638337	1645057
1637441	1640129	1642369	1639233	1643713
1645953	1639681	1640577	1641473	1635201
1645505	1641921	1638785	1641025	1635649
1636097	1636545	1644161	1642817	1643265

L10-M12

1738689	1745409	1737793	1739137	1745857
1738241	1740929	1743169	1740033	1744513
1746753	1740481	1741377	1742273	1736001
1746305	1742721	1739585	1741825	1736449
1736897	1737345	1744961	1743617	1744065

L10-M4

1649089	1655809	1648193	1649537	1656257
1648641	1651329	1653569	1650433	1654913
1657153	1650881	1651777	1652673	1646401
1656705	1653121	1649985	1652225	1646849
1647297	1647745	1655361	1654017	1654465

L10-M13

1749889	1756609	1748993	1750337	1757057
1749441	1752129	1754369	1751233	1755713
1757953	1751681	1752577	1753473	1747201
1757505	1753921	1750785	1753025	1747649
1748097	1748545	1756161	1754817	1755265

L10-M5

1660289	1667009	1659393	1660737	1667457
1659841	1662529	1664769	1661633	1666113
1668353	1662081	1662977	1663873	1657601
1667905	1664321	1661185	1663425	1658049
1658497	1658945	1666561	1665217	1665665

L10-M14

1761089	1767809	1760193	1761537	1768257
1760641	1763329	1765569	1762433	1766913
1769153	1762881	1763777	1764673	1758401
1768705	1765121	1761985	1764225	1758849
1759297	1759745	1767361	1766017	1766465

L10-M6

1671489	1678209	1670593	1671937	1678657
1671041	1673729	1675969	1672833	1677313
1679553	1673281	1674177	1675073	1668801
1679105	1675521	1672385	1674625	1669249
1669697	1670145	1677761	1676417	1676865

L10-M15

1772289	1779009	1771393	1772737	1779457
1771841	1774529	1776769	1773633	1778113
1780353	1774081	1774977	1775873	1769601
1779905	1776321	1773185	1775425	1770049
1770497	1770945	1778561	1777217	1777665

L10-M7

1682689	1689409	1681793	1683137	1689857
1682241	1684929	1687169	1684033	1688513
1690753	1684481	1685377	1686273	1680001
1690305	1686721	1683585	1685825	1680449
1680897	1681345	1688961	1687617	1688065

L10-M16

1783489	1790209	1782593	1783937	1790657
1783041	1785729	1787969	1784833	1789313
1791553	1785281	1786177	1787073	1780801
1791105	1787521	1784385	1786625	1781249
1781697	1782145	1789761	1788417	1788865

L10-M8

1693889	1700609	1692993	1694337	1701057
1693441	1696129	1698369	1695233	1699713
1701953	1695681	1696577	1697473	1691201
1701505	1697921	1694785	1697025	1691649
1692097	1692545	1700161	1698817	1699265

L11-M1

1794689	1801409	1793793	1795137	1801857
1794241	1796929	1799169	1796033	1800513
1802753	1796481	1797377	1798273	1792001
1802305	1798721	1795585	1797825	1792449
1792897	1793345	1800961	1799617	1800065

L10-M9

1705089	1711809	1704193	1705537	1712257
1704641	1707329	1709569	1706433	1710913
1713153	1706881	1707777	1708673	1702401
1712705	1709121	1705985	1708225	1702849
1703297	1703745	1711361	1710017	1710465

L11-M2

1805889	1812609	1804993	1806337	1813057
1805441	1808129	1810369	1807233	1811713
1813953	1807681	1808577	1809473	1803201
1813505	1809921	1806785	1809025	1803649
1804097	1804545	1812161	1810817	1811265

L11-M3

1817089	1823809	1816193	1817537	1824257
1816641	1819329	1821569	1818433	1822913
1825153	1818881	1819777	1820673	1814401
1824705	1821121	1817985	1820225	1814849
1815297	1815745	1823361	1822017	1822465

L11-M12

1917889	1924609	1916993	1918337	1925057
1917441	1920129	1922369	1919233	1923713
1925953	1919681	1920577	1921473	1915201
1925505	1921921	1918785	1921025	1915649
1916097	1916545	1924161	1922817	1923265

L11-M4

1828289	1835009	1827393	1828737	1835457
1827841	1830529	1832769	1829633	1834113
1836353	1830081	1830977	1831873	1825601
1835905	1832321	1829185	1831425	1826049
1826497	1826945	1834561	1833217	1833665

L11-M13

1929089	1935809	1928193	1929537	1936257
1928641	1931329	1933569	1930433	1934913
1937153	1930881	1931777	1932673	1926401
1936705	1933121	1929985	1932225	1926849
1927297	1927745	1935361	1934017	1934465

L11-M5

1839489	1846209	1838593	1839937	1846657
1839041	1841729	1843969	1840833	1845313
1847553	1841281	1842177	1843073	1836801
1847105	1843521	1840385	1842625	1837249
1837697	1838145	1845761	1844417	1844865

L11-M14

1940289	1947009	1939393	1940737	1947457
1939841	1942529	1944769	1941633	1946113
1948353	1942081	1942977	1943873	1937601
1947905	1944321	1941185	1943425	1938049
1938497	1938945	1946561	1945217	1945665

L11-M6

1850689	1857409	1849793	1851137	1857857
1850241	1852929	1855169	1852033	1856513
1858753	1852481	1853377	1854273	1848001
1858305	1854721	1851585	1853825	1848449
1848897	1849345	1856961	1855617	1856065

L11-M15

1951489	1958209	1950593	1951937	1958657
1951041	1953729	1955969	1952833	1957313
1959553	1953281	1954177	1955073	1948801
1959105	1955521	1952385	1954625	1949249
1949697	1950145	1957761	1956417	1956865

L11-M7

1861889	1868609	1860993	1862337	1869057
1861441	1864129	1866369	1863233	1867713
1869953	1863681	1864577	1865473	1859201
1869505	1865921	1862785	1865025	1859649
1860097	1860545	1868161	1866817	1867265

L11-M16

1962689	1969409	1961793	1963137	1969857
1962241	1964929	1967169	1964033	1968513
1970753	1964481	1965377	1966273	1960001
1970305	1966721	1963585	1965825	1960449
1960897	1961345	1968961	1967617	1968065

L11-M8

1873089	1879809	1872193	1873537	1880257
1872641	1875329	1877569	1874433	1878913
1881153	1874881	1875777	1876673	1870401
1880705	1877121	1873985	1876225	1870849
1871297	1871745	1879361	1878017	1878465

L12-M1

1973889	1980609	1972993	1974337	1981057
1973441	1976129	1978369	1975233	1979713
1981953	1975681	1976577	1977473	1971201
1981505	1977921	1974785	1977025	1971649
1972097	1972545	1980161	1978817	1979265

L11-M9

1884289	1891009	1883393	1884737	1891457
1883841	1886529	1888769	1885633	1890113
1892353	1886081	1886977	1887873	1881601
1891905	1888321	1885185	1887425	1882049
1882497	1882945	1890561	1889217	1889665

L12-M2

1985089	1991809	1984193	1985537	1992257
1984641	1987329	1989569	1986433	1990913
1993153	1986881	1987777	1988673	1982401
1992705	1989121	1985985	1988225	1982849
1983297	1983745	1991361	1990017	1990465

L11-M10

1895489	1902209	1894593	1895937	1902657
1895041	1897729	1899969	1896833	1901313
1903553	1897281	1898177	1899073	1892801
1903105	1899521	1896385	1898625	1893249
1893697	1894145	1901761	1900417	1900865

L12-M3

1996289	2003009	1995393	1996737	2003457
1995841	1998529	2000769	1997633	2002113
2004353	1998081	1998977	1999873	1993601
2003905	2000321	1997185	1999425	1994049
1994497	1994945	2002561	2001217	2001665

L11-M11

1906689	1913409	1905793	1907137	1913857
1906241	1908929	1911169	1908033	1912513
1914753	1908481	1909377	1910273	1904001
1914305	1910721	1907585	1909825	1904449
1904897	1905345	1912961	1911617	1912065

L12-M4

2007489	2014209	2006593	2007937	2014657
2007041	2009729	2011969	2008833	2013313
2015553	2009281	2010177	2011073	2004801
2015105	2011521	2008385	2010625	2005249
2005697	2006145	2013761	2012417	2012865

L12-M5

2018689	2025409	2017793	2019137	2025857
2018241	2020929	2023169	2020033	2024513
2026753	2020481	2021377	2022273	2016001
2026305	2022721	2019585	2021825	2016449
2016897	2017345	2024961	2023617	2024065

L12-M6

2029889	2036609	2028993	2030337	2037057
2029441	2032129	2034369	2031233	2035713
2037953	2031681	2032577	2033473	2027201
2037505	2033921	2030785	2033025	2027649
2028097	2028545	2036161	2034817	2035265

L12-M7

2041089	2047809	2040193	2041537	2048257
2040641	2043329	2045569	2042433	2046913
2049153	2042881	2043777	2044673	2038401
2048705	2045121	2041985	2044225	2038849
2039297	2039745	2047361	2046017	2046465

L12-M8

2052289	2059009	2051393	2052737	2059457
2051841	2054529	2056769	2053633	2058113
2060353	2054081	2054977	2055873	2049601
2059905	2056321	2053185	2055425	2050049
2050497	2050945	2058561	2057217	2057665

L12-M9

2063489	2070209	2062593	2063937	2070657
2063041	2065729	2067969	2064833	2069313
2071553	2065281	2066177	2067073	2060801
2071105	2067521	2064385	2066625	2061249
2061697	2062145	2069761	2068417	2068865

L12-M10

2074689	2081409	2073793	2075137	2081857
2074241	2076929	2079169	2076033	2080513
2082753	2076481	2077377	2078273	2072001
2082305	2078721	2075585	2077825	2072449
2072897	2073345	2080961	2079617	2080065

L12-M11

2085889	2092609	2084993	2086337	2093057
2085441	2088129	2090369	2087233	2091713
2093953	2087681	2088577	2089473	2083201
2093505	2089921	2086785	2089025	2083649
2084097	2084545	2092161	2090817	2091265

L12-M12

2097089	2103809	2096193	2097537	2104257
2096641	2099329	2101569	2098433	2102913
2105153	2098881	2099777	2100673	2094401
2104705	2101121	2097985	2100225	2094849
2095297	2095745	2103361	2102017	2102465

L12-M13

2108289	2115009	2107393	2108737	2115457
2107841	2110529	2112769	2109633	2114113
2116353	2110081	2110977	2111873	2105601
2115905	2112321	2109185	2111425	2106049
2106497	2106945	2114561	2113217	2113665

L12-M14

2119489	2126209	2118593	2119937	2126657
2119041	2121729	2123969	2120833	2125313
2127553	2121281	2122177	2123073	2116801
2127105	2123521	2120385	2122625	2117249
2117697	2118145	2125761	2124417	2124865

L12-M15

2130689	2137409	2129793	2131137	2137857
2130241	2132929	2135169	2132033	2136513
2138753	2132481	2133377	2134273	2128001
2138305	2134721	2131585	2133825	2128449
2128897	2129345	2136961	2135617	2136065

L12-M16

2141889	2148609	2140993	2142337	2149057
2141441	2144129	2146369	2143233	2147713
2149953	2143681	2144577	2145473	2139201
2149505	2145921	2142785	2145025	2139649
2140097	2140545	2148161	2146817	2147265

L13-M1

2153089	2159809	2152193	2153537	2160257
2152641	2155329	2157569	2154433	2158913
2161153	2154881	2155777	2156673	2150401
2160705	2157121	2153985	2156225	2150849
2151297	2151745	2159361	2158017	2158465

L13-M2

2164289	2171009	2163393	2164737	2171457
2163841	2166529	2168769	2165633	2170113
2172353	2166081	2166977	2167873	2161601
2171905	2168321	2165185	2167425	2162049
2162497	2162945	2170561	2169217	2169665

L13-M3

2175489	2182209	2174593	2175937	2182657
2175041	2177729	2179969	2176833	2181313
2183553	2177281	2178177	2179073	2172801
2183105	2179521	2176385	2178625	2173249
2173697	2174145	2181761	2180417	2180865

L13-M4

2186689	2193409	2185793	2187137	2193857
2186241	2188929	2191169	2188033	2192513
2194753	2188481	2189377	2190273	2184001
2194305	2190721	2187585	2189825	2184449
2184897	2185345	2192961	2191617	2192065

L13-M5

2197889	2204609	2196993	2198337	2205057
2197441	2200129	2202369	2199233	2203713
2205953	2199681	2200577	2201473	2195201
2205505	2201921	2198785	2201025	2195649
2196097	2196545	2204161	2202817	2203265

L13-M6

2209089	2215809	2208193	2209537	2216257
2208641	2211329	2213569	2210433	2214913
2217153	2210881	2211777	2212673	2206401
2216705	2213121	2209985	2212225	2206849
2207297	2207745	2215361	2214017	2214465

L13-M7

2220289	2227009	2219393	2220737	2227457
2219841	2222529	2224769	2221633	2226113
2228353	2222081	2222977	2223873	2217601
2227905	2224321	2221185	2223425	2218049
2218497	2218945	2226561	2225217	2225665

L13-M8

2231489	2238209	2230593	2231937	2238657
2231041	2233729	2235969	2232833	2237313
2239553	2233281	2234177	2235073	2228801
2239105	2235521	2232385	2234625	2229249
2229697	2230145	2237761	2236417	2236865

L13-M9

2242689	2249409	2241793	2243137	2249857
2242241	2244929	2247169	2244033	2248513
2250753	2244481	2245377	2246273	2240001
2250305	2246721	2243585	2245825	2240449
2240897	2241345	2248961	2247617	2248065

L13-M10

2253889	2260609	2252993	2254337	2261057
2253441	2256129	2258369	2255233	2259713
2261953	2255681	2256577	2257473	2251201
2261505	2257921	2254785	2257025	2251649
2252097	2252545	2260161	2258817	2259265

L13-M11

2265089	2271809	2264193	2265537	2272257
2264641	2267329	2269569	2266433	2270913
2273153	2266881	2267777	2268673	2262401
2272705	2269121	2265985	2268225	2262849
2263297	2263745	2271361	2270017	2270465

L13-M12

2276289	2283009	2275393	2276737	2283457
2275841	2278529	2280769	2277633	2282113
2284353	2278081	2278977	2279873	2273601
2283905	2280321	2277185	2279425	2274049
2274497	2274945	2282561	2281217	2281665

L13-M13

2287489	2294209	2286593	2287937	2294657
2287041	2289729	2291969	2288833	2293313
2295553	2289281	2290177	2291073	2284801
2295105	2291521	2288385	2290625	2285249
2285697	2286145	2293761	2292417	2292865

L13-M14

2298689	2305409	2297793	2299137	2305857
2298241	2300929	2303169	2300033	2304513
2306753	2300481	2301377	2302273	2296001
2306305	2302721	2299585	2301825	2296449
2296897	2297345	2304961	2303617	2304065

L13-M15

2309889	2316609	2308993	2310337	2317057
2309441	2312129	2314369	2311233	2315713
2317953	2311681	2312577	2313473	2307201
2317505	2313921	2310785	2313025	2307649
2308097	2308545	2316161	2314817	2315265

L13-M16

2321089	2327809	2320193	2321537	2328257
2320641	2323329	2325569	2322433	2326913
2329153	2322881	2323777	2324673	2318401
2328705	2325121	2321985	2324225	2318849
2319297	2319745	2327361	2326017	2326465

L14-M1

2332289	2339009	2331393	2332737	2339457
2331841	2334529	2336769	2333633	2338113
2340353	2334081	2334977	2335873	2329601
2339905	2336321	2333185	2335425	2330049
2330497	2330945	2338561	2337217	2337665

L14-M2

2343489	2350209	2342593	2343937	2350657
2343041	2345729	2347969	2344833	2349313
2351553	2345281	2346177	2347073	2340801
2351105	2347521	2344385	2346625	2341249
2341697	2342145	2349761	2348417	2348865

L14-M3

2354689	2361409	2353793	2355137	2361857
2354241	2356929	2359169	2356033	2360513
2362753	2356481	2357377	2358273	2352001
2362305	2358721	2355585	2357825	2352449
2352897	2353345	2360961	2359617	2360065

L14-M4

2365889	2372609	2364993	2366337	2373057
2365441	2368129	2370369	2367233	2371713
2373953	2367681	2368577	2369473	2363201
2373505	2369921	2366785	2369025	2363649
2364097	2364545	2372161	2370817	2371265

L14-M5

2377089	2383809	2376193	2377537	2384257
2376641	2379329	2381569	2378433	2382913
2385153	2378881	2379777	2380673	2374401
2384705	2381121	2377985	2380225	2374849
2375297	2375745	2383361	2382017	2382465

L14-M6

2388289	2395009	2387393	2388737	2395457
2387841	2390529	2392769	2389633	2394113
2396353	2390081	2390977	2391873	2385601
2395905	2392321	2389185	2391425	2386049
2386497	2386945	2394561	2393217	2393665

L14-M7

2399489	2406209	2398593	2399937	2406657
2399041	2401729	2403969	2400833	2405313
2407553	2401281	2402177	2403073	2396801
2407105	2403521	2400385	2402625	2397249
2397697	2398145	2405761	2404417	2404865

L14-M8

2410689	2417409	2409793	2411137	2417857
2410241	2412929	2415169	2412033	2416513
2418753	2412481	2413377	2414273	2408001
2418305	2414721	2411585	2413825	2408449
2408897	2409345	2416961	2415617	2416065

L14-M9

2421889	2428609	2420993	2422337	2429057
2421441	2424129	2426369	2423233	2427713
2429953	2423681	2424577	2425473	2419201
2429505	2425921	2422785	2425025	2419649
2420097	2420545	2428161	2426817	2427265

L15-M2

2522689	2529409	2521793	2523137	2529857
2522241	2524929	2527169	2524033	2528513
2530753	2524481	2525377	2526273	2520001
2530305	2526721	2523585	2525825	2520449
2520897	2521345	2528961	2527617	2528065

L14-M10

2433089	2439809	2432193	2433537	2440257
2432641	2435329	2437569	2434433	2438913
2441153	2434881	2435777	2436673	2430401
2440705	2437121	2433985	2436225	2430849
2431297	2431745	2439361	2438017	2438465

L15-M3

2533889	2540609	2532993	2534337	2541057
2533441	2536129	2538369	2535233	2539713
2541953	2535681	2536577	2537473	2531201
2541505	2537921	2534785	2537025	2531649
2532097	2532545	2540161	2538817	2539265

L14-M11

2444289	2451009	2443393	2444737	2451457
2443841	2446529	2448769	2445633	2450113
2452353	2446081	2446977	2447873	2441601
2451905	2448321	2445185	2447425	2442049
2442497	2442945	2450561	2449217	2449665

L15-M4

2545089	2551809	2544193	2545537	2552257
2544641	2547329	2549569	2546433	2550913
2553153	2546881	2547777	2548673	2542401
2552705	2549121	2545985	2548225	2542849
2543297	2543745	2551361	2550017	2550465

L14-M12

2455489	2462209	2454593	2455937	2462657
2455041	2457729	2459969	2456833	2461313
2463553	2457281	2458177	2459073	2452801
2463105	2459521	2456385	2458625	2453249
2453697	2454145	2461761	2460417	2460865

L15-M5

2556289	2563009	2555393	2556737	2563457
2555841	2558529	2560769	2557633	2562113
2564353	2558081	2558977	2559873	2553601
2563905	2560321	2557185	2559425	2554049
2554497	2554945	2562561	2561217	2561665

L14-M13

2466689	2473409	2465793	2467137	2473857
2466241	2468929	2471169	2468033	2472513
2474753	2468481	2469377	2470273	2464001
2474305	2470721	2467585	2469825	2464449
2464897	2465345	2472961	2471617	2472065

L15-M6

2567489	2574209	2566593	2567937	2574657
2567041	2569729	2571969	2568833	2573313
2575553	2569281	2570177	2571073	2564801
2575105	2571521	2568385	2570625	2565249
2565697	2566145	2573761	2572417	2572865

L14-M14

2477889	2484609	2476993	2478337	2485057
2477441	2480129	2482369	2479233	2483713
2485953	2479681	2480577	2481473	2475201
2485505	2481921	2478785	2481025	2475649
2476097	2476545	2484161	2482817	2483265

L15-M7

2578689	2585409	2577793	2579137	2585857
2578241	2580929	2583169	2580033	2584513
2586753	2580481	2581377	2582273	2576001
2586305	2582721	2579585	2581825	2576449
2576897	2577345	2584961	2583617	2584065

L14-M15

2489089	2495809	2488193	2489537	2496257
2488641	2491329	2493569	2490433	2494913
2497153	2490881	2491777	2492673	2486401
2496705	2493121	2489985	2492225	2486849
2487297	2487745	2495361	2494017	2494465

L15-M8

2589889	2596609	2588993	2590337	2597057
2589441	2592129	2594369	2591233	2595713
2597953	2591681	2592577	2593473	2587201
2597505	2593921	2590785	2593025	2587649
2588097	2588545	2596161	2594817	2595265

L14-M16

2500289	2507009	2499393	2500737	2507457
2499841	2502529	2504769	2501633	2506113
2508353	2502081	2502977	2503873	2497601
2507905	2504321	2501185	2503425	2498049
2498497	2498945	2506561	2505217	2505665

L15-M9

2601089	2607809	2600193	2601537	2608257
2600641	2603329	2605569	2602433	2606913
2609153	2602881	2603777	2604673	2598401
2608705	2605121	2601985	2604225	2598849
2599297	2599745	2607361	2606017	2606465

L15-M1

2511489	2518209	2510593	2511937	2518657
2511041	2513729	2515969	2512833	2517313
2519553	2513281	2514177	2515073	2508801
2519105	2515521	2512385	2514625	2509249
2509697	2510145	2517761	2516417	2516865

L15-M10

2612289	2619009	2611393	2612737	2619457
2611841	2614529	2616769	2613633	2618113
2620353	2614081	2614977	2615873	2609601
2619905	2616321	2613185	2615425	2610049
2610497	2610945	2618561	2617217	2617665

L15-M11

2623489	2630209	2622593	2623937	2630657
2623041	2625729	2627969	2624833	2629313
2631553	2625281	2626177	2627073	2620801
2631105	2627521	2624385	2626625	2621249
2621697	2622145	2629761	2628417	2628865

L15-M12

2634689	2641409	2633793	2635137	2641857
2634241	2636929	2639169	2636033	2640513
2642753	2636481	2637377	2638273	2632001
2642305	2638721	2635585	2637825	2632449
2632897	2633345	2640961	2639617	2640065

L15-M13

2645889	2652609	2644993	2646337	2653057
2645441	2648129	2650369	2647233	2651713
2653953	2647681	2648577	2649473	2643201
2653505	2649921	2646785	2649025	2643649
2644097	2644545	2652161	2650817	2651265

L15-M14

2657089	2663809	2656193	2657537	2664257
2656641	2659329	2661569	2658433	2662913
2665153	2658881	2659777	2660673	2654401
2664705	2661121	2657985	2660225	2654849
2655297	2655745	2663361	2662017	2662465

L15-M15

2668289	2675009	2667393	2668737	2675457
2667841	2670529	2672769	2669633	2674113
2676353	2670081	2670977	2671873	2665601
2675905	2672321	2669185	2671425	2666049
2666497	2666945	2674561	2673217	2673665

L15-M16

2679489	2686209	2678593	2679937	2686657
2679041	2681729	2683969	2680833	2685313
2687553	2681281	2682177	2683073	2676801
2687105	2683521	2680385	2682625	2677249
2677697	2678145	2685761	2684417	2684865

L16-M1

2690689	2697409	2689793	2691137	2697857
2690241	2692929	2695169	2692033	2696513
2698753	2692481	2693377	2694273	2688001
2698305	2694721	2691585	2693825	2688449
2688897	2689345	2696961	2695617	2696065

L16-M2

2701889	2708609	2700993	2702337	2709057
2701441	2704129	2706369	2703233	2707713
2709953	2703681	2704577	2705473	2699201
2709505	2705921	2702785	2705025	2699649
2700097	2700545	2708161	2706817	2707265

L16-M3

2713089	2719809	2712193	2713537	2720257
2712641	2715329	2717569	2714433	2718913
2721153	2714881	2715777	2716673	2710401
2720705	2717121	2713985	2716225	2710849
2711297	2711745	2719361	2718017	2718465

L16-M4

2724289	2731009	2723393	2724737	2731457
2723841	2726529	2728769	2725633	2730113
2732353	2726081	2726977	2727873	2721601
2731905	2728321	2725185	2727425	2722049
2722497	2722945	2730561	2729217	2729665

L16-M5

2735489	2742209	2734593	2735937	2742657
2735041	2737729	2739969	2736833	2741313
2743553	2737281	2738177	2739073	2732801
2743105	2739521	2736385	2738625	2733249
2733697	2734145	2741761	2740417	2740865

L16-M6

2746689	2753409	2745793	2747137	2753857
2746241	2748929	2751169	2748033	2752513
2754753	2748481	2749377	2750273	2744001
2754305	2750721	2747585	2749825	2744449
2744897	2745345	2752961	2751617	2752065

L16-M7

2757889	2764609	2756993	2758337	2765057
2757441	2760129	2762369	2759233	2763713
2765953	2759681	2760577	2761473	2755201
2765505	2761921	2758785	2761025	2755649
2756097	2756545	2764161	2762817	2763265

L16-M8

2769089	2775809	2768193	2769537	2776257
2768641	2771329	2773569	2770433	2774913
2777153	2770881	2771777	2772673	2766401
2776705	2773121	2769985	2772225	2766849
2767297	2767745	2775361	2774017	2774465

L16-M9

2780289	2787009	2779393	2780737	2787457
2779841	2782529	2784769	2781633	2786113
2788353	2782081	2782977	2783873	2777601
2787905	2784321	2781185	2783425	2778049
2778497	2778945	2786561	2785217	2785665

L16-M10

2791489	2798209	2790593	2791937	2798657
2791041	2793729	2795969	2792833	2797313
2799553	2793281	2794177	2795073	2788801
2799105	2795521	2792385	2794625	2789249
2789697	2790145	2797761	2796417	2796865

L16-M11

2802689	2809409	2801793	2803137	2809857
2802241	2804929	2807169	2804033	2808513
2810753	2804481	2805377	2806273	2800001
2810305	2806721	2803585	2805825	2800449
2800897	2801345	2808961	2807617	2808065

L16-M12

2813889	2820609	2812993	2814337	2821057
2813441	2816129	2818369	2815233	2819713
2821953	2815681	2816577	2817473	2811201
2821505	2817921	2814785	2817025	2811649
2812097	2812545	2820161	2818817	2819265

L16-M13

2825089	2831809	2824193	2825537	2832257
2824641	2827329	2829569	2826433	2830913
2833153	2826881	2827777	2828673	2822401
2832705	2829121	2825985	2828225	2822849
2823297	2823745	2831361	2830017	2830465

L16-M14

2836289	2843009	2835393	2836737	2843457
2835841	2838529	2840769	2837633	2842113
2844353	2838081	2838977	2839873	2833601
2843905	2840321	2837185	2839425	2834049
2834497	2834945	2842561	2841217	2841665

L16-M15

2847489	2854209	2846593	2847937	2854657
2847041	2849729	2851969	2848833	2853313
2855553	2849281	2850177	2851073	2844801
2855105	2851521	2848385	2850625	2845249
2845697	2846145	2853761	2852417	2852865

L16M16

2858689	2865409	2857793	2859137	2865857
2858241	2860929	2863169	2860033	2864513
2866753	2860481	2861377	2862273	2856001
2866305	2862721	2859585	2861825	2856449
2856897	2857345	2864961	2863617	2864065

L17-M1

2869889	2876609	2868993	2870337	2877057
2869441	2872129	2874369	2871233	2875713
2877953	2871681	2872577	2873473	2867201
2877505	2873921	2870785	2873025	2867649
2868097	2868545	2876161	2874817	2875265

L17-M2

2881089	2887809	2880193	2881537	2888257
2880641	2883329	2885569	2882433	2886913
2889153	2882881	2883777	2884673	2878401
2888705	2885121	2881985	2884225	2878849
2879297	2879745	2887361	2886017	2886465

L17-M3

2892289	2899009	2891393	2892737	2899457
2891841	2894529	2896769	2893633	2898113
2900353	2894081	2894977	2895873	2889601
2899905	2896321	2893185	2895425	2890049
2890497	2890945	2898561	2897217	2897665

L17-M4

2903489	2910209	2902593	2903937	2910657
2903041	2905729	2907969	2904833	2909313
2911553	2905281	2906177	2907073	2900801
2911105	2907521	2904385	2906625	2901249
2901697	2902145	2909761	2908417	2908865

L17-M5

2914689	2921409	2913793	2915137	2921857
2914241	2916929	2919169	2916033	2920513
2922753	2916481	2917377	2918273	2912001
2922305	2918721	2915585	2917825	2912449
2912897	2913345	2920961	2919617	2920065

L17-M6

2925889	2932609	2924993	2926337	2933057
2925441	2928129	2930369	2927233	2931713
2933953	2927681	2928577	2929473	2923201
2933505	2929921	2926785	2929025	2923649
2924097	2924545	2932161	2930817	2931265

L17-M7

2937089	2943809	2936193	2937537	2944257
2936641	2939329	2941569	2938433	2942913
2945153	2938881	2939777	2940673	2934401
2944705	2941121	2937985	2940225	2934849
2935297	2935745	2943361	2942017	2942465

L17-M8

2948289	2955009	2947393	2948737	2955457
2947841	2950529	2952769	2949633	2954113
2956353	2950081	2950977	2951873	2945601
2955905	2952321	2949185	2951425	2946049
2946497	2946945	2954561	2953217	2953665

L17-M9

2959489	2966209	2958593	2959937	2966657
2959041	2961729	2963969	2960833	2965313
2967553	2961281	2962177	2963073	2956801
2967105	2963521	2960385	2962625	2957249
2957697	2958145	2965761	2964417	2964865

L17-M10

2970689	2977409	2969793	2971137	2977857
2970241	2972929	2975169	2972033	2976513
2978753	2972481	2973377	2974273	2968001
2978305	2974721	2971585	2973825	2968449
2968897	2969345	2976961	2975617	2976065

L17-M11

2981889	2988609	2980993	2982337	2989057
2981441	2984129	2986369	2983233	2987713
2989953	2983681	2984577	2985473	2979201
2989505	2985921	2982785	2985025	2979649
2980097	2980545	2988161	2986817	2987265

L17-M12

2993089	2999809	2992193	2993537	3000257
2992641	2995329	2997569	2994433	2998913
3001153	2994881	2995777	2996673	2990401
3000705	2997121	2993985	2996225	2990849
2991297	2991745	2999361	2998017	2998465

L17-M13

3004289	3011009	3003393	3004737	3011457
3003841	3006529	3008769	3005633	3010113
3012353	3006081	3006977	3007873	3001601
3011905	3008321	3005185	3007425	3002049
3002497	3002945	3010561	3009217	3009665

L17-M14

3015489	3022209	3014593	3015937	3022657
3015041	3017729	3019969	3016833	3021313
3023553	3017281	3018177	3019073	3012801
3023105	3019521	3016385	3018625	3013249
3013697	3014145	3021761	3020417	3020865

L17-M15

3026689	3033409	3025793	3027137	3033857
3026241	3028929	3031169	3028033	3032513
3034753	3028481	3029377	3030273	3024001
3034305	3030721	3027585	3029825	3024449
3024897	3025345	3032961	3031617	3032065

L17-M16

3037889	3044609	3036993	3038337	3045057
3037441	3040129	3042369	3039233	3043713
3045953	3039681	3040577	3041473	3035201
3045505	3041921	3038785	3041025	3035649
3036097	3036545	3044161	3042817	3043265

L18-M1

3049089	3055809	3048193	3049537	3056257
3048641	3051329	3053569	3050433	3054913
3057153	3050881	3051777	3052673	3046401
3056705	3053121	3049985	3052225	3046849
3047297	3047745	3055361	3054017	3054465

L18-M2

3060289	3067009	3059393	3060737	3067457
3059841	3062529	3064769	3061633	3066113
3068353	3062081	3062977	3063873	3057601
3067905	3064321	3061185	3063425	3058049
3058497	3058945	3066561	3065217	3065665

L18-M3

3071489	3078209	3070593	3071937	3078657
3071041	3073729	3075969	3072833	3077313
3079553	3073281	3074177	3075073	3068801
3079105	3075521	3072385	3074625	3069249
3069697	3070145	3077761	3076417	3076865

L18-M4

3082689	3089409	3081793	3083137	3089857
3082241	3084929	3087169	3084033	3088513
3090753	3084481	3085377	3086273	3080001
3090305	3086721	3083585	3085825	3080449
3080897	3081345	3088961	3087617	3088065

L18-M5

3093889	3100609	3092993	3094337	3101057
3093441	3096129	3098369	3095233	3099713
3101953	3095681	3096577	3097473	3091201
3101505	3097921	3094785	3097025	3091649
3092097	3092545	3100161	3098817	3099265

L18-M6

3105089	3111809	3104193	3105537	3112257
3104641	3107329	3109569	3106433	3110913
3113153	3106881	3107777	3108673	3102401
3112705	3109121	3105985	3108225	3102849
3103297	3103745	3111361	3110017	3110465

L18-M7

3116289	3123009	3115393	3116737	3123457
3115841	3118529	3120769	3117633	3122113
3124353	3118081	3118977	3119873	3113601
3123905	3120321	3117185	3119425	3114049
3114497	3114945	3122561	3121217	3121665

L18-M8

3127489	3134209	3126593	3127937	3134657
3127041	3129729	3131969	3128833	3133313
3135553	3129281	3130177	3131073	3124801
3135105	3131521	3128385	3130625	3125249
3125697	3126145	3133761	3132417	3132865

L18-M9

3138689	3145409	3137793	3139137	3145857
3138241	3140929	3143169	3140033	3144513
3146753	3140481	3141377	3142273	3136001
3146305	3142721	3139585	3141825	3136449
3136897	3137345	3144961	3143617	3144065

L18-M10

3149889	3156609	3148993	3150337	3157057
3149441	3152129	3154369	3151233	3155713
3157953	3151681	3152577	3153473	3147201
3157505	3153921	3150785	3153025	3147649
3148097	3148545	3156161	3154817	3155265

L18-M11

3161089	3167809	3160193	3161537	3168257
3160641	3163329	3165569	3162433	3166913
3169153	3162881	3163777	3164673	3158401
3168705	3165121	3161985	3164225	3158849
3159297	3159745	3167361	3166017	3166465

L18-M12

3172289	3179009	3171393	3172737	3179457
3171841	3174529	3176769	3173633	3178113
3180353	3174081	3174977	3175873	3169601
3179905	3176321	3173185	3175425	3170049
3170497	3170945	3178561	3177217	3177665

L18-M13

3183489	3190209	3182593	3183937	3190657
3183041	3185729	3187969	3184833	3189313
3191553	3185281	3186177	3187073	3180801
3191105	3187521	3184385	3186625	3181249
3181697	3182145	3189761	3188417	3188865

L18-M14

3194689	3201409	3193793	3195137	3201857
3194241	3196929	3199169	3196033	3200513
3202753	3196481	3197377	3198273	3192001
3202305	3198721	3195585	3197825	3192449
3192897	3193345	3200961	3199617	3200065

L18-M15

3205889	3212609	3204993	3206337	3213057
3205441	3208129	3210369	3207233	3211713
3213953	3207681	3208577	3209473	3203201
3213505	3209921	3206785	3209025	3203649
3204097	3204545	3212161	3210817	3211265

L18-M16

3217089	3223809	3216193	3217537	3224257
3216641	3219329	3221569	3218433	3222913
3225153	3218881	3219777	3220673	3214401
3224705	3221121	3217985	3220225	3214849
3215297	3215745	3223361	3222017	3222465

L19-M1

3228289	3235009	3227393	3228737	3235457
3227841	3230529	3232769	3229633	3234113
3236353	3230081	3230977	3231873	3225601
3235905	3232321	3229185	3231425	3226049
3226497	3226945	3234561	3233217	3233665

L19-M10

3329089	3335809	3328193	3329537	3336257
3328641	3331329	3333569	3330433	3334913
3337153	3330881	3331777	3332673	3326401
3336705	3333121	3329985	3332225	3326849
3327297	3327745	3335361	3334017	3334465

L19-M2

3239489	3246209	3238593	3239937	3246657
3239041	3241729	3243969	3240833	3245313
3247553	3241281	3242177	3243073	3236801
3247105	3243521	3240385	3242625	3237249
3237697	3238145	3245761	3244417	3244865

L19-M11

3340289	3347009	3339393	3340737	3347457
3339841	3342529	3344769	3341633	3346113
3348353	3342081	3342977	3343873	3337601
3347905	3344321	3341185	3343425	3338049
3338497	3338945	3346561	3345217	3345665

L19-M3

3250689	3257409	3249793	3251137	3257857
3250241	3252929	3255169	3252033	3256513
3258753	3252481	3253377	3254273	3248001
3258305	3254721	3251585	3253825	3248449
3248897	3249345	3256961	3255617	3256065

L19-M12

3351489	3358209	3350593	3351937	3358657
3351041	3353729	3355969	3352833	3357313
3359553	3353281	3354177	3355073	3348801
3359105	3355521	3352385	3354625	3349249
3349697	3350145	3357761	3356417	3356865

L19-M4

3261889	3268609	3260993	3262337	3269057
3261441	3264129	3266369	3263233	3267713
3269953	3263681	3264577	3265473	3259201
3269505	3265921	3262785	3265025	3259649
3260097	3260545	3268161	3266817	3267265

L19-M13

3362689	3369409	3361793	3363137	3369857
3362241	3364929	3367169	3364033	3368513
3370753	3364481	3365377	3366273	3360001
3370305	3366721	3363585	3365825	3360449
3360897	3361345	3368961	3367617	3368065

L19-M5

3273089	3279809	3272193	3273537	3280257
3272641	3275329	3277569	3274433	3278913
3281153	3274881	3275777	3276673	3270401
3280705	3277121	3273985	3276225	3270849
3271297	3271745	3279361	3278017	3278465

L19-M14

3373889	3380609	3372993	3374337	3381057
3373441	3376129	3378369	3375233	3379713
3381953	3375681	3376577	3377473	3371201
3381505	3377921	3374785	3377025	3371649
3372097	3372545	3380161	3378817	3379265

L19-M6

3284289	3291009	3283393	3284737	3291457
3283841	3286529	3288769	3285633	3290113
3292353	3286081	3286977	3287873	3281601
3291905	3288321	3285185	3287425	3282049
3282497	3282945	3290561	3289217	3289665

L19-M15

3385089	3391809	3384193	3385537	3392257
3384641	3387329	3389569	3386433	3390913
3393153	3386881	3387777	3388673	3382401
3392705	3389121	3385985	3388225	3382849
3383297	3383745	3391361	3390017	3390465

L19-M7

3295489	3302209	3294593	3295937	3302657
3295041	3297729	3299969	3296833	3301313
3303553	3297281	3298177	3299073	3292801
3303105	3299521	3296385	3298625	3293249
3293697	3294145	3301761	3300417	3300865

L19-M16

3396289	3403009	3395393	3396737	3403457
3395841	3398529	3400769	3397633	3402113
3404353	3398081	3398977	3399873	3393601
3403905	3400321	3397185	3399425	3394049
3394497	3394945	3402561	3401217	3401665

L19-M8

3306689	3313409	3305793	3307137	3313857
3306241	3308929	3311169	3308033	3312513
3314753	3308481	3309377	3310273	3304001
3314305	3310721	3307585	3309825	3304449
3304897	3305345	3312961	3311617	3312065

L20-M1

3407489	3414209	3406593	3407937	3414657
3407041	3409729	3411969	3408833	3413313
3415553	3409281	3410177	3411073	3404801
3415105	3411521	3408385	3410625	3405249
3405697	3406145	3413761	3412417	3412865

L19-M9

3317889	3324609	3316993	3318337	3325057
3317441	3320129	3322369	3319233	3323713
3325953	3319681	3320577	3321473	3315201
3325505	3321921	3318785	3321025	3315649
3316097	3316545	3324161	3322817	3323265

L20-M2

3418689	3425409	3417793	3419137	3425857
3418241	3420929	3423169	3420033	3424513
3426753	3420481	3421377	3422273	3416001
3426305	3422721	3419585	3421825	3416449
3416897	3417345	3424961	3423617	3424065

L20-M3

3429889	3436609	3428993	3430337	3437057
3429441	3432129	3434369	3431233	3435713
3437953	3431681	3432577	3433473	3427201
3437505	3433921	3430785	3433025	3427649
3428097	3428545	3436161	3434817	3435265

L20-M4

3441089	3447809	3440193	3441537	3448257
3440641	3443329	3445569	3442433	3446913
3449153	3442881	3443777	3444673	3438401
3448705	3445121	3441985	3444225	3438849
3439297	3439745	3447361	3446017	3446465

L20-M5

3452289	3459009	3451393	3452737	3459457
3451841	3454529	3456769	3453633	3458113
3460353	3454081	3454977	3455873	3449601
3459905	3456321	3453185	3455425	3450049
3450497	3450945	3458561	3457217	3457665

L20-M6

3463489	3470209	3462593	3463937	3470657
3463041	3465729	3467969	3464833	3469313
3471553	3465281	3466177	3467073	3460801
3471105	3467521	3464385	3466625	3461249
3461697	3462145	3469761	3468417	3468865

L20-M7

3474689	3481409	3473793	3475137	3481857
3474241	3476929	3479169	3476033	3480513
3482753	3476481	3477377	3478273	3472001
3482305	3478721	3475585	3477825	3472449
3472897	3473345	3480961	3479617	3480065

L20-M8

3485889	3492609	3484993	3486337	3493057
3485441	3488129	3490369	3487233	3491713
3493953	3487681	3488577	3489473	3483201
3493505	3489921	3486785	3489025	3483649
3484097	3484545	3492161	3490817	3491265

L20-M9

3497089	3503809	3496193	3497537	3504257
3496641	3499329	3501569	3498433	3502913
3505153	3498881	3499777	3500673	3494401
3504705	3501121	3497985	3500225	3494849
3495297	3495745	3503361	3502017	3502465

L20-M10

3508289	3515009	3507393	3508737	3515457
3507841	3510529	3512769	3509633	3514113
3516353	3510081	3510977	3511873	3505601
3515905	3512321	3509185	3511425	3506049
3506497	3506945	3514561	3513217	3513665

L20-M11

3519489	3526209	3518593	3519937	3526657
3519041	3521729	3523969	3520833	3525313
3527553	3521281	3522177	3523073	3516801
3527105	3523521	3520385	3522625	3517249
3517697	3518145	3525761	3524417	3524865

L20-M12

3530689	3537409	3529793	3531137	3537857
3530241	3532929	3535169	3532033	3536513
3538753	3532481	3533377	3534273	3528001
3538305	3534721	3531585	3533825	3528449
3528897	3529345	3536961	3535617	3536065

L20-M13

3541889	3548609	3540993	3542337	3549057
3541441	3544129	3546369	3543233	3547713
3549953	3543681	3544577	3545473	3539201
3549505	3545921	3542785	3545025	3539649
3540097	3540545	3548161	3546817	3547265

L20-M14

3553089	3559809	3552193	3553537	3560257
3552641	3555329	3557569	3554433	3558913
3561153	3554881	3555777	3556673	3550401
3560705	3557121	3553985	3556225	3550849
3551297	3551745	3559361	3558017	3558465

L20-M15

3564289	3571009	3563393	3564737	3571457
3563841	3566529	3568769	3565633	3570113
3572353	3566081	3566977	3567873	3561601
3571905	3568321	3565185	3567425	3562049
3562497	3562945	3570561	3569217	3569665

L20-M16

3575489	3582209	3574593	3575937	3582657
3575041	3577729	3579969	3576833	3581313
3583553	3577281	3578177	3579073	3572801
3583105	3579521	3576385	3578625	3573249
3573697	3574145	3581761	3580417	3580865

L21-M1

3586689	3593409	3585793	3587137	3593857
3586241	3588929	3591169	3588033	3592513
3594753	3588481	3589377	3590273	3584001
3594305	3590721	3587585	3589825	3584449
3584897	3585345	3592961	3591617	3592065

L21-M2

3597889	3604609	3596993	3598337	3605057
3597441	3600129	3602369	3599233	3603713
3605953	3599681	3600577	3601473	3595201
3605505	3601921	3598785	3601025	3595649
3596097	3596545	3604161	3602817	3603265

L21-M3

3609089	3615809	3608193	3609537	3616257
3608641	3611329	3613569	3610433	3614913
3617153	3610881	3611777	3612673	3606401
3616705	3613121	3609985	3612225	3606849
3607297	3607745	3615361	3614017	3614465

L21-M4

3620289	3627009	3619393	3620737	3627457
3619841	3622529	3624769	3621633	3626113
3628353	3622081	3622977	3623873	3617601
3627905	3624321	3621185	3623425	3618049
3618497	3618945	3626561	3625217	3625665

L21-M5

3631489	3638209	3630593	3631937	3638657
3631041	3633729	3635969	3632833	3637313
3639553	3633281	3634177	3635073	3628801
3639105	3635521	3632385	3634625	3629249
3629697	3630145	3637761	3636417	3636865

L21-M14

3732289	3739009	3731393	3732737	3739457
3731841	3734529	3736769	3733633	3738113
3740353	3734081	3734977	3735873	3729601
3739905	3736321	3733185	3735425	3730049
3730497	3730945	3738561	3737217	3737665

L21-M6

3642689	3649409	3641793	3643137	3649857
3642241	3644929	3647169	3644033	3648513
3650753	3644481	3645377	3646273	3640001
3650305	3646721	3643585	3645825	3640449
3640897	3641345	3648961	3647617	3648065

L21-M15

3743489	3750209	3742593	3743937	3750657
3743041	3745729	3747969	3744833	3749313
3751553	3745281	3746177	3747073	3740801
3751105	3747521	3744385	3746625	3741249
3741697	3742145	3749761	3748417	3748865

L21-M7

3653889	3660609	3652993	3654337	3661057
3653441	3656129	3658369	3655233	3659713
3661953	3655681	3656577	3657473	3651201
3661505	3657921	3654785	3657025	3651649
3652097	3652545	3660161	3658817	3659265

L21-M16

3754689	3761409	3753793	3755137	3761857
3754241	3756929	3759169	3756033	3760513
3762753	3756481	3757377	3758273	3752001
3762305	3758721	3755585	3757825	3752449
3752897	3753345	3760961	3759617	3760065

L21-M8

3665089	3671809	3664193	3665537	3672257
3664641	3667329	3669569	3666433	3670913
3673153	3666881	3667777	3668673	3662401
3672705	3669121	3665985	3668225	3662849
3663297	3663745	3671361	3670017	3670465

L22-M1

3765889	3772609	3764993	3766337	3773057
3765441	3768129	3770369	3767233	3771713
3773953	3767681	3768577	3769473	3763201
3773505	3769921	3766785	3769025	3763649
3764097	3764545	3772161	3770817	3771265

L21-M9

3676289	3683009	3675393	3676737	3683457
3675841	3678529	3680769	3677633	3682113
3684353	3678081	3678977	3679873	3673601
3683905	3680321	3677185	3679425	3674049
3674497	3674945	3682561	3681217	3681665

L22-M2

3777089	3783809	3776193	3777537	3784257
3776641	3779329	3781569	3778433	3782913
3785153	3778881	3779777	3780673	3774401
3784705	3781121	3777985	3780225	3774849
3775297	3775745	3783361	3782017	3782465

L21-M10

3687489	3694209	3686593	3687937	3694657
3687041	3689729	3691969	3688833	3693313
3695553	3689281	3690177	3691073	3684801
3695105	3691521	3688385	3690625	3685249
3685697	3686145	3693761	3692417	3692865

L22-M3

3788289	3795009	3787393	3788737	3795457
3787841	3790529	3792769	3789633	3794113
3796353	3790081	3790977	3791873	3785601
3795905	3792321	3789185	3791425	3786049
3786497	3786945	3794561	3793217	3793665

L21-M11

3698689	3705409	3697793	3699137	3705857
3698241	3700929	3703169	3700033	3704513
3706753	3700481	3701377	3702273	3696001
3706305	3702721	3699585	3701825	3696449
3696897	3697345	3704961	3703617	3704065

L22-M4

3799489	3806209	3798593	3799937	3806657
3799041	3801729	3803969	3800833	3805313
3807553	3801281	3802177	3803073	3796801
3807105	3803521	3800385	3802625	3797249
3797697	3798145	3805761	3804417	3804865

L21-M12

3709889	3716609	3708993	3710337	3717057
3709441	3712129	3714369	3711233	3715713
3717953	3711681	3712577	3713473	3707201
3717505	3713921	3710785	3713025	3707649
3708097	3708545	3716161	3714817	3715265

L22-M5

3810689	3817409	3809793	3811137	3817857
3810241	3812929	3815169	3812033	3816513
3818753	3812481	3813377	3814273	3808001
3818305	3814721	3811585	3813825	3808449
3808897	3809345	3816961	3815617	3816065

L21-M13

3721089	3727809	3720193	3721537	3728257
3720641	3723329	3725569	3722433	3726913
3729153	3722881	3723777	3724673	3718401
3728705	3725121	3721985	3724225	3718849
3719297	3719745	3727361	3726017	3726465

L22-M6

3821889	3828609	3820993	3822337	3829057
3821441	3824129	3826369	3823233	3827713
3829953	3823681	3824577	3825473	3819201
3829505	3825921	3822785	3825025	3819649
3820097	3820545	3828161	3826817	3827265

L.22-M7

3833089	3839809	3832193	3833537	3840257
3832641	3835329	3837569	3834433	3838913
3841153	3834881	3835777	3836673	3830401
3840705	3837121	3833985	3836225	3830849
3831297	3831745	3839361	3838017	3838465

L.22-M8

3844289	3851009	3843393	3844737	3851457
3843841	3846529	3848769	3845633	3850113
3852353	3846081	3846977	3847873	3841601
3851905	3848321	3845185	3847425	3842049
3842497	3842945	3850561	3849217	3849665

L.22-M9

3855489	3862209	3854593	3855937	3862657
3855041	3857729	3859969	3856833	3861313
3863553	3857281	3858177	3859073	3852801
3863105	3859521	3856385	3858625	3853249
3853697	3854145	3861761	3860417	3860865

L.22-M10

3866689	3873409	3865793	3867137	3873857
3866241	3868929	3871169	3868033	3872513
3874753	3868481	3869377	3870273	3864001
3874305	3870721	3867585	3869825	3864449
3864897	3865345	3872961	3871617	3872065

L.22-M11

3877889	3884609	3876993	3878337	3885057
3877441	3880129	3882369	3879233	3883713
3885953	3879681	3880577	3881473	3875201
3885505	3881921	3878785	3881025	3875649
3876097	3876545	3884161	3882817	3883265

L.22-M12

3889089	3895809	3888193	3889537	3896257
3888641	3891329	3893569	3890433	3894913
3897153	3890881	3891777	3892673	3886401
3896705	3893121	3889985	3892225	3886849
3887297	3887745	3895361	3894017	3894465

L.22-M13

3900289	3907009	3899393	3900737	3907457
3899841	3902529	3904769	3901633	3906113
3908353	3902081	3902977	3903873	3897601
3907905	3904321	3901185	3903425	3898049
3898497	3898945	3906561	3905217	3905665

L.22-M14

3911489	3918209	3910593	3911937	3918657
3911041	3913729	3915969	3912833	3917313
3919553	3913281	3914177	3915073	3908801
3919105	3915521	3912385	3914625	3909249
3909697	3910145	3917761	3916417	3916865

L.22-M15

3922689	3929409	3921793	3923137	3929857
3922241	3924929	3927169	3924033	3928513
3930753	3924481	3925377	3926273	3920001
3930305	3926721	3923585	3925825	3920449
3920897	3921345	3928961	3927617	3928065

L.22-M16

3933889	3940609	3932993	3934337	3941057
3933441	3936129	3938369	3935233	3939713
3941953	3935681	3936577	3937473	3931201
3941505	3937921	3934785	3937025	3931649
3932097	3932545	3940161	3938817	3939265

L.23-M1

3945089	3951809	3944193	3945537	3952257
3944641	3947329	3949569	3946433	3950913
3953153	3946881	3947777	3948673	3942401
3952705	3949121	3945985	3948225	3942849
3943297	3943745	3951361	3950017	3950465

L.23-M2

3956289	3963009	3955393	3956737	3963457
3955841	3958529	3960769	3957633	3962113
3964353	3958081	3958977	3959873	3953601
3963905	3960321	3957185	3959425	3954049
3954497	3954945	3962561	3961217	3961665

L.23-M3

3967489	3974209	3966593	3967937	3974657
3967041	3969729	3971969	3968833	3973313
3975553	3969281	3970177	3971073	3964801
3975105	3971521	3968385	3970625	3965249
3965697	3966145	3973761	3972417	3972865

L.23-M4

3978689	3985409	3977793	3979137	3985857
3978241	3980929	3983169	3980033	3984513
3986753	3980481	3981377	3982273	3976001
3986305	3982721	3979585	3981825	3976449
3976897	3977345	3984961	3983617	3984065

L.23-M5

3989889	3996609	3988993	3990337	3997057
3989441	3992129	3994369	3991233	3995713
3997953	3991681	3992577	3993473	3987201
3997505	3993921	3990785	3993025	3987649
3988097	3988545	3996161	3994817	3995265

L.23-M6

4001089	4007809	4000193	4001537	4008257
4000641	4003329	4005569	4002433	4006913
4009153	4002881	4003777	4004673	3998401
4008705	4005121	4001985	4004225	3998849
3999297	3999745	4007361	4006017	4006465

L.23-M7

4012289	4019009	4011393	4012737	4019457
4011841	4014529	4016769	4013633	4018113
4020353	4014081	4014977	4015873	4009601
4019905	4016321	4013185	4015425	4010049
4010497	4010945	4018561	4017217	4017665

L.23-M8

4023489	4030209	4022593	4023937	4030657
4023041	4025729	4027969	4024833	4029313
4031553	4025281	4026177	4027073	4020801
4031105	4027521	4024385	4026625	4021249
4021697	4022145	4029761	4028417	4028865

L23-M9

4034689	4041409	4033793	4035137	4041857
4034241	4036929	4039169	4036033	4040513
4042753	4036481	4037377	4038273	4032001
4042305	4038721	4035585	4037825	4032449
4032897	4033345	4040961	4039617	4040065

L23-M10

4045889	4052609	4044993	4046337	4053057
4045441	4048129	4050369	4047233	4051713
4053953	4047681	4048577	4049473	4043201
4053505	4049921	4046785	4049025	4043649
4044097	4044545	4052161	4050817	4051265

L23-M11

4057089	4063809	4056193	4057537	4064257
4056641	4059329	4061569	4058433	4062913
4065153	4058881	4059777	4060673	4054401
4064705	4061121	4057985	4060225	4054849
4055297	4055745	4063361	4062017	4062465

L23-M12

4068289	4075009	4067393	4068737	4075457
4067841	4070529	4072769	4069633	4074113
4076353	4070081	4070977	4071873	4065601
4075905	4072321	4069185	4071425	4066049
4066497	4066945	4074561	4073217	4073665

L23-M13

4079489	4086209	4078593	4079937	4086657
4079041	4081729	4083969	4080833	4085313
4087553	4081281	4082177	4083073	4076801
4087105	4083521	4080385	4082625	4077249
4077697	4078145	4085761	4084417	4084865

L23-M14

4090689	4097409	4089793	4091137	4097857
4090241	4092929	4095169	4092033	4096513
4098753	4092481	4093377	4094273	4088001
4098305	4094721	4091585	4093825	4088449
4088897	4089345	4096961	4095617	4096065

L23-M15

4101889	4108609	4100993	4102337	4109057
4101441	4104129	4106369	4103233	4107713
4109953	4103681	4104577	4105473	4099201
4109505	4105921	4102785	4105025	4099649
4100097	4100545	4108161	4106817	4107265

L23-M16

4113089	4119809	4112193	4113537	4120257
4112641	4115329	4117569	4114433	4118913
4121153	4114881	4115777	4116673	4110401
4120705	4117121	4113985	4116225	4110849
4111297	4111745	4119361	4118017	4118465

L24-M1

4124289	4131009	4123393	4124737	4131457
4123841	4126529	4128769	4125633	4130113
4132353	4126081	4126977	4127873	4121601
4131905	4128321	4125185	4127425	4122049
4122497	4122945	4130561	4129217	4129665

L24-M2

4135489	4142209	4134593	4135937	4142657
4135041	4137729	4139969	4136833	4141313
4143553	4137281	4138177	4139073	4132801
4143105	4139521	4136385	4138625	4133249
4133697	4134145	4141761	4140417	4140865

L24-M3

4146689	4153409	4145793	4147137	4153857
4146241	4148929	4151169	4148033	4152513
4154753	4148481	4149377	4150273	4144001
4154305	4150721	4147585	4149825	4144449
4144897	4145345	4152961	4151617	4152065

L24-M4

4157889	4164609	4156993	4158337	4165057
4157441	4160129	4162369	4159233	4163713
4165953	4159681	4160577	4161473	4155201
4165505	4161921	4158785	4161025	4155649
4156097	4156545	4164161	4162817	4163265

L24-M5

4169089	4175809	4168193	4169537	4176257
4168641	4171329	4173569	4170433	4174913
4177153	4170881	4171777	4172673	4166401
4176705	4173121	4169985	4172225	4166849
4167297	4167745	4175361	4174017	4174465

L24-M6

4180289	4187009	4179393	4180737	4187457
4179841	4182529	4184769	4181633	4186113
4188353	4182081	4182977	4183873	4177601
4187905	4184321	4181185	4183425	4178049
4178497	4178945	4186561	4185217	4185665

L24-M7

4191489	4198209	4190593	4191937	4198657
4191041	4193729	4195969	4192833	4197313
4199553	4193281	4194177	4195073	4188801
4199105	4195521	4192385	4194625	4189249
4189697	4190145	4197761	4196417	4196865

L24-M8

4202689	4209409	4201793	4203137	4209857
4202241	4204929	4207169	4204033	4208513
4210753	4204481	4205377	4206273	4200001
4210305	4206721	4203585	4205825	4200449
4200897	4201345	4208961	4207617	4208065

L24-M9

4213889	4220609	4212993	4214337	4221057
4213441	4216129	4218369	4215233	4219713
4221953	4215681	4216577	4217473	4211201
4221505	4217921	4214785	4217025	4211649
4212097	4212545	4220161	4218817	4219265

L24-M10

4225089	4231809	4224193	4225537	4232257
4224641	4227329	4229569	4226433	4230913
4233153	4226881	4227777	4228673	4222401
4232705	4229121	4225985	4228225	4222849
4223297	4223745	4231361	4230017	4230465

L24-M11

4236289	4243009	4235393	4236737	4243457
4235841	4238529	4240769	4237633	4242113
4244353	4238081	4238977	4239873	4233601
4243905	4240321	4237185	4239425	4234049
4234497	4234945	4242561	4241217	4241665

L24-M12

4247489	4254209	4246593	4247937	4254657
4247041	4249729	4251969	4248833	4253313
4255553	4249281	4250177	4251073	4244801
4255105	4251521	4248385	4250625	4245249
4245697	4246145	4253761	4252417	4252865

L24-M13

4258689	4265409	4257793	4259137	4265857
4258241	4260929	4263169	4260033	4264513
4266753	4260481	4261377	4262273	4256001
4266305	4262721	4259585	4261825	4256449
4256897	4257345	4264961	4263617	4264065

L24-M14

4269889	4276609	4268993	4270337	4277057
4269441	4272129	4274369	4271233	4275713
4277953	4271681	4272577	4273473	4267201
4277505	4273921	4270785	4273025	4267649
4268097	4268545	4276161	4274817	4275265

L24-M15

4281089	4287809	4280193	4281537	4288257
4280641	4283329	4285569	4282433	4286913
4289153	4282881	4283777	4284673	4278401
4288705	4285121	4281985	4284225	4278849
4279297	4279745	4287361	4286017	4286465

L24-M16

4292289	4299009	4291393	4292737	4299457
4291841	4294529	4296769	4293633	4298113
4300353	4294081	4294977	4295873	4289601
4299905	4296321	4293185	4295425	4290049
4290497	4290945	4298561	4297217	4297665

L25-M1

4303489	4310209	4302593	4303937	4310657
4303041	4305729	4307969	4304833	4309313
4311553	4305281	4306177	4307073	4300801
4311105	4307521	4304385	4306625	4301249
4301697	4302145	4309761	4308417	4308865

L25-M2

4314689	4321409	4313793	4315137	4321857
4314241	4316929	4319169	4316033	4320513
4322753	4316481	4317377	4318273	4312001
4322305	4318721	4315585	4317825	4312449
4312897	4313345	4320961	4319617	4320065

L25-M3

4325889	4332609	4324993	4326337	4333057
4325441	4328129	4330369	4327233	4331713
4333953	4327681	4328577	4329473	4323201
4333505	4329921	4326785	4329025	4323649
4324097	4324545	4332161	4330817	4331265

L25-M4

4337089	4343809	4336193	4337537	4344257
4336641	4339329	4341569	4338433	4342913
4345153	4338881	4339777	4340673	4334401
4344705	4341121	4337985	4340225	4334849
4335297	4335745	4343361	4342017	4342465

L25-M5

4348289	4355009	4347393	4348737	4355457
4347841	4350529	4352769	4349633	4354113
4356353	4350081	4350977	4351873	4345601
4355905	4352321	4349185	4351425	4346049
4346497	4346945	4354561	4353217	4353665

L25-M6

4359489	4366209	4358593	4359937	4366657
4359041	4361729	4363969	4360833	4365313
4367553	4361281	4362177	4363073	4356801
4367105	4363521	4360385	4362625	4357249
4357697	4358145	4365761	4364417	4364865

L25-M7

4370689	4377409	4369793	4371137	4377857
4370241	4372929	4375169	4372033	4376513
4378753	4372481	4373377	4374273	4368001
4378305	4374721	4371585	4373825	4368449
4368897	4369345	4376961	4375617	4376065

L25-M8

4381889	4388609	4380993	4382337	4389057
4381441	4384129	4386369	4383233	4387713
4389953	4383681	4384577	4385473	4379201
4389505	4385921	4382785	4385025	4379649
4380097	4380545	4388161	4386817	4387265

L25-M9

4393089	4399809	4392193	4393537	4400257
4392641	4395329	4397569	4394433	4398913
4401153	4394881	4395777	4396673	4390401
4400705	4397121	4393985	4396225	4390849
4391297	4391745	4399361	4398017	4398465

L25-M10

4404289	4411009	4403393	4404737	4411457
4403841	4406529	4408769	4405633	4410113
4412353	4406081	4406977	4407873	4401601
4411905	4408321	4405185	4407425	4402049
4402497	4402945	4410561	4409217	4409665

L25-M11

4415489	4422209	4414593	4415937	4422657
4415041	4417729	4419969	4416833	4421313
4423553	4417281	4418177	4419073	4412801
4423105	4419521	4416385	4418625	4413249
4413697	4414145	4421761	4420417	4420865

L25-M12

4426689	4433409	4425793	4427137	4433857
4426241	4428929	4431169	4428033	4432513
4434753	4428481	4429377	4430273	4424001
4434305	4430721	4427585	4429825	4424449
4424897	4425345	4432961	4431617	4432065

L25-M13

4437889	4444609	4436993	4438337	4445057
4437441	4440129	4442369	4439233	4443713
4445953	4439681	4440577	4441473	4435201
4445505	4441921	4438785	4441025	4435649
4436097	4436545	4444161	4442817	4443265

L25-M14

4449089	4455809	4448193	4449537	4456257
4448641	4451329	4453569	4450433	4454913
4457153	4450881	4451777	4452673	4446401
4456705	4453121	4449985	4452225	4446849
4447297	4447745	4455361	4454017	4454465

L25-M15

4460289	4467009	4459393	4460737	4467457
4459841	4462529	4464769	4461633	4466113
4468353	4462081	4462977	4463873	4457601
4467905	4464321	4461185	4463425	4458049
4458497	4458945	4466561	4465217	4465665

L25-M16

4471489	4478209	4470593	4471937	4478657
4471041	4473729	4475969	4472833	4477313
4479553	4473281	4474177	4475073	4468801
4479105	4475521	4472385	4474625	4469249
4469697	4470145	4477761	4476417	4476865

MALKUTH

L1-M1

5173	18103	3449	6035	18965
4311	9483	13793	7759	16379
20689	8621	10345	12069	1
19827	12931	6897	11207	863
1725	2587	17241	14655	15517

L1-M10

199123	212053	197399	199985	212915
198261	203433	207743	201709	210329
214639	202571	204295	206019	193951
213777	206881	200847	205157	194813
195675	196537	211191	208605	209467

L1-M2

26723	39653	24999	27585	40515
25861	31033	35343	29309	37929
42239	30171	31895	33619	21551
41377	34481	28447	32757	22413
23275	24137	38791	36205	37067

L1-M11

220673	233603	218949	221535	234465
219811	224983	229293	223259	231879
236189	224121	225845	227569	215501
235327	228431	222397	226707	216363
217225	218087	232741	230155	231017

L1-M3

48273	61203	46549	49135	62065
47411	52583	56893	50859	59479
63789	51721	53445	55169	43101
62927	56031	49997	54307	43963
44825	45687	60341	57755	58617

L1-M12

242223	255153	240499	243085	256015
241361	246533	250843	244809	253429
257739	245671	247395	249119	237051
256877	249981	243947	248257	237913
238775	239637	254291	251705	252567

L1-M4

69823	82753	68099	70685	83615
68961	74133	78443	72409	81029
85339	73271	74995	76719	64651
84477	77581	71547	75857	65513
66375	67237	81891	79305	80167

L1-M13

263773	276703	262049	264635	277565
262911	268083	272393	266359	274979
279289	267221	268945	270669	258601
278427	271531	265497	269807	259463
260325	261187	275841	273255	274117

L1-M5

91373	104303	89649	92235	105165
90511	95683	99993	93959	102579
106889	94821	96545	98269	86201
106027	99131	93097	97407	87063
87925	88787	103441	100855	101717

L1-M14

285323	298253	283599	286185	299115
284461	289633	293943	287909	296529
300839	288771	290495	292219	280151
299977	293081	287047	291357	281013
281875	282737	297391	294805	295667

L1-M6

112923	125853	111199	113785	126715
112061	117233	121543	115509	124129
128439	116371	118095	119819	107751
127577	120681	114647	118957	108613
109475	110337	124991	122405	123267

L1-M15

306873	319803	305149	307735	320665
306011	311183	315493	309459	318079
322389	310321	312045	313769	301701
321527	314631	308597	312907	302563
303425	304287	318941	316355	317217

L1-M7

134473	147403	132749	135335	148265
133611	138783	143093	137059	145679
149989	137921	139645	141369	129301
149127	142231	136197	140507	130163
131025	131887	146541	143955	144817

L1-M16

328423	341353	326699	329285	342215
327561	332733	337043	331009	339629
343939	331871	333595	335319	323251
343077	336181	330147	334457	324113
324975	325837	340491	337905	338767

L1-M8

156023	168953	154299	156885	169815
155161	160333	164643	158609	167229
171539	159471	161195	162919	150851
170677	163781	157747	162057	151713
152575	153437	168091	165505	166367

L2-M1

349973	362903	348249	350835	363765
349111	354283	358593	352559	361179
365489	353421	355145	356869	344801
364627	357731	351697	356007	345663
346525	347387	362041	359455	360317

L1-M9

177573	190503	175849	178435	191365
176711	181883	186193	180159	188779
193089	181021	182745	184469	172401
192227	185331	179297	183607	173263
174125	174987	189641	187055	187917

L2-M2

371523	384453	369799	372385	385315
370661	375833	380143	374109	382729
387039	374971	376695	378419	366351
386177	379281	373247	377557	367213
368075	368937	383591	381005	381867

L2-M3

393073	406003	391349	393935	406865
392211	397383	401693	395659	404279
408589	396521	398245	399969	387901
407727	400831	394797	399107	388763
389625	390487	405141	402555	403417

L2-M4

414623	427553	412899	415485	428415
413761	418933	423243	417209	425829
430139	418071	419795	421519	409451
429277	422381	416347	420657	410313
411175	412037	426691	424105	424967

L2-M5

436173	449103	434449	437035	449965
435311	440483	444793	438759	447379
451689	439621	441345	443069	431001
450827	443931	437897	442207	431863
432725	433587	448241	445655	446517

L2-M6

457723	470653	455999	458585	471515
456861	462033	466343	460309	468929
473239	461171	462895	464619	452551
472377	465481	459447	463757	453413
454275	455137	469791	467205	468067

L2-M7

479273	492203	477549	480135	493065
478411	483583	487893	481859	490479
494789	482721	484445	486169	474101
493927	487031	480997	485307	474963
475825	476687	491341	488755	489617

L2-M8

500823	513753	499099	501685	514615
499961	505133	509443	503409	512029
516339	504271	505995	507719	495651
515477	508581	502547	506857	496513
497375	498237	512891	510305	511167

L2-M9

522373	535303	520649	523235	536165
521511	526683	530993	524959	533579
537889	525821	527545	529269	517201
537027	530131	524097	528407	518063
518925	519787	534441	531855	532717

L2-M10

543923	556853	542199	544785	557715
543061	548233	552543	546509	555129
559439	547371	549095	550819	538751
558577	551681	545647	549957	539613
540475	541337	555991	553405	554267

L2-M11

565473	578403	563749	566335	579265
564611	569783	574093	568059	576679
580989	568921	570645	572369	560301
580127	573231	567197	571507	561163
562025	562887	577541	574955	575817

L2-M12

587023	599953	585299	587885	600815
586161	591333	595643	589609	598229
602539	590471	592195	593919	581851
601677	594781	588747	593057	582713
583575	584437	599091	596505	597367

L2-M13

608573	621503	606849	609435	622365
607711	612883	617193	611159	619779
624089	612021	613745	615469	603401
623227	616331	610297	614607	604263
605125	605987	620641	618055	618917

L2-M14

630123	643053	628399	630985	643915
629261	634433	638743	632709	641329
645639	633571	635295	637019	624951
644777	637881	631847	636157	625813
626675	627537	642191	639605	640467

L2-M15

651673	664603	649949	652535	665465
650811	655983	660293	654259	662879
667189	655121	656845	658569	646501
666327	659431	653397	657707	647363
648225	649087	663741	661155	662017

L2-M16

673223	686153	671499	674085	687015
672361	677533	681843	675809	684429
688739	676671	678395	680119	668051
687877	680981	674947	679257	668913
669775	670637	685291	682705	683567

L3-M1

694773	707703	693049	695635	708565
693911	699083	703393	697359	705979
710289	698221	699945	701669	689601
709427	702531	696497	700807	690463
691325	692187	706841	704255	705117

L3-M2

716323	729253	714599	717185	730115
715461	720633	724943	718909	727529
731839	719771	721495	723219	711151
730977	724081	718047	722357	712013
712875	713737	728391	725805	726667

L3-M3

737873	750803	736149	738735	751665
737011	742183	746493	740459	749079
753389	741321	743045	744769	732701
752527	745631	739597	743907	733563
734425	735287	749941	747355	748217

L3-M4

759423	772353	757699	760285	773215
758561	763733	768043	762009	770629
774939	762871	764595	766319	754251
774077	767181	761147	765457	755113
755975	756837	771491	768905	769767

L3-M5

780973	793903	779249	781835	794765
780111	785283	789593	783559	792179
796489	784421	786145	787869	775801
795627	788731	782697	787007	776663
777525	778387	793041	790455	791317

L3-M6

802523	815453	800799	803385	816315
801661	806833	811143	805109	813729
818039	805971	807695	809419	797351
817177	810281	804247	808557	798213
799075	799937	814591	812005	812867

L3-M7

824073	837003	822349	824935	837865
823211	828383	832693	826659	835279
839589	827521	829245	830969	818901
838727	831831	825797	830107	819763
820625	821487	836141	833555	834417

L3-M8

845623	858553	843899	846485	859415
844761	849933	854243	848209	856829
861139	849071	850795	852519	840451
860277	853381	847347	851657	841313
842175	843037	857691	855105	855967

L3-M9

867173	880103	865449	868035	880965
866311	871483	875793	869759	878379
882689	870621	872345	874069	862001
881827	874931	868897	873207	862863
863725	864587	879241	876655	877517

L3-M10

888723	901653	886999	889585	902515
887861	893033	897343	891309	899929
904239	892171	893895	895619	883551
903377	896481	890447	894757	884413
885275	886137	900791	898205	899067

L3-M11

910273	923203	908549	911135	924065
909411	914583	918893	912859	921479
925789	913721	915445	917169	905101
924927	918031	911997	916307	905963
906825	907687	922341	919755	920617

L3-M12

931823	944753	930099	932685	945615
930961	936133	940443	934409	943029
947339	935271	936995	938719	926651
946477	939581	933547	937857	927513
928375	929237	943891	941305	942167

L3-M13

953373	966303	951649	954235	967165
952511	957683	961993	955959	964579
968889	956821	958545	960269	948201
968027	961131	955097	959407	949063
949925	950787	965441	962855	963717

L3-M14

974923	987853	973199	975785	988715
974061	979233	983543	977509	986129
990439	978371	980095	981819	969751
989577	982681	976647	980957	970613
971475	972337	986991	984405	985267

L3-M15

996473	1009403	994749	997335	1010265
995611	1000783	1005093	999059	1007679
1011989	999921	1001645	1003369	991301
1011127	1004231	998197	1002507	992163
993025	993887	1008541	1005955	1006817

L3-M16

1018023	1030953	1016299	1018885	1031815
1017161	1022333	1026643	1020609	1029229
1033539	1021471	1023195	1024919	1012851
1032677	1025781	1019747	1024057	1013713
1014575	1015437	1030091	1027505	1028367

L4-M1

1039573	1052503	1037849	1040435	1053365
1038711	1043883	1048193	1042159	1050779
1055089	1043021	1044745	1046469	1034401
1054227	1047331	1041297	1045607	1035263
1036125	1036987	1051641	1049055	1049917

L4-M2

1061123	1074053	1059399	1061985	1074915
1060261	1065433	1069743	1063709	1072329
1076639	1064571	1066295	1068019	1055951
1075777	1068881	1062847	1067157	1056813
1057675	1058537	1073191	1070605	1071467

L4-M3

1082673	1095603	1080949	1083535	1096465
1081811	1086983	1091293	1085259	1093879
1098189	1086121	1087845	1089569	1077501
1097327	1090431	1084397	1088707	1078363
1079225	1080087	1094741	1092155	1093017

L4-M4

1104223	1117153	1102499	1105085	1118015
1103361	1108533	1112843	1106809	1115429
1119739	1107671	1109395	1111119	1099051
1118877	1111981	1105947	1110257	1099913
1100775	1101637	1116291	1113705	1114567

L4-M5

1125773	1138703	1124049	1126635	1139565
1124911	1130083	1134393	1128359	1136979
1141289	1129221	1130945	1132669	1120601
1140427	1133531	1127497	1131807	1121463
1122325	1123187	1137841	1135255	1136117

L4-M6

1147323	1160253	1145599	1148185	1161115
1146461	1151633	1155943	1149909	1158529
1162839	1150771	1152495	1154219	1142151
1161977	1155081	1149047	1153357	1143013
1143875	1144737	1159391	1156805	1157667

L4-M7

1168873	1181803	1167149	1169735	1182665
1168011	1173183	1177493	1171459	1180079
1184389	1172321	1174045	1175769	1163701
1183527	1176631	1170597	1174907	1164563
1165425	1166287	1180941	1178355	1179217

L4-M16

1362823	1375753	1361099	1363685	1376615
1361961	1367133	1371443	1365409	1374029
1378339	1366271	1367995	1369719	1357651
1377477	1370581	1364547	1368857	1358513
1359375	1360237	1374891	1372305	1373167

L4-M8

1190423	1203353	1188699	1191285	1204215
1189561	1194733	1199043	1193009	1201629
1205939	1193871	1195595	1197319	1185251
1205077	1198181	1192147	1196457	1186113
1186975	1187837	1202491	1199905	1200767

L5-M1

1384373	1397303	1382649	1385235	1398165
1383511	1388683	1392993	1386959	1395579
1399889	1387821	1389545	1391269	1379201
1399027	1392131	1386097	1390407	1380063
1380925	1381787	1396441	1393855	1394717

L4-M9

1211973	1224903	1210249	1212835	1225765
1211111	1216283	1220593	1214559	1223179
1227489	1215421	1217145	1218869	1206801
1226627	1219731	1213697	1218007	1207663
1208525	1209387	1224041	1221455	1222317

L5-M2

1405923	1418853	1404199	1406785	1419715
1405061	1410233	1414543	1408509	1417129
1421439	1409371	1411095	1412819	1400751
1420577	1413681	1407647	1411957	1401613
1402475	1403337	1417991	1415405	1416267

L4-M10

1233523	1246453	1231799	1234385	1247315
1232661	1237833	1242143	1236109	1244729
1249039	1236971	1238695	1240419	1228351
1248177	1241281	1235247	1239557	1229213
1230075	1230937	1245591	1243005	1243867

L5-M3

1427473	1440403	1425749	1428335	1441265
1426611	1431783	1436093	1430059	1438679
1442989	1430921	1432645	1434369	1422301
1442127	1435231	1429197	1433507	1423163
1424025	1424887	1439541	1436955	1437817

L4-M11

1255073	1268003	1253349	1255935	1268865
1254211	1259383	1263693	1257659	1266279
1270589	1258521	1260245	1261969	1249901
1269727	1262831	1256797	1261107	1250763
1251625	1252487	1267141	1264555	1265417

L5-M4

1449023	1461953	1447299	1449885	1462815
1448161	1453333	1457643	1451609	1460229
1464539	1452471	1454195	1455919	1443851
1463677	1456781	1450747	1455057	1444713
1445575	1446437	1461091	1458505	1459367

L4-M12

1276623	1289553	1274899	1277485	1290415
1275761	1280933	1285243	1279209	1287829
1292139	1280071	1281795	1283519	1271451
1291277	1284381	1278347	1282657	1272313
1273175	1274037	1288691	1286105	1286967

L5-M5

1470573	1483503	1468849	1471435	1484365
1469711	1474883	1479193	1473159	1481779
1486089	1474021	1475745	1477469	1465401
1485227	1478331	1472297	1476607	1466263
1467125	1467987	1482641	1480055	1480917

L4-M13

1298173	1311103	1296449	1299035	1311965
1297311	1302483	1306793	1300759	1309379
1313689	1301621	1303345	1305069	1293001
1312827	1305931	1299897	1304207	1293863
1294725	1295587	1310241	1307655	1308517

L5-M6

1492123	1505053	1490399	1492985	1505915
1491261	1496433	1500743	1494709	1503329
1507639	1495571	1497295	1499019	1486951
1506777	1499881	1493847	1498157	1487813
1488675	1489537	1504191	1501605	1502467

L4-M14

1319723	1332653	1317999	1320585	1333515
1318861	1324033	1328343	1322309	1330929
1335239	1323171	1324895	1326619	1314551
1334377	1327481	1321447	1325757	1315413
1316275	1317137	1331791	1329205	1330067

L5-M7

1513673	1526603	1511949	1514535	1527465
1512811	1517983	1522293	1516259	1524879
1529189	1517121	1518845	1520569	1508501
1528327	1521431	1515397	1519707	1509363
1510225	1511087	1525741	1523155	1524017

L4-M15

1341273	1354203	1339549	1342135	1355065
1340411	1345583	1349893	1343859	1352479
1356789	1344721	1346445	1348169	1336101
1355927	1349031	1342997	1347307	1336963
1337825	1338687	1353341	1350755	1351617

L5-M8

1535223	1548153	1533499	1536085	1549015
1534361	1539533	1543843	1537809	1546429
1550739	1538671	1540395	1542119	1530051
1549877	1542981	1536947	1541257	1530913
1531775	1532637	1547291	1544705	1545567

L5-M9

1556773	1569703	1555049	1557635	1570565
1555911	1561083	1565393	1559359	1567979
1572289	1560221	1561945	1563669	1551601
1571427	1564531	1558497	1562807	1552463
1553325	1554187	1568841	1566255	1567117

L5-M10

1578323	1591253	1576599	1579185	1592115
1577461	1582633	1586943	1580909	1589529
1593839	1581771	1583495	1585219	1573151
1592977	1586081	1580047	1584357	1574013
1574875	1575737	1590391	1587805	1588667

L5-M11

1599873	1612803	1598149	1600735	1613665
1599011	1604183	1608493	1602459	1611079
1615389	1603321	1605045	1606769	1594701
1614527	1607631	1601597	1605907	1595563
1596425	1597287	1611941	1609355	1610217

L5-M12

1621423	1634353	1619699	1622285	1635215
1620561	1625733	1630043	1624009	1632629
1636939	1624871	1626595	1628319	1616251
1636077	1629181	1623147	1627457	1617113
1617975	1618837	1633491	1630905	1631767

L5-M13

1642973	1655903	1641249	1643835	1656765
1642111	1647283	1651593	1645559	1654179
1658489	1646421	1648145	1649869	1637801
1657627	1650731	1644697	1649007	1638663
1639525	1640387	1655041	1652455	1653317

L5-M14

1664523	1677453	1662799	1665385	1678315
1663661	1668833	1673143	1667109	1675729
1680039	1667971	1669695	1671419	1659351
1679177	1672281	1666247	1670557	1660213
1661075	1661937	1676591	1674005	1674867

L5-M15

1686073	1699003	1684349	1686935	1699865
1685211	1690383	1694693	1688659	1697279
1701589	1689521	1691245	1692969	1680901
1700727	1693831	1687797	1692107	1681763
1682625	1683487	1698141	1695555	1696417

L5-M16

1707623	1720553	1705899	1708485	1721415
1706761	1711933	1716243	1710209	1718829
1723139	1711071	1712795	1714519	1702451
1722277	1715381	1709347	1713657	1703313
1704175	1705037	1719691	1717105	1717967

L6-M1

1729173	1742103	1727449	1730035	1742965
1728311	1733483	1737793	1731759	1740379
1744689	1732621	1734345	1736069	1724001
1743827	1736931	1730897	1735207	1724863
1725725	1726587	1741241	1738655	1739517

L6-M2

1750723	1763653	1748999	1751585	1764515
1749861	1755033	1759343	1753309	1761929
1766239	1754171	1755895	1757619	1745551
1765377	1758481	1752447	1756757	1746413
1747275	1748137	1762791	1760205	1761067

L6-M3

1772273	1785203	1770549	1773135	1786065
1771411	1776583	1780893	1774859	1783479
1787789	1775721	1777445	1779169	1767101
1786927	1780031	1773997	1778307	1767963
1768825	1769687	1784341	1781755	1782617

L6-M4

1793823	1806753	1792099	1794685	1807615
1792961	1798133	1802443	1796409	1805029
1809339	1797271	1798995	1800719	1788651
1808477	1801581	1795547	1799857	1789513
1790375	1791237	1805891	1803305	1804167

L6-M5

1815373	1828303	1813649	1816235	1829165
1814511	1819683	1823993	1817959	1826579
1830889	1818821	1820545	1822269	1810201
1830027	1823131	1817097	1821407	1811063
1811925	1812787	1827441	1824855	1825717

L6-M6

1836923	1849853	1835199	1837785	1850715
1836061	1841233	1845543	1839509	1848129
1852439	1840371	1842095	1843819	1831751
1851577	1844681	1838647	1842957	1832613
1833475	1834337	1848991	1846405	1847267

L6-M7

1858473	1871403	1856749	1859335	1872265
1857611	1862783	1867093	1861059	1869679
1873989	1861921	1863645	1865369	1853301
1873127	1866231	1860197	1864507	1854163
1855025	1855887	1870541	1867955	1868817

L6-M8

1880023	1892953	1878299	1880885	1893815
1879161	1884333	1888643	1882609	1891229
1895539	1883471	1885195	1886919	1874851
1894677	1887781	1881747	1886057	1875713
1876575	1877437	1892091	1889505	1890367

L6-M9

1901573	1914503	1899849	1902435	1915365
1900711	1905883	1910193	1904159	1912779
1917089	1905021	1906745	1908469	1896401
1916227	1909331	1903297	1907607	1897263
1898125	1898987	1913641	1911055	1911917

L6-M10

1923123	1936053	1921399	1923985	1936915
1922261	1927433	1931743	1925709	1934329
1938639	1926571	1928295	1930019	1917951
1937777	1930881	1924847	1929157	1918813
1919675	1920537	1935191	1932605	1933467

L6-M11

1944673	1957603	1942949	1945535	1958465
1943811	1948983	1953293	1947259	1955879
1960189	1948121	1949845	1951569	1939501
1959327	1952431	1946397	1950707	1940363
1941225	1942087	1956741	1954155	1955017

L6-M12

1966223	1979153	1964499	1967085	1980015
1965361	1970533	1974843	1968809	1977429
1981739	1969671	1971395	1973119	1961051
1980877	1973981	1967947	1972257	1961913
1962775	1963637	1978291	1975705	1976567

L6-M13

1987773	2000703	1986049	1988635	2001565
1986911	1992083	1996393	1990359	1998979
2003289	1991221	1992945	1994669	1982601
2002427	1995531	1989497	1993807	1983463
1984325	1985187	1999841	1997255	1998117

L6-M14

2009323	2022253	2007599	2010185	2023115
2008461	2013633	2017943	2011909	2020529
2024839	2012771	2014495	2016219	2004151
2023977	2017081	2011047	2015357	2005013
2005875	2006737	2021391	2018805	2019667

L6-M15

2030873	2043803	2029149	2031735	2044665
2030011	2035183	2039493	2033459	2042079
2046389	2034321	2036045	2037769	2025701
2045527	2038631	2032597	2036907	2026563
2027425	2028287	2042941	2040355	2041217

L6-M16

2052423	2065353	2050699	2053285	2066215
2051561	2056733	2061043	2055009	2063629
2067939	2055871	2057595	2059319	2047251
2067077	2060181	2054147	2058457	2048113
2048975	2049837	2064491	2061905	2062767

L7-M1

2073973	2086903	2072249	2074835	2087765
2073111	2078283	2082593	2076559	2085179
2089489	2077421	2079145	2080869	2068801
2088627	2081731	2075697	2080007	2069663
2070525	2071387	2086041	2083455	2084317

L7-M2

2095523	2108453	2093799	2096385	2109315
2094661	2099833	2104143	2098109	2106729
2111039	2098971	2100695	2102419	2090351
2110177	2103281	2097247	2101557	2091213
2092075	2092937	2107591	2105005	2105867

L7-M3

2117073	2130003	2115349	2117935	2130865
2116211	2121383	2125693	2119659	2128279
2132589	2120521	2122245	2123969	2111901
2131727	2124831	2118797	2123107	2112763
2113625	2114487	2129141	2126555	2127417

L7-M4

2138623	2151553	2136899	2139485	2152415
2137761	2142933	2147243	2141209	2149829
2154139	2142071	2143795	2145519	2133451
2153277	2146381	2140347	2144657	2134313
2135175	2136037	2150691	2148105	2148967

L7-M5

2160173	2173103	2158449	2161035	2173965
2159311	2164483	2168793	2162759	2171379
2175689	2163621	2165345	2167069	2155001
2174827	2167931	2161897	2166207	2155863
2156725	2157587	2172241	2169655	2170517

L7-M6

2181723	2194653	2179999	2182585	2195515
2180861	2186033	2190343	2184309	2192929
2197239	2185171	2186895	2188619	2176551
2196377	2189481	2183447	2187757	2177413
2178275	2179137	2193791	2191205	2192067

L7-M7

2203273	2216203	2201549	2204135	2217065
2202411	2207583	2211893	2205859	2214479
2218789	2206721	2208445	2210169	2198101
2217927	2211031	2204997	2209307	2198963
2199825	2200687	2215341	2212755	2213617

L7-M8

2224823	2237753	2223099	2225685	2238615
2223961	2229133	2233443	2227409	2236029
2240339	2228271	2229995	2231719	2219651
2239477	2232581	2226547	2230857	2220513
2221375	2222237	2236891	2234305	2235167

L7-M9

2246373	2259303	2244649	2247235	2260165
2245511	2250683	2254993	2248959	2257579
2261889	2249821	2251545	2253269	2241201
2261027	2254131	2248097	2252407	2242063
2242925	2243787	2258441	2255855	2256717

L7-M10

2267923	2280853	2266199	2268785	2281715
2267061	2272233	2276543	2270509	2279129
2283439	2271371	2273095	2274819	2262751
2282577	2275681	2269647	2273957	2263613
2264475	2265337	2279991	2277405	2278267

L7-M11

2289473	2302403	2287749	2290335	2303265
2288611	2293783	2298093	2292059	2300679
2304989	2292921	2294645	2296369	2284301
2304127	2297231	2291197	2295507	2285163
2286025	2286887	2301541	2298955	2299817

L7-M12

2311023	2323953	2309299	2311885	2324815
2310161	2315333	2319643	2313609	2322229
2326539	2314471	2316195	2317919	2305851
2325677	2318781	2312747	2317057	2306713
2307575	2308437	2323091	2320505	2321367

L7-M13

2332573	2345503	2330849	2333435	2346365
2331711	2336883	2341193	2335159	2343779
2348089	2336021	2337745	2339469	2327401
2347227	2340331	2334297	2338607	2328263
2329125	2329987	2344641	2342055	2342917

L7-M14

2354123	2367053	2352399	2354985	2367915
2353261	2358433	2362743	2356709	2365329
2369639	2357571	2359295	2361019	2348951
2368777	2361881	2355847	2360157	2349813
2350675	2351537	2366191	2363605	2364467

L7-M15

2375673	2388603	2373949	2376535	2389465
2374811	2379983	2384293	2378259	2386879
2391189	2379121	2380845	2382569	2370501
2390327	2383431	2377397	2381707	2371363
2372225	2373087	2387741	2385155	2386017

L7-M16

2397223	2410153	2395499	2398085	2411015
2396361	2401533	2405843	2399809	2408429
2412739	2400671	2402395	2404119	2392051
2411877	2404981	2398947	2403257	2392913
2393775	2394637	2409291	2406705	2407567

L8M1

2418773	2431703	2417049	2419635	2432565
2417911	2423083	2427393	2421359	2429979
2434289	2422221	2423945	2425669	2413601
2433427	2426531	2420497	2424807	2414463
2415325	2416187	2430841	2428255	2429117

L8-M2

2440323	2453253	2438599	2441185	2454115
2439461	2444633	2448943	2442909	2451529
2455839	2443771	2445495	2447219	2435151
2454977	2448081	2442047	2446357	2436013
2436875	2437737	2452391	2449805	2450667

L8-M3

2461873	2474803	2460149	2462735	2475665
2461011	2466183	2470493	2464459	2473079
2477389	2465321	2467045	2468769	2456701
2476527	2469631	2463597	2467907	2457563
2458425	2459287	2473941	2471355	2472217

L8-M4

2483423	2496353	2481699	2484285	2497215
2482561	2487733	2492043	2486009	2494629
2498939	2486871	2488595	2490319	2478251
2498077	2491181	2485147	2489457	2479113
2479975	2480837	2495491	2492905	2493767

L8-M5

2504973	2517903	2503249	2505835	2518765
2504111	2509283	2513593	2507559	2516179
2520489	2508421	2510145	2511869	2499801
2519627	2512731	2506697	2511007	2500663
2501525	2502387	2517041	2514455	2515317

L8-M6

2526523	2539453	2524799	2527385	2540315
2525661	2530833	2535143	2529109	2537729
2542039	2529971	2531695	2533419	2521351
2541177	2534281	2528247	2532557	2522213
2523075	2523937	2538591	2536005	2536867

L8-M7

2548073	2561003	2546349	2548935	2561865
2547211	2552383	2556693	2550659	2559279
2563589	2551521	2553245	2554969	2542901
2562727	2555831	2549797	2554107	2543763
2544625	2545487	2560141	2557555	2558417

L8-M8

2569623	2582553	2567899	2570485	2583415
2568761	2573933	2578243	2572209	2580829
2585139	2573071	2574795	2576519	2564451
2584277	2577381	2571347	2575657	2565313
2566175	2567037	2581691	2579105	2579967

L8-M9

2591173	2604103	2589449	2592035	2604965
2590311	2595483	2599793	2593759	2602379
2606689	2594621	2596345	2598069	2586001
2605827	2598931	2592897	2597207	2586863
2587725	2588587	2603241	2600655	2601517

L8-M10

2612723	2625653	2610999	2613585	2626515
2611861	2617033	2621343	2615309	2623929
2628239	2616171	2617895	2619619	2607551
2627377	2620481	2614447	2618757	2608413
2609275	2610137	2624791	2622205	2623067

L8-M11

2634273	2647203	2632549	2635135	2648065
2633411	2638583	2642893	2636859	2645479
2649789	2637721	2639445	2641169	2629101
2648927	2642031	2635997	2640307	2629963
2630825	2631687	2646341	2643755	2644617

L8-M12

2655823	2668753	2654099	2656685	2669615
2654961	2660133	2664443	2658409	2667029
2671339	2659271	2660995	2662719	2650651
2670477	2663581	2657547	2661857	2651513
2652375	2653237	2667891	2665305	2666167

L8-M13

2677373	2690303	2675649	2678235	2691165
2676511	2681683	2685993	2679959	2688579
2692889	2680821	2682545	2684269	2672201
2692027	2685131	2679097	2683407	2673063
2673925	2674787	2689441	2686855	2687717

L8-M14

2698923	2711853	2697199	2699785	2712715
2698061	2703233	2707543	2701509	2710129
2714439	2702371	2704095	2705819	2693751
2713577	2706681	2700647	2704957	2694613
2695475	2696337	2710991	2708405	2709267

L8-M15

2720473	2733403	2718749	2721335	2734265
2719611	2724783	2729093	2723059	2731679
2735989	2723921	2725645	2727369	2715301
2735127	2728231	2722197	2726507	2716163
2717025	2717887	2732541	2729955	2730817

L8-M16

2742023	2754953	2740299	2742885	2755815
2741161	2746333	2750643	2744609	2753229
2757539	2745471	2747195	2748919	2736851
2756677	2749781	2743747	2748057	2737713
2738575	2739437	2754091	2751505	2752367

L9-M1

2763573	2776503	2761849	2764435	2777365
2762711	2767883	2772193	2766159	2774779
2779089	2767021	2768745	2770469	2758401
2778227	2771331	2765297	2769607	2759263
2760125	2760987	2775641	2773055	2773917

L9-M2

2785123	2798053	2783399	2785985	2798915
2784261	2789433	2793743	2787709	2796329
2800639	2788571	2790295	2792019	2779951
2799777	2792881	2786847	2791157	2780813
2781675	2782537	2797191	2794605	2795467

L9-M3

2806673	2819603	2804949	2807535	2820465
2805811	2810983	2815293	2809259	2817879
2822189	2810121	2811845	2813569	2801501
2821327	2814431	2808397	2812707	2802363
2803225	2804087	2818741	2816155	2817017

L9-M4

2828223	2841153	2826499	2829085	2842015
2827361	2832533	2836843	2830809	2839429
2843739	2831671	2833395	2835119	2823051
2842877	2835981	2829947	2834257	2823913
2824775	2825637	2840291	2837705	2838567

L9-M5

2849773	2862703	2848049	2850635	2863565
2848911	2854083	2858393	2852359	2860979
2865289	2853221	2854945	2856669	2844601
2864427	2857531	2851497	2855807	2845463
2846325	2847187	2861841	2859255	2860117

L9-M6

2871323	2884253	2869599	2872185	2885115
2870461	2875633	2879943	2873909	2882529
2886839	2874771	2876495	2878219	2866151
2885977	2879081	2873047	2877357	2867013
2867875	2868737	2883391	2880805	2881667

L9-M7

2892873	2905803	2891149	2893735	2906665
2892011	2897183	2901493	2895459	2904079
2908389	2896321	2898045	2899769	2887701
2907527	2900631	2894597	2898907	2888563
2889425	2890287	2904941	2902355	2903217

L9-M8

2914423	2927353	2912699	2915285	2928215
2913561	2918733	2923043	2917009	2925629
2929939	2917871	2919595	2921319	2909251
2929077	2922181	2916147	2920457	2910113
2910975	2911837	2926491	2923905	2924767

L9-M9

2935973	2948903	2934249	2936835	2949765
2935111	2940283	2944593	2938559	2947179
2951489	2939421	2941145	2942869	2930801
2950627	2943731	2937697	2942007	2931663
2932525	2933387	2948041	2945455	2946317

L9-M10

2957523	2970453	2955799	2958385	2971315
2956661	2961833	2966143	2960109	2968729
2973039	2960971	2962695	2964419	2952351
2972177	2965281	2959247	2963557	2953213
2954075	2954937	2969591	2967005	2967867

L9-M11

2979073	2992003	2977349	2979935	2992865
2978211	2983383	2987693	2981659	2990279
2994589	2982521	2984245	2985969	2973901
2993727	2986831	2980797	2985107	2974763
2975625	2976487	2991141	2988555	2989417

L9-M12

3000623	3013553	2998899	3001485	3014415
2999761	3004933	3009243	3003209	3011829
3016139	3004071	3005795	3007519	2995451
3015277	3008381	3002347	3006657	2996313
2997175	2998037	3012691	3010105	3010967

L9-M13

3022173	3035103	3020449	3023035	3035965
3021311	3026483	3030793	3024759	3033379
3037689	3025621	3027345	3029069	3017001
3036827	3029931	3023897	3028207	3017863
3018725	3019587	3034241	3031655	3032517

L9-M14

3043723	3056653	3041999	3044585	3057515
3042861	3048033	3052343	3046309	3054929
3059239	3047171	3048895	3050619	3038551
3058377	3051481	3045447	3049757	3039413
3040275	3041137	3055791	3053205	3054067

L9-M15

3065273	3078203	3063549	3066135	3079065
3064411	3069583	3073893	3067859	3076479
3080789	3068721	3070445	3072169	3060101
3079927	3073031	3066997	3071307	3060963
3061825	3062687	3077341	3074755	3075617

L9-M16

3086823	3099753	3085099	3087685	3100615
3085961	3091133	3095443	3089409	3098029
3102339	3090271	3091995	3093719	3081651
3101477	3094581	3088547	3092857	3082513
3083375	3084237	3098891	3096305	3097167

L10-M1

3108373	3121303	3106649	3109235	3122165
3107511	3112683	3116993	3110959	3119579
3123889	3111821	3113545	3115269	3103201
3123027	3116131	3110097	3114407	3104063
3104925	3105787	3120441	3117855	3118717

L10-M10

3302323	3315253	3300599	3303185	3316115
3301461	3306633	3310943	3304909	3313529
3317839	3305771	3307495	3309219	3297151
3316977	3310081	3304047	3308357	3298013
3298875	3299737	3314391	3311805	3312667

L10-M2

3129923	3142853	3128199	3130785	3143715
3129061	3134233	3138543	3132509	3141129
3145439	3133371	3135095	3136819	3124751
3144577	3137681	3131647	3135957	3125613
3126475	3127337	3141991	3139405	3140267

L10-M11

3323873	3336803	3322149	3324735	3337665
3323011	3328183	3332493	3326459	3335079
3339389	3327321	3329045	3330769	3318701
3338527	3331631	3325597	3329907	3319563
3320425	3321287	3335941	3333355	3334217

L10-M3

3151473	3164403	3149749	3152335	3165265
3150611	3155783	3160093	3154059	3162679
3166989	3154921	3156645	3158369	3146301
3166127	3159231	3153197	3157507	3147163
3148025	3148887	3163541	3160955	3161817

L10-M12

3345423	3358353	3343699	3346285	3359215
3344561	3349733	3354043	3348009	3356629
3360939	3348871	3350595	3352319	3340251
3360077	3353181	3347147	3351457	3341113
3341975	3342837	3357491	3354905	3355767

L10-M4

3173023	3185953	3171299	3173885	3186815
3172161	3177333	3181643	3175609	3184229
3188539	3176471	3178195	3179919	3167851
3187677	3180781	3174747	3179057	3168713
3169575	3170437	3185091	3182505	3183367

L10-M13

3366973	3379903	3365249	3367835	3380765
3366111	3371283	3375593	3369559	3378179
3382489	3370421	3372145	3373869	3361801
3381627	3374731	3368697	3373007	3362663
3363525	3364387	3379041	3376455	3377317

L10-M5

3194573	3207503	3192849	3195435	3208365
3193711	3198883	3203193	3197159	3205779
3210089	3198021	3199745	3201469	3189401
3209227	3202331	3196297	3200607	3190263
3191125	3191987	3206641	3204055	3204917

L10-M14

3388523	3401453	3386799	3389385	3402315
3387661	3392833	3397143	3391109	3399729
3404039	3391971	3393695	3395419	3383351
3403177	3396281	3390247	3394557	3384213
3385075	3385937	3400591	3398005	3398867

L10-M6

3216123	3229053	3214399	3216985	3229915
3215261	3220433	3224743	3218709	3227329
3231639	3219571	3221295	3223019	3210951
3230777	3223881	3217847	3222157	3211813
3212675	3213537	3228191	3225605	3226467

L10-M15

3410073	3423003	3408349	3410935	3423865
3409211	3414383	3418693	3412659	3421279
3425589	3413521	3415245	3416969	3404901
3424727	3417831	3411797	3416107	3405763
3406625	3407487	3422141	3419555	3420417

L10-M7

3237673	3250603	3235949	3238535	3251465
3236811	3241983	3246293	3240259	3248879
3253189	3241121	3242845	3244569	3232501
3252327	3245431	3239397	3243707	3233363
3234225	3235087	3249741	3247155	3248017

L10-M16

3431623	3444553	3429899	3432485	3445415
3430761	3435933	3440243	3434209	3442829
3447139	3435071	3436795	3438519	3426451
3446277	3439381	3433347	3437657	3427313
3428175	3429037	3443691	3441105	3441967

L10-M8

3259223	3272153	3257499	3260085	3273015
3258361	3263533	3267843	3261809	3270429
3274739	3262671	3264395	3266119	3254051
3273877	3266981	3260947	3265257	3254913
3255775	3256637	3271291	3268705	3269567

L11-M1

3453173	3466103	3451449	3454035	3466965
3452311	3457483	3461793	3455759	3464379
3468689	3456621	3458345	3460069	3448001
3467827	3460931	3454897	3459207	3448863
3449725	3450587	3465241	3462655	3463517

L10-M9

3280773	3293703	3279049	3281635	3294565
3279911	3285083	3289393	3283359	3291979
3296289	3284221	3285945	3287669	3275601
3295427	3288531	3282497	3286807	3276463
3277325	3278187	3292841	3290255	3291117

L11-M2

3474723	3487653	3472999	3475585	3488515
3473861	3479033	3483343	3477309	3485929
3490239	3478171	3479895	3481619	3469551
3489377	3482481	3476447	3480757	3470413
3471275	3472137	3486791	3484205	3485067

L11-M3

3496273	3509203	3494549	3497135	3510065
3495411	3500583	3504893	3498859	3507479
3511789	3499721	3501445	3503169	3491101
3510927	3504031	3497997	3502307	3491963
3492825	3493687	3508341	3505755	3506617

L11-M12

3690223	3703153	3688499	3691085	3704015
3689361	3694533	3698843	3692809	3701429
3705739	3693671	3695395	3697119	3685051
3704877	3697981	3691947	3696257	3685913
3686775	3687637	3702291	3699705	3700567

L11-M4

3517823	3530753	3516099	3518685	3531615
3516961	3522133	3526443	3520409	3529029
3533339	3521271	3522995	3524719	3512651
3532477	3525581	3519547	3523857	3513513
3514375	3515237	3529891	3527305	3528167

L11-M13

3711773	3724703	3710049	3712635	3725565
3710911	3716083	3720393	3714359	3722979
3727289	3715221	3716945	3718669	3706601
3726427	3719531	3713497	3717807	3707463
3708325	3709187	3723841	3721255	3722117

L11-M5

3539373	3552303	3537649	3540235	3553165
3538511	3543683	3547993	3541959	3550579
3554889	3542821	3544545	3546269	3534201
3554027	3547131	3541097	3545407	3535063
3535925	3536787	3551441	3548855	3549717

L11-M14

3733323	3746253	3731599	3734185	3747115
3732461	3737633	3741943	3735909	3744529
3748839	3736771	3738495	3740219	3728151
3747977	3741081	3735047	3739357	3729013
3729875	3730737	3745391	3742805	3743667

L11-M6

3560923	3573853	3559199	3561785	3574715
3560061	3565233	3569543	3563509	3572129
3576439	3564371	3566095	3567819	3555751
3575577	3568681	3562647	3566957	3556613
3557475	3558337	3572991	3570405	3571267

L11-M15

3754873	3767803	3753149	3755735	3768665
3754011	3759183	3763493	3757459	3766079
3770389	3758321	3760045	3761769	3749701
3769527	3762631	3756597	3760907	3750563
3751425	3752287	3766941	3764355	3765217

L11-M7

3582473	3595403	3580749	3583335	3596265
3581611	3586783	3591093	3585059	3593679
3597989	3585921	3587645	3589369	3577301
3597127	3590231	3584197	3588507	3578163
3579025	3579887	3594541	3591955	3592817

L11-M16

3776423	3789353	3774699	3777285	3790215
3775561	3780733	3785043	3779009	3787629
3791939	3779871	3781595	3783319	3771251
3791077	3784181	3778147	3782457	3772113
3772975	3773837	3788491	3785905	3786767

L11-M8

3604023	3616953	3602299	3604885	3617815
3603161	3608333	3612643	3606609	3615229
3619539	3607471	3609195	3610919	3598851
3618677	3611781	3605747	3610057	3599713
3600575	3601437	3616091	3613505	3614367

L12-M1

3797973	3810903	3796249	3798835	3811765
3797111	3802283	3806593	3800559	3809179
3813489	3801421	3803145	3804869	3792801
3812627	3805731	3799697	3804007	3793663
3794525	3795387	3810041	3807455	3808317

L11-M9

3625573	3638503	3623849	3626435	3639365
3624711	3629883	3634193	3628159	3636779
3641089	3629021	3630745	3632469	3620401
3640227	3633331	3627297	3631607	3621263
3622125	3622987	3637641	3635055	3635917

L12-M2

3819523	3832453	3817799	3820385	3833315
3818661	3823833	3828143	3822109	3830729
3835039	3822971	3824695	3826419	3814351
3834177	3827281	3821247	3825557	3815213
3816075	3816937	3831591	3829005	3829867

L11-M10

3647123	3660053	3645399	3647985	3660915
3646261	3651433	3655743	3649709	3658329
3662639	3650571	3652295	3654019	3641951
3661777	3654881	3648847	3653157	3642813
3643675	3644537	3659191	3656605	3657467

L12-M3

3841073	3854003	3839349	3841935	3854865
3840211	3845383	3849693	3843659	3852279
3856589	3844521	3846245	3847969	3835901
3855727	3848831	3842797	3847107	3836763
3837625	3838487	3853141	3850555	3851417

L11-M11

3668673	3681603	3666949	3669535	3682465
3667811	3672983	3677293	3671259	3679879
3684189	3672121	3673845	3675569	3663501
3683327	3676431	3670397	3674707	3664363
3665225	3666087	3680741	3678155	3679017

L12-M4

3862623	3875553	3860899	3863485	3876415
3861761	3866933	3871243	3865209	3873829
3878139	3866071	3867795	3869519	3857451
3877277	3870381	3864347	3868657	3858313
3859175	3860037	3874691	3872105	3872967

L12-M5

3884173	3897103	3882449	3885035	3897965
3883311	3888483	3892793	3886759	3895379
3899689	3887621	3889345	3891069	3879001
3898827	3891931	3885897	3890207	3879863
3880725	3881587	3896241	3893655	3894517

L12-M6

3905723	3918653	3903999	3906585	3919515
3904861	3910033	3914343	3908309	3916929
3921239	3909171	3910895	3912619	3900551
3920377	3913481	3907447	3911757	3901413
3902275	3903137	3917791	3915205	3916067

L12-M7

3927273	3940203	3925549	3928135	3941065
3926411	3931583	3935893	3929859	3938479
3942789	3930721	3932445	3934169	3922101
3941927	3935031	3928997	3933307	3922963
3923825	3924687	3939341	3936755	3937617

L12-M8

3948823	3961753	3947099	3949685	3962615
3947961	3953133	3957443	3951409	3960029
3964339	3952271	3953995	3955719	3943651
3963477	3956581	3950547	3954857	3944513
3945375	3946237	3960891	3958305	3959167

L12-M9

3970373	3983303	3968649	3971235	3984165
3969511	3974683	3978993	3972959	3981579
3985889	3973821	3975545	3977269	3965201
3985027	3978131	3972097	3976407	3966063
3966925	3967787	3982441	3979855	3980717

L12-M10

3991923	4004853	3990199	3992785	4005715
3991061	3996233	4000543	3994509	4003129
4007439	3995371	3997095	3998819	3986751
4006577	3999681	3993647	3997957	3987613
3988475	3989337	4003991	4001405	4002267

L12-M11

4013473	4026403	4011749	4014335	4027265
4012611	4017783	4022093	4016059	4024679
4028989	4016921	4018645	4020369	4008301
4028127	4021231	4015197	4019507	4009163
4010025	4010887	4025541	4022955	4023817

L12-M12

4035023	4047953	4033299	4035885	4048815
4034161	4039333	4043643	4037609	4046229
4050539	4038471	4040195	4041919	4029851
4049677	4042781	4036747	4041057	4030713
4031575	4032437	4047091	4044505	4045367

L12-M13

4056573	4069503	4054849	4057435	4070365
4055711	4060883	4065193	4059159	4067779
4072089	4060021	4061745	4063469	4051401
4071227	4064331	4058297	4062607	4052263
4053125	4053987	4068641	4066055	4066917

L12-M14

4078123	4091053	4076399	4078985	4091915
4077261	4082433	4086743	4080709	4089329
4093639	4081571	4083295	4085019	4072951
4092777	4085881	4079847	4084157	4073813
4074675	4075537	4090191	4087605	4088467

L12-M15

4099673	4112603	4097949	4100535	4113465
4098811	4103983	4108293	4102259	4110879
4115189	4103121	4104845	4106569	4094501
4114327	4107431	4101397	4105707	4095363
4096225	4097087	4111741	4109155	4110017

L12-M16

4121223	4134153	4119499	4122085	4135015
4120361	4125533	4129843	4123809	4132429
4136739	4124671	4126395	4128119	4116051
4135877	4128981	4122947	4127257	4116913
4117775	4118637	4133291	4130705	4131567

L13-M1

4142773	4155703	4141049	4143635	4156565
4141911	4147083	4151393	4145359	4153979
4158289	4146221	4147945	4149669	4137601
4157427	4150531	4144497	4148807	4138463
4139325	4140187	4154841	4152255	4153117

L13-M2

4164323	4177253	4162599	4165185	4178115
4163461	4168633	4172943	4166909	4175529
4179839	4167771	4169495	4171219	4159151
4178977	4172081	4166047	4170357	4160013
4160875	4161737	4176391	4173805	4174667

L13-M3

4185873	4198803	4184149	4186735	4199665
4185011	4190183	4194493	4188459	4197079
4201389	4189321	4191045	4192769	4180701
4200527	4193631	4187597	4191907	4181563
4182425	4183287	4197941	4195355	4196217

L13-M4

4207423	4220353	4205699	4208285	4221215
4206561	4211733	4216043	4210009	4218629
4222939	4210871	4212595	4214319	4202251
4222077	4215181	4209147	4213457	4203113
4203975	4204837	4219491	4216905	4217767

L13-M5

4228973	4241903	4227249	4229835	4242765
4228111	4233283	4237593	4231559	4240179
4244489	4232421	4234145	4235869	4223801
4243627	4236731	4230697	4235007	4224663
4225525	4226387	4241041	4238455	4239317

L13-M6

4250523	4263453	4248799	4251385	4264315
4249661	4254833	4259143	4253109	4261729
4266039	4253971	4255695	4257419	4245351
4265177	4258281	4252247	4256557	4246213
4247075	4247937	4262591	4260005	4260867

L13-M7

4272073	4285003	4270349	4272935	4285865
4271211	4276383	4280693	4274659	4283279
4287589	4275521	4277245	4278969	4266901
4286727	4279831	4273797	4278107	4267763
4268625	4269487	4284141	4281555	4282417

L13-M16

4466023	4478953	4464299	4466885	4479815
4465161	4470333	4474643	4468609	4477229
4481539	4469471	4471195	4472919	4460851
4480677	4473781	4467747	4472057	4461713
4462575	4463437	4478091	4475505	4476367

L13-M8

4293623	4306553	4291899	4294485	4307415
4292761	4297933	4302243	4296209	4304829
4309139	4297071	4298795	4300519	4288451
4308277	4301381	4295347	4299657	4289313
4290175	4291037	4305691	4303105	4303967

L14-M1

4487573	4500503	4485849	4488435	4501365
4486711	4491883	4496193	4490159	4498779
4503089	4491021	4492745	4494469	4482401
4502227	4495331	4489297	4493607	4483263
4484125	4484987	4499641	4497055	4497917

L13-M9

4315173	4328103	4313449	4316035	4328965
4314311	4319483	4323793	4317759	4326379
4330689	4318621	4320345	4322069	4310001
4329827	4322931	4316897	4321207	4310863
4311725	4312587	4327241	4324655	4325517

L14-M2

4509123	4522053	4507399	4509985	4522915
4508261	4513433	4517743	4511709	4520329
4524639	4512571	4514295	4516019	4503951
4523777	4516881	4510847	4515157	4504813
4505675	4506537	4521191	4518605	4519467

L13-M10

4336723	4349653	4334999	4337585	4350515
4335861	4341033	4345343	4339309	4347929
4352239	4340171	4341895	4343619	4331551
4351377	4344481	4338447	4342757	4332413
4333275	4334137	4348791	4346205	4347067

L14-M3

4530673	4543603	4528949	4531535	4544465
4529811	4534983	4539293	4533259	4541879
4546189	4534121	4535845	4537569	4525501
4545327	4538431	4532397	4536707	4526363
4527225	4528087	4542741	4540155	4541017

L13-M11

4358273	4371203	4356549	4359135	4372065
4357411	4362583	4366893	4360859	4369479
4373789	4361721	4363445	4365169	4353101
4372927	4366031	4359997	4364307	4353963
4354825	4355687	4370341	4367755	4368617

L14-M4

4552223	4565153	4550499	4553085	4566015
4551361	4556533	4560843	4554809	4563429
4567739	4555671	4557395	4559119	4547051
4566877	4559981	4553947	4558257	4547913
4548775	4549637	4564291	4561705	4562567

L13-M12

4379823	4392753	4378099	4380685	4393615
4378961	4384133	4388443	4382409	4391029
4395339	4383271	4384995	4386719	4374651
4394477	4387581	4381547	4385857	4375513
4376375	4377237	4391891	4389305	4390167

L14-M5

4573773	4586703	4572049	4574635	4587565
4572911	4578083	4582393	4576359	4584979
4589289	4577221	4578945	4580669	4568601
4588427	4581531	4575497	4579807	4569463
4570325	4571187	4585841	4583255	4584117

L13-M13

4401373	4414303	4399649	4402235	4415165
4400511	4405683	4409993	4403959	4412579
4416889	4404821	4406545	4408269	4396201
4416027	4409131	4403097	4407407	4397063
4397925	4398787	4413441	4410855	4411717

L14-M6

4595323	4608253	4593599	4596185	4609115
4594461	4599633	4603943	4597909	4606529
4610839	4598771	4600495	4602219	4590151
4609977	4603081	4597047	4601357	4591013
4591875	4592737	4607391	4604805	4605667

L13-M14

4422923	4435853	4421199	4423785	4436715
4422061	4427233	4431543	4425509	4434129
4438439	4426371	4428095	4429819	4417751
4437577	4430681	4424647	4428957	4418613
4419475	4420337	4434991	4432405	4433267

L14-M7

4616873	4629803	4615149	4617735	4630665
4616011	4621183	4625493	4619459	4628079
4632389	4620321	4622045	4623769	4611701
4631527	4624631	4618597	4622907	4612563
4613425	4614287	4628941	4626355	4627217

L13-M15

4444473	4457403	4442749	4445335	4458265
4443611	4448783	4453093	4447059	4455679
4459989	4447921	4449645	4451369	4439301
4459127	4452231	4446197	4450507	4440163
4441025	4441887	4456541	4453955	4454817

L14-M8

4638423	4651353	4636699	4639285	4652215
4637561	4642733	4647043	4641009	4649629
4653939	4641871	4643595	4645319	4633251
4653077	4646181	4640147	4644457	4634113
4634975	4635837	4650491	4647905	4648767

L14-M9

4659973	4672903	4658249	4660835	4673765
4659111	4664283	4668593	4662559	4671179
4675489	4663421	4665145	4666869	4654801
4674627	4667731	4661697	4666007	4655663
4656525	4657387	4672041	4669455	4670317

L14-M10

4681523	4694453	4679799	4682385	4695315
4680661	4685833	4690143	4684109	4692729
4697039	4684971	4686695	4688419	4676351
4696177	4689281	4683247	4687557	4677213
4678075	4678937	4693591	4691005	4691867

L14-M11

4703073	4716003	4701349	4703935	4716865
4702211	4707383	4711693	4705659	4714279
4718589	4706521	4708245	4709969	4697901
4717727	4710831	4704797	4709107	4698763
4699625	4700487	4715141	4712555	4713417

L14-M12

4724623	4737553	4722899	4725485	4738415
4723761	4728933	4733243	4727209	4735829
4740139	4728071	4729795	4731519	4719451
4739277	4732381	4726347	4730657	4720313
4721175	4722037	4736691	4734105	4734967

L14-M13

4746173	4759103	4744449	4747035	4759965
4745311	4750483	4754793	4748759	4757379
4761689	4749621	4751345	4753069	4741001
4760827	4753931	4747897	4752207	4741863
4742725	4743587	4758241	4755655	4756517

L14-M14

4767723	4780653	4765999	4768585	4781515
4766861	4772033	4776343	4770309	4778929
4783239	4771171	4772895	4774619	4762551
4782377	4775481	4769447	4773757	4763413
4764275	4765137	4779791	4777205	4778067

L14-M15

4789273	4802203	4787549	4790135	4803065
4788411	4793583	4797893	4791859	4800479
4804789	4792721	4794445	4796169	4784101
4803927	4797031	4790997	4795307	4784963
4785825	4786687	4801341	4798755	4799617

L14-M16

4810823	4823753	4809099	4811685	4824615
4809961	4815133	4819443	4813409	4822029
4826339	4814271	4815995	4817719	4805651
4825477	4818581	4812547	4816857	4806513
4807375	4808237	4822891	4820305	4821167

L15-M1

4832373	4845303	4830649	4833235	4846165
4831511	4836683	4840993	4834959	4843579
4847889	4835821	4837545	4839269	4827201
4847027	4840131	4834097	4838407	4828063
4828925	4829787	4844441	4841855	4842717

L15-M2

4853923	4866853	4852199	4854785	4867715
4853061	4858233	4862543	4856509	4865129
4869439	4857371	4859095	4860819	4848751
4868577	4861681	4855647	4859957	4849613
4850475	4851337	4865991	4863405	4864267

L15-M3

4875473	4888403	4873749	4876335	4889265
4874611	4879783	4884093	4878059	4886679
4890989	4878921	4880645	4882369	4870301
4890127	4883231	4877197	4881507	4871163
4872025	4872887	4887541	4884955	4885817

L15-M4

4897023	4909953	4895299	4897885	4910815
4896161	4901333	4905643	4899609	4908229
4912539	4900471	4902195	4903919	4891851
4911677	4904781	4898747	4903057	4892713
4893575	4894437	4909091	4906505	4907367

L15-M5

4918573	4931503	4916849	4919435	4932365
4917711	4922883	4927193	4921159	4929779
4934089	4922021	4923745	4925469	4913401
4933227	4926331	4920297	4924607	4914263
4915125	4915987	4930641	4928055	4928917

L15-M6

4940123	4953053	4938399	4940985	4953915
4939261	4944433	4948743	4942709	4951329
4955639	4943571	4945295	4947019	4934951
4954777	4947881	4941847	4946157	4935813
4936675	4937537	4952191	4949605	4950467

L15-M7

4961673	4974603	4959949	4962535	4975465
4960811	4965983	4970293	4964259	4972879
4977189	4965121	4966845	4968569	4956501
4976327	4969431	4963397	4967707	4957363
4958225	4959087	4973741	4971155	4972017

L15-M8

4983223	4996153	4981499	4984085	4997015
4982361	4987533	4991843	4985809	4994429
4998739	4986671	4988395	4990119	4978051
4997877	4990981	4984947	4989257	4978913
4979775	4980637	4995291	4992705	4993567

L15-M9

5004773	5017703	5003049	5005635	5018565
5003911	5009083	5013393	5007359	5015979
5020289	5008221	5009945	5011669	4999601
5019427	5012531	5006497	5010807	5000463
5001325	5002187	5016841	5014255	5015117

L15-M10

5026323	5039253	5024599	5027185	5040115
5025461	5030633	5034943	5028909	5037529
5041839	5029771	5031495	5033219	5021151
5040977	5034081	5028047	5032357	5022013
5022875	5023737	5038391	5035805	5036667

L15-M11

5047873	5060803	5046149	5048735	5061665
5047011	5052183	5056493	5050459	5059079
5063389	5051321	5053045	5054769	5042701
5062527	5055631	5049597	5053907	5043563
5044425	5045287	5059941	5057355	5058217

L15-M12

5069423	5082353	5067699	5070285	5083215
5068561	5073733	5078043	5072009	5080629
5084939	5072871	5074595	5076319	5064251
5084077	5077181	5071147	5075457	5065113
5065975	5066837	5081491	5078905	5079767

L15-M13

5090973	5103903	5089249	5091835	5104765
5090111	5095283	5099593	5093559	5102179
5106489	5094421	5096145	5097869	5085801
5105627	5098731	5092697	5097007	5086663
5087525	5088387	5103041	5100455	5101317

L15-M14

5112523	5125453	5110799	5113385	5126315
5111661	5116833	5121143	5115109	5123729
5128039	5115971	5117695	5119419	5107351
5127177	5120281	5114247	5118557	5108213
5109075	5109937	5124591	5122005	5122867

L15-M15

5134073	5147003	5132349	5134935	5147865
5133211	5138383	5142693	5136659	5145279
5149589	5137521	5139245	5140969	5128901
5148727	5141831	5135797	5140107	5129763
5130625	5131487	5146141	5143555	5144417

L15-M16

5155623	5168553	5153899	5156485	5169415
5154761	5159933	5164243	5158209	5166829
5171139	5159071	5160795	5162519	5150451
5170277	5163381	5157347	5161657	5151313
5152175	5153037	5167691	5165105	5165967

L16-M1

5177173	5190103	5175449	5178035	5190965
5176311	5181483	5185793	5179759	5188379
5192689	5180621	5182345	5184069	5172001
5191827	5184931	5178897	5183207	5172863
5173725	5174587	5189241	5186655	5187517

L16-M2

5198723	5211653	5196999	5199585	5212515
5197861	5203033	5207343	5201309	5209929
5214239	5202171	5203895	5205619	5193551
5213377	5206481	5200447	5204757	5194413
5195275	5196137	5210791	5208205	5209067

L16-M3

5220273	5233203	5218549	5221135	5234065
5219411	5224583	5228893	5222859	5231479
5235789	5223721	5225445	5227169	5215101
5234927	5228031	5221997	5226307	5215963
5216825	5217687	5232341	5229755	5230617

L16-M4

5241823	5254753	5240099	5242685	5255615
5240961	5246133	5250443	5244409	5253029
5257339	5245271	5246995	5248719	5236651
5256477	5249581	5243547	5247857	5237513
5238375	5239237	5253891	5251305	5252167

L16-M5

5263373	5276303	5261649	5264235	5277165
5262511	5267683	5271993	5265959	5274579
5278889	5266821	5268545	5270269	5258201
5278027	5271131	5265097	5269407	5259063
5259925	5260787	5275441	5272855	5273717

L16-M6

5284923	5297853	5283199	5285785	5298715
5284061	5289233	5293543	5287509	5296129
5300439	5288371	5290095	5291819	5279751
5299577	5292681	5286647	5290957	5280613
5281475	5282337	5296991	5294405	5295267

L16-M7

5306473	5319403	5304749	5307335	5320265
5305611	5310783	5315093	5309059	5317679
5321989	5309921	5311645	5313369	5301301
5321127	5314231	5308197	5312507	5302163
5303025	5303887	5318541	5315955	5316817

L16-M8

5328023	5340953	5326299	5328885	5341815
5327161	5332333	5336643	5330609	5339229
5343539	5331471	5333195	5334919	5322851
5342677	5335781	5329747	5334057	5323713
5324575	5325437	5340091	5337505	5338367

L16-M9

5349573	5362503	5347849	5350435	5363365
5348711	5353883	5358193	5352159	5360779
5365089	5353021	5354745	5356469	5344401
5364227	5357331	5351297	5355607	5345263
5346125	5346987	5361641	5359055	5359917

L16-M10

5371123	5384053	5369399	5371985	5384915
5370261	5375433	5379743	5373709	5382329
5386639	5374571	5376295	5378019	5365951
5385777	5378881	5372847	5377157	5366813
5367675	5368537	5383191	5380605	5381467

L16-M11

5392673	5405603	5390949	5393535	5406465
5391811	5396983	5401293	5395259	5403879
5408189	5396121	5397845	5399569	5387501
5407327	5400431	5394397	5398707	5388363
5389225	5390087	5404741	5402155	5403017

L16-M12

5414223	5427153	5412499	5415085	5428015
5413361	5418533	5422843	5416809	5425429
5429739	5417671	5419395	5421119	5409051
5428877	5421981	5415947	5420257	5409913
5410775	5411637	5426291	5423705	5424567

L16-M13

5435773	5448703	5434049	5436635	5449565
5434911	5440083	5444393	5438359	5446979
5451289	5439221	5440945	5442669	5430601
5450427	5443531	5437497	5441807	5431463
5432325	5433187	5447841	5445255	5446117

L16-M14

5457323	5470253	5455599	5458185	5471115
5456461	5461633	5465943	5459909	5468529
5472839	5460771	5462495	5464219	5452151
5471977	5465081	5459047	5463357	5453013
5453875	5454737	5469391	5466805	5467667

L16-M15

5478873	5491803	5477149	5479735	5492665
5478011	5483183	5487493	5481459	5490079
5494389	5482321	5484045	5485769	5473701
5493527	5486631	5480597	5484907	5474563
5475425	5476287	5490941	5488355	5489217

L16M16

5500423	5513353	5498699	5501285	5514215
5499561	5504733	5509043	5503009	5511629
5515939	5503871	5505595	5507319	5495251
5515077	5508181	5502147	5506457	5496113
5496975	5497837	5512491	5509905	5510767

L17-M1

5521973	5534903	5520249	5522835	5535765
5521111	5526283	5530593	5524559	5533179
5537489	5525421	5527145	5528869	5516801
5536627	5529731	5523697	5528007	5517663
5518525	5519387	5534041	5531455	5532317

L17-M2

5543523	5556453	5541799	5544385	5557315
5542661	5547833	5552143	5546109	5554729
5559039	5546971	5548695	5550419	5538351
5558177	5551281	5545247	5549557	5539213
5540075	5540937	5555591	5553005	5553867

L17-M3

5565073	5578003	5563349	5565935	5578865
5564211	5569383	5573693	5567659	5576279
5580589	5568521	5570245	5571969	5559901
5579727	5572831	5566797	5571107	5560763
5561625	5562487	5577141	5574555	5575417

L17-M4

5586623	5599553	5584899	5587485	5600415
5585761	5590933	5595243	5589209	5597829
5602139	5590071	5591795	5593519	5581451
5601277	5594381	5588347	5592657	5582313
5583175	5584037	5598691	5596105	5596967

L17-M5

5608173	5621103	5606449	5609035	5621965
5607311	5612483	5616793	5610759	5619379
5623689	5611621	5613345	5615069	5603001
5622827	5615931	5609897	5614207	5603863
5604725	5605587	5620241	5617655	5618517

L17-M6

5629723	5642653	5627999	5630585	5643515
5628861	5634033	5638343	5632309	5640929
5645239	5633171	5634895	5636619	5624551
5644377	5637481	5631447	5635757	5625413
5626275	5627137	5641791	5639205	5640067

L17-M7

5651273	5664203	5649549	5652135	5665065
5650411	5655583	5659893	5653859	5662479
5666789	5654721	5656445	5658169	5646101
5665927	5659031	5652997	5657307	5646963
5647825	5648687	5663341	5660755	5661617

L17-M8

5672823	5685753	5671099	5673685	5686615
5671961	5677133	5681443	5675409	5684029
5688339	5676271	5677995	5679719	5667651
5687477	5680581	5674547	5678857	5668513
5669375	5670237	5684891	5682305	5683167

L17-M9

5694373	5707303	5692649	5695235	5708165
5693511	5698683	5702993	5696959	5705579
5709889	5697821	5699545	5701269	5689201
5709027	5702131	5696097	5700407	5690063
5690925	5691787	5706441	5703855	5704717

L17-M10

5715923	5728853	5714199	5716785	5729715
5715061	5720233	5724543	5718509	5727129
5731439	5719371	5721095	5722819	5710751
5730577	5723681	5717647	5721957	5711613
5712475	5713337	5727991	5725405	5726267

L17-M11

5737473	5750403	5735749	5738335	5751265
5736611	5741783	5746093	5740059	5748679
5752989	5740921	5742645	5744369	5732301
5752127	5745231	5739197	5743507	5733163
5734025	5734887	5749541	5746955	5747817

L17-M12

5759023	5771953	5757299	5759885	5772815
5758161	5763333	5767643	5761609	5770229
5774539	5762471	5764195	5765919	5753851
5773677	5766781	5760747	5765057	5754713
5755575	5756437	5771091	5768505	5769367

L17-M13

5780573	5793503	5778849	5781435	5794365
5779711	5784883	5789193	5783159	5791779
5796089	5784021	5785745	5787469	5775401
5795227	5788331	5782297	5786607	5776263
5777125	5777987	5792641	5790055	5790917

L17-M14

5802123	5815053	5800399	5802985	5815915
5801261	5806433	5810743	5804709	5813329
5817639	5805571	5807295	5809019	5796951
5816777	5809881	5803847	5808157	5797813
5798675	5799537	5814191	5811605	5812467

L17-M15

5823673	5836603	5821949	5824535	5837465
5822811	5827983	5832293	5826259	5834879
5839189	5827121	5828845	5830569	5818501
5838327	5831431	5825397	5829707	5819363
5820225	5821087	5835741	5833155	5834017

L17-M16

5845223	5858153	5843499	5846085	5859015
5844361	5849533	5853843	5847809	5856429
5860739	5848671	5850395	5852119	5840051
5859877	5852981	5846947	5851257	5840913
5841775	5842637	5857291	5854705	5855567

L18-M1

5866773	5879703	5865049	5867635	5880565
5865911	5871083	5875393	5869359	5877979
5882289	5870221	5871945	5873669	5861601
5881427	5874531	5868497	5872807	5862463
5863325	5864187	5878841	5876255	5877117

L18-M2

5888323	5901253	5886599	5889185	5902115
5887461	5892633	5896943	5890909	5899529
5903839	5891771	5893495	5895219	5883151
5902977	5896081	5890047	5894357	5884013
5884875	5885737	5900391	5897805	5898667

L18-M3

5909873	5922803	5908149	5910735	5923665
5909011	5914183	5918493	5912459	5921079
5925389	5913321	5915045	5916769	5904701
5924527	5917631	5911597	5915907	5905563
5906425	5907287	5921941	5919355	5920217

L18-M4

5931423	5944353	5929699	5932285	5945215
5930561	5935733	5940043	5934009	5942629
5946939	5934871	5936595	5938319	5926251
5946077	5939181	5933147	5937457	5927113
5927975	5928837	5943491	5940905	5941767

L18-M5

5952973	5965903	5951249	5953835	5966765
5952111	5957283	5961593	5955559	5964179
5968489	5956421	5958145	5959869	5947801
5967627	5960731	5954697	5959007	5948663
5949525	5950387	5965041	5962455	5963317

L18-M6

5974523	5987453	5972799	5975385	5988315
5973661	5978833	5983143	5977109	5985729
5990039	5977971	5979695	5981419	5969351
5989177	5982281	5976247	5980557	5970213
5971075	5971937	5986591	5984005	5984867

L18-M7

5996073	6009003	5994349	5996935	6009865
5995211	6000383	6004693	5998659	6007279
6011589	5999521	6001245	6002969	5990901
6010727	6003831	5997797	6002107	5991763
5992625	5993487	6008141	6005555	6006417

L18-M8

6017623	6030553	6015899	6018485	6031415
6016761	6021933	6026243	6020209	6028829
6033139	6021071	6022795	6024519	6012451
6032277	6025381	6019347	6023657	6013313
6014175	6015037	6029691	6027105	6027967

L18-M9

6039173	6052103	6037449	6040035	6052965
6038311	6043483	6047793	6041759	6050379
6054689	6042621	6044345	6046069	6034001
6053827	6046931	6040897	6045207	6034863
6035725	6036587	6051241	6048655	6049517

L18-M10

6060723	6073653	6058999	6061585	6074515
6059861	6065033	6069343	6063309	6071929
6076239	6064171	6065895	6067619	6055551
6075377	6068481	6062447	6066757	6056413
6057275	6058137	6072791	6070205	6071067

L18-M11

6082273	6095203	6080549	6083135	6096065
6081411	6086583	6090893	6084859	6093479
6097789	6085721	6087445	6089169	6077101
6096927	6090031	6083997	6088307	6077963
6078825	6079687	6094341	6091755	6092617

L18-M12

6103823	6116753	6102099	6104685	6117615
6102961	6108133	6112443	6106409	6115029
6119339	6107271	6108995	6110719	6098651
6118477	6111581	6105547	6109857	6099513
6100375	6101237	6115891	6113305	6114167

L18-M13

6125373	6138303	6123649	6126235	6139165
6124511	6129683	6133993	6127959	6136579
6140889	6128821	6130545	6132269	6120201
6140027	6133131	6127097	6131407	6121063
6121925	6122787	6137441	6134855	6135717

L18-M14

6146923	6159853	6145199	6147785	6160715
6146061	6151233	6155543	6149509	6158129
6162439	6150371	6152095	6153819	6141751
6161577	6154681	6148647	6152957	6142613
6143475	6144337	6158991	6156405	6157267

L18-M15

6168473	6181403	6166749	6169335	6182265
6167611	6172783	6177093	6171059	6179679
6183989	6171921	6173645	6175369	6163301
6183127	6176231	6170197	6174507	6164163
6165025	6165887	6180541	6177955	6178817

L18-M16

6190023	6202953	6188299	6190885	6203815
6189161	6194333	6198643	6192609	6201229
6205539	6193471	6195195	6196919	6184851
6204677	6197781	6191747	6196057	6185713
6186575	6187437	6202091	6199505	6200367

L19-M1

6211573	6224503	6209849	6212435	6225365
6210711	6215883	6220193	6214159	6222779
6227089	6215021	6216745	6218469	6206401
6226227	6219331	6213297	6217607	6207263
6208125	6208987	6223641	6221055	6221917

L19-M2

6233123	6246053	6231399	6233985	6246915
6232261	6237433	6241743	6235709	6244329
6248639	6236571	6238295	6240019	6227951
6247777	6240881	6234847	6239157	6228813
6229675	6230537	6245191	6242605	6243467

L19-M3

6254673	6267603	6252949	6255535	6268465
6253811	6258983	6263293	6257259	6265879
6270189	6258121	6259845	6261569	6249501
6269327	6262431	6256397	6260707	6250363
6251225	6252087	6266741	6264155	6265017

L19-M4

6276223	6289153	6274499	6277085	6290015
6275361	6280533	6284843	6278809	6287429
6291739	6279671	6281395	6283119	6271051
6290877	6283981	6277947	6282257	6271913
6272775	6273637	6288291	6285705	6286567

L19-M5

6297773	6310703	6296049	6298635	6311565
6296911	6302083	6306393	6300359	6308979
6313289	6301221	6302945	6304669	6292601
6312427	6305531	6299497	6303807	6293463
6294325	6295187	6309841	6307255	6308117

L19-M6

6319323	6332253	6317599	6320185	6333115
6318461	6323633	6327943	6321909	6330529
6334839	6322771	6324495	6326219	6314151
6333977	6327081	6321047	6325357	6315013
6315875	6316737	6331391	6328805	6329667

L19-M7

6340873	6353803	6339149	6341735	6354665
6340011	6345183	6349493	6343459	6352079
6356389	6344321	6346045	6347769	6335701
6355527	6348631	6342597	6346907	6336563
6337425	6338287	6352941	6350355	6351217

L19-M8

6362423	6375353	6360699	6363285	6376215
6361561	6366733	6371043	6365009	6373629
6377939	6365871	6367595	6369319	6357251
6377077	6370181	6364147	6368457	6358113
6358975	6359837	6374491	6371905	6372767

L19-M9

6383973	6396903	6382249	6384835	6397765
6383111	6388283	6392593	6386559	6395179
6399489	6387421	6389145	6390869	6378801
6398627	6391731	6385697	6390007	6379663
6380525	6381387	6396041	6393455	6394317

L19-M10

6405523	6418453	6403799	6406385	6419315
6404661	6409833	6414143	6408109	6416729
6421039	6408971	6410695	6412419	6400351
6420177	6413281	6407247	6411557	6401213
6402075	6402937	6417591	6415005	6415867

L19-M11

6427073	6440003	6425349	6427935	6440865
6426211	6431383	6435693	6429659	6438279
6442589	6430521	6432245	6433969	6421901
6441727	6434831	6428797	6433107	6422763
6423625	6424487	6439141	6436555	6437417

L19-M12

6448623	6461553	6446899	6449485	6462415
6447761	6452933	6457243	6451209	6459829
6464139	6452071	6453795	6455519	6443451
6463277	6456381	6450347	6454657	6444313
6445175	6446037	6460691	6458105	6458967

L19-M13

6470173	6483103	6468449	6471035	6483965
6469311	6474483	6478793	6472759	6481379
6485689	6473621	6475345	6477069	6465001
6484827	6477931	6471897	6476207	6465863
6466725	6467587	6482241	6479655	6480517

L19-M14

6491723	6504653	6489999	6492585	6505515
6490861	6496033	6500343	6494309	6502929
6507239	6495171	6496895	6498619	6486551
6506377	6499481	6493447	6497757	6487413
6488275	6489137	6503791	6501205	6502067

L19-M15

6513273	6526203	6511549	6514135	6527065
6512411	6517583	6521893	6515859	6524479
6528789	6516721	6518445	6520169	6508101
6527927	6521031	6514997	6519307	6508963
6509825	6510687	6525341	6522755	6523617

L19-M16

6534823	6547753	6533099	6535685	6548615
6533961	6539133	6543443	6537409	6546029
6550339	6538271	6539995	6541719	6529651
6549477	6542581	6536547	6540857	6530513
6531375	6532237	6546891	6544305	6545167

L20-M1

6556373	6569303	6554649	6557235	6570165
6555511	6560683	6564993	6558959	6567579
6571889	6559821	6561545	6563269	6551201
6571027	6564131	6558097	6562407	6552063
6552925	6553787	6568441	6565855	6566717

L20-M2

6577923	6590853	6576199	6578785	6591715
6577061	6582233	6586543	6580509	6589129
6593439	6581371	6583095	6584819	6572751
6592577	6585681	6579647	6583957	6573613
6574475	6575337	6589991	6587405	6588267

L20-M3

6599473	6612403	6597749	6600335	6613265
6598611	6603783	6608093	6602059	6610679
6614989	6602921	6604645	6606369	6594301
6614127	6607231	6601197	6605507	6595163
6596025	6596887	6611541	6608955	6609817

L20-M4

6621023	6633953	6619299	6621885	6634815
6620161	6625333	6629643	6623609	6632229
6636539	6624471	6626195	6627919	6615851
6635677	6628781	6622747	6627057	6616713
6617575	6618437	6633091	6630505	6631367

L20-M5

6642573	6655503	6640849	6643435	6656365
6641711	6646883	6651193	6645159	6653779
6658089	6646021	6647745	6649469	6637401
6657227	6650331	6644297	6648607	6638263
6639125	6639987	6654641	6652055	6652917

L20-M6

6664123	6677053	6662399	6664985	6677915
6663261	6668433	6672743	6666709	6675329
6679639	6667571	6669295	6671019	6658951
6678777	6671881	6665847	6670157	6659813
6660675	6661537	6676191	6673605	6674467

L20-M7

6685673	6698603	6683949	6686535	6699465
6684811	6689983	6694293	6688259	6696879
6701189	6689121	6690845	6692569	6680501
6700327	6693431	6687397	6691707	6681363
6682225	6683087	6697741	6695155	6696017

L20-M8

6707223	6720153	6705499	6708085	6721015
6706361	6711533	6715843	6709809	6718429
6722739	6710671	6712395	6714119	6702051
6721877	6714981	6708947	6713257	6702913
6703775	6704637	6719291	6716705	6717567

L20-M9

6728773	6741703	6727049	6729635	6742565
6727911	6733083	6737393	6731359	6739979
6744289	6732221	6733945	6735669	6723601
6743427	6736531	6730497	6734807	6724463
6725325	6726187	6740841	6738255	6739117

L20-M10

6750323	6763253	6748599	6751185	6764115
6749461	6754633	6758943	6752909	6761529
6765839	6753771	6755495	6757219	6745151
6764977	6758081	6752047	6756357	6746013
6746875	6747737	6762391	6759805	6760667

L20-M11

6771873	6784803	6770149	6772735	6785665
6771011	6776183	6780493	6774459	6783079
6787389	6775321	6777045	6778769	6766701
6786527	6779631	6773597	6777907	6767563
6768425	6769287	6783941	6781355	6782217

L20-M12

6793423	6806353	6791699	6794285	6807215
6792561	6797733	6802043	6796009	6804629
6808939	6796871	6798595	6800319	6788251
6808077	6801181	6795147	6799457	6789113
6789975	6790837	6805491	6802905	6803767

L20-M13

6814973	6827903	6813249	6815835	6828765
6814111	6819283	6823593	6817559	6826179
6830489	6818421	6820145	6821869	6809801
6829627	6822731	6816697	6821007	6810663
6811525	6812387	6827041	6824455	6825317

L20-M14

6836523	6849453	6834799	6837385	6850315
6835661	6840833	6845143	6839109	6847729
6852039	6839971	6841695	6843419	6831351
6851177	6844281	6838247	6842557	6832213
6833075	6833937	6848591	6846005	6846867

L20-M15

6858073	6871003	6856349	6858935	6871865
6857211	6862383	6866693	6860659	6869279
6873589	6861521	6863245	6864969	6852901
6872727	6865831	6859797	6864107	6853763
6854625	6855487	6870141	6867555	6868417

L20-M16

6879623	6892553	6877899	6880485	6893415
6878761	6883933	6888243	6882209	6890829
6895139	6883071	6884795	6886519	6874451
6894277	6887381	6881347	6885657	6875313
6876175	6877037	6891691	6889105	6889967

L21-M1

6901173	6914103	6899449	6902035	6914965
6900311	6905483	6909793	6903759	6912379
6916689	6904621	6906345	6908069	6896001
6915827	6908931	6902897	6907207	6896863
6897725	6898587	6913241	6910655	6911517

L21-M2

6922723	6935653	6920999	6923585	6936515
6921861	6927033	6931343	6925309	6933929
6938239	6926171	6927895	6929619	6917551
6937377	6930481	6924447	6928757	6918413
6919275	6920137	6934791	6932205	6933067

L21-M3

6944273	6957203	6942549	6945135	6958065
6943411	6948583	6952893	6946859	6955479
6959789	6947721	6949445	6951169	6939101
6958927	6952031	6945997	6950307	6939963
6940825	6941687	6956341	6953755	6954617

L21-M4

6965823	6978753	6964099	6966685	6979615
6964961	6970133	6974443	6968409	6977029
6981339	6969271	6970995	6972719	6960651
6980477	6973581	6967547	6971857	6961513
6962375	6963237	6977891	6975305	6976167

L21-M5

6987373	7000303	6985649	6988235	7001165
6986511	6991683	6995993	6989959	6998579
7002889	6990821	6992545	6994269	6982201
7002027	6995131	6989097	6993407	6983063
6983925	6984787	6999441	6996855	6997717

L21-M14

7181323	7194253	7179599	7182185	7195115
7180461	7185633	7189943	7183909	7192529
7196839	7184771	7186495	7188219	7176151
7195977	7189081	7183047	7187357	7177013
7177875	7178737	7193391	7190805	7191667

L21-M6

7008923	7021853	7007199	7009785	7022715
7008061	7013233	7017543	7011509	7020129
7024439	7012371	7014095	7015819	7003751
7023577	7016681	7010647	7014957	7004613
7005475	7006337	7020991	7018405	7019267

L21-M15

7202873	7215803	7201149	7203735	7216665
7202011	7207183	7211493	7205459	7214079
7218389	7206321	7208045	7209769	7197701
7217527	7210631	7204597	7208907	7198563
7199425	7200287	7214941	7212355	7213217

L21-M7

7030473	7043403	7028749	7031335	7044265
7029611	7034783	7039093	7033059	7041679
7045989	7033921	7035645	7037369	7025301
7045127	7038231	7032197	7036507	7026163
7027025	7027887	7042541	7039955	7040817

L21-M16

7224423	7237353	7222699	7225285	7238215
7223561	7228733	7233043	7227009	7235629
7239939	7227871	7229595	7231319	7219251
7239077	7232181	7226147	7230457	7220113
7220975	7221837	7236491	7233905	7234767

L21-M8

7052023	7064953	7050299	7052885	7065815
7051161	7056333	7060643	7054609	7063229
7067539	7055471	7057195	7058919	7046851
7066677	7059781	7053747	7058057	7047713
7048575	7049437	7064091	7061505	7062367

L22-M1

7245973	7258903	7244249	7246835	7259765
7245111	7250283	7254593	7248559	7257179
7261489	7249421	7251145	7252869	7240801
7260627	7253731	7247697	7252007	7241663
7242525	7243387	7258041	7255455	7256317

L21-M9

7073573	7086503	7071849	7074435	7087365
7072711	7077883	7082193	7076159	7084779
7089089	7077021	7078745	7080469	7068401
7088227	7081331	7075297	7079607	7069263
7070125	7070987	7085641	7083055	7083917

L22-M2

7267523	7280453	7265799	7268385	7281315
7266661	7271833	7276143	7270109	7278729
7283039	7270971	7272695	7274419	7262351
7282177	7275281	7269247	7273557	7263213
7264075	7264937	7279591	7277005	7277867

L21-M10

7095123	7108053	7093399	7095985	7108915
7094261	7099433	7103743	7097709	7106329
7110639	7098571	7100295	7102019	7089951
7109777	7102881	7096847	7101157	7090813
7091675	7092537	7107191	7104605	7105467

L22-M3

7289073	7302003	7287349	7289935	7302865
7288211	7293383	7297693	7291659	7300279
7304589	7292521	7294245	7295969	7283901
7303727	7296831	7290797	7295107	7284763
7285625	7286487	7301141	7298555	7299417

L21-M11

7116673	7129603	7114949	7117535	7130465
7115811	7120983	7125293	7119259	7127879
7132189	7120121	7121845	7123569	7111501
7131327	7124431	7118397	7122707	7112363
7113225	7114087	7128741	7126155	7127017

L22-M4

7310623	7323553	7308899	7311485	7324415
7309761	7314933	7319243	7313209	7321829
7326139	7314071	7315795	7317519	7305451
7325277	7318381	7312347	7316657	7306313
7307175	7308037	7322691	7320105	7320967

L21-M12

7138223	7151153	7136499	7139085	7152015
7137361	7142533	7146843	7140809	7149429
7153739	7141671	7143395	7145119	7133051
7152877	7145981	7139947	7144257	7133913
7134775	7135637	7150291	7147705	7148567

L22-M5

7332173	7345103	7330449	7333035	7345965
7331311	7336483	7340793	7334759	7343379
7347689	7335621	7337345	7339069	7327001
7346827	7339931	7333897	7338207	7327863
7328725	7329587	7344241	7341655	7342517

L21-M13

7159773	7172703	7158049	7160635	7173565
7158911	7164083	7168393	7162359	7170979
7175289	7163221	7164945	7166669	7154601
7174427	7167531	7161497	7165807	7155463
7156325	7157187	7171841	7169255	7170117

L22-M6

7353723	7366653	7351999	7354585	7367515
7352861	7358033	7362343	7356309	7364929
7369239	7357171	7358895	7360619	7348551
7368377	7361481	7355447	7359757	7349413
7350275	7351137	7365791	7363205	7364067

L22-M7

7375273	7388203	7373549	7376135	7389065
7374411	7379583	7383893	7377859	7386479
7390789	7378721	7380445	7382169	7370101
7389927	7383031	7376997	7381307	7370963
7371825	7372687	7387341	7384755	7385617

L22-M8

7396823	7409753	7395099	7397685	7410615
7395961	7401133	7405443	7399409	7408029
7412339	7400271	7401995	7403719	7391651
7411477	7404581	7398547	7402857	7392513
7393375	7394237	7408891	7406305	7407167

L22-M9

7418373	7431303	7416649	7419235	7432165
7417511	7422683	7426993	7420959	7429579
7433889	7421821	7423545	7425269	7413201
7433027	7426131	7420097	7424407	7414063
7414925	7415787	7430441	7427855	7428717

L22-M10

7439923	7452853	7438199	7440785	7453715
7439061	7444233	7448543	7442509	7451129
7455439	7443371	7445095	7446819	7434751
7454577	7447681	7441647	7445957	7435613
7436475	7437337	7451991	7449405	7450267

L22-M11

7461473	7474403	7459749	7462335	7475265
7460611	7465783	7470093	7464059	7472679
7476989	7464921	7466645	7468369	7456301
7476127	7469231	7463197	7467507	7457163
7458025	7458887	7473541	7470955	7471817

L22-M12

7483023	7495953	7481299	7483885	7496815
7482161	7487333	7491643	7485609	7494229
7498539	7486471	7488195	7489919	7477851
7497677	7490781	7484747	7489057	7478713
7479575	7480437	7495091	7492505	7493367

L22-M13

7504573	7517503	7502849	7505435	7518365
7503711	7508883	7513193	7507159	7515779
7520089	7508021	7509745	7511469	7499401
7519227	7512331	7506297	7510607	7500263
7501125	7501987	7516641	7514055	7514917

L22-M14

7526123	7539053	7524399	7526985	7539915
7525261	7530433	7534743	7528709	7537329
7541639	7529571	7531295	7533019	7520951
7540777	7533881	7527847	7532157	7521813
7522675	7523537	7538191	7535605	7536467

L22-M15

7547673	7560603	7545949	7548535	7561465
7546811	7551983	7556293	7550259	7558879
7563189	7551121	7552845	7554569	7542501
7562327	7555431	7549397	7553707	7543363
7544225	7545087	7559741	7557155	7558017

L22-M16

7569223	7582153	7567499	7570085	7583015
7568361	7573533	7577843	7571809	7580429
7584739	7572671	7574395	7576119	7564051
7583877	7576981	7570947	7575257	7564913
7565775	7566637	7581291	7578705	7579567

L23-M1

7590773	7603703	7589049	7591635	7604565
7589911	7595083	7599393	7593359	7601979
7606289	7594221	7595945	7597669	7585601
7605427	7598531	7592497	7596807	7586463
7587325	7588187	7602841	7600255	7601117

L23-M2

7612323	7625253	7610599	7613185	7626115
7611461	7616633	7620943	7614909	7623529
7627839	7615771	7617495	7619219	7607151
7626977	7620081	7614047	7618357	7608013
7608875	7609737	7624391	7621805	7622667

L23-M3

7633873	7646803	7632149	7634735	7647665
7633011	7638183	7642493	7636459	7645079
7649389	7637321	7639045	7640769	7628701
7648527	7641631	7635597	7639907	7629563
7630425	7631287	7645941	7643355	7644217

L23-M4

7655423	7668353	7653699	7656285	7669215
7654561	7659733	7664043	7658009	7666629
7670939	7658871	7660595	7662319	7650251
7670077	7663181	7657147	7661457	7651113
7651975	7652837	7667491	7664905	7665767

L23-M5

7676973	7689903	7675249	7677835	7690765
7676111	7681283	7685593	7679559	7688179
7692489	7680421	7682145	7683869	7671801
7691627	7684731	7678697	7683007	7672663
7673525	7674387	7689041	7686455	7687317

L23-M6

7698523	7711453	7696799	7699385	7712315
7697661	7702833	7707143	7701109	7709729
7714039	7701971	7703695	7705419	7693351
7713177	7706281	7700247	7704557	7694213
7695075	7695937	7710591	7708005	7708867

L23-M7

7720073	7733003	7718349	7720935	7733865
7719211	7724383	7728693	7722659	7731279
7735589	7723521	7725245	7726969	7714901
7734727	7727831	7721797	7726107	7715763
7716625	7717487	7732141	7729555	7730417

L23-M8

7741623	7754553	7739899	7742485	7755415
7740761	7745933	7750243	7744209	7752829
7757139	7745071	7746795	7748519	7736451
7756277	7749381	7743347	7747657	7737313
7738175	7739037	7753691	7751105	7751967

L23-M9

7763173	7776103	7761449	7764035	7776965
7762311	7767483	7771793	7765759	7774379
7778689	7766621	7768345	7770069	7758001
7777827	7770931	7764897	7769207	7758863
7759725	7760587	7775241	7772655	7773517

L23-M10

7784723	7797653	7782999	7785585	7798515
7783861	7789033	7793343	7787309	7795929
7800239	7788171	7789895	7791619	7779551
7799377	7792481	7786447	7790757	7780413
7781275	7782137	7796791	7794205	7795067

L23-M11

7806273	7819203	7804549	7807135	7820065
7805411	7810583	7814893	7808859	7817479
7821789	7809721	7811445	7813169	7801101
7820927	7814031	7807997	7812307	7801963
7802825	7803687	7818341	7815755	7816617

L23-M12

7827823	7840753	7826099	7828685	7841615
7826961	7832133	7836443	7830409	7839029
7843339	7831271	7832995	7834719	7822651
7842477	7835581	7829547	7833857	7823513
7824375	7825237	7839891	7837305	7838167

L23-M13

7849373	7862303	7847649	7850235	7863165
7848511	7853683	7857993	7851959	7860579
7864889	7852821	7854545	7856269	7844201
7864027	7857131	7851097	7855407	7845063
7845925	7846787	7861441	7858855	7859717

L23-M14

7870923	7883853	7869199	7871785	7884715
7870061	7875233	7879543	7873509	7882129
7886439	7874371	7876095	7877819	7865751
7885577	7878681	7872647	7876957	7866613
7867475	7868337	7882991	7880405	7881267

L23-M15

7892473	7905403	7890749	7893335	7906265
7891611	7896783	7901093	7895059	7903679
7907989	7895921	7897645	7899369	7887301
7907127	7900231	7894197	7898507	7888163
7889025	7889887	7904541	7901955	7902817

L23-M16

7914023	7926953	7912299	7914885	7927815
7913161	7918333	7922643	7916609	7925229
7929539	7917471	7919195	7920919	7908851
7928677	7921781	7915747	7920057	7909713
7910575	7911437	7926091	7923505	7924367

L24-M1

7935573	7948503	7933849	7936435	7949365
7934711	7939883	7944193	7938159	7946779
7951089	7939021	7940745	7942469	7930401
7950227	7943331	7937297	7941607	7931263
7932125	7932987	7947641	7945055	7945917

L24-M2

7957123	7970053	7955399	7957985	7970915
7956261	7961433	7965743	7959709	7968329
7972639	7960571	7962295	7964019	7951951
7971777	7964881	7958847	7963157	7952813
7953675	7954537	7969191	7966605	7967467

L24-M3

7978673	7991603	7976949	7979535	7992465
7977811	7982983	7987293	7981259	7989879
7994189	7982121	7983845	7985569	7973501
7993327	7986431	7980397	7984707	7974363
7975225	7976087	7990741	7988155	7989017

L24-M4

8000223	8013153	7998499	8001085	8014015
7999361	8004533	8008843	8002809	8011429
8015739	8003671	8005395	8007119	7995051
8014877	8007981	8001947	8006257	7995913
7996775	7997637	8012291	8009705	8010567

L24-M5

8021773	8034703	8020049	8022635	8035565
8020911	8026083	8030393	8024359	8032979
8037289	8025221	8026945	8028669	8016601
8036427	8029531	8023497	8027807	8017463
8018325	8019187	8033841	8031255	8032117

L24-M6

8043323	8056253	8041599	8044185	8057115
8042461	8047633	8051943	8045909	8054529
8058839	8046771	8048495	8050219	8038151
8057977	8051081	8045047	8049357	8039013
8039875	8040737	8055391	8052805	8053667

L24-M7

8064873	8077803	8063149	8065735	8078665
8064011	8069183	8073493	8067459	8076079
8080389	8068321	8070045	8071769	8059701
8079527	8072631	8066597	8070907	8060563
8061425	8062287	8076941	8074355	8075217

L24-M8

8086423	8099353	8084699	8087285	8100215
8085561	8090733	8095043	8089009	8097629
8101939	8089871	8091595	8093319	8081251
8101077	8094181	8088147	8092457	8082113
8082975	8083837	8098491	8095905	8096767

L24-M9

8107973	8120903	8106249	8108835	8121765
8107111	8112283	8116593	8110559	8119179
8123489	8111421	8113145	8114869	8102801
8122627	8115731	8109697	8114007	8103663
8104525	8105387	8120041	8117455	8118317

L24-M10

8129523	8142453	8127799	8130385	8143315
8128661	8133833	8138143	8132109	8140729
8145039	8132971	8134695	8136419	8124351
8144177	8137281	8131247	8135557	8125213
8126075	8126937	8141591	8139005	8139867

L24-M11

8151073	8164003	8149349	8151935	8164865
8150211	8155383	8159693	8153659	8162279
8166589	8154521	8156245	8157969	8145901
8165727	8158831	8152797	8157107	8146763
8147625	8148487	8163141	8160555	8161417

L24-M12

8172623	8185553	8170899	8173485	8186415
8171761	8176933	8181243	8175209	8183829
8188139	8176071	8177795	8179519	8167451
8187277	8180381	8174347	8178657	8168313
8169175	8170037	8184691	8182105	8182967

L24-M13

8194173	8207103	8192449	8195035	8207965
8193311	8198483	8202793	8196759	8205379
8209689	8197621	8199345	8201069	8189001
8208827	8201931	8195897	8200207	8189863
8190725	8191587	8206241	8203655	8204517

L24-M14

8215723	8228653	8213999	8216585	8229515
8214861	8220033	8224343	8218309	8226929
8231239	8219171	8220895	8222619	8210551
8230377	8223481	8217447	8221757	8211413
8212275	8213137	8227791	8225205	8226067

L24-M15

8237273	8250203	8235549	8238135	8251065
8236411	8241583	8245893	8239859	8248479
8252789	8240721	8242445	8244169	8232101
8251927	8245031	8238997	8243307	8232963
8233825	8234687	8249341	8246755	8247617

L24-M16

8258823	8271753	8257099	8259685	8272615
8257961	8263133	8267443	8261409	8270029
8274339	8262271	8263995	8265719	8253651
8273477	8266581	8260547	8264857	8254513
8255375	8256237	8270891	8268305	8269167

L25-M1

8280373	8293303	8278649	8281235	8294165
8279511	8284683	8288993	8282959	8291579
8295889	8283821	8285545	8287269	8275201
8295027	8288131	8282097	8286407	8276063
8276925	8277787	8292441	8289855	8290717

L25-M2

8301923	8314853	8300199	8302785	8315715
8301061	8306233	8310543	8304509	8313129
8317439	8305371	8307095	8308819	8296751
8316577	8309681	8303647	8307957	8297613
8298475	8299337	8313991	8311405	8312267

L25-M3

8323473	8336403	8321749	8324335	8337265
8322611	8327783	8332093	8326059	8334679
8338989	8326921	8328645	8330369	8318301
8338127	8331231	8325197	8329507	8319163
8320025	8320887	8335541	8332955	8333817

L25-M4

8345023	8357953	8343299	8345885	8358815
8344161	8349333	8353643	8347609	8356229
8360539	8348471	8350195	8351919	8339851
8359677	8352781	8346747	8351057	8340713
8341575	8342437	8357091	8354505	8355367

L25-M5

8366573	8379503	8364849	8367435	8380365
8365711	8370883	8375193	8369159	8377779
8382089	8370021	8371745	8373469	8361401
8381227	8374331	8368297	8372607	8362263
8363125	8363987	8378641	8376055	8376917

L25-M6

8388123	8401053	8386399	8388985	8401915
8387261	8392433	8396743	8390709	8399329
8403639	8391571	8393295	8395019	8382951
8402777	8395881	8389847	8394157	8383813
8384675	8385537	8400191	8397605	8398467

L25-M7

8409673	8422603	8407949	8410535	8423465
8408811	8413983	8418293	8412259	8420879
8425189	8413121	8414845	8416569	8404501
8424327	8417431	8411397	8415707	8405363
8406225	8407087	8421741	8419155	8420017

L25-M8

8431223	8444153	8429499	8432085	8445015
8430361	8435533	8439843	8433809	8442429
8446739	8434671	8436395	8438119	8426051
8445877	8438981	8432947	8437257	8426913
8427775	8428637	8443291	8440705	8441567

L25-M9

8452773	8465703	8451049	8453635	8466565
8451911	8457083	8461393	8455359	8463979
8468289	8456221	8457945	8459669	8447601
8467427	8460531	8454497	8458807	8448463
8449325	8450187	8464841	8462255	8463117

L25-M10

8474323	8487253	8472599	8475185	8488115
8473461	8478633	8482943	8476909	8485529
8489839	8477771	8479495	8481219	8469151
8488977	8482081	8476047	8480357	8470013
8470875	8471737	8486391	8483805	8484667

L25-M11

8495873	8508803	8494149	8496735	8509665
8495011	8500183	8504493	8498459	8507079
8511389	8499321	8501045	8502769	8490701
8510527	8503631	8497597	8501907	8491563
8492425	8493287	8507941	8505355	8506217

L25-M12

8517423	8530353	8515699	8518285	8531215
8516561	8521733	8526043	8520009	8528629
8532939	8520871	8522595	8524319	8512251
8532077	8525181	8519147	8523457	8513113
8513975	8514837	8529491	8526905	8527767

L25-M13

8538973	8551903	8537249	8539835	8552765
8538111	8543283	8547593	8541559	8550179
8554489	8542421	8544145	8545869	8533801
8553627	8546731	8540697	8545007	8534663
8535525	8536387	8551041	8548455	8549317

L25-M14

8560523	8573453	8558799	8561385	8574315
8559661	8564833	8569143	8563109	8571729
8576039	8563971	8565695	8567419	8555351
8575177	8568281	8562247	8566557	8556213
8557075	8557937	8572591	8570005	8570867

L25-M15

8582073	8595003	8580349	8582935	8595865
8581211	8586383	8590693	8584659	8593279
8597589	8585521	8587245	8588969	8576901
8596727	8589831	8583797	8588107	8577763
8578625	8579487	8594141	8591555	8592417

L25-M16

8603623	8616553	8601899	8604485	8617415
8602761	8607933	8612243	8606209	8614829
8619139	8607071	8608795	8610519	8598451
8618277	8611381	8605347	8609657	8599313
8600175	8601037	8615691	8613105	8613967

www.ingramcontent.com/pod-product-compliance
Lightning Source LLC
Chambersburg PA
CBHW081136090426
42742CB00015BA/2856